Lecture Notes in Computer Science 15654

Founding Editors

Gerhard Goos
Juris Hartmanis

Editorial Board Members

Elisa Bertino, *Purdue University, West Lafayette, IN, USA*
Wen Gao, *Peking University, Beijing, China*
Bernhard Steffen, *TU Dortmund University, Dortmund, Germany*
Moti Yung, *Columbia University, New York, NY, USA*

The series Lecture Notes in Computer Science (LNCS), including its subseries Lecture Notes in Artificial Intelligence (LNAI) and Lecture Notes in Bioinformatics (LNBI), has established itself as a medium for the publication of new developments in computer science and information technology research, teaching, and education.

LNCS enjoys close cooperation with the computer science R & D community, the series counts many renowned academics among its volume editors and paper authors, and collaborates with prestigious societies. Its mission is to serve this international community by providing an invaluable service, mainly focused on the publication of conference and workshop proceedings and postproceedings. LNCS commenced publication in 1973.

Mark Manulis
Editor

Applied Cryptography and Network Security Workshops

ACNS 2025 Satellite Workshops:
AIHWS, AIoTS, QSHC, SCI, PrivCrypt, SPIQE, SiMLA, and CIMSS 2025
Munich, Germany, June 23–26, 2025
Revised Selected Papers, Part II

 Springer

Editor
Mark Manulis
Forschungsinstitut CODE
Universität der Bundeswehr München
Neubiberg, Germany

ISSN 0302-9743　　　　　　ISSN 1611-3349　(electronic)
Lecture Notes in Computer Science
ISBN 978-3-032-01805-2　　　ISBN 978-3-032-01806-9　(eBook)
https://doi.org/10.1007/978-3-032-01806-9

© The Editor(s) (if applicable) and The Author(s), under exclusive license
to Springer Nature Switzerland AG 2026

This work is subject to copyright. All rights are solely and exclusively licensed by the Publisher, whether the whole or part of the material is concerned, specifically the rights of translation, reprinting, reuse of illustrations, recitation, broadcasting, reproduction on microfilms or in any other physical way, and transmission or information storage and retrieval, electronic adaptation, computer software, or by similar or dissimilar methodology now known or hereafter developed.
The use of general descriptive names, registered names, trademarks, service marks, etc. in this publication does not imply, even in the absence of a specific statement, that such names are exempt from the relevant protective laws and regulations and therefore free for general use.
The publisher, the authors and the editors are safe to assume that the advice and information in this book are believed to be true and accurate at the date of publication. Neither the publisher nor the authors or the editors give a warranty, expressed or implied, with respect to the material contained herein or for any errors or omissions that may have been made. The publisher remains neutral with regard to jurisdictional claims in published maps and institutional affiliations.

This Springer imprint is published by the registered company Springer Nature Switzerland AG
The registered company address is: Gewerbestrasse 11, 6330 Cham, Switzerland

If disposing of this product, please recycle the paper.

Preface

These proceedings contain papers that were selected for presentation at the satellite workshops and the poster session of the 23rd International Conference on Applied Cryptography and Network Security (ACNS 2025), which took place June 23–26, 2025 in Munich, Germany.

A total of nine satellite workshops, selected through a competitive call for workshops, were held in parallel to the ACNS conference. The following eight workshops organised independent calls for papers:

- 6th ACNS Workshop on Artificial Intelligence in Hardware Security (AIHWS 2025), chaired by Lejla Batina and Shivam Bhasin
- 7th ACNS Workshop on Artificial Intelligence and Industrial Internet-of-Things Security (AIoTS 2025), chaired by Dieter Gollmann and Mujeeb Ahmed
- 1st Workshop on Quantum-Safe Hybrid Cryptography (QSHC 2025), chaired by Ludovic Perret and Christoph Striecks
- 6th ACNS Workshop on Secure Cryptographic Implementation (SCI 2025), chaired by Jingqiang Lin and Bo Luo
- 1st International Workshop on Foundations and Applications of Privacy-Enhancing Cryptography (PrivCrypt 2025), chaired by Lucjan Hanzlik and Daniel Slamanig
- 1st Workshop on Secure Protocol Implementations in the Quantum Era (SPIQE 2025), chaired by Kenneth G. Paterson and Juraj Somorovsky
- 7th ACNS Workshop on Security in Machine Learning and its Applications (SiMLA 2025), chaired by Ye Dong and Yangguang Tian
- 5th ACNS Workshop on Critical Infrastructure and Manufacturing System Security (CIMSS), chaired by Zengpeng Li and Ahmed Amro

ACNS 2025 satellite workshops received a total of 87 paper submissions. Each workshop had its own program chairs and a Program Committee (PC) in charge of the review process. The submitted papers were evaluated by respective workshop PCs based on their significance, novelty, and technical quality. The review process was double-blind and submissions received 2-3 reviews each. Ultimately, 43 papers were selected for presentation, resulting in an acceptance rate of 49%.

The award for the Best Workshop Paper went to Tishya Sarma Sarkar, Kislay Arya, Siddhartha Chowdhury, Upasana Mandal, Shubhi Shukla, Sarani Bhattacharya and Debdeep Mukhopadhyay: "NETLAM: An Automated LLM Framework to Generate and Evaluate Stealthy Hardware Trojans" from the AIHWS workshop. The winning paper was selected by voting from papers nominated by different workshops.

ACNS 2025 satellite workshops also featured 15 invited talks:

- "Trustworthy AI: Hype or Hope? Challenges of Building Resilient and Secure Machine Learning Systems" by Alexandra Dmitrienko (University of Würzburg) and "OpenTitan: Landing the Open Source Root of Trust in Production" by Johann Heyszl (Google) at AIHWS

- "ChatIoT: LLM-based Security Assistant for Internet of Things with Retrieval-Augmented Generation" by Jianying Zhou (SUTD) at the AIoTS
- "EU actions for a quantum-safe future and efforts in bringing together communities" by Fabiana Da Pieve (European Commission) and "Hybridisation from an operator's perspective" by Felix Wissel (Deutsche Telekom) at QSHC
- "How the Microarchitecture undermines Confidentiality and Integrity" by Daniel Gruss (Graz University of Technology) at SCI
- "Malicious Cryptography and Privacy Illusion" by Mirosław Kutyłowski (NASK National Research Institute) and "Privacy-Enhancing Cryptography from Lattices" by Tjerand Silde (Norwegian University of Science and Technology) at PrivCrypt
- "Combiners for low entropy cryptography" by Julia Hesse (IBM Zurich), "Lattices give us KEMs and FHE, but where are the efficient lattice PETs?" by Martin Albrecht (Sandbox AQ), "The Post-Quantum Transition at Signal: Progress and Challenges" by Rolfe Schmidt (Signal), "Lessons learned from blackbox analyses of software and hardware cryptographic implementations" by Petr Svenda (Masaryk University) and "Google's PQC Journey: An Industry Perspective" by Christiane Peters (Google) at SPIQE
- "Taming Malicious Majorities in Federated Learning using Privacy-preserving Byzantine-robust Clustering" by Rui Wang (TU Delft) at SiMLA
- "Do not attribute to malice what you can attribute to incompetence" by Dieter Gollmann (TU Hamburg) at CIMSS

The International Workshop on Cryptography, Robustness, and Provably Secure Schemes for Female Young Researchers (CrossFyre), was held in parallel with the ACNS conference, without running a competitive call for papers.

The ACNS 2025 poster session was chaired by Daniel Slamanig. The session featured nine poster presentations and corresponding short poster papers were included in these proceedings. The award for the Best Poster went to Mirko Goldmann, Leonardo Del Bino and Michael Kissner: "A path towards all-optical DDoS detection on encrypted network traffic".

The organizing of the ACNS 2025 workshops was made possible by the joint efforts of many: We thank the authors of all submissions, program chairs of individual workshops, their PC members, and additional reviewers. We acknowledge Springer-Verlag for sponsoring the awards. We thank the ACNS 2025 General Chairs, Stefan Katzenbeisser and Johannes Kinder, along with all members of their organizing team. The ACNS 2025 workshop chair would like to acknowledge Jianying Zhou for his guidance and suggestions.

Last but not least, we thank all speakers, session chairs and attendees for their contribution to the success of the ACNS 2025 satellite workshops.

June 2025   Mark Manulis

SCI 2025

Sixth ACNS Workshop on Secure Cryptographic Implementation

Program Chairs

Jingqiang Lin	University of Science and Technology of China, China
Bo Luo	University of Kansas, USA

Program Committee

Florian Caullery	HENSOLDT Cyber GmbH, Germany
Bo Chen	Michigan Technological University, USA
Yikang Chen	Chinese University of Hong Kong, China
Jiankuo Dong	Nanjing University of Posts and Telecommunications, China
Haixin Duan	Tsinghua University, China
Shanqing Guo	Shandong University, China
Honggang Hu	University of Science and Technology of China, China
Shijie Jia	Chinese Academy of Sciences, China
Rongxing Lu	Queen's University, Canada
Bingyu Li	Beihang University, China
Fengjun Li	University of Kansas, USA
Chunli Lv	China Agricultural University, China
Kui Ren	Zhejiang University, China
Jun Shao	Zhejiang Gongshang University, China
Ruisheng Shi	Beijing University of Posts and Telecommunications, China
Shifeng Sun	Shanghai Jiao Tong University, China
Qiang Tang	University of Sydney, Australia
An Wang	Beijing Institute of Technology, China
Ding Wang	Nankai University, China
Juan Wang	Wuhan University, China
Bowen Xu	Ningbo University, China
Fangyu Zheng	Chinese Academy of Sciences, China
Cong Zuo	Beijing Institute of Technology, China

Additional Reviewers

Song Bian
Long Chen
Wangchen Dai
Peigen Li
Jiqiang Lu
Yuan Ma
Wenlun Pan
Chenyang Tu
Licheng Wang
Yongjuan Wang
Weijing You
Bin Zhang

PrivCrypt 2025

First International Workshop on Foundations and Applications of Privacy-Enhancing Cryptography

Program Chairs

Lucjan Hanzlik	CISPA Helmholtz Center for Information Security, Germany
Daniel Slamanig	Universität der Bundeswehr München, Germany

Program Committee

Behzad Abdolmaleki	University of Sheffield, UK
Renas Bacho	CISPA Helmholtz Center for Information Security, Germany
Olivier Blazy	École Polytechnique, France
Jan Bobolz	University of Edinburgh, UK
Sofía Celi	Brave Software, USA
Valerio Cini	Bocconi University, Italy
Bernardo David	IT University of Copenhagen, Denmark
Thomas den Hollander	Universität der Bundeswehr München, Germany
Jesko Dujmovic	CISPA Helmholtz Center for Information Security, Germany
Scott Griffy	Brown University, USA
Shuichi Katsumata	PQShield & AIST, Japan
Stephan Krenn	AIT Austrian Institute of Technology, Austria
Mirosław Kutyłowski	NASK – National Research Institute, Poland
Omid Mir	AIT Austrian Institute of Technology, Austria
Eugenio Paracucchi	CISPA Helmholtz Center for Information Security, Germany
Octavio Perez Kempner	NTT Social Informatics Laboratories, Japan
Andy Rupp	University of Luxembourg, Luxembourg
Olivier Sanders	Orange Labs, France
Mahdi Sedaghat	KU Leuven, Belgium

Tjerand Silde	Norwegian University of Science and Technology, Norway
Erkan Tairi	ENS Paris, France
Chenzhi Zhu	University of Washington, USA

Additional Reviewers

Dung Bui

SPIQE 2025

First Workshop on Secure Protocol Implementations in the Quantum Era

Program Chairs

Kenneth G. Paterson	ETH Zurich, Switzerland
Juraj Somorovsky	Paderborn University, Germany

Program Committee

Marcus Brinkmann	Ruhr University Bochum, Germany
Sofía Celi	Brave, USA
Chitchanok Chuengsatiansup	University of Klagenfurt, Austria
Tibor Jager	University of Wuppertal, Germany
Franziskus Kiefer	Cryspen, Germany
Yong Li	Huawei, China
Robert Merget	Technology Innovation Institute, United Arab Emirates
Johannes Mittmann	Federal Office for Information Security (BSI), Germany
Thyla van der Merwe	Google, USA
Jörg Schwenk	Ruhr University Bochum, Germany
Douglas Stebila	University of Waterloo, Canada
Filippo Valsorda	https://filippo.io, USA

Contents – Part II

SCI – Secure Cryptographic Implementation

Improved PACD-Based Attacks on RSA-CRT: Breaking the Signature
Verification Countermeasure 3
   Guillaume Barbu, Laurent Grémy, and Roch Lescuyer

One Time is Enough: Chosen-Ciphertext Side-Channel Attack
on ML-KEM Cryptosystems 23
   *Yuhan Qian, Jing Gao, Yuchen Zhong, Yaoling Ding, Jingjie Wu,
Weiping Gong, Zihe Lin, and An Wang*

A Review of Lattice Cryptography Attack Cost Model 41
   Xi Hu, Yunfei Cao, and Hong Xiang

Exploring the HTTPS OCSP Ecosystem: A Comprehensive Study 61
   HengSheng Wang, ShuShang Wen, and Wei Wang

Differential Fault Analysis Against White-Box SM4 Implementations 81
   Liangju Zhao, Luoqi Chen, Yufeng Tang, and Zheng Gong

Leveled Software Implementation of Polka and Comparison
with Uniformly Masked Kyber 101
   *Thibaud Schoenauen, Clément Hoffmann, Charles Momin,
Thomas Peters, and François-Xavier Standaert*

Research on the Security Estimation Framework for Code-Based Public
Key Cryptography Algorithms 118
   Haoyue Fu, Yunfei Cao, Hong Xiang, and Congyi Zhang

Paper Document Anti-counterfeiting System Based on Digital Signatures
and Image Processing 132
   Yiyan Zhao, Jiwu Jing, Junlin He, Fangyu Zheng, and Chunjing Kou

PQMagic: Towards Secure and Efficient Post Quantum Cryptography
Implementations 152
   Yituo He, Xinpeng Hao, Juanru Li, and Yu Yu

Stateless Hash-Based Signatures for Post-Quantum Security Keys 173
   Ruben Gonzalez

ChatGPT as Preprocessing Agents: A Case Study on Cryptographic
Side-Channel Analysis 193
    Zhen Li, Anjiang Liu, An Wang, and WeiJia Wang

Improved Functional Bootstrapping of SM4 for Hybrid Homomorphic
Encryption 211
    Jin Peng, Dachao Wang, and Zheng Gong

RCE-HVE: Plausible Deniability Against Multi-snapshot Adversaries
with Amplified Storage 229
    Haoyang Xing, Chongyu Long, Anda Che, Fangyu Zheng, and Jiwu Jing

PrivCrypt – Foundations and Applications of Privacy-Enhancing Cryptography

Enhancing E-Voting with Multiparty Class Group Encryption 251
    Michele Battagliola, Giuseppe D'Alconzo, Andrea Gangemi, and Chiara Spadafora

Hierarchical Identity-Based Matchmaking Encryption 274
    Sohto Chiku, Keisuke Hara, and Junji Shikata

Silentium: Implementation of a Pseudorandom Correlation Generator
for Beaver Triples 296
    Vincent Rieder

Towards Privacy and Integrity: SNARK-Driven Verifiable FHE
for Outsourced Computation 318
    Rohitkumar R. Upadhyay, Sahadeo Padhye, Rajeev Anand Sahu, and Vishal Saraswat

SPIQE – Secure Protocol Implementations in the Quantum Era

Public Key Linting for ML-KEM and ML-DSA 337
    Evangelos Karatsiolis, Franziskus Kiefer, Juliane Krämer, Mirjam Loiero, Christian Tobias, and Maximiliane Weishäupl

Author Index 363

SCI – Secure Cryptographic Implementation

Improved PACD-Based Attacks on RSA-CRT
Breaking the Signature Verification Countermeasure

Guillaume Barbu[1], Laurent Grémy[1], and Roch Lescuyer[2(✉)]

[1] IDEMIA, Pessac, France
{guillaume.barbu,laurent.gremy}@idemia.com
[2] IDEMIA, Courbevoie, France
roch.lescuyer@idemia.com

Abstract. In this work, we use some recent developments in lattice-based cryptanalytic tools to revisit a fault attack on RSA-CRT signatures based on the Partial Approximate Common Divisor (PACD) problem. By reducing the PACD to a Hidden Number Problem (HNP) instance, we decrease the number of required faulted bits from 32 to 7 in the case of a 1024-bit RSA. With this improvement, we show that fault countermeasures based on the verification of the signature before returning it are no longer efficient. We successfully apply the attack to RSA instances up to 8192-bit. Finally, we evaluate the impact of side-channel countermeasures against this attack. The reduction from PACD to HNP might be of independent interest.

Keywords: Fault attacks · Lattice reductions · RSA-CRT · PACD · HNP · BDD with Predicate

1 Introduction

In this work, we leverage some recent advances in lattice-based attacks together with a problem reduction to break RSA-CRT signatures. In order to understand these recent advances and the problem we target, we start by surveying the usage of lattices in cryptography, in particular their use to break ECDSA, before turning our attention to RSA-CRT signatures and introducing our contributions.

Lattice reduction algorithms aim at transforming a given lattice basis into a reduced form, typically resulting in shorter and more orthogonal basis vectors. By doing so, lattice reductions facilitate the resolution of difficult problems, such as finding the shortest vector in a lattice (Shortest Vector Problem, SVP) or a vector in the lattice particularly close to another vector (Closest Vector Problem, CVP). Notably, lattice reduction algorithms like LLL [29] and BKZ [46] have found widespread applications due to their efficiency and effectiveness in reducing lattice bases [21,31,45,46]. The field of lattice reduction is still very active. For instance, recently, Ryan and Heninger proposed a novel algorithm [44] that allows to reduce lattices of a very large dimension which were previously considered out of reach, along with a public implementation called flatter [43].

A well-known application of lattices as a cryptanalytic tool is to break the ECDSA signature scheme, through a reduction to the Hidden Number Problem (HNP). The latter is to determine an integer α given many samples (a_i, t_i) where $a_i + k_i = \alpha \cdot t_i \mod N$ for which we know that $k_i < 2^l$ for some bound l, N being a public modulus. Considering an ad-hoc lattice, an HNP instance can be viewed as a CVP instance. It allows to break ECDSA signatures when a few bits of the nonce are known [34]. Indeed, an ECDSA signature (r, s) is computed as $s = k^{-1} \cdot (h + r \cdot d) \mod N$ where d is the secret key, N is the curve order, r is the x-coordinate of $[k]G$, G is the curve base point, k is the nonce and h a (hash of a) message. If we know the most significant bits u of the nonce $k = u \cdot 2^l + v$, where $v < 2^l$, for an ECDSA signature (r, s) on a message h, we have that:

$$(-s^{-1} \cdot h + u \cdot 2^l) + v = d \cdot (s^{-1} \cdot r) \mod N,$$

which is an HNP instance for the secret key d. Depending on the number of signatures and the number of known bits, such an instance might be tractable.

Bounded Distance Decoding (BDD) is a variant of CVP. It consists in finding a vector close to another vector with the additional guarantee that the target vector is not too far from a lattice element. Recently, the authors of [3] note that in some applications there is a mean to check whether the valid solution is one of the vectors returned by the lattice reduction. Hence the idea of adding a *predicate* check inside the lattice algorithm. This is called the BDD with predicate approach. In the case of the ECDSA scheme, one can check that a value α is a valid solution, since the public key $(G, P = [d]G)$ is available. The predicate in this case is basically a check that the public key is compatible with the value α, namely a check that $P \stackrel{?}{=} [\alpha]G$.

In this paper, we turn our attention to RSA signatures [42]. Given a public modulus N, a private key d and a message m, it is well-known that the generation of an RSA signature $s = m^d \mod N$ can also be computed by the so-called CRT (Chinese Remainder Theorem) trick [40] as

$$s = s_q + q \cdot [(s_p - s_q) \cdot i_q \mod p],$$

where $s_p = m^d \mod p$ and $s_q = m^d \mod q$ are the results of the modular exponentiations of the message modulo p and q, the two secret factors of the RSA modulus N, respectively, and i_q the inverse of q modulo p.

Such signatures are particularly vulnerable to fault attacks, which pose a significant threat to the security of cryptographic hardware and embedded software. Since their introduction in [6], where the authors showed that the slightest error during an RSA signature generation can allow one to factorize N with a simple *greatest common divisor* (GCD) computation, fault attacks have found countless applications, breaking all kinds of cryptosystems [8,12,16,30,39]. The literature on fault attacks and countermeasures concerning RSA implementations is very extensive [4,7,9,15,18,22,25,26,28,41,52,54].

At CHES 2012, Fouque et al. proposed a novel exploitation of faulty RSA signatures [19]. The authors see the RSA-CRT recombination as a Partial Approximate Common Divisor (Partial ACD, or PACD). By injecting a fault during one of the modular exponentiations in the RSA-CRT setting, which sets 32 bits of the result to zero, they create a setting where they can solve this PACD instance and, consequently, determine the secret factors p and q.

Contributions and Comparison with Previous Work. We first revisit the fault attack of [19, Section 5] and show that the knowledge of only 7 bits of the partial result is sufficient to factorize a 1024-bit RSA modulus (cf. Table 2 below). In [19, Appendix C, Table 4], 32 bits were needed.

We also discuss our fault model and how to defeat the verification countermeasure. Indeed, as a countermeasure to this attack, the signer might verify the signature before returning it. Reducing the number of known bits to 7 bits makes this countermeasure close to useless, as we will show.

We also show that the attack remains practical on larger RSA instances with experimental tests up to 8192-bit RSA.

In order to achieve this result, we leverage the BDD with predicate approach in the case of the RSA-CRT, and we also invoke the recent flatter tool.

Besides using these recent lattice advances, a key point, compared to [19], of our improvements is a reduction from the PACD problem to the Hidden Number Problem, in which the RSA modulus, a.k.a. the special sample of the PACD problem, becomes the modulus of the HNP instance.

After presenting our attack, we analyze this reduction in more detail and note that this is not a general result, but it suffices for the cryptanalytic purpose of our particular case.

Finally, we evaluate the robustness of popular countermeasures in the field of embedded cryptography, exhibiting some interesting solutions based on randomized blinding.

Organisation. After some preliminaries (Sect. 2) on lattices and fault injections, we describe our main procedure to attack RSA-CRT signatures (Sect. 3). Then, we discuss the effect of some standard countermeasures against our attack (Sect. 4) before we conclude (Sect. 5).

2 Preliminaries

2.1 Fault Injection

In the context of embedded systems, it is well known that an attacker can manage to skip an instruction or corrupt a machine word (e.g. set it to 0) by applying clock glitches, laser, or electromagnetic (EM) pulses on the targeted device. The exact effect of this fault may vary with the CPU architecture and the parameters of the fault injection medium. It is easy to imagine that on a 32-bit CPU, skipping an instruction may result in setting a 32-bit register to 0. This is the fault model successfully exploited by Fouque et al. in [19].

The literature on fault models demonstrates that more precise faults are achievable. For instance, Moro et al. established fault models using EM fault injections in [33]. By targeting an ARM Cortex-M3 processor executing a load instruction from Non-Volatile Memory (NVM), they showed that the EM pulse voltage can influence the number of faulted bits, ranging from 1 to 32. At CCS'17 [50], the authors also demonstrated with CLKSCREW that fault injections can be performed through software by exploiting energy management mechanisms. They showed that fine-tuning the parameters of the fault injection allows alteration of only a small number of bytes[1] in a RAM buffer, even in this context. Finally, Dutertre et al. expose in [17] the results obtained with a state-of-the-art laser targeting a 28nm CMOS node. By carefully controlling the energy transferred by the laser pulse, they demonstrated that single-bit precision is still achievable on recent technology.

2.2 Lattices

One of the primary tools to solve both the PACD and HNP problems relies on lattices, which are discrete subgroups of $\mathbb{R}^n$. The elements of a full rank-n lattice Λ are the integer linear combinations of $\mathcal{B} = \{\boldsymbol{b}_0, \boldsymbol{b}_1, \ldots, \boldsymbol{b}_{n-1}\}$, where the $\boldsymbol{b}_i$ are linearly independent. The set $\mathcal{B}$ is called a basis of Λ, often represented by a matrix $\mathbf{B}$ for which the rows are the $\boldsymbol{b}_i$. We denote by the application $\mathcal{L}$ the fact that the lattice Λ is generated by the rows of $\mathbf{B}$, i.e. $\Lambda = \mathcal{L}(\mathbf{B})$. There exists infinitely many bases of Λ, but a convenient way to solve hard lattice problems, e.g. Shortest Vector Problem (SVP) or Bounded Distance Decoding (BDD), is to work with reduced bases, informally bases with short orthogonal vectors, which can be obtained using lattice basis reduction algorithms [11,29,36,44,46].

The volume of a lattice Λ is denoted by $\det(\Lambda)$ and is equal to $\det(\mathbf{B})$, which is an invariant of the lattice. For a *random lattice* Λ [1], the Gaussian heuristic $\mathrm{gh}(\Lambda)$ gives a bound for the Euclidean length λ_1 of the shortest non-zero vector

$$\lambda_1 < \mathrm{gh}(\Lambda) = \sqrt{n/(2\pi e)} \det(\Lambda)^{1/n}.$$

A way to get (an approximation of) the shortest vector, and then solve the (approximate) SVP, is to look at the first basis vector returned by a lattice basis reduction algorithm, since usually the output basis is sorted by vector lengths. A (δ, η)-LLL reduced lattice basis [29], where $1/4 < \delta < 1$ and $1/2 < \eta < \sqrt{\delta}$, is composed of a vector $\boldsymbol{b}_0$ for which its Euclidean norm is bounded by

$$\|\boldsymbol{b}_0\| \leq (1/(\delta - \eta^2))^{(n-1)/4} \det(\Lambda)^{1/n} = R^n \det(\Lambda)^{1/n}, \tag{1}$$

where R is the root Hermite factor. The usual choice $\delta = 0.99$ and $\eta = 0.51$ gives $R \approx 1.075$, which is larger than what is practically expected in the average case where $R \approx 1.02$ [35]. The L² algorithm [36] reaches this bound, with a running time of $O(n^{4+\epsilon}(p + \log n)(p + n))$, where p is the size of the entries of the input lattice basis. Recently, Ryan and Heninger introduced the notion of an

---

[1] *"More than 80% of the faults result in 1-3 bytes being corrupted"*.

α-lattice-reduced basis [44], which is similar to a (δ, η)-LLL reduced lattice when $\alpha \approx 2\log_2(R)$ [43]. Such an α-lattice-reduced basis may be computed with the algorithm given in [44], faster than L^2 with a time complexity $O(n^\omega (p+n)^{1+\epsilon})$, where $\omega \in (2,3]$ is the matrix multiplication exponent.

These two polynomial-time algorithms may return for large dimension lattices a short vector not sufficiently accurate compared to the Gaussian heuristic prediction, which may fail to help solving the PACD or HNP problems. It is then needed to use exponential time algorithms. Two are of main interest: the enumeration algorithm, which find a short vector of norm less than $\gamma \cdot \mathrm{gh}(\Lambda)$ in $\gamma^n n^{n/(2e)+o(d)}$ steps [23], and the sieving algorithm which find $\|\boldsymbol{b}_0\| \leq \sqrt{4/3}\,\mathrm{gh}(\Lambda)$ in $2^{0.292+o(1)}$ steps [2,5].

Both algorithms may be used as SVP oracles inside BKZ [11,45,46] on blocks of dimension k. When BKZ is instantiated with the enumeration algorithm and n is sufficiently large compared to k, BKZ outputs a short vector of norm bounded by Eq. (1) where $R \approx k^{1/(2k)}$ in time $k^{k/(2e)+o(k)}$ [23]. In our context, an interested reader may refer to [3] for technical details. Practically, we can find the use of BKZ with an enumeration algorithm in [51] and BKZ with a sieving algorithm in the companion implementation of [3].

3 Attacking RSA-CRT Signatures Through PACD

In this section, we recall the definition of the ACD problem (Sect. 3.1), the principle of the PACD-based fault attack from [19] and define our attacker setting (Sect. 3.2), describe the state-of-the-art approach to solve the PACD (Sect. 3.3), show how to turn it into an HNP instance (Sect. 3.4), and report on some experiments (Sect. 3.5). Finally, we have a closer look at the impact of our attack on the signature verification countermeasure (Sect. 3.6).

3.1 The Approximate Common Divisor Problem

Informally (a formal definition is given in Sect. 3.4), an ACD instance is given by a set of samples $\{s_i\}_i$ where $s_i = r_i + \alpha \cdot p_i$ sharing the same secret integer α. The r_i values are often smaller than the integers α and p_i, and are viewed as error terms. Thus, each s_i is viewed as an approximate version of a multiple of α, the goal of an attacker being to recover the integer α from the set $\{s_i\}_i$ of approximate multiples. Such an instance is parametrized by the sizes of the target α, and of the r_i and the p_i components.

In the Partial variant of the problem, an exact multiple of the target α is also given (in other words, there exists a sample such that $r_i = 0$). The ACD problem has been thoroughly analysed in [20] where several resolution methods are compared.

3.2 RSA-CRT as a Partial ACD Instance

RSA-CRT Samples. Let us recall the recombination of the partial RSA-CRT signatures. An RSA signature $s = m^d \mod N$ can be computed as:

$$d_q = d \mod (q-1), \qquad d_p = d \mod (p-1), \qquad i_q = q^{-1} \mod p,$$

$$s_q = m^{d_q} \mod q, \qquad s_p = m^{d_p} \mod p, \qquad s = s_q + q \cdot [(s_p - s_q) \cdot i_q \mod p].$$

Gathering several signatures s_i for different m_i can be seen as an instance of the Partial ACD problem using the notation introduced in Sect. 3.1

$$s_i = \underbrace{s_q}_{r_i} + q \cdot \underbrace{[(s_p - s_q) \cdot i_q \mod p]}_{p_i}, \qquad (2)$$

where the prime factor q is the target integer, and where the special sample for which $r_i = 0$ is the public modulus N (which is indeed an exact multiple of q).

Attacker Setting. If an attacker were capable of knowing – or forcing – the most significant bits of s_q to a known value, the problem would become tractable.

We will assume in the following that an arbitrary number of bits of s_q can be faulted. Let $\tilde{s}$ be a signature for which we know that the Most Significant Bits (MSB) of $\tilde{s}_q$ are known. For simplicity, let us consider that they are null. For instance, we can consider the case of a fault injection that sets the most significant bits of s_q to zero, leading to a faulty $\tilde{s}_q$. We get the following relation for the faulty signature $\tilde{s}$:

$$\tilde{s} = \tilde{s}_q + q \cdot [(s_p - s_q) \cdot i_q \mod p].$$

Our fault imposes that $\tilde{s}_q < \frac{q}{2^l}$ for some l. With a sufficient number of signatures, it becomes possible to solve the Partial ACD and thus recover the target value q and the factorization of the RSA modulus N.

We note that a direct exploitation of such a fault is possible if $\tilde{s}_q$ is completely zeroized. In this case, computing the greatest common divisor of N and $\tilde{s}$ reveals the prime factor q.

In the rest of this section, we bound p and q such that they are η-bit primes, then the p_i are at most η-bit integers. We also bound r_i to be a ρ-bit integer, that is $\rho = \eta - l$.

3.3 The Simultaneous Diophantine Approximation Approach

Several methods are described in the state-of-the-art to solve ACD instances [20]. We can cite the Simultaneous Diophantine Approximation (SDA) approach [24], the Orthogonal based (OL) approach [37], and the Multivariate polynomial (MP) approach [13].

In our case, we choose to pick the SDA approach, for the following reasons. On the one hand, according to [20], the MP approach does not outperform the other approaches. On the other hand, the condition for success of the OL approach given in [20, Section 4] is not met in our particular case for reasonable RSA-CRT parameters and number of known bits.

According to the SDA approach, we let $\mathcal{L}(\mathbf{M})$ be the lattice in $\mathbb{Z}^{t+1}$ generated by the rows of the matrix

$$\mathbf{M} = \begin{pmatrix} 2^\rho & s_1 & \cdots & s_t \\ & -s_0 & & \\ & & \ddots & \\ & & & -s_0 \end{pmatrix}.$$

We note that $\mathcal{L}(\mathbf{M})$ contains the vector

$$\begin{aligned} \boldsymbol{v} &= (p_0, p_1, p_2, \ldots, p_t) \cdot \mathbf{M}, \\ &= (2^\rho \cdot p_0, p_0 \cdot s_1 - s_0 \cdot p_1, p_0 \cdot s_2 - s_0 \cdot p_2, \ldots, p_0 \cdot s_t - s_0 \cdot p_t), \\ &= (2^\rho \cdot p_0, p_0 \cdot r_1 - r_0 \cdot p_1, p_0 \cdot r_2 - r_0 \cdot p_2, \ldots, p_0 \cdot r_t - r_0 \cdot p_t), \end{aligned}$$

since $p_0 \cdot s_i - p_i \cdot s_0 = p_0 \cdot (q \cdot p_i + r_i) - p_i (q \cdot p_0 + r_0) = p_0 \cdot r_i - p_i \cdot r_0$. The Gaussian heuristic let us expect that the shortest vector in $\mathcal{L}(\mathbf{M})$ has norm close to

$$\sqrt{\frac{t+1}{2\pi e}} \cdot 2^\rho \cdot (s_0{}^t)^{1/(t+1)} \approx \sqrt{t+1} \cdot 2^{(\rho + 2 \cdot t \cdot \eta)/(t+1)}.$$

Depending on ρ, we can then expect that $\boldsymbol{v}$ is revealed by reducing $\mathcal{L}(\mathbf{M})$. This will give a candidate value for p_0 which will in turn allows to recover the target value $q = (s_0 - (s_0 \bmod p_0))/p_0$.

We further experiment that to maximize our chances of success, it is desirable to select the largest value s_i as s_0 (the one on the diagonal of $\mathcal{L}(\mathbf{M})$). Indeed, the larger s_0, the larger the determinant of $\mathcal{L}(\mathbf{M})$, and hence the larger the Gaussian heuristic bound. In our context, we know that all the $s_i < N$, and that N is an exact multiple of q. This lets us update our lattice basis $\mathbf{M}$ as follows

$$\mathbf{M} = \begin{pmatrix} 2^\rho & s_1 & \cdots & s_t \\ & -N & & \\ & & \ddots & \\ & & & -N \end{pmatrix},$$

and our expected small vector is then $\boldsymbol{v} = (2^\rho \cdot q, q \cdot r_1, q \cdot r_2, \ldots, q \cdot r_t)$, since $N = q \cdot p_0 + r_0$, where $p_0 = p$ and $r_0 = 0$.

3.4 The Hidden Number Problem Is Back

We now show how our PACD instance can heuristically be viewed as an HNP instance, and give a more formal analysis of this reduction.

Using the HNP in Our Attack Setting. Interestingly, the last basis $\mathbf{M}$ is similar to a basis generally used to solve HNP instances, up to a different labelling of the lines and columns of the matrix. Indeed we can also see our problem as an HNP instance. Multiplying the terms of Eq. (2) by p we have

$$s_i \cdot p = r_i \cdot p + N \cdot p_i.$$

And thus when r_i is bounded by $q/2^l$, we observe that

$$s_i \cdot p \bmod N < N/2^l,$$

where the $(s_i)_i$ are known, and p is the target hidden number. According to the Gaussian heuristic, the shortest vector in the lattice is expected to have norm

$$\mathrm{gh}(\mathcal{L}(\mathbf{M})) \leq \sqrt{\frac{t+1}{2\pi e}} (N^t \cdot 2^\rho)^{1/(t+1)}.$$

We can then study the expectation for the norm of the target vector v, to assess our chance of success depending on the number of known bits. In [20], the authors have already proved that in the generic ACD setting,

$$\mathbb{E}(\|v\|^2) < 0.47 \cdot \frac{\sqrt{t+1}}{q} \cdot 2^{\rho-1+\gamma}.$$

In our setting, the main differences are that $p_0 = p$, $r_0 = 0$ and the r_i are taken from $[0, 2^\rho)$, whereas in [20] they are taken from $(-2^\rho, 2^\rho)$. We then have

$$\mathbb{E}(\|v\|^2) = \mathbb{E}\left(\sum_{i=1}^{t}(q \cdot r_i)^2 + (q \cdot 2^{\rho+1})^2\right) = t \cdot q^2 \cdot \mathbb{E}(r_i^2) + q^2 \cdot 2^{2 \cdot \rho + 2}, \text{ and}$$

$$\mathbb{E}(r_i^2) = \frac{1}{2^{\rho+1}} \cdot \sum_{i=0}^{2^{\rho+1}} i^2 = \frac{1}{2^{\rho+1}} \cdot \left(\frac{1}{3} \cdot 2^{3\rho+3} + \frac{1}{3} \cdot 2^\rho + 2^{2 \cdot \rho+1}\right),$$

$$= \frac{1}{3} \cdot 2^{2 \cdot \rho + 2} + \frac{1}{6} + 2^\rho \approx \frac{1}{3} \cdot 2^{2 \cdot \rho + 2}. \text{ So}$$

$$\mathbb{E}(\|v\|^2) \approx t \cdot q^2 \cdot \frac{1}{3} \cdot 2^{2 \cdot \rho + 2} + q^2 \cdot 2^{2 \cdot \rho + 2} \approx \frac{1}{3} \cdot (t+1) \cdot q^2 \cdot 2^{2 \cdot \rho + 2},$$

and Jensen's inequality shows that $\mathbb{E}(\|v\|) \leq \sqrt{\mathbb{E}(\|v\|^2)} \approx 0.58 \cdot \sqrt{t+1} \cdot q \cdot 2^{\rho+1}$.

We can then confront the Gaussian heuristic with the expected norm of our target vector for different lattice dimensions and number of known bits. This is illustrated in Fig. 1 for the case of an RSA-1024 modulus and an RSA-4096 modulus. According to the curves, we can then expect to have a successful attack with a minimal number of signatures summarized in Table 1.

From a Reductionist Point of View. In this subsection, we have a closer look at the reduction we used in the previous subsection to solve the Partial ACD

Table 1. Expectation of the minimal number of signatures with respect to the number of known bits.

	32 bits	24 bits	16 bits	8 bits	4 bits
RSA-1024	16	22	35	79	214
RSA-4096	68	94	146	344	—

problem. Let us begin with some notations. Let n be a modulus[2]. Let $x \in \mathbb{Z}$ be an integer. We denote by $\lfloor x \rfloor_n$ the value x modulo n in the range $[0, n)$ and by $|x|_n$ the value x modulo n in the range $\mathbb{Z} \cap [-\frac{n}{2}, \frac{n}{2})$. The set $\text{MSB}_{\ell,n}(x)$ is the set of integers u satisfying $|x - u|_n < n/2^{\ell+1}$.

Let $\gamma, \eta, \rho \in \mathbb{N}$ be three integers. Let β be an η-bit odd integer. We have: $2^{\eta-1} < \beta < 2^\eta$. Let $\mathcal{D}$ be the following distribution, parametrized by γ, ρ.

$$\mathcal{D}_{\gamma,\rho}(\beta) := \{\beta \cdot m + r \mid m \leftarrow \mathbb{Z} \cap [0, 2^\gamma/\beta), r \leftarrow \mathbb{Z} \cap (-2^\rho, 2^\rho)\}.$$

Now we can formally state the ACD and Partial ACD problems, following [20], where *polynomial* means polynomial in the parameter η (in practice we have $\gamma = O(\eta)$).

Problem 1 (ACD). Given polynomially many samples x_i from $\mathcal{D}_{\gamma,\rho}(\beta)$, compute β.

Problem 2 (PACD). Given polynomially many samples x_i from $\mathcal{D}_{\gamma,\rho}(\beta)$, and a sample $x_0 = \beta \cdot m_0$ for a uniformly chosen $m_0 \in \mathbb{Z} \cap [0, 2^\gamma/\beta)$, compute β.

Let us now have a look at the HNP problem. Let α be a value in $\mathbb{Z}_n$, for a public modulus n. Let $\ell \in \mathbb{N}$ be an integer. Let $\mathcal{H}$ be the following distribution, parametrized by n and ℓ.

$$\mathcal{H}_{n,\ell}(\alpha) := \{(t_i, u_i) \mid t_i \leftarrow [1, n), s_i = \lfloor t_i \cdot \alpha \rfloor_n, u_i \in \text{MSB}_{\ell,n}(s_i)\}.$$

The HNP is then formulated as follows, where polynomially means here polynomial in the size of α.

Problem 3 (HNP). Given polynomially many samples (t_i, u_i) from $\mathcal{H}_{n,\ell}(\alpha)$, compute α.

The reduction from PACD to HNP we have in mind is the following one. Let $\mathcal{B}$ be an algorithm that solves the (n, ℓ)-HNP problem in time t with probability ϵ. We want to construct an algorithm $\mathcal{A}$ that solves the (γ, η, ρ)-PACD problem in time t' with probability ϵ', for some quantities to be defined.

Let $X := \{x_i\}$ be a set of samples for the Partial ACD problem. Let $n = x_0$. Construct a set of HNP samples $\{(t_i, u_i)\}$ as $t_i = x_i$, $u_i = 0$. Give the set of

---

[2] Throughout this section, we denote the modulus n instead of N since we try here to be more general than the RSA case.

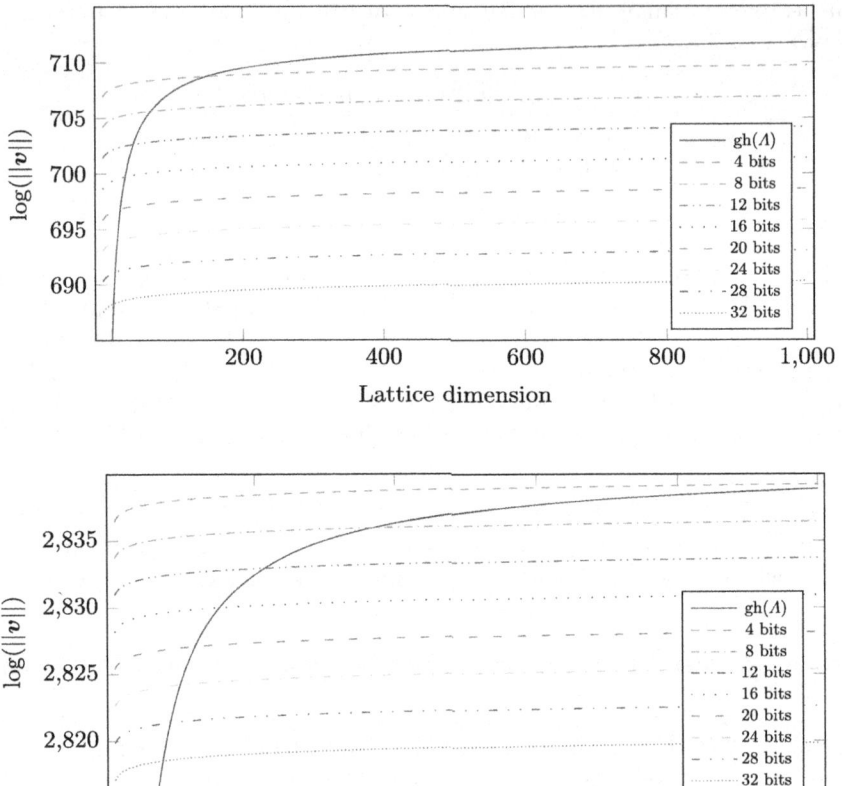

Fig. 1. Evolution of the Gaussian heuristic for various lattice dimensions (plain), compared to the evolution of the expected norm for the target vector (with different styles) for different number of known bits (from 4 to 32), for RSA-1024 (above) and RSA-4096 (below).

samples to $\mathcal{B}$, which eventually returns a value α. If α divides x_0, then algorithm $\mathcal{A}$ sets $\beta = x_0/\alpha$, otherwise $\mathcal{A}$ returns $\bot$.

For some constraints on the parameter this reduction is correct. Indeed, we know that $x_0 = \beta \cdot m_0$. If we multiply each sample x_i by m_0, we get that $x_i \cdot m_0 = \beta \cdot m_i \cdot m_0 + r_i \cdot m_0$. If we have that $|r_i| < 2^\rho < 2^{\eta-1}$, then we have that $\lfloor x_i \cdot m_0 \rfloor_n = r_i \cdot m_0$. We can bound this quantity by $r_i \cdot m_0 < 2^{\gamma+\rho}/\beta < 2^{\gamma+\rho-\eta+1}$. Hence, by setting $u_i = 0$, we have that $u_i \in \text{MSB}_{\ell,n}(m_0)$ for $n = x_0$ and $\ell < \delta + \eta - \gamma - \rho - 3$ where δ is the size in bits of x_0. Indeed:

$$\lfloor x_i \cdot m_0 \rfloor_n < 2^{\gamma+\rho-\eta+1} < 2^{\delta-1-\ell-1} < x_0/2^{\ell+1}.$$

Therefore, the $\{(t_i, u_i)\}$ are samples targetting the unknown $\alpha = m_0$. Once α is found, the target β equals x_0/α.

The problem here is that we cannot argue on the probability of success ϵ' of $\mathcal{A}$. Let us explain why. The HNP problem asks the t_i to be uniformly random. However, our t_i are clearly not uniformly random. Moreover, their structure is what makes them possibly solvable, and it is hard to randomize them before giving them to $\mathcal{B}$ without breaking this structure. So we cannot claim a reduction between those problems, in all their generality.

However, in our case we have some additional assumptions. In particular, the partial ACD modulus x_0 is greater than all the other x_i samples, which are partial RSA signatures. And, even if it is hard to argue about the distribution of the signatures, they are sufficiently random in $\mathbb{Z}_{x_0}$ so that our reduction heuristically works in our case.

3.5 Experiments

Experiments with `flatter`. The experiments with `flatter` [44] were straightforward, we simply used `flatter` to perform the lattice reduction. We repeated our attack 100 times for random RSA keys of different sizes (1024, 2048, 4096 and 8192 bits) and an increasing number of faulty signatures, and hence lattice dimensions (from 500 to 2500 by step 500). Our goal is to determine the minimal number of known bits to have a successful attack for the each key size. The results are summarized in Table 2.

Table 2. Attack success rates depending on the RSA key size, the number of known bits and the number of faulty signatures.

	RSA-1024	RSA-2048	RSA-4096	RSA-8192
Bits known	7	10	13	20
Nb. of signatures	2500	1500^a	2500	2500
Success rate (%)	63	96	11	70

^{a} The attack did not succeed for 9 known bits and 2000 or 2500 signatures. We did not go beyond 1500 signatures for 10 known bits as the success rate was already close to 100%.

The longest execution runs approximatively 70h for 100 lattice reductions of a lattice of dimension 2500, and 8192-bit elements (64 cores). Figure 2 shows the evolution of the success rate with respect to the lattice dimension for RSA 1024.

Experiments with BDD with Predicate. The experiments with the code available for BDD with Predicate [3] required some modifications. First, we adapted the code to work for RSA-CRT. We implemented a new *Solver* with a specific predicate to check. The predicate in our case is a GCD computation to check that the modulus N can be factorized by the solution. We also troubleshoot precision issues because we work with large integers.

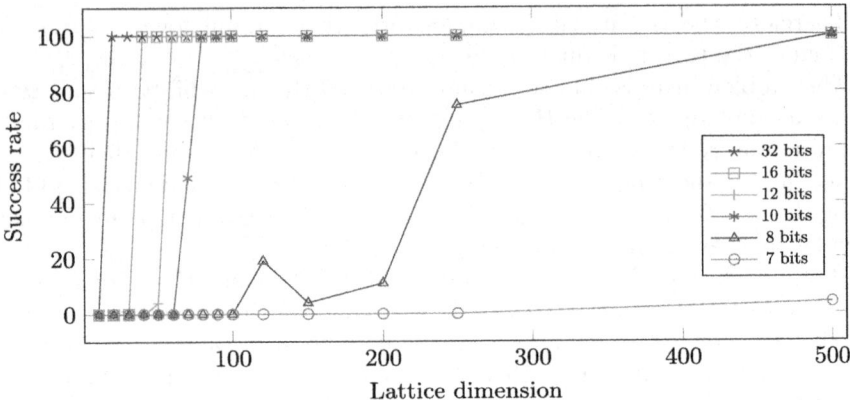

Fig. 2. Evolution of the success rate for 100 iterations when attacking RSA-1024 with a standard lattice reduction using `flatter`.

Figure 3 shows the evolution of the success rate with respect to the lattice dimension for RSA 1024.

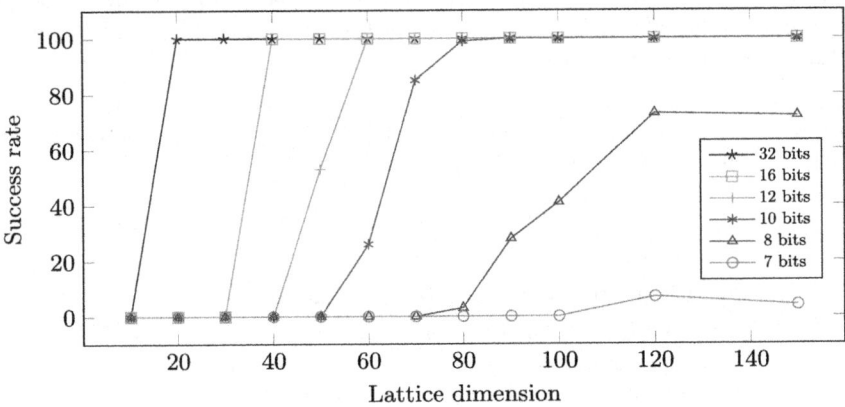

Fig. 3. Evolution of the success rate for 100 iterations when attacking RSA-1024 with the BDD with Predicate approach.

Comparison Between `flatter` and BDD with Predicate. Fig. 4 shows the difference between our experiments with `flatter` as reduction, and our experiments with the BDD with Predicate approach. When less bits are available, we see a clear gain when we add a predicate into the lattice reduction. This is understandable, given that the algorithms used in the BDD with Predicate code ensures a better reduction quality than `flatter`'s. On the other hand, the capacity of `flatter` to handle lattices of larger dimension allows to reach a 100% success rate when 8 bits are known. Nonetheless, we reach our lower bound in terms of required number of known bits with both approaches. Indeed, the attack succeeds with 7 known bits, while 32 known bits were used in the attack of [19].

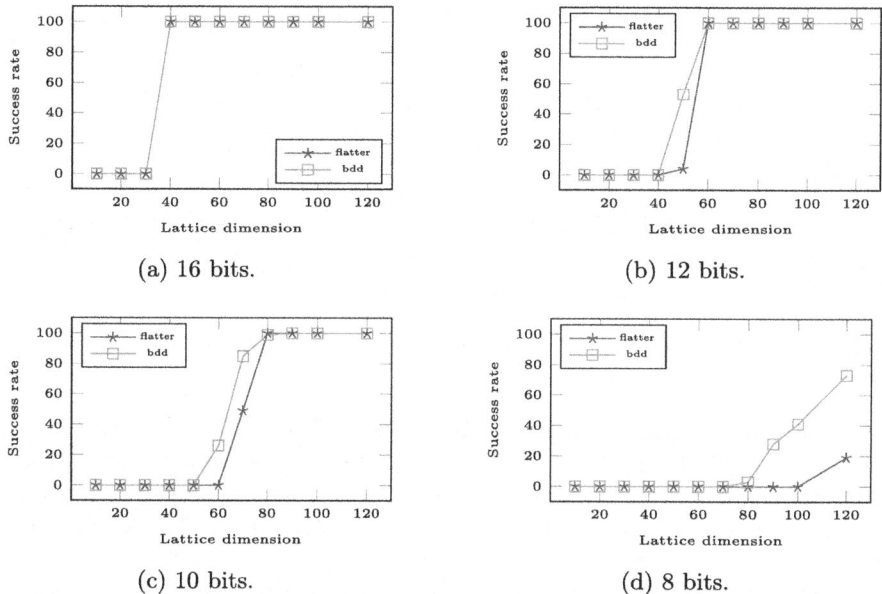

(a) 16 bits.

(b) 12 bits.

(c) 10 bits.

(d) 8 bits.

Fig. 4. Comparison between applying a standard reduction with `flatter` and the BDD with Predicate approaches.

Handling More Cases. For simplicity, we focused on the case where the MSB of the s_q partial signature is null. Standard techniques can extend this approach to cases with known MSBs or LSBs. Indeed, the BDD with Predicate repository has been adapted to handle such cases [47]. The approach involves reducing the problem to the MSB-at-0 case by (i) subtracting the known value in the MSB case, and (ii) subtracting the known value and multiplying by the inverse of 2^w in the LSB case.

In addition, we note that other variables can be targeted by our attack. Obviously, our analysis still applies when considering the other partial signature s_p. But one can also consider to fault m_q (or m_p), the reduction modulo q (or modulo p) of the message m before the exponentiation since one can also use the relation

$$\widetilde{s}^e = \widetilde{m_q} + q \cdot [(m_p - \widetilde{m_q}) \cdot i_q \bmod p].$$

3.6 Breaking the Signature Verification Countermeasure

A common countermeasure to protect RSA-CRT implementations from fault attacks consists in verifying if the signature is valid before returning it. Indeed, this is not an expensive process as it just requires to elevate s to the power of the public exponent e modulo N and check if the result is equal to the message. When the verification fails, the device either

1. returns an empty signature,
2. returns a sequence of random numbers,
3. or repeats the signing operation without the CRT trick[3].

In all cases, the attacker can tell whether the countermeasure has altered the result since it is either

1. empty,
2. an invalid signature (and she can use the public key to verify it for herself),
3. returned after a longer time than usual.

In the context of a fault attack that forces the l MSBs of s_q to 0, the signature might not be faulted with a probability of 2^{-l}. This occurs when the l MSBs of s_q *actually are* 0, a scenario referred to as a Safe-Error attack in the literature [53]. In such cases, despite the verification countermeasure, one out of 2^l signatures is released to the attacker. Consequently, the attacker only needs to fault 2^l times more signatures to collect the required number of faulted signatures.

In [19], the authors faulted 32 bits. The probability of a Safe-Error occurring in this case is extremely low: 2^{-32}. Executing enough operations to obtain the required number of Safe-Error *faulty* signatures would require an impractical amount of time. For example, consider an attack on a smartcard. According to the timings reported by JCAlgTest[4] in [49], a 1024-bit CRT RSA signature process takes an average of 100 milliseconds. An attacker would therefore need $17 \times 2^{32} \times 100.10^{-3}$ seconds – more than 230 years. As a result, the verification countermeasure is effective in this context.

Our reduction in the number of faulted bits significantly lowers the time required for a successful attack. Specifically, generating 2,500 Safe-Error *faulty* signatures with 7 known bits would take $2500 \times 2^7 \times 100.10^{-3}$ seconds – less than 9 h. In this case, the verification countermeasure becomes ineffective.

Figure 5 illustrates the expected time required to execute the attack when the verification countermeasure is implemented.

To illustrate the significance of the time required for an attack to succeed, Fig. 5 includes three time thresholds from the *Application of Attack Potential to Smartcards and Similar Devices* [48], a guideline used in the context of security evaluations within the Common Criteria[5] framework to assess attack difficulty.

---

[3] This is what is done in OpenSSL library for instance, cf `rsa_ossl_mod_exp` function in https://github.com/openssl/openssl/blob/master/crypto/rsa/rsa_ossl.c.
[4] https://github.com/crocs-muni/JCAlgTest.
[5] https://www.commoncriteriaportal.org.

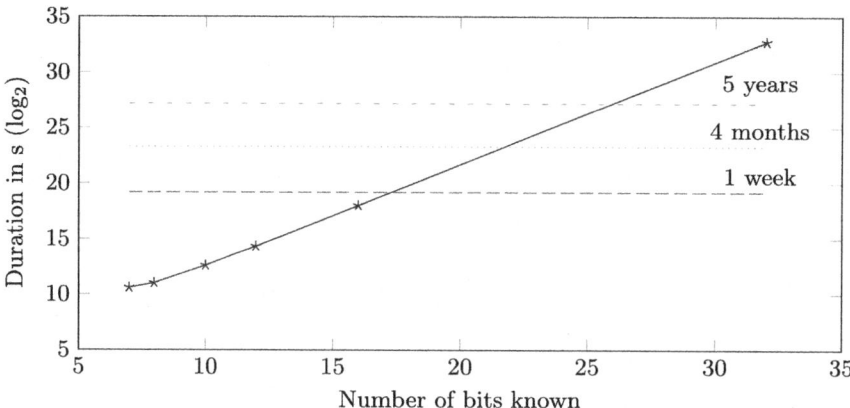

Fig. 5. Duration of the attack depending on the number of known bits.

The elapsed time needed for a successful attack is one of the key factors used to rate its feasibility.

After one week, an attack is deemed *Not practical* for individual cards, which are typically reported lost or stolen within days. After 4 months, an attack gets the maximum rating for the *elapsed time* factor. If the elapsed time exceeds 5 years, the attack is considered *Not practical* in general scenarios. In the remainder of this article, we consider the verification countermeasure effective if the 4-month threshold is exceeded – i.e. when 24 or more known bits are required for the attack to succeed.

4 Countermeasures

Several countermeasures have been proposed in the literature to protect RSA computations against side-channel attacks. In this section, we review some of them in order to assess their impact on our attack.

4.1 Additive Message Blinding

A popular countermeasure to protect RSA-CRT implementations from side-channel attacks is *additive message blinding* [14]. It may have a negative impact on the attack we present here. For the sake of clarity, we recall this masking scheme before stating how it affects the attack.

We consider that the message is blinded before the exponentiation modulo p' where p' is an extended modulus: $p' = \alpha \cdot p$ for a k-bit random value α. This is done by computing $m_p^\star = m + r_p \cdot p \bmod p'$, where r_p is a k-bit random mask. Then, $m_p^\star$ goes through the modular exponentiation modulo p' to obtain $s_p^\star = m_p^{\star d_p} \bmod p'$. And finally, after doing likewise to compute $s_p^\star$, one can recover the signature as

$$s = (s_q{}^\star + q \cdot [(s_p{}^\star - s_q{}^\star) \cdot i_q \bmod p']) \bmod N.$$

We can still see a relation of the form

$$s \cdot p = s_q{}^\star \cdot p + \lambda N.$$

However, in this case $s_q{}^\star$ is k bits larger than it is without the blinding scheme. As a result, the attacker needs to know k more bits of $s_q{}^\star$. Combined with a verification of the signature before output, this countermeasure can then be efficient against our attack, as long as k is not too small, i.e. $k \geq 16$ considering the limit established in Sect. 3.6.

4.2 Multiplicative Message Blinding

Multiplicative message blinding [27] is another blinding technique that can be found for instance in OpenSSL's implementation [38]. According to this countermeasure, the message is again blinded before the modular exponentiations, but this time it is done by multiplying it by $r^e \bmod N$, with r a random value in $\mathbb{Z}_N^*$. The modular exponentiation is then computed for $m' = m \cdot r^e \bmod N$ as usual

$$s' = s'_q + q \cdot [(s'_p - s'_q) \cdot i_q \bmod p],$$

and the signature is unmasked by multiplying it with the inverse of r. Indeed, we have

$$s' = m'^d = (m \cdot r^e)^d = m^d \cdot r \bmod N,$$

and so

$$s' \cdot r^{-1} = m^d = s \bmod N.$$

In this case, the faulty signature would still be blinded somehow, as $\tilde{s} = \tilde{s'} \cdot r^{-1} \bmod N$, and without the knowledge of r we cannot go any further.

4.3 Montgomery Representation

In 1985, Montgomery introduced a *Modular multiplication without trial division* [32]. This method is efficient when the modulus has no particular form, which is typically the case for RSA and has been widely adopted in various hardware public-key accelerators and cryptographic libraries [38].

Letting the Montgomery radix $R = r^n = 2^{wn}$ (adapted for handling integers of n w-bit words), the Montgomery multiplication takes as input A' and B' (the Montgomery representation of A and B such that $X' = X \cdot R \bmod N$) and returns

$$M(A', B', N) = A' \cdot B' \cdot R^{-1} = C' \bmod N.$$

We can note that the Montgomery representation of X can be obtained by computing $M(X, R^2, N)$, and the way back to the regular representation by $M(\tilde{X}, 1, N)$, and refer the reader to [10, Chapters 2–3] for a deeper view on Montgomery multiplication.

In our case, let us assume that the modular operations are performed in the Montgomery representation. In [19], the authors exploited faults during modular exponentiation using Montgomery arithmetic.

In contrast, we target the recombination of the two sub-exponentiations. Notably, the final two computations in Garner's formula are performed over the integers. Therefore, we assume they are processed in the regular representation. However, if a masking scheme is maintained to protect the recombination, a final modular reduction would be required. This naturally raises questions about the behaviour of our attack if the Montgomery representation were used for this step.

In the case of the multiplicative blinding, the conclusion remains that the mask prevents the attack success. In the case of the additive blinding, the faulty signature is then

$$s' = R\left(s_q{}^\star + q \cdot [(s_p{}^\star - s_q{}^\star) \cdot i_q \bmod p']\right) \bmod N.$$

To return to the regular representation, one must multiply s' by R^{-1} and reduce the result modulo N. Even with the knowledge of the Montgomery constant R, the final modular reduction results in the loss of any information on the value of $s \bmod q$.

5 Conclusion

In this work, we improved an attack against RSA-CRT signatures, using a reduction of the originally formulated problem and recent advances in lattice reductions. Following our approach, the required number of known bits drops from 32 down to 7 for 1024-bit RSA modulus. As exposed, this improvement makes the verification countermeasure alone ineffective. Besides, we have shown that larger instances of RSA can also be targeted by the PACD-based attack. Analysing the effect of standard side-channel countermeasures, we conclude that a combination of the verification of the signature with message blinding stands as a sufficient protection, provided that the random masks are not too small (i.e. at least 16-bit). Additionally, we showed that the Partial ACD problem may be solved by a reduction to the HNP problem, which does not seem to have been noticed yet in the literature and might be of independent interest.

References

1. Ajtai, M.: Generating hard instances of lattice problems (extended abstract). In: Symposium on the Theory of Computing – STOC 1996, pp. 99–108. ACM Press (1996)

2. Albrecht, M.R., Ducas, L., Herold, G., Kirshanova, E., Postlethwaite, E.W., Stevens, M.: The general sieve kernel and new records in lattice reduction. In: Ishai, Y., Rijmen, V. (eds.) EUROCRYPT 2019. LNCS, vol. 11477, pp. 717–746. Springer, Cham (2019). https://doi.org/10.1007/978-3-030-17656-3_25
3. Albrecht, M.R., Heninger, N.: On bounded distance decoding with predicate: breaking the "lattice barrier" for the hidden number problem. In: Canteaut, A., Standaert, F.-X. (eds.) EUROCRYPT 2021. LNCS, vol. 12696, pp. 528–558. Springer, Cham (2021). https://doi.org/10.1007/978-3-030-77870-5_19
4. Aumüller, C., Bier, P., Fischer, W., Hofreiter, P., Seifert, J.-P.: Fault attacks on RSA with CRT: concrete results and practical countermeasures. In: Kaliski, B.S., Koç, K., Paar, C. (eds.) CHES 2002. LNCS, vol. 2523, pp. 260–275. Springer, Heidelberg (2003). https://doi.org/10.1007/3-540-36400-5_20
5. Becker, A., Ducas, L., Gama, N., Laarhoven, T.: New directions in nearest neighbor searching with applications to lattice sieving. In: Symposium on Discrete Algorithms – SODA 2016, pp. 10–24. SIAM (2016)
6. Bellcore: New Threat Model Breaks Crypto Codes. Press Release (1996)
7. Berzati, A., Canovas, C., Goubin, L.: In(security) against fault injection attacks for CRT-RSA implementations. In: Workshop on Fault Diagnosis and Tolerance in Cryptography – FDTC 2008, pp. 101–107. IEEE Computer Society (2008)
8. Biham, E., Shamir, A.: Differential fault analysis of secret key cryptosystems. In: Kaliski, B.S. (ed.) CRYPTO 1997. LNCS, vol. 1294, pp. 513–525. Springer, Heidelberg (1997). https://doi.org/10.1007/BFb0052259
9. Boneh, D., DeMillo, R.A., Lipton, R.J.: On the importance of eliminating errors in cryptographic computations. J. Cryptol. **14**(2), 101–119 (2001)
10. Bos, J.W., Lenstra, A.K. (eds.): Topics in Computational Number Theory Inspired by Peter L. Montgomery. Cambridge University Press (2017)
11. Chen, Y., Nguyen, P.Q.: BKZ 2.0: better lattice security estimates. In: Lee, D.H., Wang, X. (eds.) ASIACRYPT 2011. LNCS, vol. 7073, pp. 1–20. Springer, Heidelberg (2011). https://doi.org/10.1007/978-3-642-25385-0_1
12. Ciet, M., Joye, M.: Elliptic curve cryptosystems in the presence of permanent and transient faults. Des. Codes Cryptogr. **36**(1), 33–43 (2005)
13. Cohn, H., Heninger, N.: Approximate common divisors via lattices. In: Algorithmic Number Theory – ANTS X. The Open Book Series, vol. 1, pp. 271–293 (2013)
14. Coron, J.-S.: Resistance against differential power analysis for elliptic curve cryptosystems. In: Koç, Ç.K., Paar, C. (eds.) CHES 1999. LNCS, vol. 1717, pp. 292–302. Springer, Heidelberg (1999). https://doi.org/10.1007/3-540-48059-5_25
15. Coron, J.-S., Joux, A., Kizhvatov, I., Naccache, D., Paillier, P.: Fault attacks on RSA signatures with partially unknown messages. In: Clavier, C., Gaj, K. (eds.) CHES 2009. LNCS, vol. 5747, pp. 444–456. Springer, Heidelberg (2009). https://doi.org/10.1007/978-3-642-04138-9_31
16. Dusart, P., Letourneux, G., Vivolo, O.: Differential fault analysis on A.E.S. In: Zhou, J., Yung, M., Han, Y. (eds.) ACNS 2003. LNCS, vol. 2846, pp. 293–306. Springer, Heidelberg (2003). https://doi.org/10.1007/978-3-540-45203-4_23
17. Dutertre, J.M., et al.: Laser fault injection at the CMOS 28 nm technology node: an analysis of the fault model. In: Workshop on Fault Diagnosis and Tolerance in Cryptography – FDTC 2018, pp. 1–6. IEEE (2018)
18. Ebeid, N.M., Lambert, R.: A new CRT-RSA algorithm resistant to powerful fault attacks. In: Workshop on Embedded Systems Security – WESS 2010, pp. 1–8. ACM (2010)

19. Fouque, P.A., Guillermin, N., Leresteux, D., Tibouchi, M., Zapalowicz, J.C.: Attacking RSA-CRT signatures with faults on montgomery multiplication. In: Cryptographic Hardware and Embedded Systems – CHES 2012. LNCS, vol. 7428, pp. 447–462. Springer (2012)
20. Galbraith, S.D., Gebregiyorgis, S.W., Murphy, S.: Algorithms for the approximate common divisor problem. LMS J. Comput. Math. **19**(A), 58–72 (2016)
21. Gama, N., Nguyen, P.Q.: Finding short lattice vectors within Mordell's inequality. In: Symposium on Theory of Computing – STOC'08, pp. 207–216. ACM Press (2008)
22. Giraud, C.: An RSA implementation resistant to fault attacks and to simple power analysis. IEEE Trans. Comput. **55**(9), 1116–1120 (2006)
23. Hanrot, G., Stehlé, D.: Improved analysis of Kannan's shortest lattice vector algorithm. In: Menezes, A. (ed.) CRYPTO 2007. LNCS, vol. 4622, pp. 170–186. Springer, Heidelberg (2007). https://doi.org/10.1007/978-3-540-74143-5_10
24. Howgrave-Graham, N.: Approximate integer common divisors. In: Silverman, J.H. (ed.) CaLC 2001. LNCS, vol. 2146, pp. 51–66. Springer, Heidelberg (2001). https://doi.org/10.1007/3-540-44670-2_6
25. Joye, M., Quisquater, J.-J., Bao, F., Deng, R.H.: RSA-type signatures in the presence of transient faults. In: Darnell, M. (ed.) Cryptography and Coding 1997. LNCS, vol. 1355, pp. 155–160. Springer, Heidelberg (1997). https://doi.org/10.1007/BFb0024460
26. Kim, C.H., Quisquater, J.-J.: Fault attacks for CRT based RSA: new attacks, new results, and new countermeasures. In: Sauveron, D., Markantonakis, K., Bilas, A., Quisquater, J.-J. (eds.) WISTP 2007. LNCS, vol. 4462, pp. 215–228. Springer, Heidelberg (2007). https://doi.org/10.1007/978-3-540-72354-7_18
27. Kocher, P.C.: Timing attacks on implementations of Diffie-Hellman, RSA, DSS, and other systems. In: Koblitz, N. (ed.) CRYPTO 1996. LNCS, vol. 1109, pp. 104–113. Springer, Heidelberg (1996). https://doi.org/10.1007/3-540-68697-5_9
28. Lenstra, A.K.: Memo on RSA signature generation in the presence of faults. Technical Report EPFL (1996)
29. Lenstra, A.K., Lesntra, H.W., Lovász, L.: Factoring polynomials with rational coefficients. Matematische Annalen **261**, 366–389 (1982)
30. Luo, P., Fei, Y., Zhang, L., Ding, A.A.: Differential fault analysis of SHA3-224 and SHA3-256. In: Workshop on Fault Diagnosis and Tolerance in Cryptography – FDTC'16, pp. 4–15. IEEE Computer Society (2016)
31. Micciancio, D., Walter, M.: Practical, predictable lattice basis reduction. In: Fischlin, M., Coron, J.-S. (eds.) EUROCRYPT 2016. LNCS, vol. 9665, pp. 820–849. Springer, Heidelberg (2016). https://doi.org/10.1007/978-3-662-49890-3_31
32. Montgomery, P.L.: Modular multiplication without trial division. Math. Comput. **44**(170), 519–521 (1985)
33. Moro, N., Dehbaoui, A., Heydemann, K., Robisson, B., Encrenaz, E.: Electromagnetic fault injection: towards a fault model on a 32-bit microcontroller. In: Workshop on Fault Diagnosis and Tolerance in Cryptography – FDTC'13, pp. 77–88. IEEE Computer Society (2013)
34. Nguyen, P.Q., Shparlinski, I.E.: The insecurity of the elliptic curve digital signature algorithm with partially known nonces. Des. Codes Cryptogr. **30**(2), 201–217 (2003)
35. Nguyen, P.Q., Stehlé, D.: LLL on the average. In: Hess, F., Pauli, S., Pohst, M. (eds.) ANTS 2006. LNCS, vol. 4076, pp. 238–256. Springer, Heidelberg (2006). https://doi.org/10.1007/11792086_18

36. Nguyen, P.Q., Stehlé, D.: An LLL algorithm with quadratic complexity. SIAM J. Comput. **39**(3), 874–903 (2009)
37. Nguyen, P.Q., Stern, J.: The two faces of lattices in cryptology. In: Silverman, J.H. (ed.) CaLC 2001. LNCS, vol. 2146, pp. 146–180. Springer, Heidelberg (2001). https://doi.org/10.1007/3-540-44670-2_12
38. OpenSSL: Cryptography and SSL/TLS toolkit (2024). https://www.openssl.org/
39. Piret, G., Quisquater, J.-J.: A differential fault attack technique against SPN structures, with application to the AES and KHAZAD. In: Walter, C.D., Koç, Ç.K., Paar, C. (eds.) CHES 2003. LNCS, vol. 2779, pp. 77–88. Springer, Heidelberg (2003). https://doi.org/10.1007/978-3-540-45238-6_7
40. Quisquater, J.J., Couvreur, C.: Fast decipherment algorithm for RSA public-key cryptosystem. Electron. Lett. **21**(18), 905–907 (1982)
41. Rauzy, P., Guilley, S.: Countermeasures against high-order fault-injection attacks on CRT-RSA. In: Workshop on Fault Diagnosis and Tolerance in Cryptography – FDTC'14, pp. 68–82. IEEE Computer Society (2014)
42. Rivest, R.L., Shamir, A., Adleman, L.M.: A method for obtaining digital signatures and public-key cryptosystems. Commun. ACM **21**(2), 120–126 (1978)
43. Ryan, K.: flatter, a (f)ast (lat)tice (r)eduction library (2023). https://github.com/keeganryan/flatter
44. Ryan, K., Heninger, N.: Fast practical lattice reduction through iterated compression. In: Advances in Cryptology – CRYPTO'23. LNCS, vol. 14083, pp. 3–36. Springer (2023)
45. Schnorr, C.: A hierarchy of polynomial time lattice basis reduction algorithms. Theoret. Comput. Sci. **53**, 201–224 (1987)
46. Schnorr, C., Euchner, M.: Lattice basis reduction: improved practical algorithms and solving subset sum problems. Math. Program. **66**, 181–199 (1994)
47. Shea, L.: Generalize ECDSA solver to work for arbitrary MSB/LSB (2021). https://github.com/malb/bdd-predicate/pull/6
48. SOG-IS: Application of Attack Potential to Smartcards and Similar Devices. Technical report, Senior Officials Group Information Systems Security (SOG-IS) (2024), version 3.2.1
49. Svenda, P., Kvasnovský, R., Nagy, I., Dufka, A.: Jcalgtest: robust identification metadata for certified smartcards. In: International Conference on Security and Cryptography – SECRYPT'22, pp. 597–604. SCITEPRESS (2022)
50. Tang, A., Sethumadhavan, S., Stolfo, S.J.: CLKSCREW: exposing the perils of security-oblivious energy management. In: USENIX Security Symposium, USENIX'17, pp. 1057–1074. USENIX Association (2017)
51. The FPLLL development team: fplll, a lattice reduction library, Version: 5.4.5 (2023). https://github.com/fplll/fplll
52. Vigilant, D.: RSA with CRT: a new cost-effective solution to thwart fault attacks. In: Oswald, E., Rohatgi, P. (eds.) CHES 2008. LNCS, vol. 5154, pp. 130–145. Springer, Heidelberg (2008). https://doi.org/10.1007/978-3-540-85053-3_9
53. Yen, S., Joye, M.: Checking before output may not be enough against fault-based cryptanalysis. IEEE Trans. Comput. **49**(9), 967–970 (2000)
54. Yen, S.-M., Kim, D., Moon, S.J.: Cryptanalysis of two protocols for RSA with CRT based on fault infection. In: Breveglieri, L., Koren, I., Naccache, D., Seifert, J.-P. (eds.) FDTC 2006. LNCS, vol. 4236, pp. 53–61. Springer, Heidelberg (2006). https://doi.org/10.1007/11889700_5

One Time is Enough: Chosen-Ciphertext Side-Channel Attack on ML-KEM Cryptosystems

Yuhan Qian[1], Jing Gao[2], Yuchen Zhong[1], Yaoling Ding[1(✉)], Jingjie Wu[3(✉)], Weiping Gong[3], Zihe Lin[1], and An Wang[1]

[1] Beijing Institute of Technology, Beijing 100081, China
{qianyuhan,dyl19,1120213514,wanganl}@bit.edu.cn
[2] China Mobile Research Institute, Beijing 100053, China
gaojingyjy@chinamobile.com
[3] Guizhou Police College, Guiyang 550005, China
wjj972@163.com

Abstract. The emergence of quantum computers threatens traditional public key cryptographic algorithms like RSA and ECDSA, driving the development of post-quantum cryptography. Among post-quantum cryptography approaches, lattice-based cryptography is a key candidate for securing embedded systems. However, post-quantum cryptography implementations remain vulnerable to side-channel attacks, which exploit physical leakages such as timing, power, and electromagnetic emissions. In this paper, we propose a one-time chosen-ciphertext simple power attack targeting ML-KEM-512 scheme. Leveraging side-channel leakages from the inverse number theoretic transform operation and the decoding process, our method enables efficient recovery of the long-term secret key with AI algorithms for automated feature extraction and classification, eliminating the need for template construction or extensive parameter tuning. We introduce an adaptive classification method for ring- or sphere-shaped data distributions, enhancing adaptability and reducing parameter dependency. Experimental results on the reference ML-KEM implementation in the pqm4 library demonstrate that, compared to previous approaches, our method reduces the number of traces needed for key recovery by 66.67%. This significant reduction improves both the efficiency and practicality of the method in real-world applications.

Keywords: Post-quantum cryptography · Lattice-based cryptography · Chosen-ciphertext attack · Side-channel attack · Key encapsulation mechanism · Public-key encryption

1 Introduction

With the development of internet of things, Public-Key Encryption (PKE) scheme is commonly used in embedded security applications such as smart cards

[15], RFID tags [8], mobile phones [6], and smart home [29]. The emergence of quantum computers presents a substantial challenge to conventional public key cryptographic algorithms. By solving problems like integer factorization and discrete logarithms in polynomial time, quantum computers can compromise the security of algorithms such as RSA and ECDSA, enabling private key recovery. To address this threat, cryptographic research has developed Post-Quantum Cryptography (PQC), which relies on mathematical problems resistant to quantum attacks, including lattice-based, code-based, and multivariate cryptography. In 2024, the National Institute of Standards and Technology (NIST) released Transition to Post-Quantum Cryptography Standards [14], aiming to adopt PQC in government encryption systems by 2035. Among them, lattice-based PQC is primarily used to replace conventional public key cryptographic algorithms in constructing encryption schemes, digital signatures, and key exchange protocols.

The security of algorithmic implementations and the resistance of cryptographic components are of paramount importance [2,9]. During the execution of PQC algorithms on embedded system devices, fluctuations in the physical state of the device are inevitable, such as timing [13,30], power consumption [12,28], and electromagnetic (EM) emission [22,24] is inevitably leaked. Side-Channel Attack (SCA) can exploit this unintended information to extract secret information during cryptographic operations, posing a significant threat to the security of embedded system devices [25].

Recovering long-term secret keys through SCA against lattice-based Key Encapsulation Mechanisms (KEMs) is a critical area of study, as such attacks present a more severe threat than those focused solely on recovering messages. These attacks can generally be divided into two categories. The first category, explored in works such as [3,10], relies on constructing an oracle to determine whether decryption was successful. The second category, pioneered by D'Anvers et al. [5], employs a message-recovery strategy by linking specific chosen messages to the entries of long-term secret key, thereby enabling key recovery.

Ueno et al. [27] introduced a SCA targeting the Fujisaki-Okamoto (FO) transform [7] in lattice-based KEMs. By leveraging trace analysis, they successfully constructed a Plaintext-Checking (PC) oracle. By integrating this with deep learning techniques, they were able to successfully attack a basic Chosen-Plaintext Attack (CPA) PKE scheme. Rajendran et al. [19] extended this approach by introducing parallel PC oracle-based side-channel attacks, which allow the recovery of a generic number P of bits of information about secret key from a single trace in ML-KEM.

Anvers et al. [5] introduced an additional decoding step for error correction codes, further improving the attack's success rate. Building on this approach, Ravi et al. [21] proposed a chosen ciphertext attack against lattice-based PKE and KEMs, focusing on exploiting error correction codes during decryption to extract the secret key.

In 2017, Primas et al. [17,18] pioneered a single trace attack on lattice-based encryption, enhancing belief propagation and focusing on encryption processes by exploiting leakage from the Number Theoretic Transform (NTT). This approach demonstrated adaptability across diverse lattice-based structures and proved effective even against advanced constant-time implementations. To further increase the attack's versatility, Hamburg et al. [11] introduced a method for generating coefficient polynomials as input to inverse NTT computation, thereby improving the attack's resistance to noise.

Tanaka et al. [26] key-recovery PC attack even if CPA secure decryption constructing the KEM is securely implemented. In the context of PC attacks, Shen et al. [23] devised a method to identify erroneous positions in the initially recovered secret key, allowing them to successfully launch an attack on ML-KEM-512.

Xu et al. [31] proposed an adaptive attack method based on EM side-channel analysis, combined with constructed ciphertext, to analyze ML-KEM-512. This attack leverages side-channel leaks, allowing an attacker to recover full key from a minimal amount of trace data using Simple Power Analysis (SPA). Ravi et al. [20] further advanced this approach by exploiting the inherent malleability properties of ciphertext in LWE/LWR-based PKE schemes, applying this to side-channel-assisted message recovery attacks. This method also proved effective in scenarios involving shuffling [1] and masking [16] countermeasures. As a result, the number of traces required for key recovery is reduced from 8 in Xu's method to just 6 traces in the case of ML-KEM.

Xu et al.'s approach employs SCA-assisted chosen-ciphertext attacks targeting both the decryption phase during the decoding process and the decoding operation. To achieve complete key recovery, the decryption phase analysis utilizes side-channel leakage from the `fqmul()` function in the `pqm4` library, requiring 4 constructed ciphertexts and 16 EM traces. For the decoding operation, the analysis exploits side-channel leakage from the `poly_frommsg()` function, necessitating 8 constructed ciphertexts and 10 EM traces. In this paper, in order to fully utilize the multiple side-channel leakages generated during the decapsulation process in a single attack, we present a one-time chosen-ciphertext SPA aimed at reducing the number of constructed ciphertexts and required traces while enhancing the automation of the recovery process, enabling the extraction of ML-KEM-512 secret key with greater efficiency.

The main contributions of this paper can be summarized as follows:

- We propose a one-time chosen-ciphertext SPA for ML-KEM, leveraging two side-channel leakages during a single decoding process: those arising from inverse NTT operation and the decoding process. This approach enables the recovery of long-term secret key by AI algorithms for automated feature extraction and classification techniques. It streamlines trace analysis by eliminating the need for template construction or extensive parameter tuning, ensuring efficient and accurate key recovery.
- To enhance adaptability, we introduce a classification method with adaptive thresholds designed for ring- or sphere-shaped data distributions. This approach classifies trace feature points to recover the key without requiring extensive parameter configuration. The threshold can be retrospectively

adjusted based on key recovery results, making the method versatile for other scenarios.
- We collected EM traces from a reference ML-KEM implementation in the pqm4 library. By crafting specific ciphertexts, we ensured each trace contained two distinct side-channel leakages. Without relying on reference traces or a profiling phase, a single selection to construct two specific ciphertexts is sufficient to fully recover the secret key. Compared to previous studies, this approach reduces the required number of traces for key recovery by at least 66.67%.

The rest of the paper is organized as follows: In Sect. 2, we review the PKE and KEM of ML-KEM, and present a previous work on chosen-ciphertext SPA for ML-KEM. Section 3 and Sect. 4 describes the methodology used in this study. In Sect. 5, the experimental results of one-time chosen-ciphertext SPA were shown and compared with previous work. Finally, Sect. 6 summarizes our method and experiments.

2 Preliminary

2.1 Module-Lattice-Based Key-Encapsulation Mechanism

ML-KEM [4] is a cryptographic scheme based on the Module-LWE problem. Its three variants ML-KEM-512, ML-KEM-768, and ML-KEM-1024 correspond to security levels 1, 3, and 5, equivalent to AES-128, AES-192, and AES-256, respectively. ML-KEM performs arithmetic operations in a fixed polynomial ring $R_q = \mathbb{Z}_q/(x^{256}+1)$, where $q = 3329$ is a prime number. ML-KEM consists of two algorithms: an IND-CPA public key encryption scheme, ML-KEM.CPAPKE, and an IND-CCA key encapsulation mechanism, ML-KEM.CCAKEM, which is built upon the former.

ML-KEM.CPAPKE includes key generation, plaintext encryption, and ciphertext decryption. During the key generation process, a polynomial matrix **A** and a polynomial vector secret key **s** are sampled from a uniform distribution and a binomial distribution, respectively. The coefficients of **s** are restricted to values within the range of -2 to 2. The public key is then computed by adding noise to the product of **A** and **s** in the NTT domain. This process involves polynomial matrix-vector multiplication, which is accelerated using the NTT algorithm.

The plaintext encryption process, as shown in Algorithm 1, involves adding the plaintext message m to the product of public key pk and a randomly sampled polynomial vector **r**, generating a polynomial v in the normal domain (line 6). Additionally, another polynomial multiplication is performed between the vector **r** and the uniformly distributed matrix **A** to compute the vector **u**. The ciphertext c, which is the output of encryption, is then computed from **u** and v (lines 7–8). Here, the functions Compress and Decompress refer to compression and decompression, respectively.

The ciphertext decryption process, as shown in Algorithm 2, involves computing the product of secret key sk and **u** to recover an approximation of v. This approximation of v is then used to recover plaintext. The process requires a set of polynomial-vector multiplication operations and an inverse NTT operation on the polynomial vectors. Additionally, this stage includes a decompression operation on the ciphertext, which restores the received ciphertext data back into its polynomial form.

Algorithm 1. Kyber.CPAPKE.Enc(pk, m, r)

1: $\hat{\mathbf{A}}^T = \text{XOF}(seed_\mathbf{A}) \in \mathcal{R}_q^{k \times k}$ /$pk = (seed_\mathbf{A} \parallel \hat{\mathbf{t}})$/
2: $\mathbf{r} \leftarrow \beta_\mu(\mathcal{R}_q^{k \times 1}; r)$
3: $\mathbf{e}_1 \leftarrow \beta_\mu(\mathcal{R}_q^{k \times 1}; r); \mathbf{e}_2 \leftarrow \beta_\mu(\mathcal{R}_q; r)$
4: $\hat{\mathbf{r}} = \text{NTT}(\mathbf{r}) \in \mathcal{R}_q^{k \times 1}$
5: $\mathbf{u} = \text{NTT}^{-1}(\hat{\mathbf{A}}^T \circ \hat{\mathbf{r}}) + \mathbf{e}_1 \in \mathcal{R}_q^{k \times 1}$
6: $v = \text{NTT}^{-1}(\hat{\mathbf{t}}^T \circ \hat{\mathbf{r}}) + \text{Decompress}_q(\text{Decode}_1(m), 1) + \mathbf{e}_2 \in \mathcal{R}_q$
7: $c_1 = \text{Encode}_{d_u}(\text{Compress}_q(\mathbf{u}, d_u))$
8: $c_2 = \text{Encode}_{d_v}(\text{Compress}_q(v, d_v))$
9: **return** $c = (c_1 \parallel c_2)$

Algorithm 2. Kyber.CPAPKE.Dec(sk, c)

1: $\mathbf{u} = \text{Decompress}_q(\text{Decode}_{d_u}(c_1))$
2: $v = \text{Decompress}_q(\text{Decode}_{d_v}(c_2))$
3: $\hat{\mathbf{s}} = \text{Decode}(sk)$
4: $m = \text{Encode}_1(\text{Compress}_q(v - \text{NTT}^{-1}(\hat{\mathbf{s}}^T \circ \text{NTT}(\mathbf{u})), 1))$
5: **return** m

ML-KEM.CCAKEM consists of two processes: key encapsulation and key decapsulation. The key encapsulation process using public-key encryption is outlined in Algorithm 3. It outputs an IND-CCA-secure ciphertext c and a session key K. The decapsulation process (Algorithm 4 takes as input the ciphertext c and the KEM secret key sk (where $sk = (sk, pk, \text{H}(pk), z)$). IND-CPA decryption is first applied to obtain the decrypted message m_0. Then, the message is re-encrypted using public key pk to produce a re-encrypted ciphertext c_0. The received ciphertext c is compared with the re-encrypted ciphertext c_0 to detect any chosen ciphertext attack. If the received ciphertext is valid, K is returned from key derivation function. Otherwise, a pseudorandom string is returned.

2.2 Chosen-Ciphertext SPA of ML-KEM

Xu et al. [31] proposed a chosen-ciphertext SPA attack targeting ML-KEM, exploiting two leakage functions: the fqmul() function involved in the modular reduction in inverse NTT during decryption, and the poly_frommsg() function called during the re-encryption phase of the decapsulation process. When

Algorithm 3. Kyber.CCAKEM.Enc(pk)

1: $m \leftarrow \mathcal{U}(\{0,1\}^{256})$
2: $m = \mathrm{H}(m)$
3: $(\bar{K}, r) = \mathrm{G}(m \| \mathrm{H}(pk))$
4: $c = \mathrm{Kyber.CPAPKE.Enc}(pk, m, r)$
5: $K = \mathrm{KDF}(\bar{K} \| \mathrm{H}(c))$.
6: **return** (c, K)

Algorithm 4. Kyber.CCAKEM.Dec(c, sk_{KEM})

1: $m' = \mathrm{Kyber.CPAPKE.Dec}(sk, c)$
2: $(\bar{K}', r') := \mathrm{G}(m' \| \mathrm{H}(pk))$
3: $c' = \mathrm{Kyber.CPAPKE.Enc}(pk, m', r')$
4: **if** $c = c'$ **then**
5:     **return** $K = \mathrm{KDF}(\bar{K}' \| \mathrm{H}(c))$.
6: **else**
7:     **return** $K = \mathrm{KDF}(z \| \mathrm{H}(c))$ /*z is random secret*/
8: **end if**

---

implementing the attack, selecting one of the leakage functions and constructing multiple specific ciphertexts, along with utilizing multiple EM traces, enables the recovery of secret key vector **s** for ML-KEM implemented on an STM32F407G development board.

Side-Channel Leakage in Inverse NTT Process. During the modular reduction in inverse NTT process (line 4 of Algorithm 2), the secret key vector **s** is multiplied with the vector **u** in NTT domain, followed by an inverse NTT. The final step of inverse NTT involves element-wise modular multiplication of the polynomial with a constant. In the reference implementation of ML-KEM-512, this process is performed using the fqmul() function.

The output value of the fqmul() function is proportional to the Hamming Weight $\mathrm{HW}(s_{\mathrm{coeff}} \cdot u_0[0] \bmod {}^{\pm}q)$, which is reflected in the Points of Interest (PoIs) in the trace. Different HW values produce distinct characteristics in the trace. By analyzing the electromagnetic (EM) trace collected from specific ciphertexts, the PoIs are classified to determine the class to which each coefficient belongs. To recover half of the secret key, u_1 is set to 0 to eliminate the influence of s_1 on the fqmul() output, where $\mathbf{s}^T = (s_0, s_1)$, $\mathbf{u}^T = (u_0, u_1)$. Simultaneously, all non-constant terms in u_0 are set to 0, and $u_0[0]$ is chosen to ensure that the output value is determined solely by the corresponding key coefficient.

Due to the small difference between $\mathrm{HW}(-2 \cdot u_0[0])$ and $\mathrm{HW}(-1 \cdot u_0[0])$, as well as between $\mathrm{HW}(1 \cdot u_0[0])$ and $\mathrm{HW}(2 \cdot u_0[0])$, analyzing traces from fqmul() function in inverse NTT stage requires multiple ciphertext selections. Five HW values related to some u_0 are clustered into two or three clusters based on the requirements. By carefully selecting u_0, the PoIs can be divided into two or three non-overlapping classes across separate attempts. Combining the classification results from all attempts ultimately determines the exact value of the coefficients of s_0.

The method for recovering s_1 is similar to that for s_0, except that u_0 is set to 0, and a specific constant term $u_1[0]$ is selected. For brevity, the details of principle for recovering s_1 are omitted here.

Side-Channel Leakage in Decapsulation Process. In the ML-KEM decapsulation process, decryption is followed by encryption to decode the same message. The decoding function poly_frommsg() generates masks with significantly different HW. The mask values and output polynomial coefficients are determined by the corresponding message bits. By analyzing the characteristics of EM traces, the message bits can be recovered, enabling the classification of s_0 coefficients into categories. However, determining the exact values of s_0 coefficients is not feasible. Therefore, an attack targeting poly_frommsg(), requires constructing multiple ciphertexts and combining the classification results from each attempt to fully recover the coefficients of s_0.

By constructing four different u_0 values and analyzing trace characteristics corresponding to message bits being "0" or "1", s_0 can be inferred. Similarly, to recover s_1, four different u_1 values are constructed, followed by the similar analysis.

3 One-Time Chosen-Ciphertext SPA on ML-KEM

In this section, we introduce a one-time chosen-ciphertext SPA targeting leakage in the reference implementation of ML-KEM during the decapsulation process. By constructing a specific ciphertext in a single attempt, leakage occurs, allowing for the recovery of half of the secret key. The other half of the key can be recovered by applying the same values to the other half of the ciphertext.

Xu et al. [31] leveraged two primary leakage: inverse NTT in decryption process and decoding during re-encryption in decapsulation process. In inverse NTT phase, two ciphertexts are constructed with $u_0[0] = 55$ and $u_0[0] = 1070$. By analyzing EM traces, half of the secret key s_0 can be recovered. Additionally, Xu et al. proposed exploiting leakage during re-encryption of decoding phase by constructing four ciphertexts and using two additional traces for profiling to recover s_0.

We combine both leakage processes by constructing a single specific ciphertext and analyzing the results from both phases, as shown in Fig. 1. This method requires only a one-time chosen ciphertext and a single trace to recover s_0. Recovery of the other half of the secret key s_1 follows a similar attack strategy. Moreover, we also considered exploiting side-channel leakage from the subtraction operation performed after the inverse NTT to recover sk. However, we found that the signal-to-noise ratio at this point is relatively low, making it infeasible to conduct effective analysis using a single trace.

In this section, we primarily describe a chosen-ciphertext attack on ML-KEM-512. As the attack methods for ML-KEM-768 and ML-KEM-1024 are identical, differing only in the selected ciphertexts, we omit their detailed descriptions.

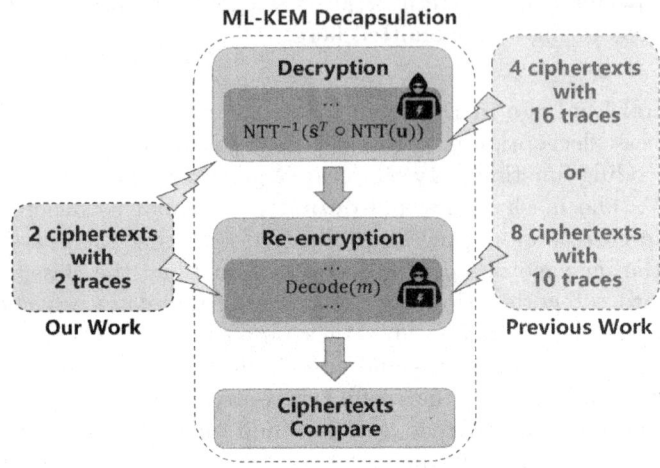

Fig. 1. Chosen-Ciphertext SPA of ML-KEM compared with previous work

3.1 Construct Ciphertexts of Inverse NTT

As described in Sect. 2.1, the fourth line of Algorithm 2 performs the multiplication of the key **s** with the vector **u** in NTT domain, followed by inverse NTT. As shown in following:

$$\mathrm{NTT}^{-1}(\mathrm{NTT}(\mathbf{s}^T) \circ \mathrm{NTT}(\mathbf{u})) \equiv \mathbf{s}^T \circ \mathbf{u} \mod {}^{\pm}q, \tag{1}$$

where $\mathbf{s}^T = (s_0, s_1)$, $\mathbf{u}^T = (u_0, u_1)$, and $q = 3329$.

This process involves invoking the fqmul() function. In the final step, each coefficient of the polynomial is modularly multiplied by a constant ($zetas\_inv[127] = 1441$), as shown in Algorithm 5. Due to the use of 16-bit wide memory for modular reduction, the hamming weight of $poly[j]$ HW($\mathbf{s}_{coeff} \cdot \mathbf{u}$ mod ${}^{\pm}q)[j]$ is linearly correlated with power consumption, where $\mathbf{s}_{coeff}$ represents the coefficients of secret key **s**. Consequently, PoIs values in the corresponding trace reveal the value of $poly[j]$. Specific values of **u**, when multiplied by the five possible secret key coefficients and reduced modulo q, produce distinct hamming weights. If these hamming weights exhibit significant differences, the variations will manifest in EM trace.

To recover s_0, only the constant term $u_0[0]$ of u_0 is constructed, while the non-constant coefficients and u_1 are set to zero. This guarantees that the hamming weight is determined solely by $u_0[0]$ and the corresponding secret key coefficient. We performed a traversal over possible values for $u_0[0]$. For certain values of

Algorithm 5. Final Step of Inverse NTT

1: **for** $j \leftarrow 0$ to 255 **do**
2: $\quad poly[j] = \mathtt{fqmul}(poly[j], zetas\_inv[127])$;
3: **end for**

$u_0[0]$, $\mathrm{HW}(s_{0_{\mathrm{coeff}}} \cdot u_0[0])$ can be categorized into two or three distinct groups based on their magnitude.

For example, when $u_0[0] = 465$, $\mathrm{HW}(s_{0_{\mathrm{coeff}}} \cdot u_0[0] \mod {}^{\pm}q)$, exhibits significant differences. Specifically, $\mathrm{HW}(-2 \cdot u_0[0] \mod {}^{\pm}q) = 11$, $\mathrm{HW}(-1 \cdot u_0[0] \mod {}^{\pm}q) = 12$, $\mathrm{HW}(1 \cdot u_0[0] \mod {}^{\pm}q) = 5$, $\mathrm{HW}(2 \cdot u_0[0] \mod {}^{\pm}q) = 5$, and $\mathrm{HW}(0 \cdot u_0[0] \mod {}^{\pm}q) = 0$. We set $u_1 = 0$, $v = 0$, and define the coefficients of s_0, $s_{0_{\mathrm{coeff}}} = \{s_0[0], s_0[1], \ldots, s_0[255]\}$, as follows:

$$s_0[i] = \begin{cases} -2, & 0 \leq i \leq 50, \\ -1, & 51 \leq i \leq 101, \\ 0, & 102 \leq i \leq 152, \\ 1, & 153 \leq i \leq 203, \\ 2, & 204 \leq i \leq 255. \end{cases} \quad (2)$$

The EM trace collected during inverse NTT operation is depicted in Fig. 2. Variations in $\mathrm{HW}(s_{0_{\mathrm{coeff}}} \cdot u_0[0])$ driven by different coefficient values are observable in the trace. Specifically, $\mathrm{HW}(-2 \cdot u_0[0])$ and $\mathrm{HW}(-1 \cdot u_0[0])$ exhibit higher values, $\mathrm{HW}(1 \cdot u_0[0])$ and $\mathrm{HW}(2 \cdot u_0[0])$ display moderate values, while $\mathrm{HW}(0 \cdot u_0[0]) = 0$ has lower value. By identifying feature points in the trace segments corresponding to each key coefficient and applying clustering analysis, the coefficients $s_{0_{\mathrm{coeff}}}$ can be grouped into three distinct categories: $\{-2, -1\}$, $\{1, 2\}$, and $\{0\}$, for $u_0[0] = 465$. Similarly, to recover $s_{1_{\mathrm{coeff}}}$, $u_1[0]$ is set to 465, u_0 is initialized to zero, and a comparable trace analysis is performed. While it is not feasible at this stage to differentiate between coefficients -2 and -1, or 1 and 2, the leakage observed during the decoding phase, as discussed in the next section, , the current classification results combined with the leakage observed

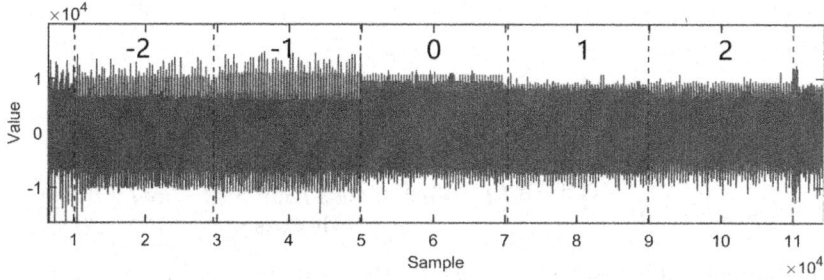

Fig. 2. The EM trace of inverse NTT operation during ML-KEM-CPAPKE decryption when $u_0[0] = 465$

during the decoding phase can enable precise classification of these coefficient values.

3.2 Construct Ciphertexts of Decoding

In ML-KEM decapsulation, the ciphertext is first decrypted to obtain the message, which is then re-encrypted. This re-encryption process decodes the message, as shown in line 6 of Algorithm 1. The decoding function poly_frommsg() exhibits significant SPA leakage, as shown in Algorithm 6. Specifically, depending on the message bits, when $((msg[i] \gg j)\&1) = 0$, the mask value is 0xffff, and when $((msg[i] \gg j)\&1) = 1$, the mask value is 0. The substantial differences in the hamming weights of these mask values lead to noticeable variations in trace characteristics.

Algorithm 6. Decoding: poly_frommsg()

Input: $msg[32]$
Output: $coeffs[]$
1: **for** $i \leftarrow 0$ to 31 **do**
2:    **for** $j \leftarrow 0$ to 7 **do**
3:       $mask = -((msg[i] \gg j)\&1);$
4:       $coeffs[8 \cdot i + j] = mask\&((q+1)/2);$
5:    **end for**
6: **end for**
7: **return** $coeffs[]$

The value of the ciphertext will affect the message bit $msg_{bin}[8i+j]$. Here, msg_{bin} represents the binary representation of the msg. Xu et al. recover s_0 using four different chosen ciphertexts. In contrast, we employ a simpler ciphertext construction method based on the analysis from the previous section. Specifically, we set $u_0[0] = 465$, with the non-constant terms of u_0, u_1, and v all set to 0. By analyzing EM traces and distinguishing the bit values of msg_{bin}, as shown in Fig. 3, we can classify the coefficients of s_0 into two categories: $\{-2, 2\}$ and $\{-1, 0, 1\}$. The method for determining the category of s_0 coefficients based on the value of msg_{bin} is shown in Eqs. (3)–(4).

$$\begin{aligned} \text{coeffs} &= v - \text{NTT}^{-1}\left(\hat{\mathbf{s}}^T \circ \text{NTT}(\mathbf{u})\right) \\ &= v - (s_0 \cdot u_0 + s_1 \cdot u_1), \end{aligned} \quad (3)$$

$$msg_{bin}[8i+j] = \begin{cases} 1, & \text{if } (q-1)/4 < coeffs[8i+j] < (3q+1)/4 \\ 0, & \text{otherwise.} \end{cases} \quad (4)$$

This ciphertext construction ensures that when $s_0[8i+j] = -2$ or 2, the binary representation of the message $msg_{bin}[8i+j] = 1$, and when $s_0[8i+j] = -1, 1,$ or 0, $msg_{bin}[8i+j] = 0$. During inverse NTT phase, the coefficients of s_0

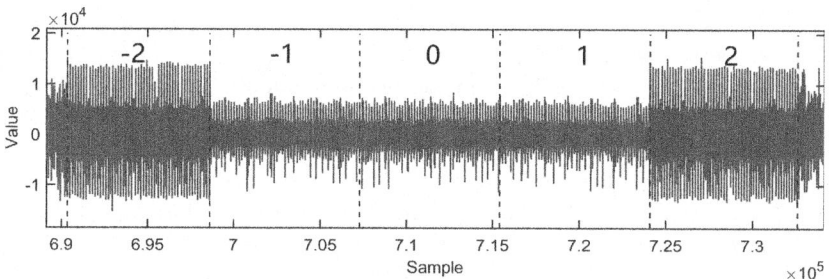

Fig. 3. The EM trace of `poly_frommsg()` function in decoding phase during ML-KEM-CPAKEM re-encrypted when $u_0[0] = 465$

can be categorized into one of three groups: $\{-2, -1\}$, $\{1, 2\}$, or $\{0\}$. By combining the SPA leakage observed during the two stages of the EM trace, s_0 can be fully reconstructed. Similarly, s_1 can be recovered using the same ciphertext as in the previous analysis. In practice, the objective of ciphertext construction is to ensure that the two analyses produce non-overlapping sets of key coefficients. The hamming weights $\text{HW}(\mathbf{s}_{\text{coeff}} \cdot u[0])$ corresponding to different coefficients during inverse NTT phase are designed to exhibit significant differences. Simultaneously, the coefficient classifications derived from decoding phase must remain distinct from those obtained in earlier analysis. Any ciphertext satisfying this condition enables the recovery of half of the secret key with just a single trace.

4 Adaptive Threshold Circle Classification for SPA

To categorize the key coefficients, we applied Principal Component Analysis (PCA) to reduce the dimensionality of traces to two or three dimensions, followed by clustering algorithms for feature classification. However, the features extracted through PCA exhibit spherical or ring-like distributions, complicating accurate classification with distance-based or density-based clustering methods. To address this challenge, this section presents an Adaptive Threshold Circle Classification (ATC) method specifically designed for SPA.

PCA reduces each message bit trace segment from the decoding phase to two dimensions. As shown in Fig. 4, the distribution of features in the two-dimensional coordinate system forms a ring-like pattern. Feature points corresponding to message bit 1 are distributed along the inner ring, while those corresponding to message bit 0 are distributed along the outer ring. There are gaps between feature points of the same category, making it difficult to accurately classify them using density-based clustering methods. We employ ATC for classification, with the steps outlined below:

1. Calculate the center of all samples and compute the distance array **D** for each feature point to the sample center. Euclidean distance, Manhattan distance, or other suitable distance metrics can be employed

2. Sort the distances from the feature points to the sample center to obtain the sorted distance array
3. Compute the differences between adjacent elements in the sorted distance array, and sort these differences in descending order to obtain the array $\mathbf{D}_{\mathrm{diff}}$
4. Use the two sample points corresponding to $\mathbf{D}_{\mathrm{diff}}[0]$ as classification threshold points. The indices of these points are referred to as $inner_{index}$ and $outer_{index}$. Feature points with distances less than $\mathbf{D}[inner_{index}]$ and greater than $\mathbf{D}[outer_{index}]$ belong to separate classes, as illustrated in Fig. 4
5. Attempt to recover the key using this classification result. If unsuccessful, update the classification threshold points by using $\mathbf{D}_{\mathrm{diff}}[1]$ as the new threshold, and reclassify. Repeat steps 4 and 5, using $\mathbf{D}_{\mathrm{diff}}[i]$ to determine the classification threshold points for the i-th update, until the key is successfully recovered.

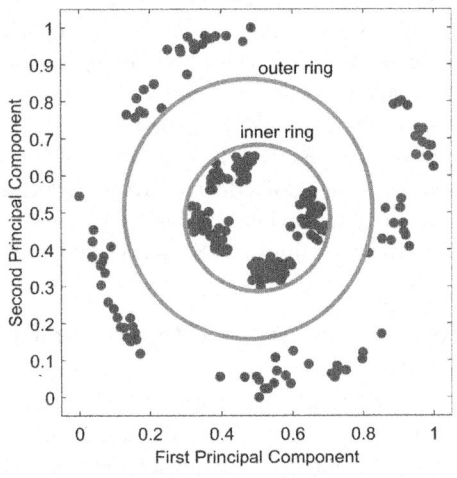

Fig. 4. The distribution of feature points after PCA on trace segments in decoding phase

5 Experiments and Comparison

5.1 Experimental Setup

We implemented ML-KEM-512 using pqm4 for the ARM Cortex-M4 on the STM32F407G discovery board. The decryption process was performed with a randomly generated key and a constructed ciphertext on the discovery board operating at a clock frequency of 168 MHz. We collected the EM traces at 2.5 GHz using a PicoScope 3404D oscilloscope with a Langer RF-U 5-2 H near-field probe. A Langer PA303 amplifier was located between the probe and oscilloscope. The traces were low-pass filtered to reduce the effect of noise.

5.2 Experiments of Key Recovery

In this section, we will detail the analysis of EM traces corresponding to the execution of inverse NTT and the `poly_frommsg()` function. During trace collection process, we randomly generated the key. To recover s_0, we set the constant term of u_0 to 465, while u_1 and v were set to 0. Figure 5(i) illustrates the whole ML-KEM decapsulation process, Fig. 5(ii) shows the trace during the execution of inverse NTT, and Fig. 5(iii) depicts the trace during the execution of `poly_frommsg()` function in decoding phase.

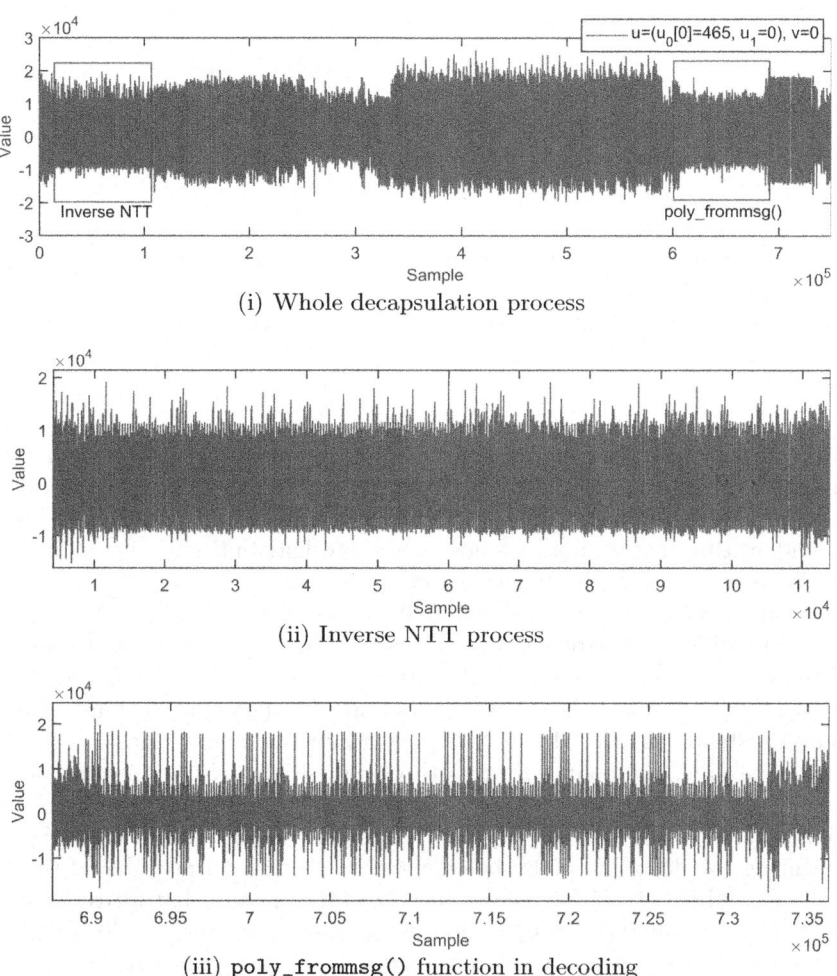

(i) Whole decapsulation process

(ii) Inverse NTT process

(iii) `poly_frommsg()` function in decoding

Fig. 5. EM traces of ML-KEM decapsulation on the STM32F407G

First, we analyzed the trace corresponding to inverse NTT process. The trace was segmented into 256 operation segments, corresponding to half the key length.

PCA was applied for dimensionality reduction, mapping each trace segment to a two-dimensional feature point. Hierarchical clustering was then employed to classify the feature points. The distribution and clustering results of feature points are illustrated in Fig. 6. The feature points were classified into three categories, corresponding to the three coefficient sets $a : \{-2, -1\}$, $b : \{1, 2\}$, and $c : \{0\}$.

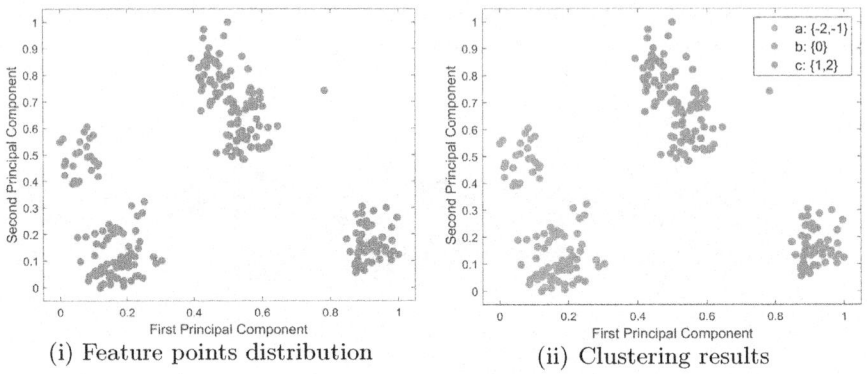

Fig. 6. Distribution and clustering results of feature points of EM trace during inverse NTT

Next, we analyzed EM traces corresponding to the decoding operation. Similarly, the traces are segmented into 256 operation segments, and PCA is applied for dimensionality reduction, with each trace segment mapped to a two-dimensional feature point. The distribution of feature points is shown in Fig. 7(i). It is evident that feature points follow a circular distribution. Using the proposed ATC, feature points are divided into two categories: $a : \{-2, 2\}$, $b : \{-1, 0, 1\}$, with a classification accuracy of 100%. We compared the classification accuracy achieved by different clustering algorithms. The hierarchical clustering algorithm and the density-based clustering algorithm, DBSCAN, both achieved an accuracy of 71.48%. Notably, DBSCAN cannot specify the expected number of clusters and instead classifies the feature points into three categories.

By combining the results from both classifications, we can recover the coefficient s_0, as shown in Table 1. For example, if the coefficient category recovered during inverse NTT phase belongs to class c, and the coefficient category recovered during the decoding phase belongs to class a, the actual value of the coefficient is -2. The method for recovering s_1 closely mirrors that for recovering s_0: we set the constant term of u_1 to 465, while setting u_0 and v to 0, then collect EM traces. We achieved a 100% key recovery accuracy, and the entire process was completed in less than one second.

5.3 Comparison

We compared our work with that of Xu et al. [31] and Ravi et al. [20]. In our chosen ciphertext SPA, we simultaneously analyze inverse NTT operation and

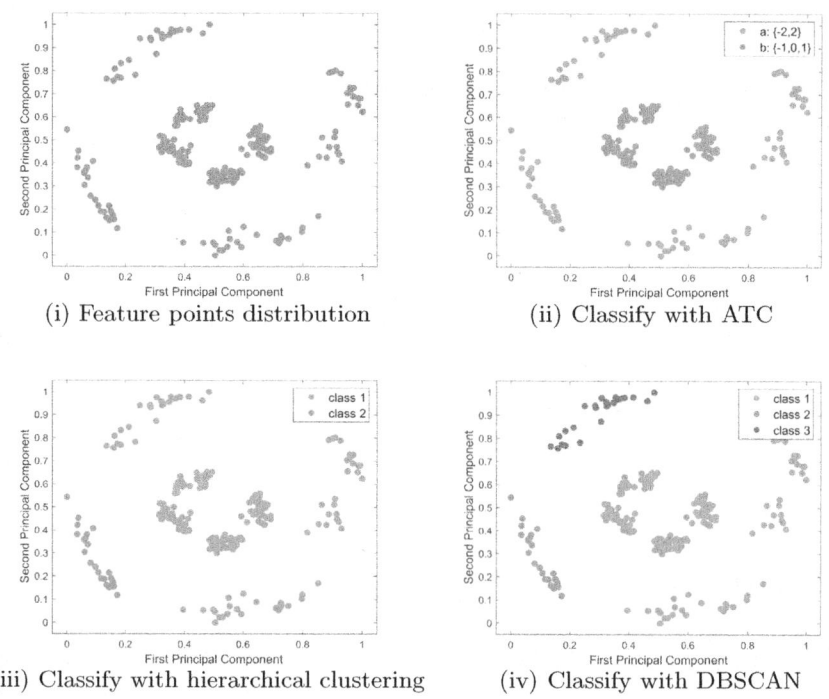

Fig. 7. Distribution and clustering results of feature points of EM trace during decoding

Table 1. Recovery of secrete key coefficients by combining the results of both classifications

Secret Coefficient	Class 1	Class 2
-2	c	a
-1	c	b
0	b	b
1	a	b
2	a	a

the decoding function in the ML-KEM key decapsulation process. With only two chosen ciphertexts (i.e. 2 traces), we achieve 100% key recovery accuracy. Furthermore, our method does not require profiling traces or manual threshold setting. In contrast, Xu et al. only analyzed either inverse NTT operation or the decoding function. When analyzing inverse NTT operation, at least 16 traces are needed to recover the key with 100% success, while for the decoding function, 2 traces are required to set thresholds, and at least 8 traces are needed for full key recovery. Ravi et al. reduced the number of traces required for key recovery from 8 traces in Xu's method to 6 traces for ML-KEM.

Our method achieves a 100% success rate while reducing the number of traces required for key recovery by a minimum of 66.67%. In the case of selecting two ciphertexts, Xu et al.'s method can only determine which coefficients in the key sequence are 0, with an accuracy of approximately 20%. In contrast, our method directly recovers the entire key, yielding an 80% improvement in accuracy (Table 2).

Table 2. Comparison of previous schemes with ours

Scheme	Implementation setting	Attack Target	Profiling traces	Attacking traces	Accuracy
[31] for NTT^{-1}	Reference (-O3)	NTT^{-1}	-	16	100%
[31] for decoding	ARM-specific (-O0)	decoding	2	8	100%
[20]	ARM-specific (-O0)	decoding	-	6	100%
Our scheme	Reference (-O0)	NTT^{-1} & decoding	-	2	100%

6 Conclusion

In this paper, we propose an efficient one-time chosen-ciphertext SPA method for ML-KEM, utilizing two side-channel leakages from inverse NTT operation and the decoding process during a single decoding. This approach enables automated key recovery through automated feature extraction and classification, simplifying trace analysis by removing the need for template construction and parameter tuning. We further introduce a classification method with adaptive thresholds for ring- or sphere-shaped data distributions, enhancing adaptability and eliminating the need for extensive parameter configuration. Experiments using the reference implementation of ML-KEM in the pqm4 library and collect EM traces demonstrate that a single selection to construct two specific ciphertexts is sufficient to fully recover the secret key, reducing the required trace count by at least 66.67% compared to previous methods.

Acknowledgments. This work is supported by National Key R&D Program of China (No. 2022YFB3103800), Beijing Natural Science Foundation (No. QY24173), Guizhou Provincial Key Technology R&D Program (No. [2023]442), Foundation of Guizhou Educational Committee (Nos. [2021]053, [2023]080), and Project for Reconstruction of Industrial Foundation and High Quality Development of Manufacturing Industry (No. 0747-2361SCCZA193).

References

1. Amiet, D., Curiger, A., Leuenberger, L., Zbinden, P.: Defeating NEWHOPE with a single trace. In: Ding, J., Tillich, J.-P. (eds.) PQCrypto 2020. LNCS, vol. 12100, pp. 189–205. Springer, Cham (2020). https://doi.org/10.1007/978-3-030-44223-1_11

2. Barbu, G., et al.: ECDSA white-box implementations: attacks and designs from CHES 2021 challenge. IACR Trans. Cryptogr. Hardw. Embed. Syst. **2022**(4), 527–552 (2022)
3. Bhasin, S., D'Anvers, J.P., Heinz, D., Pöppelmann, T., Van Beirendonck, M.: Attacking and defending masked polynomial comparison for lattice-based cryptography. IACR Trans. Cryptogr. Hardw. Embed. Syst. 334–359 (2021)
4. Bos, J., et al.: Crystals-kyber: a CCA-secure module-lattice-based KEM. In: 2018 IEEE European Symposium on Security and Privacy (EuroS&P), pp. 353–367. IEEE (2018)
5. D'Anvers, J.P., Tiepelt, M., Vercauteren, F., Verbauwhede, I.: Timing attacks on error correcting codes in post-quantum schemes. In: Proceedings of ACM Workshop on Theory of Implementation Security Workshop, pp. 2–9 (2019)
6. Dar, M.A., Askar, A., Alyahya, D., Bhat, S.A.: Lightweight and secure elliptical curve cryptography (ECC) key exchange for mobile phones. Int. J. Interact. Mob. Technol. **15**(23) (2021)
7. Fujisaki, E., Okamoto, T.: Secure integration of asymmetric and symmetric encryption schemes. In: Wiener, M. (ed.) CRYPTO 1999. LNCS, vol. 1666, pp. 537–554. Springer, Heidelberg (1999). https://doi.org/10.1007/3-540-48405-1_34
8. Gabsi, S., Kortli, Y., Beroulle, V., Kieffer, Y., Alasiry, A., Hamdi, B.: Novel ECC-based RFID mutual authentication protocol for emerging IoT applications. IEEE Access **9**, 130895–130913 (2021)
9. Gai, K., et al.: Attacking the edge-of-things: a physical attack perspective. IEEE Internet Things J. **9**(7), 5240–5253 (2021)
10. Guo, Q., Johansson, T., Nilsson, A.: A key-recovery timing attack on post-quantum primitives using the Fujisaki-Okamoto transformation and its application on FrodoKEM. In: Micciancio, D., Ristenpart, T. (eds.) CRYPTO 2020. LNCS, vol. 12171, pp. 359–386. Springer, Cham (2020). https://doi.org/10.1007/978-3-030-56880-1_13
11. Hamburg, M., et al.: Chosen ciphertext k-trace attacks on masked CCA2 secure kyber. IACR Trans. Cryptogr. Hardw. Embed. Syst. 88–113 (2021)
12. Lipp, M., et al.: PLATYPUS: software-based power side-channel attacks on x86. In: 2021 IEEE Symposium on Security and Privacy (SP), pp. 355–371. IEEE (2021)
13. Luo, C., Fei, Y., Kaeli, D.: Side-channel timing attack of RSA on a GPU. ACM Trans. Architect. Code Optim. (TACO) **16**(3), 1–18 (2019)
14. Moody, D., Perlner, R., Regenscheid, A., Robinson, A., Cooper, D.: Transition to post-quantum cryptography standards. Technical report, National Institute of Standards and Technology (2024)
15. Mumtaz, M., Akram, J., Ping, L.: An RSA based authentication system for smart IoT environment. In: 2019 IEEE 21st International Conference on High Performance Computing and Communications; IEEE 17th International Conference on Smart City; IEEE 5th International Conference on Data Science and Systems (HPCC/SmartCity/DSS), pp. 758–765. IEEE (2019)
16. Oder, T., Schneider, T., Pöppelmann, T., Güneysu, T.: Practical CCA2-secure and masked ring-LWE implementation. Cryptology ePrint Archive (2016)
17. Pessl, P., Primas, R.: More practical single-trace attacks on the number theoretic transform. In: Schwabe, P., Thériault, N. (eds.) LATINCRYPT 2019. LNCS, vol. 11774, pp. 130–149. Springer, Cham (2019). https://doi.org/10.1007/978-3-030-30530-7_7
18. Primas, R., Pessl, P., Mangard, S.: Single-trace side-channel attacks on masked lattice-based encryption. In: Fischer, W., Homma, N. (eds.) CHES 2017. LNCS,

vol. 10529, pp. 513–533. Springer, Cham (2017). https://doi.org/10.1007/978-3-319-66787-4_25
19. Rajendran, G., Ravi, P., D'anvers, J.P., Bhasin, S., Chattopadhyay, A.: Pushing the limits of generic side-channel attacks on LWE-based KEMs-parallel PC oracle attacks on kyber KEM and beyond. IACR Trans. Cryptogr. Hardw. Embed. Syst. (2023)
20. Ravi, P., Bhasin, S., Roy, S.S., Chattopadhyay, A.: On exploiting message leakage in (few) NIST PQC candidates for practical message recovery attacks. IEEE Trans. Inf. Forensics Secur. **17**, 684–699 (2021)
21. Ravi, P., Roy, S.S., Chattopadhyay, A., Bhasin, S.: Generic side-channel attacks on CCA-secure lattice-based PKE and KEMs. IACR Trans. Cryptogr. Hardw. Embed. Syst. 307–335 (2020)
22. Saito, K., Ito, A., Ueno, R., Homma, N.: One truth prevails: a deep-learning based single-trace power analysis on RSA–CRT with windowed exponentiation. IACR Trans. Cryptogr. Hardw. Embed. Syst. 490–526 (2022)
23. Shen, M., Cheng, C., Zhang, X., Guo, Q., Jiang, T.: Find the bad apples: an efficient method for perfect key recovery under imperfect SCA oracles–a case study of kyber. IACR Trans. Cryptogr. Hardw. Embed. Syst. 89–112 (2023)
24. Sigourou, A.A., Kabin, I., Langendörfer, P., Sklavos, N., Dyka, Z.: Successful simple side channel analysis: Vulnerability of an atomic pattern kP algorithm implemented with a constant time crypto library to simple electromagnetic analysis attacks. In: 2023 12th Mediterranean Conference on Embedded Computing (MECO), pp. 1–6. IEEE (2023)
25. Sravani, M., Ananiah Durai, S.: Side-channel attacks on cryptographic devices and their countermeasures—a review. In: Smart Innovations in Communication and Computational Sciences: Proceedings of ICSICCS-2018, pp. 209–226 (2019)
26. Tanaka, Y., Ueno, R., Xagawa, K., Ito, A., Takahashi, J., Homma, N.: Multiple-valued plaintext-checking side-channel attacks on post-quantum KEMs. IACR Trans. Cryptogr. Hardw. Embed. Syst. **2023**(3), 473–503 (2023)
27. Ueno, R., Xagawa, K., Tanaka, Y., Ito, A., Takahashi, J., Homma, N.: Curse of re-encryption: a generic power/EM analysis on post-quantum KEMs. IACR Trans. Cryptogr. Hardw. Embed. Syst. 296–322 (2022)
28. Wan, W., Chen, J., Zhang, S., Xia, J.: A cluster correlation power analysis against double blinding exponentiation. J. Inf. Secur. Appl. **48**, 102357 (2019)
29. Wang, L., An, H., Zhu, H., Liu, W.: Mobikey: mobility-based secret key generation in smart home. IEEE Internet Things J. **7**(8), 7590–7600 (2020)
30. Wang, Y., Paccagnella, R., He, E.T., Shacham, H., Fletcher, C.W., Kohlbrenner, D.: Hertzbleed: turning power side-channel attacks into remote timing attacks on x86. In: 31st USENIX Security Symposium (USENIX Security 2022), pp. 679–697 (2022)
31. Xu, Z., Pemberton, O., Roy, S.S., Oswald, D., Yao, W., Zheng, Z.: Magnifying side-channel leakage of lattice-based cryptosystems with chosen ciphertexts: the case study of kyber. IEEE Trans. Comput. **71**(9), 2163–2176 (2021)

A Review of Lattice Cryptography Attack Cost Model

Xi Hu[1,2], Yunfei Cao[2(✉)], and Hong Xiang[3]

[1] Beijing Institute of Mathematics Science and Applications, Beijing 101400, People's Republic of China
[2] National Key Laboratory of Security Communication, Chengdu 610041, People's Republic of China
850178519@qq.com
[3] School of Big Data and Software Engineering, Chongqing University, Chongqing 401331, People's Republic of China

Abstract. The quantum algorithm threat on the security of public key cryptography pushes people to initiate the research of post-quantum cryptography represented by lattice cryptography. Efficient lattice cryptography is based on the parameter range that dissatisfies the proven security condition, whose attack cost model depends on heuristics and experimental results, leading to a severe impact on concrete security estimation and parameter selection of lattice cryptography. This study firstly recalls some preliminary mathematics definitions and propositions of lattice cryptography and lattice hard problems, including solving algorithms of the latter. Then, cost models of these algorithms are reviewed and are partitioned into 2008 and 2016 cost models. Applications on a special type of lattice is also reviewed. This review discusses concrete security analysis of two types of lattice cryptography which are based on two distinct hard problems, which offers a criteria to parameter selection of lattice cryptography.

Keywords: Network Security · Public Key Cryptography · Lattice Cryptography · Security Estimation

1 Introduction

Public-key cryptography serves as the cornerstone for establishing trust chains in modern digital infrastructure. Its security relies on the computational intractability of mathematical problems such as integer factorization and discrete logarithms, which are widely accepted as hard by the mathematical community. However, Shor's quantum algorithm [1], proposed in 1994, reduces the complexity of solving these problems from exponential to polynomial time. This breakthrough implies that large-scale quantum computers could pose a devastating threat to conventional public-key cryptosystems. The rapid advancement of quantum computing technologies globally has significantly intensified this security concern [2].

To sustain cryptographic trust in the post-quantum era, researchers have explored alternative approaches to public-key cryptography since Shor's discovery. This effort has yielded several cryptographic families resistant to quantum attacks, including lattice-based cryptography [3], code-based cryptography [4], multivariate cryptography [5], hash-based cryptography, and isogeny-based cryptography. Collectively referred to as Post-Quantum Cryptography (PQC), these schemes derive security from mathematical problems that currently withstand quantum algorithmic attacks. Subsequent advancements in lattice-based cryptography, particularly through innovations like q-ary lattices, ideal lattices, and module lattices, have progressively optimized parameter sizes and operational efficiency to meet practical requirements. Following these developments, standardization bodies such as the National Institute of Standards and Technology (NIST) initiated PQC standardization efforts [6–8], which have garnered substantial attention from academia and industry worldwide. The finalized algorithm selections and subsequent formal standardization necessitate the migration of existing public-key infrastructures to PQC. This transition requires careful parameter set design that balances security and performance across diverse application scenarios, demanding rigorous evaluation of specific security levels and operational metrics.

For security evaluation, the prevailing methodology calculates bit security values based on the logarithmic scaling of the best-known attack complexity against the underlying hard problem. This approach underpins the security categorization framework in NIST's algorithm standardization guidelines. However, lattice-based cryptography presents unique challenges: existing efficient algorithms for solving lattice problems rely on heuristic assumptions, making it difficult to formally establish their exact complexity [9,10]. Current security analyses remain heavily dependent on empirical validations rather than provable guarantees.

To advance systematic parameter selection for lattice-based cryptosystems, this paper conducts a comprehensive survey of existing research on attack cost modeling. We first summarize fundamental mathematical definitions and results pertaining to lattice cryptography and lattice hard problems, including relevant solving algorithms. We then systematically examine cost models for these algorithms, categorizing them into two distinct classes (2008 and 2016 models) and discussing their applications to specialized lattice structures. Finally, we analyze concrete security assessments for two categories of lattice-based cryptosystems grounded in different hardness assumptions.

2 Preliminaries

A lattice is a discrete subgroup in the m-dimensional real linear space $\mathbb{R}^m$, typically represented by a set of basis vectors $B = \mathbf{b}_1, \mathbf{b}_2, \cdots, \mathbf{b}_m$. Each vector $\mathbf{x}$ in the lattice can be expressed as an integer linear combination of the basis vectors in B. The integer n is called the rank of the lattice. When $m = n$ the lattice is termed a full-rank lattice. This paper focuses exclusively on full-rank lattices.

A lattice Λ may have multiple distinct basis representations, but the determinant $\det(B)$ of the basis matrix B is an invariant of Λ. For a full-rank lattice, the geometric interpretation of $\det(B)$ can be introduced through the concept of the fundamental parallelepiped:

$$\mathcal{P}(B) := \{\mathbf{x} = x_1\mathbf{b}_1 + x_2\mathbf{b}_2 + \cdots + x_n\mathbf{b}_n \mid x_1, \cdots, x_n \in [0,1]\} \quad (1)$$

From linear algebra, $\det(B)$ equals the volume of $\mathcal{P}(B)$, denoted as $\text{vol}(\mathcal{P}(B))$. For any basis B of Λ, $\text{vol}(\mathcal{P}(B))$ remains invariant, which is abbreviated as $\text{vol}(\Lambda)$. While different basis representations are algebraically equivalent, cryptanalysis often requires finding a basis with shorter vectors that are nearly orthogonal. Gram-Schmidt orthogonalization serves as a fundamental tool for this purpose, transforming an arbitrary linearly independent vector set into an orthogonal set.

Two fundamental lattice problems are defined as follows:

Definition 1. *Given a lattice Λ and its basis B, the Shortest Vector Problem (SVP) requires finding a non-zero vector $\mathbf{x} \in \Lambda$ with the minimal Euclidean norm.*

Definition 2. *Given a lattice Λ, a real bound B, and a target vector $\mathbf{t}$, the Bounded Distance Decoding (BDD) Problem requires finding a lattice vector $\mathbf{x} \in \Lambda$ such that $\|\mathbf{x} - \mathbf{t}\| \leq B$.*

The security of lattice-based cryptography primarily relies on two foundational computational problems, both reducible to fundamental lattice hardness assumptions. Specifically, Ajtai's seminal work [11] established a reduction from the Short Integer Solution (SIS) problem to the Shortest Vector Problem (SVP), bridging the gap between average-case and worst-case hardness. This breakthrough enabled the construction of public-key cryptosystems grounded in worst-case security guarantees. Subsequently, Regev [12] introduced a reduction from the Learning with Errors (LWE) problem to SVP, innovatively integrating noise—a concept originating from communication theory—into the framework of public-key cryptography. These reductions collectively underpin the security foundations of modern lattice-based cryptographic schemes.

The security of lattice-based cryptography typically relies on two fundamental problems that can be reduced to the aforementioned hard lattice problems. Specifically, the reduction from the Short Integer Solution (SIS) problem to the Shortest Vector Problem (SVP) was established by Ajtai in his seminal lattice cryptography paper [11]. This reduction bridges the average-case to worst-case hardness, enabling the construction of public-key cryptosystems based on worst-case hardness assumptions. The reduction from the Learning With Errors (LWE) problem to SVP was introduced by Regev [12], marking the first integration of noise – a concept from communication theory – into public-key cryptography.

Definition 3 (Short Integer Solution, SIS). Given a matrix $\mathbf{A} \in \mathbb{Z}_q^{m \times n}$ and modulus q, the Short Integer Solution problem requires finding a non-zero vector $\mathbf{x} \in \mathbb{Z}^n$ satisfying:

$$\mathbf{A}\mathbf{x} \equiv \mathbf{0} \mod q \quad \text{with} \quad \|\mathbf{x}\| \leq \beta$$

where β is a predefined norm bound.

Definition 4 (Learning With Errors, LWE). Given a public matrix $\mathbf{A} \in \mathbb{Z}_q^{m \times n}$, secret vector $\mathbf{s} \in \mathbb{Z}_q^n$, error vector $\mathbf{e} \in \chi^m$ sampled from an error distribution χ, and modulus q, the LWE problem requires recovering $\mathbf{s}$ from the pair $(\mathbf{A}, \mathbf{b} = \mathbf{As} + \mathbf{e} \mod q)$.

Early lattice-based cryptosystems constructed directly from the matrix versions of the SIS and LWE problems required prohibitively large key sizes to guarantee security, rendering them impractical. This limitation was addressed by Micciancio and Lyubashevsky [13,14], who proposed constructing SIS and LWE problems over lattices with specific algebraic structures based on polynomial rings. In this framework, a single polynomial from the ring can generate an instance of SIS or LWE, reducing the key size to $O(n \log q)$ (where n is the security parameter and q the modulus). This breakthrough enabled practical lattice-based cryptography.

However, the polynomial ring variants of these hard problems correspond to lattices with special algebraic structures known as *ideal lattices*. Concerns emerged regarding potential attacks exploiting these additional algebraic properties [15]. This security uncertainty prompted subsequent lattice cryptography designers to adopt a compromise approach: constructing algorithms based on module structures over polynomial rings. The corresponding lattices, called *module lattices*, possess weaker algebraic structures than ideal lattices while maintaining higher efficiency compared to generic lattice constructions. Among the three lattice-based standards selected by NIST, both Kyber and Dilithium leverage this module lattice architecture [16,17].

The LWE problem is commonly transformed into an SVP problem on specific lattices using embedding techniques [15]. The lattice basis matrix is constructed as:

$$B = \begin{bmatrix} qI_m & \mathbf{0} & \mathbf{0} \\ \mathbf{A}^T & -\mathbf{I}_n & \mathbf{0} \\ \mathbf{b} & \mathbf{0} & 1 \end{bmatrix}$$

This technique embeds LWE instances into an $(m+n+1)$-dimensional full-rank lattice, where m denotes the dimension of the error vector and n the dimension of the secret vector. The vector $(\mathbf{s}^T, \mathbf{e}^T, 1)$ constitutes a short vector in this lattice.

The continuous optimization of SVP-solving algorithms significantly impacts cost models and security estimations in lattice-based cryptography [49]. These algorithms fall into two categories:

- **Exact solvers** (e.g., sieve algorithms and enumeration)
- **Approximate solvers** (e.g., LLL algorithm and BKZ variants)

Sieve algorithms exploit the additive closure property of lattice structures, generating new vectors through linear combinations and filtering shorter candidates [16]. Their time and space complexities are respectively $2^{cn+o(n)}$ and poly(n). Enumeration algorithms perform exhaustive search in the coefficient space of basis vectors with optimized pruning strategies [17], exhibiting time complexity $n^{cn+o(n)}$ and polynomial space complexity.

Dimension reduction strategies [33] for sieve algorithms can effectively decrease lattice dimension n, thereby reducing computational complexity. Bi et al. [47] provide a systematic review of development milestones and optimization techniques in lattice sieve algorithms.

The fundamental idea of approximate solving algorithms lies in *lattice basis reduction*, which transforms the problem of finding the shortest vector in a lattice into identifying a set of relatively short and quasi-orthogonal basis vectors. The Lenstra-Lenstra-Lovász (LLL) algorithm [18] serves as the cornerstone of this approach. This algorithm employs Gram-Schmidt orthogonalization as its core computational tool, augmented with a critical condition: if the basis vectors $\mathbf{b}_i$ and $\mathbf{b}_{i+1}$ violate the Lovász condition

$$\delta \|\widetilde{\mathbf{b}}_i\|^2 \leq \|\widetilde{\mathbf{b}}_{i+1}\|^2 + \mu_{i+1,i}^2 \|\widetilde{\mathbf{b}}_i\|^2$$

(where $\widetilde{\mathbf{b}}_i$ denotes Gram-Schmidt orthogonalized vectors and $\delta \in (0.25, 1)$ is a relaxation factor), the algorithm swaps $\mathbf{b}_i$ and $\mathbf{b}_{i+1}$, then re-executes orthogonalization.

In concrete security analysis of lattice-based cryptography, the BKZ (Block Korkine-Zolotarev) algorithm's simulation results serve as the primary reference. The BKZ algorithm operates with parameter β (block size), representing the dimension of sub-lattices where SVP solvers are invoked. Its workflow follows three phases:

- **Sub-lattice processing**: Starting from the first basis vector, create a β-dimensional projected sub-lattice basis $[\pi_i(\mathbf{b}_i), \ldots, \pi_i(\mathbf{b}_{i+\beta-1})]$ (which will be defined later)
- **SVP solving**: Apply sieving algorithms to find short vectors in the sub-lattice
- **Window sliding**: Move the processing window forward by one vector until reaching the lattice end

As illustrated in Fig. 1 (red boxes indicating SVP-solving sub-lattices), this sliding window mechanism enables progressive basis improvement. The BKZ algorithm's effectiveness fundamentally depends on the SVP oracle's performance in β-dimensional spaces, making sieving algorithms with $2^{0.292\beta + o(\beta)}$ time complexity [19] critical for practical security analysis.

The projected sublattice can be formally defined as follows. Let there be a set of k-dimensional basis vectors $\mathbf{b}_1, \ldots, \mathbf{b}_k$ spanning a linear space V, which contains a subspace U. The orthogonal complement of V is defined as $U^\perp := \{\mathbf{v} \in V \mid \langle \mathbf{v}, U \rangle = 0\}$. For $1 \leq i \leq n-1$, let π_i denote the orthogonal projection operator acting on the basis vectors $(\mathbf{b}_1, \ldots, \mathbf{b}_{i-1})$. Let $B_{i,k}$ be the basis vector group obtained by applying π_i to $\mathbf{b}_i, \ldots, \mathbf{b}_k$, specifically:

$$B_{[i,k]} := (\pi_i(\mathbf{b}_i), \ldots, \pi_i(\mathbf{b}_k))$$

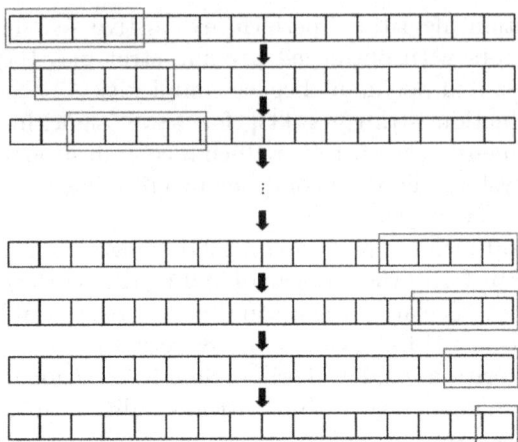

Fig. 1. BKZ algorithm (Color figure online)

The sublattice $\Lambda_{[i,k]}$ generated by the basis vector group $B_{[i,k]}$ is then called the projected sublattice.

During simulation processes, it becomes necessary to estimate the shortest vector length $\lambda_1(L)$ in lattice L without actually solving SVP. This is achieved through the following assumptions.

Assumption 1 (Gaussian Heuristic). For a full-rank lattice Λ, the expected length of the shortest non-zero vector is:

$$gh(\Lambda) = \sqrt{\frac{n}{2\pi e}} \cdot \mathrm{vol}(\Lambda)^{1/n}$$

where $\mathrm{vol}(\Lambda) = \det(\Lambda) = \det(B)$ denotes the fundamental parallelepiped volume of the lattice, equivalent to the determinant of lattice basis B.

The quality of basis vectors obtained through BKZ algorithms is typically characterized using the *Hermite factor*, defined as:

$$\delta_\beta := \frac{\|\mathbf{b}_1\|}{\mathrm{vol}(\Lambda)^{1/n}}$$

where $\|\mathbf{b}_1\|$ is the length of the first basis vector. To estimate δ, Gama and Nguyen introduced the following assumption regarding Gram-Schmidt orthogonalized basis vectors [19].

Assumption 2 (Geometric Series Assumption, GSA). For $1 \leq i \leq n-1$, the Gram-Schmidt orthogonalized basis vectors $\mathbf{b}_1^*, \ldots, \mathbf{b}_n^*$ corresponding to the BKZ-output basis $\{\mathbf{b}_1, \ldots, \mathbf{b}_n\}$ satisfy

$$\frac{\|\mathbf{b}_{i+1}^*\|}{\|\mathbf{b}_i^*\|} \approx c$$

where c is a constant related to BKZ algorithms.

3 Survey of Cost Models for Lattice Hard Problem Solving Algorithms

This section primarily discusses cost models for lattice hard problem solving algorithms. The BKZ algorithm serves as the representative lattice algorithm, and current cost models for it can be divided into two categories originating from the work of Gama and Nguyen [19] and the security analysis of the NewHope algorithm [20]. In the Lattice-Estimator work of Albrecht et al., they labeled the former as *2008 cost model* and the latter as *2016 cost model*, which are also adopted by this paper.

3.1 2008 Cost Model

Gama and Nguyen first conducted experiments on three types of SVP problems, deriving the following inequality related to BKZ parameters from their results:

$$\tau \cdot \delta_0^d \leq \frac{\lambda_2(\Lambda)}{\lambda_1(\Lambda)}$$

where δ_0 is the root Hermite factor, d is the lattice dimension, $\lambda_1(\Lambda)$ and $\lambda_2(\Lambda)$ are respectively the lengths of the shortest and second shortest vectors in lattice Λ, and $\tau \in [0.18, 0.48]$ is an experimentally determined constant. This work proposed that the above condition serves as a sufficient condition for BKZ algorithms to obtain the shortest vector with high probability. It established the first BKZ cost model consistent with experimental results, marking a pioneering contribution.

Subsequent improvements enhanced BKZ algorithm efficiency, rendering the original implementation referenced in the above work suboptimal. Chen et al. [22] introduced a series of enhancements leading to the widely adopted BKZ 2.0 algorithm. Their performance analysis provided a new cost model, with experimental results first comparing simulated outputs against actual outputs when BKZ operates at larger scales. This algorithm retains BKZ's basic execution framework but substitutes actual SVP solver executions with Gaussian heuristic assumptions to predict SVP oracle outputs. Taking basis vector lengths $\|\mathbf{b}_1\|, \ldots, \|\mathbf{b}_n\|$ and block size β as inputs, it estimates post-BKZ basis vector lengths and computes the corresponding root Hermite factor δ_β.

To reduce time costs considering the exponential time complexity of SVP oracles, Progressive-BKZ strategies gradually increase block size β during execution. As β's incremental strategy significantly impacts Progressive-BKZ's cost model, Aono et al. [23] conducted thorough research on β incrementation schemes. Building on optimizations for enumeration radius and pruning in SVP oracles, they proposed a new BKZ cost model. Subsequent works further improved Progressive-BKZ and its cost modeling [36–39].

3.2 2016 Cost Model

Alkim et al. [20] proposed a cost modeling approach based on the success condition of SVP oracles. Specifically, if the projection of the lattice's shortest vector

v (i.e., the SVP solution) onto the linear space spanned by the Gram-Schmidt vectors $\{\mathbf{b}_n^*, \mathbf{b}_{n-1}^*, \ldots, \mathbf{b}_{n-\beta+1}^*\}$ satisfies certain conditions, the SVP oracle can find the last full-block vector $\widetilde{\mathbf{v}}$. This disrupts the GSA distribution, thereby enabling solutions to the decision version of the LWE problem.

Formally, let the length of the shortest vector $\mathbf{v} = (\mathbf{s}|\mathbf{e}|1)$ in the LWE-embedded lattice Λ be $\|\mathbf{v}\| = \sigma\sqrt{n+m}$, where $\sigma \in (0,1]$ is a constant. Let β denote the block size and $\widetilde{\delta}_\beta$ the root Hermite factor. When β, σ, n, $\widetilde{\delta}_\beta$, and $\mathrm{vol}(\Lambda)$ satisfy:

$$\sigma\sqrt{\beta} \leq \widetilde{\delta}_\beta^{2\beta - n} \cdot \mathrm{vol}(\Lambda)^{\frac{1}{n}}$$

The BKZ-β algorithm can successfully find the shortest vector in Λ. By iterating $\beta \in [2, n]$ and selecting the minimal β satisfying this inequality, we obtain the required block size for solving LWE instances.

However, this work only proposed the aforementioned propositions without providing experimental results to substantiate the conclusions. This gap was addressed by subsequent work from Albrecht et al. [24], whose research group conducted a series of experiments largely supporting these propositions. Nevertheless, their results indicated that for certain lattice problem instances, actual solving costs were lower than simulation algorithm estimates.

Later, Yu and Ducas conducted a more detailed analysis of the statistical characteristics of BKZ algorithm execution [9]. Their findings revealed that prior works could only capture the first-order statistical characteristics of BKZ's performance, failing to guarantee accuracy for higher-order statistical features. This work further investigated second-order statistical characteristics of algorithmic execution costs, particularly examining behavioral differences between initial, final and normal intermediate phases during algorithm execution. This phenomenon is generally referred to as the *head-and-tail phenomenon* in existing literature. However, their modeling of the initial phase remained insufficiently precise, prompting further refinements in subsequent work by Bai et al. [25].

These observations demonstrate that the aforementioned models share a fundamental limitation: they remain heavily reliant on heuristic assumptions and experimental results from small-scale lattice problem instances. Due to computational resource constraints, current experimental findings cannot guarantee that similar results would hold when applying the same algorithms to large-scale problem instances required by efficient lattice-based cryptosystems.

3.3 Q-Ary Lattice Attack Cost Models

Current lattice cryptography relies on two fundamental hard problems: LWE and SIS. When constructing these problems using embedding techniques, the lattice basis matrix Λ typically exhibits the following structure:

$$B = \begin{pmatrix} q\mathbf{I} & * \\ \mathbf{0} & \mathbf{I} \end{pmatrix}$$

where Λ satisfies $q\mathbb{Z}^m \approx \Lambda \subset \mathbb{Z}^m$ for positive integer q. Such lattices are termed *q-ary lattices* in the literature. Due to their special structure, the Gram-Schmidt orthogonalized basis B^* obtained after executing BKZ algorithms also demonstrates distinctive characteristics. The Dilithium algorithm team provided detailed analysis of this structure in their documentation [2].

Specifically, let $B^* = (\mathbf{b}_1^* \mid \cdots \mid \mathbf{b}_n^*)$ denote the Gram-Schmidt orthogonalized vectors with lengths $\ell_i := \|\mathbf{b}_i^*\|$. For analytical convenience, we consider their logarithmic representations $\ell_i^* = \log \ell_i$.

Observing matrix B, each vector in the upper block matrix $(q\mathbf{I}|0)^\intercal$ has length q, while vectors in $(*|\mathbf{I})^\intercal$ typically exhibit lengths substantially smaller than q with high probability. Consequently, during initial BKZ execution, the vector group lengths often display abrupt slope variations. In extreme cases where the upper block matrix $*$ becomes zero, we can plot the vector length profile against dimension index i, as illustrated in Fig. 2 (left panel).

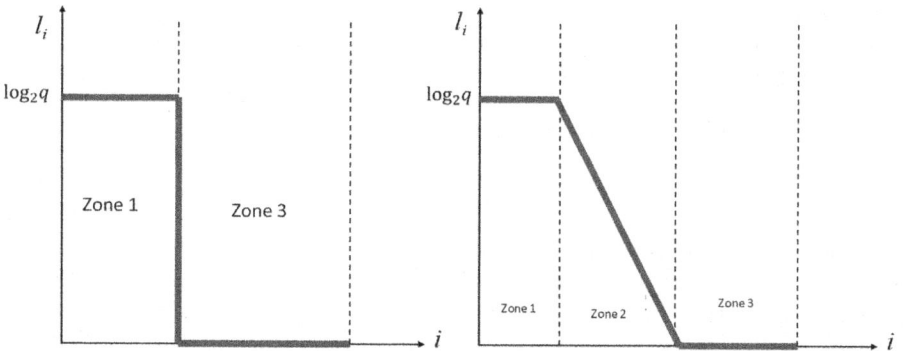

Fig. 2. Z-shape profile of q-ary lattice basis

During BKZ algorithm execution, the SVP oracle is invoked on small-dimensional sublattices to minimize the lengths of corresponding basis vectors. The strength of this effect increases with the block size parameter β. However, since BKZ operates through basis transformations within the same lattice, it preserves the determinant of the lattice. By the geometric interpretation of determinants, the sum $\sum_{i=1}^n \ell_i^*$ remains invariant under BKZ operations. Consequently, BKZ execution gradually smooths out fluctuations in basis vector lengths.

As illustrated in Fig. 2 (right panel), the resulting ℓ_i^* profile after BKZ processing exhibits a characteristic structure commonly referred to as the *Z-shape* in the literature [26]. In general cases, the number of vectors in Regions 1 and 3 may reduce to zero, corresponding to BKZ-β's more global influence on basis vectors when β increases.

3.4 BKZ Block Size and Bit Security

The preceding discussion focused on methods to determine the minimal block size β required to solve hard problems. However, the concept of *bit security* in cryptography relates to the actual runtime of attack algorithms. To bridge this gap, we must incorporate both the time complexity of SVP oracles invoked by BKZ and the number of oracle calls.

For SVP oracle time complexity, current analyses adopt state-of-the-art results such as BDGL algorithm [27] with time complexity $2^{0.292\beta + o(\beta)}$, models implemented in the Generic Sieve Kernel (G6K) [34,48], including ListSieve [41] and BGJ-Sieve [42].

Determining the number of SVP oracle invocations in BKZ remains challenging. Early BKZ studies suggested super-polynomial calls were required for full convergence. However, BKZ 2.0 [22] demonstrated that BKZ can output near-convergent basis vectors with significantly fewer calls. This led to the *early-abort strategy* [35], where BKZ execution is manually terminated after polynomial-time oracle calls.

In theoretical analyses, Alkim et al. further simplified this through the *Core-SVP methodology* [20] for NewHope security analysis. This approach fixes the number of SVP oracle calls at 1. Assuming BDGL sieving as the SVP oracle, the logarithmic BKZ runtime (i.e., bit security) becomes:

$$\log(t_{\text{BKZ}}) \approx 0.292\beta$$

Since actual BKZ executions typically require multiple oracle calls (>1), this methodology significantly underestimates attack costs and consequently overestimates cryptographic security. Current standardization processes for lattice schemes like Dilithium and Kyber [26,28] nevertheless adopt this methodology for concrete security estimation.

However, there are noteworthy optimizations on the lattice algorithms. Zhao et al. [50] proposed a memory-optimized lattice sieving implementation, leading to uncertainty for some NIST PQC candidates in that they did not ensure the security requirements. The work of Herold et al. [51] optimized tuple sieving by offering tunable time-memory trade-offs. These works indicate the importance of sub-exponential factors in the complexity of lattice algorithms, such as considerations on memory and parallel computation, which impacts the concrete security of lattice cryptography. Other directions of optimizations should also be considered, such as quantum optimizations [52,53] and novel lattice sieving algorithms [54].

4 Survey of Security Estimation Models for Lattice-Based Cryptography

As a critical step in cryptographic parameter selection, inaccurate security estimation may severely compromise algorithm security [22]. For lattice-based cryptography, the complexity of security estimation poses significant risks of human error. Meanwhile, diverse application scenarios in modern internet demand varied security-performance trade-offs. To address this challenge, Albrecht et al. [21,43] initially proposed the security estimation framework for LWE problems and implemented the LWE-Estimator tool. This tool enables users to derive security estimates from LWE instance parameters. Now rebranded as Lattice-Estimator, it comprehensively integrates security estimation methods for various lattice-based hard problems including LWE, SIS, and NTRU. Building on Albrecht's work, Bi et al. [44] systematically analyzed dual attack, decoding attack and primal attack, and providing corresponding complexity analyses and instance-specific estimations. In her doctoral dissertation [45], Bi further proposed concrete security analyses for hybrid attacks targeting LWE problems with specific secret distributions. Li [46] developed a binary search-based runtime prediction method for primal and dual attacks.

Beyond theoretical security estimation, side-channel attacks critically impact practical cryptographic implementations. Dachman-Soled et al. [29] introduced a framework incorporating quantified information leakage into security estimation, implemented through the Leaky-LWE-Estimator tool. To model information leakage, they defined a BDD variant called the *Distorted Bounded Distance Decoding* (DBDD) problem, generalizing the target vector's probability distribution to asymmetric cases for enhanced modeling flexibility.

Building upon these two established frameworks, this section surveys security estimation methodologies for the LWE and SIS computational hard problems.

4.1 LWE Security Estimation Framework

Based on previous discussions, we formalize the security estimation framework for LWE problems as follows:

$$\text{LWE} \to \text{BDD/DBDD} \to \text{SVP} \to \text{BKZ Block Size} \to \text{Bit Security}$$

The embedding technique enables constructing lattice bases corresponding to LWE instances, thus completing the first step from LWE to BDD. For the second step, we first define the *Distorted Bounded Distance Decoding* (DBDD) problem.

Let span($\cdot$) denote the linear span of a matrix, rank($\cdot$) the matrix rank, and $\Sigma^{\dagger}$ the generalized inverse of matrix Σ defined as:

$$\Sigma^{\dagger} = \left(\Sigma + \Pi_{\Sigma}^{\perp}\right)^{-1} - \Pi_{\Sigma}^{\perp}$$

where Π_{Σ} is the orthogonal projection matrix onto span(Σ). Let Y be a maximal linearly independent subset of Σ, then:

$$\Pi_{\Sigma}^{\perp} := \mathbf{I} - \mathbf{Y}^{T} \cdot (\mathbf{Y} \cdot \mathbf{Y}^{T})^{-1} \cdot \mathbf{Y}$$

Let $\sqrt{\Sigma}$ denote the Cholesky decomposition of symmetric matrix Σ. Using these notations, we formally define:

Definition 3 (DBDD Problem). Let $\Lambda \subseteq \mathbb{R}^m$ be a lattice, $\Sigma \in \mathbb{R}^{m \times m}$ a symmetric matrix, and $\mu \in \mathbb{R}^m$ a vector satisfying:

$$\mathrm{span}(\Sigma) \subset \mathrm{span}(\Sigma + \mu^T \cdot \mu) = \mathrm{span}(\Lambda)$$

The $DBDD_{\Lambda,\mu,\Sigma}$ problem requires finding vector $\mathbf{x} \in \Lambda \cap \mathcal{E}(\mu, \Sigma)$ given μ, Σ, and a basis of Λ, where:

$$\mathcal{E}(\mu, \Sigma) := \left\{ x \in \mu + \mathrm{span}(\Sigma) \mid (\mathbf{x} - \mu)^T \cdot \Sigma^\dagger \cdot (\mathbf{x} - \mu) \leq \mathrm{rank}(\Sigma) \right\}$$

Let B_d denote the d-dimensional unit ball centered at the origin. i.e. $B_d := \{x \in \mathbb{R}^d \mid \|x\| \leq d\}$. The ellipsoid $\mathcal{E}(\mu, \Sigma)$ can be geometrically interpreted as a linear transformation of the hyperball $B_{\mathrm{rank}(\Sigma)}$. The condition related with $\mathrm{span}(\Sigma)$ in the DBDD definition implies that $\mu \notin \mathrm{span}(\Sigma)$. This leads to the rank relationship:

$$\mathrm{rank}\left(\Sigma + \mu^T \mu\right) = \mathrm{rank}(\Sigma) + 1 = \mathrm{rank}(\Lambda)$$

From a probabilistic perspective, $\mathcal{E}(\mu, \Sigma)$ represents an asymmetric high-dimensional probability distribution. The DBDD-to-SVP reduction essentially performs an affine transformation converting $\mathcal{E}(\mu, \Sigma)$ into a symmetric distribution $\mathcal{E}(0, \Sigma'')$ centered at the origin. Figure 3 illustrates this transformation pipeline in two-dimensional Euclidean space.

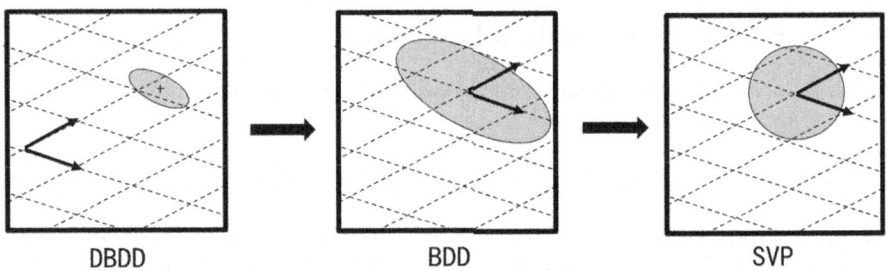

Fig. 3. Transformation of DBDD in two-dimensional Euclidean space

Specifically, we first replace $\mathcal{E}(\mu, \Sigma)$ with a larger origin-centered distribution $\mathcal{E}(0, \Sigma')$ where $\Sigma' = \Sigma + \mu^T \mu$, thereby translating the distribution center to the origin. This follows from:

$$\mathcal{E}(\mu, \Sigma) = \mu + \sqrt{\Sigma} \cdot B_{\mathrm{rank}(\Sigma)} \subset B_{\mathrm{rank}(\Sigma)+1} \cdot (\sqrt{\Sigma}, \mu)^\mathsf{T} = \mathcal{E}(0, \Sigma + \mu^\mathsf{T} \mu)$$

For the second step, we perform scaling transformation by normalizing all eigenvalues of Σ' to 1. As Σ' is symmetric, this is achieved through multiplying lattice elements by $\sqrt{\Sigma'}^\dagger$, transforming the problem instance into $(\Lambda \cdot \sqrt{\Sigma'}^\dagger, 0, \Sigma'' := \sqrt{\Sigma'^\dagger} \cdot \Sigma' \cdot (\sqrt{\Sigma'^\dagger})^\mathsf{T})$. This converts the SVP problem into finding vectors $\mathbf{v}$ in the transformed lattice.

For DBDD-to-BKZ block size estimation, either the 2008 or 2016 cost models can be employed. Using the 2016 model with origin-centered symmetric distributions, the average solution vector length becomes $\|\mathbf{v}\| = \operatorname{rank}(\Sigma'') = \sqrt{n}$. Setting $\Sigma = 1$ yields the constraint:

$$\sqrt{\beta} \leq \widetilde{\delta}_\beta^{2\beta-n} \cdot \operatorname{vol}(\Lambda)^{1/n}$$

This reveals that β depends solely on lattice dimension n and fundamental region volume $\operatorname{vol}(\Lambda)$, independent of basis vectors. Practical implementations compute $\log(\det(B))$ to mitigate precision loss in large-scale computations.

When using the 2008 cost model, BKZ simulation algorithms provide more accurate results. Additional optimizations can exploit the length distribution of projected vectors $\pi_i(\mathbf{v})$. For mainstream lattice cryptosystems, this distribution approximates symmetric Gaussian in high dimensions via the Central Limit Theorem. This approach is termed *probabilistic simulation* in literature [30].

4.2 SIS Security Estimation Framework

Existing lattice-based cryptosystems exhibit divergent requirements for SIS solution vector lengths. These constraints primarily manifest in two distinct norm spaces, i.e. Euclidean norm (ℓ_2-norm) bounded solutions and Infinity norm (ℓ_∞-norm) bounded solutions. This subsection provides separate analyses for these constraint types.

ℓ_2-Norm Model. Ruckert et al. [31] conducted pioneering work on cost modeling for SIS problems. Through extensive experimental results, they established mathematical relationships between SIS solving time T_{SIS} and the target root Hermite factor δ_0, subsequently applying these models to contemporary lattice cryptography parameter sets. However, their analysis remained surface-level, failing to reveal the reduction mechanism from SIS to underlying SVP problems or quantify the impact of critical parameters like β. This work primarily holds foundational significance.

As previously discussed, the basis matrix B_{SIS} of the q-ary lattice $\Lambda_q^\perp(A)$ associated with SIS problems can be expressed as:

$$B_{\text{SIS}} = \begin{pmatrix} q\mathbf{I}_n & -\mathbf{A}_1^{-1}\mathbf{A}_2 \\ \mathbf{0} & \mathbf{I}_{m-n} \end{pmatrix}$$

Solving SIS reduces to finding a short vector $\mathbf{v} \in \Lambda_q^\perp(A)$ satisfying $\|\mathbf{v}\| \leq B$, where B is the norm bound determined by the SIS instance.

The BKZ simulation algorithm discussed earlier enables prediction of output vector lengths $\|\mathbf{b}_1^*\|$ after basis reduction. By comparing these predicted lengths against B, we determine algorithmic success: if $\|\mathbf{b}_1^*\| < B$, the SIS solution is deemed found. This methodology bridges lattice reduction quality metrics with concrete SIS security estimation.

When $B \geq q$, non-trivial optimizations leveraging the Z-shape structure of q-ary lattices become feasible. This approach, initially proposed by Ducas et al.

[31] in their security analysis of the Mitaka variant [32] (a small-modulus Falcon variant), proceeds as follows. Firstly, execute sieve algorithms on the first β-dimensional projected sublattice within the linear descent region of the Z-shape structure to generate short vectors. Then apply lifting strategies [40] to extend these vectors to the full lattice.

This optimization reduces coordinate magnitudes in Zone 1 (see Fig. 2), consequently shrinking vector lengths. The resultant short vectors exhibit:

$$\text{Expected length: } \sqrt{\eta^2 + \frac{n_q q^2}{12}} \quad \text{and} \quad \text{Upper bound: } \sqrt{\eta^2 + \frac{n_q q^2}{4}}$$

where η^2 denotes the expected output vector length from sieving, q the modulus, and n_q the vector count in Zone 1.

Assuming Zone 1 coordinates are uniformly distributed within the n_q-dimensional hypercube $\mathcal{C}_{n_q}(q)$ (centered at origin with edge length q), the SIS solution vector length bound corresponds to a η_q-dimensional sphere with radius $\sqrt{B^2 - \eta^2}$ i.e. $\mathcal{B}_{n_q}\left(\sqrt{B^2 - \eta^2}\right)$.

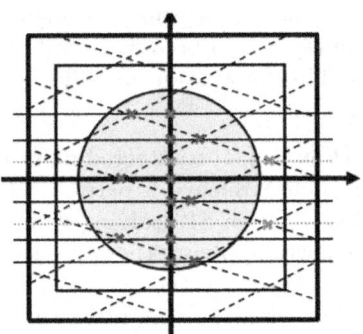

Fig. 4. A Geometric understanding of successful probability of the attack of SIS under Euclidean norm when $B \geq q$

Figure 4 visualizes this geometric interpretation in two-dimensional Euclidean space Consider the projection Λ_y of lattice Λ onto the y-axis, where coordinate magnitudes are bounded by modulus q. Valid lattice points satisfying the ℓ_2-norm constraint lie within a circle of radius B. In Fig. 4, Points in sublattice Λ_y, their lifted points (in Λ) and invalid points are marked red, blue, gray respectively. Under our assumptions, vectors reside in hypercube $\mathcal{C}_{n_q}(q)$, while those meeting the SIS norm bound B lie within the sphere $\mathcal{B}_{n_q}\left(\sqrt{B^2 - \eta^2}\right)$. The conditional probability is computed as:

$$P(B, \eta, q, n_q) = \frac{\left|\mathcal{B}_{n_q}\left(\sqrt{B^2 - \eta^2}\right) \cap \mathcal{C}_{n_q}(q)\right|}{\left|\mathcal{C}_{n_q}(q)\right|}$$

where $|\cdot|$ denotes lattice point counts within geometric regions.

Computing this probability requires determining the lattice point counts within two geometric bodies $\mathcal{C}_{n_q}(q)$ and $\mathcal{B}_{n_q}\left(\sqrt{B^2 - \eta^2}\right)$. The Gaussian heuristic enables transforming this problem into computing the volumes of these geometric bodies. For precise computation, one could employ *truncated Θ-series* methods. However, in high-dimensional lattice estimations, the computational complexity of Θ-series becomes prohibitive for practical applications. This challenge remains unresolved in current research [32].

ℓ_∞-**Norm Model.** In the lattice-based signature scheme Dilithium, the SIS problem's solution vector length bound is defined under the infinity norm (ℓ_∞-norm), whereas standard BKZ algorithms and lattice sieves are designed for Euclidean norm (ℓ_2-norm) constraints. The Dilithium Round 3 proposal [26] proposes the following strategy to adapt Euclidean norm security estimations to infinity norm settings:

Let d denote the lattice dimension and β the BKZ block size. First execute standard BKZ simulation to output basis vectors with Gram-Schmidt norms $\{\ell_i\}_{i=1}^d$. Let l and r respectively mark the start/end indices of the linear descent region in the Z-shape structure. Sieving on β-dimensional projected sublattices yields short vectors with ℓ_2-norm approximately 2^{ℓ_i}. These vectors are orthogonal to the subspace spanned by the first $l - 1$ bases, but the first $l - 1$ basis vectors of q-ary lattices are scaled standard basis vectors ($q\mathbf{e}_i$). Consequently, the first $l - 1$ components of lifted vectors (Z-shape Zone 1) are modeled as uniform distribution modulo q, while components $d-i+1$ to $d-j$ (Z-shape Zone 2) are modeled as Gaussian distribution with standard deviation $\sigma = 2^i\sqrt{j-i+1}$. Then we can compute the success probability P_{ℓ_∞}. The required number of BKZ-β executions is $\lceil 1/P_{\ell_\infty} \rceil$.

To eliminate structural biases from q-ary basis components $(q\mathbf{I}|\mathbf{0})^\mathsf{T}$, lattice basis randomization can be applied prior to BKZ execution. This *forgetting q-vector strategy* removes the Zone 1 structure, as illustrated in Fig. 5 showing vector length profiles in this case.

This model heuristically models the coordinate values of short vectors output by BKZ algorithms as Gaussian distributions. This modeling causes predicted coordinate values to shrink. Consequently, the estimated BKZ block size becomes smaller, rendering the model conservative through overestimating adversarial capabilities in parameter selection. The geometric interpretation provides references for more precise coordinate value computations, as illustrated in Fig. 6.

Figure 6 demonstrates short vectors obtained via generic SIS-solving algorithms (corresponding to ℓ_2-norm constraints), where points satisfying ℓ_∞-norm requirements are marked red and non-compliant points gray. This geometric interpretation inversely mirrors Fig. 4's scenario: generic SIS solvers acquire lattice points in high-dimensional spheres, requiring computation of their probability of falling within ℓ_∞-norm constrained hypercubes. This probability compu-

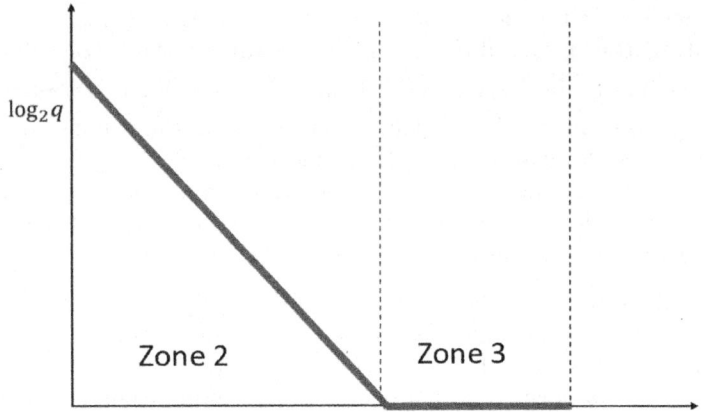

Fig. 5. Shape of q-ary lattice basis length after forgetting q-vectors

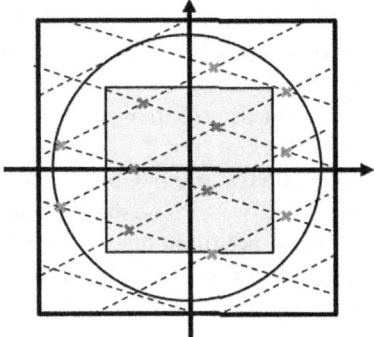

Fig. 6. A geometric understanding of success probability of SIS attacks under infinity norm

tation reduces to calculating the volumes of two geometric bodies:

$$P_{\ell_\infty} = \frac{\text{vol}\left(\mathcal{B}_n(B) \cap \mathcal{C}_n(B)\right)}{\text{vol}(\mathcal{B}_n(B))}$$

where $\mathcal{B}_n(B)$ denotes the n-dimensional sphere and $\mathcal{C}_n(B)$ the axis-aligned hypercube corresponding to the ℓ_∞-norm bound. Truncated θ-series methods can be employed for numerical computation, though practical implementations face complexity challenges in high-dimensional spaces [33].

5 Conclusion

The rapid development of quantum computing has rendered the migration to quantum-resistant cryptography urgent across industries. In the PQC era, single cryptographic algorithms and parameter sets cannot support the complexity of industrial demands. The usage of public-key cryptosystems (e.g., digital signatures) and their parameters will become increasingly diversified. Under this backdrop, security estimation for various algorithms and parameter sets emerges as a critical challenge. Given the inherent complexity of this problem, research on security estimation frameworks becomes particularly vital.

This paper surveys existing security estimation methods through two perspectives based on the security reduction hierarchy of efficient lattice-based cryptosystems: lattice hard problems such as SVP and BDD, and computational hard problems like LWE and SIS that directly underpin lattice cryptography.

Current estimation frameworks for LWE and SIS algorithms predominantly focus on ℓ_2-norm analyses. However, the MSIS problem underlying Dilithium operates under ℓ_∞-norm constraints. Remarkably, recent trends demonstrate convergence between coding theory-based and lattice-based public-key cryptosystems. Algorithms like BKZ (originally designed for lattice problems) are now being adapted to solve coding-based cryptographic problems, which typically do not rely on ℓ_2-norm constraints. Key unresolved challenges include the accuracy of modified measurement-based cost models and security estimations, as well as framework development for accurate security estimation under non-ℓ_2 norms.

Acknowledgments. This study was funded by National Key Laboratory of Security Communication Foundation (2023, 6142103042308).

References

1. Shor, P.W.: Polynomial-time algorithms for prime factorization and discrete logarithms on a quantum computer. SIAM Rev. **41**(2), 303–332 (1999)
2. Mavroeidis, V., Vishi, K., Zych, M.D., et al.: The impact of quantum computing on present cryptography. arXiv preprint arXiv:1804.00200 (2018)
3. Regev, O.: Lattice-based cryptography. In: Dwork, C. (ed.) CRYPTO 2006. LNCS, vol. 4117, pp. 131–141. Springer, Heidelberg (2006). https://doi.org/10.1007/11818175_8
4. Baldi, M., Santini, P., Cancellieri, G.: Post-quantum cryptography based on codes: state of the art and open challenges. In: 2017 AEIT International Annual Conference, pp. 1–6. IEEE (2017)
5. Ding, J.T., Gower, J.E., Schmidt, D.S.: Multivariate Public Key Cryptosystems. Springer, New York (2006)
6. National Institute of Standards and Technology: FIPS 203. Module-Lattice-based Key-Encapsulation Mechanism Standard (2024)
7. National Institute of Standards and Technology: FIPS 204. Module-Lattice-Based Digital Signature Standard (2024)
8. National Institute of Standards and Technology: FIPS 205. Stateless Hash-Based Digital Signature Standard (2024)
9. Yu, Y., Ducas, L.: Second order statistical behavior of LLL and BKZ. In: Adams, C., Camenisch, J. (eds.) SAC 2017. LNCS, vol. 10719, pp. 3–22. Springer, Cham (2018). https://doi.org/10.1007/978-3-319-72565-9_1

10. Ducas, L., Pulles, L.N.: Does the dual-sieve attack on learning with errors even work?. In: CRYPTO 2023. LNCS, vol. 14084, pp. 37–69. Springer (2023)
11. Ajtai, M., Dwork, C.: A public-key cryptosystem with worst-case/average-case equivalence. In: STOC 1997, pp. 284–293. ACM (1997)
12. Regev, O.: On lattices, learning with errors, random linear codes, and cryptography. J. ACM **56**(6), 1–40 (2009)
13. Micciancio, D.: Generalized compact knapsacks, cyclic lattices, and efficient one-way functions. Comput. Complex. **16**, 365–411 (2007)
14. Lyubashevsky, V., Peikert, C., Regev, O.: On ideal lattices and learning with errors over rings. In: Gilbert, H. (ed.) EUROCRYPT 2010. LNCS, vol. 6110, pp. 1–23. Springer, Heidelberg (2010). https://doi.org/10.1007/978-3-642-13190-5_1
15. Kannan, R.: Improved algorithms for integer programming and related lattice problems. In: STOC 1983, pp. 193–206. ACM (1983)
16. Ajtai, M., Kumar, R., Sivakumar, D.: A sieve algorithm for the shortest lattice vector problem. In: STOC 2001, pp. 601–610. ACM (2001)
17. Pohst, M.E.: On the computation of lattice vectors of minimal length, successive minima and reduced bases with applications. ACM SIGSAM Bull. **15**(1), 37–44 (1981)
18. Lenstra, A.K., Lenstra, H.W., Lovász, L.: Factoring polynomials with rational coefficients. Math. Ann. **261**, 515–534 (1982)
19. Gama, N., Nguyen, P.Q.: Finding short lattice vectors within Mordell's inequality. In: STOC 2008, pp. 207–216. ACM (2008)
20. Alkim, E., Ducas, L., Poppelmann, T., et al.: Post-quantum key exchange-a new hope. In: USENIX Security 2016, pp. 327–343 (2016)
21. Albrecht, M.R., Player, R., Scott, S.: On the concrete hardness of learning with errors. J. Math. Cryptol. **9**(3), 169–203 (2015)
22. Chen, Y., Nguyen, P.Q.: BKZ 2.0: better lattice security estimates. In: Lee, D.H., Wang, X. (eds.) ASIACRYPT 2011. LNCS, vol. 7073, pp. 1–20. Springer, Heidelberg (2011). https://doi.org/10.1007/978-3-642-25385-0_1
23. Aono, Y., Wang, Y., Hayashi, T., Takagi, T.: Improved progressive BKZ algorithms and their precise cost estimation by sharp simulator. In: Fischlin, M., Coron, J.-S. (eds.) EUROCRYPT 2016. LNCS, vol. 9665, pp. 789–819. Springer, Heidelberg (2016). https://doi.org/10.1007/978-3-662-49890-3_30
24. Albrecht, M.R., Göpfert, F., Virdia, F., Wunderer, T.: Revisiting the expected cost of solving uSVP and applications to LWE. In: Takagi, T., Peyrin, T. (eds.) ASIACRYPT 2017. LNCS, vol. 10624, pp. 297–322. Springer, Cham (2017). https://doi.org/10.1007/978-3-319-70694-8_11
25. Bai, S., Stehlé, D., Wen, W.: Measuring, simulating and exploiting the head concavity phenomenon in BKZ. In: Peyrin, T., Galbraith, S. (eds.) ASIACRYPT 2018. LNCS, vol. 11272, pp. 369–404. Springer, Cham (2018). https://doi.org/10.1007/978-3-030-03326-2_13
26. Leo, D., Eike, K., et al.: CRYSTALS-Dilithium - Algorithm Specifications and Supporting Documentation (Version 3.1) (2024). https://pq-crystals.org/dilithium/data/dilithium-specification-round3-20210208.pdf
27. Becker, A., Ducas, L., Gama, N., et al.: New directions in nearest neighbor searching with applications to lattice sieving. In: SODA 2016, pp. 10–24. SIAM (2016)
28. Roberto, A., Joppe, B., et al.: CRYSTALS-Kyber (version 3.02) - Submission to round 3 of the NIST post-quantum project (2024). https://pq-crystals.org/kyber/data/kyber-specification-round3-20210804.pdf

29. Dachman-Soled, D., Ducas, L., Gong, H., Rossi, M.: LWE with side information: attacks and concrete security estimation. In: Micciancio, D., Ristenpart, T. (eds.) CRYPTO 2020. LNCS, vol. 12171, pp. 329–358. Springer, Cham (2020). https://doi.org/10.1007/978-3-030-56880-1_12
30. Rückert, M., Schneider, M.: Estimating the security of lattice-based cryptosystems. Cryptology ePrint Archive, Report 2010/137 (2010)
31. Ducas, L., Espitau, T., Postlethwaite, E.W.: Finding short integer solutions when the modulus is small. In: CRYPTO 2023. LNCS, vol. 14084, pp. 150–176. Springer (2023)
32. Espitau, T., Fouque, P.A., Gérard, F., et al.: Mitaka: a simpler, parallelizable, maskable variant of falcon. In: EUROCRYPT 2022. LNCS, vol. 13275, pp. 222–253. Springer (2022)
33. Ducas, L.: Shortest vector from lattice sieving: a few dimensions for free. In: Nielsen, J.B., Rijmen, V. (eds.) EUROCRYPT 2018. LNCS, vol. 10820, pp. 125–145. Springer, Cham (2018). https://doi.org/10.1007/978-3-319-78381-9_5
34. Albrecht, M.R., Ducas, L., Herold, G., Kirshanova, E., Postlethwaite, E.W., Stevens, M.: The general sieve kernel and new records in lattice reduction. In: Ishai, Y., Rijmen, V. (eds.) EUROCRYPT 2019. LNCS, vol. 11477, pp. 717–746. Springer, Cham (2019). https://doi.org/10.1007/978-3-030-17656-3_25
35. Hanrot, G., Pujol, X., Stehlé, D.: Terminating BKZ. Cryptology ePrint Archive, Report 2011/198 (2011)
36. Wang, Y., Aono, Y., Takagi, T.: Hardness evaluation for search LWE problem using progressive BKZ simulator. IEICE Trans. Fundam. Electron. Commun. Comput. Sci. **101**(12), 2162–2170 (2018)
37. Postlethwaite, E.W., Virdia, F.: On the success probability of solving unique SVP via BKZ. In: Garay, J.A. (ed.) PKC 2021. LNCS, vol. 12710, pp. 68–98. Springer, Cham (2021). https://doi.org/10.1007/978-3-030-75245-3_4
38. Zhao, Z., Ding, J.: Practical improvements on BKZ algorithm. In: CSCML 2023. LNCS, vol. 13914, pp. 273–284. Springer (2023)
39. Xia, W., Wang, L., Gu, D., et al.: Improved Progressive BKZ with Lattice Sieving and a Two-Step Mode for Solving uSVP. Cryptology ePrint Archive, Report 2022/1005 (2022)
40. Babai, L.: On Lovász's lattice reduction and the nearest lattice point problem. Combinatorica **6**(1), 1–13 (1986)
41. Herold, G., Kirshanova, E., Laarhoven, T.: Speed-ups and time–memory trade-offs for tuple lattice sieving. In: Abdalla, M., Dahab, R. (eds.) PKC 2018. LNCS, vol. 10769, pp. 407–436. Springer, Cham (2018). https://doi.org/10.1007/978-3-319-76578-5_14
42. Becker, A., Gama, N., Joux, A.: Speeding-up lattice sieving without increasing the memory, using sub-quadratic nearest neighbor search. Cryptology ePrint Archive, Report 2015/522 (2015)
43. Player, R.: Parameter selection in lattice-based cryptography. Ph.D. thesis, Royal Holloway, University of London (2018)
44. Bi, L., Li, S., Liu, Y., et al.: Survey on practical security analysis of LWE problem. J. Cyber Secur. **4**(2), 1–12 (2019). (in Chinese)
45. Bi, L.: Research on practical security of learning with errors problem. Ph.D. thesis, University of Chinese Academy of Sciences (2022). (in Chinese)
46. Li, S.: Lattice basis reduction algorithms and their applications. Ph.D. thesis, University of Chinese Academy of Sciences (2022). (in Chinese)
47. Bi, L., Lu, X., Wang, K.: Research status and development trend of lattice sieve methods. J. Cryptogr. **8**(5), 735–757 (2021). (in Chinese)

48. Ducas, L., Stevens, M., van Woerden, W.: Advanced lattice sieving on GPUs, with tensor cores. In: Canteaut, A., Standaert, F.-X. (eds.) EUROCRYPT 2021. LNCS, vol. 12697, pp. 249–279. Springer, Cham (2021). https://doi.org/10.1007/978-3-030-77886-6_9
49. Albrecht, M., Ducas, L.: Lattice attacks on NTRU and LWE: a history of refinements. Cryptology ePrint Archive, Report 2021/799 (2021)
50. Zhao, Z., Ding, J., Yang, B.-Y.: Sieving with streaming memory access. IACR Trans. Cryptogr. Hardw. Embed. Syst. **2025**(2), 362–384 (2025)
51. Herold, G., Kirshanova, E., Laarhoven, T.: Speed-ups and time–memory trade-offs for tuple lattice sieving. In: Abdalla, M., Dahab, R. (eds.) PKC 2018. LNCS, vol. 10769, pp. 407–436. Springer, Cham (2018). https://doi.org/10.1007/978-3-319-76578-5_14
52. Laarhoven, T., Mosca, M., Van De Pol, J.: Finding shortest lattice vectors faster using quantum search. Des. Codes Cryptogr. **77**, 375–400 (2015)
53. Aono, Y., Nguyen, P.Q.: Random sampling revisited: lattice enumeration with discrete pruning. In: Coron, J.-S., Nielsen, J.B. (eds.) EUROCRYPT 2017. LNCS, vol. 10211, pp. 65–102. Springer, Cham (2017). https://doi.org/10.1007/978-3-319-56614-6_3
54. Albrecht, M.R., Bai, S., Fouque, P.-A., Kirchner, P., Stehlé, D., Wen, W.: Faster enumeration-based lattice reduction: root Hermite factor $k^{1/(2k)}$ time $k^{k/8+o(k)}$. In: Micciancio, D., Ristenpart, T. (eds.) CRYPTO 2020. LNCS, vol. 12171, pp. 186–212. Springer, Cham (2020). https://doi.org/10.1007/978-3-030-56880-1_7

Exploring the HTTPS OCSP Ecosystem: A Comprehensive Study

HengSheng Wang, ShuShang Wen, and Wei Wang[✉]

School of Cyber Science and Technology, University of Science and Technology of China, Hefei, China
{whsha, sswen}@mail.ustc.edu.cn, weiwang2025@ustc.edu.cn

Abstract. The widely-used HTTPS protocol relies on Transport Layer Security (TLS) to enable users to browse websites correctly and confidentially. Verifying the validity of HTTPS certificates is essential, and the Online Certificate Status Protocol (OCSP) plays a key role in checking certificate validity. However, OCSP itself faces examinations due to issues such as delays and privacy concerns. Moreover, all components involved in the OCSP protocol—web server software, OCSP responders, and browsers—often fail to adequately support Active OCSP, OCSP Stapling, and OCSP Must-Staple. To explore the current state of the OCSP ecosystem, we conducted large-scale scans of domains in the Tranco list in October 2023 and November 2024, and performed a month-long evaluation of their corresponding OCSP responders in both periods. We analyzed the support for OCSP from browsers and web server software. We found that none of the components adequately supports OCSP: Most OCSP responders experienced inaccessibility, and no web server software fully and correctly supported OCSP Stapling. Furthermore, most browsers do not respect OCSP Must-Staple and often neglect OCSP revocation checks.

Keywords: PKI · HTTPS · certificate revocation · OCSP

1 Introduction

HTTPS [26] plays an important role in communications security on the Internet. As of March 2025, 87.3% of websites have implemented HTTPS protocols [34]. The main functions of the TLS protocol include (1) authentication, (2) confidentiality, and (3) integrity. During the TLS handshake between a client and a server, the server must provide the client with an HTTPS certificate for authentication. This certificate is issued and managed within the Public Key Infrastructure (PKI) framework.

Before the HTTPS certificate expires, it may be revoked due to the leakage of the corresponding private key, changes of the certificate owner, vulnerabilities [12,37], poor implementations of cryptography [16], or other reasons [18,33]. The revocation status must be disseminated to all clients that rely on the certificate.

Otherwise, connections using a revoked certificate will be vulnerable to Man-in-the-Middle (MitM) attacks until the certificate expires. Without accurate and timely revocation checks, attackers can impersonate the server and covertly obtain passwords, financial data, and other personally identifiable information.

The Online Certificate Status Protocol (OCSP) [27] is one of the most widely adopted certificate revocation mechanisms [19]. It was originally designed to enable a browser to request the revocation status of a certificate (identified by its serial number) from the OCSP responder, which is specified in the certificate. The OCSP responder will sign an OCSP response indicating the requested certificate's revocation status. This is named *Active OCSP* in this paper. Then, to reduce communication delays and also mitigate privacy leakage, the *OCSP Stapling* technique allows a web server to proactively fetch and cache OCSP responses signed by the OCSP responder, which will be sent to browsers during the TLS handshake [24]. Recently, *OCSP Must-Staple* has been proposed to include a special certificate extension [15], instructing a browser to receive an OCSP response from the web server during the TLS handshake. It forces the web server to staple the OCSP response and send it during the TLS handshake; otherwise, a browser will terminate the handshake.

As a widely used revocation mechanism, OCSP does not work without challenges. In this paper, we explore the OCSP ecosystem, especially from the following perspectives.

- **HTTPS Servers** may choose to enable OCSP Stapling or not.
- **OCSP Responders** must sign and provide OCSP responses correctly and stably.
- **Web Server Software** shall comprehensively support different variations of OCSP (i.e., Active OCSP, OCSP Stapling, and OCSP Must-Staple).
- **Browsers** shall comprehensively support the variations of OCSP.

This paper conducted a comprehensive study on OCSP in the wild. We first performed an Internet-scale scan of HTTPS servers, collecting certificates in October 2023 and November 2024. We then initiated OCSP requests for these colleted certificates and probed OCSP responders over one month. Finally, we examined the OCSP support of 4 popular web server software and 27 browsers.

The main findings and contributions are as follows.

- Our study reveals recent OCSP promotions on the Internet. The percentage of certificates signed with OCSP Must-Staple extensions has increased from 0.02% in 2018 [10] to 0.11% in 2023, reaching 0.12% in 2024, most of which are signed by Let's Encrypt. Additionally, an increasing number of CAs now support OCSP Must-Staple. However, the adoption of OCSP Stapling varies significantly according to regions, certificate types, and domain names.
- We examined OCSP responders in two separate periods of one month, in October 2023 and November 2024, following the CA/Browser Forum (CA/B) Baseline Requirements [3]. In both assessments, more than 80% of the OCSP responders exhibited instability, and 16 OCSP responders issued incorrect OCSP responses.

- In October 2023, Nginx, Apache, OpenLiteSpeed (OLS), and Internet Information Services (IIS) were evaluated. Unfortunately, none of them supports OCSP fully and correctly. Apache even accepts OCSP responses with incorrect certificate serial numbers.
- The analysis on browsers demonstrates improved OCSP support by mobile devices in October 2023. On most platforms, Firefox actively initiates OCSP requests for all types of certificates, whereas other browsers do only for EV certificates, or even no OCSP request was found. Moreover, only Firefox respects the OCSP Must-staple extension on most platforms.

The rest of this paper is organized as below. Section 2 presents the brief background related to OCSP. Section 3 introduces related work, discussing certificate revocation methods. Section 4 presents the results of OCSP Stapling and OCSP Must-Staple obtained through large-scale scanning. In Sects. 5, 6, and 7, we discuss the supports for OCSP among OCSP responders, web server software, and browsers, respectively. Section 8 outlines the ethical considerations of our research. Section 9 concludes this work and offers recommendations.

2 Background

2.1 HTTPS and TLS

HTTPS is the de facto standard for secure communication on the Internet. Formally, HTTPS can be conceptualized as the combination of HTTP and TLS, where HTTP operates as the application-layer protocol and TLS provides a secure transport-layer channel.

The security of HTTPS communication is underpinned by the TLS protocol, which provides three fundamental guarantees to ensure secure data transmissions: (1) Authentication, whereby HTTPS certificates enable mutual identity verification, ensuring the authenticity of both communicating parties; (2) Confidentiality, achieved through encryption that prevents unauthorized access to transmitted data; and (3) Integrity, maintained through Message Authentication Codes (MACs) that detect any unauthorized modifications to data during transmission.

2.2 HTTPS Certificate

An X.509 [7] certificate is a digitally signed data structure issued by a CA. It binds a subject to a public key. The subject could be a person, a network node, or a generic entity identified by an identifier such as an email address, an IP address, or a DNS name. Certificates are issued by CAs, which themselves have certificates signed by other authorities, ultimately leading back to a few self-signed root certificates. When a client needs to verify a certificate, it must obtain the entire chain of certificates and ensure that each certificate in the chain is properly signed, within its validity period, and not revoked.

The CA/B defines three types of HTTPS certificates [1]:

- **Domain Validation (DV):** Issued upon verification of domain ownership.
- **Organization Validation (OV):** In addition to domain verification, the CA validates additional organizational information to confirm the legitimacy of the entity.
- **Extended Validation (EV):** Shares similar requirements to OV certificates but involves a stricter vetting process, often requiring a significantly longer review period.

2.3 OCSP

Figure 1 illustrates the three mechanisms of OCSP. The Active OCSP allows clients to query the CA about the revocation status of a specific certificate. The CA maintains a server called an OCSP responder to handle these requests.

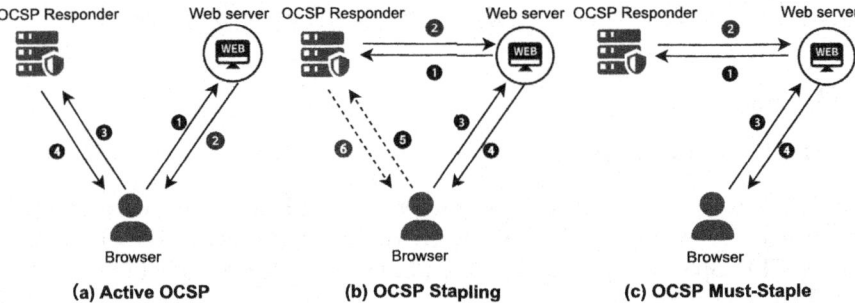

(a) Active OCSP   (b) OCSP Stapling   (c) OCSP Must-Staple

Fig. 1. (*a*) After the browser obtains the HTTPS certificate from the web server, it sends a request to the OCSP Responder to check whether the certificate is valid. (*b*) A web server prefetches an OCSP response from the OCSP Responder and caches it locally. During the TLS handshake, the server may send this response to browsers. If a browser does not receive any OCSP response, it optionally contacts the OCSP Responder. (*c*) The OCSP Must-Staple extension indicates that the web server configured with this certificate supports OCSP Stapling. So the web server must send OCSP responses during the TLS handshake, and in the case of no OCSP response a browser shall terminate the handshake.

To check a certificate's status, the client uses the URL provided in the certificate's Authority Information Access (AIA) extension to locate the OCSP responder. When making an OCSP request, the client must include the certificate's serial number along with a hash of the issuer's name and public key. However, OCSP requires the client to access the OCSP responder, which introduces additional delays in the TLS connection. Moreover, this allows the CA to know precisely when and which websites the client accesses, leading to privacy concerns. The OCSP responder returns a signed response that contains the following details:

1. certID: This is the serial number of the certificate that the client is querying about.
2. thisUpdate and nextUpdate: These fields specify the period during which the response is considered valid. The time between thisUpdate and nextUpdate is defined as the validity period.
3. producedAt: This field shows the exact time when the OCSP responder generated the response.
4. certStatus: This indicates the current revocation status of the certificate, which can be one of the following:
   - Good: The certificate is valid and has not been revoked.
   - Revoked: The certificate has been revoked. This revocation can be either temporary or permanent.
   - Unknown: The OCSP responder does not have information about the requested certificate. This usually means that the certificate is not managed by this particular responder.

OCSP Stapling was introduced to mitigate the additional latency caused by Active OCSP. A web server periodically retrieves OCSP responses for its HTTPS certificate, staples them, and includes these responses in the TLS handshake using a special TLS extension. If the server supports OCSP Stapling, it responds by sending the browser its certificate, the certificate chain (excluding the root CA certificate), and a cached OCSP response during the TLS handshake. This process eliminates the need for the client to connect to the CA's OCSP responder, thereby addressing the privacy concerns associated with Active OCSP.

OCSP Must-Staple is an X.509 certificate extension designed to address the issue of clients accepting certificates without verifying their status (i.e., soft-failures). It instructs a client to require an OCSP response to be provided in the TLS handshake whenever the certificate is encountered. When this extension is included in a certificate, it explicitly signals to the client that it must terminate the connection (i.e., hard-failures) if the server does not provide a fresh, valid OCSP response during the handshake.

3 Related Work

3.1 OCSP Ecosystem

Sosnowski et al. [31] found that obtaining a comprehensive view of certificate revocation through any single distribution mechanism—particularly the OCSP was highly challenging. Among the available methods, the Common CA Database (CCADB) offered the most complete global perspective on certificate revocation. CCADB covered nearly all valid leaf certificates and identified 44% more revoked certificates than other revocation mechanisms, while fewer than 0.3 of revocation records were observable solely through OCSP or Certificate Revocation Lists (CRLs). Liu et al. [22] found that more than 8% of revoked certificates are still configured or used on web servers due to the failure of website administrators to promptly disable or remove invalid certificates. Furthermore, only 3% of certificates are served by web servers supporting OCSP Stapling. In addition, they discovered that the CRL mechanism not only imposes significant computational overhead and additional delays on clients but also causes some CRL files to consume as much as 76MB of memory, further exacerbating transmission efficiency issues. Meanwhile, there is a lack of synchronization of revocation information between OCSP and CRL, and mobile browsers generally lack effective revocation detection mechanisms. OCSP Stapling was rarely configured in China Education and Research Network (CERNET), with no instances of OCSP Must-Staple [35]. In 2018, Chung [10] et al. conducted a comprehensive analysis of the support for OCSP Must-Staple on the Internet. Furthermore, a significant number of certificates were found [8] being used after revoked, which raises concerns regarding key compromise.

3.2 Certificate Revocation

Pull-Based Revocation: When a user visits a website and needs to check the certificate's revocation status, a request is sent to the CA, which we define as pull-based revocation. Certificate Revocation List (CRL) [7] requires the client to download and parse a list containing all revoked certificates. OCSP [27] allows real-time status queries for individual certificates, providing immediate status updates and reducing the burden of large downloads. Meanwhile, researchers have continued to optimize the performance and reliability of OCSP [9].

Push-Based Revocation: In push-based certificate revocation schemes, clients periodically download revocation information according to a predefined schedule. However, since the revocation data is typically larger than that used in pull-based methods, some strategies aim to reduce bandwidth consumption by including only a small, carefully curated subset of high-priority certificates [14,25]. Other approaches, such as Let's Revoke [30], introduce compact data structures that efficiently represent th e contents of CRLs, enabling set-membership queries to check revocation status. Nevertheless, these methods often require widespread re-issuance of existing certificates and the adoption of new extensions, which may introduce additional attack surfaces and pose challenges to practical deployment. To address these issues, schemes such as CRLite [20] and TinyCR [29] optimize the underlying data structures to minimize the size of revocation information.

Relay-Based Revocation: This approach integrates certificate revocation mechanisms directly into the TLS ecosystem. Some strategies [17,32] propose leveraging CDNs to distribute revocation information to middleboxes (a network device deployed between the client and server, capable of intercepting and processing traffic), which return certificate status to clients as part of the TLS process, reducing verification delays. However, this method requires widespread middlebox deployment, incurs CDN access costs, and necessitates a new TLS extension for both clients and servers. OCSP Stapling mitigates page load delays and privacy concerns by enabling servers to prefetch OCSP responses from the CA and deliver them to clients during the TLS handshake. While widely adopted, it depends on the cooperation of web servers and stable OCSP responder operations, leading to deployment challenges.

4 HTTPS Server Scan

In this section, we explore the situations of OCSP Stapling and OCSP Must-Staple through Internet-scale scanning.

4.1 Data Collection

We collected data on OCSP Stapling and OCSP Must-Staple on two separate occasions: October 15, 2023, and November 25, 2024. The data collection process followed these steps: (1) First, we contacted Tranco [21] to retrieve a list of 18,252,272 domains, representing major domain lists from July 1, 2022, to June 30, 2023. (2) Next, we employed MassDNS [6] to map these domains to their corresponding IP addresses. (3) Finally, we obtained 10,932,039 HTTPS certificates in 2023 and 9,262,071 certificates in 2024 utilizing ZGrab2 [38] with the obtained domain names and IP addresses. Note that some domains may correspond to the same certificate, resulting in duplicated entries within the dataset.

4.2 Results

OCSP Stapling in HTTPS Servers: Among the domains where the status of OCSP Stapling was clearly detected, Table 1 shows that the adoption rate of OCSP Stapling has increased year over year [5,36]. This significant shift, particularly from 2022, can possibly be attributed to Chrome's decision to no longer proactively initiate OCSP requests [11]. Although nearly half of the scanned domains support OCSP Stapling, only two domains among the top 10 websites supported OCSP Stapling in both 2023 and 2024. Additionally, instagram.com, which supported OCSP Stapling in 2023, no longer supports it in 2024. Therefore, OCSP Stapling is not well supported on high-traffic websites.

The OCSP Stapling Adoption Rate Varies Significantly Across Countries// Regions. Based on the IP addresses associated with domain names, we categorized domains by countryregion [28]. Figure 2 present the adoption rates of OCSP Stapling for each country/region with over 50,000 domains in 2023 and 2024, respectively. The adoption rates in both years exhibit relatively minor differences. Notably, Canada demonstrated an exceptional support rate for OCSP Stapling, consistently surpassing 90%. The United States, which has most domains, showed a gradual increase in OCSP Stapling adoption, rising from 57.66% in 2023 to 62.19% in 2024. In contrast, Iran experienced a notable decline in OCSP Stapling support, with a 25.68% drop in adoption rate. On the other hand, other countries/regions exhibited comparatively lower adoption rates. For example, in

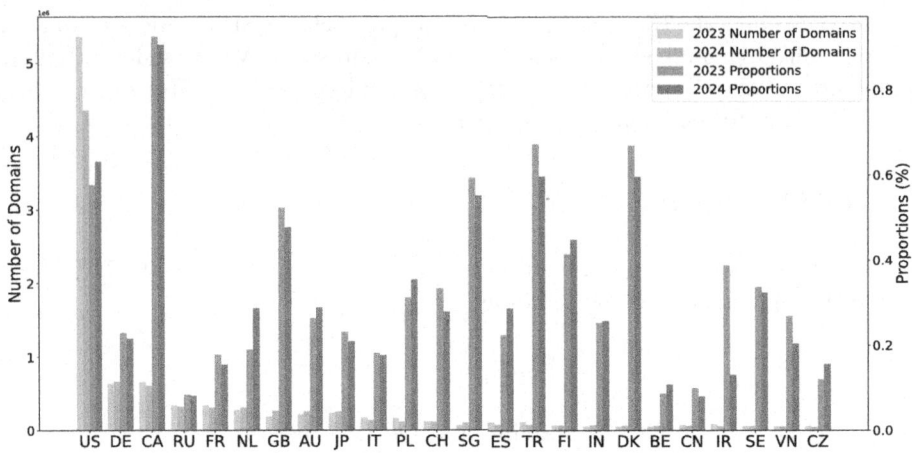

Fig. 2. OCSP Stapling Adoption by Country/Region

Russia and China, support for OCSP Stapling fell below the 10% threshold. This indicates significant regional variation in the adoption of OCSP Stapling.

The OCSP Stapling Adoption Rate Varies Significantly Across Web Servers with Different Certificate Types (i.e., OV, EV, and DV). Among the domains with OV and EV certificates, there has been a decline in OCSP Stapling adoption from October 15, 2023, to November 25, 2024. Domains with OV certificates saw a drop of over 30% in OCSP Stapling adoption. These results are unexpected, as EV certificates, which are generally associated with higher security, demonstrate the lowest rates of OCSP Stapling enablement. This trend suggests that, compared to concerns about privacy and network latency, administrators of EV certificate-based websites perhaps prioritize the ability to obtain real-time revocation information (by means of Active OCSP).

OCSP Must-Staple in HTTPS Certificates: From Table 1, we observe that the proportion of HTTPS certificates containing the OCSP Must-Staple extension among Tranco domains, as well as the proportion of such certificates after deduplication, is quite low. However, the proportion of OCSP Must-Staple adoption is gradually increasing, and the number of CAs issuing OCSP Must-Staple certificates is also on the rise.

5 OCSP Responder

In this section, we will analyze whether OCSP responders meet the following criteria: (1) accuracy, meaning that the OCSP responder must provide correct and reliable OCSP responses [3], and (2) stability, meaning that the OCSP responder must consistently respond to user OCSP requests.

Table 1. Must-Staple (domain) refers to the proportion of domains that have HTTPS certificates with the OCSP Must-Staple extension, relative to the total number of domains. Must-Staple (cert) refers to the proportion of certificates, after deduplication, that include the OCSP Must-Staple extension, relative to the total number of certificates. Data sources: 2018, 2019, and 2022 studies [5, 10].

Year	2018	2019	2022	2023	2024
OCSP Stapling	19%	27%	31%	44.45%	48.24%
Must-Staple (domain)	0.01%	-	-	0.06%	0.08%
Must-Staple (cert)	0.02%	-	-	0.11%	0.12%
EV OCSP Stapling	-	-	-	44.51%	30.16%
OV OCSP Stapling	-	-	-	74.59%	41.58%
DV OCSP Stapling	-	-	-	44.51%	48.50%

5.1 Data Collection

Large-Scale Dataset: As described in Sect. 4, we initiated OCSP requests for server certificates. Notably, some certificates from various domains lacked the AIA extension which contains the OCSP URL. We collected valid OCSP responses and obtained OCSP responses corresponding to unique certificates by performing deduplication. In the first experiment conducted on October 15, 2023, we collected 6,042,620 valid unique certificate OCSP responses. In a subsequent experiment on November 25, 2024, we obtained 5,660,604 valid unique certificate OCSP responses. This dataset is referred to as the "Large-Scale Dataset."

Hourly Dataset: To evaluate the stability of OCSP responders over time, we conducted two month-long (720-hour) measurements in year 2023 and 2024, using a probe server located in Hong Kong. The experiment proceeded in three steps: (1) We analyzed the OCSP responders corresponding to the deduplicated certificates. (2) For each responder, we randomly selected up to 50 certificates, each with a minimum of 30 days of remaining validity. If fewer than 50 such certificates were available for a given responder, all valid certificates were included. (3) OCSP requests were sent hourly for these certificates from October 15 to November 14, 2023, and from November 25 to December 25, 2024. The results are referred to as the "Hourly Dataset."

5.2 Results

Large-Scale Dataset: Errors occurred when requesting OCSP responses for 148,968 certificates in 2023 and 215,921 certificates in 2024. The majority of these errors were categorized as "unauthorized," indicating that the client was not authorized to send the query [13].

Furthermore, we observed cases where OCSP responders misconfigured the `nextUpdate` field in their responses. Specifically, http://ocsp.pki.gov.kz (2024) and http://ocsp.certservice.se (2023) incorrectly set this field to "0001-01-01," while http://sslpris.ocsp.dhimyotis.com (2023) set it to "9999-12-31." Such configuration may reflect the CA's intention to ensure that the OCSP response remains valid indefinitely until a new response is issued. Such incorrect values could lead clients or web servers to reject the OCSP response, potentially resulting in a failure to detect certificate revocations. Excluding these extreme cases, the observed errors led to a wide range of validity periods, with http://ocsp.accv.es (2023, 2024) issuing responses with the longest validity period of up to 180 days.

A validity period of such length poses a security risk in cases where a certificate is revoked but the client has cached the previous response. Under these circumstances, the client would be unable to obtain updated revocation information due to an overlong period. Conversely, OCSP responders such as http://ocsp.firmaprofesional.com (2023, 2024) and http://ocsp.catcert.cat (2023) issued responses with the shortest validity periods, some as brief as five minutes. While shorter validity periods reduce the risk of outdated revocation information, they impose a higher workload on both web servers and OCSP responders.

Hourly Dataset: The following regulations are enforced in these results. (1) If the OCSP responder is persistently unreachable during the experiment, it is considered invalid and excluded from the analysis. (2) If any certificate corresponding to an OCSP responder fails to receive an OCSP response, the responder is marked as *unstable*.

As shown in Fig. 3, we conducted experiments during two separate periods: from October 15 to November 14, 2023 (720 h) and from November 25 to December 25, 2024 (720 h). As shown in Table 2, we identified 197 valid OCSP responders and 195 valid OCSP responders, respectively. However, the majority of the OCSP responders were unstable. The worst-performing OCSP responder was only able to reliably return an OCSP response in less than 1% cases. In both experiments, fewer than 80% of OCSP responders were able to consistently provide valid OCSP responses during the worst performance period.

Additionally, while a shorter OCSP response validity period enhances security by ensuring more timely status updates, it can also impose a higher load on OCSP responders. Conversely, a longer validity period may reduce server load but increases the risk of serving outdated revocation information, thereby introducing potential security vulnerabilities. To balance security and the performance burden on OCSP responders, the CA/Browser Forum has established the following four requirements:

- **Rule 1:** The validity period of an OCSP response should be greater than or equal to eight hours.
- **Rule 2:** The validity period of an OCSP response should not exceed ten days.
- **Rule 3:** For OCSP responses with validity intervals less than sixteen hours, the CA SHALL provide an updated OCSP response prior to one-half of the validity period before the `nextUpdate`.
- **Rule 4:** For OCSP responses with validity intervals greater than or equal to sixteen hours, the CA SHALL provide an updated OCSP response at least

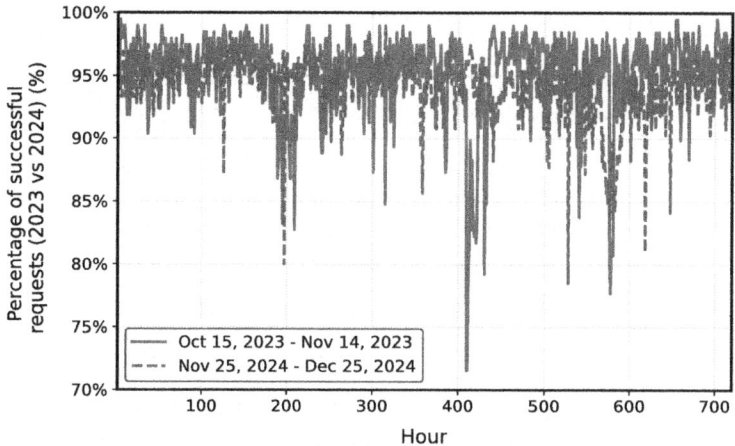

Fig. 3. During the month, the proportion of OCSP responders that successfully responded to requests every hour out of the total number of OCSP responders

eight hours prior to the nextUpdate, and no later than four days after the thisUpdate.

As observed in Table 2, over 8% of OCSP responders in both 2023 and 2024 failed to comply with the CA/B Forum rules. If an OCSP Responder is persistently unreachable or issues erroneous OCSP responses, the web server software will struggle to cache these responses for OCSP Stapling. Clients will also reject incorrect OCSP responses. In scenarios where OCSP responses are frequently unobtainable, an increasing number of browsers will opt for a soft-failures.

6 Web Server Software

In this section, we investigate the four most popular web server software to determine whether they correctly support OCSP Stapling and OCSP Must-Staple as of October 2023.

6.1 Data Collection

We conducted the following experiments within a local network (LAN): (1) we set up a web server, (2) established a CA and issued a certificate to the web server, (3) configured an OCSP responder capable of customizing response content, and (4) utilized OpenSSL with the status request extension [4] to continuously send requests to the web server.

We observed (1) the web server's requests to the OCSP responder; and (2) the web server's responses to the TLS client. We evaluated web server software based on the following aspects:

Table 2. OCSP Responder Statistics (2023 vs. 2024)

Year	2023	2024
Valid Responders	197	195
Unstable Responders	166	161
Connection Success Rate (%)	95.31%	94.41%
Responder Lowest Success Rate (%)	0.83%	0.42%
Total Error Count	32,285	64,438
Timeout Count	27,016	36,278
Unknown Errors Count	2,499	24,583
Connection Reset Count	2,005	2,429
Hourly Min. Success Rate (%)	71.57%	78.46%
Total Violations Responders	16	16
Violations Responders (Rule 1)	7	7
Violations Responders (Rule 2)	0	0
Violations Responders (Rule 3)	5	4
Violations Responders (Rule 4)	12	9

- **The Switch of OCSP Stapling**: We explored the conditions under which OCSP Stapling is expected to be switched on. All software includes this switch, which administrators can manually switch on. It should also automatically switch on when the configured server certificate contains the OCSP Must-Staple extension.
- **Prefetching of OCSP Responses**: If the web server software doesn't prefetch OCSP responses, the user's initial attempt to establish a TLS handshake with the server will either result in the absence of OCSP Stapling or encounter avoidable delays in the connection process. We analyzed the conditions under which the web server software is expected to automatically requests OCSP responses (and then replies to browsers).
- **Parsing and Processing of OCSP Responses**: We examined whether the web server software parses OCSP responses and takes corresponding actions; or simply requests, stores, and forwards them.

6.2 Results

Our results are summarized in Table 3. Most web server software does not enable OCSP Stapling by default, significantly affecting its adoption rate. Even when certificates include the OCSP Must-Staple extension, web server software does not warn about it to the administrator if OCSP Stapling is not configured. All web server software, when OCSP Stapling is enabled, fails to support regularly obtaining OCSP responses. This not only introduces additional delays during

Table 3. OCSP Stapling and Response Handling Comparison

Web Server Software		Nginx	Apache	OLS	IIS
Version		1.25.0	2.4.58	1.7.18	10.0.22621.2428
OCSP Stapling	Switch	✗	✗	✗	✓
	Certificate with OCSP Must-Staple	✗	✗	✗	✓
Active OCSP Fetching	No Response/no client request	✗	✗	✗	✗
	No Response/client request	✓	✓	✓	✓
	Response expired/no client request	✗	✗	✗	✗
	Response expired/client request	✓	✓	✓	✓
Handle OCSP Response	Delete Expired	✓	✗	✓	✗
	Wrong serial number	✓	✗	✓	✓
	Cache revoked	✗	✓	✗	✓

the initial TLS handshake between the user and the server, but also poses significant challenges to user privacy. Undoubtedly, this undermines the advantages of OCSP Stapling. These erroneous behaviors contribute to the unreliability of OCSP Stapling, thereby hindering its widespread adoption.

Nginx: Upon a client's initial connection, if the Nginx has no OCSP response in its cache, it will not provide it for this connection. In our experiment, we cleared the Nginx cache and simulated TLS connections with OpenSSL at one-second intervals. We observed that in the first few connections, Nginx failed to deliver OCSP responses to the client. It then made requests to the OCSP responder for an OCSP response, stapled the response, and delivered the response in subsequent connections. Nginx does not cache responses for revoked certificates. When a certificate is revoked, Web Server Software can inform the client during the TLS handshake that the certificate has been revoked, or it can terminate the connection to ensure security. Both actions are correct.

Apache: Apache does not prefetch OCSP responses but requests them as soon as a user tries to establish a connection, which can introduce delays during the TLS handshake. After an OCSP response expires, Apache doesn't immediately clear the cached response, continuing to offer OCSP Stapling for some time. Apache accepts OCSP responses with the wrong serial number and serves them to clients. Additionally, Apache caches and provides OCSP responses of revoked certificate.

OpenLiteSpeed: OLS rejects OCSP responses with incorrect serial numbers, does not cache revoked OCSP responses, and fails to offer Stapling on initial connections.

Internet Information Services: IIS does not prefetch OCSP responses but accesses the OCSP responder when the OCSP Stapling switch is triggered, which may be considered unnecessary when switching off OCSP Stapling. In the last 10 min before the cached response expires, if a user accesses the server, IIS requests a new OCSP response. Whether the request succeeds or not, the old cache is cleared. Issues may arise when IIS fails to obtain a newer response while having removed the older but unexpired one. Additionally, if the certificate includes the OCSP Must-Staple extension, IIS will enable OCSP Stapling even if it is disabled by administrators manually.

7 Browser

In this section, we investigate whether browsers support Active OCSP, OCSP Stapling, and OCSP Must-Staple as of October 2023.

7.1 Data Collection

In case different browsers may share OCSP responses through some form of cache, we employed a one-time detection strategy. Using Wireshark, we observed whether each domain name could trigger the browser to initiate OCSP requests.

Additionally, to ensure the consistency of certificate attributes for domain names during the testing process, we verified the OCSP status online using another device before testing each domain name, through adjusting OCSPchecker [23]. This included checking whether the domain enabled OCSP Stapling, the type of certificate used, and the support for OCSP Must-Staple. This step ensured the timeliness and reliability of the testing process, grounding our study in the current state of domain names.

Notably, understanding the certificate revocation detection mechanisms of browsers is not an easy task. Each browser exhibits unique behavior when handling OCSP. The complexity of these behaviors includes the use of whitelists, handling different certificate types, website caching, and the influence of CRLset and OneCRL libraries maintained by Chrome and Firefox. Due to the numerous factors influencing browser behavior, we could only observe specific, measurable behaviors during the testing period. All measurements were conducted on physical devices.

We investigated the OCSP ecosystem of browsers from the following aspects:

- **Active OCSP:** We examined whether browsers across different systems initiate OCSP requests for different certificate types.
- **The Respect for OCSP Stapling:** We assessed whether OCSP Stapling during the TLS handshake eliminates redundant OCSP requests by browsers, identifying such redundancy as a form of disrespect for OCSP Stapling.
- **The Respect for OCSP Must-Staple:** We evaluated whether browsers terminate the TLS connection when the certificate includes OCSP Must-Staple but the TLS handshake does not include Stapling.

7.2 Results

Our results are summarized in Table 4. Browsers should fully respect OCSP Stapling and OCSP Must-Staple. Unfortunately, we have found that some browsers still initiate OCSP requests even when OCSP Stapling is present, rendering OCSP Stapling meaningless. Additionally, only a few platforms of Firefox adhere to OCSP Must-Staple by terminating the connection when OCSP Stapling is unavailable but the certificate includes OCSP Must-Staple. This behavior indirectly leads to the slow deployment of OCSP Must-Staple.

Windows, Linux, and MacOS: Firefox actively sends OCSP requests for various types of certificates and allows users to adjust this behavior through settings. It avoids additional OCSP requests when detecting OCSP Stapling, thus improving performance. However, Firefox still initiates OCSP requests when encountering OCSP Must-Staple certificates without OCSP Stapling, which wastes resources. Although QQ Browser and Safari only initiate OCSP requests for EV certificates, they avoid making additional OCSP requests when OCSP Stapling is detected.

HarmonyOS and Android: Our research shows that browsers like Firefox proactively send OCSP requests for EV certificates. When web server software provides OCSP Stapling, Firefox avoids unnecessary requests. Additionally, for OCSP Must-Staple certificates without Stapling, Firefox terminates the connection instead of issuing further OCSP requests.

iOS: Our analysis of various browsers on iOS revealed no stable or consistent patterns in their OCSP behavior. A speculation is that the OCSP behavior may be determined by the system. According to Apple's documentation for SecPolicyCreateRevocation [2], creating a revocation policy manually is usually unnecessary unless there is a need to override the default behavior. All iOS browsers initiate OCSP requests for EV certificates when there is no OCSP Stapling. Firefox and QQ Browser do not initiate OCSP requests when OCSP Stapling is implemented. Despite this, all browsers fail to terminate connections with the OCSP Must-Staple extension if no Stapling is provided.

Table 4. In the "Active OCSP" column, ✓ indicates an OCSP request was initiated, while ✗ denotes it was not. In the "OCSP Stapling" column, ✓ means no duplicate OCSP requests were made, whereas ✗ indicates duplicate requests were initiated, - indicates that the browser does not have "Active OCSP," and therefore, it is not necessary to perform measurements related to the "OCSP Stapling" column. For the "OCSP Must-staple" column, ✗ indicates that when the certificate includes OCSP Must-Staple but the web server does not provide OCSP Stapling, the browser does not terminate the connection. ✓ means the browser disconnects without initiating an OCSP request, while △ signifies disconnection after making an OCSP request.

OS	Browser	Version	Active OCSP			OCSP Stapling	OCSP Must-staple
			EV	OV	DV		
Windows	Chrome	118.0.5993.71	✗	✗	✗	-	✗
	Firefox	118.0.2	✓	✓	✓	✓	△
	Edge	118.0.2088.76	✗	✗	✗	-	✗
	QQ	12.0	✓	✗	✗	✓	✗
	Opera	102.0	✗	✗	✗	-	✗
HarmonyOS	Firefox	118.0	✓	✗	✗	✓	✓
	Chrome	117.0.5938.154	✗	✗	✗	-	✗
	QQ	14.3.6	✗	✗	✗	-	✗
	Edge	117.0.2045.53	✗	✗	✗	-	✗
Linux	Chrome	117.0.5938.149	✗	✗	✗	-	✗
	Firefox	118.0.2	✓	✓	✓	✓	△
Android	Firefox	118.1.1	✓	✗	✗	✓	✓
	Chrome	117.0.5938.154	✗	✗	✗	-	✗
	QQ	14.3.6	✗	✗	✗	-	✗
	Edge	117.0.2045.53	✗	✗	✗	-	✗
iOS	Chrome	118.0.5993.69	✓	✗	✗	✗	✗
	Firefox	118.2	✓	✗	✗	✓	✗
	Safari	iOS:17.0.3	✓	✗	✗	✗	✗
	Edge	118.0.2088.46	✓	✗	✗	✗	✗
	Opera	3.3.7	✓	✗	✗	✗	✗
	QQ	14.3.7	✓	✗	✗	✓	✗
macOS	Chrome	118.0.5973.1	✗	✗	✗	-	✗
	Firefox	118.0.2	✓	✓	✓	✓	△
	Safari	macOS:12.6	✓	✗	✗	✓	✗
	Edge	117.0.2045.55	✗	✗	✗	-	✗
	Opera	102.0	✗	✗	✗	-	✗
	QQ	5.0	✓	✗	✗	✓	✗

Additional Observations: During testing, we observed that the same domain might correspond to multiple servers with varying OCSP Stapling configurations.

8 Ethical Concerns and Responsible Disclosure

All our experiments were conducted on publicly accessible services without collecting any personal or sensitive information. For the large-scale dataset, scanning was performed twice during the study period. For the hourly dataset, each OCSP responder was queried no more than once per hour, and for each query, a maximum of 50 certificates were selected. This approach ensures minimal impact on the performance and availability of the OCSP responders.

During our experiments, we identified several inconsistencies and errors in the OCSP responses issued by certain OCSP responders. Additionally, we discovered implementation flaws in OCSP Stapling and OCSP Must-Staple by some web server software. In adherence to responsible disclosure and research ethics, we reported these issues to the relevant parties, including the CAs operating the affected OCSP responders, the web server software vendors, the CA/B Forum, and major browser vendors.

9 Conclusions and Recommendations

In recent years, the OCSP ecosystem has experienced significant progress. The adoption rates of OCSP Stapling and OCSP Must-Staple have continued to rise, with increasing support from both web server software and major browsers. Currently, all tested web server software has implemented OCSP Stapling functionality, and some desktop and mobile browsers have also gained the capability to actively initiate OCSP requests.

However, our study reveals that the OCSP ecosystem still faces numerous challenges. The adoption of OCSP Stapling is significantly influenced by factors such as region and certificate type, with OCSP Stapling adoption rates in certain countries or regions falling below 10%. During two extended 720-hour monitoring periods, the majority of OCSP responders experienced conditions where OCSP responses were unavailable, and some even returned incorrect responses. Moreover, no existing web server software fully and correctly supports both OCSP Stapling and OCSP Must-Staple. Notably, Apache servers have been observed to accept expired or incorrect OCSP responses. Meanwhile, browser support for OCSP remains inadequate. Most browsers do not proactively initiate OCSP requests or only perform OCSP queries when using EV certificates. Additionally, some browsers unnecessarily send redundant OCSP requests to responders even after successfully obtaining an OCSP response through Stapling, leading to resource wastage. At present, only Firefox on certain platforms strictly adheres to the OCSP Must-Staple extension specifications.

OCSP Stapling can eliminate user-side latency and prevent the leakage of user privacy, while OCSP Must-Staple can further enforce a hard-failure strategy. To better promote the adoption of OCSP Stapling and OCSP Must-Staple, we propose the following recommendations:

- **OCSP responders** should ensure their global accessibility and stability. At the same time, they must rigorously verify the accuracy of the OCSP responses they issue. These two aspects are critical for the widespread adoption of the hard-failure strategy. Additionally, when issuing certificates, CAs should promote the issuance of OCSP Must-Staple certificates and inform certificate applicants about this option.
- **Web server software** must correctly handle OCSP responses, respect the `nextupdate`, and reject erroneous OCSP responses. It must regularly prefetch OCSP responses to prevent delays and privacy leaks during a user's first visit to a website. Ideally, web server software should enable OCSP Stapling by default, as most website administrators may overlook this option. When web server software configures certificates with OCSP Must-Staple, it can choose to automatically configure OCSP Stapling or prompt the administrator.
- **Browsers** should respect OCSP Stapling and OCSP Must-Staple settings. If the web server provides OCSP Stapling, browsers should not initiate redundant OCSP requests unnecessarily. If a certificate includes the OCSP Must-Staple extension but does not receive OCSP Stapling, browsers should enforce a hard-failure by terminating the connection.

References

1. Ca/browser forum extended validation guidelines. https://cabforum.org/working-groups/server/extended-validation/documents/CA-Browser-Forum-EV-Guidelines-2.0.1.pdf, version 2.0.1
2. Secpolicycreaterevocation. https://developer.apple.com/documentation/security/1400026-secpolicycreaterevocation
3. Baseline requirements for the issuance and management of publicly-trusted certificates. Technical report, CA/Browser Forum (2023). https://cabforum.org/uploads/CA-Browser-Forum-BR-v2.0.1.pdf
4. 3rd, D.E.E.: Transport Layer Security (TLS) Extensions: Extension Definitions. RFC 6066 (2011)
5. Berbecaru, D.G., Lioy, A.: An evaluation of x.509 certificate revocation and related privacy issues in the web PKI ecosystem. IEEE Access **11** (2023)
6. Blechschmidt, S.: Massdns (2023). https://github.com/blechschmidt/massdns
7. Boeyen, S., Santesson, S., Polk, T., Housley, R., Farrell, S., Cooper, D.: Internet X.509 Public Key Infrastructure Certificate and Certificate Revocation List (CRL) Profile. RFC 5280. https://www.rfc-editor.org/info/rfc5280
8. Cerenius, D., Kaller, M., Bruhner, C.M., Arlitt, M., Carlsson, N.: Trust issue(r)s: certificate revocation and replacement practices in the wild. In: Passive and Active Measurement Conference (PAM) (2024)
9. Chariton, A.A., Degkleri, E., Papadopoulos, P., Ilia, P., Markatos, E.P.: CCSP: a compressed certificate status protocol. In: IEEE INFOCOM 2017-IEEE Conference on Computer Communications (2017)
10. Chung, T., et al.: Is the web ready for OCSP must-staple? In: Internet Measurement Conference (IMC) (2018)
11. Dickson, R.: Revocation checking for EV server certificates in chrome (2022). https://groups.google.com/a/mozilla.org/g/dev-security-policy/c/S6A14e-X-T0/m/T4WxWgajAAAJ?pli=1

12. Durumeric, Z., et al.: The matter of heartbleed. In: Proceedings of the 2014 Conference on Internet Measurement Conference (2014)
13. Galperin, S., Adams, D.C., Myers, M., Ankney, R., Malpani, A.N.: X.509 Internet Public Key Infrastructure Online Certificate Status Protocol - OCSP. RFC 2560. https://www.rfc-editor.org/info/rfc2560
14. Goodwin, M.: Revoking intermediate certificates: introducing onecrl. https://blog.mozilla.org/security/2015/03/03/revoking-intermediate-certificates-introducing-onecrl/
15. Hallam-Baker, P.: X.509v3 Transport Layer Security (TLS) Feature Extension. RFC 7633 (2015). https://doi.org/10.17487/RFC7633. https://www.rfc-editor.org/info/rfc7633
16. Heninger, N., Durumeric, Z., Wustrow, E., Halderman, J.A.: Mining your PS and QS: detection of widespread weak keys in network devices. In: 21st USENIX Security Symposium (USENIX Security 2012) (2012)
17. Hu, Q., Asghar, M.R., Brownlee, N.: Certificate revocation guard (CRG): an efficient mechanism for checking certificate revocation. In: 2016 IEEE 41st Conference on Local Computer Networks (LCN) (2016)
18. KeyChest: Let's encrypt revokes 3,000,000 certificates (2020). https://keychest.net/stories/lets-encrypt-revokes-3000000-certs
19. Khan, S., et al.: A survey on x.509 public-key infrastructure, certificate revocation, and their modern implementation on blockchain and ledger technologies. IEEE Commun. Surv. Tutor. (2023)
20. Larisch, J., Choffnes, D., Levin, D., Maggs, B., Mislove, A., Wilson, C.: Crlite: a scalable system for pushing all TLS revocations to all browsers. In: IEEE Symposium on Security and Privacy (SP) (2017)
21. Le Pochat, V., Van Goethem, T., Tajalizadehkhoob, S., Korczyński, M., Joosen, W.: Tranco: a research-oriented top sites ranking hardened against manipulation. In: Network and Distributed System Security Symposium (NDSS) (2019)
22. Liu, Y., et al.: An end-to-end measurement of certificate revocation in the web's PKI. In: Internet Measurement Conference (IMC) (2015)
23. MetLife: Ocspchecker. https://github.com/MetLife/OCSPChecker
24. Pettersen, Y.N.: The Transport Layer Security (TLS) Multiple Certificate Status Request Extension. RFC 6961. https://www.rfc-editor.org/info/rfc6961
25. Project, C.: Crlsets. https://www.chromium.org/Home/chromium-security/crlsets/
26. Rescorla, E.: RFC2818: HTTP over TLS (2000)
27. Santesson, S., Myers, M., Ankney, R., Malpani, A., Galperin, S., Adams, D.C.: X.509 Internet Public Key Infrastructure Online Certificate Status Protocol - OCSP. RFC 6960 (2013)
28. Sapics: IP-location-DB. https://github.com/sapics/ip-location-db/tree/main/asn-country
29. Shi, X., Shi, S., Wang, M., Kaunisto, J., Qian, C.: On-device IoT certificate revocation checking with small memory and low latency. In: Proceedings of the 2021 ACM SIGSAC Conference on Computer and Communications Security (2021)
30. Smith, T., Dickinson, L., Seamons, K.: Let's revoke: scalable global certificate revocation. In: Network and Distributed Systems Security (NDSS) Symposium (2020)
31. Sosnowski, M., Zirngibl, J., Sattler, P., Aulbach, J., Lang, J., Carle, G.: An internet-wide view on https certificate revocations: observing the revival of CRLs via active TLS scans. In: 2024 IEEE European Symposium on Security and Privacy Workshops (EuroS&PW). IEEE (2024)

32. Szalachowski, P., Chuat, L., Lee, T., Perrig, A.: RITM: revocation in the middle. In: 2016 IEEE 36th International Conference on Distributed Computing Systems (ICDCS) (2016)
33. The Register: Trustico and digicert in symantec spat (2018). https://www.theregister.com/2018/03/01/trustico_digicert_symantec_spat/
34. W3Techs: Usage statistics of default protocol https for websites. https://w3techs.com/technologies/details/ce-httpsdefault
35. Wang, W., Li, Y., Wang, C., Yan, Y., Li, J., Gu, D.: Re-check your certificates! experiences and lessons learnt from real-world https certificate deployments. In: Network and System Security (NSS) (2021)
36. Wazan, A.S., et al.: On the validation of web x. 509 certificates by TLS interception products. IEEE Trans. Dependable Secure Comput. **19**(1), 227–242 (2020)
37. Zhang, L., et al.: Analysis of SSL certificate reissues and revocations in the wake of heartbleed. In: Proceedings of the 2014 Conference on Internet Measurement Conference (2014)
38. ZMap. https://github.com/zmap/zgrab2

Differential Fault Analysis Against White-Box SM4 Implementations

Liangju Zhao[1], Luoqi Chen[1], Yufeng Tang[1,2], and Zheng Gong[1(✉)]

[1] School of Computer Science, South China Normal University, Guangzhou, China
cis.gong@gmail.com
[2] School of Physical and Mathematical Sciences, Nanyang Technological University, Singapore, Singapore

Abstract. Side-channel analyses like differential computation analysis (DCA) and differential fault analysis (DFA) become one of the primary threat to white-box cryptography. Yet the proposed encoding-based white-box SM4 implementations (based on CEJO and self-equivalence framework) have not been systematically evaluated against fault attacks. Therefore, we conduct a comprehensive DFA study targeting encoding-based white-box SM4, under at most a single remotely handled external encoding situation. Our results demonstrate that any white-box SM4 implementation utilizing 32-bit internal encodings without output external encoding is inherently vulnerable to DFA.

In Boolean circuit-based software implementations, masking is commonly used to protect sensitive bits by distributing them across secret shares. While prior research has focused primarily on evaluating the resistance of masking-based white-box designs against computation analyses, their robustness against fault analysis remains largely unexplored. To address this gap, we examine the vulnerability of the non-linear masking scheme proposed at ASIACRYPT 2018 and the SEL masking scheme introduced at CHES 2021 under fault injection.

Through a systematic analysis of fault propagation across masking shares, we show that masking-based white-box SM4 implementations do not provide sufficient resistance against fault analysis. Our theoretical analysis and experimental validation demonstrate that the master keys of both encoding-based and masking-based white-box SM4 implementations can be successfully recovered with as few as 8 and 32 injected faults, respectively.

Keywords: white-box cryptography · SM4 · differential fault analysis · encoding · masking schemes

1 Introduction

White-box cryptography (WBC) addresses scenarios in which an adversary has full control over the execution environment of a cryptographic implementation. This process enables the adversary to potentially extract sensitive information, such as secret keys, through memory dumps or by manipulating the algorithm via reverse engineering. In this context, traditional cryptographic methods become vulnerable. In 2003, Chow *et al.* [12] introduced the white-box context, where attackers fully control the algorithm's environment and possess complete knowledge of its design. In a white-box context, the attackers can dynamically observe algorithm execution, modify intermediate values, and debug the program. To prevent such attacks, Chow textitet al. [12] introduced white-box cryptography. They proposed the first white-box implementations of AES [12] and DES [11] to mitigate key extraction attacks in white-box environments. Their white-boxing method for ciphers is known as the CEJO framework. Its core idea is transforming subround functions into a sequence of lookup tables (LUTs) with embedded subkeys. Each LUT is subsequently combined with random encodings to obfuscate key information. The encodings are categorized as internal or external. Internal encodings can be pairwise canceled between successive LUTs, while external encodings are applied to the algorithm's input and output. Based on CEJO, numerous white-box implementations [9,18,25] have been introduced. However, these implementations are proven vulnerable against algebraic analysis [5,14,21,28].

In addition to CEJO framework, McMillion *et al.* [27] introduced an alternative white-box framework, known as the self-equivalence (SE) framework, initially applied to AES. This framework embeds the secret key into a full-round affine layer, thereby obfuscating key information via large affine self-equivalence encodings. However, Ranea and Preneel's analysis [30] revealed that the AES S-box exhibits limited self-equivalences, with merely 2,040 self-equivalence pairs. Based on affine equivalence problems, they proposed an algebraic analysis against self-equivalence white-box AES.

Algebraic attacks, requiring exploiting the algebraic structure of white-box implementations, can bypass both internal and external encodings. These attacks do not depend on the specifics of the encoding schemes but require detailed knowledge of the algorithm's implementation. However, in practical white-box implementations, software obfuscation techniques are often employed, making the internal implementation details and encoding methods inaccessible or obscured. This lack of transparency significantly reduces the feasibility of algebraic attacks in real-world scenarios.

On the other hand, differential computation analysis (DCA) [8] and differential fault analysis (DFA) [31] offer a more practical alternative for attacking white-box ciphers, as they do not require reverse engineering of the internal encoding. Both DCA and DFA rely on different assumptions about the exposure of encoded data. Specifically, DFA requires the final output of the implementation to be available in a non-encoded form, while DCA depends on unprotected access to either the input or the output [1]. These conditions are met in practical applications where only one side of the encoding is externally managed. For instance, in DRM systems, the input may be securely encoded and processed server-side, but the output–intended for local playback–must eventually be decoded on the client side. This configuration is commonly referred to as *at most a single remotely handled external encoding.* At the CHES 2017 and CHES 2019 Capture the Flag Challenges [13,29], attackers primarily used DCA and DFA to recover the keys of white-box AES, without the details of the internal encodings.

In software, a cryptographic algorithm can be implemented as a bit-sliced Boolean circuit. Masking utilizes secret shares to hide sensitive bits in Boolean circuit, which follows the idea of adapting the obfuscation methods [7]. Linear masking splits a sensitive variable into shares and processes them without leakage of any information. Unfortunately, the linear masking has been proven vulnerable against Higher-Order DCA [7] and Algebraic DCA [6]. At ASIACRYPT 2018, Biryukov and Udovenko [6] proposed a non-linear masking scheme. At CHES 2021, Seker *et al.* [32] proposed a combined masking scheme (SEL masking). Both non-linear masking and SEL masking are proven vulnerable against DCA-like attacks [16,35]. Notably, existing literature primarily evaluates masking schemes against computational analysis. The critical question of their security under fault analysis remains substantially underexplored.

SM4 is a block cipher developed by the Office of State Commercial Cryptography Administration of China, published as a national cryptographic industry standard in 2012 [34]. The first white-box implementation of SM4, known as the Xiao-Lai white-box SM4 [39], was designed using CEJO framework. This implementation applied transformations and obfuscations to the SM4 algorithm, attempting to protect it from key extraction attacks in a white-box environment. However, in 2013, Lin *et al.* [24] successfully broke the Xiao-Lai white-box SM4 scheme, demonstrating the vulnerabilities in its design. In response, Shi *et al.* [33] proposed a novel white-box SM4 scheme in 2015, embedding SM4 operations into LUTs and securing them with random obfuscation to enhance resistance to attacks. Additionally, in the same year, Bai *et al.* [3] introduced the Bai-Wu white-box SM4 implementation, which enhanced security by adding complexity to the linear encodings in the Xiao-Lai approach. Despite these advancements, Pan *et al.* [38] successfully analyzed both the Xiao-Lai and Bai-Wu white-box SM4 schemes in 2018, revealing their key space sizes and demonstrating the limited security gain provided by complex linear encodings. Wang *et al.* [37] based on collision attack optimized the analysis against white-box SM4 to 2^{23}. Lu *et al.* [26] mentioned that Lepoint *et al.* 's collision attack is infeasible to apply to some WBSM4 implementations. Yang *et al.* [40] proposed a dynamic white-box implementation of SM4, which updates key information regularly to improve the security. In 2024, Gong *et al.* [15] modified the self-equivalence implementation and applied it to SM4. In the same year, Chen *et al.* [10] proposed a white-box SM4 based on the self-equivalence framework by transforming SM4 into an SPN-like cipher.

To the best of our knowledge, no specific fault analysis methods or results have been reported for existing white-box SM4 implementations. Furthermore, the security of masking schemes against DFA remains unexplored. This paper aims to bridge the gap by investigating the application of DFA to white-box SM4, examining how the encoding and masking techniques affect its security and exploring potential countermeasures to strengthen the algorithm's resistance to such attacks.

Our Contributions. This paper systematically evaluates the DFA resistance on proposed SM4 white-box implementations. Given the diversity of existing encoding-based white-box SM4 implementations and masking-based white-box SM4, we selected representative schemes to assess their DFA vulnerability. Specifically, for the CEJO framework, we analyzed the Xiao-Lai (XL-WBSM4) and Bai-Wu (BW-WBSM4) schemes. For the self-equivalence framework, we examined Gong et al.'s implementation (GTY-WBSM4). For masking schemes, Biryukov et al.'s non-linear masking and Seker et al.'s masking are evaluated. The master keys of both encoding-based and masking-based white-box SM4 implementations can be successfully extracted with 8 and 32 fault injections respectively, achieving an attack in time complexity of 2^{14}.

2 Preliminaries

2.1 Notions

In this paper, let $X = (x_{n-1}, ..., x_1, x_0)$ represent an n-bit vector, where x_{n-1} is the most significant bit (MSB). Let $\oplus$ and $\lll$ represent the bitwise exclusive-or and left rotation operations, respectively. An (n, m)-bit function is defined as a mapping $f : F_2^n \mapsto F_2^m$. For simplicity, an n-bit function refers to a mapping $f : F_2^n \mapsto F_2^n$. Specifically, an $(n, 1)$-bit function is referred to as a Boolean function. The composition of two functions is represented by $\circ$. Let X be a 32-bit word, and $X[i]$ denote the i-th byte of X, where $i = 0, 1, 2, 3$.

2.2 White-Box Cipher Based on Encodings

Given an n-bit iterated block cipher, the encryption function for a fixed key k is denoted by $E_k = E_{k^{(n_r)}}^{(n_r)} \circ E_{k^{(n_r-1)}}^{(n_r-1)} \circ \cdots \circ E_{k^{(1)}}^{(1)}$, where $E_{k^{(i)}}^{(i)}$ denotes the i-th round function. For simplicity, we omit the round key subscript of the round functions.

Definition 1. [12] *Let F be an (n,m)-bit function and (I, O) denote a pair of n-bit and m-bit permutations. The function $\overline{F} = O \circ F \circ I$ is called an encoded F, where I and O are called the input and output encoding, respectively.*

Definition 2. [30] *Let $E_k = E^{(n_r)} \circ ... \circ E^{(1)}$ be the encryption function of an iterated n-bit cipher with fixed key k. A white-box implementation $\overline{E^{(n_r)}}$ is an encoded E_k composed of encoded round functions, that is,*

$$\overline{E_k} = \overline{E^{(n_r)}} \circ ... \circ \overline{E^{(1)}} = (O^{(n_r)} \circ E^{(n_r)} \circ I^{(n_r)}) \circ ... \circ (O^{(1)} \circ E^{(1)} \circ I^{(1)}),$$

where the n-bit round encodings $(I^{(1)}, O^{(1)}), (I^{(2)}, O^{(2)}), ..., (I^{(n_r)}, O^{(n_r)})$ are n-bit permutation pairs s.t. $I^{(i+1)} = (O^{(i)})^{-1}$ for $i = 1, 2, ..., n_r - 1$.

Since the intermediate round encodings are cancelled out, $\overline{E_k}$ can be also written as $\overline{E_k} = O^{(n_r)} \circ E_k \circ I^{(1)}$. The encodings $(I^{(1)}, O^{(n_r)})$ are called the external encodings, where $I^{(1)}$ and $O^{(n_r)}$ are the input and output external encoding.

Let $E_k = E^{(n_r)} \circ ... E^{(1)}$ be the encryption of an SPN cipher with the round function $E^{(r)} = LL \circ SL \circ \oplus_{k^{(r)}}$, where SL and LL denote the non-linear and linear layer. The intermediate affine layers are defined by $AL^{(r)} = \oplus_{k^{(r)}} \circ LL$.

Definition 3. [30] *Let F be an n-bit function. A pair of n-bit affine permutations (A, B) such that $F = B \circ F \circ A$ is called an affine self-equivalence of F, and $(A, B) \in SE(F)$, where $SE(F)$ denotes the set of affine self-equivalences of F. And A, B are called left and right self-equivalence of F.*

Definition 4. [30] *A self-equivalence implementation is an encoded E_k given by*

$$\overline{E_k} = \overline{AL^{(n_r+1)}} \circ SL \circ \overline{AL^{(n_r)}} \circ SL \circ \overline{AL^{(n_r-1)}} \circ ... \circ \overline{AL^{(2)}} \circ SL \circ \overline{AL^{(1)}}$$

where the intermediate encodings of the affine layers are affine self-equivalences of the non-linear layer, i.e.,

$$\overline{AL^{(r)}} = O^{(r)} \circ AL^{(r)} \circ I^{(r)}, (O^{(r)}, I^{(r+1)}) \in \text{self-equivalences of } SL.$$

2.3 Masking-Based White-Box Implementations

To defend against DCA, Biryukov and Udovenko [6] introduced a non-linear masking technique for Boolean circuit-based white-box block ciphers. Key-related intermediate computational values are decomposed into multiple mutually independent random values. As a form of white-box implementation, this approach incurs significantly lower storage overhead compared to lookup table-based white-box implementations.

Linear Masking (Boolean Masking). Isha et al. [17] defined that an order-n masking splits a sensitive variable x into $n + 1$ shares satisfying

$$x = x_0 \oplus x_1 \oplus x_2 \oplus \cdots \oplus x_n.$$

The variables $x_0, \cdots x_{n-1}$ are generated uniformly and independently, and $x_n = x \oplus x_0 \oplus \cdots x_{n-1}$. Linear masking ensures that any combination of less than $n + 1$ shares cannot reveal any information about x.

Non-Linear Masking. Non-linear masking scheme splits a sensitive variable x into a, b and c satisfying

$$x = ab \oplus c,$$

where a and b are randomly generated bits, and c is computed as $c = x \oplus ab$ while the probability of $x \oplus ab = x$ is $\frac{3}{4}$.

SEL Masking. In CHES 2021, Seker *et al.* [32] proposed the SEL masking which consists of linear shares of order n and non-linear shares of degree d. It follows two security notions, *probing security* [17,19] and *prediction security* [6]. The former model states that every tuple of n or less intermediate variables cannot reveal any information about the sensitive variable. The latter focuses on the probability of an adversary to predict the secret value of any degree-d function over intermediate values. Let $x \in \mathbb{F}_2$ be a sensitive variable. The sensitive variable of SEL masking can be described as

$$x = \prod_{j=0}^{d} \tilde{x}_j \oplus \bigoplus_{i=1}^{n} x_i.$$

The variables $\tilde{x}_0, \cdots, \tilde{x}_d, \cdots, x_1, \cdots, x_{n-1} \in \mathbb{F}_2$ are chosen randomly and independently, and $x_n = x \oplus \prod_{j=0}^{d} \tilde{x}_j \oplus \bigoplus_{i=1}^{n-1} x_i$.

Masked Implementations. In masked implementations, the algorithm is transformed into *bit-sliced Boolean circuits*, where sensitive variables are split into shares via masking schemes. Key components include:

- **XOR Gadgets**: Securely compute $\oplus$ operations while preserving share independence.
- **AND Gadgets**: Compute multiplications between masked variables without leakage.
- **Refresh Gadgets**: Re-randomize shares to prevent glitch-induced leakage.

Each gadget adheres to the masking scheme's security properties. For detailed designs, see [6,32].

2.4 Description of SM4 Algorithm

SM4 is a 128-bit block cipher using 128-bit master keys and 32-round unbalanced Feistel structure, with identical encryption/decryption procedures (decryption uses reversed round keys). Given a plaintext $(X_0, X_1, X_2, X_3) \in (\mathbb{F}_2^{32})^4$, the iteration of the states are

$$\begin{cases} X_{i+4} = X_i \oplus T(X_{i+1} \oplus X_{i+2} \oplus X_{i+3} \oplus RK_i) \\ (X_i, ..., X_{i+3}) \mapsto (X_{i+1}, X_{i+2}, X_{i+3}, X_{i+4}) \end{cases}$$

The round function $T : \mathbb{F}_2^{32} \to \mathbb{F}_2^{32}$ combines three operations:

$$T(\cdot) = L \circ \tau \circ \text{AddRoundKey}(\cdot)$$

- **AddRoundKey**: $A \oplus RK_i = (a_0 \oplus k_0, ..., a_3 \oplus k_3)$
- **Non-linear Layer**: $\tau(A) = (S(a_0), S(a_1), S(a_2), S(a_3))$ where S is the 8-bit S-box
- **Linear Layer**: $L(B) = B \oplus (B \lll 2) \oplus (B \lll 10) \oplus (B \lll 18) \oplus (B \lll 24)$

2.5 Differential Fault Analysis on Regular SM4

Differential fault analysis, first proposed by Biham and Shamir in [4], is an active attack where faults are injected to perform differential cryptanalysis. Several differential fault analysis (DFA) methods target SM4, in white-box model, [23]'s attack is particularly effective.

Assume a byte fault is injected into the second word (X_{32}) of the last-round input. Let the input and output of the last round encryption be: $(X_{31}, X_{32}, X_{33}, X_{34})$ and $(Y_0, Y_1, Y_2, Y_3) = (X_{35}, X_{34}, X_{33}, X_{32})$. And the faulty execution yields: $Enc_{RK_{31}}(X_{31}, X_{32}^*, X_{33}, X_{34}) = (X_{35}^*, X_{34}, X_{33}, X_{32}^*)$. For i-th byte fault in X_{32}^*, we have the following differential:

- Input differential: $\alpha = X_{32}^*[i] \oplus X_{32}[i]$
- Output differential: $\beta = L^{-1}(X_{35}[i]) \oplus L^{-1}(X_{35}^*[i])$

Using the differential pair $\alpha \to \beta$, the attacker can enumerate all possible values of $RK_{31}[i]$ for the byte. A value qualifies as a valid key candidate if it satisfies the following conditions:

$$\begin{cases} S(X_{32}[i] \oplus X_{33}[i] \oplus X_{34}[i] \oplus RK_{31}[i]) = S_a \\ S(X_{32}[i] \oplus X_{33}[i] \oplus X_{34}[i] \oplus RK_{31}[i] \oplus \alpha) = S_b \\ S_a \oplus S_b = \beta \end{cases}$$

where S denotes SM4's S-box. By injecting 2 single-byte fault, the value of $RK_{31}[i]$ can be determined.

If injecting Faults into X_{33} or X_{34}, similar results can be obtained by injecting faults into a byte of X_{33}, X_{34}, or both X_{32} and X_{33}. However, if the faults are injected into X_{31}, it would result in a simple XOR operation on the output.

2.6 Adversary Model of White-Box DFA

In order to perform DFA attack on white-box cryptographic implementations, one fundamental requirement needs to be satisfied: the output of the implementation needs to be available in a non-encoded form. This requirement is satisfied whenever the white-box implementation under attack does not make use of external encodings to protect the output of the algorithm implemented. For example, in DRM applications, the server may take care of the input external encoding remotely, but the client needs to revert the output encoding to finalize the content decryption. This situation in real life is also referred to *at most a single remotely handled external encoding*.

Though Amodori et al. [2] successfully mounted a DFA against output external encodings, their attack was only available on AES and required the size of external output encodings to be 8 bits. In the case of SM4, the size of external encodings is 32 bits. Hence, this paper focuses on mounting attacks on implementations without external encodings.

Once the output of the white-box implementation is available in a non-encoded form, to perform DFA, the attacker also requires the ability to inject faults into the cryptographic process at the right locations within the algorithm. In the classic DFA where the algorithm is implemented in hardware, faulting can be difficult. For example, faulting a smart card might cause the chip to self-destruct if it detects an injection, which is why recent DFA research focus on minimizing the number of faults for analysis. However, in the software attack model where white-box cryptography is implemented, faults are very cheap and easy to perform, and do not lead to the program to self-destruct. Further, in the case of white-box attack model, the adversary has stronger capabilities than in black-box attacks. Combining static and dynamic code analysis, the adversary is able to locate the appropriate locations of the intermediate values of specific rounds. Also the attacker has the access to lookup tables of the algorithm and can even directly and precisely inject faults into the tables. To address the ability of such an adversary, we formulate the attack model of a white-box DFA adversary as follows:

- The adversary is capable of altering entries in lookup tables or intermediate values at specific rounds. Both types of modifications are considered forms of fault injection in white-box implementations.
- The adversary can repeatedly invoke the white-box implementation with random plaintexts and obtain the corresponding ciphertexts, both in fault-free and fault-injected scenarios. It is assumed that ciphertexts are either unprotected by external encodings or that such encodings have been removed.
- The adversary leverages the differential relationship between correct and faulty ciphertexts to conduct key recovery attacks via differential cryptanalysis.

3 DFA Against Encoding-based White-Box SM4

Although adversaries in the white-box DFA model are assumed to have the capability to inject faults at arbitrary locations, the presence of internal encodings can obscure the effects of such injections, necessitating careful analysis before the attack. In this section, we first introduce encoding-based white-box SM4 implementations. We then analyze fault injections in the final round of XL-WBSM4, and subsequently extend the analysis to BW-WBSM4 and GTY-WBSM4.

3.1 Three Types of Encoding-Based White-Box SM4

XL-WBSM4: Xiao and Lai's Implementation. Xiao and Lai [39] proposed the first white-box SM4 implementation (XL-WBSM4) based on the CEJO framework. The round function of XL-WBSM4 is depicted in Fig. 1. It is based on secret affine permutations P_i to protect each internal states of SM4 X_i. The round keys are embedded in lookup tables combining S-boxes, AddRoundKey operations, and random affine encodings.

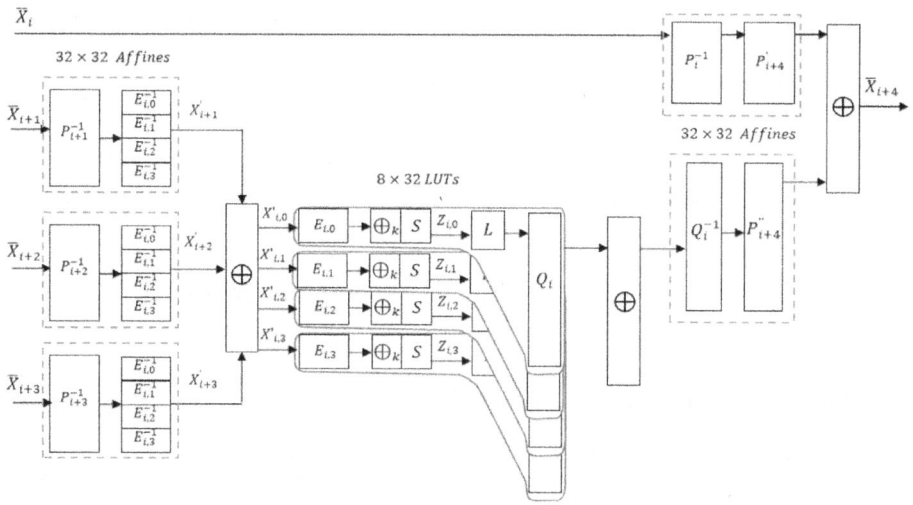

Fig. 1. XL-WBSM4 iterated state function.

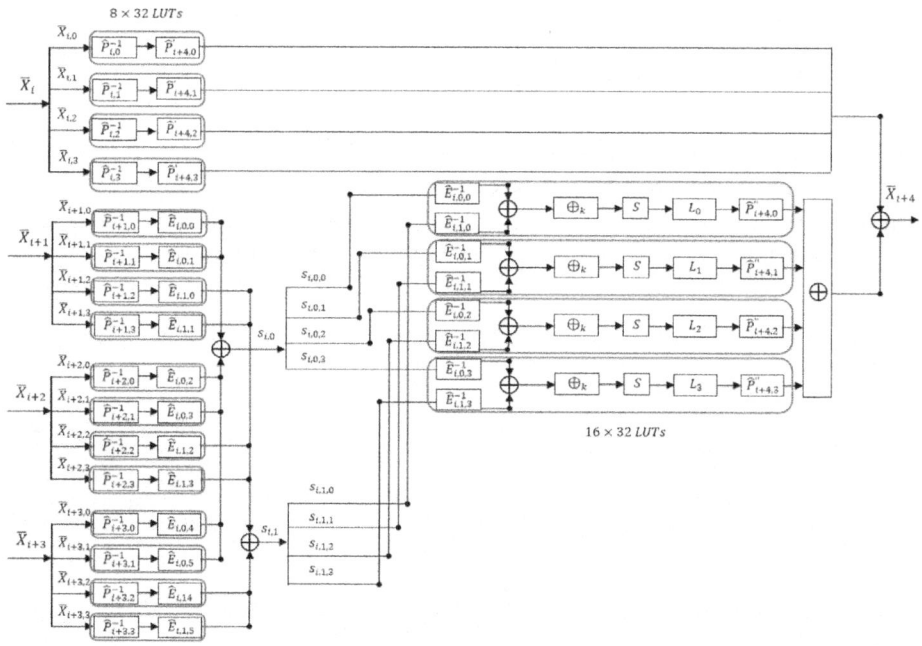

Fig. 2. BW-WBSM4 iterated state function.

BW-WBSM4: Bai and Wu's Implementation. Similar to XL-WBSM4, Bai and Wu's White-box SM4 implementation (BW-WBSM4) [3] is based on CEJO framework which also employ a 32×32 secret affine encodings to protect each internal states of SM4 as depicted in Fig. 2. And the key values are also embedded in look up tables. Unlike XL-WBSM4, in order to increase the randomness of encodings protecting key values, it uses a concatenation of two 8×8 random affine permutations.

GTY-WBSM4: Gong et al.'s Implementation. Gong et al. [15] proposed a white-box SM4 implementation (GTY-WBSM4) based on self-equivalence framework. Using the self-equivalence permutations of the S-boxes, GTY-WBSM4 protects the the internal states with secret permutations P_i and self-equivalences (A, B). As depicted in Fig. 3, the non-linear layer is exposed explicitly while affine layers are protected by encodings.

3.2 Fault Injection on XL-WBSM4

When injecting fault in CEJO framework, both faulting LUTs and faulting intermediate values are legal fault injections. However, in theory, the effects of faulting LUTs can be viewed as injecting faults to the input values before LUTs. Thus, our analysis mainly focus on fault injections on the exposed intermediate values. In the last round encryption of XL-WBSM4, the exposed intermediate values that can perform fault injections are:

1. The encoded round inputs $(\overline{X}_i, \overline{X}_{i+1}, \overline{X}_{i+2}, \overline{X}_{i+3})$;
2. The inputs of 8×32 look up tables $(X'_{i,0}, X'_{i,1}, X'_{i,2}, X'_{i,3})$;
3. The inputs of the last 32×32 affine permutation.

In the case of 3, where the faults injected before the last secret affine permutation, the secrecy of the affine permutation does not provide any leakage of key information. Because the difference between faulty ciphertext and correct ciphertext would not go through the round key addition. Therefore, the position

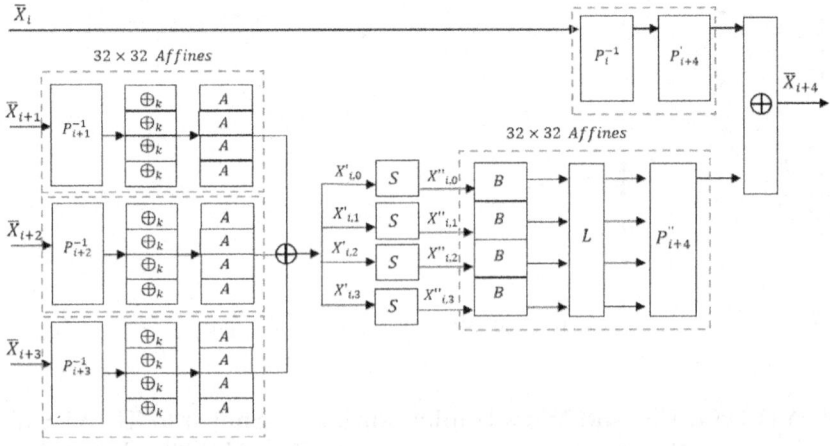

Fig. 3. GTY-WBSM4 iterated state function.

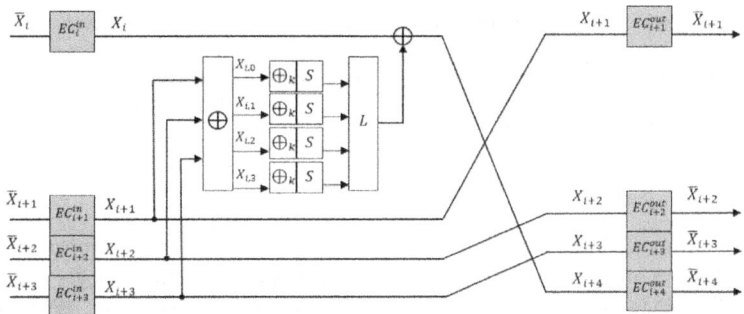

Fig. 4. Encoded round encryption of WBSM4.

is not suitable for key recovery. In the case of 2, if the adversary choose to inject a fault into any of the bytes of input value before 8×32 look up tables, the fault model can be viewed as injecting a byte fault into the input before round key addition. Due to the protection of secret 8 bits internal encoding $E_{i,j}$, the input difference of the S-box is unknown. While random byte fault models can enable a key recovery in scenario using DFA in [22], we demonstrate a stronger attack through Case 1 injections.

In case 1, the faults are injected to the round inputs $(\overline{X}_i, \overline{X}_{i+1}, \overline{X}_{i+2}, \overline{X}_{i+3})$. In this case, the white-box SM4 can be viewed as encoded SM4, as depicted in Fig. 4 where EC_i^{in} and EC_i^{out} denote the input and output encodings i-th round and $\overline{X}_i, \overline{X}_{i+1}, \overline{X}_2, \overline{X}_{i+3}, \overline{X}_{i+4}$ are the encoded values. These encoded values are exposed and vulnerable to adversarial fault injections, the resulting fault affecting the algorithm remains unknown. Therefore, when injecting fault into the encoded value, the actual fault affecting the algorithm is unknown. For further analysis, we call the faults injected known to the attacker to be *local faults*, and the faults that actually and directly affecting the algorithm to be *encoded fault*. In this case, injecting a byte *local fault* would consequently result in injecting a random 32 bits *encoded fault* due to the presence of 32 bits random affine encodings.

As we stated in Sect. 3.2 our analysis is based on the premise that the output of the algorithm is not protected by the external encodings. EC_{i+1}^{out}, EC_{i+2}^{out}, EC_{i+3}^{out} and EC_{i+4}^{out} can be viewed as identity permutations. Hence, as we can see from the encoded SM4, if the fault is injected to any of $X_{i+1}, X_{i+2}, X_{i+3}$, the difference caused by the *encode fault* can be directly obtained using the ciphertexts. Therefore, the presence of the internal encodings does not prevent the adversary to obtain the input difference of the S-boxes, which means the DFA introduced in Sect. 3.1 is still valid in XL-WBSM4. In fact, the random affine 32 bits encoding even magnify the difference of *local fault*, since injecting a byte *local fault* would likely to affect 4 bytes of the input difference, resulting in leaking 4 bytes information of the round key. Thus, injecting two *local faults* uniquely determines the round key.

3.3 Fault Injection on BW-WBSM4 and GTY-WBSM4

In BW-WBSM4, the exposed intermediates in the last round encryption are:

1. The encoded round inputs $(\overline{X}_i, \overline{X}_{i+1}, \overline{X}_{i+2}, \overline{X}_{i+3})$;
2. The inputs of 16×32 look up tables $(s_{i,0,0}, s_{i,0,1}, s_{i,0,2}, s_{i,0,3})$, $(s_{i,1,0}, s_{i,1,1}, s_{i,1,2}, s_{i,1,3})$.

Different from XL-WBSM4, the selections of fault injection are less. However, the encodings that protect the round inputs are the same, both XL-WBSM4 and BW-WBSM4 make use of 32 bits secret affine permutation. BW-WBSM4's reduction to encoded SM4 is identical to XL-WBSM4. In this case the attack using fault injections to the encoded round inputs can be applied to it as well.

In GTY-WBSM4, the implementations are quite different with XL-WBSM4 and BW-WBSM4, which is based on the self-equivalence framework. In this implementation, instead of using LUTs, round keys are concealed within affine permutations guarded by secret self-equivalences of the nonlinear layer. The fault injectable intermediates are:

1. The encoded round inputs $(\overline{X}_i, \overline{X}_{i+1}, \overline{X}_{i+2}, \overline{X}_{i+3})$;
2. The inputs of the S-boxes $(X'_{i,0}, X'_{i,1}, X'_{i,2}, X'_{i,3})$;
3. The inputs of 32×32 affine permutations $(X''_{i,0}, X''_{i,1}, X''_{i,2}, X''_{i,3})$.

Similar to the other 2 implementations, GTY-WBSM4 also uses a secret 32 bits affine permutation to protect each encoded round input. The use of self-equivalences (A, B) is a protection of the permutation P_i^{-1}. However, round inputs remain protected by 32-bit affine permutations. Therefore, the attack is on the same case as the previous 2 implementations.

Algorithm 1 outlines the general DFA procedure for encoded SM4. The input of the algorithm contains the number of required faults N, the targeting round number rc, the list of values of the local fault $localfault[]$, and the injected byte index of the input of the targeting round $byteindex$. The output of the algorithm is the value of the 32 bits round key.

Furthermore, our attack indicates that any white-box SM4 implementation reducible to the structure shown in Fig. 4 is vulnerable, regardless of whether the 32-bit internal encodings are linear or non-linear. This vulnerability arises not only because all three implementations we analyzed conform to this structure, but also due to the fact that, under 32-bit internal encodings, a fault affects only the inputs to the S-boxes within a single round. The corresponding input difference can be directly inferred from the affected output branch. When the internal encoding size is smaller than 32 bits, the attack remains feasible as fault propagation is narrower. However, if the internal encoding exceeds 32 bits, the fault may propagate across multiple branches, potentially affecting X_i. If X_i is altered, the resulting output difference of the S-boxes becomes unpredictable, failing the attack.

Algorithm 1. DFA on encoded SM4

Input: $N, rc, localFault[], byteindex$
Output: K
1: $\mathbb{T} \Leftarrow \varnothing$ ▷ Fault Injection Stage
2: **for** $i = 0; i < N; i++$ **do**
3:      $(P_0^i, P_1^i, P_2^i, P_3^i) = RandomPT()$
4:      $(C_0^i, C_1^i, C_2^i, C_3^i) = Enc_K(P_i)$
5:      $(C_0^{*i}, C_1^{*i}, C_2^{*i}, C_3^{*i}) = InjectFault(Enc_K(P_i), rc, localFault[i], byteindex)$
6:      $x^i = C_0^i \oplus C_1^i \oplus C_2^i$
7:      $\alpha^i = C_0^i \oplus C_1^i \oplus C_2^i \oplus C_0^{*i} \oplus C_1^{*i} \oplus C_2^{*i}$
8:      $\beta^i = L^{-1}(C_3^i \oplus C_3^{*i})$
9:      Append triplet (x^i, α^i, β^i) to $\mathbb{T}$
10: **end for**
11: **for** each bytes k_j in K **do** ▷ Fault Analysis stage
12:     **for** $k_j = 0; k_j < 256; k_j++$ **do**
13:         **for** each j-th byte of triplet $(x^i, \alpha^i, \beta^i) \in \mathbb{T}$ **do**
14:             $S_i^a = S(k_i \oplus x_j^i)$
15:             $S_i^b = S(k_i \oplus x_j^i \oplus \alpha_j^i)$
16:         **end for**
17:         **if** all $S_i^a \oplus S_i^b == \beta_j^i$ **then**
18:             The value of key byte is determined, and we can break the loop.
19:         **end if**
20:     **end for**
21: **end for**
22: **return** K

4 DFA Against Masking-Based White-Box SM4

This section analyzes DFA on masking-based White-box SM4, using the same attack model defined in the previous analysis. To facilitate key recovery, we focus on injecting faults into the inputs of the final encryption round. We begin by examining the fault propagation characteristics of SM4 under both non-linear masking and SEL masking schemes. Based on these observations, we then present a general DFA approach applicable to both masking strategies.

4.1 Fault Injection Under the Effect of Non-linear Masking

In non-linear masking, the inputs of the last round encryption of SM4 (X_i, X_{i+1}, X_{i+2}, X_{i+3}) are presented as ($a_i b_i \oplus c_i$, $a_{i+1} b_{i+1} \oplus c_{i+1}$, $a_{i+2} b_{i+2} \oplus c_{i+2}$, $a_{i+3} b_{i+3} \oplus c_{i+3}$). Therefore, unlike attacking encoding-based white-box SM4, the adversary injects fault into shares of ($X_i, X_{i+1}, X_{i+2}, X_{i+3}$) instead of their encoded versions. In DFA, the adversary always needs to invoke the encryption twice on the same plaintext to get at least one correct ciphertext and its faulty version. Thus, the difference between the correct ciphertext and the faulty would only be introduced by the fault behaviours. However, in masking schemes, each invocation contains different randomness. In this case, the 2 invocations of encryption on the same plaintext would generate 2 different shares of the same inputs of the last round.

Let x be the correct variable in the first invocation of encryption, where $x = ab \oplus c$, and x' be the variable in the second invocation before the fault injection, where $x' = a'b' \oplus c'$. Since x and x' come from the same plaintext, therefore, $x = x'$. For a DFA attacker, the fault can be introduced into a', b' and c'.

Naturally, the effect of fault injection differs due to injecting to different shares. If the attacker choose to inject to a' or b', and since a', b' are commutative in forming x', without loss of generosity, we pick a' to be the injected share and its faulty version to be a^*. Let the fault difference to be α where $\alpha = a^* \oplus a'$, the variable after fault injection to be x^* which would satisfy $x^* = a^*b' \oplus c'$.

The fault difference would be

$$\begin{aligned} x \oplus x^* &= x' \oplus x^* \\ &= a^*b' \oplus c' \oplus a'b' \oplus c' \\ &= (a' \oplus \alpha)b' \oplus c' \oplus a'b' \oplus c' \\ &= \alpha b'. \end{aligned}$$

The results indicates that difference introduced by fault injection being non-zero based on $b' \neq 0$. In the case of Boolean circuit, where each share is bit size, the success rate of injecting non-zero fault would be $\frac{1}{2}$. If the fault is injected to c', then the faulty variable x^* would satisfy $x^* = a'b' \oplus c' \oplus \alpha$. In this case, the difference introduced by fault would be $x \oplus x^* = \alpha$. Thus, injecting fault to c' would guarantee the success of non-zero difference fault injection.

Unlike internal encoding, masking does not inherently affect fault propagation. Thus, injecting a bit fault into the input of last round encryption would only result in changing one bit of input of S-box which only reveals information of one byte in the round key. Full recovery of the 32-bit round key requires fault injections across all four byte positions. Since in our attack model, the adversary can precisely inject faults. Each byte requires two distinct fault injections, totaling eight faults for full key recovery.

4.2 Fault Injection Under the Effect of SEL Masking

In SEL masking, the sensitive variable x is presented as $x = \prod_{j=0}^{d} \tilde{x}_j \oplus \bigoplus_{i=1}^{n} x_i$. Let x be the correct sensitive variable in the first invocation of encryption, where $x = \prod_{j=0}^{d} \tilde{x}_j \oplus \bigoplus_{i=1}^{n} x_i$, and x' be the sensitive variable in the second invocation before fault injection, where $x' = \prod_{j=0}^{d} \tilde{x}'_j \oplus \bigoplus_{i=1}^{n} x'_i$.

If the fault is injected to $\tilde{x}'_p (1 \leq p \leq n)$, and the fault difference be α, then the faulty variable x^* would satisfy:

$$x^* = (\tilde{x}'_p \oplus \alpha) \prod_{j=0, j \neq p}^{d} \tilde{x}'_j \oplus \bigoplus_{i=1}^{n} x'_i$$

$$= \prod_{j=0}^{d} \tilde{x}'_j \oplus \alpha \prod_{j=0, j \neq p}^{d} \tilde{x}'_j \oplus \bigoplus_{i=1}^{n} x'_i$$

$$= x \oplus \alpha \prod_{j=0, j \neq p}^{d} \tilde{x}'_j.$$

The difference introduced by fault injection $x \oplus x^*$ would be $\alpha \prod_{j=0, j \neq p}^{d} \tilde{x}'_j$. Thus, to successfully injecting a non-zero difference, $\prod_{j=0, j \neq p}^{d} \tilde{x}'_j \neq 0$ must be satisfied. Given that variables $\tilde{x}'_j$, where $j = 0, \cdots, d$ are randomly generated, the probability of injecting non-zero difference would be $(\frac{1}{2})^d$. Therefore, it is insufficient to inject fault into $\tilde{x}'_p$.

If fault injection happens to x_p, where $p = 1, \cdots, n$, with with the fault difference being α, then the faulty variable x^* would satisfy:

$$x^* = \prod_{j=0}^{d} \tilde{x}'_j \oplus \bigoplus_{i=1, i \neq p}^{n} x'_i \oplus (x'_p \oplus \alpha)$$

$$= x \oplus \alpha.$$

It shows that injecting fault to x_p would guarantee the success of non-zero difference fault injection. And also similar to white-box SM4 with non-linear masking, we need to inject 2 faults on each byte to fully recover the round key, requiring 8 faults in total.

Algorithm 2 summarize the attack procedure on both non-linear masking and SEL masking. In fault injection, both schemes are targeting linear part of the share, which are C' in non-linear masking and x'_i in SEL masking. Different from the algorithm targets encoding-based white-box SM4, the fault injections require the index of bit share instead of value. The adversary needs to use different indexes of bit to achieve faulting different values which denoted as *faultindex*[] in the algorithm. From the algorithm we can see, to recover a 32 bits round key, the time complexity of enumerating possible key values is 2^{12}.

Algorithm 2. DFA on SM4 with masking

Input: $N, rc, faultindex[], byteindex$
Output: K

1:   $\mathbb{T} \Leftarrow \varnothing$ ▷ Fault Injection Stage
2:   **for** $i = 0; i < N; i++$ **do**
3:       $(P_0^i, P_1^i, P_2^i, P_3^i) = RandomPT()$
4:       $(C_0^i, C_1^i, C_2^i, C_3^i) = Enc_K(P_i)$
5:       $(C_0^{*i}, C_1^{*i}, C_2^{*i}, C_3^{*i}) = InjectFault(Enc_K(P_i), rc, faultindex[i], byteindex)$
6:       $x^i = C_0^i \oplus C_1^i \oplus C_2^i$
7:       $\alpha^i = C_0^i \oplus C_1^i \oplus C_2^i \oplus C_0^{*i} \oplus C_1^{*i} \oplus C_2^{*i}$
8:       $\beta^i = L^{-1}(C_3^i \oplus C_3^{*i})$
9:       Append triplet (x^i, α^i, β^i) to $\mathbb{T}$
10: **end for**
11: **for each bytes** k_j **in** K **do**   ▷ Fault Analysis stage
12:     **for** $k_j = 0; k_j < 256; k_j++$ **do**
13:         **for each** j-th byte of triplet $(x^i, \alpha^i, \beta^i) \in \mathbb{T}$ **do**
14:             $S_i^a = S(k_i \oplus x_j^i)$
15:             $S_i^b = S(k_i \oplus x_j^i \oplus \alpha_j^i)$
16:         **end for**
17:         **if** all $S_i^a \oplus S_i^b == \beta_j^i$ **then**
18:             The value of key byte is determined, and we can break the loop.
19:         **end if**
20:     **end for**
21: **end for**
22: **return** K

5 Experimental Results and Countermeasures

5.1 Experimental Results

We validate DFA against five implementations: encoding-based white-box SM4 (XL-WBSM4, BW-WBSM4, GTY-WBSM4), masking-based white-box SM4 with non-linear masking (WBSM4-NL), and SM4 with SEL masking (WBSM4-SEL). For WBSM4-SEL, we evaluate degree-1 ($d = 1$) and degree-2 ($d = 1$) instances. To perform the attack on SM4 with encodings, following the our attack model, precise faults are injected into the second 32-bit block of the final round's input. For masked implementations, each fault injection perturbs a single bit due to share isolation. In order to generate different fault differences, we select different indexes to perform fault injections in practice. The attack recovers individual round keys. Full master key extraction requires faulting four consecutive rounds. To fully recover the master key, the attack must perform on several rounds. For the case of SM4, to determine the master key, the attack needs to perform for 4 consecutive rounds. Table 1 summarizes experimental results. Parts of the experimental codes are available in[1].

Due to the fault magnification produced by 32-bit internal encodings, the master key of all the encoding-based white-box SM4 can be determined with 8

---
[1] https://github.com/Uboan/DFA-on-WBSM4..

Table 1. Differential Fault Analysis on Protected SM4 Variants: Master Key Recovery

Cipher	Framework	Degree	Faults	Time Complexity
XL-WBSM4	CEJO	–	8	2^{14}
BW-WBSM4	CEJO	–	8	2^{14}
GTY-WBSM4	Self-equivalence	–	8	2^{14}
WBSM4-NL	Masking	1	32	2^{14}
WBSM4-SEL	Masking	1	32	2^{14}
WBSM4-SEL	Masking	2	32	2^{14}

faults, while in masking schemes, 32 faults are required to uniquely recover the master key. The time complexity of all the attacks are 2^{14}.

5.2 Countermeasures

To counteract fault analysis in WBC, Lee et al. proposed the table redundancy method [20]. which makes use of multiple branches of LUTs for the vulnerable rounds (e.g., in the case of AES, the sixth to ninth rounds) and XOR the outputs to obfuscate the fault injection. Applying such method to SM4, redundant implementations of the final four rounds could theoretically prevent single-point fault injection. However, Tang et al. [36] demonstrated that adaptive attackers injecting synchronized faults into both primary and redundant branches can bypass this protection.

An alternative defense involves larger width of internal encoding. The idea of our attack is to use the ciphertexts to obtain the input and output differences of the S-boxes to perform key recovery. When injecting fault into the second 32 bits of $(\overline{X}_i, \overline{X}_{i+1}, \overline{X}_{i+2}, \overline{X}_{i+3})$ in the last round input, one can obtain the input difference from the output of the first 32 bits, and obtain the output difference from the fourth 32 bits. However, if a single byte fault can affect 4 branches of the input, the attacker cannot obtain the output differences of the S-boxes since the outputs of S-boxes are XOR-ed by the encoded fault of the first branch. Therefore, the attack is not available. Besides enlarging the size of internal encodings, merging the last several rounds is also useful, which simply blocks the attacker from fault injecting to the last round of the encryption. However, these two methods may not be practical at the moment, so we leave them in future work.

6 Conclusion

This paper examined the effectiveness of DFA on white-box SM4 implementations in CEJO frameworks and self-equivalence framework under at most a single remotely handled external encoding. Our theoretical analysis and experimental results reveal that white-box implementations—including XL-WBSM4,

BW-WBSM4, and GTY-WBSM4—are vulnerable to DFA, with internal encodings amplifying the impact of fault injections. Further, the attack suggests that any white-box SM4 implementations that can be reduced to an encoded structure with 32-bit internal encodings are vulnerable. Additionally, we evaluate the resistance of masking-based white-box SM4. Our investigation demonstrates that both non-linear and SEL masking fail to resist DFA. Furthermore, we discuss that table redundancy cannot resist such an attack if the attack model is adjusted to an adaptive side-channel analysis model. Enlarging the size of internal encodings that protect round inputs and compressing the last several rounds in the white-box SM4 implementations are considered theoretically resisting such an attack. However, the practical implementations of the two countermeasures require further security analysis, which would be a direction for future work.

Acknowledgments. This work was supported by National Natural Science Foundation of China (62072192, U2336209), Guangdong Basic and Applied Basic Research Foundation (2022A1515140090). Yufeng Tang was also supported by China Scholarship Council Grant (202406750040).

References

1. Alpirez Bock, E., et al.: White-box cryptography: don't forget about grey-box attacks. J. Cryptol. **32**, 1095–1143 (2019)
2. Amadori, A., Michiels, W., Roelse, P.: A DFA attack on white-box implementations of AES with external encodings. In: International Conference on Selected Areas in Cryptography, pp. 591–617. Springer (2019)
3. Bai, K., Wu, C.: A secure white-box SM4 implementation. Sec. and Commun. Netw. **9**(10), 996–1006 (2016). https://doi.org/10.1002/sec.1394
4. Biham, E., Shamir, A.: Differential fault analysis of secret key cryptosystems. In: Kaliski, B.S. (ed.) CRYPTO 1997. LNCS, vol. 1294, pp. 513–525. Springer, Heidelberg (1997). https://doi.org/10.1007/BFb0052259
5. Billet, O., Gilbert, H., Ech-Chatbi, C.: Cryptanalysis of a white box AES implementation. In: Selected Areas in Cryptography: 11th International Workshop, SAC 2004, Waterloo, Canada, August 9-10, 2004, Revised Selected Papers 11, pp. 227–240. Springer (2005)
6. Biryukov, A., Udovenko, A.: Attacks and Countermeasures for White-box Designs. In: Peyrin, T., Galbraith, S. (eds.) ASIACRYPT 2018. LNCS, vol. 11273, pp. 373–402. Springer, Cham (2018). https://doi.org/10.1007/978-3-030-03329-3_13
7. Bogdanov, A., Rivain, M., Vejre, P.S., Wang, J.: Higher-Order DCA against Standard Side-Channel Countermeasures. In: Polian, I., Stöttinger, M. (eds.) COSADE 2019. LNCS, vol. 11421, pp. 118–141. Springer, Cham (2019). https://doi.org/10.1007/978-3-030-16350-1_8
8. Bos, J.W., Hubain, C., Michiels, W., Teuwen, P.: Differential Computation Analysis: Hiding Your White-Box Designs is Not Enough. In: Gierlichs, B., Poschmann, A.Y. (eds.) CHES 2016. LNCS, vol. 9813, pp. 215–236. Springer, Heidelberg (2016). https://doi.org/10.1007/978-3-662-53140-2_11
9. Bringer, J., Chabanne, H., Dottax, E.: White box cryptography: another attempt. Cryptology ePrint Archive, Paper 2006/468 (2006). https://eprint.iacr.org/2006/468

10. Chen, J., Luo, Y., Liu, J., Wang, C., Zhang, Y., Dong, X.: A white-box implementation of SM4 with self-equivalence encoding. Comput. J. **67**(3), 1087–1098 (2023).https://doi.org/10.1093/comjnl/bxad044, https://doi.org/10.1093/comjnl/bxad044
11. Chow, S., Eisen, P., Johnson, H., Van Oorschot, P.C.: A white-box DES implementation for DRM applications. In: ACM Workshop on Digital Rights Management, pp. 1–15. Springer (2002)
12. Chow, S., Eisen, P., Johnson, H., Van Oorschot, P.C.: White-box cryptography and an AES implementation. In: Selected Areas in Cryptography: 9th Annual International Workshop, SAC 2002 St. John's, Newfoundland, Canada, August 15–16, 2002 Revised Papers 9, pp. 250–270. Springer (2003)
13. CryptoExperts, Cybercrypt: Ches 2019 capture the flag challenge-the whibox contest (2019). https://whibox.io/contests/2019/
14. Derbez, P., Fouque, P.A., Lambin, B., Minaud, B.: On recovering affine encodings in white-box implementations. IACR Trans. Cryptographic Hardware and Embedded Syst. **2018**(3), 121–149 (2018). https://doi.org/10.13154/tches.v2018.i3.121-149, https://tches.iacr.org/index.php/TCHES/article/view/7271
15. Gong, Z., Tang, Y., Yi, N.: SM4 White-box implementation using self-equivalence encoding and its implicit functions. No. 21-115, 55 Xinye Road, Haizhu District, Guangzhou City, Guangdong Province, 510000, cn117997513a edn. (2024)
16. Goubin, L., Rivain, M., Wang, J.: Defeating state-of-the-art white-box countermeasures with advanced gray-box attacks. IACR Trans. Cryptographic Hardware Embedded Syst. **2020**(3), 454–482 (2020). https://doi.org/10.13154/tches.v2020.i3.454-482, https://tches.iacr.org/index.php/TCHES/article/view/8597
17. Ishai, Y., Sahai, A., Wagner, D.: Private Circuits: Securing Hardware against Probing Attacks. In: Boneh, D. (ed.) CRYPTO 2003. LNCS, vol. 2729, pp. 463–481. Springer, Heidelberg (2003). https://doi.org/10.1007/978-3-540-45146-4_27
18. Karroumi, M.: Protecting white-box AES with dual ciphers. In: Rhee, K.H., Nyang, D. (eds.) Information Security and Cryptology - ICISC 2010, pp. 278–291. Springer, Berlin Heidelberg, Berlin, Heidelberg (2011)
19. Kim, H., Hong, S., Lim, J.: A fast and provably secure higher-order masking of AES S-box. In: Preneel, B., Takagi, T. (eds.) Cryptographic Hardware and Embedded Systems - CHES 2011, pp. 95–107. Springer, Berlin Heidelberg, Berlin, Heidelberg (2011)
20. Lee, S., Jho, N.S., Kim, M.: Table redundancy method for protecting against fault attacks. IEEE Access **9**, 92214–92223 (2021)
21. Lepoint, T., Rivain, M., De Mulder, Y., Roelse, P., Preneel, B.: Two attacks on a white-box AES implementation. In: International conference on selected areas in cryptography, pp. 265–285. Springer (2013)
22. Li, R., Sun, B., Li, C., You, J.: Differential fault analysis on SMS4 using a single fault. Cryptology EPrint Archive, Paper 2010/063 (2010). https://eprint.iacr.org/2010/063
23. Li, W., Gu, D., Wang, Y., Liu, Y., Liu, Z.: An extension of differential fault analysis on SMS4. In: 2010 2nd International Conference on E-business and Information System Security, pp. 1–4 (2010). https://doi.org/10.1109/EBISS.2010.5473514
24. Lin, T., Lai, X.: Efficient attack to white-box SMS4 implementation (in chinese). J. Softw. **24**(9), 2238–2249 (2013). in Chinese
25. Link, H.E., Neumann, W.D.: Clarifying obfuscation: improving the security of white-box encoding. Cryptology ePrint Archive, Paper 2004/025 (2004). https://eprint.iacr.org/2004/025

26. Lu, J., Wang, C.: Cryptanalysis of two white-box implementations of the CLEFIA block cipher. In: Information and Communications Security: 25th International Conference, ICICS 2023, Tianjin, China, November 18–20, 2023, Proceedings, pp. 51–68. Springer-Verlag, Berlin, Heidelberg (2023). https://doi.org/10.1007/978-981-99-7356-9-4, https://doi.org/10.1007/978-981-99-7356-9-4
27. McMillion, B., Sullivan, N.: Attacking white-box AES constructions. In: Proceedings of the 2016 ACM Workshop on Software PROtection, pp. 85–90 (2016)
28. Michiels, W., Gorissen, P., Hollmann, H.D.: Cryptanalysis of a generic class of white-box implementations. In: Selected Areas in Cryptography: 15th International Workshop, SAC 2008, Sackville, New Brunswick, Canada, August 14-15, Revised Selected Papers 15, pp. 414–428. Springer (2009)
29. Prouff, E., et al.: Ches 2017 capture the flag challenge-the whibox contest, an ecrypt white-box cryptography competition (2017). https://whibox.io/contests/2017/
30. Ranea, A., Preneel, B.: On self-equivalence encodings in white-box implementations. In: Selected Areas in Cryptography: 27th International Conference, Halifax, NS, Canada (Virtual Event), October 21-23, 2020, Revised Selected Papers 27, pp. 639–669. Springer (2021)
31. Sanfelix, E., Mune, C., de Haas, J.: Unboxing the white-box: practical attacks against obfuscated ciphers. presentation at blackhat europe (2015)
32. Seker, O., Eisenbarth, T., Liskiewicz, M.: A white-box masking scheme resisting computational and algebraic attacks. Cryptology ePrint Archive, Paper 2020/443 (2020). https://eprint.iacr.org/2020/443
33. Shi, Y., He, Z.: A lightweight white-box symmetric encryption algorithm against node capture for WSNs. In: 2014 IEEE Wireless Communications and Networking Conference (WCNC), pp. 3058–3063 (2014). https://doi.org/10.1109/WCNC.2014.6952994
34. Shuwang, L., et al.: SM4 block cipher algorithm (2012)
35. Tang, Y., Gong, Z., Chen, J., Xie, N.: Higher-order DCA attacks on white-box implementations with masking and shuffling countermeasures. IACR Trans. Cryptographic Hardw. Embed. Syst. **2023**(1), 369–400 (2022). https://doi.org/10.46586/tches.v2023.i1.369-400, https://tches.iacr.org/index.php/TCHES/article/view/9956
36. Tang, Y., Gong, Z., Sun, T., Chen, J., Zhang, F.: Adaptive side-channel analysis model and its applications to white-box block cipher implementations. In: Information Security and Cryptology: 17th International Conference, Inscrypt 2021, Virtual Event, August 12–14, 2021, Revised Selected Papers 17, pp. 399–417. Springer (2021)
37. Wang, R., Guo, H., Lu, J., Liu, J.: Cryptanalysis of a white-box SM4 implementation based on collision attack. IET Inf. Secur. **16**(1), 18–27 (2022). https://doi.org/10.1049/ise2.12045
38. Pan, W., Tihong Qin, Y.J.L.Z.: Cryptanalysis of two white-box SM4 implementations. J. Cryptologic Res. **5**(6), 651 (2018). https://doi.org/10.13868/j.cnki.jcr.000274, http://www.jcr.cacrnet.org.cn/CN/10.13868/j.cnki.jcr.000274
39. Xiao, Y., Lai, X.: White-box cryptography and a SMS4 implementation (in chinese). In: Proceedings of 2009 Annual Conference of the Chinese Association of Cryptologic Research, pp. 24–34. China (2009), in Chinese
40. Yatao Yang, Hui Dong, Y.Z.Y.Z.: Wbdl: improved SM4 dynamic white-box cryptographic algorithm. J. Cryptologic Res. **10**(4), 796 (2023). https://doi.org/10.13868/j.cnki.jcr.000629, http://www.jcr.cacrnet.org.cn/CN/10.13868/j.cnki.jcr.000629

Leveled Software Implementation of Polka and Comparison with Uniformly Masked Kyber

Thibaud Schoenauen[(✉)], Clément Hoffmann, Charles Momin, Thomas Peters, and François-Xavier Standaert

Crypto Group, ICTEAM Institute, UCLouvain, Louvain-la-Neuve, Belgium
thibaud.schoenauen@uclouvain.be

Abstract. POLKA is a post-quantum public-key encryption scheme from PKC 2023, designed in order to be efficiently protected against side-channel attacks. Its motivation arises from the acknowledged difficulty of protecting KYBER against such attacks. Concretely, the structure of POLKA aims to allow so-called leveled implementations, so that protecting its long-term key requires strong and expensive countermeasures (like masking) for a part of its operations only. This contrasts with KYBER, for which preventing side-channel attacks requires to uniformly protect all its operations. The good leakage-resilience features of POLKA nevertheless come with performance overheads in an unprotected implementation context. Since no concrete implementations of POLKA were proposed so far, it left the question of the number of shares for which it can become an interesting alternative to KYBER open. We bridge this gap by proposing a leveled software implementation of POLKA and show that, already for two shares, it leads to significant performance gains over the state-of-the-art uniformly masked implementations of KYBER (Bos et al., TCHES 2021, Bronchain and Cassiers, TCHES 2022).

1 Introduction

CRYSTALS-KYBER (short: KYBER) is a new standard for key encapsulation and public-key encryption [1]. While it is expected to provide strong security even in the presence of quantum computers, securing its implementations against side-channel attacks has been shown to be very challenging. Informally, one of the main reasons of this difficulty is that the security of KYBER against Chosen-Ciphertext Attacks (CCA) relies on the so-called Fujisaki-Okamoto (FO) transform [17], which essentially checks that ciphertexts are well formatted by decrypting and re-encrypting them. As a result, a side-channel adversary can perform a chosen-ciphertext attack against the part of KYBER that is only secure against Chosen-Plaintext Attacks (CPA), by observing the leakage of a decryption before the re-encryption step [27,31,32,35,36,38]. This is a severe weakness since exploiting it only requires to target the confidentiality of the re-encrypted message with a distinguishing attack, a task that is considerably easier than performing a key-recovery [34]. Informally, this is because message distinguishing attacks can directly exploit the leakage of all the target operations of a leaking implementation, without key guessing. As a result, the traditional intuitions prevailing when analyzing the implementation of symmetric cryptographic primitives against leakage may not extend to the post-quantum asymmetric setting. For example, the aforementioned message distinguishing attack is a Simple Power Analysis (SPA) exploiting the measurement of a single manipulation of an ephemeral secret. Yet, it frequently turns out to be more powerful (hence, harder to prevent) than a Differential Power Analysis (DPA) attacks against KYBER's decryption, which exploits multiple manipulations of the long-term secret [2].

Given the anticipated cost to secure KYBER with standard countermeasures like masking [6,7,11,13,14], POLKA was introduced as an alternative CCA-secure post-quantum public-key encryption scheme [20]. It embeds a number of features aimed at simplifying secure implementation. First, POLKA is designed in such a way that CCA security is obtained without relying on the FO transform. Second, its decryption process is randomized in order to remove adversarial control on intermediate computations that can facilitate side-channel attacks. Third, it leverages key-homomorphic computations that are easy to mask. Finally, it can rely on hard physical learning problems to argue about the security of some (unmasked) operations [16,21]. As a result, POLKA is expected to enable leveled implementations, as popular in symmetric cryptography [5]. That is, it aims to be implemented securely without uniformly masking all its operations.

It is important to emphasize that a leveled implementation of POLKA and a uniformly masked implementation of KYBER lead to different security guarantees. Borrowing the terminology used in symmetric cryptography [19], a leveled implementation of POLKA is *leakage-resilient*: its ephemeral secrets may be compromised in the presence of leakage, but security is restored once leakage is removed from the adversary's view. In other words, a leveled implementation of POLKA only protects its long-term secret key. By contrast, a uniformly protected implementation of KYBER is *leakage-resistant* and also protects its ephemeral secrets. In this work, we are therefore concerned with the situation where implementers want to efficiently ensure leakage-resilience. This is a natural first step since, for example, all the aforementioned attacks against KYBER's FO-transform target its long-term secret key. But if implementers want leakage-resistance guarantees, the interest of POLKA over KYBER currently vanishes.

Given this cautionary note, the interesting consequence of POLKA's design, that we want to investigate, is that the asymptotic performances of its leveled implementation scale linearly in the number of shares used for its masked computations. By contrast, the performances of a uniformly masked KYBER scale quadratically in the number of shares. Since this trend comes at the cost of some overheads for POLKA's unprotected implementation, it raises the question of *when (i.e., for which number of shares) can* POLKA *become an interesting alternative to* KYBER *(assuming that only leakage-resilience is required)?*

In order to answer this question, we describe a leveled software implementation of POLKA taking advantage of standard optimization techniques for post-quantum cryptography. Doing so, we also instantiate the few components that its authors left unspecified and slightly tweak the proposal of [20] in order to further reduce the side-channel attack surface. As a result, we put forward that despite the overheads of its unprotected implementation, a leveled implementation of POLKA leads to better performances than a uniformly masked implementation of KYBER on an ARM Cortex-M4 device, already with $d = 2$ shares.

We then wrap up the paper by discussing the remaining challenges in order to turn this improved but qualitative "performances vs. number of shares tradeoff" into an improved quantitative "performances vs. side-channel security tradeoff". Conjecturing that key recovery attacks against POLKA should be significantly more difficult to perform than message distinguishing attacks against KYBER, we conclude that POLKA, or more generally alternative encryption schemes tailored for improved side-channel security, have a strong potential to considerably improve this tradeoff for post-quantum public-key encryption schemes. We complete this discussion with a number of interesting open problems.

2 Background

We start with some preliminaries needed for the understanding of the paper. Namely, we give more details about the POLKA algorithm that we will fully instantiate and implement in subsect. 2.1, and about the NTT that will be the main tool for the polynomial arithmetic operations of our implementation in subsect. 2.2. We do not provide details about Kyber that we do not re-implement and for which various comprehensive descriptions can be found online. The most relevant references for our purposes are the masked implementations in [6,7], of which we will extract performance tables for our comparisons.

2.1 Polka

POLKA is a CCA-secure post-quantum public-key encryption scheme tailored for efficiency when implemented with side-channel security guarantees [20]. Its black-box security relies on the Ring Learning With Errors (RLWE) assumption [24] in the Quantum Random Oracle Model (QROM), while its side-channel efficiency stems from heuristic design tweaks aimed at lowering the overheads of countermeasures. The scheme comes with two noise distribution variants over the coefficients of the polynomials: either centered Gaussian or centered binomial distributions. Here, we focus on the latter version, like KYBER.

While the structure of POLKA follows the KEM-DEM paradigm by deriving an ephemeral secret key from an asymmetric key encapsulation part (KEM) to encrypt the message with a symmetric deterministic encryption (DEM), the way its decryption rejects ill-formed ciphertexts differs from most post-quantum public-key encryption schemes designed for practical use. POLKA rejects ciphertexts through norm checks on re-extracted noises to confer a rigidity property without relying on the FO transform [17]. This eliminates KYBER's critical re-encryption step and the associated attacks listed in introduction.

POLKA also includes additional tricks in its black-box design to ease side-channel countermeasures. For example, its KEM part leverages the bounded additive homomorphy of RLWE ciphertexts to randomize the intermediate values in the decryption step, and ensures that the long-term key is only used in linear operations that can be masked with linear overheads. Besides, POLKA can leverage a structured version of the Learning With Physical Rounding (LWPR) problem [16,21], a physical learning problem of which the heuristic hardness is used to further increase its opportunities of leveled implementation.

Algorithmic Description. We define a noise distribution, to be used over integer vector coefficients, as $\{\sum_{i=1}^{2}(u_i - v_i) \mod 3 \mid u_i, v_i \leftarrow \{0,1\}\}$, where mod 3 means the integer representative over $\{-1, 0, 1\}$. The resulting ternary distribution over $\mathcal{R} = \mathbb{Z}_q[X]/(X^n + 1)$ is denoted as $\mathcal{D}_{n,B}^{\text{coeff}}$, where $B = 1$. For any $r \leftarrow \mathcal{D}_{n,B}^{\text{coeff}}$, we have $\|r\| \leq B$ for the infinity norm over the vector of coefficients. We refer to [20] for the key generation, which produces $b = p(as + e) \in \mathcal{R}^*$ from $s, e \leftarrow \mathcal{D}_{n,B}^{\text{coeff}}$ and $p \geq 2B + 1 \in \mathbb{Z}$, and defines the secret key as s. Next, we describe the encryption and decryption steps of POLKA:

Encrypt: Given a public key (n, q, p, a, b) and a message $M \in \{0,1\}^{\ell_m}$:

1. Sample $r, e_1, e_2 \leftarrow \mathcal{D}_{n,B}^{\text{coeff}}$ and compute the KEM part

$$c_1 = a \cdot r + e_1 \in \mathcal{R}, \qquad c_2 = b \cdot r + e_2 \in \mathcal{R}$$

together with $K = \mathsf{H}(r, e_1, e_2) \in \{0, 1\}^\kappa$.

2. Compute $c_0 = \mathsf{E}_K(M)$ as the DEM part.

Output the ciphertext $C = (c_0, c_1, c_2)$.

Decrypt: Given a secret key $s \in \mathcal{R}$ and $C = (c_0, c_1, c_2)$, do the following:

1. Sample $r', e_1', e_2' \leftarrow \mathcal{D}_{n,B}^{\text{coeff}}$ and compute $c_1' = a \cdot r' + e_1'$ and $c_2' = b \cdot r' + e_2'$.
2. Compute $\bar{c}_1 = c_1 + c_1'$ and $\bar{c}_2 = c_2 + c_2'$.
3. Compute $\bar{\mu} = \bar{c}_2 - p \cdot \bar{c}_1 \cdot s$ over $\mathcal{R}$.
4. Compute $\bar{e}_2 = \bar{\mu} \mod p \in \{-\frac{p-1}{2}, \ldots, \frac{p-1}{2}\}$. If $\|\bar{e}_2\| > 2B$, return $\bot$.
5. Compute $\bar{r} = (\bar{c}_2 - \bar{e}_2) \cdot b^{-1} \in \mathcal{R}$. If $\|\bar{r}\| > 2B$, return $\bot$.
6. Compute $\bar{e}_1 = \bar{c}_1 - a \cdot \bar{r} \in \mathcal{R}$. If $\|\bar{e}_1\| > 2B$, return $\bot$.
7. Compute $r = \bar{r} - r'$, $e_1 = \bar{e}_1 - e_1'$ and $e_2 = \bar{e}_2 - e_2'$. If $\|r\| > B$, or $\|e_1\| > B$, or $\|e_2\| > B$, then return $\bot$.
8. Compute $K = \mathsf{H}(r, e_1, e_2) \in \{0,1\}^\kappa$ and return

$$M = \mathsf{D}_K(c_0) \in \{0,1\}^{\ell_m} \cup \{\bot\}.$$

As suggested in [20], we choose to pre-compute the inverse of b and store it in the public key to avoid computing it on the decryption step.

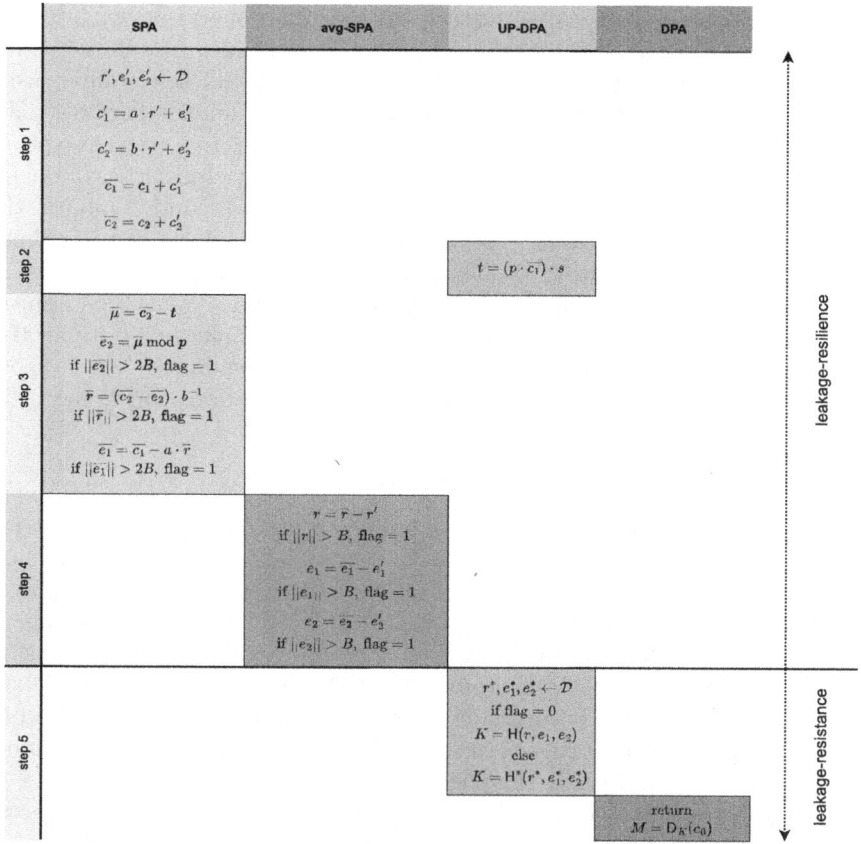

Fig. 1. Leveled implementation of POLKA, from [20].

Leveled Implementation. We now describe the protected implementation of POLKA's decryption proposed in [20], for which we re-use the visual description of Fig. 1. The color codes indicate the type of side-channel attacks that must be prevented by implementers. Light green means SPA security for randomized values, dark green means "SPA with repetition" security for non-randomized values (i.e., SPA with repeated measurements of the same value), light blue means DPA security for key-homomorphic operations manipulating unknown (randomized) inputs and dark blue is for standard DPA security. As discussed in introduction, our focus in this paper is on the leakage-resilience guarantees of POLKA (i.e., the upper part of the figure, where the long-term secret is manipulated).

The general structure of POLKA, that rejects ill-formed ciphertexts without FO transform thanks to norm checks, directly removes one critical attack vector that severely affects the side-channel security of KYBER. We next describe the other design features that support the leveled implementation of POLKA.

Dummy Ciphertexts. When many traces of the same operation with identical inputs are collected, adversaries can combine them in order to reduce the noise in the leakage measurements (e.g., thanks to averaging). In POLKA, intermediate values are expressed as RLWE samples of the form $c = a \cdot r + e$, where a is public, and r and e are small secret values that the adversary aims to retrieve. To prevent such an averaging, POLKA introduces randomized dummy ciphertexts of the form $c' = a \cdot r' + e'$, where r' and e' are small random values, and combines them with the original ciphertext as a pseudorandom $\bar{c} = c + c'$, which is unknown to the adversary. The security proofs are then adjusted in order to account for the new norms of these randomized intermediate values. While this approach incurs some mild overheads for generating the dummy ciphertexts, it effectively transforms a SPA with repetition attack path into a regular SPA attack path, significantly simplifying the task of protecting the operations concerned.

Key-Homomorphic Operations and (Ring-)LWPR. Despite having a DPA attack path seems unavoidable in any decryption scheme that must manipulate a long-term secret key, POLKA is designed in such a way that the main operation manipulating this long-term secret (i.e., s in step 2 of Fig. 1) is key-homomorphic. As a result, it can be efficiently performed share by share (i.e., with overheads that scale linearly in the number of shares). Furthermore, under the LWPR assumption, it is possible to unmask the value of t so that all the norm checks of steps 3 and 4 can be performed on unshared values. The LWPR assumption is a physical learning problem that has been heuristically shown to be computationally ard [16,21]. Standard LWPR samples have the form $(r, \mathsf{L}(r \cdot s))$, where r is a random public vector, s is a secret vector, and the leakage function L acts as an injective rounding function. In POLKA, the polynomial product involving the long-term secret naturally suggests a ring variant of the LWPR problem.

2.2 NTT

Let Φ_N be the N-th cyclotomic polynomial and q be a prime number. Since $\Phi(X)$ has integer coefficients, we can consider the polynomial ring $\mathcal{R} = \mathbb{Z}_q[X]/(\Phi(X))$, where $\mathbb{Z}_q$ is the field of integers with addition and multiplication modulo q, i.e., $\mathbb{Z}/(q)$. As $\Phi(X)$ factors into coprime irreducible polynomials $f_i(X)$ of degree δ in $\mathcal{R}$ if the order of q modulo N is δ, the well-known Chinese Reminder Theorem ensures that we have the ring isomorphism $\mathcal{R} \approx \mathcal{R}_1 \times \cdots \times \mathcal{R}_{\varphi(N)/\delta}$, where $\mathcal{R}_i = \mathbb{Z}_q[X]/(f_i(X))$ with $\mathcal{R} \to \mathcal{R}_i; a \to a \bmod f_i(X)$. The naive multiplication in $\mathcal{R}$ has an asymptotic cost of n^2 multiplications in $\mathbb{Z}_q$, where $n = \varphi(N)$ is the degree of Φ_N. Assuming that q is chosen given N so that δ is constant, the corresponding multiplication can be carried out using only around δ^2 multiplications modulo q in each $\mathcal{R}_i$, leading to $\mathcal{O}(n)$ such multiplications. For well-chosen N values, typically a power of 2, the Number Theoretic Transform (NTT) then allows applying the above isomorphism back and forth in $\mathcal{O}(n \log n)$ operations in $\mathbb{Z}_q$, with the same complexity to perform multiplications over $\mathcal{R}$.

For KYBER, we have $N = 512$ and the prime $q = 3329$ of order 2 modulo N. For POLKA, we have $N = 2048$ and the prime $q = 59393$ of order 1, thus a fully splitting ring $\mathcal{R}$. In both cases, we have $2n = N$ and $\Phi_N(X) = X^n + 1$.

3 Instantiation and Tweaks

In this section, we first complete the specifications of POLKA by instantiating the few components that were left open by its authors in subsect. 3.1. We next bring relevant clarifications to the leveled implementation of Fig. 1 and slightly tweak it in order to further reduce the side-channel attack surface.

3.1 Choice of Symmetric Primitives

Step 5 of POLKA requires a hash function. As standard in post-quantum cryptography, we use SHA-3 for this purpose.[1] As a new standard, it benefits from various open implementations. It is also natural given our goal to compare the performances of POLKA with the ones of KYBER (which relies on SHA-3).

Besides, Step 5 of POLKA requires an Authenticated Encryption (AE) scheme. The authors of [20] proposed an instantiation based on a key-homomorphic MAC, which may be interesting in order to upgrade the leakage-resilience guarantees of POLKA towards leakage-resistance ones. Yet, as is, this solution is specialized to fixed-length messages which makes POLKA less comparable to KYBER. It is also not sufficient to make POLKA leakage-resistant (since DPA can anyway target its hash function). Given our restricted goal of leakage-resilient implementation, we therefore stepped back to a more standard choice, which is to select an AE from the NIST lightweight cryptography competition. Among the candidates, Saturnin appeared as a natural choice, due to its focus on post-quantum security which we also target [9]. Our implementations rely on the (unprotected) C implementation made available with its submission to the NIST.

3.2 Clarifications and Improvements

Despite Fig. 1 highlights the security requirements of a leveled implementation of POLKA, it does not directly clarify which parts of the computations are masked, nor which operations are performed in the NTT domain. The updated Fig. 2 provides such clarifications. First, we use the "widehat" notation for all the operations that are performed in the NTT domain. Changes from hatted to non-hatted variables (and vice-versa) therefore indicate where NTTs and inverse NTTs must be computed. Second, we use subscripts in Step 2 of the figure in order to clarify the operations that are computed per share due to masking.

We note that while the impact of masking and unmasking on side-channel vulnerability is evident, NTT conversions can also have an impact in this respect.

---

[1] https://csrc.nist.gov/pubs/fips/202/final.

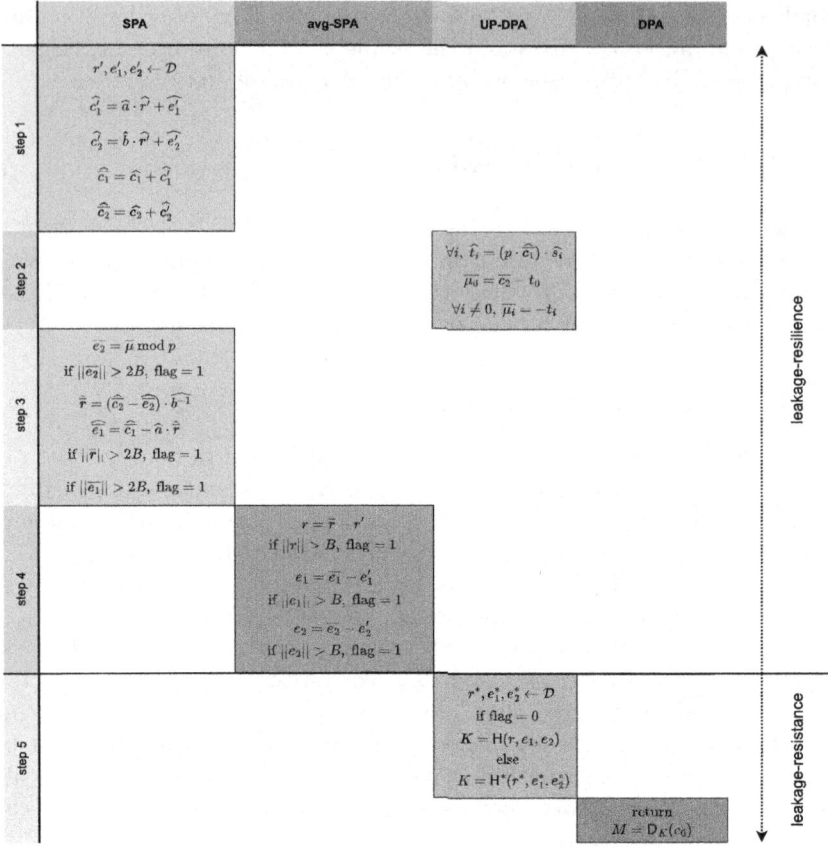

Fig. 2. Tweaked leveled implementation of POLKA.

Specifically, the result of the product in Step 2 must not remain in its NTT representation when unmasked. The hardness analysis of LWPR indeed relies on classical polynomial multiplication [16,21], as the algebraic structure of pointwise multiplication in the NTT domain offers weaker key mixing. For efficiency, the product can still be computed in the NTT domain. However, the result must undergo a masked inverse NTT before unmasking. In POLKA, this constraint aligns naturally with the subsequent operation (i.e., a modular reduction) which cannot be performed in the NTT domain anyway. Interestingly, this observation suggests a slight improvement of POLKA's leveled implementation that is also reflected in Fig. 2. Namely, since we need to exit the NTT domain before unmasking, we can perform the subsequent subtraction operation in the masked domain. Such a change comes at no additional cost (since the subtraction applies to a single share) and further minimizes the exposition of sensitive values.

4 Implementation Choices

In this section, we outline the implementation choices made for POLKA, focusing on polynomial multiplication and modular arithmetic techniques.

4.1 Polynomial Multiplication

As with all RLWE-based schemes, POLKA's computations rely heavily on polynomial multiplications in rings. This operation constitutes a significant portion of the overall computation cost. When performed using a naive method, the complexity is in $\mathcal{O}(n^2)$, where n is the polynomial degree. Fortunately, POLKA's ring structure is chosen to allow the use of the NTT (described in subsect. 2.2). The NTT converts polynomials to their image in the NTT domain. The naive implementation of the NTT runs in $\mathcal{O}(n^2)$ but using the Cooley-Tukey butterfly algorithm [10] (and the Gentleman-Sande one for the inverse NTT [18]) this complexity becomes $\mathcal{O}(n \log n)$. Once in the NTT domain, polynomial multiplications can be performed point-wise, reducing the complexity to $\mathcal{O}(n)$.

4.2 Switches Between Representations

The polynomial operations in POLKA include additions, multiplications, norm checks, and small modular reductions. Additions can be performed in either representation, as long as all terms share the same domain. However, for efficiency reasons, multiplications must be carried out in the NTT representation, whereas norm checks and modular reductions require the polynomials to be in their natural representation. In order to minimize the number of representation switches, the polynomials in the public and secret keys are stored directly in their NTT representations. From Fig. 2, we can then directly count that POLKA's decryption requires 4 NTT and $3 + d$ inverse NTT operations, where d represents the number of shares used for the masked computations of Step 2.

4.3 Modular Arithmetic

Most of POLKA's operations ultimately reduce to perform modular arithmetic over the integers. However, the default implementation of modular operations in C neither runs in constant time nor achieves optimal performance. In order to address these inefficiencies, we employ Montgomery's and Barrett's reduction algorithms, both widely used in cryptographic implementations.

Montgomery's Reduction. Montgomery's reduction is an efficient algorithm for modular multiplication [26]. Its key insight is that performing divisions and modular operations with powers of two is significantly faster than with arbitrary values. To leverage this, we first compute the number m of multiples of q that need to be added to an input T to make it divisible by $R = 2^{32}$. We then efficiently divide $(T + m \cdot q)$ by R to obtain a result in the range $[0, 2q)$. The original algorithm includes a final step to subtract q if necessary, ensuring that the output strictly lies within $[0, q)$. However, depending on subsequent operations in POLKA, this step can often be skipped, allowing the result to remain in $[0, 2q)$. This procedure yields the value TR^{-1} (mod q) instead of T (mod q). To recover the desired result, we pre-multiply T by R (mod q), which comes for free if T arises from a product between a value and a constant, as in the NTT.

Barrett's Reduction. While Montgomery reduction is highly efficient, it has two drawbacks: it performs poorly when reducing overflowed values (e.g., sums), and its output can exceed q. In cases where these issues are problematic, we use Barrett's reduction [4] instead. Barrett's reduction replaces division by the modulus q with a cheaper multiplication and bit-shift operation. Although it is slower than Montgomery's reduction, it guarantees the output remains in the range $[0, q)$, making it preferable when strict modular bounds are required.

Both for Montgomery's and Barret's reductions, we actually rely on improved versions that are able to deal with signed inputs, proposed by Seiler [33].

4.4 Small Hash Function Input

A naive approach to organize the hash function input in Step 5 of Fig. 2 would be to concatenate the coefficients of r, $e1$ and $e2$ in a big array. However, this approach would make the input of this hash function quite large (about 100 kilobits) and therefore long to process. A better way to organize this input is to stack several coefficients per register. Indeed, r, $e1$ and $e2$ are guaranteed to be small polynomials with coefficients among three values. Therefore, it is possible to represent every of those coefficients with only two bits and to construct our hash input by storing chunks of coefficients in single variables. This technique allows us to reduce the size of the hash input to roughly 6 kilobits.

5 Results and Discussions

In this section, we finally benchmark both POLKA and KYBER, analyze POLKA's performances per decryption step and operation and compare the performances of the two algorithms, in the unprotected and protected settings.

5.1 Experimental Setup

In order to perform our measurements, we ran our code on the NUCLEO-L4R5ZI board with an ARM Cortex-M4 32-bit micro-controller as required by the framework pqm4 [23], and more specifically the fork pqm4_masked [7]. The measurements of KYBER were done using the code from [7] for Kyber768. The pqm4_masked framework allows defining personalized bench cases. In addition to the bench cases related to Encrypt and Decrypt, we defined one bench case per decryption step, one per polynomial operator (addition, substraction, multiplication, scalar product, randomization, NTTs, inverse NTTs, norm computation, mask refreshing, modular reduction), one for Saturnin and one for Keccak.

5.2 Analysis of Polka' Performances

We first focus on POLKA's decryption step, which is the most sensitive from the side-channel analysis viewpoint. We therefore observe the cycle counts and their evolution as the number of shares increases, first per step in Decrypt and then per type of operation in Decrypt, in Fig. 3 and Fig. 4, respectively.[2]

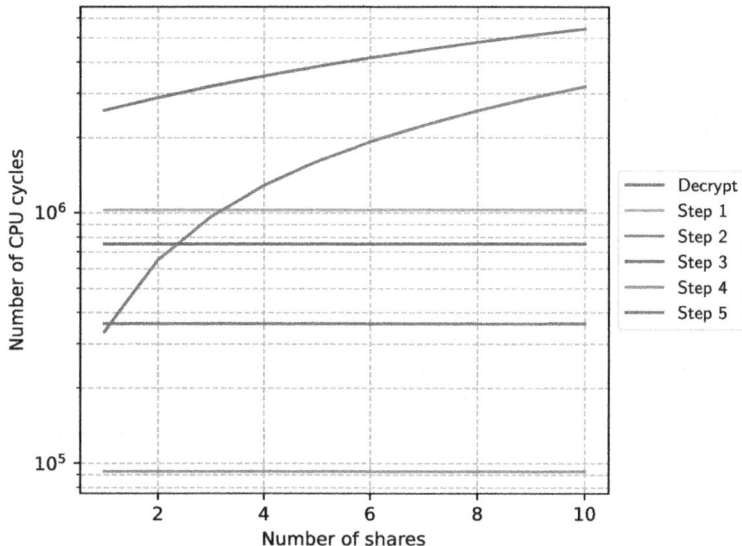

Fig. 3. Cycle counts for each decryption step in POLKA.

Fig. 3 leads to the expected observation that the performances of a leveled implementation of POLKA's decryption scale linearly with the number of shares used to protect its long-term key, which is a direct outcome of key-homomorphic computations. For the rest, we note that when the number of shares is low ($d < 4$), most of the computation time is spent in the first and third steps, which are the steps dealing with dummy ciphers. We observe that the cost of those steps is constant, since they are performed on unmasked data. Beyond 4 shares, the time spent in the second step (i.e., the masked multiplication) starts to dominate as it is the only step performed on masked data.

Fig. 4 offers a complementary view. It highlights that most of the computation time is spent on the NTTs and inverse NTTs. It also shows that only the cycles spent to perform the inverse NTT, refreshing, multiplication and subtraction

---

[2] Our implementations are not perfectly constant time, mostly due to the randomness generation and the implementation of Saturnin not being constant time. Yet, the standard deviations observed are three orders of magnitude smaller than the mean values we report, so they do not affect our conclusions regarding the performance trends of POLKA implementations when their number of shares increases.

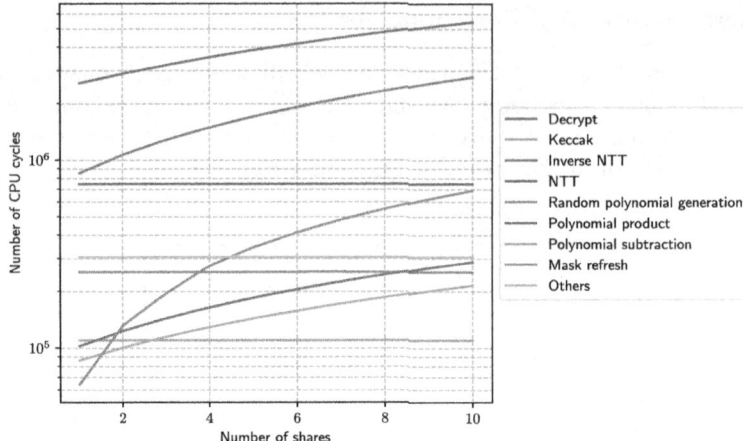

Fig. 4. Cycle counts for the main operations in POLKA's decryption.

operations (i.e., the operations of Step 2 in Fig. 2) increase linearly with the number of shares. We note that the refresh step is increasing faster than the other routines. This is due to the fact that refreshing a mask requires $d-1$ polynomial randomizations, $d-1$ additions and $d-1$ subtractions.

5.3 Comparison with Kyber

We finally compare the performances of POLKA and KYBER, first for unprotected implementations in Table 1, then for their protected decryption in function of the number of shares, in Fig. 5. We recall that the physical security guarantees targeted by both implementations are different: leakage-resistance for the uniformly masked KYBER, leakage-resilience for the leveled POLKA.

Table 1. Cycle counts for KYBER and POLKA's unprotected implementation.

	KYBER	POLKA
Encrypt	957, 176	880, 201
Decrypt	707, 827	2, 571, 178

Table 1 shows that, as expected, the leakage-resilience features of POLKA come with overheads in the unprotected setting: its decryption is about four times slower than the one of KYBER. We note that the POLKA's encryption is slightly faster, which we assume is due to KYBER's compression step.

Fig. 5 shows that these overheads are rapidly compensated when side-channel protections are needed. Already for $d=2$ shares, POLKA is twice faster than KYBER. This factor grows with d and improves to 8 for 8 shares. We discuss the expected quantitative impact of these figures in the next conclusions.

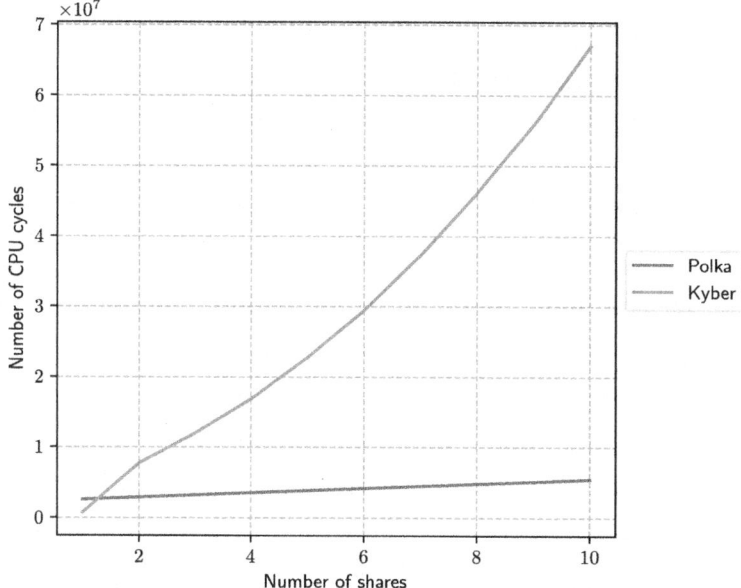

Fig. 5. Cycle counts for KYBER and POLKA's protected decryption.

6 Conclusion and Open Problems

Our results essentially confirm the conjecture from [20] that leveled implementations of schemes like POLKA can rapidly lead to better performances than a uniformly masked implementation of KYBER. It turns out this is already true for $d = 2$ shares. It also raises interesting open problems that we now detail.

First, both the uniformly masked implementations of KYBER in [6,7] and the leveled implementation of POLKA in this paper focus on masking the necessary operations. While this is an important first step, it remains that SPA attack paths need to be prevented (at the share level for KYBER, both at the share level and after Step 2 for POLKA). Such SPA protections are expected to be cheap. We nevertheless list the operations that should require special care.

Starting with KYBER, it is for example well-known that single-trace (SPA) attacks against the (share by share implementation of the) NTT may be a threat [29,30]. If successful, such attacks indeed cancel the impact of masking. A natural option to prevent this issue is to rely on a hardware coprocessor. Alternatively, shuffling can be used as a surrogate to emulate parallelism [37].

A similar issue pops up in POLKA. In particular, it is important that the inverse NTT operations in Step 2 of Fig. 2 are secure against SPA (which, again, is calling for parallelism or shuffling). Besides, the security of the LWPR assumption that we leverage in order to unmask the computations after this Step 2 also requires that the operations in Step 3 do not leak "too much" about t [16,21]. Once more, parallelism and shuffling appear as natural options. Yet, it is also worth noticing that POLKA embeds design features to minimize this leakage. Namely, the LWPR assumption was so far studied for a public vector multiplied with a secret key (as it is usually the case for hard learning problems). But the leveled implementation of Fig. 2 multiplies a secret (randomized) vector, of which the adversary only sees the leakage with a shared key. Hence, studying how much this hardens the problem is an interesting open problem. Second, Step 3 in the same figure starts with a modular reduction which turns 16-bit values into 3-bit values, substantially reducing the leakage on t that subsequent operations can provide. Finally, LWPR was so far studied in a conservative setting where leakages are assumed to be noise-free. So it is another interesting open problem to find out whether there is a gap to exploit between the LWPR assumption and a more realistic "learning with physical rounding and noise" assumption.

Next, the "security vs. performance" tradeoff that we study is so far qualitative. Again, this appears to be a necessary first step and, for example, a similar tradeoff was also first studied for masked implementations of KYBER. But it also suggests investigating how this qualitative analysis can be translated into a quantitative one as an important extension. This will likely be a non-trivial task, since it implies understanding in depth how to assess the worst-case (quantitative) security guarantees of KYBER and POLKA, which both have multiple (SPA and DPA) attack paths. There are nevertheless reasons to believe that the turn to a quantitative analysis will further amplify the impact of POLKA. First, and as already mentioned, the absence of FO transform removes the possibility of a message distinguishing attack which is, in many cases, the most critical one for KYBER [2]. Concretely, it leads implementations with large number of shares to be breakable [15]. Second, it is already well documented that key-homomorphic primitives bring significant advantages in terms of dealing with physical defaults [8,16]. So it is expected that translating the number of shares into a "statistical security order" will be easier for POLKA than KYBER: both in software, due to transitions [3,12], and in hardware due to glitches [25,28].

In order to stimulate research in these directions, we make our baseline implementation of POLKA available at the following address:

https://github.com/uclcrypto/pqm4_polka.

While such an implementation is not expected to directly satisfy the aforementioned security requirements, we believe it is relevant to assess the severity of different attack paths given the randomized nature of POLKA's decryption.

As mentioned in the introduction, the leveled implementation of POLKA in this paper provides security for its long-term secret key (i.e., leakage-resilience). While this is a practically-relevant guarantee given that the most critical side-channel attacks against KYBER target its long-term key, finding out whether leakage-resistance could be obtained in a more efficient manner than by masking Step 5 in Fig. 2 instantiated with standard hash functions and authenticated encryption schemes is a natural next step. The original description of [20] suggests that key-homomorphic primitives could be used for a part of this final step. Yet, for now, it does not remove the need to securely mask a cryptographic hash function, which would incur quadratic overheads. So it is yet another promising scope for further research efforts to improve POLKA on this front.

Besides, the recent work of Hövelmanns et al. introduced an alternative framework to proving the security of post-quantum encryption schemes ensuring rigidity via norm checks [22]. It would be interesting to study whether it applies to POLKA (or variations thereof), and whether it can lead to prove the security of its KEM component rather than encryption scheme as a whole.

Eventually, the physical security guarantees of POLKA remain heuristic so far. So a comprehensive proof of leakage-resilience or leakage-resistance, under weak and falsifiable physical assumptions is a challenging long-term goal.

Acknowledgments. Thibaud Schoenauen is a PhD student funded by the FSR project PQShield. Thomas Peters and François-Xavier Standaert are respectively senior research associate and research director of the Belgian Fund for Scientific Research (F.R.S.-FNRS). This work has been funded in part by the European Research Council (ERC) Advanced Grant BRIDGE (number 101096871) and by the Walloon Region through the project CyberExcellence (convention number 2110186). Views and opinions expressed are those of the authors and do not necessarily reflect those of the European Union or the ERC. Neither the European Union nor the granting authority can be held responsible for them.

References

1. Avanzi, R., et al.: and Damien Stehlé. Algorithm specifications and supporting documentation. NIST Post-Quantum Cryptography Standard, CRYSTALS-Kyber (2022)
2. Azouaoui, M., Bronchain, O., Hoffmann, C., Kuzovkova, Y., Schneider, T., Standaert, F.: Systematic study of decryption and re-encryption leakage: the case of kyber. In: COSADE, volume 13211 of Lecture Notes in Computer Science, pp. 236–256. Springer, 2022
3. Balasch, J., Gierlichs, B., Grosso, V., Reparaz, O., Standaert, F.: On the cost of lazy engineering for masked software implementations. In: CARDIS, volume 8968 of Lecture Notes in Computer Science, pp. 64–81. Springer, 2014
4. Barrett, P.: Implementing the rivest shamir and adleman public key encryption algorithm on a standard digital signal processor. In: CRYPTO, volume 263 of Lecture Notes in Computer Science, pp. 311–323. Springer (1986)
5. Bellizia, D., et al.: Mode-Level vs. Implementation-Level Physical Security in Symmetric Cryptography. In: Micciancio, D., Ristenpart, T. (eds.) CRYPTO 2020. LNCS, vol. 12170, pp. 369–400. Springer, Cham (2020). https://doi.org/10.1007/978-3-030-56784-2_13
6. Bos, J.W., Gourjon, M., Renes, J., Schneider, T., Vredendaal, C.: Masking kyber: first- and higher-order implementations. IACR Trans. Cryptogr. Hardw. Embed. Syst. **2021**(4), 173–214 (2021)
7. Bronchain, O., Cassiers, G.: Bitslicing arithmetic/boolean masking conversions for fun and profit with application to lattice-based kems. IACR Trans. Cryptogr. Hardw. Embed. Syst. **2022**(4), 553–588 (2022)
8. Bronchain, O., Schneider, T., Standaert, F.-X.: Reducing risks through simplicity: high side-channel security for lazy engineers. J. Cryptogr. Eng. **11**(1), 39–55 (2021)

9. Canteaut, A., et al.: Saturnin: a suite of lightweight symmetric algorithms for post-quantum security. IACR Trans. Symmetric Cryptol. **2020**(S1), 160–207 (2020)
10. Cooley, J., Tukey, J.: An algorithm for the machine calculation of complex fourier series. Math. Comput. **19**(90), 297–301 (1965)
11. Coron, J.-S., Gérard, F., Montoya, S., Zeitoun, R.: High-order polynomial comparison and masking lattice-based encryption. IACR Trans. Cryptogr. Hardw. Embed. Syst. **2023**(1), 153–192 (2023)
12. Coron, J.-S., Giraud, C., Prouff, E., Renner, S., Rivain, M., Vadnala, P.K.: Conversion of Security Proofs from One Leakage Model to Another: A New Issue. In: Schindler, W., Huss, S.A. (eds.) COSADE 2012. LNCS, vol. 7275, pp. 69–81. Springer, Heidelberg (2012). https://doi.org/10.1007/978-3-642-29912-4_6
13. D'Anvers, J.: One-hot conversion:towards faster table-based A2B conversion. In: EUROCRYPT (4), volume 14007 of Lecture Notes in Computer Science, pp. 628–657. Springer (2023)
14. D'Anvers, J.-P., Heinz, D., Pessl, P., Beirendonck, M., Verbauwhede, I.: Higher-order masked ciphertext comparison for lattice-based cryptography. IACR Trans. Cryptogr. Hardw. Embed. Syst. **2022**(2), 115–139 (2022)
15. Dubrova, E., Ngo, K., Gärtner, J., Wang, R.: Breaking a fifth-order masked implementation of crystals-kyber by copy-paste. In APKCAsiaCCS, pp. 10–20. ACM (2023)
16. Duval, S., Méaux, P., Momin, C., Standaert, F.-X.: Exploring crypto-physical dark matter and learning with physical rounding towards secure and efficient fresh re-keying. IACR Trans. Cryptogr. Hardw. Embed. Syst. **2021**(1), 373–401 (2021)
17. Fujisaki, E., Okamoto, T.: Secure integration of asymmetric and symmetric encryption schemes. In: CRYPTO, volume 1666 of Lecture Notes in Computer Science, pp. 537–554. Springer (1999)
18. Gentleman,M.W., Sande. G.: Fast fourier transforms: for fun and profit. In: AFIPS Fall Joint Computing Conference, volume 29 of AFIPS Conference Proceedings, pp. 563–578. AFIPS / ACM / Spartan Books, Washington D.C., 1966
19. Guo, C., Pereira, O., Peters, T., Standaert, F.-X.: Authenticated Encryption with Nonce Misuse and Physical Leakage: Definitions, Separation Results and First Construction. In: Schwabe, P., Thériault, N. (eds.) LATINCRYPT 2019. LNCS, vol. 11774, pp. 150–172. Springer, Cham (2019). https://doi.org/10.1007/978-3-030-30530-7_8
20. Hoffmann, C., Libert, B., Momin, C., Peters, T., Standaert, F.: POLKA: towards leakage-resistant post-quantum CCA-secure public key encryption. In: Public Key Cryptography (1), volume 13940 of Lecture Notes in Computer Science, pp. 114–144. Springer, 2023
21. Hoffmann, C., Méaux, P., Momin, C., Rotella, Y., Standaert, F., Udvarhelyi, B.: Learning with physical rounding for linear and quadratic leakage functions. In: CRYPTO (3), volume 14083 of Lecture Notes in Computer Science, pp. 410–439. Springer, 2023
22. Hövelmanns, K., Hülsing, A., Majenz, C., Sisinni, F.: (un)breakable curses - re-encryption in the fujisaki-okamoto transform. In: EUROCRYPT (2), volume 15602 of Lecture Notes in Computer Science, pp. 245–274. Springer, 2025
23. Kannwischer, M.J., Petri, R., Rijneveld, J., Schwabe, P., Stoffelen, K.: PQM4: post-quantum crypto library for the ARM Cortex-M4. https://github.com/mupq/pqm4
24. Lyubashevsky, V., Peikert, C., Regev, O.: On Ideal Lattices and Learning with Errors over Rings. In: Gilbert, H. (ed.) EUROCRYPT 2010. LNCS, vol. 6110, pp. 1–23. Springer, Heidelberg (2010). https://doi.org/10.1007/978-3-642-13190-5_1

25. Mangard, S., Pramstaller, N., Oswald, E.: Successfully Attacking Masked AES Hardware Implementations. In: Rao, J.R., Sunar, B. (eds.) CHES 2005. LNCS, vol. 3659, pp. 157–171. Springer, Heidelberg (2005). https://doi.org/10.1007/11545262_12
26. Montgomery, P.L.: Modular multiplication without trial division. Math. comput. **44**(170), 519–521, 1985
27. Ngo, K., Dubrova, E., Guo, Q., Johansson, T.: A side-channel attack on a masked IND-CCA secure saber KEM implementation. IACR Trans. Cryptogr. Hardw. Embed. Syst. **2021**(4), 676–707 (2021)
28. Nikova, S., Rijmen, V., Schläffer, M.: Secure hardware implementation of nonlinear functions in the presence of glitches. J. Cryptol. **24**(2), 292–321 (2011)
29. Pessl, P., Primas, R.: More Practical Single-Trace Attacks on the Number Theoretic Transform. In: Schwabe, P., Thériault, N. (eds.) LATINCRYPT 2019. LNCS, vol. 11774, pp. 130–149. Springer, Cham (2019). https://doi.org/10.1007/978-3-030-30530-7_7
30. Primas, R., Pessl, P., Mangard, S.: Single-Trace Side-Channel Attacks on Masked Lattice-Based Encryption. In: Fischer, W., Homma, N. (eds.) CHES 2017. LNCS, vol. 10529, pp. 513–533. Springer, Cham (2017). https://doi.org/10.1007/978-3-319-66787-4_25
31. Rajendran, G., Ravi, P., D'Anvers, J.-P., Bhasin, S., Chattopadhyay, A.: Pushing the limits of generic side-channel attacks on lwe-based kems - parallel PC oracle attacks on kyber KEM and beyond. IACR Trans. Cryptogr. Hardw. Embed. Syst. **2023**(2), 418–446 (2023)
32. Ravi, P., Roy, S.S., Chattopadhyay, A., Bhasin, S.: Generic side-channel attacks on cca-secure lattice-based PKE and KEMS. IACR Trans. Cryptogr. Hardw. Embed. Syst. **2020**(3), 307–335 (2020)
33. Seiler, G.: Faster AVX2 optimized NTT multiplication for ring-lwe lattice cryptography. IACR Cryptol. ePrint Arch, page 39, 2018
34. Standaert, F.: Towards and Open Approach to Secure Cryptographic Implementations (Invited Talk). In: EUROCRYPT I, volume 11476 of LNCS, pages xv 2019. https://www.youtube.com/watch?v=KdhrsuJT1sE
35. Tanaka, Y., Ueno, R., Xagawa, K., Ito, A., Takahashi, J., Homma, N.: Multiple-valued plaintext-checking side-channel attacks on post-quantum kems. IACR Trans. Cryptogr. Hardw. Embed. Syst. **2023**(3), 473–503 (2023)
36. Ueno, R., Xagawa, K., Tanaka, Y., Ito, A., Takahashi, J., Homma, N.: Curse of re-encryption: A generic power/em analysis on post-quantum kems. IACR Trans. Cryptogr. Hardw. Embed. Syst. **2022**(1), 296–322 (2022)
37. Veyrat-Charvillon, N., Medwed, M., Kerckhof, S., Standaert, F.-X.: Shuffling against Side-Channel Attacks: A Comprehensive Study with Cautionary Note. In: Wang, X., Sako, K. (eds.) ASIACRYPT 2012. LNCS, vol. 7658, pp. 740–757. Springer, Heidelberg (2012). https://doi.org/10.1007/978-3-642-34961-4_44
38. Xu, Z., Pemberton, O., Roy, S., Oswald, D.F., Yao, W., Zheng, Z.: Magnifying side-channel leakage of lattice-based cryptosystems with chosen ciphertexts: the case study of kyber. IEEE Trans. Computers, **71**(9), 2163–2176 (2022)

Research on the Security Estimation Framework for Code-Based Public Key Cryptography Algorithms

Haoyue Fu[1], Yunfei Cao[1(✉)], Hong Xiang[2], and Congyi Zhang[2]

[1] National Key Laboratory of Security Communication, Chengdu 610041, People's Republic of China
`1345093538@qq.com`
[2] School of Big Data and Software Engineering, Chongqing University, Chongqing 401331, People's Republic of China

Abstract. Since the advent of Shor's algorithm, the demand for quantum-resistant security has gained significant attention across industries. While the exact timeline for the complete obsolescence of first-generation public-key cryptography remains uncertain, designers of network products and protocols must familiarize themselves with potential quantum-resistant alternatives and prepare contingency plans in advance. This paper focuses on code-based public key cryptography algorithms, providing an overview of their research background and detailing the current status of code-based algorithms active in multiple rounds of NIST evaluations, including eliminated candidates and their shortcomings. Additionally, we review security analysis methodologies for code-based algorithms, covering coding theory, associated hard problems, analytical approaches, and major attack algorithms.

Keywords: Post-quantum cryptography · Code-based algorithms · Public-key cryptography

1 Introduction

With the advent of Shor's algorithm [1] and the accelerated development of quantum computers by major global powers, quantum computers pose a significant threat to the security foundations of existing classical computer communication networks, namely first-generation public-key cryptography (RSA, ECC, DH, SM2, etc.). Consequently, the replacement of current public-key cryptosystems with quantum-resistant alternatives has become a critical concern for the global cybersecurity community, including standardization bodies, academia, IT industries, and key application domains such as finance, telecommunications, and power grids.

To address this, the U.S. national standards institution initiated a global call for post-quantum cryptographic algorithms. On July 5, 2022, NIST finalized four lattice-based schemes for standardization: CRYSTALS-KYBER [2] (encryption), CRYSTALS-Dilithium [3], FALCON [4], and the hash-based SPHINCS+ [5] (signatures). Additionally, four candidate schemes were selected for further evaluation: code-based BIKE [6], Classic McEliece [7], HQC [8], and the isogeny-based SIKE [9] (later modified). Notably, CRYSTALS-KYBER is the sole encryption algorithm among the standardized selections, while the candidates are all encryption schemes.

After the fourth round of submissions, NIST launched an additional call for signature algorithms [10] due to the lack of diversified candidates and the dominance of lattice-based schemes. Code-based algorithms, which originated in the 1970s and rely on the NP-Complete problem of random linear code decoding, emerged as a major focus. Despite their longstanding security reputation (nearly 50 years without successful attacks), code-based schemes face challenges in practical adoption due to excessively large public keys. For example, in TLS protocol integration [11], CRYSTALS-KYBER requires public keys ranging from 800 bytes (Kyber-512) to 1568 bytes (Kyber-1024), while Classic McEliece demands 261,120 bytes (Classic McEliece-348864) to 1,357,824 bytes (Classic McEliece-8192128). Transmitting such large keys would occupy at least four TCP packets per communication, rendering Classic McEliece impractical for TLS. However, its unparalleled security heritage (since 1978) [12] and theoretical robustness compelled NIST to retain it as a contingency option against potential breaches in standardized algorithms.

This paper analyzes the hard problems underpinning code-based algorithms, evaluates their security foundations, and critiques the security claims in algorithm specifications.

2 Security Foundations of Code-Based Algorithms

Coding theory studies the properties of codes and their performance in practical applications, commonly used in data compression, encryption, error correction, and network coding. The mathematical theory of communication [13] states that appropriate error-correcting codes can transmit messages over various channels with minimal bit error rates. This is because any communication channel has a defined capacity C. If the required transmission rate R is less than C, there exists a coding method where the error probability can be made arbitrarily small when the code length n is sufficiently large and maximum likelihood decoding (MLD) is applied. However, the complexity of MLD increases exponentially with n or N, making it physically infeasible for large n or N.

In 1978, Robert McEliece proposed the McEliece cryptosystem, whose security is based on error-correcting codes introduced by the Russian scholar Valerii Denisovich Goppa in his 1970 paper [12]. Its application context addressed data security issues in large-scale distributed multi-user systems, such as NASA-managed satellite networks, and it was the first scheme proven equivalent to an NP-Complete problem. Building on this, Niederreiter [14] proposed the Niederreiter cryptosystem in 1986 using generalized Reed–Solomon (GRS) codes, applying the same idea to the parity-check matrix H of linear codes. The security of McEliece and Niederreiter schemes is fundamentally equivalent. However, in 1992, Sidelnikov and Shestakov demonstrated that Niederreiter's GRS-based scheme was insecure. Subsequent improvements ([15–19], etc.) to the original McEliece scheme aimed to reduce public key sizes for efficiency, but most were later proven insecure or inefficient. By 2001, Kobara and Imai [20] proposed a conversion achieving IND-CCA2 security while maintaining the original McEliece security and nearly identical transmission rates.

Despite improvements, McEliece and Niederreiter schemes have not achieved widespread practical adoption like RSA or ECC due to excessively large public keys. However, their resistance to Shor's algorithm—and more generally, to Fourier sampling attacks on coset states—has positioned them as prominent candidates in post-quantum cryptography. Common McEliece variants include schemes combining Goppa codes to obscure the code structure, addressing vulnerabilities in Niederreiter's original version. Recent research explores structured codes to optimize efficiency, such as Quasi-Cyclic (QC) Codes [17], Low-Density Parity-Check (LDPC) Codes [21], Quasi-Dyadic (QD) Codes [22], Quasi-Cyclic LDPC (QC-LDPC) Codes [23].

Let $\mathbb{F} = \{0,1\}$ be the binary field. An n-dimensional vector space V over $\mathbb{F}$ is constructed, where C is a subspace of V, termed a binary linear block code. Elements of C are codewords. From a vector space perspective, a linear block code $C(n,k,d)$ can be viewed as a k-dimensional subspace of the n-tuple vector space C, with k linearly independent codewords, and d denoting the minimum Hamming distance between codewords.

Decoding $C(n,k,d)$ involves finding the codeword c closest to the received vector. Specifically, given a parity-check matrix H and a syndrome s, solving the syndrome decoding problem (SDP) requires finding a binary vector e of length n with Hamming weight $\text{wt}(e) \leq t$ such that $He^\top = s$. The name derives from the fact that by computing a given concomitant s, solving that concomitant decoding problem, and adding the resulting vector e, it is possible to decode the given and find the codeword c with the smallest distance to it.

Two decision problems in coding theory, proven NP-Complete in [11], underpin security:

1. **Coset Weight Problem:** Given a random $r \times n$ binary matrix H, an r-bit vector s, and a positive integer t, determine whether there exists an n-bit vector e with $\text{wt}(e) \leq t$ such that:

$$He^\top = s.$$

This is also termed the Decisional Syndrome Decoding Problem (DSDP).

2. **Subspace Weight Problem:** Given a random $r \times n$ binary matrix H and a positive integer w, determine whether there exists an n-bit vector e with $\text{wt}(e) = w$ such that:

$$He^\top = \mathbf{0}_{r \times 1}.$$

This is known as the Decisional Codeword Finding Problem (DCFP).

Code-based algorithms rely on variants of these hard problems. The SDP seeks an error vector with weight $\leq t$, while the Codeword Finding Problem (CFP) requires finding a codeword with weight w. The equivalence between search and decision versions of these problems ensures their NP-Complete hardness.

The CFP, reformulated as finding a binary vector c with $\text{wt}(c) = w$ satisfying $H_{\text{pub}} c^\top = \mathbf{0}$, is also called the Homogeneous Syndrome Decoding Problem (HSDP).

3 Security Analysis Methods for Code-Based Algorithms

3.1 Security Analysis Methods

Although NP-Complete problems are widely believed to be unsolvable in polynomial time, the best-known methods for solving codeword finding and syndrome decoding problems still have computable time complexities, which grow exponentially with the weight of the target codeword or error vector.

Generally, message recovery attacks (MRAs), or side-channel attacks, are more effective for codeword finding problems. This is evident in attacks against LEDAcrypt and BIKE algorithms during NIST's second round of evaluations. However, under the assumption that system-specific and random parity-check matrices are indistinguishable, solving an instance of the syndrome decoding problem (SDP) is required to perform an MRA when given a generator matrix G. Under these conditions, both attack methods share identical computational complexities. Taking the original McEliece scheme [12] as an example, its ciphertext corresponds to the sum of a public codeword and an error vector e with weight t. The message can be encoded either as e or m. In the latter case, an MRA can be executed by searching for e and adding it to the intercepted ciphertext. By computing a valid parity-check matrix H from G, and then solving the syndrome of the intercepted ciphertext via H, this attack is effectively transformed into an SDP instance.

The optimal strategy for solving SDP depends on the relationship between the instance parameters. When t exceeds the Gilbert-Varshamov (GV) distance, the generalized birthday algorithm (GBA) [24] is currently the best-known method for solving SDP, as corroborated by early studies on code-based algorithm security mentioned in Sect. 1. However, in practical scenarios addressed here, t is significantly smaller than the GV distance. In such cases, information set decoding (ISD) algorithms are the most prominent methods for solving SDP. Beyond Prange's original algorithm, improved ISD variants can also address codeword finding problems due to their structural similarity.

All ISD algorithms involve iterative processes to retrieve an error vector corresponding to a given syndrome. Let $P_s uc$ denote the reciprocal of the success probability per attempt. The overall complexity of any ISD variant can be expressed as the product of the computational cost C per attempt and the average number of required attempts. Thus, the time complexity for solving SDP using existing ISD variants is:

$$T(n) = \frac{Cost \times Avg\_Num}{P\_suc}.$$

This work relies on the ideas of [25] and combines the descriptions in the previous two sections to arrive at the following security analysis method.

3.2 Security Assessment Framework Design

Based on the analyses in previous sections, the security assessment framework for code-based algorithms is designed as shown in Fig. 1.

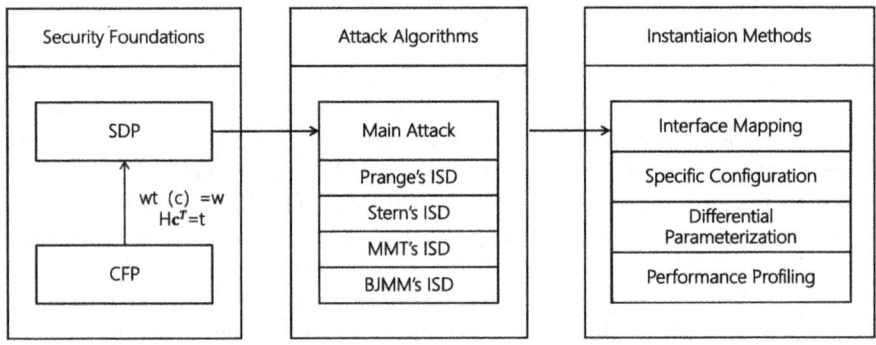

Fig. 1. Design Diagram of Security Estimation Framework.

The security assessment framework is divided into three modules to achieve systematic evaluation:

1. **Mapping Fundamental Hard Problems for Code-Based Algorithms:** Security evaluation begins with converting codeword finding problems into syndrome decoding problems. This ensures compatibility across code-based post-quantum algorithms with diverse designs. The syndrome decoding problem (SDP) requires finding an error vector with weight $\leq t$, while the codeword finding problem (CFP) seeks a codeword with weight w. Since CFP can be reformulated as finding a binary vector c with $\text{wt}(c) = w$, it can be transformed into an SDP instance.
2. **Code-Based Algorithm Solving via Information Set Decoding (ISD):** Section 4 details the advantages of ISD over other attack algorithms and explains the design principles of mainstream ISD variants. By applying the generalized ISD framework summarized in Sect. 3.1, a comprehensive attack algorithm suite is implemented to test the performance of code-based algorithms.
3. **Formula-Based Simulation:** Beyond generic ISD algorithms, the framework incorporates security analyses under specialized memory constraints (e.g., logarithmic or cube-root conditions). These analyses are computationally derived using formula-based methods during experiments.

4 Main Attack Algorithms

4.1 Prange Algorithm

The Prange algorithm [12] is the origin of information set decoding (ISD) and the earliest ISD method. Its core idea is to guess a set I of k error-free positions in the error vector e for syndrome decoding. Prange's algorithm forms the foundation for all subsequent ISD variants.

The algorithm begins by applying a random permutation to the columns of the parity-check matrix H. For any permutation matrix $P \in \mathbb{F}_2^{n \times n}$, we compute $(HP)(P^{-1}e) = s$. Gaussian elimination is then applied to the row vectors of the result via multiplication by an invertible matrix $Q \in \mathbb{F}_2^{(n-k) \times (n-k)}$, yielding:

$$QHP = \hat{H}I_{n-k},$$

where $H \in \mathbb{F}_2^{(n-k) \times k}$. Let $(P^{-1}e) = (e', e'') \in \mathbb{F}_2^k \times \mathbb{F}_2^{n-k}$, and $Qs = \hat{s} \in \mathbb{F}_2^{n-k}$. This leads to the identity:

$$Q(HP)(P^{-1}e) = \hat{H}(e' + e'') = \hat{s}.$$

Assuming $\text{wt}(e) = w$ and $\text{wt}(e') = p$, the goal is to find $e' \in \mathbb{F}_2^k$ with weight p such that:

$$\text{wt}(\hat{H}e' + s) = \text{wt}(e'') = w - p.$$

Once a suitable permutation P and vector e' are determined, the solution to the syndrome decoding problem is:

$$e = P(e', \hat{H}e' + \hat{s}).$$

The algorithm workflow is summarized in Table 1.

Prange's algorithm sets $p = 0$ for e', eliminating the need to solve approximate matching problems. Subsequent variants address this by allowing $p > 0$.

4.2 Stem Algorithm

The Stem algorithm [13] is an improved ISD method based on Prange's approach. It introduces "1-windows" of zeros into the error vector e'', modifying the step in Prange's algorithm where $(P^{-1}e) = (e', e'') \in \mathbb{F}_2^k \times \mathbb{F}_2^{n-k}$ by setting $e'' = (0', \delta)$. This redistributes the weight, aligning $f(e)$ with the syndrome on the first coordinate of 1, expressed as:

$$\hat{He'} = \hat{s} + e'' = \hat{s} + (0', \delta) = (\hat{s}_1, \hat{s}_2 + \hat{e}),$$

where $s = (s_1, s_2) \in \mathbb{F}_2^k \times \mathbb{F}_2^{n-k-1}$. This improvement draws from Leo's algorithm [27], which addresses large minimum weight problems by probabilistic methods for shorter extended binary linear codes. Though initially proposed for binary codes, it generalizes to codes over $\text{GF}(q)$ with $q > 2$. Additionally, Stem's algorithm employs a meet-in-the-middle (MITM) strategy on e using $(\hat{H}e')_{[l]} = \hat{s}_1$.

Table 1. Prange Information Set Decoding Algorithm

Algorithm	Prange Information Set Decoding Algorithm
Input	s: An r-bit syndrome
	H: An $r \times n$ binary parity-check matrix
	w: Target weight of the error vector
Output	e: An n-bit error vector satisfying $He^\top = s$, $\text{wt}(e) = w$
1.	**repeat**
2.	Select random permutation matrix $P \in \mathbb{F}_2^{n \times n}$
3.	$\hat{H} \leftarrow (QHP)[k]$
4.	$(P^{-1}e) = (e', e'') \in \mathbb{F}_2^k \times \mathbb{F}_2^{n-k}$
5.	$s \leftarrow Qs$, ensuring $\hat{H}(e' + e'') = s$
6.	**for** $e' \in \mathbb{F}_2^k$ **do**
7.	$e = P(e', \hat{H}e' + s)$
8.	**if** $\text{wt}(e) = w$ **then**
9.	**BREAK**
10.	**end if**
11.	**end for**
12.	**until** $\text{wt}(e) = w$

By splitting e' as $e' = (e_1, 0^{k/2}) + (0^{k/2}, e_2)$, two lists are constructed: $\hat{H}(x, 0^{k/2})$ and $\hat{H}(0^{k/2}, y)$, where:

$$x, y \in \mathbb{B}_{\frac{p}{2}}^{\frac{k}{2}}.$$

The algorithm searches for pairs in these lists whose sum matches s_1 on the first coordinate, verifying if each pair $(x', 0)(0, y')$ satisfies:

$$\text{wt}(f(x', y') + s) = w - p.$$

The workflow is outlined in Table 2.

4.3 MMT Algorithm

The MMT algorithm [28], proposed by May, Meurer, and Thomae, differs from Stem and Leon variants by avoiding splitting e and instead utilizing four MMT components. Its preprocessing step resembles Dumer's algorithm [29], which eliminates "1-windows" and increases the dimension of e to $k + 1$. Dumer's approach is defined as:

$$QHP = \begin{bmatrix} H_1 & 0 \\ H_2 & I_{n-k-1} \end{bmatrix},$$

where $H_1 \in \mathbb{F}_2^{1 \times (k+1)}$ and $H_2 \in \mathbb{F}_2^{(n-k-1) \times (k+1)}$. For $(P^{-1}e) = (e', e'') \in \mathbb{F}_2^{k+1} \times \mathbb{F}_2^{n-k-1}$, assume $\text{wt}(e') = p$. The equation becomes:

$$QHP(e', e'') = (H_1 e', H_2 e' + e'') = (\hat{s}_1, \hat{s}_2) = \hat{s},$$

Table 2. Stem Information Set Decoding Algorithm

Algorithm	Stem Information Set Decoding Algorithm
Input	s: An r-bit syndrome
	H: An $r \times n$ binary parity-check matrix
	w: Target weight of the error vector
Output	e: An n-bit error vector satisfying $He^\top = s$, $\text{wt}(e) = w$
1.	**repeat**
2.	Select random permutation matrix $P \in \mathbb{F}_2^{n \times n}$
3.	$\hat{H} \leftarrow (QHP)[k]$
4.	$(P^{-1}e) = (e', e'') \in \mathbb{F}_2^k \times \mathbb{F}_2^{n-k}$, $e'' = (0', \delta)$
5.	$s \leftarrow Qs$, ensuring $f(e) = s + e''$
6.	Split $e' = (e_1, 0^{k/2}) + (0^{k/2}, e_2)$
7.	**for** e_1, e_2 with coordinate sum 1 **do**
8.	$e = P(e', \text{wt}(\hat{H}(e_1, e_2) + s))$
9.	**if** $\text{wt}(e) = w$ **then**
10.	**BREAK**
11.	**end if**
12.	**end for**
13.	**until** $\text{wt}(e) = w$

with $(\hat{s}_1, \hat{s}_2) \in \mathbb{F}_2^1 \times \mathbb{F}_2^{n-k-1}$. The algorithm uses a meet-in-the-middle (MTM) strategy to search for e', compute candidate x, and check if $\text{wt}(H_2 x + \hat{s}_2) = w - p$. If satisfied, the solution $P(x, H_2 x + \hat{s}_2)$ is output.

MMT diverges from Dumer by splitting e' into four components using MTM:

$$e_1 = (a_1, 0^2) + (0^2, a_2),$$
$$e_2 = (a_3, 0^2) + (0^2, a_4),$$
$$e' = e_1 + e_2,$$

where $a_i \in \mathbb{B}_p^1$ for $i = 1, 2, 3, 4$. Lists L_1, L_2, L_3, L_4 are constructed by enumerating all possible values of a_i.

A random $t \in \mathbb{F}_2^1$ is selected. For $l \leq 1$, a filtered list L_{12} is built from $L_1 \times L_2$, retaining pairs (x, y) satisfying:

$$(H_1(x+y))_{[l_1]} = t.$$

Similarly, L_{34} is constructed. Merging L_{12} and L_{34} yields L_{1234}, where elements $z \in L_{1234}$ must satisfy:

$$\text{wt}(\hat{H}_2 z + \hat{s}_2) = w - p.$$

If valid, the algorithm terminates. The workflow is summarized in Table 3.

Table 3. MMT Information Set Decoding Algorithm

Algorithm	Algorithm 3: MMT Information Set Decoding Algorithm
Input	s: An r-bit syndrome
	H: An $r \times n$ binary parity-check matrix
	w: Target weight of the error vector
Output	e: An n-bit error vector satisfying $\mathbf{H}e^\top = s$, wt$(e) = w$
1.	repeat
2.	Select random permutation matrix $P \in \mathbb{F}_2^{n \times n}$
3.	$\hat{H} \leftarrow (QHP)[k]$
4.	$e' \in \mathbb{F}_2^k \times \mathbb{F}_2^{n-k}$, $e'' = (0^t, \delta)$
5.	$(P^{-1}e) = (e', e'')$
6.	$\hat{s} \leftarrow Qs$, ensuring $\mathbf{H}e' = \hat{s} + e''$
7.	Split $e_1 = (a_1, 0^{\frac{k+1}{2}}) + (0^{\frac{k+1}{2}}, a_2)$
8.	Split $e_2 = (a_3, 0^{\frac{k+1}{2}}) + (0^{\frac{k+1}{2}}, a_4)$
9.	$e' = e_1 + e_2$
10.	Construct $L_{12} = \{(x+y) \mid (\mathbf{H}_1(x+y))_{[l_1]}, t \in \mathbb{F}_2^{l_1}\}$
11.	Construct $L_{34} = \{(x+y) \mid (\mathbf{H}_2(x+y))_{[l_2]}, t \in \mathbb{F}_2^{l_2}\}$
12.	Merge $L_{1234} = \{z = z_1 + z_2 \mid z_1 \in \mathbb{F}_2^1, z_2 \in \mathbb{F}_2^2\}$
13.	for $t_0 = t + (\hat{s}_1)_{[l_1]} = (v, w) \in \mathbf{H}_1(v+w) = (\hat{s}_1)_{[l_1]}$ do
14.	if wt$(\hat{\mathbf{H}}_2 z + \hat{s}_2) =$ wt$(e'') = w - p$ then
15.	BREAK
16.	end if
17.	end for
18.	until wt$(e) = w$

4.4 BJMM Algorithm

The BJMM algorithm [30], proposed by Becker, Joux, May, and Meurer, improves the MMT algorithm in two key aspects: recursive application of list construction strategies and modifications to the generation of list elements.

BJMM represents a vector e with weight wt$(e) = p$ and length $k+1$ as the sum of two vectors e_1, e_2 of equal length, where $(\mathrm{P}^{-1}e) = (e', e'') \in \mathbb{F}_2^{k+1} \times \mathbb{F}_2^{n-k-1}$. Unlike MMT, which strictly requires wt$(e_1) =$ wt$(e_2) = p/2$, BJMM allows wt$(e_1) =$ wt$(e_2) = p/2 + \varepsilon$, where the excess weight ε cancels during computation. This relaxation increases the number of valid (e_1, e_2) pairs by a factor of $(k+1-p)/2$, reducing the list size required for subsequent meet-in-the-middle (MTM) searches. The recursive list construction strategy further enhances efficiency by introducing two distinct reduction factors through its depth.

The second improvement modifies the recursive application of MTM strategies inherited from Stem and earlier ISD variants. By pre-filtering partially compliant candidates at each recursion level, BJMM significantly optimizes the search process. Unlike Stem's meet-in-the-middle approach, which reformulates $\hat{H}(e' + e'') = \hat{s}$ as $\hat{H}e' = \hat{s} + e''$, the BJMM algorithm constructs two pairing lists similar to MMT. For all possible e_1, BJMM builds lists $(e_1, \hat{H}_1 e_1)$ and $(e_2, \hat{H}_1 e_2 + s_1)$, followed by linear searches based on list lengths.

The workflow is detailed in Table 4.

Table 4. BJMM Information Set Decoding Algorithm

Algorithm	Algorithm 4: BJMM Information Set Decoding Algorithm
Input	s: An r-bit syndrome
	H: An $r \times n$ binary parity-check matrix
	w: Target weight of the error vector
Output	e: An n-bit error vector satisfying $He^\top = s$, $\text{wt}(e) = w$
1.	repeat
2.	Select random permutation matrix $P \in \mathbb{F}_2^{n \times n}$
3.	$\hat{H} \leftarrow (QHP)[k]$
4.	$e' \in \mathbb{F}_2^k \times \mathbb{F}_2^{n-k}, e'' = (0', \delta)$
5.	$(P^{-1}e) = (e', e'')$
6.	$\hat{s} \leftarrow Qs$, ensuring $\hat{H}e' = \hat{s} + e''$
7.	Split $e' = e_1 + e_2$
8.	for (e_1, e_2) do
9.	if $\text{wt}(e_1) = \text{wt}(e_2) = \frac{p}{2} + \varepsilon$ then
10.	$L_{12} \leftarrow \{(x+y) \mid (H_1(x+y))_{[l_1]} \in \mathbb{F}_2^{l_1}\}$
11.	$L_{34} \leftarrow \{(x+y) \mid (H_2(x+y))_{[l_2]} \in \mathbb{F}_2^{l_2}\}$
12.	$L_{1234} \leftarrow \{z = z_1 + z_2 \mid z_1 \in \mathbb{F}_2^{l_1}, z_2 \in \mathbb{F}_2^{l_2}\}$
13.	for $t_0 = t + (\hat{s}_1)_{[l_1]} = (v, w) \in H_1(v+w) = (\hat{s}_1)_{[l_1]}$ do
14.	if $\text{wt}(\hat{H}_2 z + \hat{s}_2) = \text{wt}(e') = w - p$ then
15.	BREAK
16.	end if
17.	end for
18.	end if
19.	end for
20.	until $\text{wt}(e) = w$

4.5 Instantiation Methods

Based on the descriptions in the previous section, this section instantiates algorithms such as MMT, BJMM, and May-Ozerov into framework interface functions to demonstrate their hierarchical structure and implementation differences. The algorithm hierarchy and differential implementations are illustrated in Fig. 2.

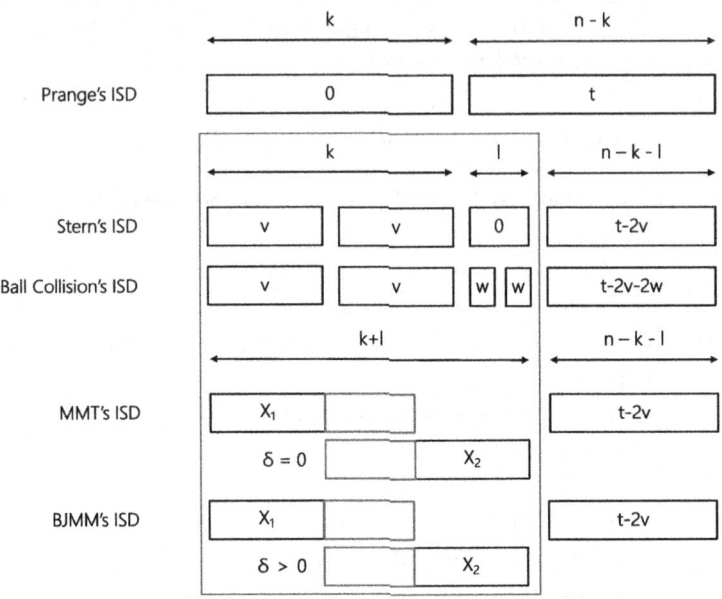

Fig. 2. Hierarchical Structure of Information Set Decoding Algorithms.

Key Implementation Steps

1. **Interface Mapping:** Define unified interface functions for syndrome decoding (e.g., SolveSDP()) and codeword finding (e.g., SolveCFP()) to encapsulate algorithmic logic while preserving parameterization flexibility.
2. **Algorithm-Specific Configuration:**
   - **MMT:** Implement the four-component splitting strategy with meet-in-the-middle list filtering.
   - **BJMM:** Integrate recursive list construction and weight relaxation $(\text{wt}(e_i) = p/2 + \varepsilon)$.
   - **May-Ozerov:** Optimize subspace weight constraints using advanced combinatorial pruning.
3. **Differential Parameterization:** Configure algorithm-specific parameters (e.g., error weight distribution p, recursion depth d) through modular input structures to isolate implementation variations.
4. **Performance Profiling:** Attach runtime and memory monitoring modules to benchmark computational complexity $(C(n,r,t))$ and validate theoretical security claims.

Hierarchical Differentiation

1. **Core Layer:** Shared ISD operations (e.g., permutation, Gaussian elimination).
2. **Variant Layer:** Algorithm-specific optimizations (e.g., MMT's 1-windows, BJMM's recursion).
3. **Interface Layer:** Unified function calls (e.g., Attack(code_params, alg_variant)).

5 Conclusion

This paper investigates and analyzes the mainstream information set decoding problem, provides a security analysis framework for post-quantum cryptographic algorithms and evaluates and analyzes the security of the involved algorithms. Firstly, based on the structural commonality between the algorithms, we provide a generalized framework to realize the above information set decoding algorithms, and then we analyze the principles and improvement ideas of the representative information set decoding algorithms of Stern, MMT, and DOOM, and give the corresponding strength of the algorithms. This research aids the work of analyzing the security of the encoding algorithms, and the practical application should be considered in combination with the execution details, target platform, possible hardware acceleration and many other factors.

Acknowledgments. This study was funded by National Key Laboratory of Security Communication Foundation (2023, 6142103042308).

References

1. Shor, P.W.: Polynomial-time algorithms for prime factorization and discrete logarithms on a quantum computer. SIAM Rev. **41**(2), 303–332 (1999)
2. Bos, J., Ducas, L., Kiltz, E., et al.: CRYSTALS-Kyber: a CCA-secure module-lattice-based KEM. In: 2018 IEEE European Symposium on Security and Privacy (EuroS&P), pp. 353–367. IEEE (2018)
3. Ducas, L., Lepoint, T., Lyubashevsky, V., et al.: CRYSTALS-Dilithium: Digital signatures from module lattices. Cryptology ePrint Archive, Report 2017/633 (2018)
4. Prest, T., Fouque, P.A., Hoffstein, J., et al.: Falcon. NIST Post-Quantum Cryptography Project (2020). https://csrc.nist.gov/projects/post-quantum-cryptography
5. Soni, D., Basu, K., Nabeel, M., Aaraj, N., Manzano, M., Karri, R.: SPHINCS$^+$. In: Soni, D., Basu, K., Nabeel, M., Aaraj, N., Manzano, M., Karri, R. (eds.) Hardware Architectures for Post-Quantum Digital Signature Schemes, pp. 141–162. Springer, Cham (2021). https://doi.org/10.1007/978-3-030-57682-0_9
6. Aragon, N., Barreto, P., Bettaieb, S., et al.: BIKE. NIST PQC Round 1 Submission (2019)
7. Singh, H.: Code based cryptography: Classic McEliece. arXiv preprint arXiv:1907.12754 (2019)

8. Melchor, C.A., Aragon, N., Bettaieb, S., et al.: Hamming Quasi-Cyclic (HQC). NIST PQC Round 2 Submission (2018)
9. Seo, H., Anastasova, M., Jalali, A., et al.: Supersingular isogeny key encapsulation (SIKE) round 2 on ARM Cortex-M4. IEEE Trans. Comput. **70**(10), 1705–1718 (2020)
10. NIST CSRC: NIST announces additional digital signature candidates for the PQC standardization process (2023). https://csrc.nist.gov/News/2023/additional-pqc-digital-signature-candidates
11. Zhang, F., Pan, T., Zhao, Y.: TLS1.3 post-quantum secure migration scheme, implementation and performance evaluation. J. Cryptol. Res. **9**(1), 143–163 (2022)
12. Berlekamp, E., McEliece, R., Van Tilborg, H.: On the inherent intractability of certain coding problems. IEEE Trans. Inf. Theory **24**(3), 384–386 (1978)
13. Shannon, C.E.: A mathematical theory of communication. ACM SIGMOBILE Mob. Comput. Commun. Rev. **5**(1), 3–55 (2001)
14. Niederreiter, H.: Knapsack-type cryptosystems and algebraic coding theory. Probl. Control Inf. Theory **15**(2), 157–166 (1986)
15. Gabidulin, E.M., Ourivski, A.V., Honary, B., et al.: Reducible rank codes and their applications to cryptography. IEEE Trans. Inf. Theory **49**(12), 3289–3293 (2003)
16. Gabidulin, E.M., Paramonov, A.V., Tretjakov, O.V.: Ideals over a non-commutative ring and their application in cryptology. In: Davies, D.W. (ed.) EUROCRYPT 1991. LNCS, vol. 547, pp. 482–489. Springer, Heidelberg (1991). https://doi.org/10.1007/3-540-46416-6_41
17. Gaborit, P.: Shorter keys for code based cryptography. In: Proceedings of International Workshop Coding Cryptography (WCC 2005), pp. 81–91 (2005)
18. Janwa, H., Moreno, O.: McEliece public key cryptosystems using algebraic-geometric codes. Des. Codes Cryptogr. **8**(3), 293–307 (1996)
19. Sidelnikov, V.M.: A public-key cryptosystem based on binary Reed-Muller codes. Discrete Math. Appl. **4**(3), 191–207 (1994)
20. Kobara, K., Imai, H.: Semantically secure McEliece public-key cryptosystems - conversions for McEliece PKC. In: Kim, K. (ed.) PKC 2001. LNCS, vol. 1992, pp. 19–35. Springer, Heidelberg (2001). https://doi.org/10.1007/3-540-44586-2_2
21. Monico, C., Rosenthal, J., Shokrollahi, A.: Using low density parity check codes in the McEliece cryptosystem. In: IEEE ISIT 2000, p. 215. IEEE (2000)
22. Misoczki, R., Barreto, P.S.L.M.: Compact McEliece keys from Goppa codes. In: Jacobson, M.J., Rijmen, V., Safavi-Naini, R. (eds.) SAC 2009. LNCS, vol. 5867, pp. 376–392. Springer, Heidelberg (2009). https://doi.org/10.1007/978-3-642-05445-7_24
23. Baldi, M., Bodrato, M., Chiaraluce, F.: A new analysis of the McEliece cryptosystem based on QC-LDPC codes. In: Ostrovsky, R., De Prisco, R., Visconti, I. (eds.) SCN 2008. LNCS, vol. 5229, pp. 246–262. Springer, Heidelberg (2008). https://doi.org/10.1007/978-3-540-85855-3_17
24. Kirchner, P.: Improved generalized birthday attack. Cryptology ePrint Archive, Report 2011/377 (2011)
25. Esser, A., Bellini, E.: Syndrome decoding estimator. In: PKC 2022, pp. 112–141. Springer (2022)
26. Prange, E.: The use of information sets in decoding cyclic codes. IRE Trans. Inf. Theory **8**(5), 5–9 (1962)
27. Stern, J.: A method for finding codewords of small weight. In: Cohen, G., Wolfmann, J. (eds.) Coding Theory 1988. LNCS, vol. 388, pp. 106–113. Springer, Heidelberg (1989). https://doi.org/10.1007/BFb0019850

28. Leon, J.S.: A probabilistic algorithm for computing minimum weights of large error-correcting codes. IEEE Trans. Inf. Theory **34**(5), 1354–1359 (1988)
29. May, A., Meurer, A., Thomae, E.: Decoding random linear codes in $\tilde{\mathcal{O}}(2^{0.054n})$. In: Lee, D.H., Wang, X. (eds.) ASIACRYPT 2011. LNCS, vol. 7073, pp. 107–124. Springer, Heidelberg (2011). https://doi.org/10.1007/978-3-642-25385-0_6
30. Dumer, I.: On minimum distance decoding of linear codes. In: 5th International Workshop Information Theory, pp. 1–10 (1991)
31. Becker, A., Joux, A., May, A., Meurer, A.: Decoding random binary linear codes in $2^{n/20}$: how 1+1=0 improves information set decoding. In: Pointcheval, D., Johansson, T. (eds.) EUROCRYPT 2012. LNCS, vol. 7237, pp. 520–536. Springer, Heidelberg (2012). https://doi.org/10.1007/978-3-642-29011-4_31

Paper Document Anti-counterfeiting System Based on Digital Signatures and Image Processing

Yiyan Zhao, Jiwu Jing, Junlin He, Fangyu Zheng, and Chunjing Kou(✉)

University of Chinese Academy of Sciences, Beijing, China
kouchunjing@ucas.ac.cn

Abstract. With the advancement of information technology, counterfeit methods for paper documents have become increasingly sophisticated. Traditional anti-counterfeiting technologies suffer from issues such as ease of replication, difficulty in verification, and poor real-time performance, making them inadequate for modern security needs. This paper presents a novel anti-counterfeiting system for paper documents, leveraging digital signatures and image processing. By integrating digital certificates and USB Key technologies, the system provides an efficient and reliable solution. Anti-counterfeiting information is embedded into the document using grid encoding and SM2 digital signatures. Verification can be performed through a mobile phone app, making it both accessible and convenient. Experimental results demonstrate that the system achieves 96% verification accuracy, ensuring strong security and scalability for other document anti-counterfeiting applications.

Keywords: paper documents · anti-counterfeiting · digital signatures · image processing

1 Introduction

Paper documents play a crucial role in society as the core medium for information transmission and rights verification. They are widely used in fields such as education, finance, healthcare, and law, including admission letters, passports, forensic documents, and financial instruments. Despite the increasing trend toward digitization, paper documents retain an irreplaceable position due to their formality and immunity to issues like electronic device failures or network problems. However, with the proliferation of digital printing technologies and the advancement of forgery techniques, the security of paper documents faces significant challenges [1]. Counterfeiting and tampering have become prevalent, seriously infringing on the legitimate rights of stakeholders and undermining social trust.

Traditional anti-counterfeiting methods, including watermarks, fluorescent inks, and specialized paper, provide basic security features but fall short in addressing modern document fraud challenges. These approaches suffer from high implementation costs due to the need for specialized materials and equipment, making them unsuitable for large-scale applications. Furthermore, static features such as watermarks are vulnerable to replication and mimicry. In addition, traditional verification processes often rely on costly, specialized equipment and expert personnel, resulting in inefficiencies. By contrast, our proposed system integrates the dynamic capabilities of digital signatures with image processing technologies, offering a cost-effective, scalable, and more efficient solution that meets the demands of modern, high-speed information systems.

In recent years, digital signature and image processing technologies have provided innovative solutions for paper document security, effectively addressing document counterfeiting. Digital signatures generate unique cryptographic identifiers for documents, ensuring content integrity and authenticity. We employ SM2 digital signatures, leveraging the security of elliptic curve cryptography (ECC), which offers superior performance over traditional RSA methods in both security and computational efficiency. Additionally, we integrate two image processing techniques—binarization and grid-based enlargement. These techniques transform the document into a structured image pattern, improving its recognizability during verification, similar to the scanning process of QR codes. We also apply HSV color space and geometric approximation algorithms for vertex localization, further enhancing the system's accuracy [2,3]. These innovations lead to anti-counterfeiting documents that are not only secure and cost-effective but also scalable for real-time document authentication.

In view of the current situation, this paper designs and implements an anti-counterfeiting system based on digital signatures and image processing technology, supporting the generation and verification of anti-counterfeit paper documents. Additionally, we develop a prototype system using admission letters as an example. As a crucial document in the university admission process, admission letters hold irreplaceable legal validity and societal significance. However, frequent cases of forgery have led to infringements on candidates' rights, disrupted admission order, and damaged the reputation of institutions. Based on this, this paper provides an efficient and low-cost solution for the anti-counterfeiting and authenticity verification of university admission letters. The proposed solution is highly versatile and can serve as a reference for the anti-counterfeiting of other types of paper documents, contributing to the development of a more efficient and reliable anti-counterfeiting system.

Our main contributions are as follows:

- Based on USB Key and SM2 digital signatures, a hardware-level security mechanism is implemented to ensure the secure storage of private keys, effectively preventing key leakage and document tampering, thereby enhancing the security of anti-counterfeit documents.
- A mobile offline verification scheme based on public key cryptography (PKI) is proposed, which requires no database or network connection, ensuring an efficient and secure verification process.

– In the application scenario of university admission letters, system evaluation shows that the generated anti-counterfeit documents can effectively resist forgery and tampering, achieving a verification accuracy of 96%.

2 Preliminaries

2.1 USB Key

A USB Key is a hardware encryption device used for identity authentication, digital signatures, and secure key storage. It stores private keys and certificates in an isolated chip, ensuring keys never leave the device, which reduces leakage risks. In our system, the ePass3000GM USB Key is adopted to generate and verify SM2 signatures and supports the PKCS#11 standard for integration [5].

To prevent key leakage, it includes PIN-based access, hardware-isolated storage, and defenses against side-channel attacks like electromagnetic shielding and randomized power usage. Repeated incorrect PIN entries trigger lockout, and private keys remain non-extractable even under physical attack. These features ensure strong protection for high-security cryptographic operations.

2.2 SM2 Digital Signature Algorithm

SM2 is a Chinese national digital signature algorithm based on Elliptic Curve Cryptography (ECC), offering strong security and efficiency due to the hardness of the Elliptic Curve Discrete Logarithm Problem (ECDLP). It uses the SM3 hash algorithm and generates a signature pair (r, s).

– **Signature Generation**: Given a message M, compute the hash value $e = \text{Hash}(M)$. Choose a random integer k such that $1 \leq k \leq n - 1$, where n is the order of the elliptic curve group. Compute the elliptic curve point $(x_1, y_1) = kG$, where G is the base point. Define $r = (e + x_1) \mod n$, and if $r = 0$ or $r+k = n$, select another k and repeat. Compute $s = (k-r \cdot d) \cdot (1+d)^{-1} \mod n$, where d is the private key. If $s = 0$, restart with a new k. The final signature is (r, s).
– **Signature Verification**: Given a signature (r, s) and the public key P, first compute $t = (r + s) \mod n$. If $t = 0$, reject the signature. Compute the elliptic curve point $(x_2, y_2) = sG + tP$. Compute $R = (e + x_2) \mod n$, where $e = \text{Hash}(M)$. If $R = r$, the signature is valid; otherwise, it is rejected.

In our system, SM2 ensures document integrity and authenticity, with private keys securely stored in the USB Key to prevent forgery and tampering.

2.3 Image Processing

LAB Color Space. LAB (CIELAB) is a device-independent color space representing human visual perception using three channels: L (lightness), a (greenâĂŞred), and b (blueâĂŞyellow). In this study, LAB is used for color classification with the CIE76 formula to measure perceptual differences [6].

CIE76 calculates the Euclidean distance between two LAB values as:

$$\Delta E_{76} = \sqrt{(L_1 - L_2)^2 + (a_1 - a_2)^2 + (b_1 - b_2)^2}$$

where L_1, a_1, b_1 and L_2, a_2, b_2 are the LAB values of two colors. A larger ΔE indicates greater color difference.

Geometric Approximation Techniques. Geometric approximation simplifies complex shapes using fewer representative points while preserving essential features. A classic method is the Ramer-Douglas-Peucker (RDP) algorithm [2,3], which reduces the number of points in a curve or polygon.

The algorithm connects the start and end points of a curve and identifies the point with the maximum perpendicular distance to the line. If the distance exceeds a set threshold, the point is kept and the curve is split recursively; otherwise, the line replaces the segment. The result is a simplified curve composed of key points. This recursive process balances efficiency and approximation accuracy.

3 Related Work

3.1 Traditional Paper Document Anti-counterfeiting Methods

Traditional anti-counterfeiting methods include special paper, inks, watermarks, and labels.

Anti-counterfeiting Paper. Fluorescent materials and fibers are embedded in paper for security. Szczeszak et al. developed paper with up-conversion nanoparticles visible only under specific lighting conditions [7]. Laser engraving also creates micro-marks on paper surfaces to enhance security [8]. These techniques use specialized materials and equipment, which are usually costly.

Anti-counterfeiting Ink. Special inks produce unique effects under specific conditions, such as color-shifting [9], fluorescence [10,11], and pH sensitivity [12]. Magnetic additives can also enable verification via card readers [13]. These inks enhance security but remain costly.

Watermarks. Patterns or text are embedded in paper, visible under transmitted light. Though effective, watermarks are complicated to produce and increasingly vulnerable to replication due to advancements in printing technology [14].

Anti-counterfeiting Labels. Labels are added for quick identification. Chen et al. proposed dynamic labels that change color and luminescence under external stimuli [15]. These labels are easy to use but may degrade over time.

3.2 Emerging Paper Document Anti-counterfeiting Methods

In recent years, biometric recognition, Radio Frequency Identification(RFID), QR code, and computer vision have been applied to the anti-counterfeiting of paper documents.

Biometric Recognition. Biometric recognition verifies identity by embedding biological features such as fingerprints and facial structure. Zhang et al. proposed using document creator fingerprints for forensic anti-counterfeiting [16], while Wang S. et al. applied similar techniques to polymer banknotes [17]. Choudhury et al. introduced a passport authentication system using hand geometry and facial markers, encrypting multimodal biometric data with AES and SHA-256 before embedding it into a QR code [18]. Although effective, biometric recognition is constrained by device precision and the degradation of physiological features [19].

RFID Technology. RFID technology encodes personal information into RFID tags, which are verified using a reader. Mudraganam C.S. proposed an RFID-based method for anti-counterfeiting in degree certificates, where RFID tags embedded in the certificates contain the holder's name, graduation date, and biometric information. The tags are digitally signed by the issuing university, and verifiers use readers to authenticate the holder's identity and the certificate's validity [20]. This technology is also widely used in identity cards and tickets but is limited in large-scale applications for paper document anti-counterfeiting due to high costs.

QR Code. QR codes are widely used in anti-counterfeiting applications due to their low production costs and ease of integration. Yahya et al. embedded encrypted student information into a QR code on academic certificates, allowing verification of the certificate's authenticity through scanning [21]. Li C.M. et al. stored a JSON copy of the paper document in the QR code, which was compressed using the Deflate algorithm and digitally signed by the issuer. Verification was performed by scanning the QR code on the document [22]. Ahmed et al. designed a QR code document authentication system based on dual encryption. The system involves scanning the QR code with a smartphone application, sending the encrypted data to a central system for verification, and returning detailed information to the smartphone application upon successful verification [23].

Computer Vision. Through the extraction and analysis of image features, computer vision effectively identifies and verifies the authenticity of documents. Auberson M. et al. proposed a method utilizing digital image classification technology to analyze and classify counterfeit identity documents [24]. Mehrjardi F.Z. et al. systematically reviewed image forgery detection techniques in the field of computer vision, with a focus on the application of deep learning methods in this area [25]. Zheng Z. et al. developed an anti-counterfeiting identification system based on random texture patterns, leveraging a supervised guided segmentation algorithm and a Bone Width Transformation (BWT) algorithm to locate key image regions for authenticity verification [26].

4 Anti-counterfeiting Method

4.1 Overview of Method

Our anti-counterfeit admission letter can be verified on mobile devices without an internet connection. We generate a digital signature based on all the information in the anti-counterfeit area of the notice and place the signature at the bottom of the notice. The verifier takes photos of the notice and uses our dedicated verification program to check its authenticity. The authentication method for the admission letter includes two parts: generating the anti-counterfeit admission letter and verifying the anti-counterfeit admission letter. The overall process is shown in Fig. 1.

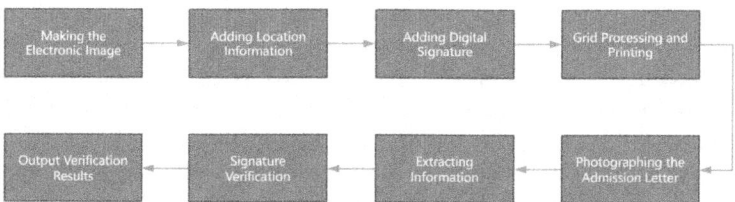

Fig. 1. The overall process of authentication method for the admission letter.

In the admission letter generation stage, we process all the content on the notice into a grid of uniform size, then apply binary encoding to each grid cell. This converts the notice into a binary array. We use a USB Key to perform SM3 hashing and SM2 signing on the array, and the signature is drawn in a grid format at the bottom of the notice. To quickly generate a large number of admission letters, we developed an easy-to-use admission letter generator for users.

In the admission letter verification stage, the binary array stored in the admission letter can only be read by our verification program. The verifier takes multiple photos of the admission letter and submits them to the verification program. The program reads each grid cell of the notice and extracts the binary array. It then reads the signature information, performs SM3 hashing on the array, and verifies the signature using the SM2 public key. Finally, it outputs whether the notice is real or counterfeit.

Our anti-counterfeiting system for paper documents combines digital signatures and image processing technologies to provide a reliable and low-cost solution, overcoming the limitations of traditional methods. Traditional systems rely on special materials and equipment for verification, leading to high production costs. In contrast, this system allows verification via a smartphone camera, with no need for specialized equipment, offering simplicity and low cost. Traditional technologies, like watermarks and anti-counterfeit labels, are susceptible to duplication and wear, reducing their effectiveness over time. This system uses digital signatures to ensure document immutability, preventing forgery and ensuring long-term stability. Unlike traditional QR-signature systems, our method integrates visual encoding and authentication in one layout. The anti-counterfeiting region conveys both visual structure and signed content, offering tamper-evidence that is human-perceivable and machine-verifiable, without relying on external markers like QR codes.

Security Considerations and Threat Model. To better characterize the system's resilience against attacks, we introduce a basic threat model and outline potential adversary capabilities.

We consider an adversary who has access to printed anti-counterfeiting documents and attempts to forge new documents or modify existing ones without access to the original private key or generation tools. The attacker may attempt pixel-level editing, partial image reconstruction, or signature transplantation.

Our system resists such tampering attempts due to the strong cryptographic binding between the binary array and the SM2 digital signature. Even slight modifications in the grid content or structure will result in a signature mismatch during verification. The use of a USB Key for private key storage further strengthens resistance to key leakage and unauthorized document generation.

Although we do not provide a formal security proof, the use of a well-established digital signature scheme (SM2) and the immutability of grid-encoded data ensures that tampering attacks without access to the signing key are computationally infeasible under standard ECC assumptions. Future work will include formal modeling and proof of resistance to forgery and reconstruction attacks.

4.2 Production Method

Step 1: Making the Electronic Image. The user creates an electronic admission letter image, referred to as the template, which is divided into a message area and a signature area. For an image of cols × rows pixels, the top messageLine rows define the message area, and the rest form a white signature area (RGB: 255, 255, 255). The message area contains user-designed elements such as text, patterns, school emblems, and stamps, with blank fields for student details like name and major.

After creation, we performance finite-value mapping process on the message area of the electronic image. The information section, which includes user-designed text, patterns, school emblems, stamps, and other elements, as well as student details such as name and major filled by the system, is converted into two fixed colors: red (255, 0, 0) and blue (0, 0, 255), while the background section is processed as white (255, 255, 255). The processed electronic image is shown in Fig. 2. If the image's width or height is an even number of pixels, an extra pixel is added to make it an odd dimension. The added pixel does not store any content and serves only as a preparation for subsequent operations.

Dear ,
Congratulations! You have been admitted to our university as a Master's student in . Please report to our university with this notice on September 1, 2025 to complete your registration.
We look forward to welcoming you.

Fig. 2. A sample electronic image.

Step 2: Adding Location Information. To ensure that the array stored in the admission letter can be recognized after a photo is taken, location information needs to be added. The method involves performing binarization on the white pixels in the image, alternating the white areas between green and white based on the parity of the sum of the pixel's horizontal and vertical coordinates. The green and white pixels will still represent the background section.

The location adding information algorithm begins by duplicating the input image to preserve the original. It then traverses each pixel, identifying pure white pixels (RGB: 255, 255, 255). For each such pixel, it calculates the sum of its row and column indices: if even, the pixel is set to green (RGB: 0, 255, 0); if odd, it remains white. This results in an output image with a background patterned in alternating green and white pixels.

Step 3: Adding Digital Signature. In this step, the algorithm reads the array stored in the message area of the anti-counterfeit admission letter's electronic image. The message area is subjected to SM3 hashing and SM2 signing to generate a digital signature. The resulting signature is converted into a 512-bit binary array, which consists of two parts: r and s. The signature is then drawn by representing "1" with red pixels and "0" with white pixels.

The drawing of the signature begins from a designated column on the signLine-th row of the signature area in the anti-counterfeit admission letter. The red and white pixels are used to encode the signature in a way that is visually distinguishable.

Step 4: Grid Processing and Printing. The electronic image is enlarged in a grid pattern, with each pixel expanded into a $d \times d$ block of identical pixels. After enlargement, the background area becomes a pattern of alternating white and green grids, forming a checkerboard-like effect. Since the width and height of the electronic image are odd-numbered pixels, the four corners will be green grids, which helps in identifying the vertices of the anti-counterfeit area during subsequent steps. The main steps of the grid enlargement algorithm are as follows:

1. **Create Enlarged Image Space:** Based on the input image size and the enlargement factor d, calculate the dimensions of the enlarged image and create a new image.
2. **Pixel-by-Pixel Traversal:** Sequentially traverse each pixel to extract its color values.
3. **Fill Enlarged Pixel Blocks:** For each original pixel, create a $d \times d$ pixel block in the enlarged image at the corresponding position, and fill it with the original pixel's color.
4. **Generate the Enlarged Image:** After all pixel blocks are filled, output the enlarged image.

To reduce color diffusion caused by printing and photographing, isolation grids need to be added. We designate blue and red grids as information grids, storing "1"; white and green grids are called background grids, storing "0"; and white grids are added around the information grids, also storing "0". The electronic image stores a binary array of size rows × cols.

According to printing resolution and paper size, a canvas is created and the grid-based anti-counterfeiting image is centered. This region is referred to as the anti-counterfeiting area. The final admission letter (Fig. 3) is printed using a laser printer with high-weight coated paper, "fit to page" disabled, and high-resolution settings. When distributing the letters, make sure the paper is flat and free of wrinkles.

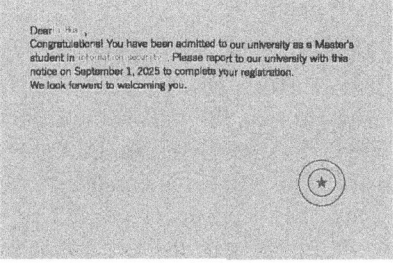

Fig. 3. The final admission letter.

4.3 Verification Method

Step 1: Photographing the Admission Letter. When taking a photo of the admission letter, try to maintain a perpendicular angle to the image so that the top and bottom edges, as well as the left and right edges of the anti-counterfeiting area, are approximately parallel. Ensure sufficient lighting to avoid large shadows. At least 5 photos meeting these requirements should be captured to ensure data accuracy.

To enhance usability and reduce reliance on user precision during photo capture, our verification app provides an on-screen framing guide. Users are instructed to align the clearly distinguishable green anti-counterfeiting area with the viewfinder border, eliminating the need for manual angle estimation or paper alignment.

Furthermore, the app supports five framing modes—top, bottom, left, right, and center-aligned—to guide users in capturing the anti-counterfeiting region from slightly varied positions. This design improves robustness against shadows, blur, and minor misalignment. During verification, multiple captured images are analyzed individually, and if needed, fused via a majority-voting mechanism to reconstruct a reliable binary pattern.

Step 2: Extracting Information. To extract the two-dimensional array stored in the photo and retrieve the information from the message and signature areas, each grid cell must be precisely located and classified by color. Blue and red grid cells serve as information grids, representing "1", while white and green grid cells function as background grids, representing "0". It is essential to ensure that the extracted data remains consistent with the original data.

The size of the grid cells in the photo may differ from the $d \times d$ cells in the original electronic image, as their dimensions depend on factors such as the phone's resolution, shooting angle, and distance. Although the shape of the grid cells may undergo slight deformation due to these variables, they can still be approximated as squares. Since the top and bottom edges of the anti-counterfeiting area in the photo are required to be nearly horizontal and parallel, it can be assumed that the grid cells within the same row have approximately equal side lengths. Based on this property, a formula for calculating the side length can be derived for precise positioning.

When extracting the grid array from the photo, it is necessary to determine the pixel coordinates of the top-left corner of each grid cell, hereinafter referred to as "grid points". Due to possible irregularities in the grid arrangement, the cells in each row may not be perfectly aligned horizontally, meaning the grid points do not always lie on the same horizontal line. Consequently, their coordinates cannot be directly obtained through simple calculations. A more accurate positioning method is required to ensure precise extraction of the array.

Among all grid cells, only background grids possess positioning functionality. Specifically, green grid cells always serve as positioning references. The positioning capability of white grid cells depends on their adjacent grid colors: when neither the top nor bottom adjacent grid cells are white, the white cell has vertical positioning functionality; when neither the left nor right adjacent grid cells are white, the white cell has horizontal positioning functionality. Therefore, before positioning, a color classification process is necessary to determine which grid cells have positioning functions accurately.

The color classification method can be described as follows:
First, it is necessary to maintain pixel mean templates for green and white grid cells. The initial value of the white template is set to (255, 255, 255), and the green template is set to (0, 255, 0). In subsequent processing, these templates are dynamically updated based on the pixel mean values of green or white grid cells in the surrounding area. Before performing color classification, the position of the current grid cell must be determined. If the row and column indices have the same parity, the position is likely a green grid cell or an isolated white grid cell; if the row and column indices have different parity, the position is a regular white grid cell.

The criteria for determining a green grid are as follows: The average values of the blue channel (B) and red channel (R) of the grid's pixels are calculated and compared with the green grid template. If the B or R value exceeds 80% of the corresponding color value in the template, the grid is judged as non-green. If the green channel (G) value of the grid is less than either the B or R value, it is also judged as non-green. Additionally, in the LAB color space, if the color difference calculated using the CIE76 method between the grid's pixel average and the green grid template exceeds 60, the grid is judged as non-green. Otherwise, the grid is recognized as green.

The criteria for determining a white grid are as follows: If the B, G, and R average values of the grid's pixels are all less than or equal to 50% of the corresponding values in the white grid template, the grid is judged as non-white. Additionally, in the LAB color space, if the color difference calculated using the CIE76 method between the grid's pixel average and the white grid template exceeds 60, the grid is judged as non-white. Otherwise, the grid is recognized as white.

The grid positioning method can be described as follows:
Based on the process of creating the anti-counterfeiting admission letter, the anti-counterfeiting area is the green region in the center of the photo. First, we need to determine the pixel coordinates of the four vertices of the green area. The specific method is as follows: convert the image from the BGR color space to the HSV color space; set the HSV range for green and generate a mask that only retains the pixels that meet the green conditions; perform contour detection on the mask of the green area to identify all contours in the image, then select the largest contour as the target anti-counterfeiting area; apply the Ramer-Douglas-Peucker (RDP) algorithm to approximate this contour as a quadrilateral with four vertices, ordered as top-left, bottom-left, top-right, and bottom-right; return the coordinates of the four vertices for subsequent use.

After vertex positioning is completed, the side length of each grid row in the photo can be calculated. The formulas for calculating the side length are as follows,

$$x_1 = \frac{topD}{photoCols}, \qquad (1)$$

$$x_{\text{photoRows}} = \frac{\text{bottomD}}{\text{photoCols}} \quad (2)$$

$$x_k = \frac{(\text{bottomD} - \text{topD}) \times \text{xsum} + \text{topD} \times \text{verticalD}}{(\text{photoCols}) \times \text{verticalD} - \text{bottomD} + \text{topD}} \quad (3)$$

Among them, x_1 represents the side length of the first row, $x_{\text{photoRows}}$ represents the side length of the last row, and x_k represents the side length of the k-th row, where k is an integer between 1 and photoRows. topD represents the distance between the top-right and top-left vertices, bottomD represents the distance between the bottom-right and bottom-left vertices, and verticalD represents the distance between the top-left and bottom-left vertices. photoRows represents the number of grid rows in the anti-counterfeiting area of the photo, photoCols represents the number of grid columns in the anti-counterfeiting area of the photo, and x_{sum} represents the sum of the grid side lengths from row 1 to row $k-1$.

After the side length is calculated, the grid points of the first row are determined. The pixel coordinates of the top-left corner are already known, meaning the grid point of the first grid in the first row is fixed. For the other grid points in the first row, the starting position of the next grid point is calculated based on the coordinates of the previous grid point and the grid's side length. This starting position may not be precise. If the grid has a positioning function, the position will be adjusted based on the scoring function, moving the grid point to the pixel coordinates with the highest score, i.e., the optimal position. If the grid does not have a positioning function, the starting position calculated from the previous grid will be retained, and subsequent positioning will follow this adjustment rule.

For the remaining rows, the first step is to determine the position of the starting green grid point in the current row. The position of the first green grid point in the current row is estimated based on the coordinates of the first green grid point from the previous row. The optimal position of this grid point is then determined by calculating the green score, followed by the calculation of the first white grid point's position. Subsequently, the remaining grid points in the current row are positioned, where the horizontal coordinate of the starting position is the same as the previous grid point in the same column, and the vertical coordinate is the same as the previous grid point in the same row. Then, the positioning capability of each grid point is assessed, and its position is adjusted to ensure accuracy. Finally, the grids are classified based on their colors to determine the binary information they store.

The formulas for calculating the green grid score and the white grid score are as follows,

$$scoreG = \sum_{i=0}^{x_k} \sum_{j=0}^{x_k} \left(weightG[i][j] \times brightG \times (255\sqrt{2} - distanceG) \right) \quad (4)$$

$$scoreW = \sum_{i=0}^{x_k} \sum_{j=0}^{x_k} \left(weightW[i][j] \times brightW \times \left(255\sqrt{\frac{2}{3}} - distanceW\right)\right) \quad (5)$$

Among them, k represents the row number of the grid, W_x and W_y represent the weight matrices of the same size as the grid, and $P_{i,j}$ represents the brightness of the pixel in the i-th row and j-th column within the grid. We treat the RGB color space as a cube, where distanceG and distanceW represent the distances from the pixel at (r, g, b) to the corresponding color lines. Specifically, distanceG represents the distance from the point (r, g, b) to the line "Red = 0, Blue = 0", which represents green. distanceW represents the distance from the point (r, g, b) to the line "Red = Blue = Green", which represents white.

The formula for calculating the brightness of a pixel (r, g, b) is:

$$brightG = \frac{g}{b + g + r} \quad (6)$$

$$brightW = \frac{\min(b, g, r)}{255} \quad (7)$$

The formula for calculating the distance from a pixel (r, g, b) to the corresponding color line is:

$$distanceG = \sqrt{b^2 + r^2} \quad (8)$$

$$distanceW = \sqrt{(r-g)^2 + (r-b)^2 + (g-b)^2} \quad (9)$$

Step 3: Signature Verification. The verification program performs a signature check on the extracted admission letter array. First, each photo is individually verified. If any photo successfully passes the SM2 signature check, the process stops. If none of the 5 photos pass the verification, a "majority voting" mechanism is used to generate the final photo array, from which the message and signature are extracted for verification.

The "majority voting" process is as follows: for each corresponding position across the 5 arrays, the values are compared. If the majority of photos have a grid value of 1 at a specific position, that position is set to 1; if the majority value is 0, the position is set to 0.

Step 4: Output Verification Results. Based on the results of the signature verification, the system outputs the corresponding message to the user, determining whether the admission letter is authentic.

Robustness to Grid Distortion. To reduce the potential impact of resolution variation and minor grid distortion during photo capture, the system incorporates two design strategies.

First, users are guided to take five images of the admission letter using different framing positions, while maintaining a perpendicular shooting angle. If all individual verifications fail, the system applies a majority-voting mechanism to the binary arrays extracted from the multiple images, thereby reducing recognition errors caused by local blurring, slight deformation, or color inconsistency.

Second, the system performs image segmentation on the anti-counterfeiting area to extract its contour and estimate the vertex positions and grid unit dimensions. This enables the system to adapt to mild perspective distortion and scaling variations caused by resolution changes during photography.

Nevertheless, we acknowledge that under non-ideal conditions—such as low resolution, insufficient lighting, or non-perpendicular shooting angles—the verification accuracy may still be affected. In future work, we plan to enhance the system's environmental adaptability through the integration of image enhancement algorithms and real-time feedback mechanisms.

5 Implementation

5.1 Generator

The software and hardware environment used for the admission letter generator is outlined in the following Table 1.

Table 1. Software and hardware environment of the admission letter generator

Operating System	Windows 11
Processor	12th Gen Intel(R) Core(TM) i5-12500H 2.50 GHz
Memory	16.0 GB
Running Software	Visual Studio 2019, MFC
Programming Language	C++

Architecture. The admission letter generator adopts a modular design, as shown in Fig. 4. It includes the following main modules:

1. **User Interaction Module.** The interface includes areas for upload, settings, and generation, supporting the user to upload the student information sheet and template image. All column names from the student information sheet are displayed in a drop-down menu, allowing the user to select the text field positions. The module also supports the selection and preview of font, size, color, and other attributes. Additionally, the system provides error prompts and operational guidance to prevent issues caused by format errors or incorrect settings during the operation.
2. **Data Processing Module.** This module parses the student information sheet, extracts column names, and helps the user select the data to be filled in. It reads the specified columns from the student information sheet row

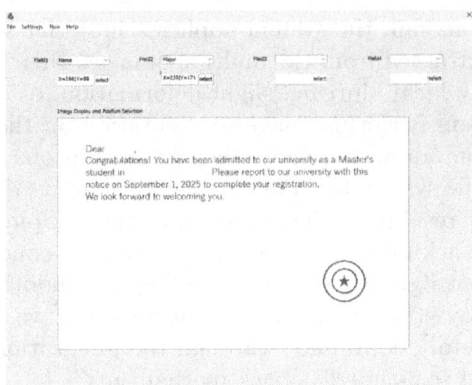

Fig. 4. The interface of the admission letter generator.

by row and dynamically associates the data with the positions defined in the template. The module provides functions for detecting empty values or format errors in the information sheet to assist the user in making corrections.
3. **Image Processing Module.** This module fills the student data into the template according to the user-specified font, size, and color, along with a series of image operations as described in Sect. 4.1. It supports common image formats such as PNG, JPEG, and others.
4. **Digital Signature Module.** The module reads the private key from a USB Key for digital signing, using the SM2 algorithm and SM3 hashing to ensure the authenticity and security of the file. The signature result is appended to the anti-counterfeit image.
5. **Export and Generation Module.** This module performs necessary image processing on the signed image files, generating the final admission letter and saving it to the specified directory for easy printing and distribution.

Workflow. The workflow design of the admission letter generator emphasizes simplicity and efficiency, and includes the following stages:
1. **Upload Phase.** Users upload the student information sheet and template image via the interactive interface.
2. **Setting Phase.** Users set the correspondence between the template fields and the columns in the student information sheet. Users select the column names to be filled from the drop-down menu in the combo box, then choose the position for the information to be added in the template by clicking with the mouse. The system also allows customization of font, size, and color to meet personalized needs.
3. **Generation Phase.** Users click the "Run" button to start the batch generation process. The system reads the student information sheet data row by row and dynamically fills it into the template image, then invokes the digital signature module to sign the generated file with the SM2 algorithm.

4. **Save Phase.** The system saves the generated admission letters with the record number to the user-specified directory and displays a prompt showing the number of successfully generated files and any error messages after the operation is completed.

5.2 Verification App

The software and hardware environment used for the admission letter verification App is outlined in the following Table 2.

Table 2. Software and hardware environment of the admission letter verification App

Development Operating System	MacOS Sonoma 14.6.1
Development Tools	Xcode
Programming Language	Objective-C++
Device	iPhone 13
Camera	12 MP
Operating Platform	iOS

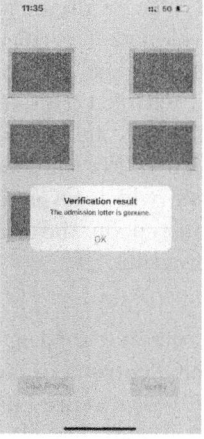

Fig. 5. The interface for successful verification.

Architecture. The admission letter verification app is mainly divided into the following three modules: User Interaction Module, Signature Verification Module, and Result Feedback Module. The interface for successful verification is shown in Fig. 5.

1. **User Interaction Module.** This module is responsible for photo upload, deletion, and task initiation. Users click the "Take Photo" button to upload up to 5 admission letter photos, either by capturing or selecting them from the local album. The uploaded images are displayed as thumbnails, supporting click-to-delete and re-upload. Users click the "Verify" button to start the verification process.
2. **Signature Verification Module.** As the core of the app, this module uses OpenCV to scan the image line by line, extracting the stored binary array and parsing the message and signature. Then, it reads the signature public key from the digital certificate and uses the SM2 algorithm from the GMSSL library for signature verification. The entire process is completed locally to ensure user data privacy and security.
3. **Result Feedback Module.** This module is responsible for displaying the verification result. The system processes the 5 uploaded photos and provides a determination of either "The admission letter is genuine" or "The admission letter is fake".

5.3 Experiment

Experimental Environment. To evaluate the effectiveness of the method designed in this paper, we developed a verification program on the PC side according to the method described in Sect. 4.2 for testing. The experiments were conducted on a laptop equipped with a 12th Gen Intel(R) Core(TM) i5-12500H processor (2.50 GHz), 16 GB of RAM, and a 64-bit Windows operating system. Additionally, an iPhone 13 (with a 12 MP camera) was used to capture photos of anti-counterfeit admission letters, which formed the experimental dataset. The system was implemented and tested on the corresponding hardware platform using a dedicated verification program.

Dataset. When creating the electronic images, we selected a print resolution of 300 dpi with A4 paper size. The electronic image has dimensions of 750 pixels × 500 pixels, with the top 470 rows representing the message area and the bottom 30 rows representing the signature area. After enlargement, the grid-based anti-counterfeit image was centered on a 3508 × 2480 pixel canvas. Letters were printed using a laser printer on high-weight coated paper, with border-fit disabled to preserve grid clarity.

During photography, lighting was carefully controlled to avoid shadows. The camera was kept as perpendicular as possible to the page, ensuring that the top-bottom and left-right edges of the anti-counterfeit region appeared nearly parallel.

The dataset includes two parts. The first comprises 1,000 real admission letter photos, grouped into five images each. The second is a forged dataset generated by altering only the name field while keeping the layout unchanged, also containing 1,000 images in five-image groups.

Experimental Results. This experiment validated 1000 real admission letter photos, with 960 letters successfully passing the verification, resulting in an overall verification accuracy of 96%. Furthermore, to assess the stability and consistency of the verification method, we conducted 10 independent experiments, each validating 100 admission letters, as shown in the Fig. 6. The accuracy for each experiment ranged from 94% to 97%, demonstrating the method's consistency and reliability across different trials. The experiment validated 1,000 forged admission letter photos, none of which passed verification, resulting in a false positive rate of 0%.

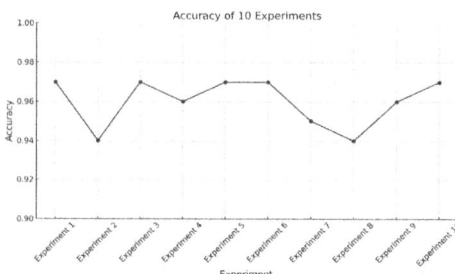

Fig. 6. Accuracy distribution of experiment results.

6 Conclusions and Future Work

This research designed and implemented an innovative anti-counterfeiting system for paper documents by integrating image processing and digital signature technologies. Experimental results show excellent performance in verifying admission letters, significantly enhancing document authenticity. Compared to traditional methods, the system greatly improves anti-counterfeiting effectiveness while offering high scalability and usability, making it suitable for widespread application to critical paper documents.

Despite initial success, further improvement is possible. This work mainly targets admission letters; future applications may extend to identity documents, financial credentials, and contracts, each with distinct requirements demanding tailored anti-counterfeiting strategies. Advancements in image and encryption algorithms—such as deep learning for better recognition and stronger cryptography for faster, more secure signatures—could further boost system performance.

Enhancing usability is also vital: simplifying operations and offering online verification would improve user experience and adaptability.

A notable advantage is the layout-agnostic design. By treating the entire electronic document as a color image and interpreting each pixel through a binary-valued color mapping scheme, the system supports diverse formats without relying on templates. However, current validation is limited to admission letters. Applying the system to visually complex documents (e.g., tabular layouts) may introduce new challenges, such as grid positioning errors. Addressing these through adaptive layout modeling and large-scale testing is a key direction for future work. With continued development, this system can provide secure, generalizable solutions to ensure the authenticity and integrity of a wide range of paper documents.

References

1. Baechler, S.: Document fraud: will your identity be secure in the twenty-first century? Eur. J. Crim. Policy Res. **26**(3), 379–398 (2020)
2. Ramer, U.: An iterative procedure for the polygonal approximation of plane curves. Comput. Graphics Image Process. **1**(3), 244–256 (1972). https://doi.org/10.1016/S0146-664X(72)80017-0
3. Douglas, D.H., Peucker, T.K.: Algorithms for the reduction of the number of points required to represent a digitized line or its caricature. Cartographica Int. J. Geogr. Inf. Geovisualization **10**(2), 112–122 (1973)
4. MeiHong, L., JiQiang, L.: USB key-based approach for software protection. In: 2009 International Conference on Industrial Mechatronics and Automation, pp. 151–153. IEEE (2009)
5. RSA Laboratories: PKCS #11: Cryptographic token interface standard. RSA Laboratories (2004). https://www.oasis-open.org/committees/pkcs11/
6. International Commission on Illumination (CIE): Colorimetry, 2nd ed. CIE Publication No. 15.2. CIE Central Bureau, Vienna, Austria (1986)
7. Szczeszak, A., Skwierczyńska, M., Przybylska, D., et al.: Upconversion luminescence in cellulose composites (fibres and paper) modified with lanthanide-doped SrF_2 nanoparticles. J. Mater. Chem. C **8**(34), 11922–11928 (2020)
8. Shenzhen Emperor Technology Company Limited.: Colored Anti-Counterfeiting Identification Card Manufacturing Method and Colored Anti-Counterfeiting Identification Card. EP18938017.3 (2020)
9. Piatriková, L., Tarábek, P., Cimrák, I.: Digital verification of optically variable ink feature on identity cards. In: 2023 33rd Conference of Open Innovations Association (FRUCT), pp. 210–218. IEEE (2023)
10. Mardani, H., Roghani-Mamaqani, H., Shahi, S., et al.: Anti-counterfeiting inks based on forster resonance energy transfer in microcrystalline cellulose-grafted poly(amidoamine) for artificial industries. ACS Appl. Polym. Mater. **5**(2), 1092–1102 (2023)
11. Mardani, H., Bayrak, E., Zelik, E., et al.: Anti-counterfeiting ink based on polymer nanoparticles containing spiropyran and Aza-BODIPY for artificial industries. React. Funct. Polym. (2023)
12. Muthamma, K., Sunil, D., Shetty, P., et al.: Eco-friendly flexographic ink from fluorene-based Schiff base pigment for anti-counterfeiting and printed electronics applications. Prog. Org. Coat. **161**, 106463 (2021)

13. Wu, J., Ge, H.: Review of patented technology of magnetic ink anti-counterfeiting. In: Zhao, P., Ye, Z., Xu, M., Yang, L. (eds.) Advanced Graphic Communication, Printing and Packaging Technology. LNEE, vol. 600, pp. 387–394. Springer, Singapore (2020). https://doi.org/10.1007/978-981-15-1864-5_54
14. Tang, Y.L., Huang, Y.T.: Print-and-scan resilient watermarking for authenticating paper-based certificates. In: 2010 First International Conference on Pervasive Computing, Signal Processing and Applications, pp. 357–361. IEEE (2010)
15. Chen, H., Hu, H., Sun, B., et al.: Dynamic anti-counterfeiting labels with enhanced multi-level information encryption. ACS Appl. Mater. Interfaces **15**(1), 2104–2111 (2022)
16. Zhang, Y., Gao, C., Li, Z., et al.: A method of fingermark anti-counterfeiting for forensic document identification. Pattern Recogn. Lett. **152**, 86–92 (2021)
17. Wang, S., Toreini, E., Hao, F.: Anti-counterfeiting for polymer banknotes based on polymer substrate fingerprinting. IEEE Trans. Inf. Forensics Secur. **16**, 2823–2835 (2021)
18. Choudhury, Z.H., Rabbani, M.M.A.: Biometric passport for national security using multibiometrics and encrypted biometric data encoded in the QR code. J. Appl. Secur. Res. **15**(2), 199–229 (2020)
19. Drahanský, M., Kanich, O.: Vulnerabilities of biometric systems. In: Conference on Security and Protection of Information, Brno, Czech Republic, pp. 53–60 (2015)
20. Mudraganam, C.S.: SmartDEGREE from TCS to combat certificate malpractices. RFID J. (2009)
21. Yahya, Z., Kamarzaman, N.S., Azizan, N., et al.: A new academic certificate authentication using leading edge technology. In: Proceedings of the 1st International Conference on E-commerce, E-Business and E-Government, pp. 82–85 (2017)
22. Li, C.M., Hu, P., Lau, W.C.: Authpaper: protecting paper-based documents and credentials using authenticated 2D barcodes. In: 2015 IEEE International Conference on Communications (ICC), pp. 7400–7406. IEEE (2015)
23. Ahmed, H.A., Jang, J.W.: Document certificate authentication system using digitally signed QR code tag. In: Proceedings of the 12th International Conference on Ubiquitous Information Management and Communication, pp. 1–5 (2018)
24. Auberson, M., Baechler, S., Zasso, M., et al.: Development of a systematic computer vision-based method to analyse and compare images of false identity documents for forensic intelligence purposes–Part I: acquisition, calibration and validation issues. Forensic Sci. Int. **260**, 74–84 (2016)
25. Mehrjardi, F.Z., Latif, A.M., Zarchi, M.S., et al.: A survey on deep learning-based image forgery detection. Pattern Recogn. (2023). https://doi.org/10.1016/j.patcog.2023.109778
26. Zheng, Z., Zheng, H., Ju, J., et al.: A system for identifying an anti-counterfeiting pattern based on the statistical difference in key image regions. Expert Syst. Appl. **183**, 115410 (2021). https://doi.org/10.1016/j.eswa.2021.115410

PQMagic: Towards Secure and Efficient Post Quantum Cryptography Implementations

Yituo He[1(✉)], Xinpeng Hao[1], Juanru Li[3], and Yu Yu[1,2]

[1] Shanghai Qi Zhi Institute, Shanghai, China
yituohe@163.com, haoxinpeng@sqz.ac.cn
[2] Shanghai Jiao Tong University, Shanghai, China
yyuu@sjtu.edu.cn
[3] Feiyu Tech, Shanghai, China
mail@lijuanru.com

Abstract. Quantum computing threatens current public-key cryptosystems, driving the need for post-quantum cryptography (PQC). However, PQC implementations face additional risks. We find implementation issues in existing PQC libraries (e.g., pq-crystals and liboqs), while they also fail to fully leverage modern processors. To address these issues, we propose four optimization strategies: Branch Optimization, Register Allocation, Vectorized Execution, and Secure and Efficient Pipelining. These strategies minimize execution branches, instruction counts, and memory accesses while enhancing security, mitigating the implementation from side-channel attack risk. We implement these in PQMAGIC, a high-performance PQC library for ML-KEM and ML-DSA, and it significantly outperforms state-of-the-art libraries. For ML-KEM-1024, it achieves efficiency gains of up to 1.77x, 1.79x, and 1.52x for Keygen, Encaps, and Decaps, while reducing instruction counts and memory access overhead by up to 47.1% and 60.1%. For ML-DSA-87, it improves Keygen, Sign, and Verify by up to 2.24x, 1.89x, and 2.04x, with instruction counts and memory access reduced by up to 44.4% and 64.5%. Additionally, PQMAGIC eliminates up to 90.9% of branch operations in matrix expansion for ML-DSA. Besides, PQMAGIC also outperforms traditional cryptographic algorithm combinations (RSA-2048/ECDSA-256 + ECDH) selected from OpenSSL. It only has a slight gap at the highest level L5 compared to ECDSA-256 + ECDH combination. Our work shows that combining modern hardware capabilities with careful instruction scheduling enables secure and efficient PQC implementations, paving the way for post-quantum cryptographic migration.

Keywords: Post-Quantum Crypto · Crypto Engineering · PQMagic

1 Introduction

Quantum computing threatens to break many public-key cryptosystems currently in use. Consequently, research into post-quantum cryptography (PQC)

focuses on developing cryptosystems secure against both quantum and classical computers. Unfortunately, not all threats against PQC come from quantum computing. As an empirical study [6] demonstrated, systems-level bugs—rather than inherent flaws in the underlying ciphers—are a major contributor to security vulnerabilities in many widely used cryptographic libraries. This conclusion also applies to PQC libraries. Since PQC implementations must interoperate with existing processors, operating systems, and networks, software security issues like memory corruption remain a critical concern. Moreover, PQC libraries remain vulnerable to traditional side-channel attacks (e.g., those exploiting timing leaks to extract secret-key information). Thus, it is critical to develop secure, efficient PQC software components and integrate them into modern cryptographic infrastructure to mitigate both quantum and conventional threats.

PQC software especially PQC libraries, like other crypto software, need to apply a rigorous security standard for their implemented code. We argue that although many current crypto libraries have deployed various code securing strategies (e.g., using specific hardware ISA such as AES-NI and SHA-NI to secure the crypto operations, using formal verification to avoid non-constant time execution), PQC libraries are less concerned. Even though a variety of PQC crypto libraries have been developed, to the best of our knowledge, seldom work thoroughly examined to what extent these libraries adopted secure code implementation to protect them against common attacks. In this paper, we first demonstrate the implementation issues in current PQC libraries and discuss the risks. We found that our investigated PQC libraries (pq-crystals [7,10] and liboqs [19]) did not fully leverage the features of modern processors, hence led to a not-that-optimal code implementation that potentially increased the risks of timing side-channel or secret information disclosure.

In response, we propose a series of code securing strategies that mainly utilize four strategies to generate secure and efficient implementations of current PQC ciphers such as ML-KEM and ML-DSA. We have implemented PQMAGIC, a PQC library that followed the proposed code securing strategies and demonstrated that our implementation significantly reduced execution branches, instruction counts, and memory accesses. In comparison with state-of-the-art optimized PQC libraries, the optimal implementation of PQMAGIC achieves significant reductions in instruction counts and memory access overhead. For ML-KEM-1024, these reductions reach up to 47.1% and 60.1%, respectively. Similarly, for ML-DSA-87, PQMAGIC reduces instruction counts and memory access overhead by up to 44.4% and 64.5%, respectively. Additionally, PQMAGIC successfully eliminates branch operations in matrix expansion for ML-DSA by up to 90.9% compared to state-of-the-art libraries. In terms of performance, PQMAGIC significantly outperforms state-of-the-art optimized PQC libraries. For ML-KEM-1024, PQMAGIC achieves efficiency gains of up to 1.77x, 1.79x, and 1.52x for Keygen, Encaps, and Decaps operations, respectively. Similarly, for ML-DSA-87, PQMAGIC demonstrates improvements of 2.24x, 1.89x, and 2.04x for Keygen, Sign, and Verify operations, respectively. Notably, we evaluate PQMAGIC by combining ML-KEM and ML-DSA together against traditional cryptographic algorithm combinations (RSA-2048/ECDSA-256 + ECDH) selected from OpenSSL. PQMAGIC outperforms the RSA-2048 + ECDH combination across all security levels, achieving efficiency improvements of 4.77x at L1, 3.25x at L3, and 2.67x at L5. When compared to ECDSA-256 + ECDH, PQMAGIC maintains superior performance at L1 and L3 (1.58x and 1.07x, respectively), with only a slight efficiency gap (0.88x) at the highest security level L5. These results showed that security of PQC software implementation could benefit from both new hardware ISAs and proper instruction scheduling.

2 Security Issues in Current PQC Implementations

The rapid evolution of modern CPU architectures has provided developers with substantial hardware resources [4,8,12,18], such as vector instruction sets (e.g., AVX512), multi-level cache hierarchies, out-of-order execution, and superscalar pipelines. These resources not only significantly improve the performance of code implementations but also help mitigate security risks.

However, through extensive analysis of existing works [7,10,14,19–21], we have found that many implementations of ML-KEM and ML-DSA often overlook security issues in the pursuit of performance optimization, fail to fully utilize the features and resources of modern CPUs. For instance, the pq-crystals library [7, 10] optimizes ML-KEM and ML-DSA using only the AVX2 instruction set, while liboqs [19] provides further encapsulation based on this work. Although these open-source libraries have made some progress in performance optimization, they still fall short in mitigating the security risk of algorithm implementations. Its frequent memory accesses and branch-heavy code structures not only hinder further performance improvements but also introduce risks such as timing side-channel attacks and memory exposure. Moreover, as these libraries do not fully leverage the architectural advantages of modern CPUs, there remains significant room for performance optimization. As for some closed-source optimizations [20, 21], while they claim to utilize the AVX512 instruction set for performance gains, they also lack a thorough consideration of algorithm security and fail to fully exploit instruction pipeline optimizations to enhance both security and computational efficiency.

To provide a more concrete illustration of the security risks in existing algorithm implementations, we analyzed the implementation details of the state-of-the-art open-source libraries, pq-crystals [7,10] and liboqs [19]. As shown in Fig. 1, both pq-crystals and liboqs use switch-case structures in their source code. The switch-case structure generates multiple branch instructions after compilation. When branch prediction fails, the CPU must flush the pipeline and reload instructions, incurring performance penalties. Beyond these computational inefficiencies, the current implementation exhibits suboptimal design characteristics. This branch-heavy pattern represents poor programming practice, as its adoption in other code contexts could potentially introduce additional side-channel security risk.

To further verify the potential security risks introduced by the branching structure in the source code, we conducted a comprehensive reverse engineering

```
static inline void polyvec_matrix_expand_row (/* ... */) {
  switch(i) {
    case 0:
      polyvec_matrix_expand_row0 (buf, buf + 1, rho);
      *row = buf;
      break;
    case 1:
      polyvec_matrix_expand_row1 (buf + 1, buf, rho);
      *row = buf + 1;
      break;
    /* Many Other Cases */
    case 7:
      polyvec_matrix_expand_row7 (buf + 1, buf, rho);
      *row = buf + 1;
      break;
  }
}
```

Fig. 1. Risky Branch-Prone Control Flow Pattern in pq-crystal [10] and liboqs [19]

analysis of binaries compiled with *O3* optimization. We found that the compiler retained the switch-case branch structures in all cases except the lowest security level parameter set (i.e., ML-DSA-44), failing to optimize them. This indicates that switch-case structures will truly risk the algorithms in real-world deployments.

Additionally, Fig. 2 shows that these implementations involve extensive memory read/write operations. Each macro function is called four times and contains multiple memory operations. This design introduces high memory access overhead, which also suffers a significant risk of memory exposure. The high frequency of memory accesses increases the risk of cache side-channel vulnerabilities, through which sensitive data could potentially be extracted by attackers.

3 Method

To mitigate security issues in the code optimization process while further improving algorithm execution efficiency, we propose the following four optimization strategies:

- **Branch Optimization**: Reducing complex branches to reduce the impact of misprediction while demonstrating a coding paradigm that inherently mitigates side-channel risks across all coding scenarios.
- **Register Allocation**: Maximizing data residency in registers to reduce memory accesses, thereby lowering the risk of data leakage through cache access patterns.
- **Vectorized Parallel Execution**: Leveraging SIMD instructions to accelerate computations, reducing the total number of instructions required for the

```
.macro levels2t7 off                .macro levels0t1 off
/* level 2 */                       /* level 0 */
vmovdqa /*offset*/(%rdi),%ymm4      vpbroadcastd
/* 7 More vmovdqa */                    /*offset*/(%rsi),%ymm1
vpbroadcastd                        vpbroadcastd
    /*offset*/(%rsi),%ymm1              /*offset*/(%rsi),%ymm2
vpbroadcastd                        vmovdqa /*offset*/(%rdi),%ymm4
    /*offset*/(%rsi),%ymm2          /* 7 More vmovdqa */
/* Other Operations */              /* Other Operations */

/* level 3 */                       /* level 1 */
vmovdqa /*offset*/(%rsi),%ymm1      vpbroadcastd
vmovdqa /*offset*/(%rsi),%ymm2          /*offset*/(%rsi),%ymm1
/* Other Operations */              /* 3 More vpbroadcastd */
                                    /* Other Operations */
/* level 4 */
vmovdqa /*offset*/(%rsi),%ymm1      vmovdqa %ymm4,/*offset*/(%rdi)
vmovdqa /*offset*/(%rsi),%ymm2      /* 7 More vmovdqa */
/* Other Operations */              .endm

/* ... */                           .text
                                    .global cdecl(ntt_avx)
/* level 7 */                       cdecl(ntt_avx):
/* ... */                           vmovdqa _8XQ*4(%rsi),%ymm0
                                    levels0t1       0
/* Store the Result Back */         /* 3 more levels0t1 */
vmovdqa %ymm9,/*offset*/(%rdi)      levels2t7       0
/* 7 More vmovdqa */                /* 3 more levels2t7 */
.endm                               ret
```

Fig. 2. Risky Memory Access Patterns in NTT Implementations in pq-crystal and liboqs

same operation as well as improving data parallelism, and thus shortening execution time. This helps mitigate certain security threats, such as timing side-channel attacks, by minimizing the time window available for adversarial observation.
- **Secure and Efficient Pipelining**: Mitigating the risk of the compiler introducing unsafe data dependencies or control dependencies that could inadvertently leak information [16] by directly writing assembly codes, while optimizing execution order to better align with CPU pipeline structures for both security and performance.

This section will detail how these optimization strategies work together to enhance algorithm security while fully leveraging the performance potential of modern hardware architectures.

3.1 Branch Optimization

Our design employs a branch optimization strategy that systematically eliminates unnecessary branching dependencies. This architectural decision stems from the performance challenges associated with conditional branching, where variable execution timing can disrupt pipeline efficiency and computational predictability.

By replacing conventional switch-case constructs with dedicated function implementations for each logical path, we achieve more deterministic execution behavior. The branch-free design not only ensures consistent processing timelines but also establishes a better coding paradigm.

The optimized architecture consolidates all polynomial sampling operations into a unified function implementation. By eliminating branching constraints, this approach achieves full utilization of AVX512 instruction sets, enabling simultaneous processing of eight polynomials with enhanced compiler optimization opportunities. Furthermore, the reduction in function call overhead also contributes to overall execution efficiency and system stability.

3.2 Register Allocation

Memory access latency is a critical bottleneck in secure and high-performance computing. To mitigate this issue, we prioritize storing critical data (e.g., polynomial coefficients) in registers, minimizing memory accesses and reducing the risk of data leakage through cache access patterns.

Modern AVX512 registers provide robust hardware support for secure and efficient computation. Each register can store 512 bits of data, and with AVX512 instruction set, the number of available registers is expanded to 32. This allows us to retain more data in registers, reducing reliance on memory and mitigating potential side-channel vulnerabilities.

For the ML-KEM algorithm, every polynomial contains 256 coefficients, with each coefficient being 12 bits long (stored as 16-bit values). This requires only 8 AVX512 registers to store all coefficients. Similarly, for the ML-DSA algorithm, every polynomial consists of 256 coefficients, with each coefficient being 23 bits long (stored as 32-bit values), requiring only 16 AVX512 registers. Even after allocating registers for coefficient storage, there remain 24/16 available 512-bit registers for ML-KEM/ML-DSA, which can be leveraged for intermediate computations. By preloading polynomial coefficients into registers, we minimize memory access patterns that could otherwise be exploited in cache-based side-channel attacks.

3.3 Vectorized Parallel Execution

Modern CPUs provide SIMD instruction sets such as AVX512, which allow us to process multiple data elements in configurations like 32×16-bit or 16×32-bit simultaneously. This capability is particularly beneficial for cryptographic algorithms such as Keccak-1600 and polynomial arithmetic in ML-KEM as well as ML-DSA, where efficient parallelism not only accelerates computation but also enhances security by reducing exposure to timing-based side-channel attacks.

For Keccak-1600, AVX512 enables up to 8-way parallel processing of independent hash operations, allowing multiple 64-bit state computations to be performed simultaneously within a single instruction cycle. Similarly, ML-KEM and ML-DSA rely heavily on polynomial arithmetic, where coefficients are stored as 32-bit and 16-bit values, respectively. Since computations on different coefficients exhibit minimal data dependency, they are well-suited for vectorized execution. By utilizing AVX512, multiple coefficients can be processed in parallel within a single register, effectively reducing the total number of instructions required for the same operation. This not only improves execution efficiency but also narrows the attack window for adversaries, further mitigating the risk of side-channel attacks.

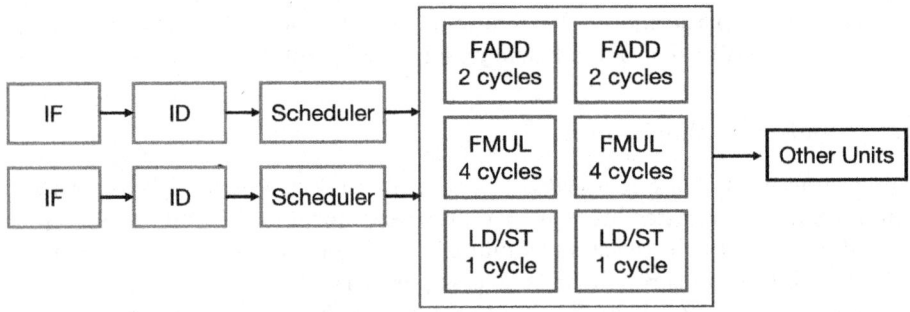

Fig. 3. Illustration of Modern CPU Pipeline

3.4 Secure and Efficient Pipelining

Instruction pipelining is a fundamental mechanism for achieving instruction-level parallelism (ILP) [1,2]. We directly use assembly code to implement algorithm components, controlling instruction scheduling order. Then we take advantage of multiple execution units in modern superscalar processors, optimally arranging similar types of assembly instructions together, rather than simply interleaving different types of instructions. Therefore, we reduce potential security risks introduced by compilers [16] while improving the ILP.

Specifically, modern processors (e.g., AMD and Intel CPUs) enhance parallelism through superscalar architecture [8,12,18], which provides the following key features:

- **Multiple Execution Units**: Independent functional units (e.g., integer ALUs, FPUs, load/store units) allow concurrent execution of heterogeneous operations, reducing control dependencies that could leak execution timing variations.

– **Multi-Issue Capability**: Modern CPUs can fetch, decode, and dispatch multiple instructions per cycle, enabling higher throughput while minimizing compiler-induced timing variations.

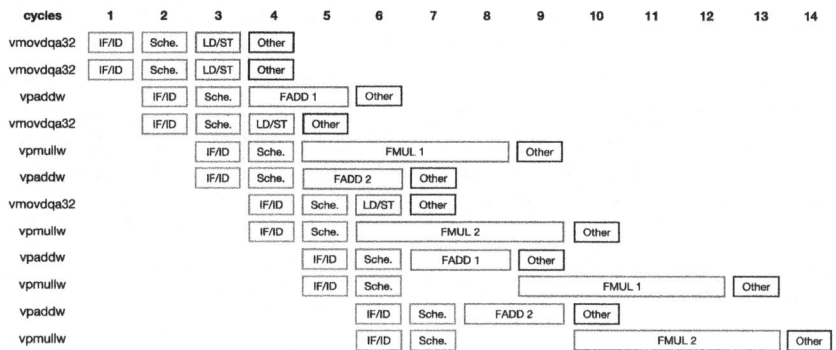

(a) Instruction Scheduling with Low Parallelism

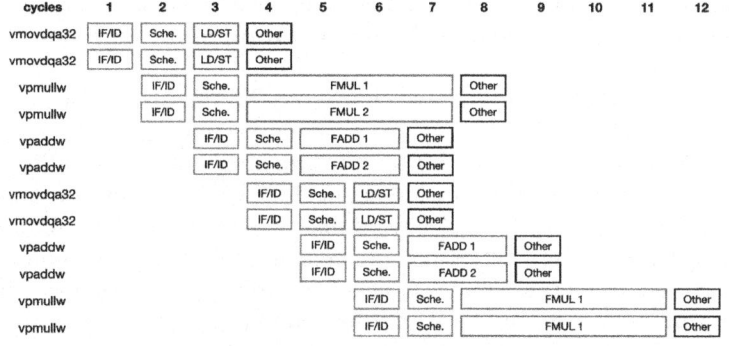

(b) Optimized Instruction Scheduling with Improved Parallelism

Fig. 4. Comparison of Instruction-Level Parallelism Before and After Optimization on a Superscalar CPU

Figure 3 shows a simplified diagram of a modern superscalar CPU pipeline structure, including two instruction fetch (IF) units, two instruction decode (ID) units, two instruction scheduler units, and six execution units with three different types (i.e., FADD, FMUL, and LD/ST).

To illustrate the security and performance benefits of increasing ILP on superscalar CPUs, we designed a toy example consisting of 12 instructions, as shown in Fig. 4. We aim to compare different instruction scheduling schemes on our simplified CPU architecture (Fig. 3). We then ensure that the optimized scheduling scheme achieves improved performance while mitigating compiler-introduced security risks at the same time.

In Fig. 4a, although instructions are interleaved to facilitate parallel execution across different execution unit types, the lack of consideration for parallelism within the same type of execution units leads to 2 pipeline stalls, requiring 14 cycles to complete.

In contrast, the optimized secure instruction scheduling scheme in Fig. 4b carefully arranges instructions to balance execution across different execution units. By overlapping instructions of the same type and filling idle cycles of high-latency instructions with other types, the schedule eliminates pipeline stalls successfully. This approach reduces the total cycle count to 12, improving performance by 14.3%. Besides that, manually scheduling the instruction pipeline using hand-writing assembly directly could naturally mitigate the risk of timing side-channel attacks introduced by compilers.

4 PQMAGIC

In this section, we present our PQC library, PQMAGIC[1]. It applies optimization strategies proposed in Sect. 3 and systematically reduces the risk of security issues while improving computational efficiency for ML-KEM/ML-DSA implementation. The implementation of PQMAGIC focuses on securing three critical operations: **polynomial arithmetic**, **hash components**, and **matrix expansion**.

For **polynomial arithmetic**, we employed the *Register Allocation* to maximize data residency, *Vectorized Parallel Execution* to accelerate computations, and *Secure and Efficient Pipelining* to optimize instruction scheduling, ensuring both efficiency and mitigation to side-channel attacks. For **hash components**, we leveraged *Vectorized Parallel Execution* to process multiple data elements simultaneously, reducing the total number of instructions and minimizing the time window for potential timing attacks. For **matrix expansion**, we applied *Branch Optimization* to eliminate complex conditional branches introduced by switch-case structure, which reduces the risk of timing side-channel attacks. Besides, it gives an opportunity for parallelism sampling in matrix expansion and avoids performance penalties caused by frequent branch mispredictions.

The remainder of this section provides a detailed explanation of how these strategies are applied to optimize the implementation of the three critical operations.

4.1 Polynomial Arithmetic

Polynomial arithmetic remains one of the most computationally intensive core operations in both ML-KEM and ML-DSA algorithms, and its performance and security significantly impact the overall efficiency of these cryptographic schemes. Among the components of polynomial arithmetic, the Number Theoretic Transform (NTT) and its inverse operation (INTT) are particularly critical, as they

---

[1] https://pqcrypto.dev/.

not only dominate the computational cost but also present a potential attack surface. Therefore, to enhance both the security and efficiency of polynomial arithmetic, we focused on optimizing NTT operations, aiming to reduce their vulnerability to side-channel attacks while improving their execution efficiency.

Modern processors widely support the AVX512 instruction set, which provides 512-bit registers and expands the number of registers to 32. Leveraging this capability, we apply *Register Allocation* and *Vectorized Parallel Execution* strategies to PQMAGIC. First, we maximized the advantages of AVX512 by preloading all coefficients required for NTT operations into the registers, thereby reducing the risk of memory exposure and eliminating the performance overhead caused by repeated memory access. Specifically, in the ML-KEM algorithm, a polynomial consists of 256 coefficients of 12 bits each, which can be entirely stored in just 8 AVX512 registers. Similarly, in the ML-DSA algorithm, a polynomial contains 256 coefficients of 23 bits, requiring only 16 AVX512 registers for storage.

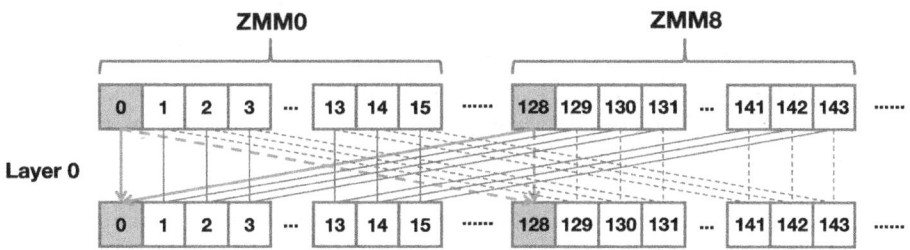

Fig. 5. NTT Layer 0 For ML-DSA

By consolidating all coefficient data into registers, this approach improves data locality and cache hit rates. As a result, by leveraging the data storage capabilities of AVX512 registers, the optimized NTT/INTT operations require only a single memory read for each coefficient and each root value, and a single memory write to store the results after computation. All other computations are performed entirely within the registers, eliminating additional memory access. Therefore PQMAGIC could minimize the risk of memory data exposure and improve the execution efficiency.

In addition to enhancing data parallelism, we further applied *Secure and Efficient Pipelining* strategy to directly use assembly code, optimizing instruction scheduling and improving ILP. As shown in Fig. 5, the first layer of NTT operations in ML-DSA reveals that only two coefficient registers (e.g., ZMM0 and ZMM8) exhibit data dependencies during execution, while the remaining registers operate independently. Leveraging this feature, we could interleave operations of different coefficient registers, fully utilizing the parallel capabilities of the instruction pipeline and the out-of-order execution capabilities of modern processors.

Furthermore, we carefully considered the features of modern superscalar processors, aiming to utilize multiple execution units. By referencing [3,13], we ana-

Table 1. Instruction CPI on Different CPU platforms.

Instruction	CPI (Intel CPU)	CPI (AMD CPU)
vmovdqa32	0.5	0.5
vpaddw/vpsubw	0.5	0.25
vpaddd/vpsubd	0.5	0.25
vpmullw/vpmulhw	0.5/1.0	0.5
vpmuldq	0.5/1.0	0.5

lyzed the number of parallel execution units for vector instructions in modern CPUs. Table 1 lists the CPI (Cycles Per Instruction) values for key instructions frequently used in NTT operations across common CPU platforms. CPI reflects the average number of cycles required to execute the instruction. It also indirectly indicates the number of parallel execution units. Based on this data, we further optimized the instruction scheduling strategy. When the CPI value is small, it indicates more parallel execution units. In this case, we carefully arranged identical instructions together to fully utilize hardware resources. When the CPI value is large, we filled gaps between such instructions with other operations to prevent pipeline stalls. This strategy maximizes ILP, while also reducing time-window for adversaries. Besides, using assembly code directly allows us to avoid compiler-induced execution variations that could lead to security issues [16] naturally.

4.2 Hash Components

The SHAKE hash function serves as a core cryptographic primitive in both ML-KEM and ML-DSA, and its computational efficiency and security directly impact the overall performance and robustness of these algorithms. We thus applied *Vectorized Parallel Execution* strategies for optimizing the Keccak-1600 structure in SHAKE, focusing on enhancing parallel computation while mitigating timing-based side-channel risks.

By leveraging the 512-bit wide vector registers provided by AVX512, we can enable parallel processing of up to 8 independent hash operations within a single instruction cycle. The degree of parallelism is doubled compared to the AVX2 version, increasing from 4-way to 8-way. This optimization not only increases throughput but also reduces the total number of instructions required for the same amount hash operation. Fewer instructions mean a shorter execution time, which naturally narrows the time window available for adversaries to observe and exploit timing variations, thereby reducing the risk of timing-based side-channel attacks.

Additionally, our strategy helps to minimize data loading and storage latency by processing multiple data elements simultaneously within registers, reducing the frequency of memory accesses when doing hash operations, further mitigating the risk of cache-based side-channel attacks.

4.3 Matrix Expansion

In the implementation of matrix expansion, we applied *Branch Optimization* to eliminate complex conditional branches introduced by switch-case structures. The optimized implementation demonstrates superior programming practices by employing uniform execution paths across all operations. This design choice not only enhances code reliability but also eliminates performance fluctuations caused by conditional branch mispredictions.

By unrolling the switch-case operations, we achieve both more efficient compiler optimization potential and better parallel processing capabilities. Specifically, through branch optimization, we consolidate all polynomial sampling operations into a single unified function. This integrated approach processes the entire matrix by grouping polynomials in sets of eight, fully leveraging the parallel processing capabilities of AVX512 instructions. The implementation not only enhances execution consistency and stability, but also significantly reduces function call overhead. Therefore, this approach achieves improved performance for matrix expansion while showing a better coding paradigm that inherently reduces potential side-channel risks across all execution scenarios.

5 Evaluation

In this section, we conducted a comprehensive evaluation of the strategies implemented in PQMAGIC, focusing on security risk mitigation, performance improvements and practical applicability with a case study.

5.1 Experimental Setup

We evaluated PQMAGIC on an x64 platform featuring an AMD Ryzen 5 9600X processor and 256 GB RAM, with a Debian 12 OS. For our comparative evaluation, we conducted a comprehensive survey of existing implementations and identified: two state-of-the-art open-source libraries (pq-crystals [7,10] and liboqs [19]), as well as two recent works employing AVX-512 optimizations [20,21]. To ensure both reproducibility and fair comparison, we ultimately selected implementations with publicly available source code as our benchmark targets, i.e., the pq-crystals and liboqs libraries. From these libraries, we derived three datasets for evaluation:

- **pq-crystals-portable**: The baseline implementation from pq-crystals, representing an unoptimized version of ML-KEM and ML-DSA. Note that the commit versions we selected for these two algorithms are *4768bd37* and *444cdcc8* respectively.
- **pq-crystals-opt**: An optimized version from pq-crystals, leveraging AVX2 instructions to enhance performance. The commit versions for both ML-KEM and ML-DSA are the same as **pq-crystals-portable**.
- **liboqs**: A further refined version from liboqs, which integrates and encapsulates pq-crystals' implementations while providing additional component-level adjustments. The selected commit version is *5450d7c2*.

To maximize the performance of the comparison targets in our dataset, we compiled each project with the highest optimization level (-*O3*) and enabled architecture-specific optimizations by specifying -*march=native*. This compilation setting allows the compiler to fully utilize all available CPU instruction sets (including AVX-512) for optimal code generation.

Table 2. Comparison of Branch Operation Numbers in Matrix Expansion Function Across Libraries.

	pq-crystals-portable	pq-crystals-opt	liboqs	PQMAGIC
ML-DSA-44	2	1	1	1
ML-DSA-65	2	9	9	1
ML-DSA-87	2	11	11	1

5.2 Evaluation of Security Strategies in PQMAGIC

To validate the effectiveness of our optimization strategies, we designed to compare PQMAGIC's branch number in matrix expansion operation, total instruction number and memory operations against three implementations in our dataset.

Branch Reduction in Matrix Expansion. First, we compared the number of branches in the matrix expansion operation across all implementations. All code was compiled with the highest optimization flags (-*O3*, -*march=native*), and the resulting binaries were comprehensively reverse-engineered to count the branches in the matrix expansion operation. The results are shown in Table 2. PQMAGIC achieved the fewest branches: for ML-DSA-87 parameter set, the highest security level (L5), the branch count was reduced from 11 in both pq-crystals-opt and liboqs to just 1 in PQMAGIC. This reduction is attributed to the elimination of nested loops in the sampling process, which typically generate two branches. For the ML-DSA-65 parameter set, PQMAGIC reduced the branch count from 9 in pq-crystals-opt and liboqs to 1. For the ML-DSA-44 parameter set, compiler optimizations result in pq-crystals-opt and liboqs achieving a branch count of 1, matching PQMAGIC's performance in this regard. In contrast, the unoptimized pq-crystals-portable implementation retained 2 branches due to its nested loop structure. These results demonstrate that PQMAGIC's branch optimization strategy successfully minimizes branch counts, reducing the risk of timing side-channel attacks and improving execution stability by mitigating branch misprediction penalties.

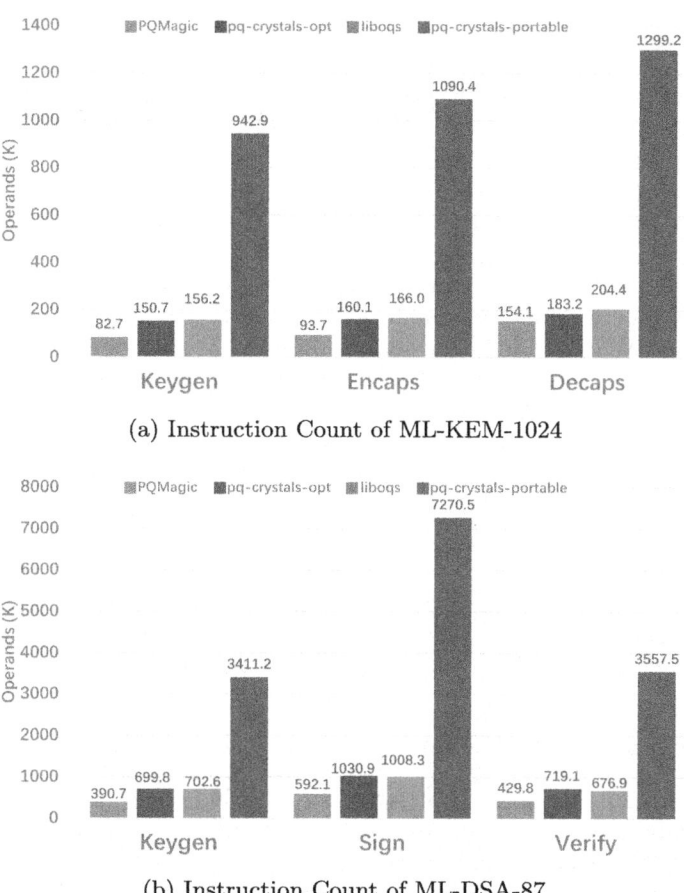

Fig. 6. Compare the number of instructions of PQMagic's implementation of ML-KEM and ML-DSA under the highest security parameters with other open source library implementations

Instruction Count and Memory Access Reduction. Then, we compared the number of instructions and memory access operations in PQMAGIC against the other implementations. To ensure fairness in testing, we fixed identical input values for all test cases, including random numbers, signed messages, and signature contexts. This design guarantees that each implementation performs the same operation routines.

Figures 6 and 7 shows the results for ML-KEM and ML-DSA at their highest security levels (L5). Compared to the performance-optimized pq-crystals-opt implementation, PQMAGIC reduced the instruction count for ML-KEM's

Keygen, Encaps, and Decaps operations by 45.1%, 41.5%, and 15.9%, respectively, while memory access overhead was reduced by 44.5%, 40.7% and 9.8%. Compared to liboqs, PQMAGIC achieved reductions of 47.1%, 43.6%, and 24.6% in instruction count and 60.1%, 56.9%, and 32.3% in memory access overhead for the same operations. Against the unoptimized pq-crystals-portable implementation, PQMAGIC reduced instruction counts by 91.2%, 91.4%, and 88.1%, and memory access overhead by 94.6%, 94.7%, and 92.2% for Keygen, Encaps, and Decaps respectively.

For ML-DSA, PQMAGIC outperformed pq-crystals-opt by reducing instruction counts for Keygen, Sign, and Verify operations by 44.2%, 42.6%, and 40.2%, respectively, and memory access overhead by 61.6%, 51.2%, and 64.5%. Compared to liboqs, PQMAGIC achieved reductions of 44.4%, 41.3%, and 36.5% in instruction count and 50.8%, 38.2%, and 50.9% in memory access overhead for Keygen, Sign, and Verify respectively. Against the unoptimized pq-crystals-portable implementation, PQMAGIC reduced instruction counts by 88.5%, 91.9%, and 87.9%, and memory access overhead by 90.0%, 92.7%, and 91.3% for each operation.

These results highlight that we lower the risk of data leakage through memory access patterns and minimize the time window available for adversarial observation. As a result, these strategies raise the bar for potential attackers, making it more challenging to exploit side-channel vulnerabilities.

5.3 Performance Analysis of ML-KEM Implementation

In the performance evaluation of the ML-KEM algorithm, we adopt the same testing methodology as described in Sect. 5.4. As illustrated in Fig. 8, PQMAGIC achieves significant performance improvements compared to other implementations. Against pq-crystals, PQMAGIC demonstrates speedups of 1.27x, 1.24x, and 1.19x in Keygen, Encaps, and Decaps operations, respectively. Compared to liboqs, PQMAGIC increase the performance by 1.77x, 1.79x, and 1.52x for the same operations. When compared to the unoptimized pq-crystals-portable implementation, PQMAGIC delivers even more substantial gains, with performance improvements of 8.05x, 7.83x, and 8.53x in Keygen, Encaps, and Decaps, respectively.

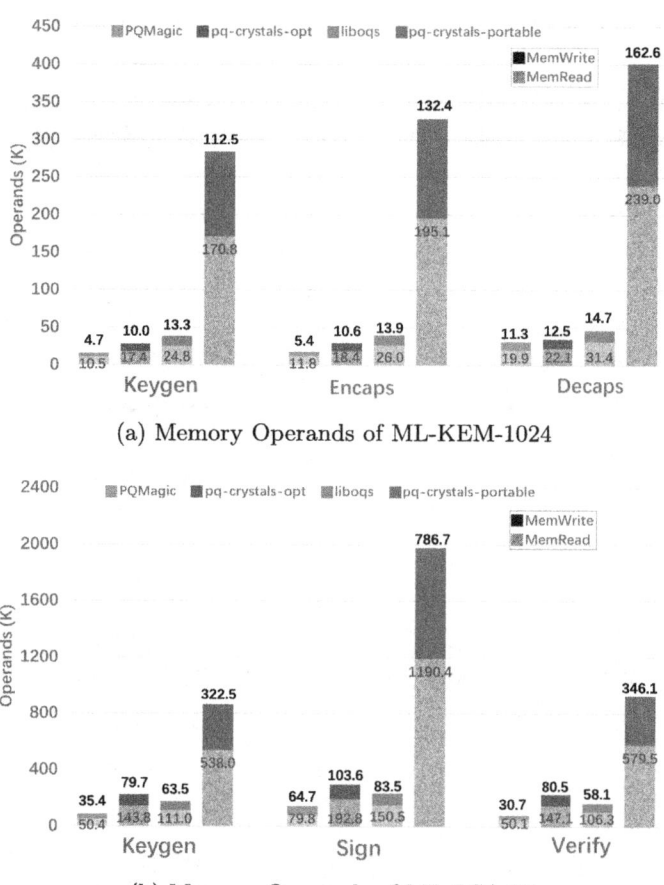

Fig. 7. Compare the number of memory operations of PQMagic's implementation of ML-KEM and ML-DSA under the highest security parameters with other open source library implementations

5.4 Performance Analysis of ML-DSA Implementation

In this section, we conduct a performance evaluation of the PQMAGIC ML-DSA implementation. We ran each benchmark binary within 3 s, recording the number of algorithm executions for each test. The results of the ML-DSA comparison with the highest level of security parameters [9] are shown in Fig. 8. The results demonstrate that PQMAGIC significantly outperforms other implementations. Compared to pq-crystals, PQMAGIC achieves performance improvements of approximately 1.90x in Keygen, 1.74x in Sign, and 1.83x in Verify. When compared to liboqs, PQMAGIC shows even greater gains, with speedups of 2.24x, 1.89x, and 2.04x for Keygen, Sign, and Verify, respectively. Against the

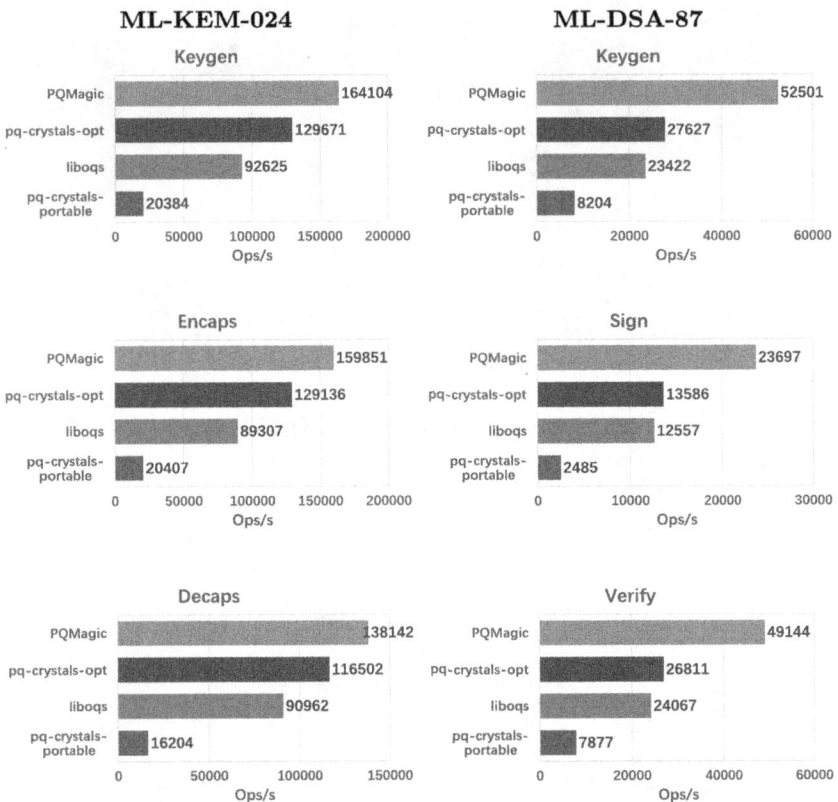

Fig. 8. Comparison of operations per second for PQMagic implementation of ML-KEM and ML-DSA at highest security parameters with other open source library implementations

unoptimized pq-crystals-portable implementation, PQMAGIC delivers remarkable improvements of 6.40x, 9.54x, and 6.24x for the same operations.

5.5 Case Study

Post-quantum cryptographic algorithms are inherently more complex than traditional cryptographic algorithms, inevitably introducing higher computational and storage overhead, which poses significant challenges for post-quantum cryptographic migration. To evaluate the contributions of PQMAGIC to post-quantum cryptographic migration, we designed the following experiments to assess the performance of the migrated algorithms.

We selected the widely used TLS 1.3 protocol to evaluate the impact of cryptographic algorithms on handshake performance and designed a simplified model for establishing secure connections. Specifically, this model retains only the core processes of key exchange and authentication while excluding external interference factors such as network latency and packet loss.

In our experiments, we simulated key exchange and authentication workflows using post-quantum cryptographic algorithms (ML-DSA + ML-KEM) and traditional algorithms (RSA-2048/ECDSA-256 + ECDH), conducting a comparative analysis between PQMAGIC implementations at L1/L3/L5 security levels and traditional algorithm implementations from the state-of-the-art library OpenSSL [15]. Note that, ML-DSA-44 is at L2 security level, while ML-KEM-512 only reaches L1. So, we treated ML-DSA-44 + ML-KEM-512 as the minimal security level of its components, i.e., L1. As shown in Fig. 9, the results demonstrate that PQMAGIC outperforms the RSA-2048 + ECDH combination across all security levels. At the L1 security level, PQMAGIC achieves a 4.77x efficiency improvement over RSA-2048 + ECDH. At the L3 and L5 security levels, the improvements are 3.25x and 2.67x, respectively. When compared to the more efficient ECDSA-256+ECDH combination, PQMAGIC still shows superior performance at the L1 and L3 security levels, with efficiency improvements of 1.58x and 1.07x, respectively. At the highest L5 security level, PQMAGIC's efficiency is slightly lower, at 0.88x compared to ECDSA-256 + ECDH.

Given that the L3 security level already meets NIST's recommended requirements and the performance gap at L5 is only 9 microseconds, these results highlight PQMAGIC's strong practicality and its potential to facilitate the transition to post-quantum cryptography.

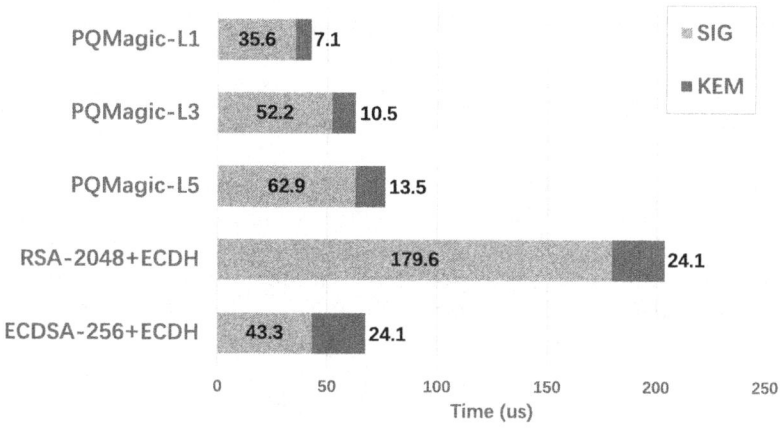

Fig. 9. The TLS 1.3 handshake latency of PQMagic post-quantum algorithm compared to traditional cryptographic algorithms

6 Related Work

The optimization of post-quantum cryptographic algorithms has been widely studied. Gueron et al. [11] proposed a vectorized sampling step for accelerating lattice-based key exchange, laying the groundwork for efficient implementations of post-quantum primitives. Seiler [17] introduced an AVX2-optimized implementation of the Number Theoretic Transform (NTT) for ring-LWE-based cryptography, which became a cornerstone for subsequent optimizations. These techniques were further adopted and extended in the pq-crystals library, which implemented the Kyber [7] and Dilithium [10] algorithms (later standardized as ML-KEM [5] and ML-DSA [9] by NIST) using AVX2 instructions for core operations.

Recent advancements have focused on leveraging the AVX512 instruction set for further optimizations. Lei et al. [14] proposed parallel polynomial sampling and arithmetic operations using AVX512, improving the efficiency of ML-DSA. Zheng et al. [21] introduced PSPM-TEE, an optimized vectorization approach for polynomial multiplication for ML-DSA. Besides that, Zheng et al. [20] also optimize ML-KEM using AVX512, integrating it into the TLS 1.3 protocol. However, these works did not fully exploit the capabilities of modern superscalar CPU pipelines or discuss potential security risks in their implementations.

7 Conclusion

In this paper, we first identify several security issues in existing PQC implementations, which also fail to fully leverage the resource advantages of modern CPUs to enhance performance. To address these issues, we propose four optimization strategies that reduce branch counts, instruction counts, and memory access operations. Based on these optimization strategies, we implement PQMAGIC, demonstrating that it not only achieves lower security risks compared to state-of-the-art implementations but also delivers superior performance. Notably, PQMAGIC even surpasses the execution efficiency of traditional cryptographic algorithms, showcasing its strong practicality and providing robust support for the transition to post-quantum cryptography.

While our optimization approach delivers significant performance gains, it has inherent limitations regarding portability and maintainability. The AVX-512 dependency limits portability to other architectures, and assembly codes reduce code readability. These trade-offs make our approach best suited for performance-critical scenarios with fixed hardware targets.

Acknowledgments. The authors would like to thank the reviewers for their valuable feedback. This work was partially supported by Shanghai Science and Technology Innovation Action Plan Special Project (23511100900).

References

1. Abdulrahman, A., Becker, H., Kannwischer, M.J., Klein, F.: Fast and clean: auditable high-performance assembly via constraint solving. IACR Trans. Cryptographic Hardware Embed. Syst. **2024**(1), 87–132 (2024)
2. Abdulrahman, A., Kannwischer, M.J., Lim, T.H.: Enabling microarchitectural agility: taking ml-kem & ml-dsa from cortex-m4 to m7 with slothy. Cryptology ePrint Archive (2025)
3. Abel, A., Reineke, J.: Uops info. http://www.uops.info, Accessed 13 Mar 2025
4. Abel, A., Reineke, J.: uops. info: Characterizing latency, throughput, and port usage of instructions on intel microarchitectures. In: Proceedings of the Twenty-Fourth International Conference on Architectural Support for Programming Languages and Operating Systems, pp. 673–686 (2019)
5. Alagic, G., Dang, Q., Moody, D., Robinson, A., Silberg, H., Smith-Tone, D., et al.: Module-lattice-based key-encapsulation mechanism standard (2024)
6. Blessing, J., Specter, M.A., Weitzner, D.J.: Cryptography in the wild: an empirical analysis of vulnerabilities in cryptographic libraries. In: Proceedings of the 19th ACM Asia Conference on Computer and Communications Security, pp. 605–620 (2024)
7. Bos, J., et al.: Crystals-kyber: a cca-secure module-lattice-based kem. In: 2018 IEEE European Symposium on Security and Privacy (EuroS&P), pp. 353–367. IEEE (2018)
8. Cohen, B., Subramony, M., Clark, M.: Next generation "zen 5" core. In: 2024 IEEE Hot Chips 36 Symposium (HCS), pp. 1–27. IEEE (2024)
9. Dang, T., et al.: Module-lattice-based digital signature standard (2024)
10. Ducas, L., et al.: Crystals-dilithium: a lattice-based digital signature scheme. In: IACR Transactions on Cryptographic Hardware and Embedded Systems, pp. 238–268 (2018)
11. Gueron, S., Schlieker, F.: Speeding up r-lwe post-quantum key exchange. In: Nordic Conference on secure IT Systems, pp. 187–198. Springer (2016)
12. Intel: Intel 64 and ia-32 architectures optimization reference manual. https://www.intel.com/content/www/us/en/content-details/821612/intel-64-and-ia-32-architectures-optimization-reference-manual-volume-1.html, Accessed 13 Mar 2025
13. Intel: Intel intrinsics guide. https://www.intel.com/content/www/us/en/docs/intrinsics-guide/index.html, Accessed 13 Mar 2025
14. Lei, D., He, D., Peng, C., Luo, M., Liu, Z., Huang, X.: Faster implementation of ideal lattice-based cryptography using avx512. ACM Trans. Embed. Comput. Syst. **22**(5), 1–18 (2023)
15. OpenSSL: Openssl. https://github.com/openssl/openssl, Accessed 13 Mar 2025
16. Schneider, M., Lain, D., Puddu, I., Dutly, N., Capkun, S.: Breaking bad: how compilers break constant-time⁻ implementations. arXiv preprint arXiv:2410.13489 (2024)
17. Seiler, G.: Faster avx2 optimized ntt multiplication for ring-lwe lattice cryptography. Cryptology ePrint Archive (2018)
18. Singh, T., et al.: "zen 5": the amd high-performance 4nm x86-64 microprocessor core. In: 2025 IEEE International Solid-State Circuits Conference (ISSCC), vol. 68, pp. 1–3. IEEE (2025)

19. Stebila, D., Mosca, M.: Post-quantum key exchange for the internet and the open quantum safe project. In: Avanzi, R., Heys, H. (eds.) Selected Areas in Cryptography (SAC) 2016, LNCS, vol. 10532, pp. 1–24. Springer, October 2017, https://openquantumsafe.org
20. Zheng, J., et al.: Faster post-quantum tls 1.3 based on ml-kem: implementation and assessment. In: European Symposium on Research in Computer Security, pp. 123–143. Springer (2024)
21. Zheng, J., Zhu, H., Song, Z., Wang, Z., Zhao, Y.: Optimized vectorization implementation of crystals-dilithium. arXiv preprint arXiv:2306.01989 (2023)

Stateless Hash-Based Signatures for Post-Quantum Security Keys

Ruben Gonzalez[1,2](✉)

[1] Neodyme AG, München, Germany
mail@ruben-gonzalez.de
[2] Max Planck Institute for Security and Privacy, Bochum, Germany

Abstract. The U.S. National Institute of Standards and Technology (NIST) recently standardized the first set of post-quantum cryptography algorithms. Two of the three NIST-selected signature algorithms are lattice based, offering good performance but posing challenges due to complex implementation and intricate security assumptions. A more conservative choice for quantum-safe authentication are hash-based signature systems, such as the also-standardized SLH-DSA, which is based on the SPHINCS+ construction. However, due to large signature sizes and low signing speeds, hash-based systems have only found use in niche applications. In this work we combine different approaches to show that the SPHINCS+ signature system can be optimized in its parameters and implementation to be high performing, even when signing in an embedded setting. We demonstrate this in the context of user authentication using hardware security keys within FIDO and show that our SPHINCS+-based implementation can outperform lattice-based solutions from the literature while remaining highly portable. Due to conservative security assumptions, it does not require a hybrid construction and can be used as a drop-in replacement to perform authentication on current security keys. For reproducibility and to encourage further research, we publish our implementation and a framework for benchmarking tailored SPHINCS+ instantiations on Cortex-M4 MCUs.

Keywords: PQC · SPHINCS+ · Hash · LWC · FIDO

1 Introduction

Shor's algorithm [51] and recent advances in quantum computing [18,20] jeopardize the security of most widely used asymmetric cryptosystems. In response to this growing threat, researchers and standardization bodies have worked together to find suitable post-quantum cryptography (PQC) algorithms. The U.S. National Institute of Standards and Technology (NIST) has recently standardized one key encapsulation mechanism (KEM) and three digital signature systems with post-quantum security. Two out of three of these standardized signature schemes rely on lattice-based constructions. That is not surprising, as lattice-based signatures offer high performance at comparatively small key and signature size. However, trust in these lattice-based PQC algorithms grows only slowly due to their novelty, complexity and tangled security assumptions [16,25]. Consequently, lattice-based algorithms are usually deployed in so-called *hybrid* mode, combining them with pre-quantum algorithms to ensure continued security against both classical and quantum adversaries. A class of PQC algorithms that do not suffer from this lack of trust are hash-based constructions [42]. In fact, the only NIST standardized PQC algorithm that isn't based on structured-lattice constructions is the hash-based SLH-DSA signature system [45]. SLH-DSA is an instantiation of the SPHINCS+ signature framework [13]. A major drawback of SPHINCS+ is its slow signing speed and very large signature size. This seems to make it a rather poor choice for many applications, especially for applications that require signing in resource-constraint environments. On the other hand, hash-based systems offer the possibility of using PQC without hybrid constructions, reducing complexity and resource overhead.

In this work we adjust SPHINCS+, by carefully tuning its parameters and primitives, for a use case it might seem unfit for: FIDO. FIDO (Fast Identity Online) is an authentication standard for endusers, designed to avoid reliance on passwords and defeat phishing [1]. We demonstrate that a SPHINCS+ signature system can be instantiated for use in a resource constrained FIDO security key, adhering tough resource and time constrains. We further compare the performance and resource consumption of our implementation to previous FIDO experiments employing lattice-based hybrid PQC constructions and show that our SPHINCS+-based solution can outperform them.

Our contributions are:

- We show that SPHINCS+ signature systems can be instantiated to perform well in embedded settings that require signing and relatively short signatures, even outperforming lattice-based PQC systems. We compare the performance to results previously acquired in the same setting (FIDO authentication) and on the same hardware (the nRF52840 development board). Furthermore, we show that in contrast to previous work utilizing lattice-based schemes, no complex implementation-level optimization tricks or hybrid constructions are necessary for this resource constrained environment.
- We release a Client to Authenticator Protocol (CTAP) implementation for use in FIDO, based on Google's OpenSK, employing various adjusted SPHINCS+ instantiations. The released code package includes a framework for systematically testing and benchmarking custom SPHINCS+ instantiations on Cortex-M4. For portability and compatibility with OpenSK, the code is written in Rust. As part of the experiments conducted, the hardware-based hash accelerator (CryptoCell 310) was used for comparison, but is not necessary to achieve the documented results. The released code can therefore be used across platforms.
- We further release a tool for quickly identifying suitable SPHINCS+ parameter sets for specific requirements, such as speed or signature size.

1.1 Related Work

Post-Quantum FIDO Implementation. In [28] Ghinea et al. implement CTAP using the, now standardized [47], lattice-based CRYSTALS-Dilithium signature system for FIDO-based authentication. Their work implements a hybrid approach using the post-quantum Dilithium and pre-quantum ECDSA algorithms. The authors chose Dilithium over the other now standardized PQC signature systems Falcon and SPHINCS+ for three reasons: speed, complexity and size. Dilithium has a much faster key generation than Falcon. This is relevant in CTAP, as the keys have to be generated on the embedded device. Additionally, Dilithium has a less complex implementation than Falcon as it does not rely on floating-point arithmetic. SPHINCS+ was not chosen for their experiment due to large signature sizes and poor signing performance. To reduce required storage space their implementation does not actually save a private key, but a small 32 byte seed that can be used to compute the private key on the fly. Moreover, they invest significant engineering effort to tweak their Dilithium implementation to recompute certain parts of the private key and intermediate results during every signing operation. This is done to reduce Dilithium's memory footprint, trading worse runtime for reduced memory consumption similar to [17]. In their paper they also introduce requirements for runtime, memory consumption and message size within a FIDO security key setting. In our work we adhere to these requirements, making a direct comparison possible. As both implementations are based on OpenSK, we could reuse parts of their setup in our experiments.

SHPINCS+ Instantiations and Optimization. SPHINCS+ was submitted to the NIST PQC competition in 2017 [13]. Since 2024 it is standardized in the Federal Information Processing Standard (FIPS) 205 under the name SLH-DSA. As over 90% of computation in SPHINCS+ is spend inside the underlying hash function [36], most research has focused on optimizing that hash function e.g. in hardware [40,50]. Karl et al. recently analysed the impact of hardware-accelerated SPHINCS+ and reviewing possible architectures for such hardware [37]. The authors also include estimates of communication costs for using such hardware acceleration. In this work we complement that study, as we use hardware acceleration for a hash primitive. In another paper, Kölbl and Philipoom take note of the possibility to tweak SPHINCS+ parameter sets for custom use cases [38]. They show that SPHINCS+ signature sizes and verification speeds can be drastically reduced if the maximum amount of allowed signings per private key is reduced. While NIST mandated that 2^{64} signatures should be possible for a single private key without compromising security [46], this threshold is unnecessarily high for many use cases. Based on this, Kölbl and Philipoom present a SPHINCS+ parameterization that allows for fast verification on embedded devices and offers relatively short signatures. They show experimentally, that this enables firmware verification using SPHINCS+ on an embedded device. Their parameters maintain compatibility to SLH-DSA, except for the requirement of allowed signatures per private key. The allowed signatures per key are drastically reduced to 2^{10} or 2^{20}, which is more than enough for firmware signing. Our work complements their work in the sense that it also approaches an embedded use case for which SPHINCS+ seems unfit at first sight. However, their work focuses exclusively on verification on an embedded device, which is arguably the much easier problem for SPHINCS+. They further state: *"Compared to other post-quantum signature schemes like Dilithium, the signing speed will always be significantly worse"*. Our work tackles this more difficult case of key generation and signing within the embedded device.

2 Background

This section details the background needed to understand the implementation and results. First we describe FIDO, a widely-used, signature-based user authentication standard. We then detail the necessary background on PQC and hash-based signatures in particular.

2.1 FIDO-Based Authentication

The FIDO2 standard defines a signature-based and phishing-resistant user authentication mechanism. It can be used for single or second-factor authentication. As FIDO2 is a vast standard, this section details only its aspects relevant for this work. Within FIDO, users authenticate themselves by signing login data. For that purpose the user stores a public key in the application upon registration. During registration, the user either stores only the public key in the application, this is referred to as *resident key*[1] setting, or the symmetrically encrypted private key alongside it, which is referred to as *non-resident key* setting. Specifically, the FIDO standard explicitly allows to include the encrypted private key into metadata stored in the application. Figure 1 shows the high-level difference between the two options during authentication.

An advantage of the *non-resident key* setting is that the private key (amongst other metadata) does not need to be stored on the user's side. This is very relevant as FIDO otherwise requires the private keys to be stored in *secure storage* within a trusted platform module (TPM) [1], where storage is sparse and expensive. The main advantage of the *resident key* setting is that it allows for username-less authentication, as the TPM holds a table with user ID (*User Handle*), application domain (*Relying Party ID*) and private key. The downside of *resident key* is that it requires *secure storage* on the user's side for every application the user registered. FIDO defines three communication parties for authentication: authenticator, client and the relying party. The client is an application connecting the authenticator and the relying party, usually a web browser or operating system. The relying party is the application that requires authentication. The authenticator securely stores the user's key material and signs authentication requests. Authenticators communicate only with the client. They

---

[1] The FIDO standard now refers to *resident key* as *"discoverable credential"*. However, as much of the literature and code still refer to *resident key*, we retain that term.

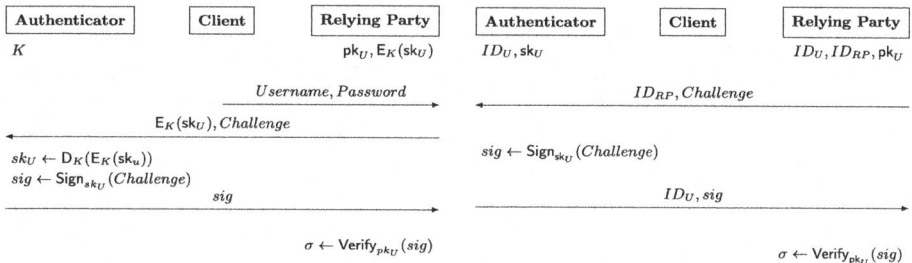

Fig. 1. Simplified protocol flow diagrams of FIDO instantiations of *non-resident key* (left) and the *resident key* (right) authentication. K denotes the symmetric encryption key stored inside the authenticator, sk_U and pk_U the users private and public key, ID_U, ID_{RP} the user's and relying party's IDs. Authentication succeeds if $\sigma = 1$.

do so via CTAP, the Client to Authenticator Protocol, which is a part of the FIDO standard. Authenticators can be either roaming (external device) or bound (internal device). Roaming authenticators are allowed to communicate via Bluetooth, NFC or USB.

2.2 Post-Quantum Cryptography

NIST recognized the quantum threat in 2015 and soon after launched a multiyear standardization effort to identify so called post-quantum cryptography schemes for key encapsulation and digital signatures [46]. In 2022 NIST slected one key encapsulation mechanism and three signature algorithms for standardization. Table 1 shows the selected signature algorithms with their claimed security level, key, signatures sizes and performance on a Cortex-M4 embedded processor [36]. The table reveals that post-quantum cryptography is much more expensive than its state-of-the-art pre-quantum counterpart: keys and signatures are much larger and operations require more computational time. Memory limitations can also be problematic for PQC [36], which is of course especially relevant for embedded use cases where bandwidth, storage, memory and CPU time are sparse. A suitable choice in algorithm is therefore integral for FIDO security keys.

Post-Quantum Adoption. The three standardized PQC signature algorithms rely on different assumptions. Dilithium's [22] and Falcon [26]'s security claims are based on the difficulty of solving large instances of structured-lattice problems. These claims are much discussed and sometimes contested in the academic discourse [14,15,21]. Because of these debates and the novelty of the algorithms, most implementers, such as Google [30], Cloudflare [52], Signal [39] or Apple [24], chose to use lattice-based PQC only in conjunction with a pre-quantum algorithm. This ensures that even if the PQC algorithm contains a major flaw, a pre-quantum attacker will not be able to exploit the system. Combining pre- and

Table 1. Comparison of NIST PQC signature algorithms selected for standardization. The timings refer to the non-optimized, hence portable, reference implementation taken from PQM4 [36] running on a Cortex-M4. The table is divided into security level I, III and V, as defined by NIST. The listed algorithms claim **at least** the security level detailed. SPHINCS+ benchmarks use the SHAKE256 extendable output function (XOF) as hash primitive.

	Sizes (bytes)			Computation ($\approx$Kcycles)		
	privkey	pubkey	signature	keygen	sign	verify
Level I $\approx$ **AES128**						
Ed25519[a]	32	32	64	200	240	720
Dilithium2	2 528	1 312	2 420	1 874	7 925	2 063
Falcon-512	1 281	897	666	229 742	62 255	834
SPHINCS+-128	64	32	17 088	50 505	1 182 422	70 501
Level III $\approx$ **AES192**						
Dilithium3	4 000	1 952	3 293	3 205	12 359	3 377
SPHINCS+-192	96	48	35 664	74 890	1 937 690	103 305
Level V $\approx$ **AES256**						
Dilithium5	4 864	2 592	4 595	5 341	15 579	5 610
Falcon-1024	1 281	1 793	1 280	602 066	136 241	1 678
SPHINCS+-256	128	64	49 856	200 110	4 026 533	108 394

[a] Pre-Quantum algorithm for comparison. Benchmarks taken from Owens et al. [49].

post-quantum algorithms into so-called *hybrid constructions* is therefore quite common. However, also *hybrid constructions* are debated. Famously, in 2022 the Natioal Security Agency (NSA) even stated that it *"does not expect to approve"* hybrid constructions for national security citing complexity, interoperability and maintenance concerns [48].

SPHINCS+, on the other hand is *hash based* and its security is solely based on well-understood assumptions of the utilized hash primitive [32]. As these assumptions are easier to analyze than their structured-lattice counterparts and since hash-based cryptography has been studied since the early 1970s, it does not seem to suffer from the same trust issues. Exemplary of this is the French Cybersecurity Agency's (ANSSI) position paper on PQC, stating *"any product that includes post-quantum mitigation shall implement hybridation except if the quantum mitigation only relies on hash-based signatures like [...] SPHINCS+ [...]"* [12]. The German Federal Office for Information Security (BSI) comes to the same conclusion [34]. The downsides of SPHINCS+ are apparent in Table 1. Signing is slow and signatures are large, which is especially problematic for embedded use cases.

2.3 SPHINCS+

Hash-based signature schemes were first described as One Time Signature (OTS) schemes by Lamport in 1979 [42] and further refined by Winternitz the same year [44]. Lamport's scheme relies solely on the properties of the employed one-way function at the expense of being *"one time"*. This means that every private/public key pair can only by used once, as parts of the private key are revealed in the signature. Merkle built up on Lamport's idea by using hash trees to administer multiple OTS public keys under a common root node [44]. This comes at the expense of larger signatures, as the *authentication path* between OTS public key, which is a leaf node, and the root node has to be included. Much more problematic, however, is that a global state has to be kept per key. Maintaining the correct state globally is very challenging and often times impossible, which is why *stateful hash-based signature systems* have mainly seen adoption in niche applications [43]. Using stateful hash-based signature in FIDO is not an option, as the *non-resident key* authenticator does not hold a state and would have to trust the relying party to not send him a previously used state. In its call for PQC schemes, NIST explicitly called for *stateless* contributions, excluding the otherwise already quantum secure stateful hash based signature schemes.

SPHINCS+ is a *stateless* hash-based signature scheme. It's built mainly on the ideas of the Extended Merkle Signature Scheme (XMSS) [19]. Both rely on the Winternitz One-Time Signature Plus (WOTS+) [31] OTS scheme. Just as XMSS, SPHINCS+ relies on a binary hash tree at its core. However, to become *stateless*, SPHINCS+ needs to have a hash tree so enormous, that choosing a leaf node (private/public key pair) at random is sufficient to exclude any realistic possibility of key reuse. To accomplish this, two tricks are used. First, a so-called *"hypertree"* is utilized. This hypertee contains several layers of XMSS binary hash trees. Each hash tree root within the hypertree is used to authenticate the hypertrees below it. The trees of the lowest hypertee level have key pairs associated to their leaf nodes. This is equivalent to the approach described for multi-tree XMSS in [33]. The novel idea behind SPHINCS+ is to drastically reduce the hypertree's size by authenticating few time signature (FTS) instead of OTS key pairs in its leaf nodes. SPHINCS+ utilizes the Forest of Random Subsets (FORS) FTS for this purpose. Reusing a FORS key pair decreases security only gradually, instead of immediately as in OTS schemes. FORS uses its own tree structure, containing sets of private keys in its leaf nodes for that purpose. As authentication paths shrink due to the much smaller hypertree, using FORS allows for much better signature sizes without impacting security. The exact inner workings of WOTS, XMSS and FORS are detailed in the SPHINCS+ NIST submission [13]. The subprimitives, WOTS+, hypertree and FORS allow SPHINCS+ to be stateless, but they also offer many options for parameterization. As the SPHINCS+ NIST submission states *"SPHINCS+ can be viewed as a signature template. It is a way to build a signature scheme [...]."*.

SPHINCS+ Parameters. SPHINCS+ instantiations can be fine tuned using six parameters:

- n: The security parameter. Refers to virtually all hash function input, output and tree node sizes in bytes. Commonly used values are 16, 24 and 32 reflecting NIST security levels I, III and V.
- w: The Winternitz parameter specifying how often a message is split during encoding for WOTS+. This does not impact security.
- h: The overall height (layers of nodes) of the hypertree.
- d: Number of layers of subtrees in the hypertree.
- k: Number of trees per FORS public key.
- t: Number of leaves in a FORS tree.

The Winternitz parameter (w) and number of hypertree layers (d) only specify performance tradeoffs. Larger values of w lead to shorter signatures, but more hash function invocations. The number of subtree layers (d) is proportional to the signature size, but inversely proportional to the number of hash function invocation during key generation and signing. All remaining parameters are security relevant. Optimizing these parameters therefore has to be done with caution. The generic quantum security level (bit security) of SPHINCS+ is captured in (1) [13]:

$$b = -\frac{1}{2}\log\left(\frac{1}{2^{8n}} + \sum_{\gamma}\left(1 - \left(1 - \frac{1}{t}\right)^{\gamma}\right)^{k}\binom{q}{\gamma}\left(1 - \frac{1}{2^h}\right)^{q-\gamma}\frac{1}{2^{h\gamma}}\right) \quad (1)$$

The equation ties together all configurable, security-critical parameters with the maximum number of signatures that can securely be produced using the scheme (q) and the number of times an FTS key pair would have to be reused before security is degrading (γ). From the equation it is clear that reducing the maximum allowed number of signatures per SPHINCS+ key pair (q) greatly affects the possibility to further optimize security-relevant parameters. To make equations more concise, we further specify the values $h' = \frac{h}{d}$ as the height of an XMSS tree within the hypertree and l as the number of n-bytes elements in a WOTS+ private key which solely depends on w with $l = \lfloor \frac{\log(\lceil \frac{8n}{log(w)} \rceil (w-1))}{\log(w)} \rfloor + 1$.

SPHINCS+ Runtime. The aforementioned parameters affect runtime, size and security. More than 90% of the SPHINCS+ runtime is spent inside the hash primitive [36]. Reducing the number of hash-function calls should therefore be a prime objective for optimizing SPHINCS+ instantiations to our use case. The number of hash-function calls for key generation and signing are given in (2) and (3).

$$\#_{\text{KeyGen}} = 2^{h/d}(lw + l + 2) - 1 \quad (2)$$

$$\#_{\text{Sign}} = d\left(2^{h/d}(lw + l + 2) - 1\right) + k(3t - 1) \quad (3)$$

It is important to note here, that these equations specify the number of computed hash values. The number of consumed bytes per hash function call, and

Table 2. Key and signature sizes for SPHINCS+.

	Private Key	Public Key	Signature
Bytes	$4n$	$2n$	$n(h + k(\log t + 1) + dl + 1)$

hence the number of round/compression function invocations are not reflected. These numbers, while performance relevant, depend on the employed hash function and are therefore further discussed in Sect. 4. However, as we will see, the number of computed hash values provides a good enough estimate for runtime.

SPHINCS+ Key and Signature Sizes. CPU time, bandwidth and storage are a concern when using PQC schemes. SPHINCS+ comes with very competitive key sizes, but large signatures. A SPHINCS+ public key contains the n-byte hypertree root and an n-byte seed needed for deterministic computation of tree elements. The private key contains the public key as well as an n-byte seed for WOTS and FORS private key generation and an n-byte random value needed for randomization in message hashing. The signature contains a randomness value (n bytes), a FORS signature consisting of FORS leaves with their associated authentications paths ($nk(\log t + 1)$ bytes) and an XMSS-like signature containing WOTS+ signatures and corresponding authentication paths ($dn(l + h')$ bytes). Table 2 shows the overall length of keys and signatures given these parameters. From the table it becomes apparent that the overall signature size depends on hypertree height (h), number of hypertree layers (d), number of FORS trees (k) and leaves (t) as well as the Winternitz length parameter (l).

3 Implementation

This section details our implementation of a USB-based CTAP authenticator for use in FIDO, employing PQC signatures in the form of adjusted SPHINCS+ signatures. To allow for comparison of results we use the same hardware and software stack as in the work of Ghinea et al. [28]. We use the nRF52840 development kit [10] with a Cortex-M4F MCU running at 32 MHz. As in [28], we limit our implementation to 64kB of RAM and keep it generic enough to be easily portable to other platforms. In contrast to Ghinea et al., we also employ the nRF52850's cryptography hardware accelerator CryptoCell 310 [11]. However, the CryptoCell is only used for comparison and not required by the implementation. Benchmarks were conducted using the experimental OpenSK [5] security key firmware CTAP2 implementation. OpenSK is based on the TockOS [6] embedded operating system. Our SPHINCS+ implementation is based on the C reference implementation. To benchmark within the OpenSK/TockOS environment, we wrote a SPHINCS+ wrapper for the Rust programming language. All major components, such as OpenSK, TockOS and the SPHINCS+ wrapper are written in Rust and published under a permissive license. A repository[2] with

---

[2] Located at: https://github.com/rugo/fido-sphincs-experiments/tree/acns-sci.

benchmarking framework, helper scripts and Rust code is published for reproducibility and to encourage further research. Both *resident* and *non-resident key* scenarios are supported in our implementation. As our SPHINCS+ approach is not a hybrid solution and has very short keys, changes to the OpenSK CTAP implementation are limited to including SPHINCS+ and adding a new algorithm identifier.

3.1 Requirements

For comparability we follow the requirements described in [28]. These requirements stem from the FIDO specification [3]:

- User presence and user verification tokens usually timeout after 30 s, but are guaranteed to be valid for at least 10 s.
- The size of a CTAP message over USB cannot exceed 7609 bytes.

We therefore aim for commands to finish within 10 s and CTAP messages smaller than 7609 bytes. The latter limit stems from the fact that CTAP2 uses a *signed char* (7-bit) value as its length field. Allowing for larger messages (and hence larger signatures) would be a trivial change in the OpenSK firmware. Changing the length field to an *unsigned char* (8 bit) allows for a payload/message size of 15 161 bytes [1]. For completeness we also include SPHINCS+ instantiations with signatures larger than the CTAP payload maximum in the results, but mark them explicitly as non-compliant. From this we follow priorities as in [28]:

R1 Key generation must finish in less than 10 s.
R2 Key pairs must be smaller than 7 kB.
R3 The private key should be small to allow storing additional credentials.
A1 The login operation is more frequent than registration. Signing should be as fast as possible.
A2 A private key and signature together must fit into a CTAP message.

As [28], we further limit ourselves to 64 kB of RAM and require our implementation to be as portable as the underlying CTAP implementation written in Rust. The NIST-submitted SPHINCS+ parameter sets all fail to achieve A1 and A2. Key generation (R1) and key sizes (R2 & R3) however aren't a problem. Our FIDO adjusted SPHINCS+ instantiations should therefore optimize signing speed and signature size.

Side Channel Resilience. Just as in [28], we follow the attacker model described in FIDO's security assumptions [4]. We assume the FIDO client to be trustworthy and acting in the user's interest. This is a necessary requirement for FIDO anyway. Local attacks, such as fault injection [27] or power side-channel attacks [35] on SPHINCS+, are therefore out of scope. We only consider timing-based side channels that could be triggered remotely. Here it is important to note that SPHINCS+ is constant time via its construction [13]. Time-based side channels therefore do not take specific effors to be mitigated.

3.2 Adjusting SPHINCS+

Given the lowest acceptable security level I, the public and private key are only 32 and 64 bytes large respectively and could be used as a drop-in replacement for elliptic curve keys [8] without the need for alterations in e.g. database columns of the relying party. Therefore, only signature size (A2) and signing speed (A1) have to be optimized using Eqs. (1), (2) and (3). A core variable to tune our SPHINCS+ parameter sets is the number of allowed signatures per SPHINCS+ private key q. Reducing q affects security as defined in (1) and further detailed in [13] and [38]. The NIST-submitted parameter sets allow, by NIST specification, for $q = 2^{64}$ signatures per key. Given a user performing one authentication per relying party per day, such a key could be used for far more than a trillion (10^{12}) years, which is clearly overkill. Similar to the approach in [38] we therefore lower the maximum amount of allowed signatures to a more realistic level.

Adjusting the Number of Allowed Signatures. In our analysis we allow for $q = 2^8$, $q = 2^{10}$ and $q = 2^{16}$ signatures/authentications. FIDO seems to be a good choice for reducing this number, as every signature has to be approved manually (usually with a tap) by the user. A scenario with real-time constraints or a high volume of signatures can be ruled out. Additionally, FIDO-based authentication is commonly connected to applications with long-running sessions. Google web sessions for example last for 14 days by default [7], Cloudflare's for 3 [2], Microsoft's for 5 (Sharepoint) to 90 (Entra) days [9]. For simplicity we assume a somewhat worst case with respect to the key duration, where a user authenticates to the same relying party every day. Even with the lowest setting of $q = 2^8 = 256$, this user could authenticate using the same key for approximately every workday in a year. After this key expires, a new key would have to be registered. For the user that would mean tapping the authenticator once more during authentication, which is quite cheap. For the best-case scenario with authenticating to Google every 14 days, the same key could be used for around 10 years. With an authentication every day, the settings $q = 2^{10}$ and $q = 2^{16}$ would delay re-registering by around 3 and 180 years respectively. Table 3 shows how different settings in q would affect the key lifetimes when used with popular FIDO-ready applications. To store the number of computed signatures, the *"signCount"* variable already included in the FIDO standard [4] can be employed in the implementation.

Adjusting Parameters. To optimize the parameters discussed in Sect. 2.3 we follow a similar approach to Kölbl et al. [38], but optimize for signing speed and signature size instead of verification speed. We employ an explorative approach and built a tool inspired by the SAGE script included in the SPHINCS+ NIST submission package [13]. This leads to a multitude of parameters with different tradeoffs further discussed in Sect. 4.1.

Table 3. SPHINCS+ key lifetimes based on common session expiration times of popular web services supporting FIDO. Lifetimes are presented in years based on the number of allowed signature q.

q	Google	Sharepoint	Cloudflare	Daily
2^8	9.8	3.5	2.1	0.7
2^{10}	39.3	14	8.4	2.8
2^{16}	2,513.7	897.7	538.7	179.6

Adjusting Hash Functions. The SPHINCS+ NIST submission includes SHA256, SHAKE256 and Haraka instantiations. Haraka is an AES-based construct optimized for use in x86 CPU architectures with AES-NI extension. On our embedded platform Haraka leads to much runtime overhead and was therefore not investigated further. Additionally to SHA256 and SHAKE256, the ASCON hash primitive was used in benchmarks. ASCON is a lightweight hash function scheduled for standardization by NIST. We employed the ASCON C reference implementation. The CryptoCell 310 hardware accelerator on our evaluation board supports the SHA256 hash function. For comparison, SHA256 was benchmarked in both hard and software.

4 Results

In this section we first culminate all previous considerations into adjusted SPHINCS+ instantiations for FIDO-friendly values of q. We then benchmark different hash functions relevant to our construction and compare hardware SHA256 to its software version. Next, we present benchmarks to the FIDO-relevant operations *KeyGen* and *Sign* as well as the FIDO operations *MakeCredential* and *GetCredential*. All benchmarks are then discussed and compared to previous work on the same platform.

4.1 SPHINCS+ Instantiations

To fulfill the requirements detailed in Sect. 3.1, we utilized our parameter discovery tool. We filtered parameter choices that could lead to a good speed/size tradeoff. The filter starts by sorting all parameter choices by signature size. It then calculates the number of computed hashes and selects a new parameter set if the number of computed hashes is smaller than that of the previously selected. It then outputs a list of all selected parameter sets. The output shows that level I instantiations offer signature sizes lower than the previously described CTAP USB message size limit. For level III and V there also exist parameter choices with small enough signatures to fit this limit. However, as they require significantly more hash computations and increasing the message size limit is a technical triviality (see Sect. 3.1), the increased message size was set as threshold for them. The value $q = 2^8$ offers only very marginal improvement over $q = 2^{10}$.

Table 4. Cycles spent calculating the minimum amount of hashes required for signing in a given security level. Numbers are given in kilocycles (10^3), averaged over 1000 runs when compiled with *-O3*.

Level	SHA256 (soft)	SHA256 (hard)	ASCON	SHAKE256
I	93 268	130 997	197 534	488 680
III	209 141	293 743	442 940	1 095 792
V	283 664	398 413	600 774	1 486 258

Using $q = 2^{10}$ therefore seems like a good tradeoff for FIDO. However, we benchmark all relevant choices of $q = \{2^8, 2^{10}, 2^{16}\}$ for completeness. Larger signatures lead to fewer hash calculations but also longer transmission times during FIDO authentication.

4.2 Hash Functions

SPHINCS+ spends the vast majority of its CPU time inside the hash function. Choosing an appropriate hash function for our use case is therefore integral for performance. SPHINCS+, as submitted to NIST, employs the secure SHA256, SHAKE256 and Haraka one way functions. In their work [37], Karl et al. suggest to include the lightweight crypto scheme ASCON [23] which was recently selected for standardization by NIST. This seems to fit our embedded use case. We therefore focus our performance comparison on SHA256, SHAKE256 and ASCON. Table 4 shows the amount of cycles needed on our embedded platform to compute the number of hashes required per security level. It comes with no surprise that software SHA256 is much faster than software SHAKE256 on a 32 bit platform. What might be surprising at first sight, is that SHA256 in software also outperforms software ASCON and hardware-backed SHA256 on our platform.

Hardware vs. Software. However, as Karl. et al. [37] note, not only hardware accelerators themselves, but also the application including data transfer to those accelerators have to be taken into account. In the case of SPHINCS+, a large amount of very small messages (usually a small multiple of n) have to be hashed. This provides a somewhat worst-case scenario for the CryptoCell 310 hardware accelerator, as short messages have to constantly be written into a specific memory segment followed by a relatively slow call to the CryptoCell. This is similar to the observation by van der Lann et al. for SPHINCS+ running on Java Cards [41]. ASCON on the other hand was designed with a very small hardware footprint, not software performance, in mind.

The software version of SHA256 was therefore used for further benchmarks. However, results with other hash functions can easily be extrapolated from the results in Table 4. The employed SHA256 implementation is the C implementation taken from the SPHINCS+ submission package. This was done to keep the implementation portable and comes at little cost, as previous work has shown that assembly-optimized SHA256 does not outperform portable code compiled with a modern compiler [36].

4.3 Adjusted SPHINCS+ Benchmarks

For FIDO, the runtime of the following four functions is relevant. *KeyGen*: the key generation time in the authenticator (hardware security key). *Sign*: the time needed to sign an authentication request in the authenticator. *MakeCredential*: the time needed to create a new credential (key pair), when requested by the FIDO client. *GetCredential*: the time needed to deliver a signed authentication request to the FIDO client.

As *KeyGen* is a subroutine of *MakeCredential*, and *Sign* of *GetCredential*, their respective runtimes are strongly correlated. However, a parameter set with large signatures might lead to a fast *Sign*, but a slow *GetCredential*, due to transmission latency. For better analysis we therefore benchmarked the four functions individually. The results of *MakeCredential* and *GetCredential* are discussed in the next section. Table 5 shows benchmark results of security level I parameter choices for $q = 2^{10}$ that have a small enough signature for use in vanilla FIDO.

Runtimes in the table are captured in milliseconds instead of cycles. This was done to be comparable to previous work, mainly Ghinea et al. [28]. Estimates of cycle counts can, however, be acquired by multiplying the time with the MCUs frequency, which was configured to 32 768kHz. Unsurprisingly, the number of hashes computed during signing is strongly correlated with the runtime of the signing algorithm. The table also shows that the signature size is inversely proportional to both key generation and signing time. Larger signature sizes also lead to more stack space consumed. Stack space could be drastically reduced, as SPHINCS+ signatures are computed front to back and can be streamed [29]. However, since the consumed stack space is well within the requirements, this is not needed. Compiling the code with *-O3* leads to much improved runtimes, which is consistent with previous work [36]. The largest signature listed (7456B) still fits into the technical context, complies with RAM/stack requirements and adheres to the requirements $A1$ and $A2$ previously defined. We therefore focus on the largest signature still fitting into the technical context.

Table 6 shows a direct comparison between the SPHINCS+ results and the Dilithium-based hybrid approach from [28]. In the table, SPHINCS+ instantiations are denoted as SPHINCS+-*b*-*q*, with *b* being the quantum bit security as defined above. The Dilithium private keys are small, as the implementation stores only a seed value and computes the private key on every signing operation to save expensive TPM storage. Table 6 shows that SPHINCS+ levels I and III with $q = \{2^8, 2^{10}\}$ outperform the lattice-based approach on the board in terms of signing speed at the cost of larger signatures. In security level V, SPHINCS+ has competitive speed but would require a relaxation in signature-size constraints.

Table 5. Various SPHINCS+ parameter choices for security level I and $q = 2^{10}$ with their performance results averaged over 1000 runs on an nRF52480 board. Values of t are specified in $\log_2$. All parameters were instantiated with a software-only version of SHA256 and use a Winternitz parameter of $w = 16$.

Signature (Bytes)	Hashes (#)	Params.				KeyGen			Sign		
		h	d	k	t	Runtime (ms) -Oz	-O3	Stack (kB)	Runtime (ms) -Oz	-O3	Stack (kB)
3968	102528	12	2	15	10	3476.1	2332.3	3.3	11385.5	7631.3	14.0
4048	89216	12	2	17	9	3445.0	2320.0	3.3	9378.3	6310.5	14.2
4208	82048	12	2	20	8	3444.1	1161.9	3.3	8349.9	5620.7	14.7
4288	70720	10	2	17	10	1748.6	1176.7	3.3	8548.1	5665.1	14.9
4336	55360	10	2	19	9	1748.1	585.0	3.3	6316.1	4247.7	15.1
4608	44336	12	3	17	9	857.4	585.0	3.2	5037.8	3432.9	15.8
4768	37168	12	3	20	8	866.8	589.7	3.2	4065.8	2724.3	16.3
5088	33328	12	3	25	7	871.0	589.7	3.2	3531.2	2386.6	17.3
5296	32288	8	2	28	8	866.8	293.8	3.2	3790.3	2553.7	17.9
5328	28192	12	4	20	8	432.7	292.5	3.2	3186.4	2156.5	17.9
5440	26264	9	3	25	8	433.0	292.2	3.2	3124.8	2156.5	18.3
5648	24352	12	4	25	7	434.9	292.3	3.2	2650.9	1775.0	18.9
6032	22048	12	4	32	6	439.3	292.2	3.2	2343.4	1553.7	20.0
6064	21912	9	3	33	7	436.9	147.6	3.2	2524.8	1683.1	20.1
6688	18644	10	5	29	7	218.9	147.6	3.2	2150.1	1439.9	21.9
7152	17560	12	6	32	6	221.1	148.4	3.1	1907.3	1264.4	23.3
7456	16340	10	5	40	6	218.9	147.6	3.2	1820.4	1225.5	24.2

4.4 FIDO Benchmarks

Finally, we conclude with benchmarks on the FIDO-relevant CTAP commands *MakeCredential* and *GetCredential*. All benchmarks were conducted via USB transport. *MakeCredential* generates a new key and sends both public and (encrypted) private key to the client. This is the *non-resident key* setting as introduced in Sect. 2.1. *GetCredential* on the other hand signs an authentication request and returns a signature to the client. Table 7 shows the results of these benchmarks. Runtimes for the hybrid construction were reproduced using the code from [28]. A first conclusion is that all previously defined requirements are met for security level I and III. All CTAP commands finish within 10 s and execute well within the RAM requirements. The SPHINCS+-based aproach even outperforms the lattice-based, hybrid approach from [28] in these levels. With a relaxation of the maximum message size, our SPHINCS+ solution could also outperform their approach in the highest security level.

Table 6. Performance of tailored SPHINCS+ instantiations and the Dilithium-based hybrid construction from [28] on the nRF52840 board. Both implementations are compiled with -O3. Runtimes are averaged over 1000 runs.

	Sizes (bytes)			Runtime (ms)	
Level I	privkey	pubkey	signature	keygen	sign
Dilithium2-Hybrid	32	1 344	2 420	197.5	1 320.5
SPHINCS+-129-2^8	64	32	6 864	148.3	1 079.6
SPHINCS+-129-2^{10}	64	32	7 456	147.6	1 225.5
SPHINCS+-130-2^{16}	64	32	7 280	292.3	2 261.8
Level III					
Dilithium3-Hybrid	32	1 984	3 293	245.6	2 298.4
SPHINCS+-193-2^8	96	48	14 256	147.5	1 735.6
SPHINCS+-193-2^{10}	96	48	13 080	292.3	2 169.8
SPHINCS+-195-2^{16}	96	48	14 928	292.3	3 410.8
Level V					
Dilithium5-Hybrid	32	2 624	4 595	345.3	2 797.2
SPHINCS+-258-2^8 †	128	64	25 120	296.2	2 075.7
SPHINCS+-258-2^{10} †	128	64	24 352	292.1	2 638.0
SPHINCS+-258-2^{16} †	128	64	28 832	292.0	3 216.6

†: Instantiation's signature too large for requirements.

4.5 Discussion

A reason for the good performance of SPHINCS+ in this setting could be the required portability. MCU-specific assembly-level optimizations are not possible when aiming for portable code, which is often times a requirement. Dilithium seems to suffer from this portability requirement much more than SPHINCS+. Another reason why Dilithium-backed *GetCredential* commands are slower on average is the command's very long tail. Dilithium's signing operation has a retry loop that discards insecure parameters. This makes its runtime non-deterministic. Ghinea et al. even state that 3% of their Dilithium5 *GetCredential* commands fail to complete within the 10 s requirement due to this retry loop. SPHINCS+ does not suffer from this, as it is constant time by design and the runtimes showed virtually no variance.

Much of the current literature seems to focus on optimizing hardware implementations for SPHINCS+/SLH-DSA [37,50]. While these hardware-backed systems promise impressive performance improvements, they might be able to perform even better when allowing (or mandating) custom SPHINCS+ instantiations. Comparing and combining adjusted SPHINCS+ parameter sets with custom hardware seems like an interesting avenue for future research.

Table 7. Runtime benchmarks in milliseconds of the *MakeCredential* and *GetCredential* CTAP commands in the *non-resident key* setting, averaged over 1000 iterations. Standard deviation of *GetCredential* runtime denoted as σ.

	Make	Get	
Level I	duration	duration	σ
Dilithium2-Hybrid	547.3	1 808.7	933.8
SPHINCS+-129-2^8	283.4	1 595.9	0.2
SPHINCS+-129-2^{10}	283.7	1 791.8	0.1
SPHINCS+-130-2^{16}	429.2	2 687.9	0.1
Level III			
Dilithium3-Hybrid	668.3	2 861.1	1 865.2
SPHINCS+-193-2^8	283.2	2 099.9	0.2
SPHINCS+-193-2^{10}	429.6	2 751.8	0.2
SPHINCS+-195-2^{16}	426.3	3 967.3	0.1
Level V			
Dilithium5-Hybrid	799.2	4029.2	2 437.4
SPHINCS+-258-2^8 †	425.7	2 803.9	0.2
SPHINCS+-258-2^{10} †	429.4	3 406.0	0.1
SPHINCS+-258-2^{16} †	432.2	4 075.8	0.1

†: Instantiation's signature too large for requirements.

5 Conclusion

In this paper we proposed a practical, post-quantum solution for hardware-security-key-based authentication using tailored stateless hash-based signatures. The results show that adjusting SPHINCS+ to specific embedded applications that require signing can yield very competitive results that rely on only few, well-understood assumptions. Especially in an embedded setting, where resources are sparse this opens many possibilities. Furthermore, our solution is highly portable and reduces complexity as it does not require sophisticated implementation tricks and can be used without a hybrid construction. These results emphasize that SPHINCS+ should not be seen as a signature scheme, but as a very flexible framework for creating signature schemes.

We implemented and benchmarked our solution with various parameterizations and showed that it can even outperform lattice-based solutions from the literature. Our implementation and benchmarking framework was published to encourage further research in this direction.

References

1. Authentication Specifications - FIDO Alliance — fidoalliance.org. https://fidoalliance.org/specifications/download/, Accessed 03 Feb 2025

2. Cloudflare - manage active sessions. https://developers.cloudflare.com/fundamentals/setup/account/account-security/manage-active-sessions/, Accessed 29 Jan 2025
3. Fido alliance - ctap2 specification. https://fidoalliance.org/specs/fido-v2.0-ps-20190130/fido-client-to-authenticator-protocol-v2.0-ps-20190130.html, Accessed 29 Jan 2025
4. Fido security reference. https://fidoalliance.org/specs/common-specs/fido-security-ref-v2.1-rd-20210525.html, Accessed 29 Jan 2025
5. GitHub - google/OpenSK: OpenSK. https://github.com/google/OpenSK, Accessed 29 Jan 2025
6. Github - tockos. https://github.com/tock/tock, Accessed 29 Jan 2025
7. Google - session length for google services. https://support.google.com/a/answer/7576830, Accessed 29 Jan 2025
8. Libsodium - ed25519 implementation. https://github.com/jedisct1/libsodium/blob/59a98bc7f9d507175f551a53bfc0b2081f06e3ba/src/libsodium/include/sodium/crypto_sign_ed25519.h#L34, Accessed 29 Jan 2025
9. Microsoft - session timeouts for ms 365. https://learn.microsoft.com/en-us/microsoft-365/enterprise/session-timeouts, Accessed 29 Jan 2025
10. Nordic nrf52840 dk brief. https://www.nordicsemi.com/-/media/Software-and-other-downloads/Product-Briefs/nRF52840-DK-product-brief.pdf, Accessed 29 Jan 2025
11. Nordic semiconductor - arm trustzone cryptocell 310. https://docs.nordicsemi.com/bundle/ps_nrf52840/page/cryptocell.html, Accessed 29 Jan 2025
12. ANSSI: Anssi views on the post-quantum cryptography transition (2024), ttps://cyber.gouv.fr/sites/default/files/document/follow_up_position_paper_on_post_quantum_cryptography.pdf, Accessed 24 Jan 2025
13. Aumasson, J., et al.: Sphincs+-submission to the nist post-quantum project, v3. 1. NIST PQC Round **3** (2022)
14. Bernstein, D.J.: Multi-ciphertext security degradation for lattices. Cryptology ePrint Archive (2022)
15. Bernstein, D.J.: Asymptotics of hybrid primal lattice attacks. Cryptology ePrint Archive (2023)
16. Bernstein, D.J., et al.: Kyberslash: exploiting secret-dependent division timings in kyber implementations. Cryptology ePrint Archive (2024)
17. Bos, J.W., Renes, J., Sprenkels, A.: Dilithium for memory constrained devices. In: International Conference on Cryptology in Africa, pp. 217–235. Springer (2022)
18. Bravyi, S., Cross, A.W., Gambetta, J.M., Maslov, D., Rall, P., Yoder, T.J.: High-threshold and low-overhead fault-tolerant quantum memory. Nature **627**(8005), 778–782 (2024)
19. Buchmann, J., Dahmen, E., Hülsing, A.: Xmss-a practical forward secure signature scheme based on minimal security assumptions. In: Post-Quantum Cryptography: 4th International Workshop, PQCrypto 2011, Taipei, Taiwan, November 29–December 2, 2011. Proceedings 4, pp. 117–129. Springer (2011)
20. Campbell, E.: A series of fast-paced advances in quantum error correction. Nat. Rev. Phys. **6**(3), 160–161 (2024)
21. Chen, Y.: Quantum algorithms for lattice problems. Cryptology ePrint Archive (2024)
22. Contributors, D.: Crystals-dilithium specification v3.1. https://pq-crystals.org/dilithium/data/dilithium-specification.pdf (2021), Accessed 03 Feb 2025
23. Dobraunig, C., Eichlseder, M., Mendel, F., Schläffer, M.: Ascon v1. 2: Lightweight authenticated encryption and hashing. J. Cryptology **34**, 1–42 (2021)

24. Engineering, A.S.: iMessage with PQ3: the new state of the art in quantum-secure messaging at scale. https://security.apple.com/blog/imessage-pq3/ (2024), Accessed 03 Feb 2025
25. Firmin, C.: PQShield plugs timing leaks in Kyber/ML-KEM to improve PQC implementation maturity | PQShield — pqshield.com. https://pqshield.com/pqshield-plugs-timing-leaks-in-kyber/, Accessed 03 Feb 2025
26. Fouque, P.A., et al.: Falcon: fast-fourier lattice-based compact signatures over ntru. Submission to the NIST's Post-Quantum Cryptography Standardization Process **36**(5), 1–75 (2018)
27. Genêt, A., Kannwischer, M.J., Pelletier, H., McLauchlan, A.: Practical fault injection attacks on sphincs. Cryptology ePrint Archive (2018)
28. Ghinea, D., et al.: Hybrid post-quantum signatures in hardware security keys. In: International Conference on Applied Cryptography and Network Security, pp. 480–499. Springer (2023)
29. Gonzalez, R., et al.: Verifying post-quantum signatures in 8 kb of ram. In: Post-Quantum Cryptography: 12th International Workshop, PQCrypto 2021, Daejeon, South Korea, 20–22 July 2021, Proceedings 12, pp. 215–233. Springer (2021)
30. Hansen, R.: Post-quantum cryptography: standards and progress — security.googleblog.com. https://security.googleblog.com/2024/08/post-quantum-cryptography-standards.html (2024), Accessed 03 Feb 2025
31. Hülsing, A.: W-ots+–shorter signatures for hash-based signature schemes. In: Progress in Cryptology–AFRICACRYPT 2013: 6th International Conference on Cryptology in Africa, Cairo, Egypt, 22–24 June 2013, Proceedings 6, pp. 173–188. Springer (2013)
32. Hülsing, A., Kudinov, M.: Recovering the tight security proof of sphincs+. In: International Conference on the Theory and Application of Cryptology and Information Security, pp. 3–33. Springer (2022)
33. Hülsing, A., Rausch, L., Buchmann, J.: Optimal parameters for xmss mt. In: Security Engineering and Intelligence Informatics: CD-ARES 2013 Workshops: MoCrySEn and SeCIHD, Regensburg, Germany, 2–6 September 2013, Proceedings 8, pp. 194–208. Springer (2013)
34. for Information Security, F.O.: Kryptografie quantensicher gestalten - quantum secure cryptography (german). https://www.bsi.bund.de/SharedDocs/Downloads/DE/BSI/Publikationen/Broschueren/Kryptografie-quantensicher-gestalten.pdf (2024), Accessed 17 Feb 2025
35. Kannwischer, M.J., Genêt, A., Butin, D., Krämer, J., Buchmann, J.: Differential power analysis of xmss and sphincs. In: Constructive Side-Channel Analysis and Secure Design: 9th International Workshop, COSADE 2018, Singapore, 23–24 April 2018, Proceedings 9, pp. 168–188. Springer (2018)
36. Kannwischer, M.J., Rijneveld, J., Schwabe, P., Stoffelen, K.: PQM4: post-quantum crypto library for the ARM Cortex-M4, https://github.com/mupq/pqm4
37. Karl, P., Schupp, J., Sigl, G.: The impact of hash primitives and communication overhead for hardware-accelerated sphincs+. In: International Workshop on Constructive Side-Channel Analysis and Secure Design, pp. 221–239. Springer (2024)
38. Kölbl, S., Philipoom, J.: A note on sphincs+ parameter sets. Cryptology ePrint Archive (2022)
39. Kret, E.: Quantum resistance and the signal protocol — signal.org. https://signal.org/blog/pqxdh/ (2024), Accessed 03 Feb 2025
40. Kwak, J., Jang, Y., Park, J., Lee, H.: Slh-dsa-based digital signature and verification fpga system. Trans. Semicond. Eng. **2**(4), 69–77 (2024)

41. van der Laan, E., Poll, E., Rijneveld, J., de Ruiter, J., Schwabe, P., Verschuren, J.: Is java card ready for hash-based signatures? In: International Workshop on Security, pp. 127–142. Springer (2018)
42. Lamport, L.: Constructing digital signatures from a one way function (1979)
43. Lange, T.: Hash-based signatures. In: Encyclopedia of Cryptography, Security and Privacy, pp. 1110–1112. Springer (2025)
44. Merkle, R.C.: A certified digital signature. In: Conference on the Theory and Application of Cryptology, pp. 218–238. Springer (1989)
45. NIST: FIPS205: stateless hash-based digital signature standard. https://nvlpubs.nist.gov/nistpubs/FIPS/NIST.FIPS.205.pdf, Accessed 03 Feb 2025
46. NIST: submission requirements and evaluation criteria for the post-quantum cryptography standardization process. https://csrc.nist.gov/CSRC/media/Projects/Post-Quantum-Cryptography/documents/call-for-proposals-final-dec-2016.pdf, Accessed 03 Feb 2025
47. Nist, G.M.D.: Fips 204: module-lattice-based digital signature standard (2024)
48. NSA: the commercial national security algorithm suite 2.0 and quantum computing faq, September 2022, The Commercial National Security Algorithm Suite 2.0 and Quantum Computing FAQ
49. Owens, D., El Khatib, R., Bisheh-Niasar, M., Azarderakhsh, R., Kermani, M.M.: Efficient and side-channel resistant ed25519 on arm cortex-m4. IEEE Trans. Circ. Syst. I: Regul. Papers (2024)
50. Saarinen, M.J.O.: Accelerating slh-dsa by two orders of magnitude with a single hash unit. In: Annual International Cryptology Conference, pp. 276–304. Springer (2024)
51. Shor, P.W.: Algorithms for quantum computation: discrete logarithms and factoring. In: Proceedings 35th Annual Symposium on Foundations of Computer Science, pp. 124–134. IEEE (1994)
52. Westerbaan, B.: Cloudflare now uses post-quantum cryptography to talk to your origin server — blog.cloudflare.com. https://blog.cloudflare.com/post-quantum-to-origins/ (2023), Accessed 03 Feb 2025

ChatGPT as Preprocessing Agents: A Case Study on Cryptographic Side-Channel Analysis

Zhen Li[1], Anjiang Liu[2], An Wang[3(✉)], and WeiJia Wang[1]

[1] School of Cyber Science and Technology, Shandong University, Qingdao, China
[2] School of Computer Science (National Pilot Software Engineering School), Beijing University of Posts and Telecommunications, Beijing, China
[3] School of Cyberspace Science and Technology, Beijing Institute of Technology, Beijing, China
wanganl@bit.edu.cn

Abstract. Side-channel analysis techniques extract cryptographic keys by analyzing physical or electrical characteristics generated during the encryption process. When performing correlation power analysis and simple power analysis on raw traces, challenges such as noise interference necessitate effective trace preprocessing–a task that traditionally relies on domain expertise, specialized tools, and extensive experience. Meanwhile, ChatGPT has gained widespread attention for its intelligent interaction capabilities and effectiveness in assisting users with task-specific operations. However, its potential for trace preprocessing remains underexplored and calls for systematic investigation. In this paper, we propose three expert-strategy prompt templates to explore and assess ChatGPT's capabilities in trace preprocessing. We validate the effectiveness of ChatGPT in performing six categories of trace preprocessing methods through expert-strategy prompts at varying abstraction levels. Furthermore, we evaluate the impact of ChatGPT-assisted preprocessing on traces across various platforms and cryptographic algorithms, analyzing its influence on the overall performance of side-channel analysis.

Keywords: Cryptography · Machine Learning · Side-Channel Analysis · Large Language Model

1 Introduction

Currently, artificial intelligence technology is advancing rapidly, and the world is being profoundly transformed by Large Language Models (LLMs) [7]. Propelled by leading companies such as OpenAI and Meta, LLMs have ushered in a transformative era in artificial intelligence. Today, various LLMs have achieved remarkable success and play vital roles across diverse domains, including code generation and refactoring, software development assistance, and data analysis operations. Among these, ChatGPT, as a leading LLM, is at the forefront of this revolution. With its outstanding natural language processing capabilities and multimodal learning proficiency, ChatGPT has emerged as a benchmark product in the industry, garnering widespread recognition and attention [8].

Side-Channel Analysis (SCA) is a class of techniques that infer cryptographic keys or sensitive data by collecting physical leakage information (e.g., power consumption, electromagnetic radiation) during cryptographic device operation [2]. SCA was first proposed by Paul Kocher in 1999, revealing the gap between the physical implementation of cryptographic algorithms and their theoretical security models. By employing timing analysis (measuring execution time differences) and Simple Power Analysis (SPA), attackers were able to compromise implementations of public-key algorithms such as RSA. These breakthroughs marked a paradigm shift in cryptographic security research—from relying solely on mathematical models to incorporating physical-layer defenses. SCA thus highlighted the fundamental gap between theoretical security and practical implementation.

In SCA, trace acquisition and subsequent processing are essential operational prerequisites. However, in practice, the raw traces obtained from physical measurements—such as power consumption or electromagnetic emissions—are often noisy, misaligned, or incomplete due to environmental interference, measurement inaccuracies, or hardware constraints. As a result, these raw traces are typically unsuitable for direct analysis or attack procedures. To ensure data quality and reliability, trace preprocessing is therefore a critical step. However, such operations often heavily rely on specialized tools and expert knowledge. Given the superior natural language processing and feedback capabilities of ChatGPT-based LLMs, whether they can be leveraged to perform trace preprocessing in a simple yet efficient manner is a question worth exploring [22].

To address this issue, this paper explores whether ChatGPT can effectively assist side-channel analysts in trace preprocessing through designed prompts, thereby enhancing the accuracy and efficiency of SCA. Specifically, we aim to investigate whether ChatGPT can perform trace preprocessing operations accurately and efficiently. Furthermore, considering the impact of existing prompt engineering methods, we categorize expert-strategy prompts into three types to guide ChatGPT in executing diverse preprocessing tasks, thereby evaluating its capability under varying levels of prompt generality. Finally, we evaluate the effectiveness of ChatGPT-assisted SCA by assessing key recovery performance using SPA and Correlation Power Analysis (CPA) with different trace preprocessing methods.

2 Preliminaries

2.1 Side-Channel Analysis

SCA exploits physical leakages—such as power consumption, electromagnetic emissions, or timing information—to extract sensitive information from cryptographic devices. Among various SCA techniques, SPA and CPA are two foundational and widely studied approaches. While they differ in methodology, both share the common goal of recovering secret keys.

SPA is a direct and intuitive form of attack that analyzes the power consumption trace from a single or a small number of cryptographic operations. It is based on the observation that certain operations, instructions, or data-dependent branches in an implementation produce distinguishable patterns in the power trace [19]. By visually inspecting the trace or applying simple signal processing techniques, an attacker with knowledge of the algorithm's structure may identify key-dependent behavior and extract the secret key. Traditionally, SPA required expert-level manual analysis, but recent advancements have introduced automated techniques to improve scalability. Common methods include trace segmentation (to isolate relevant operations), dimensionality reduction (e.g., Principal Component Analysis or Linear Discriminant Analysis) to extract informative features, and clustering such as K-means or DBSCAN to group similar patterns for easier interpretation [9,18]. In contrast, CPA is a statistical approach that analyzes a large set of traces using hypothesis testing to correlate predicted intermediate values with actual measurements [3]. It assumes a leakage model—commonly Hamming weight or Hamming distance—to estimate how internal data influences power consumption. For each key hypothesis, the attacker calculates the correlation between the predicted leakage and observed traces, typically using Pearson's correlation coefficient. The hypothesis with the highest correlation is considered the most likely candidate. To improve attack effectiveness, CPA often incorporates preprocessing steps such as trace alignment, noise filtering and point of interest selection. These steps enhance the signal-to-noise ratio and improve the chances of successful key recovery.

In this work, we conduct experiments using both SPA and CPA to evaluate the effectiveness of trace preprocessing performed by ChatGPT. By applying these two representative SCA techniques, we assess whether the processed traces preserve meaningful leakage and support successful key recovery.

2.2 Trace Preprocessing

Collected traces contain three main components: the desired information signal, noise, and constant offsets [6]. The noise originates from external environmental interference, signal conversion inaccuracy, and other sources, all of which can significantly affect the effectiveness of SCA. Trace preprocessing aims to enhance the quality of the physical signals collected during SCA [14,16]. Its key objectives include: attenuating or eliminating random noise to enhance the signal-to-noise ratio; correcting timing misalignment to ensure synchronization across traces; filtering out interference in specific frequency bands while retaining useful signal components [10]. The trace preprocessing methods investigated in this study are described as follows.

1. **Row Average.** Calculate the mean of all traces at each time sampling point.
2. **Standard Deviation.** Calculate the standard deviation at each time sampling point.
3. **Absolute Value.** Negative values in the trace are replaced with their absolute values, ensuring that the entire trace is non-negative.

4. **Vertical Alignment.** Calculate the average of the first n points of each trace. Adjust each trace to match the target value, allowing vertical alignment across multiple traces.
5. **Sliding Window Average.** Compute a moving average by sliding a fixed-size window along each trace. At each position, the average of the points within the window is calculated, resulting in a smoothed version of the original trace that reduces high-frequency fluctuations.
6. **Low-Pass Filtering.** Given a weight w, each point is updated sequentially from left to right using the formula $x_i = \frac{(x_i + W \cdot x_{i-1})}{w+1}$. Subsequently, the intermediate values are smoothed from right to left using $x_i = \frac{(x_i + W \cdot x_{i+1})}{w+1}$ [5].

2.3 ChatGPT

ChatGPT is a state-of-the-art language model developed by OpenAI, based on the Generative Pre-trained Transformer architecture [17]. Specifically, it leverages deep learning techniques and large-scale transformer networks trained on massive amounts of text data to understand and generate human-like language [21]. The model excels in various natural language processing tasks, including text generation, translation, summarization, and question answering [13]. ChatGPT has found applications in numerous domains, such as virtual assistance, content creation, education, and programming support, demonstrating remarkable adaptability and generalization [1,20].

One of the key strengths of ChatGPT is its ability to process complex language prompts and generate coherent and contextually relevant responses. This capability forms the foundation of "prompt engineering", a practice where users design effective input prompts to guide the model toward specific behaviors or outputs. Prompt engineering is crucial in adapting ChatGPT for domain-specific tasks, enabling it to mimic expert reasoning or perform analytical operations in unfamiliar contexts [4,12].

Given its strong generalization and reasoning capabilities, an intriguing question arises: can ChatGPT be applied to specialized technical domains such as SCA? While ChatGPT was not explicitly trained on SCA data, its ability to interpret patterns, explain code, and generalize from examples opens potential avenues for leveraging it in trace analysis and strategy design [11]. This chapter aims to provide foundational insights into ChatGPT's capabilities and explores the rationale behind considering its use in the SCA context [15].

3 Trace Processing Based on LLM

3.1 Research Pipeline

The research pipeline is illustrated in Fig. 1, and consists of three main stages: ① dataset preparation and prompt template design; ② evaluation of trace preprocessing under different prompt; ③ evaluation of SCA results on real datasets.

In stage ①, inspired by methods such as Zero-Shot Prompting and Chain-of-Thought Reasoning, we designed three prompt strategies with varying levels of abstraction based on a generic template. Each strategy was paired with corresponding output formats, and multiple sets of traces were collected. The design and optimization details of these strategies are discussed in Sect. 3.2 and Sect. 4.2. In stage ②, guided by the prompt strategies, ChatGPT was directed to perform six differentiated trace preprocessing operations, and its output data were systematically collected. In stage ③, the optimized prompt strategies were applied to real-world datasets in SCA scenarios. By comparing ChatGPT-processed traces with original traces, we validated the effectiveness of prompt engineering in enhancing preprocessing quality for SPA and CPA tasks.

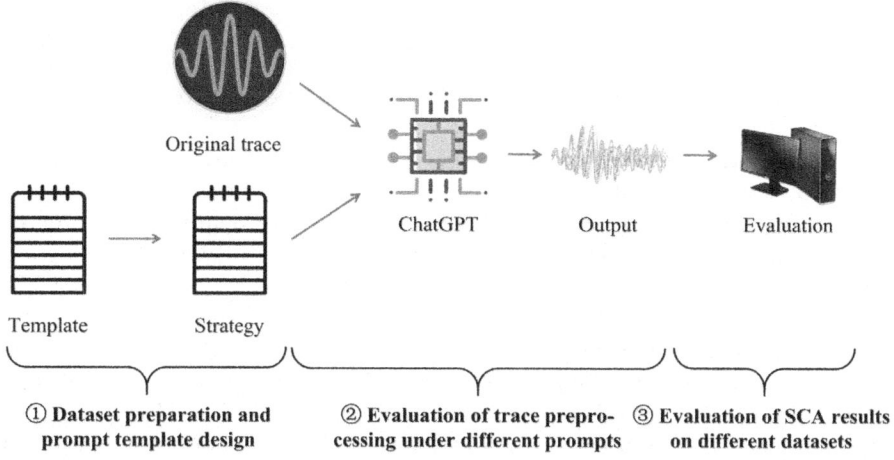

Fig. 1. Research pipeline

3.2 Expert Strategy Design

To facilitate effective interaction with ChatGPT for trace preprocessing tasks, we designed a structured prompt strategy that includes both a fixed prompt header (named "common head") and multiple levels of expert strategies, as shown in Table 1. The common head of each prompt is crafted to establish the role of ChatGPT as an expert in SCA and signal processing. It also provides necessary contextual information about the input data, such as the format of the trace file and important constraints (e.g., absence of a header row).

The three expert strategies we propose to guide ChatGPT's behavior are as follows.

- **The Summary-Level strategy** Directly provide the specific method name to ChatGPT, relying on its own interpretation to generate processing results

Table 1. Strategy design

Common Head		I would like you to act as an expert in SCA and signal processing, helping me perform specific operations. During the analysis process, please do not ask me any questions; instead, proceed step by step until you provide the final answer. The file contains a large dataset of traces with multiple rows. The value of each point represents its height. Please note that this file does not have a header row—this is critical. To complete this task, for each trace, you may need to follow these steps:
Expert Strategy	Summary-Level	Perform <method name>. Then specify <output format>.
	Extended-Level	Perform <method name> with <method parameter> and <brief steps>. Then specify <output format>.
	Detailed-Level	Perform <specific step> with <method parameterer>. Then specify <output format>.
Output Format		Finally, generate the adjusted file.

without additional constraints or prompts. Example: "Perform moving average operation."

- **The Extended-Level strategy** Decompose target operations into generalized procedural steps. Execute forward propagation operation. Perform backward propagation operation. Specify concrete implementation parameters. Example: Moving average window size: 10. Forward/backward propagation weights: 0.52.
- **The Detailed-Level strategy** Building upon the extended-level instructions, thoroughly elaborate on and standardize the complete computational procedures by fully specifying each generalized operational step. For example, "calculate the average of ten numbers" should be detailed as: "First sum these ten numbers to obtain the total sum value, then divide this sum value by 10 to derive the average value."

Through the above design, a prompt consists of common head, specific-level expert strategy and output format in sequence. By applying different prompts, we further assess ChatGPT's ability to understand natural language and specialized information, thereby enabling more effective use of ChatGPT for trace preprocessing.

4 Experiments

This section presents the selection of prompt strategies and evaluates ChatGPT's effectiveness in SCA tasks involving both SPA and CPA. By investigating the impact of expert-designed strategies across different prompt levels and analyzing the number of traces required for successful key recovery, we assess the feasibility of leveraging ChatGPT for trace preprocessing in the context of SCA. We will conduct a comparative analysis between the outcomes achieved through ChatGPT-based implementation of conventional methods versus those obtained through manual human implementation of traditional approaches, aiming to validate the straightforward effectiveness of employing such signal processing tasks.ward effectiveness of employing such signal processing tasks.

4.1 Datasets

We accessed ChatGPT through the OpenAI web interface and selected the GPT-4o model for experiments based on task characteristics. To ensure experimental independence, each prompt-based operation was conducted in a new session with the model's memory function disabled.

To fully explore the capabilities of ChatGPT, the datasets used in our study are summarized in Table 2. The first two datasets are based on the asymmetric encryption algorithm ECC, which is typically analyzed using SPA. These datasets involve large files and long traces, presenting additional challenges for effective processing by ChatGPT. Typically, due to significant electromagnetic noise, Dataset 2 contains a larger number of traces for key recovery. In contrast, symmetric cryptographic algorithms are also included in our evaluation. The latter two datasets involve AES algorithm, which is generally analyzed using CPA. In summary, our datasets encompasses various algorithms, platforms, and SCA analysis methods, aiming to provide a comprehensive evaluation of ChatGPT's capabilities.

Table 2. Information of datasets

Name	Algorithm	Platform	Physical Leakage	Trace Number	Features
Dataset 1	AES-256	STC89C52RC	Power	100	8,500
Dataset 2	AES-256	STC89C52RC	Electromagnetic	400	8,500
Dataset 3	ECC-256	Smart Card	Power	1	3,200,000
Dataset 4	RSA-1024	Smart Card	Power	1	5,000,000

4.2 Performance of Expert Strategy

This section presents six trace preprocessing methods that are the focus of our study, each accompanied by a prompt strategy informed by expert knowledge at different levels. Specifically, each prompt consists of three parts: a common head, a level-specific expert strategy, and an output format. The common head defines ChatGPT's role, specifies that each line in the file represents a trace, and sets constraints on ChatGPT's responses. Building on this, the expert strategy outlines the steps required to perform the specific operation, and finally, the output format standardizes ChatGPT's response structure.

We stored each trace in the dataset as a row in a CSV file, effectively forming a matrix. The dataset, along with three different prompt strategies, was then submitted to ChatGPT while we simultaneously implemented the same experimental operations through manual coding. By comparing the outcomes of both approaches, we were able to validate the effectiveness of ChatGPT. This methodology was consistently applied in all six subsequent trace preprocessing experiments.

For sliding window average preprocessing, the prompts used are shown in Table 3. At the summary level, ChatGPT selected a relatively small window size on its own but followed the required steps accurately. The extended level explicitly included the window size for the moving average, and the detailed level broke down each computational step. All prompt levels proved to be effective in guiding ChatGPT to perform this preprocessing method correctly.

Table 3. Specific strategies for sliding window average

Summary-Level	Extended-Level	Detailed-Level
"Common Head"*		
Perform an appropriate window average on each trace.	Perform a sliding window average operation with a window size of ten points.	(a) Calculate the average height of it and the nine points after it, denoted as h. (b) Replace the height of this point with h.
Finally, generate the adjusted file.		

* "Common Head" refers to the content corresponding to the "Common Head" row in Table 1.

For vertical alignment preprocessing, the prompts used are listed in Table 4. At the summary level, ChatGPT misunderstood vertical alignment as horizontal alignment, failing to meet the requirement. In the extended level, the inclusion of instructions for shifting upward and downward helped guide ChatGPT correctly, while the detailed level provided commonly used mathematical methods. Both extended and detailed levels produced results consistent with expectations.

For row averaging preprocessing, the prompts used are listed in Table 5, the summary level prompt failed to convey the intended meaning accurately to ChatGPT. However, both the extended and detailed level prompts successfully guided ChatGPT to achieve the desired results.

For standard deviation and absolute value preprocessing, the prompts used are listed in Table 6 and Table 7. ChatGPT correctly understood both terms across all prompt levels. It was able to execute the preprocessing steps exactly as expected under summary, extended, and detailed level instructions.

For low-pass filtering, the prompts used are listed in Table 8, the summary level prompt produced only a minor effect. At the extended level, due to the variety of possible implementation methods, ChatGPT selected an effective filtering approach, though the result was slightly less effective than the detailed level.

Table 4. Specific strategies for vertical alignment

Summary-Level	Extended-Level	Detailed-Level
"Common Head"*		
You need to align each trace vertically as much as possible.	You need to add or subtract all points on each trace to align them as closely as possible.	(a) Calculate the average height of the first ten points in the trace, denoted as h_2. (b) Compute the average height of the first ten points in the first trace, denoted as h_1. (c) Subtract the difference ($h_2 - h_1$) from every point in the current trace.
Finally, generate the adjusted file.		

* "Common Head" refers to the content corresponding to the "Common Head" row in Table 1

Table 5. Specific strategies for row average

Summary- Level	Extended- Level	Detailed-Level
"Common Head"*		
Perform row averaging operation.	Calculate the average height.	(a) Calculate the sum of all points for this trace, denoted as sum. (b) Divide sum by the number of points on this trace to obtain the average value of the trace.
Arranging these averages into a single trace.		

* "Common Head" refers to the content corresponding to the "Common Head" row in Table 1

When provided with mathematical formulas in the detailed prompt, ChatGPT was able to achieve significantly better trace denoising and smoothing.

All operations demonstrate optimal performance under Detailed-Level strategies. For different operations implemented with Summary-Level and Extended-Level prompt strategies, ChatGPT exhibits varying degrees of effectiveness due to implementation diversity. The specific manifestations are as follows: In most cases involving high-consistency and relatively simple tasks, employing generalized language allowing ChatGPT to operate autonomously yields optimal results. However, for complex operations, parameter specification and procedural descriptions become essential requirements. Through this approach, superior trace preprocessing outcomes can be systematically achieved. Partial experimental results are shown in the Fig. 2 and Fig. 3.

The vertical alignment operations performed by ChatGPT on the trace all proved to be effective. Both the Extended-Level and Detailed-Level operations were consistently executed in accordance with the prompt instructions. The discrepancy between the Extended-Level results and expectations stemmed from the longitudinal alignment specified in the prompts being restricted to only the first ten data points. Nevertheless, at the Summary-Level, ChatGPT successfully achieved vertical alignment through optimized parameter selection or improved algorithmic implementation.

Table 6. Specific strategies for standard deviation

Summary-Level	Extended-Level	Detailed-Level
"Common Head"*		
Calculate the standard deviation of each trace.	(a) Calculate the variance of the trace. (b) Root the variance to obtain the standard deviation of the trace.	(a) Calculate the average value v of the trace. (b) Calculate the difference between each data point and the mean and square it, and record it as X_i. (c) Sum all X_i and divide by the number of trace data points to obtain variance w. (d) Take the square root of variance w.
Arranging these points into a single trace.		

* "Common Head" refers to the content corresponding to the "Common Head" row in Table 1

Table 7. Specific strategies for absolute value

Summary-Level	Extended-Level	Detailed-Level
"Common Head"[a]		
Calculate the absolute value of each point in each trace and replace that point.	—[b]	Transform all negative numbers into their own inverse numbers.
Arrange the points of each trajectory in a row instead of placing them in one position.		

[a] "Common Head" refers to the content corresponding to the "Common Head" row in Table 1
[b] — indicates that there is no design for the Extended-Level prompt.

The trace processed with Summary-Level low-pass filtering shows no significant changes. After Extended-Level processing, the noise in the trace is noticeably reduced, though some interference remains visible. In contrast, the Detail-Level processing proves highly effective, with noise becoming extremely faint and the key informational features clearly preserved. A comparative analysis reveals that while the Extended-Level prompt provides significant improvement over the Summary-Level when specific parameters are defined, it still falls short compared to the Detail-Level. Fundamentally, although the Extended-Level and Detail-Level are intended to perform similar operations, their preprocessing results differ. This suggests that when faced with generalized operational terms, ChatGPT may choose from multiple available methods to complete the task—choices that may not align with those used in the Detail-Level approach. We provide detailed steps for each operation in the proposed method, along with comprehensive explanations of the algorithms used at each stage. While ChatGPT demonstrates strong performance in interpreting summary-level prompts, certain deviations were observed in specific contexts. For instance, during vertical alignment, it misinterpreted the term "vertical alignment" as horizontal translation, resulting in incorrect outputs. In the case of low-pass filtering with extended-level prompts, suboptimal parameter selection led to reduced preprocessing effectiveness. These

Table 8. Specific strategies for low-pass filtering

Summary- Level	Extended- Level	Detailed-Level
"Common Head"*		
Perform low-pass filtering using an appropriate method.	For each trace, perform the Forward Pass operation and then perform the Backward Pass operation with the weight set to 10.	I will use 'w' to represent the value 52. First: (a) For each trace, starting from the second point, traverse sequentially to the last point. (b) The height of the current point plus w multiplied by the height of the previous point, and then divided by $w + 1$. Second: (a) For each trace, starting from the second to last point, traverse sequentially to the first point. (b) The height of the current point plus w multiplied by the height of the next point, and then divided by $w + 1$.
Finally, generate the adjusted file.		

* "Common Head" refers to the content corresponding to the "Common Head" row in Table 1

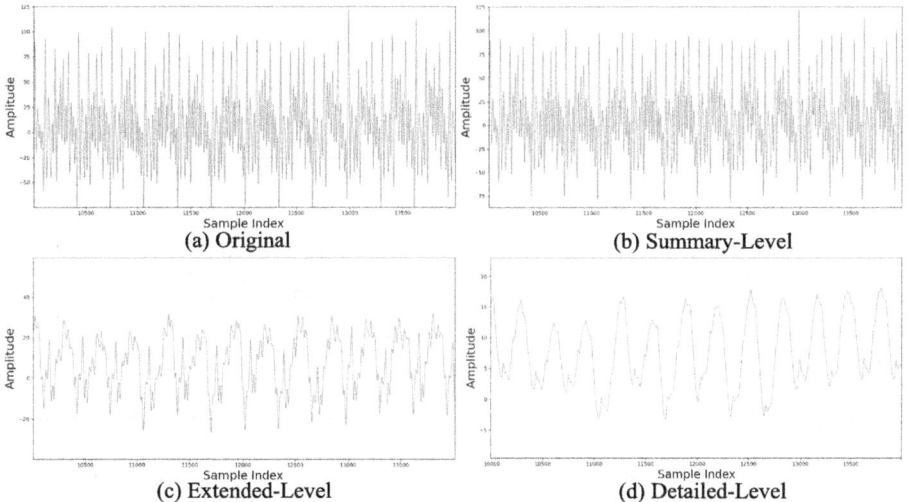

(a) Original (b) Summary-Level (c) Extended-Level (d) Detailed-Level

Fig. 2. Results of low-pass filtering in trace preprocessing across strategy levels

issues required human intervention to define precise steps and fine-tune parameters to achieve optimal performance. The final validation results are presented in Table 9

The "✓" symbol indicates that the trace processed by ChatGPT demonstrates significant effective noise reduction or alignment compared to the original trace, while the "−" symbol denotes no processing at this stage. Some instructions may not achieve optimal results due to manually set parameters, but if they produce correct and effective modifications to the trace, they are still marked with "✓".

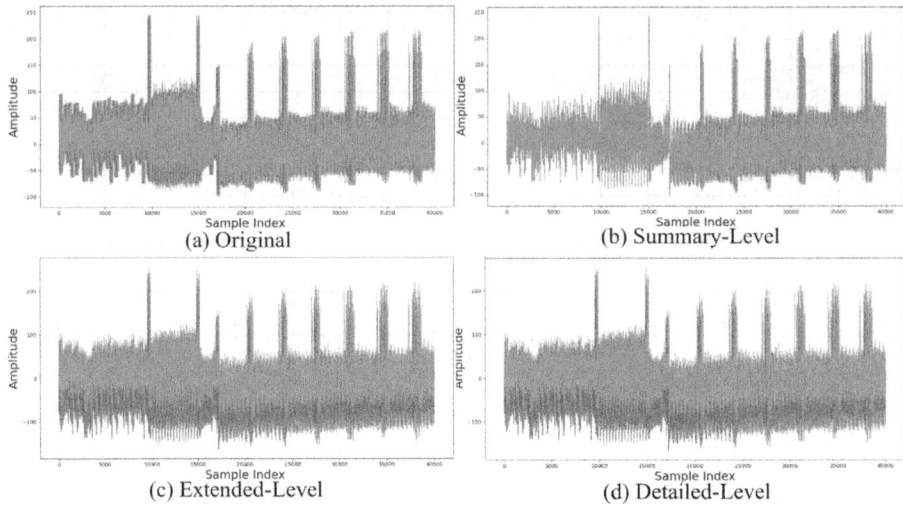

Fig. 3. Results of vertical alignment across strategy levels

Table 9. Effectiveness of Strategy Results

	Vertical Alignment	Sliding Window Average	Low-pass Filtering	Row Average	Standard Deviation	Absolute Value
Summary-Level	×	✓	×	×	✓	✓
Extended-Level	✓	✓	✓	✓	✓	–
Detailed-Level	✓	✓	✓	✓	✓	✓

We also evaluated the high-dimensional data handling capabilities of Chat-GPT and found that it can process CSV files with up to 500,000 columns and 50,000 rows, provided the total file size does not exceed approximately 50MB. When dealing with trace data, a single trace can be split across multiple rows. To ensure continuity during analysis, prompts can be constructed such that the beginning of the next row is treated as the continuation of the previous row's end.

Despite occasional semantic misunderstandings, ChatGPT outperformed manual preprocessing when tasks were fully comprehended. While low-pass filtering with extended level did not achieve optimal results, it still provided valid preprocessing results. Overall, ChatGPT demonstrated robust problem-solving capabilities under extended-level prompts, validating the practicality and efficacy of moderately abstract prompts for domain-specific tasks.

4.3 Performance in Side-Channel Analysis

Whether trace preprocessing performed by ChatGPT can improve the effectiveness of SCA is worth exploring. To this end, we applied detailed-level prompts for preprocessing across four datasets. Specifically, we conducted CPA on the first S-box output of the AES datasets, and performed segmentation, dimensionality reduction, and K-means clustering on the datasets involving asymmetric cryptographic algorithms. The results were used to evaluate the impact of ChatGPT-based trace preprocessing on the overall effectiveness of the analysis.

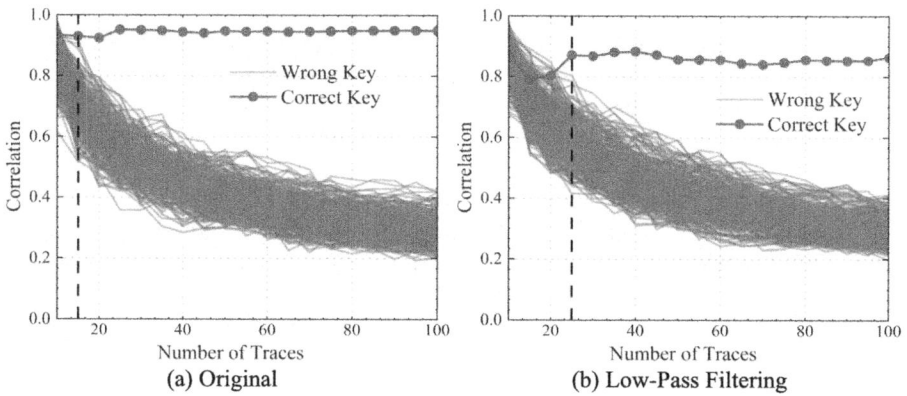

Fig. 4. Results of CPA with low-pass filtering on Dataset 1

Figure 4 and Fig. 5 illustrate the effectiveness of CPA applied to both raw and preprocessed traces on Dataset 1 and Dataset 2 respectively. The horizontal axis represents the number of power traces used for analysis, while the vertical axis indicates the correlation coefficient. The blue lines depict the maximum correlation across all key hypotheses as the number of traces increases. The red line shows the correlation trend of the correct key, and the black dashed line marks the first point where the correct key achieves the highest correlation. When a separation emerges between the correlation of the correct key and that of incorrect key, we define the corresponding number of traces as the minimum trace count required by CPA to successfully recover the key.

As shown in Fig. 4, for Dataset 1, the raw traces required 20 traces to successfully recover the key using CPA. In contrast, only 15 traces were needed after ChatGPT-based preprocessing. In Fig. 5, for Dataset 2, the raw traces required 340 traces for successful key recovery, whereas only 200 traces were needed after low-pass filtering by ChatGPT. These results demonstrate that ChatGPT-based preprocessing can effectively enhance the performance of CPA. In both datasets, the number of traces required for successful key recovery was significantly reduced after applying the ChatGPT-generated preprocessing steps. This indicates that, even without professional experience, language model-guided

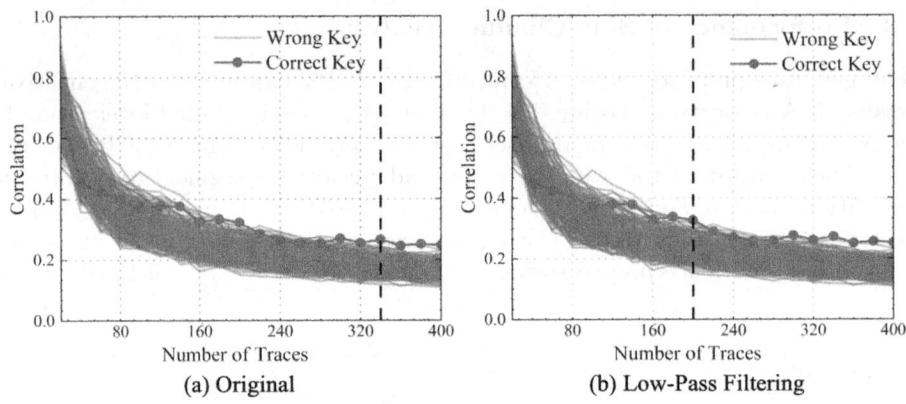

Fig. 5. Results of CPA with low-pass filtering on Dataset 2

preprocessing can preserve or amplify critical leakage features in power traces. Such improvements suggest the potential of integrating large language models into the SCA workflow as intelligent, automated assistants for trace preprocessing.

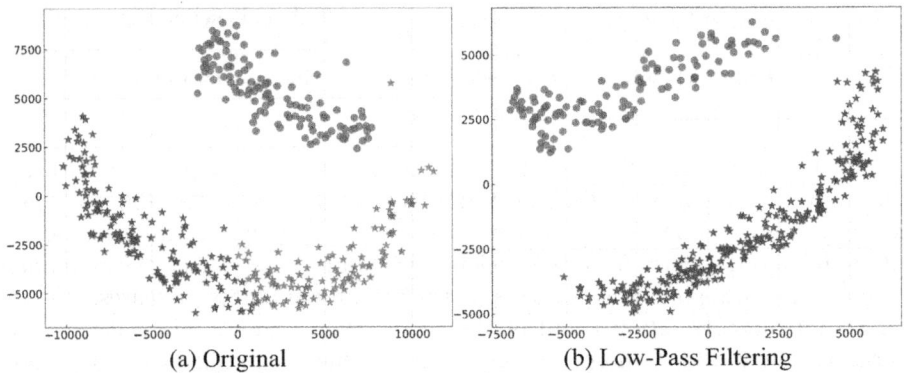

Fig. 6. Results of SPA with low-pass filtering on Dataset 3

Figure 6 and Fig. 7 demonstrate the results on both raw and preprocessed traces using Dataset 3 and Dataset 4. After dimensionality reduction and clustering, the traces are classified into two groups, with all data points assigned different colors and shapes. Colors represent the mappings derived from SPA, while shapes correspond to the correct operation associated with each trace. The expected outcome is that the SPA-derived mappings and the actual operation mappings align—meaning points of the same color should also share the same shape.

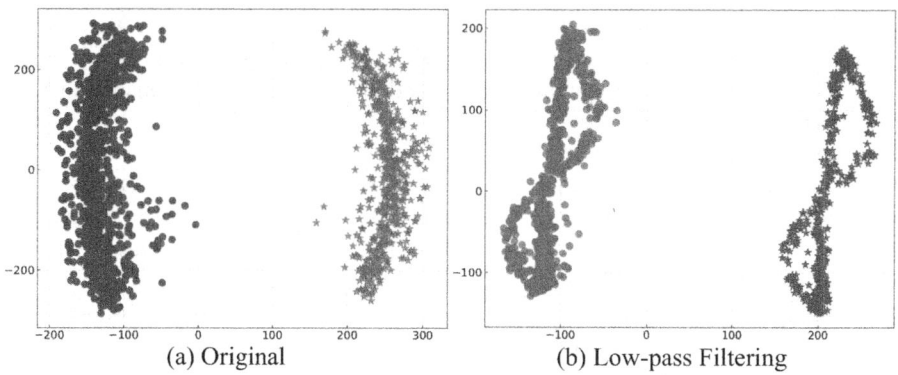

Fig. 7. Results of SPA with low-pass filtering on Dataset 4

In Fig. 6, the colors of the star-shaped points in the raw trace plot are not uniform, indicating suboptimal SPA performance. In contrast, the plot of the preprocessed traces fully meets expectations, showing that SPA was successfully performed after preprocessing. Figure 7 shows that both raw and low-pass filtered traces perform reasonably well in SPA. However, the clustering patterns are different, demonstrating that ChatGPT has effectively and correctly preprocessed the raw traces, enhancing the quality of the analysis.

In conclusion, ChatGPT demonstrates strong performance in trace preprocessing on real-world datasets. With the use of prompt templates and expert strategies, non-experts can easily and effectively perform trace preprocessing for SCA, without requiring extensive domain-specific knowledge. The experimental results underscore the practical utility of ChatGPT in this context. By leveraging ChatGPT for trace preprocessing, we successfully recovered the secret key from the experimental data. A comparative analysis of the number of traces required for AES implementations and recovery accuracy in implementing asymmetric cryptographic algorithms show that the ChatGPT-preprocessed approach significantly outperforms direct attacks on raw traces, demonstrating its effectiveness in enhancing the success rate of SCA.

4.4 Summary of Experimental Process

Our evaluation and analysis yield several important insights regarding the use of ChatGPT in trace preprocessing for SCA. The training data for large language models like ChatGPT typically encompasses academic papers, technical documentation, industry reports, and specialized forums, encompassing domain-specific knowledge in fields such as SCA. Through systematic exposure to terminology, logical relationships, and case studies embedded in these texts, the models acquire tacit knowledge from specialized domains. By learning general patterns from massive datasets, they effectively transfer these insights to trace preprocessing tasks. When combined with context-aware instruction tuning—a critical component of in-context learning—ChatGPT demonstrates strong capabilities in both the understanding mechanisms and processing methods of signals. First, ChatGPT has demonstrated the capability to perform a variety of trace preprocessing tasks—including filtering, segmentation, and clustering—with a reasonable degree of accuracy and consistency. This suggests that large language models can be effectively adapted for technical signal processing tasks, even without explicit training in this domain. Additionally, by applying structured, expert-crafted prompt strategies, we were able to guide ChatGPT through the preprocessing pipeline in a reproducible and interpretable manner. This highlights the potential for non-expert users to leverage such prompt templates to assist with CPA and SPA attacks, significantly lowering the barrier to entry for practical SCA.

Furthermore, our results indicate that the level of detail in prompts plays a crucial role in the model's performance. While more detailed procedural descriptions generally lead to more precise and effective outputs, overly verbose or complex instructions can introduce problems such as memory limitations, response truncation, or misunderstanding of intent—particularly in multi-step operations. These issues can reduce the reliability of the model and potentially bias the analysis. As such, future work should focus on balancing prompt informativeness with brevity, ensuring that essential operations are communicated clearly without overwhelming the model. Mitigating hallucination and addressing the contextual memory limitations of language models remain important directions for further investigation.

5 Conclusions

In this work, we explored the feasibility of employing ChatGPT as an assistant for trace preprocessing in the context of SCA. By designing a set of expert-inspired prompt templates, we enabled ChatGPT to perform various trace preprocessing operations, such as segmentation, filtering, and alignment, with simple user input. These prompts were structured across different levels of specificity, allowing for flexible interaction and control over the preprocessing process.

Through a series of experiments conducted on multiple datasets spanning different platforms, cryptographic algorithms, and physical leakage types, we evaluated the effectiveness of ChatGPT-assisted preprocessing using SPA and CPA. The results demonstrate that, in both symmetric and asymmetric cryptographic scenarios, ChatGPT-preprocessed traces significantly reduced the number of samples required for successful key recovery, compared to attacks on raw traces. This highlights the model's potential to enhance the efficiency of SCA without relying on highly specialized human expertise.

Our work highlights the feasibility and promising future of applying LLMs to SCA. By leveraging their ability to encode domain knowledge through prompt-based interaction, LLMs offer an intelligent, user-friendly solution for automating trace analysis. This not only reduces reliance on expert knowledge and traditional complex workflows but also enables broader participation in hardware security research. The demonstrated adaptability of LLMs to domain-specific signal processing tasks suggests a valuable direction for continued exploration and integration of AI-driven tools in real-world SCA scenarios.

Acknowledgement. This work is supported by National Key R&D Program of China (No. 2022YFB3103800), Beijing Natural Science Foundation (No. QY24173), Guizhou Provincial Key Technology R&D Program (No. [2023]442).

References

1. Baktash, J.A., Dawodi, M.: Gpt-4: a review on advancements and opportunities in natural language processing. CoRR abs/ arXiv: 2305.03195 (2023)
2. Bogdanov, A.: Improved side-channel collision attacks on AES. In: Adams, C., Miri, A., Wiener, M. (eds.) SAC 2007. LNCS, vol. 4876, pp. 84–95. Springer, Heidelberg (2007). https://doi.org/10.1007/978-3-540-77360-3_6
3. Brier, E., Clavier, C., Olivier, F.: Correlation power analysis with a leakage model. In: Joye, M., Quisquater, J.-J. (eds.) CHES 2004. LNCS, vol. 3156, pp. 16–29. Springer, Heidelberg (2004). https://doi.org/10.1007/978-3-540-28632-5_2
4. Clavié, B., Ciceu, A., Naylor, F., Soulié, G., Brightwell, T.: Large language models in the workplace: a case study on prompt engineering for job type classification. In: Métais, E., Meziane, F., Sugumaran, V., Manning, W., Reiff-Marganiec, S. (eds.) Natural Language Processing and Information Systems - 28th International Conference on Applications of Natural Language to Information Systems, NLDB 2023, Derby, UK, 21-23 June 2023, Proceedings. LNCS, vol. 13913, pp. 3–17. Springer (2023). https://doi.org/10.1007/978-3-031-35320-8_1
5. Conejo, A.J.O., Lederer, A., Hirche, S.: Adaptive low-pass filtering using sliding window gaussian processes. In: European Control Conference, ECC 2022, London, United Kingdom, 12-15 July 2022, pp. 2234–2240. IEEE (2022). https://doi.org/10.23919/ECC55457.2022.9838285
6. Debande, N., Souissi, Y., Elaabid, M.A., Guilley, S., Danger, J.: Wavelet transform based pre-processing for side channel analysis. In: 45th Annual IEEE/ACM International Symposium on Microarchitecture, MICRO 2012, Workshops Proceedings, Vancouver, BC, Canada, 1-5 December 2012, pp. 32–38. IEEE Computer Society (2012). https://doi.org/10.1109/MICROW.2012.15
7. Gao, S., Wen, X., Gao, C., Wang, W., Zhang, H., Lyu, M.R.: What makes good in-context demonstrations for code intelligence tasks with llms? In: 38th IEEE/ACM International Conference on Automated Software Engineering, ASE 2023, Luxembourg, 11-15 September 2023. pp. 761–773. IEEE (2023). https://doi.org/10.1109/ASE56229.2023.00109
8. He, H.: Sequential Decisions and Predictions in Natural Language Processing. Ph.D. thesis, University of Maryland, College Park, MD, USA (2016). https://doi.org/10.13016/M28Z2J, https://hdl.handle.net/1903/18580
9. Mesterharm, C., Izmailov, R., Alexander, S., Tsang, S.: Automated clustering of em side-channel emissions to detect anomalous device behavior. In: Cyber Sensing 2020, vol. 11417, pp. 59–68. SPIE (2020)
10. Ninan, M., et al.: A second look at the portability of deep learning side-channel attacks over EM traces. In: Losiouk, E., Brighente, A., Conti, M., Aafer, Y., Fratantonio, Y. (eds.) The 27th International Symposium on Research in Attacks, Intrusions and Defenses, RAID 2024, Padua, Italy, 30 September 2024- 2 October 2024. pp. 630–643. ACM (2024). https://doi.org/10.1145/3678890.3678900

11. Panoff, M., Yu, H., Shan, H., Jin, Y.: A review and comparison of AI enhanced side channel analysis. CoRR abs/ arxiv: 2402.02299 (2024)
12. Park, D., An, G., Kamyod, C., Kim, C.G.: A study on performance improvement of prompt engineering for generative AI with a large language model. J. Web Eng. **22**(8), 1187–1206 (2023). https://doi.org/10.13052/JWE1540-9589.2285
13. Patel, A., Li, B., Rasooli, M.S., Constant, N., Raffel, C., Callison-Burch, C.: Bidirectional language models are also few-shot learners. In: The Eleventh International Conference on Learning Representations, ICLR 2023, Kigali, Rwanda, 1-5 May 2023. OpenReview.net (2023)
14. Picek, S., Perin, G., Mariot, L., Wu, L., Batina, L.: Sok: deep learning-based physical side-channel analysis. ACM Comput. Surv. **55**(11), 227:1–227:35 (2023). https://doi.org/10.1145/3569577
15. Randolph, M., Diehl, W.: Power side-channel attack analysis: a review of 20 years of study for the layman. Cryptogr. **4**(2), 15 (2020). https://doi.org/10.3390/CRYPTOGRAPHY4020015
16. Robissout, D., Bossuet, L., Habrard, A.: Scoring the predictions: a way to improve profiling side-channel attacks. J. Cryptogr. Eng. **14**(3), 513–535 (2024). https://doi.org/10.1007/S13389-024-00346-4
17. Sufi, F.K.: Generative pre-trained transformer (GPT) in research: a systematic review on data augmentation. Inf. **15**(2), 99 (2024). https://doi.org/10.3390/INFO15020099
18. Wang, A., He, S., Wei, C., Sun, S., Ding, Y., Wang, J.: Using convolutional neural network to redress outliers in clustering based side-channel analysis on cryptosystem. In: International Conference on Smart Computing and Communication. pp. 360–370. Springer (2022)
19. Wang, Z., et al.: SPA-GPT: general pulse tailor for simple power analysis based on reinforcement learning. IACR Trans. Cryptogr. Hardw. Embed. Syst. **2024**(4), 40–83 (2024). https://doi.org/10.46586/TCHES.V2024.I4.40-83
20. Xia, C.S., Wei, Y., Zhang, L.: Automated program repair in the era of large pre-trained language models. In: 45th IEEE/ACM International Conference on Software Engineering, ICSE 2023, Melbourne, Australia, 14-20 May 2023, pp. 1482–1494. IEEE (2023). https://doi.org/10.1109/ICSE48619.2023.00129
21. Yenduri, G., et al.: GPT (generative pre-trained transformer) - a comprehensive review on enabling technologies, potential applications, emerging challenges, and future directions. IEEE Access **12**, 54608–54649 (2024). https://doi.org/10.1109/ACCESS.2024.3389497
22. Zhou, W., Wang, A., Ding, Y., Wei, C., Zhang, J., Zhu, L.: One solves all: Exploring chatgpt's capabilities for fully automated simple power analysis on cryptosystems. IACR Cryptol. ePrint Arch. p. 2069 (2024)

Improved Functional Bootstrapping of SM4 for Hybrid Homomorphic Encryption

Jin Peng[1], Dachao Wang[2], and Zheng Gong[1](✉)

[1] South China Normal University, Guangzhou, China
pengjin250@gmail.com, cis.gong@gmail.com
[2] Lund University, Lund, Sweden
dachao.wang@eit.lth.se

Abstract. Fully Homomorphic Encryption (FHE) enables to evaluate arbitrary functions on encrypted data, where the noise to protect the security also results in the ciphertext expansion problem. Hybrid Homomorphic Encryption (HHE), also called transciphering, utilizes symmetric ciphers to address the expansion problem. But HHE also increases the transciphering computational costs on the server side. Therefore, how to design an efficient homomorphic decryption circuit plays a pivotal role for practical HHE. In the literature, researchers proposed several decryption circuits for block cipher SM4, which has been standardized for commercial cryptography in China. However, those proposals still have the practical issues about high latency, memory, and communication overhead.

In this paper, we propose an HHE scheme with an improved functional bootstrapping of SM4, which reduces the time and memory costs for the ciphertext transformation. Specifically, we construct homomorphic circuit for the lookup table (LUT) implementation of SM4, which are integrated from two homomorphic decryption circuits (Circuit 1 and 2). Circuit 1 follows the standard LUT implementation, whilst Circuit 2 optimizes the homomorphic evaluation. Compare to the bootstrapped version of Brakerski Gentry Vaikuntanathan (BGV) scheme of transciphering, the latency of Circuit 2 improves from 1.6 h to 285.5 s. The memory costs of our proposal are also reduced from 2 GB to 0.5 GB with respect to the Fully Homomorphic Encryption over the Torus (TFHE) scheme.

Keywords: Hybrid Homomorphic Encryption · Fully Homomorphic Encryption over the Torus · Functional Bootstrapping · SM4

1 Introduction

Homomorphic Encryption (HE) allows to compute functions on encrypted data without decryption before, introduced by Rivest et al. [39] in 1978. Subsequently, Partially Homomorphic Encryption (PHE) [16,37,42] and SomeWhat Homomorphic Encryption (SWHE) [4] schemes were proposed, where PHE only allows to compute either addition or multiplication operation and SWHE allows to compute both operations with limited times. But how to construct Fully Homomorphic Encryption (FHE) remained an open challenge until Gentry proposed bootstrapping technique [21] in 2009. Bootstrapping can refresh the noise of ciphertexts to avoid decryption failure, making FHE schemes conduct functions with unlimited times. This technique is then widely used in FHE schemes, including BGV [6], BFV [5], CKKS [10], and TFHE [11].

However, the noise for security also causes the ciphertext expansion, significantly increasing communication overhead when transmitting FHE ciphertexts. To make the FHE scheme practical, Hybird Homomorphic Encryption (HHE), also called transciphering, is firstly proposed by Naehrig et al. [36]. Unlike FHE, in the HHE scenario, the data owner employs a symmetric encryption algorithm E to encrypt data, and the computation server homomorphically evaluates the decryption E^{-1} circuit to transform the symmetric ciphertext $E(m)$ to $FHE(m)$. Thus, the server enables to compute on ciphertexts. Compared with FHE, the HHE scheme introduces a homomorphic decryption operation for symmetric ciphertexts, which makes a trade-off between the communication overhead and the server transciphering costs.

Research on HHE begins from the standard block cipher AES [14,19,22], while AES is not well-suited for HHE scheme due to the high multiplicative depth and multiplicative complexity. Thus, some FHE-friendly symmetric ciphers are proposed, including LowMC [2], MiMC [1], Rasta-like ciphers [13,17,18,25,27,29], FLIP-like ciphers [15,34,35], HERA [12], Chaghri [3], Rubato [28], and Yux [31]. Nonetheless, the security cannot be guaranteed [20,24,32,33]. However, a majority of data in dataset is encrypted by standard ciphers, using the FHE-friendly ciphers in HHE can result in the compatibility issue. It requires to transform ciphertexts from FHE-friendly symmetric ciphers into standardized ciphers. Thus, the effective homomorphic decryption circuit of standard ciphers, specifically AES, remains interest for the HHE community.

The application of homomorphic AES decryption circuit focus on three type bootstrapping of the TFHE scheme, including gate bootstrapping [44], functional bootstrapping [40] and circuit bootstrapping [41,43,44]. However, the SM4 algorithm, a widely used standard symmetric block cipher in China, garnering fewer concentration. For BGV scheme, Xue [45] proposed the first homomorphic evaluation of SM4, where the leveled and bootstrapped version requires 6 and 1.58 h, respectively. For TFHE, Wei et al. [44] utilized three-level circuit bootstrapping to achieve homomorphic SM4 decryption with an evaluation latency of 78 s. Unfortunately, transitions between these three layers introduce communication overhead due to the KeySwitch operation, which requires $(N \times B_{KS} \times t)$ TRLWE ciphertexts for the KeySwitchKey. In [44], the KeySwitch parameters for level 1 to 0 and 2 to 1 are ($N = 1024, B_{KS} = 2^2 = 4, t = 7$) and ($\bar{N} = 2048, \bar{B}_{KS} = 2^3 = 8, \bar{t} = 10$), respectively, resulting in a total KeySwitchKey size of approximately 2GB. In HHE scenario, the data owner must generate and transmit the KeySwitchKey to the communication server, thus increasing the communication burden.

1.1 Contribution

This paper presents two homomorphic circuits for the LUT implementation of SM4, containing 32-bit XOR evaluation and four 8-bit-to-32-bit T_i lookup table operations. Since 4-bit precision messages offer optimal performance for functional bootstrapping, we generate a 4-bit-to-4-bit XOR table for homomorphic 32-bit XOR evaluation and decompose each 8-bit-to-32-bit T_i table into eight 8-bit-to-4-bit sub-tables for homomorphic T_i operation. We describe the detailed process to transform the plaintext evaluation to the FHE ciphertext evaluation. Specifically, we design two circuits, where Circuit 1 fully follows the LUT implementation, and Circuit 2 optimizes the number of the homomorphic evaluation. Compare to the bootstrapped version of BGV scheme of transciphering, the latency of Circuit 2 improves from 1.6 h to 285.5 s. The memory costs of our proposal are also reduced from 2GB to 0.5GB with respect to the TFHE.

Organization. We first review the TFHE scheme, functional bootstrapping (FBS), multi-values functional bootstrapping (MVBS), tree-based MVBS in Sect. 2. In Sect. 3, we provide a short specification of the lookup implementation of SM4. Two homomorphic decryption circuits are proposed in Sect. 4. Environment setting and performance analysis are provided in Sect. 5. The paper concludes in Sect. 6.

2 The TFHE Cryptosystem

TFHE cryptosystem is a fully homomorphic scheme with security based on Learning with Errors (LWE) problem [38]. In this section, we review the fundamental concepts and bootstrapping technique necessary for the understanding of this paper.

The 'T' in TFHE means the Real Torus $\mathbb{T} = \mathbb{R}/\mathbb{Z}$, the set of real number modulo 1, where $\mathbb{T}^n$ represents a vector with n elements in $\mathbb{T}$. We denote by $\mathbb{Z}_N[X]$ the ring of polynomials $\mathbb{Z}[X]/(X^N + 1)$, where $\mathbb{T}_N[X]$ denotes the polynomials $\mathbb{R}[X]/(X^N + 1) \bmod 1$, and $\mathbb{T}_N[X]^n$ denotes n polynomials in $\mathbb{T}_N[X]$. Let $\mathbb{B} = \{0, 1\}$ and $\mathbb{B}_N[X]^n$ denote n polynomials in $\mathbb{Z}_N[X]$ with coefficients in $\mathbb{B}$.

TFHE scheme defines the general LWE problem (TLWE) and general scale invariant version of the GSW scheme [23] (TRGSW). To differ with the Ring mode with TLWE, it also introduces the notation TRLWE. These three ciphertexts are summarize below.

- **TLWE sample**: Given a random vector $\boldsymbol{a}$ sampled from $\mathbb{T}^n$, a random error e sampled from a Gaussian distribution with mean 0 and standard deviation σ, and secret key $\boldsymbol{s}$ sampled from $\mathbb{B}^n$. For a message $m \in \mathbb{T}$, the TLWE ciphertext $c = (\boldsymbol{a}, b) \in \mathbb{T}^{n+1}$. Specifically, $b = \langle \boldsymbol{a}, \boldsymbol{s} \rangle + m + e \in \mathbb{T}$, where $\langle \, , \, \rangle$ is an inner product.
- **TRLWE sample**: Given a random polynomial $a(X)$ sampled from $\mathbb{T}_N[X]^k$, a error polynomial $e(X)$ with the coefficients randomly sampled from a Gaussian distribution with mean 0 and standard deviation σ, and secret key polynomial $s(X)$ with coefficients from $\mathbb{B}$. For a message polynomial $m(X) \in$

$\mathbb{T}_N[X]$, the TRLWE ciphertext $c(X)$ is encrypted as $c(X) = (a(X), b(X)) \in \mathbb{T}_N[X]^2$. Specifically, $b(X) = a(X)s(X) + m(X) + e(X) \in \mathbb{T}_N[X]$.

- **TRGSW sample**: Given a message $m \in \mathbb{B}$, the TRGSW ciphertext C is encrypted as follows:

$$\mathcal{C} = \begin{pmatrix} a_1(X) & b_1(X) \\ a_2(X) & b_2(X) \\ \vdots & \vdots \\ a_\ell(X) & b_\ell(X) \\ a_{\ell+1}(X) & b_{\ell+1}(X) \\ \vdots & \vdots \\ a_{2\ell}(X) & b_{2\ell}(X) \end{pmatrix} + m \cdot \begin{pmatrix} 1/B_g & 0 \\ 1/B_g^2 & 0 \\ \vdots & \vdots \\ 1/B_g^\ell & 0 \\ 0 & 1/B_g \\ \vdots & \vdots \\ 0 & 1/B_g^\ell \end{pmatrix},$$

where $(a_i(X), b_i(X))$, $i \in [1..2\ell]$ are fresh TRLWE ciphertexts encrypted by the same secret key $s(X)$. TRGSW ciphertexts are the public evaluation key used in bootstrapping.

2.1 TFHE Bootstrapping

Bootstrapping is a crucial technique to manage the ciphertext noise for further homomorphic evaluations, including several fundamental operations, briefly introduced in this section.

- **BlindRotate**: Given a test-polynomial $T(X)$ encrypted as a TRLWE ciphertext $c = \text{TRLWE}(T(X))$, an encrypted LWE ciphertext $\text{TLWE}(m) = (\boldsymbol{a}, b)$, and a TRGSW ciphertext encrypting the secret key $\boldsymbol{s}$. The BlindRotate algorithm outputs a TRLWE ciphertext $c' = \text{TRLWE}(T(X) \cdot X^{\langle \boldsymbol{a}, \boldsymbol{s} \rangle - b})$. Essentially, this performs a rotation of $T(X)$ based on the index m.
- **SampleExtract**: Given a TRLWE ciphertext $c = \text{TRLWE}(M(X))$ and an index $p \in \{0, \cdots, N-1\}$. The SampleExtract algorithm outputs a TLWE ciphertext $\text{TLWE}(m_p)$, where m_p is the $p-th$ coefficient of the polynomial $M(X)$.
- **KeySwitch**: Given p TLWE ciphertexts $\text{TLWE}(m_i)$ encrypted by the same secret key $\boldsymbol{s}$. The KeySwitch algorithm outputs $\text{TRLWE}(f(m_0, \cdots, m_{p-1}))$, encrypted by another secret key $\boldsymbol{s'}$, where $f : \mathbb{T}^p \to \mathbb{T}_N[X]$ is a public linear morphism. The KeySwitch algorithm allows to packing of TLWE ciphertexts in one TRLWE ciphertext, and evaluates a function f on these input TLWE ciphertext. The KeySwitch operation can be used to pack multiple TLWE ciphertexts into a TRLWE ciphertext, while SampleExtract can unpack reversely.

2.2 Functional Bootstrapping and Multi-value Bootstrapping

Functional Bootstrapping (FBS), also called Programmable Bootstrapping (PBS), refreshes the ciphertext noise, concurrently homomorphically evaluating arbitrary functions on encrypted inputs. The idea is to embed the value of function $f: \mathbb{Z}_t \to \mathbb{Z}_t$ into a test polynomial $T(X)$, such that

$$T(X) = \sum_{i=0}^{N-1} f(\lceil \frac{i \cdot t}{N} \rceil) \cdot X^i.$$

We note that the TRLWE ciphertext of $T(X)$ contains N/t slots with same plaintext for BlindRotate operation. $T(X)$ is depicted in Fig. 1.

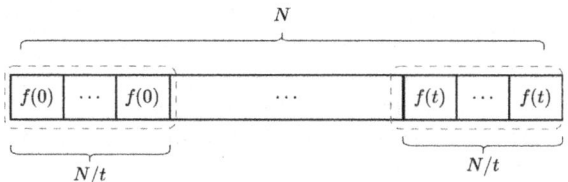

Fig. 1. Test polynomial

Furthermore, multi-value functional bootstrapping (MVBS) [7] supports to compute several functions on the same input while only consuming one FBS. For each function F_i, the corresponding test polynomial TV_{F_i} can be split into two sub polynomials $(TV^{(0)}, TV^{(1)}_{F_i}(X))$ by Eq. (1), where $TV^{(0)}$ individuals to the functions F_i.

$$(1 + X + \cdots + X^{N-1}) \cdot (1 - X) \equiv 2 \mod (X^N + 1). \tag{1}$$

Each $TV_{F_i} = \sum_{i=1}^{N-1} t_i \cdot X^i$ is equivalent to

$$TV_{F_i} = \frac{1}{2} \cdot (1 + X + \cdots + X^{N-1}) \cdot (1 - X) \cdot TV_{F_i} \mod (X^N + 1).$$

where

$$TV^{(0)} = \frac{1}{2} \cdot (1 + X + \cdots + X^{N-1}) = \frac{1}{2} \cdot \sum_{i=0}^{N-1} X^i,$$

$$TV^{(1)}_{F_i}(X) = (1 - X) \cdot TV_{F_i} = (1 - X) \cdot \sum_{i=1}^{N-1} t_i \cdot X^i$$

Therefore, to conduct MVBS for multi-functions on the same encrypted input, it requires to initialize the test-polynomial $TV^{(0)}$, use BlindRotate operation with input TLWE to obtain a new TRLWE sample called accumulator (ACC). Then, multiply ACC by each $TV^{(1)}_{F_i}(X)$ to obtain the results of these functions.

2.3 Tree-Based MVBS

Tree-based MVBS [26] structures multiple functional bootstraps to a tree and uses the output of a lookup table to construct a new table.

Firstly, the origin table is split to multiple sub-tables with B elements, each sub-table is packed into a test-polynomial. Then the column index for original table, a TLWE with B precision of the corresponding plaintext, is a selector to locating the position of these test-polynomials. The BlindRotate operation blindly rotates the values of position to the constant coefficient of all test-polynomials, extracted into B TLWE ciphertexts by SampleExtract operation. These separate TLWEs are packed into a TRLWE ciphertext, where the corresponding plaintext is like a new LUT with B values. The packing process is also called LWEs-to-RLWE operation. Finally, the TLWE of the row index for original table is rotated to obtain the LUT result in a TLWE ciphertext. The total process is depicted in Fig. 2.

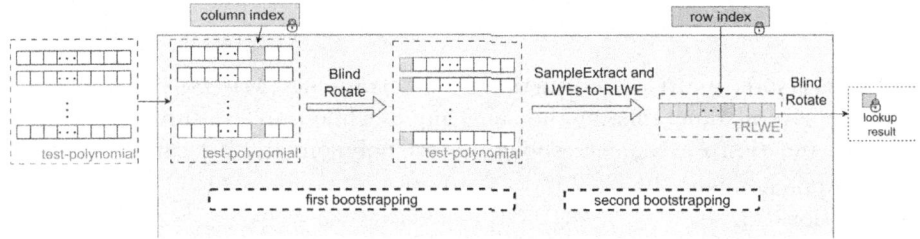

Fig. 2. Tree-based MVB technique

The LWEs-to-RLWE operation in [26] requires $(N \times B_{KS} \times t \times B)$ TRLWE ciphertexts KeySwitchKey, where the basis B significantly influence the key size. Hao et al. [9] employ the automorphism $\tau(\cdot)$ and EvalAuto operation to achieve the PackLWEs procedure. To pack $B = 2^\ell$ TLWE ciphertexts to a TRLWE ciphertext, it requires ℓ EvalAuto operations with ℓ keys. Thus, the keyswitch key decreases to $(N \times B_{KS} \times t \times log_2 B)$ TRLWE ciphertexts.

3 A Brief Description of SM4

SM4 algorithm is a standard block cipher of China, which comprises 32 round functions, defined as

$$F(X_i, X_{i+1}, X_{i+2}, X_{i+3}, rk_i) = X_i \oplus T(X_{i+1} \oplus X_{i+2} \oplus X_{i+3} \oplus rk_i), \ i \in [0..31]$$

The structure of SM4 is described in Fig. 3.

The input of SM4 represents as (X_0, X_1, X_2, X_3). Each function receives a 128-bit intermediate state $(X_i, X_{i+1}, X_{i+2}, X_{i+3})$ and i-th round key rk_i as inputs, and produces a 32-bit value X_{i+4} used to compose the $(i + 1)$-th round

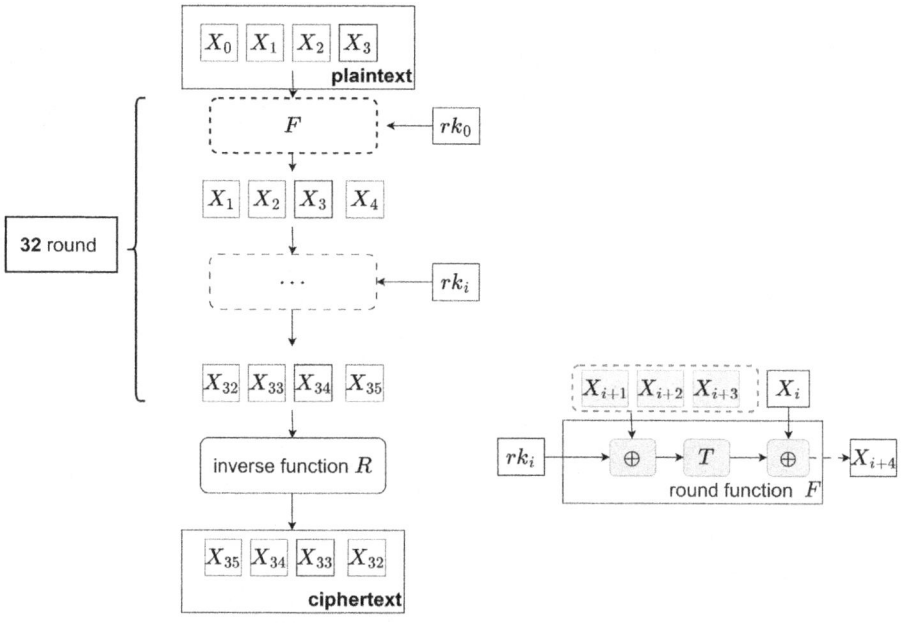

Fig. 3. SM4 algorithm

state as output. The transformation T is composed of a non-linear transformation τ followed by a linear transformation L. The non-linear transformation τ applies four parallel Sboxes

$$B = \tau(x_0, x_1, x_2, x_3) = (\text{Sbox}(x_0), \text{Sbox}(x_1), \text{Sbox}(x_2), \text{Sbox}(x_3)),$$

where $x_i \in \mathbb{Z}_8$, $i \in [0..3]$ and $B \in \mathbb{Z}_{32}$. Subsequently, B serves as the input to the linear transformation L to obtain the output C.

$$C = L(B) = B \oplus (B \lll 2) \oplus (B \lll 10) \oplus (B \lll 24).$$

Finally, X_{i+4} is calculated as $X_0 \oplus (L \circ \tau) = X_0 \oplus C$. After the 32 round function, the result is the reverse sequence of the output of 32 function. The integral procedure is described below.

$$X_{i+4} = X_i \oplus T(X_{i+1} \oplus X_{i+2} \oplus X_{i+3} \oplus rk_i) \qquad (2)$$
$$(Y_0, Y_1, Y_2, Y_3) = R(X_{32}, X_{33}, X_{34}, X_{35}) = (X_{35}, X_{34}, X_{33}, X_{32}).$$

Key Expansion. Key expansion generates 32 round keys from the 128-bit secret key (MK_0, MK_1, MK_2, MK_3). Initially, the secret key is initialized as $(rk_0, rk_1, rk_2, rk_3) = (MK_0 \oplus FK_0, MK_1 \oplus FK_1, MK_2 \oplus FK_2, MK_3 \oplus FK_3)$, where $FK_i \in \mathbb{Z}_{3}2$, $i \in [0..3]$ are constant values. The key expansion is similar to the round function F:

$$rk_{i+4} = rk_i \oplus T'(rk_{i+1} \oplus rk_{i+2} \oplus rk_{i+3} \oplus CK_i), \ i \in [0..31],$$

where $CK_i \in \mathbb{Z}_{32}$ is a constant value. The transformation T' consists of the non-linear transformation τ and a linear transformation $L'(B) = B \oplus (B \lll 13) \oplus (B \lll 23)$

We consider the lookup table implementation of SM4 proposed by [30], the main idea is to compose the four Sbox with the followed cyclic shift transformation L, as defined

$$L(S(x_0), S(x_1), S(x_2), S(x_3))$$
$$= L(S(x_0) \lll 24) \oplus L(S(x_1) \lll 16) \oplus L(S(x_2) \lll 8) \oplus L(S(x_3)).$$

Four table T_i with 8-bit input and 32-bit output is defined :

$$T_0(x) = L(S(x_0) \lll 24)$$
$$T_1(x) = L(S(x_1) \lll 16)$$
$$T_2(x) = L(S(x_2) \lll 8)$$
$$T_3(x) = L(S(x_3))$$

Thus, the Eq.(2) is equivalence as

$$(x_0, x_1, x_2, x_3) = X_{i+1} \oplus X_{i+2} \oplus X_{i+3} \oplus rk_i \tag{3}$$
$$X_{i+4} = X_i \oplus T_0(x_0) \oplus T_1(x_1) \oplus T_2(x_2) \oplus T_3(x_3) \tag{4}$$

The transformation in (3) involves three 32-to-32 bitwise XOR operations, and the Eq. (4) requires four 8-to-32 lookup tables T_i and four 32-to-32 bitwise XOR operations. Specifically, Eq. (3) splits a 32-bit values into four 8-bit values. These values are then utilized as inputs to the four T tables, resulting in four 32-bit output, as shown in Eq. (4).

4 Homomorphic Decryption Circuit of SM4 Algorithm

While homomorphic evaluation of standard symmetric ciphers has primarily focused on AES, there has been less attention given to SM4. The decryption structure of SM4 is identical to its encryption, except for the order of the round keys sequence. Consequently, homomorphic evaluation of SM4, transforming SM4 ciphertext $c = E(m)$ into FHE(m), only requires designing a homomorphic circuit for the round function, without considering a specific decryption circuit like AES.

The linear transformation L operates on a 32-bit input, applying left shifts of $(0, 2, 10, 24)$ bits before three bitwise XOR operations on these results. The constraint arises from the fixed precision of encrypted messages in TFHE schemes. Directly implementing L would restrict the plaintext precision to 1-bit or 2-bit. However, homomorphic evaluation of TFHE achieves optimal efficiency with 4-bit precision. Therefore, we focus on the LUT implementation of SM4 and design a homomorphic circuit via functional bootstrapping technique.

4.1 Homomorphic Evaluation of Round Function

To maximize the efficiency of TFHE functional bootstrapping, we implement all operations in homomorphic circuit via LUT method.

In the TFHE scheme, the message precision p must be predefined before encryption, ranging the message in $[0..B-1]$, where $B = 2^p$ is basis. Although the decryped value may exceed the range after the ciphertext computation, a decoding process adjusts the value to fall with this range. Since a higher precision requires larger parameters of TFHE, resulting in a significant increase in computational overhead, the choice of B is limited in $(2^0, \cdots, 2^8)$. Consequently, if a message x requires more than p bits for representation, a decomposition method must be employed before encrypted. The decomposition of x is expressed below.

$$x = \sum_{j=0}^{w} x_j \cdot B^j \text{ with } x_j \in \{0, \cdots, B-1\}, \ w \geq 1. \tag{5}$$

The SM4 round function involves 32-bit intermediate value X_i, round key rk_i, and T table output, which exceed the supported capacity of TFHE scheme. To address it, a basis B is predefined to decompose plaintext messages before TFHE encryption and evaluation. The experimental finding presented in [40] demonstrate that 4-bit precision messages achieved peak efficiency in homomorphic AES evaluation, surpassing 2-bit, 8-bit, and 16-bit precisions.

When setting basis $B = 2^4 = 16$, a 32-bit message is decomposed into $m = m_0 + m_1 \cdot 16 + \cdots + m_7 \cdot 16^7$. and the corresponding ciphertext is of the form

$$c = (c_0, c_1, \cdots, c_7) = (\text{FHE}(m_0), \text{FHE}(m_1), \cdots, \text{FHE}(m_7)).$$

For two ciphertexts c and c' with the corresponding plaintext m and m', the XOR operation between plaintexts represents as $m \oplus m' = (m_0, m_1, \cdots, m_7) \oplus (m'_0, m'_1, \cdots, m'_7) = (m_0 \oplus m'_0, m_1 \oplus m'_1, \cdots, m_7 \oplus m'_7)$. Then, the homomorphic XOR operation can be represented as

$$c \oplus c' = (c_0, c_1, \cdots, c_7) \oplus (c'_0, c'_1, \cdots, c'_7) = (c_0 \oplus c'_0, c_1 \oplus c'_1, \cdots, c_7 \oplus c'_7). \tag{6}$$

We transform a 32-bits XOR operation on ciphertexts to eight times 4-bits XOR operations. As TFHE does not natively support 4-bit XOR operation on ciphertexts, a LUT T_{XOR} is required. The generation is represented below.

$$T_{\text{XOR}}(x) = (x \ \& \ 0xf) \oplus ((x \gg 4) \ \& \ 0xf), \quad x \in [0..255].$$

Then the $c_i \oplus c'_i$ is the output of the homomorphic XOR circuit through the $Eval$ algorithm supported by FHE

$$c_i \oplus c'_i = Eval((\text{FHE}(m_i), \text{FHE}(m'_i)), T_{\text{XOR}}). \tag{7}$$

For two ciphertexts c_i and c'_i, we apply the MVB optimization to evaluate T_{XOR} and output the result $\text{FHE}(m_i \oplus m'_i)$ in only two bootstrapping. We represent c_i (resp. c'_i) as the column index, while c'_i (resp. c_i) as the row index.

The first bootstrapping blindly rotates c_i to obtain 16 TLWE ciphertexts, where the corresponding plaintexts are in the m_i-th column of T_{XOR}. These values are then composed into a TRLWE ciphertext, which requires 16 keyswitching keys. The second bootstrapping is role on the TRLWE ciphertext, blindly rotating c_i' to obtain one TLWE ciphertext, which is the m_i'-th row of m_i-th column. The TLWE ciphertext is $\text{FHE}(m_i \oplus m_i')$. The comparison of XOR evaluation between two plaintexts and ciphertexts is shown as Fig. 4.

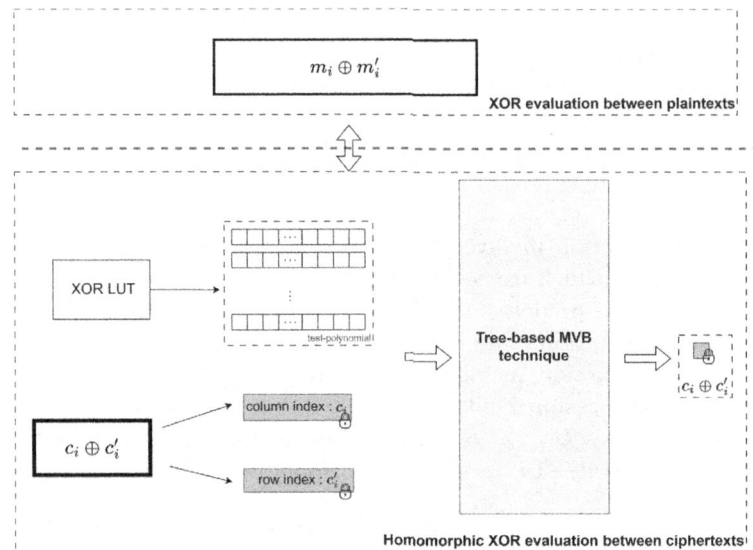

Fig. 4. Comparison of XOR evaluation between plaintexts and ciphertexts

Homomorphic evaluation of the T tables differs slightly from homomorphic XOR evaluation. Each T_i table maps an 8-bit value to a 32-bit value. For homomorphic evaluation, both input and output are FHE ciphertexts, with the encrypted messages represented in 4-bit precision (for $B = 2^4 = 16$). To facilitate this, each 8-to-32 T_i is decomposed into eight 8-to-4 sub-tables. The process is outline below:

$$T_{i,j}(x) = (T_i(x) \gg (32 - (4 \times j))) \ \& \ 0xf, \ i \in [0..3], \ j \in [1..8].$$

For an 8-bit input m, LUT operation is to extract the value in position m via $T_{i,j}(m)$. Using the basis $B = 2^4$, the 8-bit message can be decomposed as $m = m_0 + m_1 \cdot 16$. The corresponding ciphertext is of the form

$$c = (c_0, c_1) = (\text{FHE}(m_0), \text{FHE}(m_1))$$

The homomorphic evaluation of $T_{i,j}$ is represented by

$$T_{i,j}(c) = Eval(\text{FHE}(m_0), \text{FHE}(m_1)), T_{i,j}).$$

Homomorphic XOR evaluation operates on components from two distinct ciphertexts c and c', whereas the homomorphic $T_{i,j}$ evaluation uses components derived from a ciphertext c. Moreover, the column index is defined as $\text{FHE}(m_0)$ and the row index as $\text{FHE}(m_1)$, and this sequence is non-interchangeable. The comparison of lookup $T_{i,j}$ table between a plaintext and ciphertext is illustrated in Fig. 5.

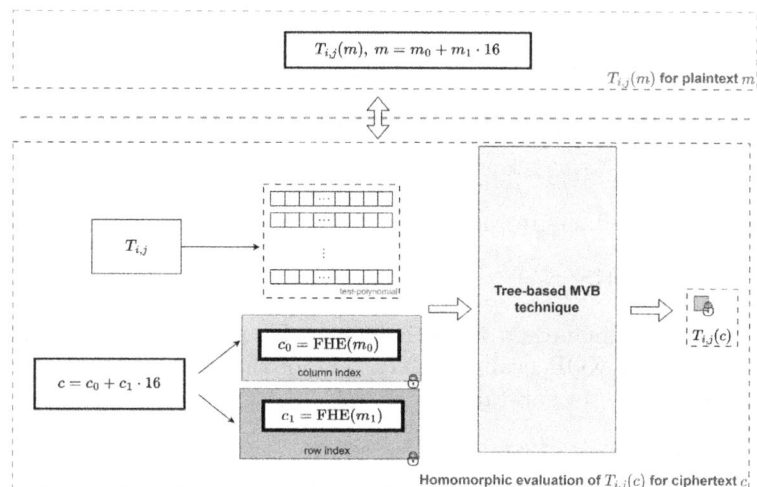

Fig. 5. Comparison of $T_{i,j}$ evaluation between plaintexts and ciphertexts

4.2 Going Homomorphic for Real Numbers

To homomorphically evaluate the SM4 decryption circuit, the 128-bit ciphertext $c = \text{SM4}(m)$ and the 32 encrypted round keys $\text{FHE}(rk_i), i \in [0..31]$ via TFHE scheme should be sent from the data owner to the homomorphic evaluation.

Let $X_i = (c \gg (128 - 32 * i))\ \&\ (2^{32} - 1) \in \mathbb{Z}_{32}, i \in [0..3]$. In the first round of homomorphic evaluation, X_0, X_1, X_2, X_3 are encrypted by SM4, $\text{FHE}(rk_0)$ is encrypted by FHE. The Eq. (3) $X_1 \oplus X_2 \oplus X_3 \oplus \text{FHE}(rk_0)$ conducts via two bitwise XOR operations and one homomorphic XOR evaluation. The intermediate result $X' = X_1 \oplus X_2 \oplus X_3$ should be split into eight blocks of 4-bit nibbles and encrypted in FHE ciphertexts.

$$\text{FHE}(X') = (\text{FHE}(X'_0), \cdots, \text{FHE}(X'_7)), \tag{8}$$

$$X' \in \mathbb{Z}_{32},\ X'_j = (X' \gg (32 - 4 * j))\ \&\ 0xf,\ j \in [0..7]. \tag{9}$$

The homomorphic XOR evaluation between FHE(X') and FHE(rk_0), where FHE(rk_i) consists of eight FHE ciphertexts

$$\text{FHE}(rk_i) = (\text{FHE}(rk_{i,0}), \cdots, \text{FHE}(rk_{i,7})), \ i \in [0..31]$$
$$rk_0 \in \mathbb{Z}_{32}, \ rk_{0,j} = (rk_0 \gg (32 - 4*j)) \ \& \ 0xf, \ j \in [0..7],$$

The homomorphic XOR evaluation is represented as

$$\text{FHE}(X'_j) \oplus \text{FHE}(rk_{0,j}) = Eval((\text{FHE}(X'_j), \text{FHE}(rk_{0,j})), T_{\text{XOR}}). \tag{10}$$

The output of Eq.(3) in the first round is four FHE array:

$$\text{FHE}(x_i) = (\text{FHE}(x_{i,0}), \text{FHE}(x_{i,1})), \ i \in [0..3]$$
$$x_i \in \mathbb{Z}_4, x_{i,k} = x_i \gg (8 - 4*k) \ \& \ 0xf, \ k \in [0..1].$$

Equation (4) conducts in the homomorphic encryption:

$$\text{FHE}(X_0) \oplus T_0(\text{FHE}(x_0)) \oplus T_1(\text{FHE}(x_1)) \oplus T_2(\text{FHE}(x_2)) \oplus T_3(\text{FHE}(x_3)).$$

This evaluation includes 4 times homomorphic evaluation of T table and 4 times homomorphic XOR evaluation. In the homomorphic evaluation of T_i, T_i has been split into eight sub-tables

$$T_i(\text{FHE}(x_i)) = (T_{i,0}(\text{FHE}(x_i)), \cdots, T_{i,7}(\text{FHE}(x_i))), \ i \in [0..3],$$

where FHE($x_{i,0}$) and FHE($x_{i,1}$) are defined as the row and column index for MVBS, respectively. The process if

$$T_{i,j}(\text{FHE}(x_i)) = Eval(\text{FHE}(x_{i,0}), \text{FHE}(x_{i,1}), T_{i,j}) \ j \in [0..7]. \tag{11}$$

4.3 Parallelization

In HHE, a homomorphic computation has more computing resource, which can efficiency run on several cores to conduct the parallelization and optimize execution times. In addition, the construction of SM4 is suitable for parallelization, where it can evaluate the T_i tables and several XOR operations in parallel. We use the OpenMP [8] to parallelize our homomorphic SM4.

To homomorphically evaluate Eq. (3), we parallelize the evaluation of FHE(rk_i) $\oplus$FHE(X_{i+1}) and FHE(X_{i+2}) $\oplus$FHE(X_{i+3}) for round 2 to 31. This involves $2 \times 8 = 16$ homomorphic evaluation of 4-bit XOR operations. Furthermore, the result of FHE(X_{i+2})$\oplus$FHE(X_{i+3}) from an even round i can be reused in the $(i+1)$-th round. Consequently, two consecutive rounds require $3 \times 8 = 24$ homomorphic evaluations of 4-bit XOR.

To homomorphically evaluate Eq. (4), we simultaneously evaluate all T_i tables for full-round, requiring $4 \times 8 = 32$ homomorphic evaluations of 4-bit $T_{i,j}$ table. Additionally, we parallelize the evaluation of FHE($T_0(x_0)$)$\oplus$FHE($T_1(x_1)$) and FHE($T_2(x_2)$)$\oplus$FHE($T_3(x_3)$), which involves $2 \times 8 = 16$ homomorphic evaluations of 4-bit XOR operations. The total process is described in Fig. 6.

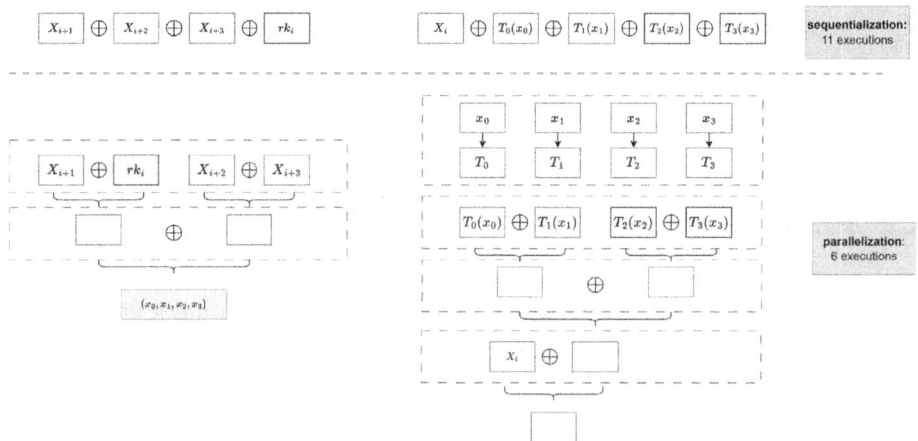

Fig. 6. SM4 parallelization

5 Experiments on the Homomorphic Decryption of SM4

In this section, we implement the homomorphic evaluation of two SM4 decryption circuits through functional bootstrapping based on the TFHE library [11] with optim" build. All experiments are conducted on Intel(R) Xeon(R) Gold 6226R CPU @ 2.90 GHz using Ubuntu 22.04 LTS with 80 GB memory. The implementation source code is compiled with GCC 11.4.0.

5.1 Parameter Selection

We set the messages precision basis $B = 2^4 = 16$ for the circuits, with the necessary parameters for bootstrapping technique. Parameters are shown in Table 1, same as [44].

Table 1. Parameters for homomorphic SM4 decryption circuit

Security Level	B	LWE		RLWE			Bootstrapping		KeySwitch	
		n	σ	N	k	σ	l	$log_2(B_g)$	B_{KS}	t
127	4	630	2^{-15}	1024	1	2^{-25}	3	6	4	7

To homomorphically decrypt SM4 ciphertexts, the data owner sends necessary keys to the computation server, where the size of KeySwitchKey dominates the total evaluation key. Table 2 compares the size of KeySwitchKey in our work with [44].

Table 2. Key Size used in the WB-HHE framework.

work	KeySwitchKey size
[44]	2 GB
our	0.5 GB

5.2 Performance Analysis

In this section, we analyze the performance of two homomorphic SM4 decryption circuits based on TFHE scheme in HHE framework. Our circuits are designed base on the lookup table implementation of the SM4 algorithm, including two operations: homomorphic 4-bit XOR and homomorphic $T_{i,j}, (0 \leq i \leq 3, 0 \leq j \leq 7)$ tables.

In the first two rounds of Circuit 1, there exists the XOR operations of SM4 ciphertexts and homomorphic 4-bit XOR with corresponding round key FHE(rk). The evaluation of round 1 contains 2 XOR operations in $X_1 \oplus X_2 \oplus X_3$, 40 homomorphic 4-bit XOR and 32 homomorphic $T_{i,j}$ operations, outputting the FHE ciphertext of X_4. The operations of round 2 contains 1 XOR operation in $X_2 \oplus X_3$, 48 homomorphic 4-bit XOR and 32 homomorphic $T_{i,j}$ operations, outputting the FHE ciphertext of X_5. The followed 30 rounds only consist of homomorphic evaluation, including 56 homomorphic 4-bit XOR and 32 homomorphic $T_{i,j}$ operations.

Since some intermediate values in two consecutive rounds can be reused, we design the Circuit 2, where round $i+1$ employs the value FHE($X_{i+2} \oplus X_{i+3}$) calculated in round i. We summarize the number of homomorphic lookup table in Table 3.

Table 3. Number of Homomorphic LUT in SM4

Circuit	Table	Number
1	4-bit XOR	1768
	$T_{i,j}$	1024
2	4-bit XOR	1648
	$T_{i,j}$	1024

The computation server in HHE scheme enables complex computations, supporting parallelization on the homomorphic evaluation circuit. Thus we use "#pragma omp parallel for num_threads(16)" instruction to conduct the parallelization to test the latency for Circuit 2. The experimental result is illustrated in Table

Compared with the TFHE circuit in [44] composed by CBS bootstrapping, the homomorphic SM4 decryption circuit consists of FBS bootstrapping is much slower. It is because the latter one calls the Tree-based MVB function more than 2600 times. The Circuit 1, fully following with the lookup table implementation, consumes 290.1 s, while reusing some intermediate FHE ciphertexts, the latency

Table 4. Latency of Homomorphic Evaluation of SM4 decryption circuit

FHE scheme	Circuit	Bootstrapping	Latency	Thread
BGV	[45]	-	6h	1
BGV	[45]	bootstrapped	1.6h	1
TFHE	[44]	CBS	78s	1
	1	FBS	**290.1s**	1
	2		**285.5s**	1
	Parallelization 2		**54.3s**	16

[1] **FBS** means the functional bootstrapping technique in TFHE scheme.

[2] **CBS** means the circuit bootstrapping technique in TFHE scheme.

reduces to 285.5 s. Finally, the parallelization version can improves the latency 5.28x.

6 Conclusion

The public two homomorphic SM4 decryption circuits are based on BGV algorithm and the circuit bootstrapping technique in TFHE scheme, while the former is too slow, and then latter requires 2 GB storage and communication overhead. For trade-off these two aspect, we design two homomorphic decryption circuits(Circuit 1 and 2) of SM4 based on the functional bootstrapping in TFHE scheme. Experimental results show that the latency of Circuit 2 improves from 1.6 h to 285.5 s compared with the circuit in BGV scheme. The memory costs of our proposal are also reduced from 2 GB to 0.5 GB with respect to the TFHE scheme.

The multiplicative depth of symmetric block ciphers mainly influence the latency of homomorphic decryption. One possible future work is to reduce the number of bootstrapping in the circuit.

References

1. Albrecht, M., Grassi, L., Rechberger, C., Roy, A., Tiessen, T.: MiMC: efficient encryption and cryptographic hashing with minimal multiplicative complexity. In: Cheon, J.H., Takagi, T. (eds.) ASIACRYPT 2016. LNCS, vol. 10031, pp. 191–219. Springer, Heidelberg (2016). https://doi.org/10.1007/978-3-662-53887-6_7
2. Albrecht, M.R., Rechberger, C., Schneider, T., Tiessen, T., Zohner, M.: Ciphers for MPC and FHE. In: Oswald, E., Fischlin, M. (eds.) EUROCRYPT 2015. LNCS, vol. 9056, pp. 430–454. Springer, Heidelberg (2015). https://doi.org/10.1007/978-3-662-46800-5_17
3. Ashur, T., Mahzoun, M., Toprakhisar, D.: Chaghri - a fhe-friendly block cipher. In: Proceedings of the 2022 ACM SIGSAC Conference on Computer and Communications Security, CCS 2022, pp. 139–150. Association for Computing Machinery, New York (2022). https://doi.org/10.1145/3548606.3559364

4. Bonnoron, G., et al.: Somewhat/fully homomorphic encryption: implementation progresses and challenges. In: El Hajji, S., Nitaj, A., Souidi, E.M. (eds.) C2SI 2017. LNCS, vol. 10194, pp. 68–82. Springer, Cham (2017). https://doi.org/10.1007/978-3-319-55589-8_5
5. Brakerski, Z.: Fully homomorphic encryption without modulus switching from classical GapSVP. In: Safavi-Naini, R., Canetti, R. (eds.) CRYPTO 2012. LNCS, vol. 7417, pp. 868–886. Springer, Heidelberg (2012). https://doi.org/10.1007/978-3-642-32009-5_50
6. Brakerski, Z., Gentry, C., Vaikuntanathan, V.: (leveled) fully homomorphic encryption without bootstrapping. In: Proceedings of the 3rd Innovations in Theoretical Computer Science Conference, ITCS 2012, pp. 309–325. Association for Computing Machinery, New York (2012). https://doi.org/10.1145/2090236.2090262
7. Carpov, S., Izabachène, M., Mollimard, V.: New techniques for multi-value input homomorphic evaluation and applications. In: Matsui, M. (ed.) CT-RSA 2019. LNCS, vol. 11405, pp. 106–126. Springer, Cham (2019). https://doi.org/10.1007/978-3-030-12612-4_6
8. Chapman, B., Mehrotra, P.: OpenMP and HPF: integrating two paradigms. In: Pritchard, D., Reeve, J. (eds.) Euro-Par 1998. LNCS, vol. 1470, pp. 650–658. Springer, Heidelberg (1998). https://doi.org/10.1007/BFb0057912
9. Chen, H., Dai, W., Kim, M., Song, Y.: Efficient homomorphic conversion between (Ring) LWE Ciphertexts. In: Sako, K., Tippenhauer, N.O. (eds.) ACNS 2021. LNCS, vol. 12726, pp. 460–479. Springer, Cham (2021). https://doi.org/10.1007/978-3-030-78372-3_18
10. Cheon, J.H., Kim, A., Kim, M., Song, Y.: Homomorphic encryption for arithmetic of approximate numbers. In: Takagi, T., Peyrin, T. (eds.) ASIACRYPT 2017. LNCS, vol. 10624, pp. 409–437. Springer, Cham (2017). https://doi.org/10.1007/978-3-319-70694-8_15
11. Chillotti, I., Gama, N., Georgieva, M., Izabachène, M.: TFHE: fast fully homomorphic encryption over the torus. J. Cryptol. **33**(1), 34–91 (2020). https://doi.org/10.1007/S00145-019-09319-X
12. Cho, J., et al.: Transciphering framework for approximate homomorphic encryption. In: Tibouchi, M., Wang, H. (eds.) ASIACRYPT 2021. LNCS, vol. 13092, pp. 640–669. Springer, Cham (2021). https://doi.org/10.1007/978-3-030-92078-4_22
13. Cid, C., Indrøy, J.P., Raddum, H.: FASTA – a stream cipher for Fast FHE evaluation. In: Galbraith, S.D. (ed.) CT-RSA 2022. LNCS, vol. 13161, pp. 451–483. Springer, Cham (2022). https://doi.org/10.1007/978-3-030-95312-6_19
14. Coron, J.-S., Lepoint, T., Tibouchi, M.: Scale-invariant fully homomorphic encryption over the integers. In: Krawczyk, H. (ed.) PKC 2014. LNCS, vol. 8383, pp. 311–328. Springer, Heidelberg (2014). https://doi.org/10.1007/978-3-642-54631-0_18
15. Cosseron, O., Hoffmann, C., Méaux, P., Standaert, F.X.: Towards case-optimized hybrid homomorphic encryption. In: Agrawal, S., Lin, D. (eds.) Advances in Cryptology – ASIACRYPT 2022, pp. 32–67. Springer Nature Switzerland, Cham (2022). https://doi.org/10.1007/978-3-031-22969-5_2
16. Desmedt, Y.: Elgamal public key encryption. In: van Tilborg, H.C.A., Jajodia, S. (eds.) Encyclopedia of Cryptography and Security, pp. 396–396. Springer US, Boston, MA (2011). https://doi.org/10.1007/978-1-4419-5906-5_318
17. Dobraunig, C., et al.: Rasta: a cipher with low ANDdepth and few ANDs per Bit. In: Shacham, H., Boldyreva, A. (eds.) CRYPTO 2018. LNCS, vol. 10991, pp. 662–692. Springer, Cham (2018). https://doi.org/10.1007/978-3-319-96884-1_22

18. Dobraunig, C., Grassi, L., Helminger, L., Rechberger, C., Schofnegger, M., Walch, R.: Pasta: A case for hybrid homomorphic encryption. IACR Trans. Cryptogr. Hardw. Embed. Syst. **2023**(3), 30–73 (2023). https://doi.org/10.46586/TCHES.V2023.I3.30-73
19. Doröz, Y., Hu, Y., Sunar, B.: Homomorphic AES evaluation using the modified LTV scheme. Des. Codes Cryptogr. **80**(2), 333–358 (2016). https://doi.org/10.1007/S10623-015-0095-1
20. Duval, S., Lallemand, V., Rotella, Y.: Cryptanalysis of the FLIP family of stream ciphers. In: Robshaw, M., Katz, J. (eds.) CRYPTO 2016. LNCS, vol. 9814, pp. 457–475. Springer, Heidelberg (2016). https://doi.org/10.1007/978-3-662-53018-4_17
21. Gentry, C.: A Fully Homomorphic Encryption Scheme. Ph.D. thesis, Stanford University, USA (2009). https://searchworks.stanford.edu/view/8493082
22. Gentry, C., Halevi, S., Smart, N.P.: Homomorphic evaluation of the AES circuit. In: Safavi-Naini, R., Canetti, R. (eds.) CRYPTO 2012. LNCS, vol. 7417, pp. 850–867. Springer, Heidelberg (2012). https://doi.org/10.1007/978-3-642-32009-5_49
23. Gentry, C., Sahai, A., Waters, B.: Homomorphic encryption from learning with errors: conceptually-simpler, asymptotically-faster, attribute-based. In: Canetti, R., Garay, J.A. (eds.) CRYPTO 2013. LNCS, vol. 8042, pp. 75–92. Springer, Heidelberg (2013). https://doi.org/10.1007/978-3-642-40041-4_5
24. Gilbert, H., Heim Boissier, R., Jean, J., Reinhard, J.R.: Cryptanalysis of elisabeth-4. In: Guo, J., Steinfeld, R. (eds.) Advances in Cryptology – ASIACRYPT 2023, pp. 256–284. Springer Nature Singapore, Singapore (2023). https://doi.org/10.1007/978-981-99-8727-6_9
25. Grassi, L., Liu, F., Rechberger, C., Schmid, F., Walch, R., Wang, Q.: Minimize the randomness in rasta-like designs: how far can we go? In: Eichlseder, M., Gambs, S. (eds.) Selected Areas in Cryptography – SAC 2024, pp. 207–238. Springer Nature Switzerland, Cham (2025). https://doi.org/10.1007/978-3-031-82841-6_9
26. Guimarães, A., Borin, E., Aranha, D.F.: Revisiting the functional bootstrap in TFHE. IACR Trans. Cryptogr. Hardw. Embed. Syst. **2021**(2), 229–253 (2021). https://doi.org/10.46586/TCHES.V2021.I2.229-253
27. Ha, J., et al.: Masta: an he-friendly cipher using modular arithmetic. IEEE Access **8**, 194741–194751 (2020). https://doi.org/10.1109/ACCESS.2020.3033564
28. Ha, J., Kim, S., Lee, B., Lee, J., Son, M.: Rubato: noisy ciphers for approximate homomorphic encryption. In: Dunkelman, O., Dziembowski, S. (eds.) Advances in Cryptology – EUROCRYPT 2022, pp. 581–610. Springer International Publishing, Cham (2022). https://doi.org/10.1007/978-3-031-06944-4_20
29. Hebborn, P., Leander, G.: Dasta-alternative linear layer for rasta. IACR Trans. Symmetric Cryptol. **2020**(3), 46–86 (2020). https://doi.org/10.13154/TOSC.V2020.I3.46-86
30. Li, X., Xie, M., Huang, C.: Fast software implementation of the sm4 algorithm. In: Proceedings of the 2024 8th International Conference on High Performance Compilation, Computing and Communications, HP3C 2024, pp. 127–132. Association for Computing Machinery, New York (2024). https://doi.org/10.1145/3675018.3675028
31. Liu, F., Li, Y., Chen, H., Jiao, L., Luo, M., Wang, M.: Yux: finite field multiplication based block ciphers for efficient FHE evaluation. IEEE Trans. Inf. Theory **70**(5), 3729–3749 (2024). https://doi.org/10.1109/TIT.2024.3349414
32. Liu, F., Anand, R., Wang, L., Meier, W., Isobe, T.: Coefficient grouping: breaking chaghri and more. In: Hazay, C., Stam, M. (eds.) Advances in Cryptology – EURO-

CRYPT 2023, pp. 287–317. Springer Nature Switzerland, Cham (2023). https://doi.org/10.1007/978-3-031-30634-1_10
33. Liu, F., Sarkar, S., Meier, W., Isobe, T.: algebraic attacks on rasta and dasta using low-degree equations. In: Tibouchi, M., Wang, H. (eds.) ASIACRYPT 2021. LNCS, vol. 13090, pp. 214–240. Springer, Cham (2021). https://doi.org/10.1007/978-3-030-92062-3_8
34. Méaux, P., Carlet, C., Journault, A., Standaert, F.-X.: Improved filter permutators for efficient FHE: better instances and implementations. In: Hao, F., Ruj, S., Sen Gupta, S. (eds.) INDOCRYPT 2019. LNCS, vol. 11898, pp. 68–91. Springer, Cham (2019). https://doi.org/10.1007/978-3-030-35423-7_4
35. Méaux, P., Journault, A., Standaert, F.-X., Carlet, C.: Towards stream ciphers for efficient FHE with low-noise ciphertexts. In: Fischlin, M., Coron, J.-S. (eds.) EUROCRYPT 2016. LNCS, vol. 9665, pp. 311–343. Springer, Heidelberg (2016). https://doi.org/10.1007/978-3-662-49890-3_13
36. Naehrig, M., Lauter, K.E., Vaikuntanathan, V.: Can homomorphic encryption be practical? In: Cachin, C., Ristenpart, T. (eds.) Proceedings of the 3rd ACM Cloud Computing Security Workshop, CCSW 2011, Chicago, IL, USA, 21 October 2011, pp. 113–124. ACM (2011). https://dl.acm.org/citation.cfm?id=2046682
37. Paillier, P.: Paillier encryption and signature schemes. In: van Tilborg, H.C.A., Jajodia, S. (eds.) Encyclopedia of Cryptography and Security, 2nd Ed, pp. 902–903. Springer (2011). https://doi.org/10.1007/978-1-4419-5906-5_488
38. Regev, O.: On lattices, learning with errors, random linear codes, and cryptography. J. ACM **56**(6), 34:1–34:40 (2009). https://doi.org/10.1145/1568318.1568324
39. Rivest, R.L., Adleman, L., Dertouzos, M.L.: On data banks and privacy homomorphisms. Foundations of Secure Computation, pp. 169–179. Academia Press (1978)
40. Trama, D., Clet, P., Boudguiga, A., Sirdey, R.: A homomorphic AES evaluation in less than 30 seconds by means of TFHE. In: Brenner, M., Costache, A., Rohloff, K. (eds.) Proceedings of the 11th Workshop on Encrypted Computing & Applied Homomorphic Cryptography, Copenhagen, Denmark, 26 November 2023. pp. 79–90. ACM (2023). https://doi.org/10.1145/3605759.3625260
41. Wang, R., Wen, Y., Li, Z., Lu, X., Wei, B., Liu, K., Wang, K.: Circuit bootstrapping: faster and smaller. In: Joye, M., Leander, G. (eds.) Advances in Cryptology - EUROCRYPT 2024 - 43rd Annual International Conference on the Theory and Applications of Cryptographic Techniques, Zurich, Switzerland, 26-30 May 2024, Proceedings, Part II. LNCS, vol. 14652, pp. 342–372. Springer (2024). https://doi.org/10.1007/978-3-031-58723-8_12
42. Wardlaw, W.P.: The RSA public key cryptosystem. In: Joyner, D. (ed.) Coding Theory and Cryptography, pp. 101–123. Springer Berlin Heidelberg, Berlin, Heidelberg (2000). https://doi.org/10.1007/978-3-642-59663-6_6
43. Wei, B., Lu, X., Wang, R., Liu, K., Li, Z., Wang, K.: Thunderbird: efficient homomorphic evaluation of symmetric ciphers in 3gpp by combining two modes of TFHE. IACR Trans. Cryptogr. Hardw. Embed. Syst. **2024**(3), 530–573 (2024). https://doi.org/10.46586/TCHES.V2024.I3.530-573
44. Wei, B., Wang, R., Li, Z., Liu, Q., Lu, X.: Fregata: faster homomorphic evaluation of AES via TFHE. In: Athanasopoulos, E., Mennink, B. (eds.) Information Security - 26th International Conference, ISC 2023, Groningen, The Netherlands, 15-17 November 2023, Proceedings. LNCSe, vol. 14411, pp. 392–412. Springer (2023). https://doi.org/10.1007/978-3-031-49187-0_20
45. Xue, Y.: Homomorphic evaluation of the SM4. IACR Cryptol. ePrint Arch. p. 1340 (2020). https://eprint.iacr.org/2020/1340

RCE-HVE: Plausible Deniability Against Multi-snapshot Adversaries with Amplified Storage

Haoyang Xing[✉], Chongyu Long, Anda Che, Fangyu Zheng, and Jiwu Jing

University of Chinese Academy of Sciences, Yuquan Road 19A, Beijing 100049, China
xinghaoyang22@mails.ucas.ac.cn

Abstract. Our disks and USB flash drives often store sensitive information, making them vulnerable to coercive adversaries, such as oppressive regimes, who can force users to disclose encryption keys. Traditional disk encryption methods are insufficient in such scenarios. Plausible deniability encryption addresses this issue by allowing users to convincingly deny the existence of specific private data on their storage devices. A notable example is the now defunct TrueCrypt [1], which effectively resists single-snapshot adversaries, those who can access the storage device only once. In academic research, methods like HIVE and DataLair have been proposed to counter multi-snapshot adversaries, who can access the device multiple times, by leveraging ORAM constructions. However, these approaches impose significant limitations on the usable storage space. To address these challenges, we propose RCE-HVE, a comprehensive optimization of the HIVE method that enhances both performance and storage efficiency. Compared to existing solutions, RCE-HVE is more concise, efficient, and provides substantially larger usable storage space.

Keywords: Plausible deniability · Disk encryption · ORAM

1 Introduction

Hard drives and USB flash drives often store sensitive information. Although common full-disk encryption methods, such as dm-crypt, provide a basic level of data protection, they fail against coercive adversaries, entities that can compel users to disclose their encryption keys. In such scenarios, traditional encryption alone is not sufficient to protect sensitive data.

Plausible Deniability (PD) offers a promising solution to counter coercive adversaries. PD enables users to convincingly deny the existence of specific private data on their storage devices. A notable example is TrueCrypt, which implements PD by initially filling disk space with random data and then allowing users to create two volumes: a public volume and a hidden volume. The public volume stores seemingly private data (which can be disclosed under coercion), while the hidden volume contains the actual sensitive data. Both volumes are encrypted using distinct keys derived from different passwords in a randomized and semantically secure encryption scheme. When coerced, users can reveal the key to the public volume while denying the existence of the hidden volume. Without the hidden volume's key, the encrypted data remain indistinguishable from random noise, making it impossible for adversaries to prove the existence of the hidden volume. TrueCrypt effectively achieves PD against *single-snapshot* adversaries—those who can access the storage device only once.

However, as Czeskis et al. [3] point out, TrueCrypt fails against *multi-snapshot* adversaries who can access the disk at multiple time points (e.g., during repeated border crossings). This limitation arises because TrueCrypt relies on static randomness: the disk is filled with random data only at the time of volume creation. If an adversary compares disk snapshots taken at different times and observes changes in supposedly random sectors, they can infer the existence of a hidden volume.

To address this vulnerability, we need to introduce dynamic randomness—a mechanism that plausibly explains changes in disk data over time. This can be achieved by using a simulator that injects randomness into the disk at appropriate intervals, typically triggered by operations on the public volume. The goal is to obscure the user's access patterns to hidden data, making them indistinguishable from access patterns to the public volume. Oblivious RAM (ORAM) [4] inherently provides such dynamic randomness by concealing access patterns, thereby ensuring the security of hidden data. Building on this, Blass et al. proposed HIVE [5], the first effective PD scheme against multi-snapshot adversaries. HIVE employs a write-only ORAM construction to conceal access patterns, ensuring that hidden writes are indistinguishable from public reads.

Despite its innovative design, HIVE experiences significant performance overhead due to its recursive map storage and the necessity to clear metadata blocks after each read/write operation. Consequently, HIVE only achieves a throughput of 1 MB/s.

Existing PD schemes based on ORAM constructions, such as HIVE and DataLair, impose substantial space overhead. For instance, HIVE reserve at least half of the physical storage space to facilitate rapid selection of free blocks, while DataLair employs a similar protocol. We observed that free blocks can be selected from non-public volume blocks rather than the entire physical storage space. This approach ensures that the amount of free space exceeds the size of the hidden volume, enabling efficient block selection without compromising security. To implement this, we introduce a table to track physical block usage allocated to the public volume. This design is discussed in the following sections.

This paper makes the following contributions:

- We propose a novel free block selection strategy for PD ORAM constructions, which significantly increases the usable space for both public and hidden volumes without compromising throughput efficiency.
- We present RCE-HVE (Rapid, Capacious, and Efficient Hidden Volume Encryption), a new PD scheme that integrates our free block selection strat-

egy and replaces metadata and map operations with efficient in-memory operations. RCE-HVE allows the public volume to occupy the entire physical storage or the hidden volume to utilize up to half of the total space, but not both simultaneously.
- We implement RCE-HVE as a fully functional prototype in the Linux kernel and conduct comprehensive performance evaluations, demonstrating its practical usability and superior efficiency.

2 The Model of PD Integrating Multiple-Volume FDE + ORAM

Existing PD schemes generally share similar security requirements, though with slight variations. In HIVE [5], Blass et al. define security levels based on snapshot frequency and access pattern restrictions. DataLair [6] introduces the PD-CPA game, incorporating the ratio of hidden to public operations and granting the adversary the ability to choose storage devices. Invisiline [12] proposes Plausible Invisibility, which ensures both deniability and readability with off-the-shelf software (OTSS Readability).

Multi-snapshot PD schemes fundamentally require that adversaries cannot detect the existence of hidden volumes. In the absence of a public volume key, a hidden volume cannot be distinguished from random noise, which implies that hidden volume write operations and *dummy writes* that generate random noise are computationally indistinguishable. Based on this observation, HIVE sequentially appends either dummy writes or legitimate hidden-volume writes after public read operations, creating indistinguishable I/O patterns that prevent adversaries from determining whether hidden-volume writes have occurred. This operational methodology provides provable resistance against multi-snapshot attacks while maintaining strict plausible deniability guarantees.

2.1 Preliminaries

Before defining our security game, we introduce the notation.

A user $\mathcal{U}$ interacts with a block storage device (e.g. hard drives, USB drives) through encryption software. Let N denote the total number of blocks, each of size B. The system supports n_p public volumes and n_h hidden volumes, encrypted using keys $\{K_p^i\}_{i\in[1,n_p]}$ and $\{K_h^i\}_{i\in[1,n_h]}$, each with at least s bits of entropy. The corresponding encrypted volumes are denoted as $\{V_p^i\}_{i\in[1,n_p]}$ and $\{V_h^i\}_{i\in[1,n_h]}$.

The hidden volumes are allocated following the public volumes:

- $V_{i,i\in[1,n_p]}$: Public volumes.
- $V_{i,i\in[n_p+1,n_p+n_h]}$: Hidden volumes.
- $V_{i,i\in[1,n_p+n_h]}$: All volumes.

Similarly to HIVE [5], an *access* is defined as $o = (\text{op}, b, V_i, d)$, where $\text{op} \in \{\text{pub\_w}, \text{pub\_r}, \text{hid\_w}, \text{hid\_r}\}$. Here, pub_w and pub_r denote write and read operations on public volumes, while hid_w and hid_r apply to hidden volumes. An *access pattern* is a sequence of accesses $O = \langle o_1, \ldots, o_n \rangle$.

The concept of *write traces* has been widely explored in the ORAM literature [13,14]. Chakraborti et al. [6] define a write trace as "the actual modifications to physical blocks due to an access pattern." We adopt this definition but highlight that write traces also include recursive ORAM modifications, which may impact deniability.

2.2 Security Game

For adversary $\mathcal{A}$, it possesses the following capabilities:

- **Computational Power**: $\mathcal{A}$ is bounded to the probabilistic polynomial-time (PPT) computation.
- **Snapshot Ability**: $\mathcal{A}$ can capture multiple snapshots D of devices through repeated observations.
- **Key Knowledge**: $\mathcal{A}$ has obtained the public volume's decryption key $\{K_p^i\}_{i \in [1, n_p]}$.

The security goal is that the adversary cannot determine whether a hidden volume exists.

Building upon IND-CPA, we define the PD-CPA security game (see Fig. 1):

1. Adversary $\mathcal{A}$ selects n_p, n_h and sends them to challenger $\mathcal{C}$.
2. $\mathcal{C}$ selects a random bit b and generates encryption keys $\{K_p^i\}_{i \in [1, n_p]}$ and $\{K_h^i\}_{i \in [1, n_h]}$.
3. $\mathcal{C}$ initializes public and hidden volumes on the storage device $\mathcal{D}$ using these keys.
4. $\mathcal{C}$ takes a snapshot D_0 of $\mathcal{D}$ and sends it along with public keys $\{K_p^i\}_{i \in [1, n_p]}$ to $\mathcal{A}$.
5. $\mathcal{A}$ selects access patterns O_0 and O_1 with *certain constraints* and sends them, along with a bit d, to $\mathcal{C}$. If $d = 1$, $\mathcal{C}$ will return an updated snapshot.
6. $\mathcal{C}$ executes O_b. If $d = 1$, it returns snapshot D to $\mathcal{A}$.
7. Steps 5–6 repeat $p = \text{poly}(s)$ times.
8. $\mathcal{A}$ outputs a guess b'. If $b' = b$, $\mathcal{A}$ wins.

Definition 1. *A storage scheme satisfies PD if no probabilistic polynomial-time adversary can win the PD-CPA game with non-negligible advantage. Formally, there exists a negligible function $\epsilon(s)$ such that:*

$$\Pr[\mathcal{A} \text{ wins PD-CPA}] \leq \frac{1}{2} + \epsilon(s). \tag{1}$$

We impose constraints on access patterns O. Specifically:

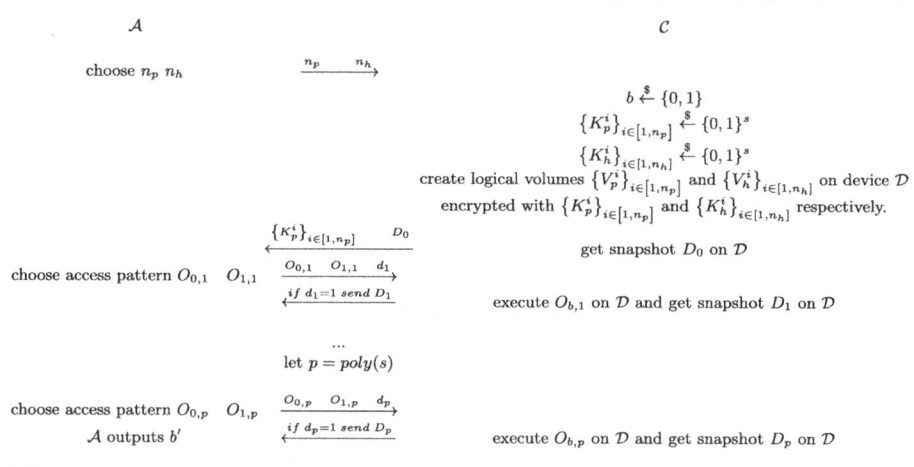

Fig. 1. PD-CPA game

- $O_0 = \langle o_{0,1}, \ldots, o_{0,n} \rangle$ includes read/write operations on both public and hidden volumes, while $O_1 = \langle o_{1,1}, \ldots, o_{1,n} \rangle$ only includes public volume operations.
- Unlike PD-DM [11] and DataLair [6], we prohibit $\perp$ operations, ensuring that O_0 and O_1 are the same length. This restriction avoids delaying hidden writes indefinitely, making the scheme more practical. In PD-DM and DataLair, the worst-case scenario occurs when no public volume operations are executed, resulting in hidden write data never being persisted to disk.
- Public write operations must be identical in O_0 and O_1 to prevent trivial adversary wins through public volume decryption.

3 A Novel Method for Allocating Free Blocks

In ORAM-based PD schemes, the selection of free blocks for new incoming data is crucial for both performance and security. Many existing studies have explored free block allocation [5,6]. Based on HIVE, we propose a novel free block allocation scheme that ensures PD while significantly increasing the available space for both public and hidden volumes. Moreover, our approach improves efficiency by reducing unnecessary data movements and minimizing performance overhead.

3.1 Defeating Multi-snapshot Adversaries in the Block Device Layer

Implementing a PD scheme (e.g., HIVE) at the block device (BD) layer typically requires a mapping mechanism to translate logical block addresses into physical block addresses. As illustrated in Fig. 2, the read/write operations for the b-th logical block of the public volume V_1 are translated by the block device layer into read/write operations for the β-th physical block.

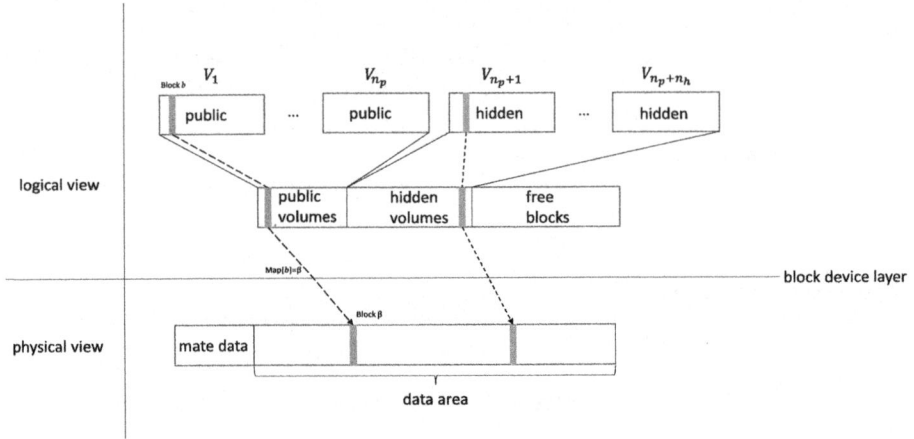

Fig. 2. Translation View. The logical addresses $(1, b)$ are translated into physical addresses β by the block device layer.

To implement a PD scheme that is resistant to multi-snapshot attacks, the access pattern must be concealed. Specifically, any operation performed on a hidden volume must be *plausibly explained* as an operation on the public volume. Since the adversary acknowledges and accepts the existence of a public volume, every modification observed in a disk snapshot must be justifiable through plausible public volume operations, ensuring that hidden volume activity *remains indistinguishable* from legitimate public volume usage.

Since the adversary possesses the public volume's key, public write operations can be trivially distinguished by the adversary. Therefore, we consider using public read operations to obfuscate hidden volume activity. Furthermore, because hidden reads do not modify the snapshot of the disk, the key challenge is to ensure computational indistinguishability between public reads and hidden writes.

A fundamental technique [5] involves appending dummy writes after public read operations to conceal hidden writes. According to the restrictions of PD-CPA, for two access patterns O_0 and O_1 provided by $\mathcal{A}$, the existence of $\perp$ operations is not allowed, and public writing must remain identical. This constraint ensures that the write trace generated by O_0's hidden read/write and public read operations is indistinguishable from that generated by O_1's public read. Fortunately, pure read operations (without appending dummy write) do not leave any write traces on disk snapshots. Based on the computational indistinguishability between dummy writes and hidden writes (proved by Lemma 1), a straightforward method to obfuscate hidden reads/writes is to *append a dummy write* to each read operation (Algorithms 1 and 2). This discussion does not yet consider the impact of map updates on security.

Note that the disk locations of dummy writes and hidden writes must remain indistinguishable. If hidden data persists on disk without being overwritten, an adversary may reasonably suspect it contains meaningful ciphertext. In contrast, blocks written by dummy writes are always free blocks that can be arbitrarily overwritten. Based on this observation, both dummy writes and hidden writes select their disk locations via the `GetFreeBlock` function.

Algorithm 1. Read-PD

Input: Logical volume V_i, logical address b
Output: Data d
1: $\beta := \text{map}_i[b]$
2: $d := \text{DiskRead}(\beta)$
3: $\beta' := \text{GetFreeBlock}()$
4: $s \xleftarrow{\$} \{0,1\}^B$
5: /* Dummy write to mask access pattern */
6: $\text{DiskWrite}(\beta', s)$
7: **return** d

Algorithm 2. Write-PD

Input: Logical volume V_i, logical address b, data d
1: $\beta := \text{GetFreeBlock}()$
2: $\text{UpdateMap}(i, b, \beta)$
3: $\text{DiskWrite}(\beta, \text{Enc}(d))$
4: **return**

Lemma 1. *For disks with identical snapshots, the write trace generated by a dummy write is indistinguishable from the write trace generated by a hidden write operation.*

Proof. Since both dummy writes and hidden writes invoke `GetFreeBlock` function, the adversary cannot distinguish them based on the write location (β' and β). Furthermore, as hidden data is encrypted using a semantically secure encryption scheme, it is indistinguishable from a random string s. Therefore, the lemma holds.

3.2 Randomly Selecting Non-public Blocks

In this section, we focus on `GetFreeBlock` function. The sole requirement of PD for `GetFreeBlock` is to avoid implying the existence of hidden data. The

Fig. 3. PBR & FBB. The block querying trick reduces the time complexity to $O(\sqrt{N})$.

approach adopted by HIVE involves randomly selecting blocks from the entire global space, which inherently does not suggest the presence of hidden data. We propose a novel free block allocation scheme where free blocks are randomly selected from non-publicly occupied blocks. This approach also complies with PD, as it categorizes blocks into two distinct types: public blocks and non-public blocks, treating hidden blocks and free blocks equally without distinction. In the worst-case scenario under HIVE, if `GetFreeBlock` retrieves only public data blocks, it must read, decrypt, enqueue, dequeue, encrypt, and write public data, resulting in significant performance overhead. However, this process provides no additional deniability, as the adversary already possesses the public volume key.

Observing that hidden occupied blocks and free blocks are indistinguishable from the adversary's perspective, `GetFreeBlock` must not rely on the hidden volume's distribution when selecting free blocks. However, since the adversary can obtain public volume keys, `GetFreeBlock` can partially rely on the public data distribution without compromising PD. Based on this observation, we propose a scheme that selects free blocks only from non-publicly occupied blocks. This approach improves performance by preventing unnecessary enqueuing of public data while maintaining PD.

Public Block Record and Free Block Bucket. To implement our scheme, we introduce a data structure that records whether each disk block is publicly occupied, referred to as the *Public Block Record* (PBR) (Fig. 3). Given that a single bit can represent the occupation status of a 4096-byte block, the space overhead is $1/32768$ of the total disk capacity. For a 1 TB disk, this amounts to approximately 30 MB, which is acceptable.

When executing the `GetFreeBlock` function, a random element with value 0 is selected from the PBR, and its index is returned as the free block's physical address. Since PBR is a large array, a simple traversal would be inefficient. Therefore, we employ a *Free Block Bucket* (FBB) to accelerate the query process. By dividing N bits into $\sqrt{N}$ blocks and recording the number of 0 in each block, the complexity of selecting a free block is reduced from $O(N)$ to $O(\sqrt{N})$.

Public Block Record and BIT A more sophisticated yet efficient approach involves leveraging the Fenwick Tree [15] to maintain the PBR. The Fenwick Tree, also known as the Binary Indexed Tree (BIT), is a data structure optimized for efficient prefix sum queries on dynamic arrays. When combined with binary search, it enables the identification of the index of the n-th free block with a time complexity of $O(\log^2 N)$.

To achieve this, we first negate the elements in the PBR, transforming the problem of locating the x-th free block into finding the x-th occurrence of the value 1. This reformulation allows us to efficiently determine the desired index using binary search. The process begins by computing the prefix sum of the first $N/2$ elements. If this sum is greater than or equal to x, it indicates that the x-th 1 lies within the first $N/2$ elements, prompting further refinement by computing the prefix sum of the first $N/4$ elements. Conversely, if the sum is smaller than x, the x-th 1 must be in the latter $N/2$ elements, requiring a recalculation of the prefix sum for the first $\frac{3}{4}N$ elements. This iterative process continues until the exact position of the x-th 1 is determined.

The GetFreeBlock algorithm is presented in Algorithm 3. FenwickTree Query function operates with a time complexity of $O(\log N)$ and is invoked repeatedly within the binary search procedure. As a result, the overall time complexity of GetFreeBlock is $O(\log^2 N)$. The BIT is dynamically allocated and deallocated in memory when the device is opened and closed, respectively. The BIT array has a length of $N+1$, leading to a space complexity of $O(N)$. Furthermore, whenever the distribution of the public volume on the disk changes, the FenwickTreeUpdate function must be executed, incurring an update time complexity of $O(\log N)$.

Algorithm 3. GetFreeBlock - BIT

Input: PBR=$[r_1, ..., r_N]$, BIT=$[0, b_1, ..., b_N]$, total physical block number N, publicly occupied block number u_p
Output: a free physical block β
1: $u_{non\text{-}pub} := N - u_p$
2: $x \xleftarrow{\$} [1, u_{non\text{-}pub}]$
3: $l := 1$
4: $h := N$
5: **while** $l < h$ **do**
6:   $m = (L + h)/2$
7:   **if** FenwickTreeQuery(BIT, m)$\geq x$ **then**
8:     $h := m$
9:   **else**
10:    $l := m + 1$
11: **end if**
12: **end while**
13: **return** l.

Bounding the Stash Size. Under our approach, the GetFreeBlock function may return either a free block or a hidden occupied block. If a free block is returned, data is written directly. If a hidden occupied block is returned, its hidden data is moved to an in-memory stash to be written back later. To prevent memory overflow, it is crucial to maximize the probability of selecting genuinely free blocks. A simple strategy is to maintain a higher proportion of free blocks relative to hidden occupied blocks, as validated by HIVE [5].

HIVE demonstrates that as long as the number of free blocks accounts for at least half of the selectable blocks, the stash size remains bounded, preventing memory overflow.

Since HIVE randomly selects blocks from the global space, the free blocks must constitute at least 50% of the total capacity. In other words, HIVE can utilize at most 50% of the global space.

In contrast, RCE-HVE selects free blocks only from non-publicly occupied blocks. Therefore, RCE-HVE only requires free blocks to occupy half of the non-publicly occupied blocks, achieving space utilization that far exceeds 50% of total capacity.

4 Practical Hidden Volume Encryption with RCE-HVE

4.1 RCE-HVE Algorithms

We now present the core algorithms of RCE-HVE: **RCE-HVERead** (Algorithm 4) and **RCE-HVEWrite** (Algorithm 5).

Algorithm 4. RCE-HVERead

Input: Logical volume V_v, logical address b;
Output: Data d
1: $\text{map}_v[b] := \beta$;
2: $d := \text{DiskRead}(\beta)$;
3: $d := \text{Dec}_{k_v}(d)$;
4: RCE-HVEWrite($\perp$);
5: **return** d;

Algorithm 5. RCE-HVEWrite

Input: Logical volume V_v, logical address b, data d, number of public volumes n_p, number of hidden volumes n_h, number of publicly occupied blocks u_p, number of hidden occupied blocks u_h, PBR=$[r_1, ..., r_N]$, FBB=$[b_1, ..., b_{\sqrt{N}}]$.
Output:
1: /* Step 1: Enqueue the incoming block (if not $\perp$). */
2: **if** $d \neq \perp$ **then**
3:    Enqueue(Stash$_v$, (b, d));
4:    $\beta := \text{map}_v[b]$;
5:    UpdateMap($v, b, \perp$);
6:    UpdateReverseMap($\beta, \perp, \perp$);
7:    **if** $v \leq n_p$ **then**

8:    UpdatePBR($\beta, 0$);
9:    $u_p := u_p - 1$;
10:   else
11:      $u_h := u_h - 1$;
12:   end if
13: end if
14:
15: /* Step 2: Select RCE-K non-public blocks. */
16: for $i \leftarrow 1$ to RCE-K do
17:    $\beta_i :=$ GetFreeBlock(R, B, N, u_p);
18: end for
19: for $i \leftarrow 1$ to RCE-K do
20:    $b_t, l :=$ ReverseMap[β_i];
21:    if $b_t \neq \bot$ then
22:       $d_t :=$ DiskRead(β_i);
23:       $d_t :=$ Dec$_{k_l}(d_t)$;
24:       /* Enqueue blocks occupied by hidden volumes. */
25:       Enqueue(Stash$_l, (b_t, d_t)$);
26:       UpdateMap($l, b_t, \bot$);
27:       UpdateReverseMap($\beta_i, \bot, \bot$);
28:       $u_h := u_h - 1$;
29:    end if
30: end for
31:
32: /* Step 3: Dequeue in the order of public blocks, hidden blocks, and random strings. */
33: for $i \leftarrow 1$ to RCE-K do
34:    flag := true;
35:    for $j \leftarrow 1$ to $n_p + n_h$ do
36:       if Stash$_j \neq \bot$ then
37:          $(b_t, d_t) :=$ Dequeue(Stash$_j$);
38:          UpdateMap(j, b_t, β_i);
39:          UpdateReverseMap(β_i, j, b_t);
40:          if $j \leq n_p$ then
41:             UpdatePBR($\beta_i, 1$);
42:             $u_p := u_p + 1$;
43:          else
44:             $u_h := u_h + 1$;
45:          end if
46:          DiskWrite(β_i, Enc$_{k_j}(d_t)$);
47:          flag := false;
48:       end if
49:    end for
50:    if flag = true then
51:       $s \xleftarrow{\$} \{0,1\}^B$;

52:        DiskWrite(β_i, s);
53:    **end if**
54: **end for**
55: **return**;

RCE-HVERead. The **RCE-HVERead** algorithm maps the logical block b of volume V_v to a physical block β, reads and decrypts the data stored at β, and returns the decrypted data d. At the end of the read operation, a dummy **RCE-HVEWrite**($\bot$) is executed. This serves two purposes: (1) it ensures that public reads are indistinguishable from hidden writes, and (2) it provides additional opportunities for the stash to dequeue, preventing stash overflow.

RCE-HVEWrite. The **RCE-HVEWrite** algorithm handles dummy, hidden, and public writes. Its execution can be divided into the following steps:

- **Step 1: Enqueue Incoming Data (if applicable)**
    - If the write operation is not a dummy write (i.e., $d \neq \bot$), enqueue the incoming block (b, d) into the stash of the corresponding volume.
    - Update the `Map` and `ReverseMap` to reflect the block's new state.
    - If the block belongs to a public volume, update the Public Block Record (PBR) and decrement the count of publicly occupied blocks (u_p).
    - If the block belongs to a hidden volume, decrement the count of hidden occupied blocks (u_h).
- **Step 2: Select RCE-K Non-Public Blocks**
    - Similar to parameter k in HIVE which determines the number of selected blocks, we set RCE-K=3 in our system.
    - Use `GetFreeBlock` function to select RCE-K non-public blocks. These blocks may be free blocks or belong to hidden volumes.
    - For each selected block, check the `ReverseMap` to determine if it is occupied by a hidden volume.
    - If the block is occupied by a hidden volume, read and decrypt the data, then enqueue it into the stash of the corresponding hidden volume.
    - Update the `Map` and `ReverseMap` to release the physical block for future use.
- **Step 3: Dequeue and Write Data**
    - For each of the RCE-K selected blocks, perform a dequeue operation in the following order:
        * Public blocks (from public volumes).
        * Hidden blocks (from hidden volumes).
        * Random strings (if no data is available in the stashes).
    - Write the dequeued data back to the disk, encrypting it with the appropriate volume key.
    - Update the `Map`, `ReverseMap`, and PBR to reflect the new block assignments.

This step-by-step process ensures that hidden data operations are indistinguishable from random writes, maintaining plausible deniability. By prioritizing public blocks during the dequeue phase, RCE-HVE further obscures access patterns, making it difficult for adversaries to infer the existence of hidden volumes.

Map and ReverseMap. The Map and ReverseMap are essential data structures for RCE-HVE. The Map translates logical block addresses to physical block addresses, while the ReverseMap performs the inverse mapping. These structures are loaded into memory when the volume is opened and saved to disk when the volume is closed. During operation, they are updated in memory using the UpdateMap and UpdateReverseMap functions.

4.2 Algorithm Analysis

Physical Space Utilization. RCE-HVE maximizes physical space utilization by ensuring that the number of hidden occupied blocks (u_h) does not exceed the number of free blocks. Specifically, the disk distribution must satisfy $2u_h \leq N - u_p$, where u_p is the number of publicly occupied blocks. This constraint ensures that the stash does not overflow and that free blocks are always available for allocation.

When $u_h = 0$, the public volume can utilize up to 100% of the storage space ($u_p = N$). When $u_p = 0$, the hidden volume can utilize up to 50% of the storage space ($u_h = N/2$). However, these two parameters cannot simultaneously reach their maximum values.

Avoiding Enqueuing Public Data. The new free block allocation strategy avoids the costly process of enqueuing publicly occupied blocks. By maintaining the BIT and PBR, RCE-HVE ensures that public blocks are not selected for enqueueing, reducing the expected number of non-free blocks selected. This constitutes the fundamental reason for RCE-HVE's dual advantages in both throughput and storage efficiency.

Memory Overhead. To minimize memory overhead, HIVE employs a technique suggested by Shi et al. [16], which stores the position map of the data ORAM in a recursive map ORAM on disk. While this approach reduces memory usage, it introduces a vulnerability: the recursive storage of the map ORAM generates distinguishable write traces. These traces can be exploited by adversaries to infer the existence of hidden volumes. We refer to this vulnerability as the Access Pattern Propagation (APP) attack.

RCE-HVE addresses this issue by eliminating the use of recursive ORAM for the position map. Instead, the map is stored entirely in memory, preventing the APP attack and enhancing both security and performance. This approach reduces I/O overhead and ensures that all map-related operations are handled efficiently.

The position map uses 8 bytes to represent a 4,096-byte block, resulting in a memory overhead of 1/512 of the disk capacity. For example, a 1 TB disk requires 2 GB of memory, which is manageable on modern computing devices.

4.3 Security

In this section, we formally establish the security theory of RCE-HVE and provide a comprehensive proof.

Theorem 1. *PD-CPA security is achieved in the RCE-HVE framework.*

Proof. According to the security game defined in Sect. 2, the length of operation sequence must be identical, and all public write operations must remain identical. Consequently, when O_0 performs hidden read/write operations, the corresponding O_1 operation must necessarily be a public read. Thus, the security proof reduces to demonstrating the computational indistinguishability between public reads and hidden reads/writes given identical initial snapshots.

Since both public reads and hidden reads invoke RCE-HVERead, they are computationally indistinguishable. Therefore, the security proof reduces to demonstrating the indistinguishability between public reads and hidden writes.

The proof can be completed by extending Lemma 1 to the case of selecting RCE-HVE free blocks.

Although hidden writes enqueue hidden volume data and modify the stash's state, the stash resides in memory and remains unobservable to adversaries. Moreover, when dequeuing, hidden volume data is indistinguishable from random noise. In fact, for O_1 and O_2, it suffices to ensure that the stash contains identical public data. Since the dequeue policy always prioritizes the removal of public volume data first, this requirement is trivially satisfied.

5 Implementation and Evaluation

We implemented RCE-HVE as a kernel module device mapper, enabling it to operate between the Linux block I/O layer and the underlying physical devices. This design allows RCE-HVE to map logical blocks to physical blocks efficiently.

Using RCE-HVE, we created two logical volumes on a physical device partition (e.g., '/dev/sdb1'): a public volume and a hidden volume. The public volume can utilize up to the entire partition size, while the hidden volume is limited to 50% of the partition size. We compared the throughput of RCE-HVE with HIVE, a practical, open-source PD scheme implemented at the block device layer.

5.1 Benchmarks

Our experiments were conducted on a standard Linux system equipped with an Intel i7-10750 CPU, 4 GB of RAM, and a 1 TB WD Green SN350 SSD. The system ran Ubuntu 14.04 LTS with kernel version 3.13.0. We allocated a 50 GB physical partition for testing, allowing the public volume to use up to 50GB and the hidden volume up to 25 GB. Both volumes were formatted with the ext4 file system, and throughput was measured using bonnie++ 1.97 [2].

Table 1. Throughput Comparison (MB/s). Higher is better. RCE-HVE demonstrates slightly better performance compared to in-memory HIVE, while being at least four times faster than HIVE in all access types.

Access	HIVE	RCE-HVE	HIVE (in-memory)
Public Read	0.4	2.21	1.82
Public Write	0.47	3.02	2.91
Hidden Read	4.64	21.66	23.1
Hidden Write	0.43	3.49	3.423

5.2 Throughput

Table 1 compares the throughput of RCE-HVE with HIVE and an in-memory version of HIVE. The in-memory HIVE, derived from the original HIVE open-source code, transfers map and metadata operations to memory to avoid potential APP attacks and high I/O overhead, albeit at the cost of increased memory usage.

RCE-HVE achieves performance comparable to in-memory HIVE while being at least 4× faster than the original HIVE across all access types. This performance improvement stems from RCE-HVE's in-memory map management, which eliminates additional I/O overhead. Furthermore, RCE-HVE's free block allocation scheme contributes to its efficiency, as it avoids selecting publicly occupied blocks, thereby reducing unnecessary enqueue operations. Notably, RCE-HVE even slightly outperforms in-memory HIVE, particularly as the size of the public volume increases, highlighting the advantages of our free block allocation strategy.

5.3 Performance Under Different Public Volume Distributions

To further demonstrate the benefits of our free block allocation scheme, we conducted experiments under varying public volume distributions. Using the Linux 'dd' command, we continuously wrote files to the public volume and measured the performance of both in-memory HIVE and RCE-HVE (Fig. 4).

As the public volume occupancy increased, the throughput of in-memory HIVE gradually declined: public write throughput decreased by 18% (0.58 MB/s), public read by 15% (0.43 MB/s), and hidden write by 22% (0.77 MB/s). In contrast, RCE-HVE's throughput remained stable. The difference plots (Fig. 4(d)–(f)) clearly illustrate that RCE-HVE's performance advantage over in-memory HIVE grows linearly with the size of the public volume, further validating the efficiency of our free block allocation scheme.

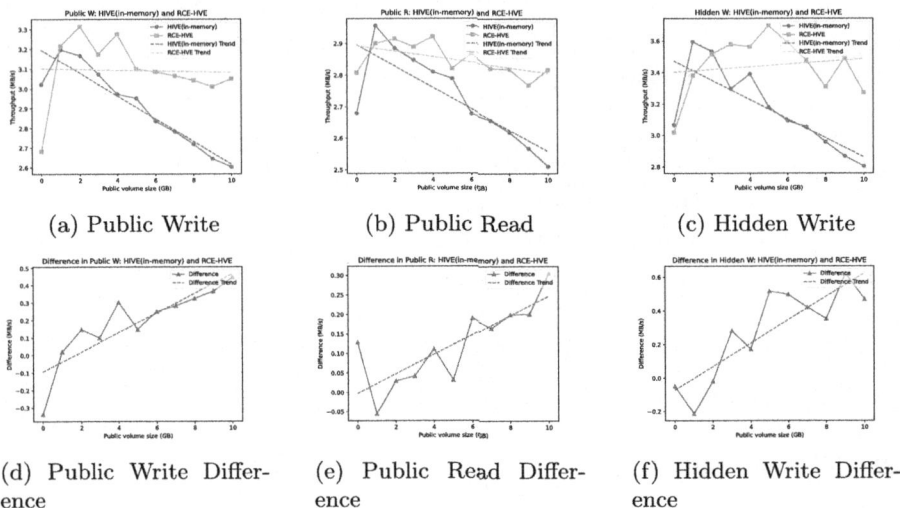

Fig. 4. Performance under different Public Volume Distributions. Figure 4(a)–(c) show the throughput of HIVE (in-memory) and RCE-HVE as the size of the public volume changes. Fig 4(d)–(f) show the throughput difference between RCE-HVE and HIVE (in-memory) as the size of the public volume changes.

6 Discussion

RCE-HVE utilizes `Map` and `ReverseMap` to maintain the mapping relationships between logical blocks and physical blocks. As shown in Algorithm 5, blocks that logically belong to the hidden volume can be selected by the `GetFreeBlock` function, subsequently written into the *Stash*, and then disassociated from their corresponding physical blocks via `UpdateMap` and `UpdateReverseMap`. The state of these physical blocks is then updated to free.

Note that hidden blocks written into the stash are only temporarily managed in memory and will soon be written back to disk. The purpose of this mechanism is to plausibly deny the existence of the hidden volume blocks belonging to the hidden volume appearing as free blocks and remain readily available.

In contrast, the public volume does not require such operations. Blocks allocated to the public volume need not be reclaimed, and the system does not conceal whether a block belongs to the public volume. Importantly, in RCE-HVE, the number of blocks occupied by both the public and hidden volumes is monotonically increasing once allocated. This implies that excessive public volume data will permanently occupy the space reserved for hidden volumes, which constitutes a noteworthy issue warranting further discussion.

7 Related Work

Plausible Deniability was first introduced by Anderson et al. [7] as a powerful property that allows users to convincingly deny the existence of sensitive data on a storage device. By ensuring that adversaries cannot obtain evidence of hidden data, PD prevents coercion attacks where users might be forced to reveal encryption keys. Anderson et al. proposed two steganographic file system designs to achieve PD: one representing hidden files as linear combinations of cover files, and another storing hidden files at locations determined by cryptographic hashes of their filenames. While these methods achieve PD, they suffer from high performance overhead, low space utilization, and potential data loss risks.

TrueCrypt [1] later popularized PD by implementing it at the block device layer. TrueCrypt fills the entire disk with random noise, making free space indistinguishable from encrypted hidden volumes. This approach effectively prevents adversaries from proving the existence of hidden volumes. TrueCrypt's success inspired subsequent works, such as Skillen et al. [8], who adapted the technique for mobile devices, and Jia et al. [9], who applied it to NAND flash storage. More recently, Anzuoni et al. [10] introduced Shufflecake as a "spiritual successor" to TrueCrypt, supporting multiple volumes with varying security levels on a single device. Under coercion, users can unlock lower-security volumes, leaving adversaries unable to determine the total number of volumes on the device.

However, these solutions are vulnerable to multi-snapshot adversaries, who can access the storage device multiple times. To defend against such adversaries, hiding user access patterns becomes essential. Oblivious RAM (ORAM) [4] provides a natural solution for this purpose. Blass et al. [5] proposed HIVE, the first PD scheme resilient to multi-snapshot adversaries. HIVE combines TrueCrypt-like hidden volume techniques with ORAM to ensure indistinguishability between hidden data and free blocks. It uses in-memory stashes to queue incoming data blocks, which are later dequeued when free blocks are selected. The dequeuing process is simulated by writing random data, effectively masking hidden write operations.

Building on HIVE, DataLair [6] observed that public data operations need not be hidden and proposed DL-ORAM. By pairing hidden operations with public writes, DataLair accelerates public operations by two orders of magnitude while optimizing hidden operations. Despite these improvements, both HIVE and DataLair suffer from significant space overhead, as their free block allocation strategies require reserving half of the storage space.

PD-DM [11] takes a different approach, arguing that hiding access locations is unnecessary. Inspired by log-structured file systems, PD-DM sequentially increases physical addresses for writes and embeds hidden data within public data payloads. This design reduces seek times for random accesses and minimizes the number of physical blocks per logical write. However, PD-DM sacrifices storage efficiency for performance, further highlighting the trade-offs in existing PD schemes.

In 2024, Pinjala et al. [12] introduced the concept of "plausibly invisible," which combines PD with Readability using Off-the-Shelf Software (OTSS). Their system, INVISILINE, stores hidden data within the initialization vectors used by dm-crypt to encrypt public data. Under coercion, users can access public data through dm-crypt without additional software. While INVISILINE achieves OTSS compatibility, its hidden data capacity is limited to 19 GB on a 1 TB disk. Nonetheless, INVISILINE opens a promising research direction: concealing the use of PD schemes themselves.

Compared to these works, RCE-HVE addresses the limitations of existing PD schemes by introducing a novel free block selection strategy that maximizes storage utilization while maintaining throughput efficiency. Unlike HIVE and DataLair, which reserve half of the storage space, RCE-HVE dynamically allocates free blocks from non-public volume areas, significantly increasing usable space for both public and hidden volumes. Additionally, RCE-HVE replaces metadata and map operations with in-memory operations, further enhancing performance. Our experimental results demonstrate that RCE-HVE achieves superior space efficiency and usability compared to prior approaches.

Compared to existing PD schemes, RCE-HVE introduces a novel free block selection strategy that maximizes storage utilization while maintaining throughput efficiency. Unlike HIVE and DataLair, which reserve half of the storage space, RCE-HVE dynamically allocates free blocks from non-public volume areas, significantly increasing usable space for both public and hidden volumes. Additionally, RCE-HVE replaces metadata and map operations with in-memory operations, further enhancing performance.

8 Conclusion

RCE-HVE is a rapid, efficient, and high-capacity PD scheme designed to withstand multi-snapshot attacks. By ensuring that publicly occupied blocks are excluded during free block allocation, it eliminates the need for costly public data enqueue operations, thereby maintaining stable I/O performance regardless of public volume distribution. Moreover, RCE-HVE imposes more flexible space constraints, allowing the public volume to potentially utilize the entire physical device while enabling the hidden volume to occupy up to half of the available storage. Finally, RCE-HVE enhances performance by offloading HIVE's mapping operations to memory, effectively mitigating the risk of APP attacks.

Acknowledgements. This work was supported by the National Key Research and Development Program of China under Grant No. 2023YFB3105801.

References

1. TrueCrypt: Free open-source on-the-fly encryption (2014). http://www.truecrypt.org/
2. Coker, R.: Bonnie++. http://www.coker.com.au/bonnie++. Accessed 16 June 2024
3. Czeskis, A., Hilaire, D.J.St., Koscher, K., Gribble, S.D., Kohno, T., Schneier, B.: Defeating Encrypted and Deniable File Systems: TrueCrypt v5.1a and the Case of the Tattling OS and Applications (2008)
4. Goldreich, O., Ostrovsky, R.: Software protection and simulation on oblivious RAMs. J. ACM (JACM) **43**(3), 431–473 (1996)
5. Blass, E.-O., Mayberry, T., Noubir, G., Onarlioglu, K.: Toward robust hidden volumes using write-only oblivious ram, pp. 203–214 (2014)
6. Chakraborti, A., Chen, C., Sion, R.: DataLair: efficient block storage with plausible deniability against multi-snapshot adversaries. arXiv preprint arXiv:1706.10276, 2017
7. Anderson, R., Needham, R., Shamir, A.: The steganographic file system, pp. 73–82 (1998)
8. Skillen, A., Mannan, M.: On implementing deniable storage encryption for mobile devices (2013)
9. Jia, S., Xia, L., Chen, B., Liu, P.: DEFTL: implementing plausibly deniable encryption in flash translation layer, pp. 2217–2229 (2017)
10. Anzuoni, E., Gagliardoni, T.: ShuffleCake: Plausible Deniability for Multiple Hidden Filesystems on Linux, pp. 3033–3047 (2023)
11. Chen, C., Chakraborti, A., Sion, R.: PD-DM: an efficient locality-preserving block device mapper with plausible deniability. In: Proceedings on Privacy Enhancing Technologies (2019)
12. Pinjala, S.K., Carbunar, B., Chakraborti, A., Sion, R.: INVISILINE: Invisible Plausibly-Deniable Storage, p. 18 (2023)
13. Maas, M., et al.: Phantom: Practical oblivious computation in a secure processor, pp. 311–324 (2013)
14. Stefanov, E., et al.: Path ORAM: an extremely simple oblivious RAM protocol. J. ACM (JACM) **65**(4), 1–26 (2018)
15. Fenwick, P.M.: A new data structure for cumulative frequency tables. Softw. Pract. Exper. **24**(3), 327–336 (1994)
16. Shi, E., Chan, T.-H.H., Stefanov, E., Li, M.: Oblivious RAM with O ((log N) 3) worst-case cost, pp. 197–214 (2011)

PrivCrypt – Foundations and Applications of Privacy-Enhancing Cryptography

Enhancing E-Voting with Multiparty Class Group Encryption

Michele Battagliola[1(✉)], Giuseppe D'Alconzo[2], Andrea Gangemi[2], and Chiara Spadafora[3]

[1] Department Information Engineering, Marche Polytechnic University, Ancona, Italy
m.battagliola@staff.univpm.it
[2] Department of Mathematical Sciences, Polytechnic University of Turin, Turin, Italy
{giuseppe.dalconzo,andrea.gangemi}@polito.it
[3] Department of Mathematics, University of Trento, Trento, Italy
chiara.spadafora@unitn.it

Abstract. CHide is one of the most prominent e-voting protocols, which, while combining security and efficiency, suffers from having very long encrypted credentials. In this paper, starting from CHide, we propose a new protocol, based on multiparty Class Group Encryption (CGE) instead of discrete logarithm cryptography over known order groups. We achieve a computational complexity of $O(nr)$, for n votes and r voters, while calling the MixNet algorithm one time. The homomorphic properties of CGE allow for credentials that are shorter by a factor of 20 while maintaining the same level of security, at the cost of a small slowdown in efficiency.

Keywords: Class Group Encryption · Threshold Encryption · Coercion Resistance · E-voting

1 Introduction

E-voting protocols are usually based on discrete logarithm cryptography; in particular, the most widely used encryption scheme is ElGamal (e.g., [2,24,35,36]), due to its homomorphic properties. However, protocols often require both sum and multiplication to be computed efficiently, and ElGamal is not suitable for this purpose, leading to protocols that are often computationally [30] or memory inefficient [4,18].

A possible alternative to ElGamal is the multiparty Class Group Encryption (CGE) [10,11]. Introduced in 2015 by Castagnos and Laguillaumie [13], CGE is the first discrete logarithm-based scheme that allows for an unlimited number of linear operations on plaintexts, without losing the ability to decrypt. Recently, Braun et al. introduced the notion of threshold CGE [10,11], which allows efficient multiplication of plaintexts using a multiparty protocol. This feature is particularly helpful for designing e-voting protocols, as it allows a wider range of computations. In particular, our attention is focused on the CHide voting protocol: proposed by Cortier et al. in [18], CHide is an efficient [4,18] and secure protocol, as it achieves the strongest notion of coercion resistance.

1.1 E-Voting Protocols

Internet voting, often referred to as remote electronic voting (e-voting), enables voters to cast their votes via the Internet, removing the need for physical polling stations. Since its introduction in the early 2000s in Estonia and in the United States, its popularity has grown and it is now implemented to various degrees in several countries, including Switzerland [25], Canada [12] and Australia [27].

To be considered secure, an election must ensure vote and voter privacy, vote verifiability and the correctness of the final results. Cryptographic protocols are well-suited for this task, and numerous protocols, as Helios [3], Selene [34] and Civitas [15], have been recently developed to secure Internet-based elections.

However, there is one additional property that is equally crucial to address in a fair and democratic electoral process: resistance to coercion. In other words, a voting protocol must protect voters from being forced into voting in a specific way, either through threats or rewards. This threat becomes even greater in the context of e-voting, due to its remote nature. This greatly expands the range of possible coercion-attacks compared to in-person voting at polling stations.

1.2 Related Work

One of the first e-voting protocols that counters coercion is [30] by Juels, Catalano and Jakobsson (JCJ). They proposed the first mathematical formalization of coercion resistance, which is still the benchmark for research in the field. However, the real security of JCJ was recently questioned: the paper [18] critically examines the definition of coercion resistance given in [30] and identifies a weakness that stems from the procedure preceding the tally, in which trustees remove ballots that should not be counted.

Thus, the authors proposed a new definition of coercion resistance which overcomes the weaknesses of the one proposed by JCJ and designed CHide, a new protocol that achieves it. In addition of being more secure than JCJ, CHide is also more efficient, having a computational complexity of $O((n+r)\log(n+r)^2)$, where n denotes the number of votes and r is the number of voters, instead of the quadratic complexity of the JCJ protocol. Parallel to CHide, Aranha et al. [4] used a very similar approach to solve the security issue of JCJ, achieving a better computational complexity of $O((n+r)\log(n+r))$, at the price of an additional mixnet. However, both of them suffer from the fact that the encrypted credentials are very long: in fact, instead of the "standard" ElGamal encryption, the credentials are encrypted bit-by-bit, so that a k bits credential is expanded in k ElGamal ciphertexts. This negatively impacts performance, resulting in very space-consuming protocols and causing big constant factor in the computational complexity.

Table 1. Comparison between our proposal and the JCJ and CHide voting schemes. **Tally compl.** is the asymptotic complexity of the Tally Phase, where n denotes the number of cast votes and r the number of credentials; **MixNets** is the number of calls to the MixNet subroutine; **Enc. cred.** is the size of the encryption of a credential for a security parameter $\lambda = 128$ and **Security** is the type of security provided by the scheme: with *CHide* we mean that the scheme achieves the Coercion Resistance property of Definition 2, while *JCJ* denotes the weaker notion from [30].

Protocol	Tally compl.	MixNets	Enc. cred.	Security
JCJ [30]	$O(n^2 + nr)$	2	95.6 B	JCJ
CHide [18]	$O\left((n+r)\log_2(n+r)^2\right)$	1	8160 B	CHide
Aranha et al. [4]	$O\left((n+r)\log_2(n+r)\right)$	2	8160 B	CHide
This work	$O(nr)$	1	390.6 B	CHide

Other Notions of Coercion Resistance. Besides the definition proposed by JCJ in [30], other definitions have been used, such as the one utilized by NetVote and ReVote [1,39] and by VoteAgain [31]. Comparing these definitions is often hard, but in general the (patched) JCJ one is regarded as the strongest [26]. For this reason we focus our analysis on protocols that achieve it.

1.3 Our Contribution

This paper combines the advantages of the JCJ protocol [30] and the CHide variants [4,18]. Our contribution is twofold. First, we propose an alternative version of [4,18] with shorter credentials, modifying the encryption scheme from ElGamal to CGE. The greater flexibility offered by CGE allows us to avoid encrypting credentials bit-by-bit, resulting in a protocol that requires much less memory: as shown in Table 1 our protocols require about 20 times less memory than [4,18], while achieving the same security level. However, by doing so, we lose the advantage of bit-by-bit encryption, which is the possibility to sort credentials, so our protocol suffers a slowdown compared to CHide. As a second contribution, to limiting this slowdown we propose an optimized version of our proposal, obtaining a tally that, while not as efficient as [4], requires less than quadratic time. Specifically, the idea is to "amortize" the time required to compute the final count by performing some precomputation during the voting phase, instead of waiting until the end of the election. While the overall computational complexity is the same, the time interval between the end of the election and the publication of results is significantly shorter.

Table 1 shows a comparison between the various protocols: for JCJ and CHide (both versions), to compute the length of an encrypted credential we assume that ElGamal is performed on Curve25519 [8], while we use [9] for CGE.

Organization. The paper is organized as follows: Sect. 2 recaps the cryptographic tools that are later used in Sect. 3, where our new voting protocol is described. This section also presents all the zero-knowledge protocols that are necessary.

Section 4 is devoted to security proofs, while Sect. 5 describes two optimizations of the base protocol.

2 Preliminaries

In the course of this paper, we denote with λ the security parameter. In the pseudocode " $\leftarrow\$$ " denotes the random sampling, " $\leftarrow$ " is a variable assignment and " $=$ " is an equality check.

2.1 Proofs and Arguments of Knowledge

An interactive protocol for a relation $\mathbb{L} \subseteq \mathbb{Y} \times \mathbb{W}$ is a protocol between a prover, who holds a statement-witness pair $(y, w) \in \mathbb{L}$, and a verifier, who knows only the statement y. At the end of the interaction, we want an honest prover to be able to convince the verifier, possibly without leaking any additional information. On the other hand, we want a dishonest prover (not knowing w) to be unable to convince the verifier. The sequence of exchanged messages is said *transcript*.

Definition 1. *[37] An interactive protocol Π between a Prover P and a Verifier V proving a relation $\mathbb{L}$ can satisfy the following properties.*

- Completeness: *if P follows the protocol on input $(y, w) \in \mathbb{L}$, the verifier accepts with overwhelming probability.*
- Soundness: *for every $y \in \mathbb{Y}$ such that does not exist $w \in \mathbb{W}$ for which $(y, w) \in \mathbb{L}$, a Prover P having input y is accepted by a Verifier V with negligible probability.*
- Special Soundness: *there exists an efficient deterministic algorithm $\mathcal{E}$, called extractor, with the following property: whenever $\mathcal{E}$ is given as input the statement $y \in \mathbb{Y}$ and two accepting transcripts (com, ch, resp) and (com, ch′, resp′), with ch $\neq$ ch′, $\mathcal{E}$ outputs $w \in \mathbb{W}$ such that $(y, w) \in \mathbb{L}$.*
- Honest-Verifier Zero Knowledge *(HVZK): there exists a polynomial-time algorithm $\mathcal{S}$, called* simulator, *which on input $y \in \mathbb{Y}$ and a random challenge* ch, *outputs an accepting transcript* (com, ch, resp) *with the same probability distribution as the transcripts between an honest P and V on input y.*

An interactive protocol having completeness, special soundness and HVZK is called zero-knowledge proof of knowledge. *An interactive protocol satisfying completeness, soundness and HVZK is said* zero-knowledge argument of knowledge.

To ease the notation, in the rest of the paper we will refer both to proofs and arguments using the term "proofs". However, it will be specified when an interactive protocol is an argument and not a proof. An interactive protocol is said to be *public coin* if the message of the verifier is taken from a random source. For such class of protocols, the Fiat-Shamir transform [23] allows to remove the interaction between the prover and the verifier. We will use this method to produce non-interactive zero-knowledge proofs and arguments from the interactive ones in Sect. 3.1.

Given a zero-knowledge proof Π for the relation $\mathbb{L} \subseteq \mathbb{Y} \times \mathbb{W}$, we denote the protocol performed on witness $w \in \mathbb{W}$ and statement $y \in \mathbb{Y}$ as $\Pi[y, w]$.

Proofs and arguments of knowledge can be composed to perform AND and OR proofs of the relations they prove. The AND proof of two protocols Π_1 and Π_2 is simply given by their parallel composition, and the AND proof is accepting if both are accepting; we write $\Pi_1 \wedge \Pi_2$. The standard construction of an OR proof can be found in [21, Sect. 4] and we denote it with $\Pi_1 \vee \Pi_2$.

2.2 Cryptography from Class Groups

Class Group Encryption (CGE) is a public key encryption scheme introduced in [13]. This construction is *linearly homomorphic*: given ciphertexts $c_1 = \mathsf{Enc}(m_1)$, ..., $c_k = \mathsf{Enc}(m_k)$ and public values $\mu_0, \mu_1, \ldots, \mu_k$, there exists a procedure Linear such that

$$\mathsf{Linear}(c_1, \ldots, c_k; \mu_0, \mu_1, \ldots, \mu_k) = \mathsf{Enc}\left(\mu_0 + \sum_{i=1}^{k} \mu_i m_i\right).$$

To build such a scheme, we follow the construction from [13]. For a security parameter λ, consider an abelian finite group $\hat{G}$ of unknown order having a cyclic subgroup $F = \langle f \rangle$ of order $p > 2^\lambda$, where computing the discrete logarithm of any element is easy. The order of $\hat{G}$ is then $\hat{s}p$ for some integer $\hat{s}$. Let $h = x^p$ for a random $x \in \hat{G}$, and define $g = hf$ and $G = \langle g \rangle$. We can see that $G \cong H \times F$ where $H = \{y^p \mid y \in G\}$ and $H = \langle h \rangle$. Then, let $\epsilon \in \mathbb{N}$ be a statistical distance parameter and let $\mathcal{D}_H$ be a distribution over the integers. We assume that the distributions $\{h^x \mid x \leftarrow_\$ \mathcal{D}_H\}$ and the uniform distribution in H have negligible statistical distance. Suppose to know a bound $\tilde{s} > \hat{s}$, then $\mathcal{D}_H$ can be instantiated as the uniform distribution on $[0, 2^{\epsilon-2}\tilde{s}[$. The public parameters of the encryption scheme are given by the tuple $\mathsf{pp} = (\hat{G}, \tilde{s}, g, h, f)$. The secret key is given by $\mathsf{sk} \leftarrow_\$ \mathcal{D}_H$, while the public key is $\mathsf{pk} = h^{\mathsf{sk}}$. Then, to encrypt a message m in $\mathbb{Z}/p\mathbb{Z}$, the sender samples a random r from $\mathcal{D}_H$ and computes

$$\mathsf{Enc}(\mathsf{pk}, m, r) = (h^r, \mathsf{pk}^r f^m) = (\mathsf{ct}_1, \mathsf{ct}_2) = \mathsf{ct}.$$

From now on, the ciphertexts will be denoted as pairs $\mathsf{ct} = (\mathsf{ct}_1, \mathsf{ct}_2)$, i.e., a list of ciphertexts will have the indexes as superscripts $\mathsf{ct}^{(1)}, \ldots, \mathsf{ct}^{(\ell)}$, and each entry is a pair $(\mathsf{ct}_1^{(i)}, \mathsf{ct}_2^{(i)})$. To decrypt, the receiver computes $\mathsf{ct}_2/\mathsf{ct}_1^{\mathsf{sk}} = f^m$ and then retrieves m since $f^m \in F$ and the discrete logarithm in F is easy. We denote $m = \mathsf{Dec}(\mathsf{sk}, \mathsf{ct}_1, \mathsf{ct}_2)$. This encryption scheme is linearly homomorphic: given two ciphertexts $\mathsf{ct} = (\mathsf{ct}_1, \mathsf{ct}_2)$ and $\mathsf{ct}' = (\mathsf{ct}'_1, \mathsf{ct}'_2)$ which encrypt $m, m' \in \mathbb{Z}/p\mathbb{Z}$ respectively, we have that $(\mathsf{ct}_1 \cdot \mathsf{ct}'_1, \mathsf{ct}_2 \cdot \mathsf{ct}'_2)$ is an encryption of $m + m'$, and $(\mathsf{ct}_1^a, \mathsf{ct}_2^a)$ is an encryption of am for any $a \in \mathbb{Z}$.

Threshold Encryption and Multiparty Computation from CGE. In [11], a threshold CGE and a multiparty computation protocol are presented. In particular, secret keys are shared with a t-out-of-n secret sharing scheme, meaning that every subset of $t-1$ users does not obtain any information on the secrets. Then, this threshold scheme is employed to allow an efficient algorithm for plaintext multiplication that does not require any decryption. We will use the arithmetic functionalities presented in [11] as the basis of the operations used in the voting protocol. Namely, the functionalities Init, KeyGen, Decrypt from [11, Sect. 6.1] and the arithmetic black-box functionalities Init, Input, Output, Linear and Multiply from [11, Sect. 7]. For the sake of readability, since CGE is already linearly homomorphic and linear operations do not require communication, in our protocols, instead of calling Linear, they are executed directly. Differently, when a homomorphic multiplication between two ciphertexts is needed, we will use the Multiply functionality. Recently, the paper [10] improves on [11], by presenting a new key generation algorithm with lower communication complexity and new methods to batch zero-knowledge proofs in unknown order groups.

Mixnet from CGE. A *Mixnet* is a protocol that takes as input an ordered set of k ciphertexts $(C_1, \ldots, C_k)$ and returns another ordered set of ciphertexts $(C'_1, \ldots, C'_k)$ such that C'_i is a re-encryption of the plaintext from $C_{\pi^{-1}(i)}$ for a random permutation π. In the e-voting scenario, mixnets are used to randomize the list of valid encrypted votes. In this way, the link between the voter and their preference is broken and the secrecy is ensured.

A well-known mixnet that works with ElGamal encryption has been defined in [5] by Bayer and Groth. Later, Beaugrand et al. [6] adapted the protocol from [5] to work with the class group framework, providing a mixnet with sublinear communication complexity. In our construction, we will use the proposal from [6]: the functionality Mixnet takes as input a list of class group ciphertexts and returns the permuted and re-encrypted list, with a proof π_{Mixnet} of its correctness.

Cryptographic Assumptions. It has been shown that the CGE public key encryption scheme is IND-CPA secure in [14] under the *Hard Subgroup Membership* assumption (HSM) [14], stating that distinguishing between elements of the form h^a from elements of the form g^b is intractable. In this context, $a \leftarrow_\$ \mathcal{D}_H$ and b is sampled from a distribution on integers $\mathcal{D}_G$ such that the statistical distance between the uniform distribution on G and $\{g^a \mid a \leftarrow_\$ \mathcal{D}_G\}$ is negligible.

In groups of unknown order, to prove statements in zero-knowledge, it is not known how to use Schnorr-like proofs since, to show the soundness of the protocol, some exponents need to be inverted. Thus, to overcome the limitation of the unknown order of $\hat{G}$ in the soundness proofs, we rely on the *C-rough assumption* (RO$_C$) [11], which informally states that class groups $\hat{G}$ having order $q \nmid \mathrm{ord}(\hat{G})$ for each prime $q < C$ are indistinguishable from class groups not having this property.

Another assumption needed in our protocol is the *Unknown Order* (ORD) one [20], where it must be intractable to compute an element $h \in \hat{G} \setminus F$ and a non-zero integer e such that $h^e = 1$. In other words, it must be infeasible to find an element in $\hat{G} \setminus F$ and a multiple of its order.

The threshold CGE between N parts presented in [11] is secure and tolerates up to $t < N/2$ corruptions under the ORD and RO_{N+1} assumptions. Finally, the CGE-based mixnet presented in [6] is secure under the RO_C assumption.

All the assumptions presented here are formally defined in Appendix A.

2.3 Security Properties of E-Voting Protocols

In order to be considered secure, an e-voting protocol with algorithms (Setup, Reg, Vote, Tally) should enforce the following properties: *correctness* [30], *fairness* [19], *vote privacy* [38], individual verifiability (usually expressed in terms of *cast-as-intended* [22], *recorded-as-cast* [32], *tallied-as-recorded* [33]), *universal verifiability* [38], *eligibility verifiability* [17]) and coercion resistance [18,30].

Coercion resistance is one of the most challenging properties to achieve when designing e-voting protocols. In this paper, we use the definition proposed in [18], which is an improvement of [30]. In simple words, in the registration phase, every voter is provided with a voting credential and a way to produce *fake credentials* that are indistinguishable from real ones. Votes cast with fake credentials are subsequently discarded. To evade coercion, voters can handle to the coercer the fake credential, without losing the ability to cast a valid vote. In the following, we report its formal definition.

We consider a distribution $\mathbb{D}$ of sequence of pairs (j, ν) where j is a voter and ν is a voting option in $[1, n_V]$. Additionally, fake votes are modeled as pairs where $j \notin [1, n_V]$. The definition of coercion resistance follows the standard real-ideal world paradigm: in the real world, the adversary controls some authority and participates in the protocol, while in the ideal world, at the end of the voting phase, the tally is done by a trusted third party. We say that a voting protocol is secure if and only if for every adversary in the real world there is an equivalent adversary in the ideal world. With reference to [18], we have the following definition.

Definition 2 (Coercion Resistance [18]). *A voting protocol with algorithms* (Setup, Reg, Vote, Tally) *is* coercion resistant *if there exists an algorithm* Fake *that, on input a credential σ outputs a random credential $\tilde{\sigma}$ such that for every adversary $\mathcal{A}$, for all parameters $n_T, t, n_V, n_\mathcal{A}, n_C$ and for all distributions $\mathbb{D}$, there exists a simulator $\mathcal{S}$ such that*

$$\Pr(\text{Ideal}_\mathcal{S}^{\text{CR}}(\lambda, n_V, n_\mathcal{A}, n_C, \mathbb{D}) = 1) - \Pr(\text{Real}_\mathcal{A}^{\text{CR}}(\lambda, n_T, t, n_V, n_\mathcal{A}, n_C, \mathbb{D}) = 1)$$

is negligible, where Ideal^{CR} *and* Real^{CR} *are defined in Fig. 1.*

3 The Voting Protocol

The participants in the voting protocol are:

- The *public board* $\mathcal{BB}$, an honest append-only list of data, where all the participants can write and read.

$\text{Real}^{\text{CR}}(\mathcal{A}, k, n_T, t, n_V, n_\mathcal{A}, n_C, \mathcal{BB})$	$\text{Ideal}^{\text{CR}}(\mathcal{A}, k, n_V, n_\mathcal{A}, n_C, \mathcal{D})$
1: $\mathcal{BB} \leftarrow \emptyset$	1:
2: $\text{pk}, \text{sk}_i, h_i \leftarrow \text{Setup}^\mathcal{A}(k, n_T, t)$	2:
3: $\{\sigma^i\}_{i \in V}, R \leftarrow \text{Reg}(k, \text{pk}, n_V)$	3:
4: $V_\mathcal{A} \leftarrow \mathcal{A}()$	4: $V_\mathcal{A} \leftarrow \mathcal{A}()$
5: $(j, \beta) \leftarrow \mathcal{A}(\{\sigma^i\}_{i \in V}, R)$	5: $(j, \beta) \leftarrow \mathcal{A}()$
6: **if** $|V_\mathcal{A}| \neq n_\mathcal{A}$ or $j \notin V \setminus V_\mathcal{A}$ or $\beta \notin [0, n_C]$	6: **if** $|V_\mathcal{A}| \neq n_\mathcal{A}$ or $j \notin V \setminus V_\mathcal{A}$ or $\beta \notin [0, n_C]$
7: **return** 0	7: **return** 0
8: $B \leftarrow \mathcal{D}(n_V - n_\mathcal{A}, n_C)$	8: $B \leftarrow \mathcal{D}(n_V - n_\mathcal{A}, n_C)$
9: **for** $(i, *) \in B, i \notin [1, n_V]$ **do**	9:
10: $\quad \sigma^i \leftarrow \text{Fake}(\sigma^i)$	10:
11: $b \leftarrow_\$ \{0, 1\}$	11: $b \leftarrow_\$ \{0, 1\}$
12: $\tilde{\sigma} \leftarrow \sigma^j$	12:
13: **if** $b == 1$	13: **if** $b = 1$
14: $\quad$ remove all $(j, *)$ from B	14: $\quad$ Remove all $(j, *)$ from B
15: **else**	15: **else**
16: $\quad$ Remove all $(j, *)$ from B but the last	16: $\quad$ Remove all $(j, *)$ from B but the last
17: $\quad$ Replace it with (j, β)	17: $\quad$ Replace it with (j, β)
18: $\quad \tilde{\sigma} \leftarrow \text{Fake}(\sigma^j)$	18:
19: $\mathcal{A}(\tilde{\sigma})$	19:
20: **for** $(i, \alpha) \in B$ **do**	20: $(\nu_i)_{i \in V_\mathcal{A}}, \beta' \leftarrow \mathcal{A}(|B|)$
21: $M \leftarrow \mathcal{A}(\mathcal{BB})$	21: **if** $b = 1$ and $\beta \neq \emptyset$
22: $\mathcal{BB} \leftarrow \mathcal{BB} \cup \{m \in M | m \text{ valid}\}$	22: $\quad B \leftarrow B \cup \{(j, \beta')\}$
23: $\mathcal{BB} \leftarrow \{\text{Vote}(\sigma^i, \alpha, \text{pk})\}$	23: $B \leftarrow B \cup \{(i, \nu_i) | i \in V_\mathcal{A}, \nu_i \in [1, n_C]\}$
24: $M \leftarrow \mathcal{A}(\mathcal{BB})$	24:
25: $\mathcal{BB} \leftarrow \mathcal{BB} \cup \{m \in M | m \text{ valid}\}$	25:
26: $X, \Pi \leftarrow \text{Tally}^\mathcal{A}(\mathcal{BB}, R, \text{pk}, \{h_i, \text{sk}_i\}, t)$	26: $X \leftarrow \text{Result}(\text{Cleanse}(B))$
27: $b' \leftarrow \mathcal{A}()$	27: $b' \leftarrow \mathcal{A}(X)$
28: **return** $b = b'$	28: **return** $b = b'$

Fig. 1. Security game of coercion resistance. λ is the security parameter, n_T the number of talliers, t the threshold, n_V the number of voters, $n_\mathcal{A}$ the number of corrupted voters, n_C the number of voting options and $\mathbb{D}$ the distribution. The algorithm Reg generates the public-private credential pair for each voter, while Result returns the tally and Cleanse removes votes from invalid voters and re-votes. For more details, refer to [18].

- The election *trustees*, a set $\mathcal{T}$ of $n_\mathcal{T}$ authorities that performs the tally. We allow corruptions up to the threshold $t < n_\mathcal{T}$ of the encryption scheme.
- The set of *voters* $\mathcal{V}$. There are $n_\mathcal{V}$ voters and at least 2 of them are honest.

- The *auditors*, a set of parties that checks the consistency of the data published on the board and the validity of all the zero-knowledge proofs (ZKPs). Since every check involves only public data, any party could serve as an auditor.
- The *registrars*, a second set $\mathcal{R}$ of $n_\mathcal{R}$ authorities that issue credentials to voters. For coercion resistance, we require that all the registrars are honest.

The voting protocol is composed by four phases.

1. **Setup Phase:** the authorities generate the public data and the parameters for the election (e.g. the public key, the hash function used for the non-interactive ZKPs, etc.).
2. **Registration Phase:** voters authenticate themselves with the relevant authorities and receive voting materials, usually containing their voting credentials and a proof of their correctness. For coercion resistance we required that the voting material allows for an *Evasion Strategy*, to be used in case of coercion.
3. **Voting Phase:** voters vote using the obtained credentials. Voters can vote more than once (usually, re-voting invalidates previous votes). During this phase, voters should be able to verify the correctness of the protocol, checking that the vote was cast-as-intended and recorded-as-cast. This is usually done via a combination of ZKP, the usage of a public board and device auditing techniques like the Benaloh Challenge [7].
4. **Tally Phase:** the election result is computed, and published along with a ZKP about its correctness.

Setup Phase. A security parameter λ is chosen. The $n_\mathcal{T}$ election trustees jointly execute the distributed key generation protocol presented in [10]. They use the Init and the KeyGen functionalities, producing a public key pk and private shares sk_i for $i = 1, ..., n_\mathcal{T}$, one for each trustee. A commitment h_i for the private share of sk_i is published by the i-th trustee on the public board, in addition to pk.

Registration Phase. Credentials are created by registrars and their encryptions are published on the public bulletin board $\mathcal{BB}$. Each credential is sent privately to the voter, with designated verifier zero-knowledge proofs (DVZKP) to ensure its validity.[1] We denote with σ a credential and with $\mathbb{R}_\sigma$ the list of all the authorized (encrypted) credentials. We refer to elements in $\mathbb{R}_\sigma$ as the "public credentials".

Evasion Strategy. To evade coercion a voter can simply lie about their credential σ, generate a random fake credential $\tilde{\sigma}$ and give it to the coercer, manipulating the DVZKP accordingly. In this way, voters are also able to vote with their correct credential.

---

[1] Voter authentication is out of the scope of this paper but, for example, it could be done via a digital signature by the user with a long-term key pair.

Voting Phase. To cast a vote for candidate ν, voter V computes an encryption of their voting choice $\mathsf{ct}^V = \mathsf{Enc}(\mathsf{pk}, \nu, \rho_\nu)$ and an encryption of their credential $\mathsf{ct}^C = \mathsf{Enc}(\mathsf{pk}, \sigma, \rho_\sigma)$. Additionally, the voter computes two proofs: π_{Vote}, the proof produced by the protocol Π_{Vote} to prove that ν is a valid voting option, and π_{Cred} produced by Π_{Cred} to prove the knowledge of σ in ct^C. These proofs are also used to link together ct^V and ct^C, making the pair $(\mathsf{ct}^V, \mathsf{ct}^C)^2$ non-malleable. To link these two proofs we apply the Fiat-Shamir transform to the AND (i.e. concatenation) of them. We call the tuple $(\mathsf{ct}^V, \mathsf{ct}^C, \pi_{\mathsf{Vote}}, \pi_{\mathsf{Cred}})$ a "ballot". This ballot is then published by the voter V on $\mathcal{BB}$ using an anonymous channel.

During the Voting Phase, each voter V can vote multiple times. For simplicity, the policy we implement is that we count only the last vote cast with each credential. This is implicit in how the Update function in the tally phase is designed. During this step the auditors verify the uniqueness of each ballot and that every published proof is valid. Votes that fail these checks are discarded and are not processed further.

Tally Phase. The tally procedure is a multiparty protocol between the n_T trustees. In order to tally the votes, we need the equality Eq and update Update functionalities presented later. From now on, we refer to $\mathsf{Enc}(\sigma) = \mathsf{Enc}(\mathsf{pk}, \sigma, \rho)$. The equality functionality Eq is used to check whether two ciphertexts encrypt the same credential or not: it takes as input two ciphertexts $(\mathsf{Enc}(\sigma), \mathsf{Enc}(\bar\sigma))$ and returns the encryption of 1 if $\sigma = \bar\sigma$ and an encryption of 0 otherwise. It is presented in Fig. 2 and uses the exponentiation functionality Exp, which, in turn, needs the multiparty multiplication protocol Multiply from [11]. The protocol for equality Eq is correct, since when $\sigma = \bar\sigma$ we have that $b = 0$, otherwise $b = 1$, due to $x^p = 1$ for all $x \in (\mathbb{Z}/p\mathbb{Z})^*$. Observe that the exponentiation procedure Exp, shown in Fig. 2, is performed using the square-and-multiply procedure, i.e. using $O(\log_2(p))$ multiplications.

$\mathsf{Exp}(\mathsf{Enc}(x), s)$	$\mathsf{Eq}(\mathsf{Enc}(\sigma), \mathsf{Enc}(\bar\sigma))$
1: $(s_0, \ldots, s_\ell) \leftarrow \mathsf{Binary}(s)$	1: $y \leftarrow \mathsf{Enc}(\sigma) \cdot \mathsf{Enc}(\bar\sigma)^{-1}$
2: $Y \leftarrow \mathsf{Enc}(1)$	2: $b \leftarrow \mathsf{Exp}(y, p)$
3: for $i = \ell, \ldots, 0$ do	3: return $\mathsf{Enc}(1) \cdot b^{-1}$
4: $\quad Y \leftarrow \mathsf{Multiply}(Y, Y)$	
5: $\quad$ if $k_i = 1$	
6: $\quad\quad Y \leftarrow \mathsf{Multiply}(Y, \mathsf{Enc}(x))$	
7: return Y	

Fig. 2. Exponentiation and Equality procedures. Here p is the order of F. Multiply is the multiplication functionality from in [11].

---

[2] Notice that each ciphertext of the couple is a couple itself, as per defined in Sect. 2.2.

Now, we present the Update functionality (Fig. 3) for the update of the votes. It takes as input two pairs of vote-credential encryptions $(\mathsf{Enc}(\nu), \mathsf{Enc}(\sigma))$ and $(\mathsf{Enc}(\bar{\nu}), \mathsf{Enc}(\bar{\sigma}))$, and it returns a ciphertext $\mathsf{ReEnc}(\nu^*)$, where $\nu^* = \nu$ if $\sigma \neq \bar{\sigma}$ and $\nu^* = \bar{\nu}$ otherwise. Here, $\mathsf{ReEnc}(x)$ is the encryption of x using a different randomness.

Finally, we describe the Tally protocol (Fig. 3). The idea is to start with a list R of null votes, encoded by the element 0, one for each credential in $\mathbb{R}_\sigma$ and update it with all the ballots in $\mathcal{BB}$, so that, at end, R contains the last vote made with each credential. Formally, at the beginning of Tally Phase, we have

$$R = \{(\mathsf{Enc}(0), \mathsf{Enc}(\sigma_i)) \mid \sigma_i \in \mathbb{R}_\sigma\}.$$

For each ballot in $\mathcal{BB}$, the whole list R is updated using Update, such that the entry corresponding to the credential in the considered ballot is changed, while the others are simply re-encrypted. Note that it is impossible to distinguish whether an entry is simply re-encrypted or changed. Also, note that when a vote is cast with a fake credential, it means that the entire R is re-encrypted, since no entry in R correspond to a fake credential. This is done to avoid leaking the number of fake votes. In order to do this, first, the $n_\mathcal{T}$ trustees create the list R as described above. Note that this is a copy and not a re-encryption of the credentials σ_i's. Then, for each entry $\mathcal{BB}_i$ of the public bulletin board $\mathcal{BB}$ and for each entry R_j of the list R the Update function is performed, so that, after this computation, the first entry of R_j is the encryption of the last vote made with the credential σ_j. Let $R[1]$ be the list of the first entries of every element in R: at the end of the procedure this is the list of valid votes. The mixnet is performed on this list using the functionality Mixnet from [6], obtaining a permuted list of valid votes, breaking the link between the voter and his preference. The Mixnet procedure additionally produces a proof π_{Mixnet} that has to be checked in order to verify the correctness of the shuffle. Finally, the trustees can decrypt the permuted list via the functionality Decrypt from [11], getting the valid preferences in clear.

3.1 Zero-Knowledge Proofs

Apart from the proofs of knowledge needed and produced by the multiparty protocol from [10,11] and the mixnet from [6], the voting system, in its voting phase, uses two different zero-knowledge proofs. Let $(\mathsf{ct}^\mathsf{V}, \mathsf{ct}^\mathsf{C})$ be the pair of ciphertexts where $\mathsf{ct}^\mathsf{V} = \mathsf{Enc}(\mathsf{pk}, \nu, \rho_\nu)$ is the encryption of a voting preference ν and $\mathsf{ct}^\mathsf{C} = \mathsf{Enc}(\mathsf{pk}, \sigma, \rho_\sigma)$ is an encryption of their credential σ. The first argument of knowledge, denoted with Π_{Vote} proves that ν is a valid voting option. The second proof Π_{Cred} is needed to prove the knowledge of σ in the ciphertext ct^C.

The zero-knowledge proofs will be presented as a 3-move interactive protocols which can be made non-interactive by the Fiat-Shamir transform [23] by computing the verifier message as a hash function of the concatenation of the statement and the first message. For all the upcoming protocols, $\mathsf{pp} = \left(\hat{G}, \tilde{s}, g, h, f\right)$ is the tuple of public parameters, where $\hat{G}$ has unknown order and it has a subgroup

Update($B,\bar{B}$)	Tally($\mathcal{BB},\mathbb{R}_\sigma$)
1: $(\mathsf{Enc}(v), \mathsf{Enc}(\sigma)) \leftarrow B$	1: **for** $i = 1\ldots, \|\mathbb{R}_\sigma\|$ **do**
2: $(\mathsf{Enc}(\bar{v}), \mathsf{Enc}(\bar{\sigma})) \leftarrow \bar{B}$	2: $\quad R_i \leftarrow (\mathsf{Enc}(\bot), \mathbb{R}_{\sigma i})$
3: $b \leftarrow \mathsf{Eq}(\mathsf{Enc}(\bar{\sigma}), \mathsf{Enc}(\sigma))$	3: **for** $i = 1,\ldots, \|\mathcal{BB}\|$ **do**
4: $m_1 \leftarrow \mathsf{Multiply}(b, \mathsf{Enc}(\bar{v}))$	4: $\quad$ **for** $j = 1,\ldots, \|R\|$ **do**
5: $m_2 \leftarrow \mathsf{Multiply}(\mathsf{Enc}(1) \cdot b^{-1}, \mathsf{Enc}(v))$	5: $\quad\quad \mathsf{Enc}(v^*) \leftarrow \mathsf{Update}(\mathcal{BB}_i, R_j)$
6: **return** $m_1 \cdot m_2$	6: $\quad\quad R_j[1] \leftarrow \mathsf{Enc}(v^*)$
	7: $\quad (V, \pi_{\mathsf{Mixnet}}) \leftarrow \mathsf{Mixnet}(R[1])$
	8: $\quad$ **if** $\mathsf{Verify}(\pi_{\mathsf{Mixnet}}) = \bot$ **return** $\bot$
	9: $\quad y \leftarrow \mathsf{Decrypt}(V)$
	10: **return** y

Fig. 3. Update and Tally procedures.

$G \cong H \times F$, with H a cyclic group generated by h and F the unique subgroup of G of order p, which is generated by f. Furthermore, the public key used to encrypt is $\mathsf{pk} = h^{\mathsf{sk}}$, where sk is the corresponding secret key. More details can be found in Sect. 2.2.

The starting point to design both Π_{Vote} and Π_{Cred} is the *proof of plaintext knowledge* Π_{PoPK} from [6, Sect. 3], which demonstrates plaintext knowledge of a public ciphertext, in particular, given a public key pk, it is an interactive protocol for the following relation

$$\{(\mathsf{ct}, (m, \rho)) \mid \mathsf{ct} = \mathsf{Enc}(\mathsf{pk}, m, \rho)\}.$$

For completeness, the protocol is described in Fig. 4, and its security is based on the RO_C assumption. Note that the integer C that appears in the protocol is exactly the C used in the definition of this assumption. More details about how to prove the soundness and the special soundness properties of interactive protocols with unknown group order can be found in [6].

The zero-knowledge proof Π_{Cred} is exactly the proof of plaintext knowledge given in Fig. 4 for a ciphertext $\mathsf{ct}^{\mathsf{C}} = \mathsf{Enc}(\mathsf{pk}, \sigma, \rho_\sigma)$ encrypting a credential σ with randomness ρ_σ

$$\Pi_{\mathsf{Cred}}\left[\mathsf{ct}^{\mathsf{C}}, (\sigma, \rho_\sigma)\right] = \Pi_{\mathsf{PoPK}}\left[\mathsf{ct}^{\mathsf{C}}, (\sigma, \rho_\sigma)\right].$$

The proof Π_{Vote} proves that, given ct^{V}, the voter 1) knows the plaintext, i.e. the vote, and 2) the vote is an admissible vote. Indeed, Π_{Vote} can be viewed as an AND proof of the two statements above. The first one is directly given by the proof of plaintext knowledge Π_{PoPK} from Fig. 4, while, for the second, a slightly involved proof is needed.

We want to design a protocol to prove that the vote ν given in $\mathsf{ct}^{\mathsf{V}} = \mathsf{Enc}(\mathsf{pk}, \nu, \rho_\nu)$ is a correct vote, i.e. it belongs to the set of valid votes $\{\nu_1, \ldots, \nu_k\}$.

Π_{PoPK}

Prover(pp, (ct$_1$, ct$_2$), m, ρ)		**Verifier**(pp, (ct$_1$, ct$_2$))
$\tilde{\rho} \leftarrow\!\!\$\ [0, 2^{2\epsilon} C \tilde{s}[,\ \tilde{m} \leftarrow\!\!\$\ \mathbb{Z}/\mathbb{Z}p$,		
$\tilde{\mathsf{ct}} \leftarrow \mathsf{Enc}(\mathsf{pk}, \tilde{m}, \tilde{\rho})$	$\xrightarrow{\tilde{\mathsf{ct}}}$	
	$\xleftarrow{x}$	$x \leftarrow\!\!\$\ [0, C[$
$\hat{\rho} \leftarrow \tilde{\rho} + \rho x,\ \hat{m} \leftarrow \tilde{m} + mx$	$\xrightarrow{\hat{m}, \hat{\rho}}$	accept if
		$\tilde{\mathsf{ct}}_1 \cdot \mathsf{ct}_1^x = h^{\hat{\rho}},\ \tilde{\mathsf{ct}}_2 \cdot \mathsf{ct}_2^x = \mathsf{pk}^{\hat{\rho}} f^{\hat{m}}$

Fig. 4. Interactive protocol Π_{PoPK} to prove knowledge of m and ρ from [6].

The building block of this proof is an *argument of randomness knowledge* Π_{AoRK}, proving the relation

$$\{((m, \mathsf{ct}), \rho) \mid \mathsf{ct} = \mathsf{Enc}(\mathsf{pk}, m, \rho)\}.$$

Observe that in this case the message m is part of the statement. We can design an argument of randomness knowledge slightly modifying the proof of plaintext knowledge from Fig. 4. The protocol is given in Fig. 5.

Π_{AoRK}

Prover(pp, $(m, (\mathsf{ct}_1, \mathsf{ct}_2)), \rho$)		**Verifier**(pp, $((\mathsf{ct}_1, \mathsf{ct}_2), m)$)
$\tilde{\rho} \leftarrow\!\!\$\ [0, 2^{2\epsilon} C \tilde{s}[$		
$\tilde{\mathsf{ct}} \leftarrow \mathsf{Enc}(\mathsf{pk}, 0, \tilde{\rho})$	$\xrightarrow{\tilde{\mathsf{ct}}}$	
	$\xleftarrow{x}$	$x \leftarrow\!\!\$\ [0, C[$
$\hat{\rho} \leftarrow \tilde{\rho} + \rho x$	$\xrightarrow{\hat{\rho}}$	accept if
		$\tilde{\mathsf{ct}}_1 \cdot \mathsf{ct}_1^x = h^{\hat{\rho}},\ \tilde{\mathsf{ct}}_2 \cdot \mathsf{ct}_2^x = \mathsf{pk}^{\hat{\rho}} f^{xm}$

Fig. 5. Interactive protocol Π_{AoRK} to prove knowledge of ρ such that $(\mathsf{ct}_1, \mathsf{ct}_2) = \mathsf{Enc}(\mathsf{pk}, m, \rho)$, for a public message m.

Remark 1. There are some technical difficulties to design a *proof* of randomness knowledge. As noted in [6], the proof of plaintext knowledge Π_{PoPK} from Fig. 4 is *partial extractable*; this means that only a part of the witness (m, ρ) can be efficiently extracted, namely, the message m. However, even if we cannot extract the randomness ρ in the protocol of Fig. 5, it is complete, sound, and honest-verifier zero-knowledge, showing that it is an *argument* of knowledge. This is enough for our purposes, as we show later in Sect. 4. Indeed, the protocol is only used during the voting phase to identify and discard invalid votes, and in the security proof we do not need to extract the randomness used.

Theorem 1. *The protocol Π_{AoRK} for randomness knowledge described in Fig. 5 is a zero-knowledge argument, i.e., it is complete, sound and honest-verifier zero-knowledge under the RO_C assumption.*

The proof of Theorem 1 can be found in Appendix B and it follows the one of [6, Th. 2].

On top of the argument of randomness knowledge Π_{AoRK}, we can build an *argument of plaintext equality* Π_{AoPE} for the relation

$$\{((\mathsf{ct},\mathsf{ct}'),(m,\rho,\rho')) \mid \mathsf{ct} = \mathsf{Enc}(\mathsf{pk},m,\rho) \wedge \mathsf{ct}' = \mathsf{Enc}(\mathsf{pk},m,\rho')\}.$$

We can then show that two ciphertexts $\mathsf{ct} = \mathsf{Enc}(\mathsf{pk},m,\rho)$ and $\mathsf{ct}' = \mathsf{Enc}(\mathsf{pk},m,\rho')$ share the same public message m showing that, due to the homomorphic properties of the CGE, the ciphertext ct/ct' is an encryption of 0. This is done using Π_{AoRK}, setting ct/ct' as the ciphertext, 0 as the message and $\rho - \rho'$ as randomness. Following the notation from above, we set

$$\Pi_{\mathsf{AoPE}}\left[(m,\mathsf{ct},\mathsf{ct}'),(\rho,\rho')\right] = \Pi_{\mathsf{AoRK}}\left[(0,\mathsf{ct}/\mathsf{ct}'),\rho - \rho'\right].$$

At this point, we have the ingredients to design the argument of knowledge Π_{Vote}. It is obtained by using the OR construction of k argument of plaintext equality, each of which proves that the plaintext in ct^C is ν_i for $i \in [k]$. Observe that the standard construction for OR proof given in [21, Sect. 4] has communication linear in the number of clauses, in our case k. Recall that the AND of two interactive protocols is simply given by their concatenation. Hence, the proof Π_{Vote}, proving the relation

$$\{(\mathsf{ct},(\nu,\rho_\nu)) \mid \mathsf{ct} = \mathsf{Enc}(\mathsf{pk},\nu,\rho_\nu) \wedge \nu \in \{\nu_1,\ldots,\nu_k\}\},$$

for public ρ_i's, is given by

$$\Pi_{\mathsf{Vote}}\left[\mathsf{ct}^\mathsf{V},(\nu,\rho_\nu)\right] = \Pi_{\mathsf{PoPK}}\left[\mathsf{ct}^\mathsf{V},(\nu,\rho_\nu)\right] \bigwedge \left(\bigvee_{i=1}^{k} \Pi_{\mathsf{AoPE}}\left[(\nu_i,\mathsf{ct}^\mathsf{V},\mathsf{Enc}(\mathsf{pk},\nu_i,\rho_i)),(\rho_\nu,\rho_i)\right]\right).$$

The argument of knowledge Π_{Vote} and the proof of knowledge Π_{Cred} are then linked together to make them non-malleable: when using the Fiat-Shamir transform, for each proof the challenge is computed using the first messages and statements of the two proofs together.

3.2 Designated Verifier Re-encryption Proof

For the security proof, a last zero-knowledge proof is needed. We present Π_{DVRE}, a Designated Verifier Re-Encryption proof [28] which can be faked by the Designated Verifier Ver in order to validate a fake credential. In short, it is an OR proof of 1) a proof of a Re-Encryption, i.e. given $\mathsf{ct}^{(0)}, \mathsf{ct}^{(1)}$, one proves that they are two encryptions of the same message, and 2) the proof of knowledge of a secret key $\mathsf{sk}_{\mathsf{Ver}}$ linked to a publicly known public key $\mathsf{pk}_{\mathsf{Ver}}$.

For the sake of clarity, we first show the proof Π_{RE} of Re-Encryption for the relation

$$\left\{ \left((\mathsf{ct}^{(0)}, \mathsf{ct}^{(1)}), \tilde{\rho} \right) \mid \mathsf{ct}^{(1)} = (h^{\tilde{\rho}} \mathsf{ct}_1^{(0)}, \mathsf{pk}^{\tilde{\rho}} \mathsf{ct}_2^{(0)}) \right\}$$

in Fig. 6. Here, we use a standard parallel repetition with λ binary challenges, where λ is the security parameter.

Prover $\left(\mathsf{pp}, \mathsf{ct}^{(0)}, \mathsf{ct}^{(1)}, \tilde{\rho} \right)$ **Verifier** $\left(\mathsf{pp}, \mathsf{ct}^{(0)}, \mathsf{ct}^{(1)} \right)$

$(d_1, \ldots, d_\lambda) \leftarrow\!\!\!\$\ [0, 2^{\varepsilon-2} \tilde{s}[^\lambda$

$I_i \leftarrow \left(\mathsf{ct}_1^{(0)} h^{d_i}, \mathsf{ct}_2^{(0)} h^{d_i} \right)$ for $i = 1, \ldots, \lambda$ $\xrightarrow{\quad I_1, \ldots, I_\lambda \quad}$

$\xleftarrow{\quad c_1, \ldots, c_\lambda \quad}$ $(c_1, \ldots, c_\lambda) \leftarrow\!\!\!\$\ \{0, 1\}^\lambda$

$z_i \leftarrow d_i - \tilde{\rho} c_i$ for $i = 1, \ldots, \lambda$ $\xrightarrow{\quad z_1, \ldots, z_\lambda \quad}$ **accept if for** $i = 1, \ldots, \lambda$

$I_i = \left(h^{z_i} \mathsf{ct}_1^{(c_i)}, h^{z_i} \mathsf{ct}_2^{(c_i)} \right)$

Fig. 6. Protocol to prove that $\mathsf{ct}^{(1)}$ is a re-encryption of $\mathsf{ct}^{(0)}$.

Theorem 2. *The interactive protocol Π_{RE} described in Fig. 6 is complete, special sound and honest-verifier zero-knowledge.*

The proof of Theorem 2 is a standard proof for a parallel repetition protocol with binary challenge and it can be found in Appendix B.

For the second part, observe that the key pair $(\mathsf{sk}_{\mathsf{Ver}}, \mathsf{pk}_{\mathsf{Ver}})$ does not have to be related to CGE. However, we can still use a discrete logarithm-based keypair. In particular, suppose that there exists a public element $\mathfrak{g}$ of order q such that $\mathsf{pk}_{\mathsf{Ver}} = \mathfrak{g}^{\mathsf{sk}_{\mathsf{Ver}}}$. This implies that we can use known order groups, allowing us to use more efficient protocols, such as Schnorr. However, since the two challenge spaces must be equal, for the proof of knowledge of $\mathsf{sk}_{\mathsf{Ver}}$, we use λ parallel repetitions with binary challenges for simplicity. The DVZKP is then an OR proof, obtained using standard techniques and is included in the full version of the paper.

4 Security Analysis

The security proof for our voting protocol is very similar to the ones presented in [4,18]. Hence, here we just sketch the proof.

Theorem 3. *Under the HSM, the RO_C and the ORD assumptions, the voting system presented in Sect. 3 is coercion-resistant.*

Proof. Let $\mathcal{A}$ be an adversary for the real game. We give to $\mathcal{A}$ the power to impersonate t among $n_\mathcal{T}$ election trustees and up to $n_\mathcal{A}$ voters. Our goal is to build an adversary $\mathcal{S}$ for the ideal game using $\mathcal{A}$ as a subroutine. In particular, $\mathcal{S}$ controls the remaining $n_\mathcal{T} - t$ trustees and needs to simulate both the Setup and the Tally.

First of all, $\mathcal{S}$ and $\mathcal{A}$ run the Setup algorithm to generate a common public key pk, secret shares of the private key $\mathsf{sk}_1, ..., \mathsf{sk}_{n_\mathcal{T}}$ and the public commitments $h_1, ..., h_{n_\mathcal{T}}$. During this step, $\mathcal{S}$ is also able to reconstruct the secret key sk by extracting $\mathcal{A}$'s secrets. The simulation of the key generation is shown in Sect. 6.2 of [11]. Then, $\mathcal{S}$ follows the real game normally, getting the set of corrupted voters $V_\mathcal{A}$, the coerced voter j and the voting choice β from the adversary. In the ideal game, $\mathcal{S}$ sends the same choices for $V_\mathcal{A}, j, \beta$.

When asking for the credential of voter j, $\mathcal{S}$ provides to $\mathcal{A}$ the real credential σ^j. From the ideal game, $\mathcal{S}$ learns the size $|B|$ of the ideal board and uses it to simulate the voting process. For $|B|$ times:

- $\mathcal{S}$ calls $\mathcal{A}$ with input B getting $\mathbb{M}$, a list of ballots the adversary wants to make.
- $\mathcal{S}$ decrypts all the valid votes and credentials in $\mathbb{M}$. For every authorized credential σ^i, $\mathcal{S}$ saves the tuple (σ^i, ν) or updates a previously saved (σ^i, ν').
- $\mathcal{S}$ adds all valid ballots in $\mathbb{M}$ to B.
- $\mathcal{S}$ chooses a random voter and a valid voting option and casts a valid vote, adding it to B.

At the end of the voting process, $\mathcal{S}$ adds the same votes in the ideal game.

$\mathcal{S}$ learns the result of the election X at the end of the ideal game and uses it to simulate the tallying process in the real game:

- $\mathcal{S}$ simulates all the Update procedure, due to the UC security of threshold CGE.
- $\mathcal{S}$ simulates the MixNet controlling the honest authorities, while $\mathcal{A}$ uses the dishonest ones.
- $\mathcal{S}$ chooses $|X|$ entries at random and simulates its partial decryption: every entry not chosen is decrypted to 0, while such $|X|$ entries are decrypted such that the result is exactly X.

At this point $\mathcal{A}$ makes its guess b and $\mathcal{S}$ forwards the same guess in the ideal game. The differences between a real execution and the simulation are:

- In the real game $\mathcal{A}$ can get either the real credential σ^j or a fake one. In the simulation $\mathcal{A}$ always receives σ^j. Since in both the real and ideal worlds fake credentials have uniformly random distribution and the DVZKP could be simulated, $\mathcal{A}$ can only distinguish a real execution from a simulated one if and only if it is able to distinguish whether the received credential is a plaintext of one of the encrypted credentials in $\mathbb{R}_\sigma$ or not. Since CGE is IND-CPA due to the HSM assumption, this is impossible.
- During the simulation of the voting loop $\mathcal{S}$ adds random ballots, while in the real game ballots are drawn according to $\mathbb{D}$. As before, since the ballots are encrypted, the simulation is indistinguishable from the real game.

- During the tally, $\mathcal{S}$ simulates the execution of the Update procedure. Due to the UC security of the MPC class group encryption, the simulation is indistinguishable from a real execution, as shown in [11].
- In the simulation, the result always includes all the last valid ballots cast by honest voters. In a real execution, the adversary may change it by casting ballots on behalf of an honest voter. However, to do so, the adversary must be able to create a valid proof about the credential used, and this is unfeasible.
- $\mathcal{S}$ simulates the decryption protocol at the end. This simulation is indistinguishable under the ORD and the RO_C assumptions, as shown in [11].

□

4.1 Notes About Privacy and Verifiability

Here, we provide an informal discussion about privacy and verifiability, with a sketch of the proof. Before that, however, we need to define IND-PA0 security, that is indistinguishability under parallel chosen plaintext attack. It is a stronger property than security under chosen plaintext attack (IND-CPA), where the adversary has also access to a list of decrypted ciphertexts. For a formal definition, see [18]. It is possible to show that the voting map of Sect. 3.

$$(\nu, \sigma) \to (\mathsf{Enc}(\mathsf{pk}, \nu, \rho_\nu), \mathsf{Enc}(\mathsf{pk}, \sigma, \rho_\sigma), \pi_{\mathsf{Vote}}, \pi_{\mathsf{Cred}})$$

is an IND-PA0 encryption scheme, where π_{Vote} and π_{Cred} are the proofs produced by Π_{Vote} and Π_{Cred}, the protocols described in Sect. 3.1. In particular, π_{Vote} is a proof that the vote ν is known and correct and π_{Cred} proves the plaintext knowledge of σ.

Privacy. Informally, privacy means that it is impossible to guess which option a voter chose. Formally, in the privacy game, the adversary $\mathcal{A}$ chooses two voting options ν_0, ν_1 and an "observed voter" v_o, who picks a random bit b and votes ν_b. The adversary, controlling $t - 1$ trustees, wins if they guess b. See Appendix C of [18] for a formal definition. To prove it, we make a reduction to the IND-PA0 security of the encryption protocol used.

Sketch. Suppose that $\mathcal{A}$ is an adversary that wins the privacy game with non-negligible advantage. We show how to build an adversary $\mathcal{S}$ for the IND-PA0 that wins with non-negligible advantage. Indeed, $\mathcal{S}$ chooses ν_0, ν_1 as the plaintext for the IND-PA0 game. Before the tally, $\mathcal{S}$ uses the whole board $\mathcal{BB}$ as a query in the IND-PA0 game, except for the vote cast by v_o, for which $\mathcal{S}$ chooses randomly one of the two voting options. At this point, $\mathcal{S}$ can simulate the whole tally knowing the end result and guesses whatever bit b $\mathcal{A}$ guesses. When $\mathcal{S}$ chooses correctly the vote for v_o, the simulation is perfect and $\mathcal{S}$ wins every time $\mathcal{A}$ wins, which happens with probability $\frac{1}{2}$ + negl. Instead, if $\mathcal{S}$ picks the wrong choice, which happens $\frac{1}{2}$ of the times, $\mathcal{S}$ wins with probability $\frac{1}{2}$. Overall, the winning probability of $\mathcal{S}$ is $\frac{1}{2}$ + negl which is non negligible. □

Verifiability. Universal verifiability is granted by the proofs produced by the trustees and by the honesty of the bulletin board. Cast-as-intended instead is more tricky, since it should require to design algorithms for voters to inquire about their own devices. Many protocols, such as the Benaloh challenge [7], are suitable, however, they usually rely more on "responsible behaviour" from the user, without having a solid security proof. Moreover, they often fall short when analyzed from a game theory standpoint, like in [29] where the authors suggest that the optimal strategy is to (almost) always ignore the audit step and cast the vote immediately. For this reason, we left cast-as-intended out of our scope and we suggest to employ one of the various established solutions since our protocol can support many of them [16].

5 Performance and Optimizations

The main advantage of our protocol is the compactness of the encrypted credentials, which are k times shorter than in [4,18], since we only need a single ciphertext instead of k for a k-bit credential. The complexity of Tally Phase is $O(nr)$, where n is the number of votes and r is the number of registered credentials. Although not optimal and higher than the complexity of the protocols presented in [4,18], our complexity is still better than that of many coercion resistance protocols, whose execution typically takes place in $O(n^2 + nr)$. Furthermore, it is worth noting that having shorter credentials has a large impact on the actual execution time of the protocol, since the execution time of [4,18] is linear with respect to the number of ciphertexts.

We propose two improvements in order to achieve a better execution time while, unfortunately, maintaining the same asymptotic complexity $O(nr)$.

Online Tally. To further optimize the Tally procedure (see Fig. 3), a possibility would be to perform the Update procedure every time a new vote is added to $\mathcal{BB}$. While the overall complexity would remain the same, this would allow for distribute the workload throughout the entire voting process, rather than only at the end, resulting in an overall reduction of the delay between the end of the voting phase and the publication of the results.

Removing the MixNet. If the number N of candidates is small enough, an optimization can be implemented to avoid the mixnet. The principle is the following. Suppose that the votes are cast in $\mathbb{Z}/p\mathbb{Z}$, where $p \simeq 2^M$. A preference for the i-th candidate is encoded in the vote $2^{(i-1)\frac{M}{N}}$. In the tally phase, instead of decrypting all the votes (after the MixNet), we can simply compute $T = \Pi_{i=1}^{|R|} R_i[1]$ and then decrypt T. Notice that $T = \sum_{i=0}^{N-1} 2^{(i-1)\frac{M}{N}} x_i$, where x_i is the number of votes for the i-th candidate. From the knowledge of T, one can easily retrieve all the x_i's using its representation in base $2^{\frac{M}{N}}$. To avoid an overflow of votes, an upper bound to the number of voters is $2^{\frac{M}{N}}$.

Acknowledgments. The first author is supported by the Italian Ministry of University's PRIN 2022 program under the "Mathematical Primitives for Post Quantum Digital Signatures" (P2022J4HRR) and by the FISA project "Quantum-sate cryptographic tools for the protection of national data and information technology assets" (QSAFEIT). The second and the third authors are members of the INdAM Research group GNSAGA and CrypTO, the group of Cryptography and Number Theory of the Politecnico di Torino. The work of the fourth author has been supported by a joint laboratory between Fondazione Bruno Kessler and the Italian State Mint and Polygraphic Institute.

A Cryptographic Assumptions

In this section, we report the cryptographic assumptions on which the proposed e-voting scheme relies.

Definition 3 (Hard Subgroup Membership assumption (HSM)). *Let $\mathcal{D}_G$ and $\mathcal{D}_H$ two distributions over the integers such that*

1. *$\{g^x \mid x \twoheadleftarrow\$\ \mathcal{D}_G\}$ is at distance less than $2^{-\lambda}$ from the uniform distribution on G and*
2. *$\{h^x \mid x \twoheadleftarrow\$\ \mathcal{D}_H\}$ is at distance less than $2^{-\lambda}$ from the uniform distribution on G.*

Let $\mathsf{pp} = (\hat{G}, \tilde{s}, g, h, f)$ be the public parameters, then the Hard Subgroup Membership *assumption states that*

$$\left| \Pr\left[b = b' : x \twoheadleftarrow\$\ \mathcal{D}_G,\ x' \twoheadleftarrow\$\ \mathcal{D}_H,\ b \twoheadleftarrow\$\ \{0,1\},\ Z_0 = g^x,\ Z_1 = h^{x'},\ b' \twoheadleftarrow\$\ \mathcal{A}(\mathsf{pp}, Z_b) \right] - \frac{1}{2} \right|$$

is negligible in λ for every PPT adversary $\mathcal{A}$.

Definition 4 (C-rough assumption (RO_C)). *Let C be a natural number. Define CLGen as the algorithm taking as input the security parameter λ, a prime p and some randomness $\rho \in \{0,1\}^\lambda$ and returning the public parameters $\mathsf{pp} = (\hat{G}, \tilde{s}, g, h, f)$. Let $\mathcal{D}_C^{\mathsf{rough}}$ be the uniform distribution over the set*

$$\{\rho \in \{0,1\}^\lambda \mid \mathsf{pp} = \mathsf{CLGen}(1^\lambda, p, \rho) \vee \forall q < C,\ q \nmid ord(\hat{G})\}.$$

The C-rough assumption states that

$$\left| \Pr\left[1 \twoheadleftarrow\$\ \mathcal{A}\left(1^\lambda, \rho_0\right) : \rho_0 \twoheadleftarrow\$\ \{0,1\}^\lambda \right] - \Pr\left[1 \twoheadleftarrow\$\ \mathcal{A}\left(1^\lambda, \rho_1\right) : \rho_1 \twoheadleftarrow\$\ \mathcal{D}_C^{\mathsf{rough}} \right] \right|$$

is negligible in λ for every PPT adversary $\mathcal{A}$.

Definition 5 (Unknown Order assumption ORD). *Let $\mathsf{pp} = (\hat{G}, \tilde{s}, g, h, f)$ be the public parameters, then the Unknown Order assumption states that*

$$\Pr\left[(h, e) \twoheadleftarrow\$\ \mathcal{A}(1^\lambda, \mathsf{pp}) : h \in \hat{G} \setminus F,\ e \neq 0,\ h^e = 1 \right]$$

is negligible in λ for every PPT adversary $\mathcal{A}$.

B Missing Proofs

Proof of Theorem 1. The correctness follows from direct inspection.

The soundness property is proven following the same arguments from [6]. Assume that one can extract two accepting transcripts $(\tilde{\mathsf{ct}}, x, \hat{\rho})$ and $(\tilde{\mathsf{ct}}, x', \hat{\rho}')$ from a prover P^* which is accepted with non-negligible probability, with $x \neq x'$. Then, since they are accepting, we have that

$$(\tilde{\mathsf{ct}}_1 \cdot \mathsf{ct}_1^x, \tilde{\mathsf{ct}}_2 \cdot \mathsf{ct}_2^x) = (h^{\hat{\rho}}, \mathsf{pk}^{\hat{\rho}} f^{xm}) \text{ and } (\tilde{\mathsf{ct}}_1 \cdot \mathsf{ct}_1^{x'}, \tilde{\mathsf{ct}}_2 \cdot \mathsf{ct}_2^{x'}) = (h^{\hat{\rho}'}, \mathsf{pk}^{\hat{\rho}'} f^{x'm}).$$

Hence, dividing the two equations, we have

$$(\mathsf{ct}_1^{x-x'}, \mathsf{ct}_2^{x-x'}) = (h^{\hat{\rho}-\hat{\rho}'}, \mathsf{pk}^{\hat{\rho}-\hat{\rho}'} f^{(x-x')m}) = \mathsf{Enc}(\mathsf{pk}, (x-x')m, \hat{\rho} - \hat{\rho}').$$

By the C-rough assumption, since $0 < |x - x'| < C$, the element $x - x'$ is invertible modulo $q\hat{s}$, the order of $\hat{G}$ and denote its inverse with z. Then, we have

$$(\mathsf{ct}_1, \mathsf{ct}_2) = (\mathsf{ct}_1^{(x-x')z}, \mathsf{ct}_2^{(x-x')z}) = \mathsf{Enc}(\mathsf{pk}, m, z(\hat{\rho} - \hat{\rho}'))$$

and hence, there exists the randomness $z(\hat{\rho} - \hat{\rho}')$ for the ciphertext $(\mathsf{ct}_1, \mathsf{ct}_2)$ with plaintext m.

For the honest-verifier zero-knowledge property, we refer to [6, Th. 2]. □

Proof of Theorem 2. The correctness follows from direct inspection since, if $\mathsf{ct}^{(1)}$ is a re-encryption of $\mathsf{ct}^{(0)}$ using randomness $\tilde{\rho}$, then we have that

$$\mathsf{ct}^{(1)} = (\mathsf{ct}_1^{(1)}, \mathsf{ct}_2^{(1)}) = (h^{\tilde{\rho}} \mathsf{ct}_1^{(0)}, h^{\tilde{\rho}} \mathsf{ct}_2^{(0)}).$$

To prove special soundness, consider two accepting transcripts $(\{I_i\}, \{c_i\}, \{z_i\})_i$ and $(\{I_i\}, \{c'_i\}, \{z'_i\})_i$ with different challenges such that there exist an index j with $c_j \neq c'_j$. For instance, suppose that $c_j = 0$ and $c'_j = 1$. Then, the extractor computes the witness $\tilde{\rho}$ as $z'_j - z_j$.

The following simulator $\mathcal{S}_{\mathsf{RE}}$ provides the honest-verifier zero-knowledge property. For each i from 1 to λ, the simulator samples a random bit challenge c_i, then it picks a random z_i from $[0, 2^{\epsilon-2}\tilde{s}[$ and computes $I_i = (h^{z_i} \mathsf{ct}_1^{(c_i)}, h^{z_i} \mathsf{ct}_2^{(c_i)})$. The produced transcript has the same distribution of a honest-generated one. □

References

1. Achenbach, D., Kempka, C., Löwe, B., Müler-Quade, J.: Improved Coercion-Resistant electronic elections through deniable Re-Voting. USENIX J. Election Technol. Syst. (JETS) **3**(2), 26–45 (2015). https://www.usenix.org/jets/issues/0302/achenbach
2. Adida, B.: Helios: web-based open-audit voting. In: USENIX Security Symposium, vol. 17, pp. 335–348 (2008)
3. Adida, B.: Helios: web-based open-audit voting. In: USENIX Security Symposium, pp. 335–348. USENIX Association (2008)

4. Aranha, D.F., Battagliola, M., Roy, L.: Faster coercion-resistant e-voting by encrypted sorting. E-Vote-ID 2023 (2023). https://doi.org/10.18420/e-vote-id2023_03
5. Bayer, S., Groth, J.: Efficient zero-knowledge argument for correctness of a shuffle. In: Pointcheval, D., Johansson, T. (eds.) EUROCRYPT 2012. LNCS, vol. 7237, pp. 263–280. Springer, Heidelberg (2012). https://doi.org/10.1007/978-3-642-29011-4_17
6. Beaugrand, A., Castagnos, G., Laguillaumie, F.: Efficient succinct zero-knowledge arguments in the cl framework. J. Cryptol. 38(1) (2025). https://doi.org/10.1007/s00145-024-09534-1
7. Benaloh, J.: Simple verifiable elections. In: Workshop on Accurate Electronic Voting Technology, EVT 2006, p. 5. USENIX Association (2006)
8. Bernstein, D.J.: Curve25519: new Diffie-Hellman speed records. In: Yung, M., Dodis, Y., Kiayias, A., Malkin, T. (eds.) PKC 2006. LNCS, vol. 3958, pp. 207–228. Springer, Heidelberg (2006). https://doi.org/10.1007/11745853_14
9. Bouvier, C., Castagnos, G., Imbert, L., Laguillaumie, F.: I want to ride my bicycl: Bicycl implements cryptography in class groups. J. Cryptol. 36(3) (2023). https://doi.org/10.1007/s00145-023-09459-1
10. Braun, L., et al.: An improved threshold homomorphic cryptosystem based on class groups. In: Galdi, C., Phan, D.H. (eds.) Security and Cryptography for Networks, pp. 24–46. Springer, Cham (2024)
11. Braun, L., Damgård, I., Orlandi, C.: Secure multiparty computation from threshold encryption based on class groups. In: Handschuh, H., Lysyanskaya, A. (eds.) Advances in Cryptology - CRYPTO 2023, pp. 613–645. Springer, Cham (2023)
12. Cardillo, A., Akinyokun, N., Essex, A.: Online voting in Ontario municipal elections: a conflict of legal principles and technology? In: Krimmer, R., et al. (eds.) E-Vote-ID 2019. LNCS, vol. 11759, pp. 67–82. Springer, Cham (2019). https://doi.org/10.1007/978-3-030-30625-0_5
13. Castagnos, G., Laguillaumie, F.: Linearly homomorphic encryption from DDH. In: Nyberg, K. (ed.) CT-RSA 2015. LNCS, vol. 9048, pp. 487–505. Springer, Cham (2015). https://doi.org/10.1007/978-3-319-16715-2_26
14. Castagnos, G., Laguillaumie, F., Tucker, I.: Practical fully secure unrestricted inner product functional encryption modulo p. In: Peyrin, T., Galbraith, S. (eds.) ASIACRYPT 2018. LNCS, vol. 11273, pp. 733–764. Springer, Cham (2018). https://doi.org/10.1007/978-3-030-03329-3_25
15. Clarkson, M.R., Chong, S., Myers, A.C.: Civitas: toward a secure voting system. In: IEEE Symposium on Security and Privacy, pp. 354–368. IEEE Computer Society (2008)
16. Cortier, V., Dreier, J., Gaudry, P., Turuani, M.: A simple alternative to Benaloh challenge for the cast-as-intended property in Helios/Belenios. In: HAL (2019)
17. Cortier, V., Gaudry, P., Glondu, S.: Belenios: a simple private and verifiable electronic voting system. In: Guttman, J.D., Landwehr, C.E., Meseguer, J., Pavlovic, D. (eds.) Foundations of Security, Protocols, and Equational Reasoning. LNCS, vol. 11565, pp. 214–238. Springer, Cham (2019). https://doi.org/10.1007/978-3-030-19052-1_14
18. Cortier, V., Gaudry, P., Yang, Q.: Is the JCJ voting system really coercion-resistant? (2024). https://doi.org/10.1109/CSF61375.2024.00003
19. Recommendation CM/Rec(2017)5 of the Committee of Ministers to member States on standards for e-voting. https://search.coe.int/cm/Pages/result_details.aspx?ObjectID=0900001680726f6f

20. Couteau, G., Klooß, M., Lin, H., Reichle, M.: Efficient range proofs with transparent setup from bounded integer commitments. In: Canteaut, A., Standaert, F.-X. (eds.) EUROCRYPT 2021. LNCS, vol. 12698, pp. 247–277. Springer, Cham (2021). https://doi.org/10.1007/978-3-030-77883-5_9
21. Damgård, I.: On σ-protocols. Lecture Notes, University of Aarhus, Department for Computer Science **84** (2002)
22. Escala, A., Guasch, S., Herranz, J., Morillo, P.: Universal cast-as-intended verifiability. In: Clark, J., Meiklejohn, S., Ryan, P.Y.A., Wallach, D., Brenner, M., Rohloff, K. (eds.) FC 2016. LNCS, vol. 9604, pp. 233–250. Springer, Heidelberg (2016). https://doi.org/10.1007/978-3-662-53357-4_16
23. Fiat, A., Shamir, A.: How to prove yourself: practical solutions to identification and signature problems. In: Odlyzko, A.M. (ed.) CRYPTO 1986. LNCS, vol. 263, pp. 186–194. Springer, Heidelberg (1987). https://doi.org/10.1007/3-540-47721-7_12
24. Glondu, S.: Belenios specification. Technical report, Belenios Project (2024). https://www.belenios.org/specification.pdf. Accessed 30 May 2025
25. Haines, T., Pereira, O., Teague, V.: Running the race: a swiss voting story. In: E-Vote-ID. LNCS, vol. 13553, pp. 53–69. Springer (2022)
26. Haines, T., Smyth, B.: Surveying definitions of coercion resistance. IACR ePrint Arch., p. 822 (2019). https://eprint.iacr.org/2019/822
27. Halderman, J.A., Teague, V.: The New South Wales iVote system: security failures and verification flaws in a live online election. In: Haenni, R., Koenig, R.E., Wikström, D. (eds.) VOTELID 2015. LNCS, vol. 9269, pp. 35–53. Springer, Cham (2015). https://doi.org/10.1007/978-3-319-22270-7_3
28. Hirt, M., Sako, K.: Efficient receipt-free voting based on homomorphic encryption. In: Preneel, B. (ed.) EUROCRYPT 2000. LNCS, vol. 1807, pp. 539–556. Springer, Heidelberg (2000). https://doi.org/10.1007/3-540-45539-6_38
29. Jamroga, W.: Pretty good strategies for Benaloh challenge. In: Volkamer, M., et al. (eds.) Electronic Voting, pp. 106–122. Springer, Cham (2023)
30. Juels, A., Catalano, D., Jakobsson, M.: Coercion-resistant electronic elections. In: Proceedings of the 2005 ACM Workshop on Privacy in the Electronic Society, pp. 61–70 (2005)
31. Lueks, W., Querejeta-Azurmendi, I.n., Troncoso, C.: Voteagain: a scalable coercion-resistant voting system. In: Proceedings of the 29th USENIX Conference on Security Symposium, SEC 2020. USENIX Association, USA (2020)
32. Müller, J., Truderung, T.: CAISED: a protocol for cast-as-intended verifiability with a second device. In: International Joint Conference on Electronic Voting, pp. 123–139. Springer (2023)
33. Popoveniuc, S., Kelsey, J., Regenscheid, A., Vora, P.: Performance requirements for End-to-End verifiable elections. In: 2010 Electronic Voting Technology Workshop/Workshop on Trustworthy Elections (EVT/WOTE 10). USENIX Association, Washington, DC (2010). https://www.usenix.org/conference/evtwote-10/performance-requirements-end-end-verifiable-elections
34. Ryan, P.Y.A., Rønne, P.B., Iovino, V.: Selene: voting with transparent verifiability and coercion-mitigation. In: Clark, J., Meiklejohn, S., Ryan, P.Y.A., Wallach, D., Brenner, M., Rohloff, K. (eds.) FC 2016. LNCS, vol. 9604, pp. 176–192. Springer, Heidelberg (2016). https://doi.org/10.1007/978-3-662-53357-4_12
35. State Electoral Office of Estonia: Ivxv protocols: Specification. Technical report Dok IVXV-PR-EN-1.8.0, State Electoral Office of Estonia (2022). https://www.valimised.ee/sites/default/files/2023-02/IVXV-protocols.pdf. Accessed 30 May 2025

36. Swiss Post: Swiss post e-voting system documentation (2025). https://gitlab.com/swisspost-evoting/e-voting/e-voting-documentation/-/tree/master/System. Accessed 30 May 2025
37. Thaler, J., et al.: Proofs, arguments, and zero-knowledge. Found. Trends® Priv. Secur. **4**(2–4), 117–660 (2022)
38. U.S. Election Assistance Commission: Voluntary Voting System Guidelines (VVSG) version 2.0 (2021). https://www.eac.gov/voting-equipment/voluntary-voting-system-guidelines
39. Weber, S.G., Araujo, R., Buchmann, J.: On coercion-resistant electronic elections with linear work. In: The Second International Conference on Availability, Reliability and Security (ARES 2007), pp. 908–916 (2007). https://doi.org/10.1109/ARES.2007.108

Hierarchical Identity-Based Matchmaking Encryption

Sohto Chiku[1,2](✉)[iD], Keisuke Hara[1,2][iD], and Junji Shikata[1][iD]

[1] Yokohama National University, Yokohama, Japan
chiku-sohto-tw@ynu.jp, shikata-junji-rb@ynu.ac.jp
[2] National Institute of Advanced Industrial Science and Technology (AIST),
Tokyo, Japan
hara-keisuke@aist.go.jp

Abstract. Identity-based matchmaking encryption (IB-ME) is an advanced encryption scheme that allows both the sender and the receiver to specify their respective identities. We study the notion of *hierarchical IB-ME (HIB-ME)*, which augments IB-ME with delegation capabilities.

Specifically, we first formalize HIB-ME and construct it based on hierarchical identity-based encryption and hierarchical identity-based signature. Moreover, as applications of the HIB-ME, we show two chosen ciphertext secure (H)IB-ME constructions for different security levels.

1 Introduction

1.1 Background and Motivation

Identity-Based Matchmaking Encryption. Identity-based matchmaking encryption (IB-ME), proposed by Ateniese et al. [2], is a novel extension of the ordinary encryption system. In this system, both the sender and receiver can specify appropriate identities, which must be satisfied for the message to be revealed. More specifically, in IB-ME, as a setup phase, each sender (resp., receiver) is provided a secret encryption (resp., decryption) key associated to its identity σ (resp., ρ) by the authority called the key generation center (KGC). Then, when a sender generates a ciphertext ct using encryption key ek_σ, in addition to a plaintext m, it selects the target identity of receiver ρ. Upon receiving a ciphertext ct from the sender with his identity σ, a receiver who has a decryption key of ρ and selects a sender identity σ can decrypt the ciphertext ct. As security requirements, IB-ME should satisfy two properties: *privacy* and *authenticity*. Roughly, if identity requirements by senders and receivers do not match, privacy guarantees that any information of a plaintext and an identity does not leak from a ciphertext. Also, authenticity ensures that only the sender who has an encryption key associated with his identity σ can generate a ciphertext associated with σ. To show the usefulness of IB-ME, Ateniese et al. [2] demonstrated that a privacy-preserving bulletin board system[1] (over a Tor network) could be realized based on IB-ME. In that system, users who might belong to different organizations can communicate secretly through this bulletin board or collect information from anonymous sources.

Prior Works. Following the seminal work [2,3], research on various flavors of IB-ME has been carried out. Francati et al. [14] proposed a mismatch-cases privacy and gave a construction from a q-type assumption in the plain model. Chen et al. [11] dismantle q-type assumption and proposed the first IB-ME construction from the standard assumption in the standard model. Wang et al. [24] proposed a generic construction of IB-ME based on a 2-level anonymous HIBE and an identity-based signature scheme. Boyen and Li [7] constructed IB-ME that satisfy enhanced privacy under standard assumptions using an anonymous IBE, an identity-based signature, an average-case randomness extractor, and a reusable computational extractor. Belfiore et al. [4] constructed IB-ME that achieves the notion of enhanced privacy using as building blocks an anonymous IBE, a homomorphic signature, and a reusable computational extractor. There exists some works [12,19,24] by taking another approach to achieve CCA secure IB-ME as follows. Chiku et al. [12] towards CCA secure IB-ME schemes by taking two other approaches. One is based on combining Boneh and Franklin IBE scheme [6], Sakai et al.'s identity-based non-interactive key exchange protocol [21], and Fujisaki-Okamoto transformation [15]. Another one is depending on a CCA secure IBE scheme, an IBS scheme, and a hash function modeled as a random oracle. These constructions are toward not only CCA security but also enhanced privacy. Lin et al. [19] towards a CCA secure IB-ME scheme using the CHK conversion technique. This study applies the CHK technique to specific pairing-based IBE and constructs a pairing-based CCA secure IB-ME construction. Wang et al. [24] insist on their IB-ME towards CCA security by replacing CPA secure HIBE with CCA secure HIBE, but there is no security proof for CCA privacy.

Motivation. In this paper, we aim to formulate a model and give a general construction for *hierarchical IB-ME (HIB-ME)*, thereby providing a basis for further exploration of its theoretical applications. Incorporating hierarchical structures into identity-based primitives is a natural and important step in the evolution of advanced cryptographic primitives with centralized authority. This extension enables the distribution of key generation tasks across multiple levels, reducing the burden on central authorities and improving overall efficiency. Additionally, this extension has a potential for an application to achieve CCA security (e.g., [9]).

---

[1] A bulletin board is an online platform where users can post messages, share information, and engage in discussions on various topics. It allows for asynchronous communication, enabling users to interact at their convenience.

1.2 Our Contribution

Based on the above motivation, this paper gives the following three technical contributions.

A New Primitive: Hierarchical Identity-Based Matchmaking Encryption. We devise a new extension of IB-ME called *hierarchical identity-based matchmaking encryption (HIB-ME)*. Roughly, HIB-ME is an extension of IB-ME in the sense that it enables senders (resp., receivers) to generate encryption keys (resp., decryption keys) for their children's identities. Regarding security aspects, we define CPA privacy, CCA privacy, tweaked CCA privacy, and authenticity. We show that a CPA secure HIB-ME scheme can be obtained by combining hierarchical identity-based encryption (HIBE) and hierarchical identity-based signature (HIBS) by extending the Wang et al.'s CPA secure IB-ME construction [24].

Table 1. Comparison between our IB-ME scheme and the existing CCA secure IB-ME schemes. "Anon IBE" stands for anonymous identity-based encryption, "IBS" stands for identity-based signature, "2-HIB-ME" stands for HIB-ME with 2-level receiver delegation, "OTS" stands for one-time strong signature, and "(Q)ROM" (resp., "StdM") stands for (quantum) random oracle model (resp., standard model).

Schemes	Privacy Level	Crypto. Primitives	Assumption	Model
Chiku et al. [12]	CCA		BDH	ROM
Chiku et al. [12] + [13,20]	CCA	Anon IBE + IBS	NTRU	QROM
Lin et al. [19]	CCA		SXDH	StdM
CHK w/ OTS (Sect. 4.1) + [5]	CCA	2-HIB-ME + OTS	k-lin	StdM
CHK w/ OTS (Sect. 4.1) + [1]	CCA	2-HIB-ME + OTS	LWE	StdM
CHK w/o OTS (Sect. 4.2) + [5]	tweaked CCA	2-HIB-ME	k-lin	StdM
CHK w/o OTS (Sect. 4.2) + [1]	tweaked CCA	2-HIB-ME	LWE	StdM

Extension of CHK Conversion in HIB-ME. As an application of HIB-ME, we propose a CCA secure (H)IB-ME scheme in the standard model. Specifically, we offer a systematic analysis of the Canetti-Halevi-Katz (CHK) conversion technique [9] within the (H)IB-ME framework and propose two distinct variants of the CHK conversion tailored for (H)IB-ME (one is for CCA security and the other is for tweaked CCA security). The resulting schemes are summarized in Table 1.

First, we show a natural extension of the CHK conversion, where a CCA secure (H)IB-ME is derived from CPA secure HIB-ME and one-time signatures. Regarding the efficiency, for example, the ciphertext size is almost the same as the underlying CPA secure (H)IB-ME scheme. From the previous works [1,5,8,10,18,22], we can realize our generic construction over bilinear groups or lattices.

Moreover, we introduce a slightly weak but reasonable CCA security notion, called *tweaked CCA security*, for (H)IB-ME. Roughly, tweaked CCA security is the same as (standard) CCA security except that the (secret) encryption key used in generating challenge ciphertexts is not allowed to be leaked. As an advantage of tweaked CCA security, we show that a tweaked CCA secure (H)IB-ME scheme can be constructed solely based on a CPA secure HIB-ME scheme (without strong one-time signature) by leveraging privacy and authenticity of the underlying HIB-ME scheme. (That is, regarding the ciphertext size, our tweaked CCA secure (H)IB-ME scheme does not have an overhead occurred by strong one-time signature).

2 Preliminaries

Notations. In this paper, we use the following notations. For $n \in \mathbb{N}$, we denote $[n] = \{1, .., n\}$. Let $\lambda \in \mathbb{N}$ denote the security parameter. $x \leftarrow X$ denotes the operation of sampling an element x from a finite set X. $y \leftarrow \mathcal{A}(x; r)$ denotes that a probabilistic Turing machine $\mathcal{A}$ outputs y for an input x using a randomness r, and we simply denote $y \leftarrow \mathcal{A}(x)$ when we do not need to write the internal randomness explicitly. PPT stands for probabilistic polynomial time. $x := y$ denotes that x is defined by y. We say a function $\varepsilon(\lambda)$ is negligible in λ, if $\varepsilon(\lambda) = o(1/\lambda^c)$ for every $c \in \mathbb{Z}$, and we write $negl(\lambda)$ to denote a negligible function in λ. $\emptyset$ denotes the empty set. If $\mathcal{O}$ is a function or an algorithm and $\mathcal{A}$ is an algorithm, $\mathcal{A}^{\mathcal{O}}$ means $\mathcal{A}$ has oracle access to $\mathcal{O}$. For a bit string x, $\text{len}(x)$ denotes the length of x.

2.1 One-Time Digital Signature

Let Sig denote a digital signature scheme. Sig consists of the following three algorithms (KGen, Sign, Ver):

KGen(1^λ) → (vk, sk): The key generation algorithm takes the security parameter 1^λ as input, and outputs a verification key vk and signing key sk.
Sign(sk, m) → Σ: The signing algorithm takes a sk and plaintext m ∈ $\mathcal{M}$ as input, and outputs a signature Σ.
Ver(vk, Σ, m) → 1/0: The verifying algorithm takes vk, and Σ as input, and outputs 1 (meaning "accept") or 0 (meaning "reject").

Correctness. The correctness for Sig requires that for all $\lambda \in \mathbb{N}$, (vk, sk) ← KGen(1^λ) and m ∈ $\mathcal{M}$, it holds that

$$\Pr\left[1 = \text{Ver}(\text{vk}, \Sigma, \text{m}) \mid \Sigma \leftarrow \text{Sign}(\text{sk}, \text{m})\right] = 1.$$

Security. Next, we define a one-time strong unforgeability (sEUF-CMA security) for a digital signature scheme.

Definition 1 (One-time sEUF-CMA Security). *Let* Sig *be a digital signature scheme. We say that* Sig *satisfies one-time* sEUF-CMA *security if for all PPT adversaries* $\mathcal{A}$, *it holds that*

$$\mathsf{Adv}_{\mathsf{Sig},\mathcal{A}}^{\mathsf{seuf\text{-}cma}}(\lambda) := \Pr\left[\begin{array}{l}((\mathsf{m},\Sigma)\neq(\mathsf{m}^*,\Sigma^*))\wedge \\ (\mathsf{Ver}(\mathsf{vk},\Sigma,\mathsf{m})=1)\end{array} \middle| \begin{array}{l}(\mathsf{vk},\mathsf{sk})\leftarrow\mathsf{KGen}(1^\lambda); \\ \mathsf{m}^* \leftarrow \mathcal{A}(\mathsf{vk}); \\ \Sigma^* \leftarrow \mathsf{Sign}(\mathsf{sk},\mathsf{m}^*); \\ (\Sigma,\mathsf{m}) \leftarrow \mathcal{A}(\mathsf{vk},\Sigma^*);\end{array}\right] \leq \mathsf{negl}(\lambda).$$

2.2 Hierarchical Identity-Based Encryption

Let HIBE denote a hierarchical identity-based encryption (HIBE) [16,17,23]. HIBE for identity space $\mathcal{ID}$ and message space $\mathcal{M}$ consists of following five algorithms (Setup, KGen, KDel, Enc, Dec):

Setup($1^\lambda, l$) → (mpk, msk): The setup algorithm takes the security parameter 1^λ and the maximum hierarchical depth l as input, and outputs a master public key mpk and a master secret key msk.

KGen(mpk, msk, ID) → $\mathsf{sk}_{\mathsf{ID}}$: The key generation algorithm takes mpk, msk, and a user identity ID, and outputs a user secret key $\mathsf{sk}_{\mathsf{ID}}$.

KDel(mpk, $\mathsf{sk}_{\mathsf{ID}'}$, ID) → $\mathsf{sk}_{\mathsf{ID}'|\mathsf{ID}}$: The key delegation algorithm takes mpk, $\mathsf{sk}_{\mathsf{ID}'}$, and a user identity ID, and outputs a user secret key $\mathsf{sk}_{\mathsf{ID}'|\mathsf{ID}}$ for the $d+1$ depth identity ID'|ID.

Enc(mpk, ID, m) → ct: The encryption algorithm takes mpk, ID, and a plaintext m as input, and outputs a ciphertext ct.

Dec(mpk, $\mathsf{sk}_{\mathsf{ID}}$, ct) → m/⊥: The decryption algorithm takes mpk, $\mathsf{sk}_{\mathsf{ID}}$, and ct as input, and outputs m or ⊥.

Correctness. For correctness, we require that for all $\lambda \in \mathbb{N}$, (mpk, msk) ← Setup($1^\lambda, l$), ID $\in \mathcal{ID}$, $\mathsf{sk}_{\mathsf{ID}}$ ← KGen(mpk, msk, ID), and m $\in \mathcal{M}$,

$$\Pr[\mathsf{Dec}(\mathsf{mpk},\mathsf{sk}_{\mathsf{ID}},\mathsf{Enc}(\mathsf{mpk},\mathsf{ID},\mathsf{m})) = \mathsf{m}] = 1.$$

Moreover, we also require the distribution of $\mathsf{sk}_{\mathsf{ID}'|\mathsf{ID}}$ ← KDel(mpk, $\mathsf{sk}_{\mathsf{ID}'}$, ID) is identical to the one from KGen(mpk, msk, ID'|ID).

Security. Next, we define IND-hID-CPA security for a HIBE scheme.

Definition 2 (IND-hID-CPA Security). *Let* HIBE *be an l-level HIBE scheme. We say that* HIBE *satisfies* IND-hID-CPA *security if for all PPT adversaries* $\mathcal{A}$, *it holds that*

$$\mathsf{Adv}_{\mathsf{HIBE},\mathcal{A}}^{\mathsf{ind\text{-}hid\text{-}cpa}}(\lambda, l) := \left|\Pr\left[b = b' \middle| \begin{array}{l} b \leftarrow_\$ \{0,1\}, \mathcal{L}_{\mathsf{sk}} := \emptyset; \\ (\mathsf{mpk},\mathsf{msk}) \leftarrow \mathsf{Setup}(1^\lambda, l); \\ (\mathsf{ID}_0^*, \mathsf{ID}_1^*, \mathsf{m}_0^*, \mathsf{m}_1^*) \leftarrow \mathcal{A}^{\mathcal{O}_{\mathsf{KGen}}, \mathcal{O}_{\mathsf{KDel}}, \mathcal{O}_{\mathsf{sk}}}(\mathsf{mpk}); \\ \mathsf{ct}_b^* \leftarrow \mathsf{Enc}(\mathsf{mpk}, \mathsf{ID}_b^*, \mathsf{m}_b^*); \\ b' \leftarrow \mathcal{A}^{\mathcal{O}_{\mathsf{KGen}}, \mathcal{O}_{\mathsf{KDel}}, \mathcal{O}_{\mathsf{sk}}}(\mathsf{ct}_b^*);\end{array}\right] - \frac{1}{2}\right|$$

$$= \mathsf{negl}(\lambda),$$

with restriction $(\mathsf{ID}_b^*, \cdot) \in \mathcal{L}_{\mathsf{sk}} \wedge (\mathtt{prefix}(\mathsf{ID}_b^*), \cdot) \in \mathcal{L}_{\mathsf{sk}}$ for $b \in \{0, 1\}$, and $\mathcal{O}_{\mathsf{KGen}}$ is queried only once for the same ID. Now, we define three type of oracles that $\mathcal{A}$ can access as follows:

- **Key Generation** $\mathcal{O}_{\mathsf{KGen}}(\mathsf{mpk}, \mathsf{msk}, \cdot)$: On input ID, the challenger runs $\mathsf{sk}_{\mathsf{ID}} \leftarrow \mathsf{KGen}(\mathsf{mpk}, \mathsf{msk}, \mathsf{ID})$ and updates $\mathcal{L}_{\mathsf{sk}} := \mathcal{L}_{\mathsf{sk}} \cup \{(\mathsf{ID}, \mathsf{sk}_{\mathsf{ID}})\}$.
- **Key Delegate** $\mathcal{O}_{\mathsf{KDel}}(\mathsf{mpk}, \cdot, \cdot)$: On input $(\mathsf{ID}', \cdot) \in \mathcal{L}_{\mathsf{sk}}$, ID, the challenger extracts $\mathsf{sk}_{\mathsf{ID}'}$ from $\mathcal{L}_{\mathsf{sk}}$, runs $\mathsf{sk}_{\mathsf{ID}'|\mathsf{ID}} \leftarrow \mathsf{KDel}(\mathsf{mpk}, \mathsf{sk}_{\mathsf{ID}'}, \mathsf{ID})$, and updates $\mathcal{L}_{\mathsf{sk}} := \mathcal{L}_{\mathsf{sk}} \cup \{(\mathsf{ID}'|\mathsf{ID}, \mathsf{sk}_{\mathsf{ID}'|\mathsf{ID}})\}$.
- **Key Reveal** $\mathcal{O}_{\mathsf{sk}}(\cdot)$: On input $(\mathsf{ID}, \cdot) \in \mathcal{L}_{\mathsf{sk}}$, the challenger extracts $\mathsf{sk}_{\mathsf{ID}}$ from $\mathcal{L}_{\mathsf{sk}}$, and returns $\mathsf{sk}_{\mathsf{ID}}$ to $\mathcal{A}$. In addition, the challenger updates $\mathcal{L}_{\mathsf{sk}} := \mathcal{L}_{\mathsf{sk}} \setminus \{(\mathsf{ID}, \mathsf{sk}_{\mathsf{ID}})\}$.

2.3 Hierarchical Identity-Based Signature

Let HIBS denote a hierarchical identity-based signature (HIBS) [16,23]. HIBS consists of following five algorithms (Setup, KGen, KDel, Sign, Ver):

$\mathsf{Setup}(1^\lambda, l) \to (\mathsf{mpk}, \mathsf{msk})$: The setup algorithm takes the security parameter 1^λ and the maximum hierarchical depth l as input, and outputs a master public key mpk and a master secret key msk.

$\mathsf{KGen}(\mathsf{mpk}, \mathsf{msk}, \mathsf{ID}) \to \mathsf{sk}_{\mathsf{ID}}$: The key generation algorithm takes mpk, msk, and a user identity ID, and outputs a user secret key $\mathsf{sk}_{\mathsf{ID}}$.

$\mathsf{KDel}(\mathsf{mpk}, \mathsf{sk}_{\mathsf{ID}'}, \mathsf{ID}) \to \mathsf{sk}_{\mathsf{ID}'|\mathsf{ID}}$: The key delegation algorithm takes mpk, $\mathsf{sk}_{\mathsf{ID}'}$, and a user identity ID, and outputs a user secret key $\mathsf{sk}_{\mathsf{ID}'|\mathsf{ID}}$ for the $d+1$ depth identity $\mathsf{ID}'|\mathsf{ID}$.

$\mathsf{Sign}(\mathsf{mpk}, \mathsf{sk}_{\mathsf{ID}}, \mathsf{m}) \to \Sigma$: The signing algorithm takes a mpk, $\mathsf{sk}_{\mathsf{ID}}$, and a message $\mathsf{m} \in \mathcal{M}$ as input, and outputs a signature Σ.

$\mathsf{Ver}(\mathsf{mpk}, \mathsf{ID}, \Sigma, \mathsf{m}) \to 1/0$: The verifying algorithm takes mpk, $\mathsf{ID} \in \mathcal{ID}$, Σ, and m as input, and outputs 1 (meaning "accept") or 0 (meaning "reject").

Correctness. For corectness, we require that for all $\lambda \in \mathbb{N}$, $(\mathsf{mpk}, \mathsf{msk}) \leftarrow \mathsf{Setup}(1^\lambda, l)$, $\mathsf{ID} \in \mathcal{ID}$, $\mathsf{sk}_{\mathsf{ID}} \leftarrow \mathsf{KGen}(\mathsf{mpk}, \mathsf{msk}, \mathsf{ID})$, $\mathsf{m} \in \mathcal{M}$, and $\Sigma \leftarrow \mathsf{Sign}(\mathsf{mpk}, \mathsf{sk}_{\mathsf{ID}}, \mathsf{m})$,

$$\Pr\left[\mathsf{Ver}(\mathsf{mpk}, \mathsf{ID}, \Sigma, \mathsf{m}) = 1\right] = 1.$$

Moreover, we also require the distribution of $\mathsf{sk}_{\mathsf{ID}'|\mathsf{ID}} \leftarrow \mathsf{KDel}(\mathsf{mpk}, \mathsf{sk}_{\mathsf{ID}'}, \mathsf{ID})$ is identical to the one from $\mathsf{KGen}(\mathsf{mpk}, \mathsf{msk}, \mathsf{ID}'|\mathsf{ID})$.

Security. Next, we define EUF-hID-CMA security for a HIBS scheme.

Definition 3. *Let HIBS be an l-level HIBS scheme. We say that HIBS satisfies EUF-hID-CMA security if for all PPT adversary $\mathcal{A}$, it holds that*

$$\mathsf{Adv}_{\mathsf{HIBS},\mathcal{A}}^{\mathsf{euf\text{-}hid\text{-}cma}}(\lambda, l) := \Pr\left[\begin{array}{l|l} (\mathsf{ID}^*, \cdot) \in \mathcal{L}_{\mathsf{sk}} \wedge & \mathcal{L}_{\mathsf{sk}}, \mathcal{L}_\Sigma := \emptyset; \\ (\mathtt{prefix}(\mathsf{ID}^*), \cdot) \in \mathcal{L}_{\mathsf{sk}} \wedge & (\mathsf{mpk}, \mathsf{msk}) \leftarrow \mathsf{Setup}(1^\lambda, l); \\ ((\mathsf{ID}^*, \mathsf{m}^*, \cdot) \notin \mathcal{L}_\Sigma) \wedge & (\mathsf{ID}^*, \Sigma^*, \mathsf{m}^*) \\ (\mathsf{Ver}(\mathsf{mpk}, \mathsf{ID}^*, \Sigma^*, \mathsf{m}^*) \neq 0) & \leftarrow \mathcal{A}^{\mathcal{O}_{\mathsf{KGen}}, \mathcal{O}_{\mathsf{KDel}}, \mathcal{O}_{\mathsf{sk}}, \mathcal{O}_{\mathsf{Sign}}}(\mathsf{mpk}); \end{array}\right]$$

$$= \mathsf{negl}(\lambda),$$

with restriction $\mathcal{O}_{\mathsf{KGen}}$ is queried only once for the same ID. Now, we define four type of oracles that $\mathcal{A}$ can access as follows:

- **Key Generation** $\mathcal{O}_{\mathsf{KGen}}(\mathsf{mpk}, \mathsf{msk}, \cdot)$: Same as Definition 2.
- **Key Delegate** $\mathcal{O}_{\mathsf{KDel}}(\mathsf{mpk}, \cdot, \cdot)$: Same as Definition 2.
- **Key Reveal** $\mathcal{O}_{\mathsf{sk}}(\cdot)$: Same as Definition 2.
- **Signature Generation** $\mathcal{O}_{\mathsf{Sign}}(\cdot, \cdot)$: On input $\mathsf{ID} \in \mathcal{L}_{\mathsf{sk}}$ and m, the challenger extracts $\mathsf{sk}_{\mathsf{ID}}$ from $\mathcal{L}_{\mathsf{sk}}$, runs $\Sigma \leftarrow \mathsf{Sign}(\mathsf{mpk}, \mathsf{sk}_{\mathsf{ID}}, \mathsf{m})$, and returns Σ to $\mathcal{A}$. In addition, the challenger updates $\mathcal{L}_\Sigma := \mathcal{L}_\Sigma \cup \{(\mathsf{ID}, \mathsf{m}, \Sigma)\}$.

3 Hierarchial Identity-Based Matchmaking Encryption

In this section, we introduce a new cryptographic primitive called hierarchical identity-based matchmaking encryption (HIB-ME).

3.1 Formalization of HIB-ME

In this section, we provide the syntax, correctness, and security definitions for HIB-ME. Informally, HIB-ME is an extension of IB-ME in the sense that it enables senders (resp., receivers) to generate encryption keys (resp., decryption keys) for their children's identities. Let (k, l)-level HIB-ME denote an HIB-ME scheme with a maximum depth k for sender keys and depth l for receiver keys. (k, l)-level HIB-ME consists of the following seven algorithms (Setup, SKGen, SKDel, RKGen, RKDel, Enc, Dec):

Setup($1^\lambda, k, l$) → (mpk, msk): The setup algorithm takes the security parameter 1^λ and the maximum hierarchical sender depth k and receiver depth l as input, and outputs a master public key mpk and a master secret key msk.

SKGen(mpk, msk, σ) → ek_σ: The sender key generation algorithm takes mpk, msk, and a sender identity σ, and outputs a encryption key ek_σ.

SKDel(mpk, $\mathsf{ek}_{\sigma'}, \sigma$) → $\mathsf{ek}_{\sigma'|\sigma}$: The sender key delegation algorithm takes mpk, $\mathsf{ek}_{\sigma'}$, and a sender identity σ, and outputs a encryption key $\mathsf{ek}_{\sigma'|\sigma}$ for the $d+1$ depth identity $\sigma'|\sigma$.

RKGen(mpk, msk, ρ) → dk_ρ: The receiver key generation algorithm takes mpk, msk, and a receiver identity ρ, and outputs a decryption key dk_ρ.

RKDel(mpk, $\mathsf{dk}_{\rho'}, \rho$) → $\mathsf{dk}_{\rho'|\rho}$: The receiver key delegation algorithm takes mpk, $\mathsf{dk}_{\rho'}$, and a receiver identity ρ, and outputs a decryption key $\mathsf{dk}_{\rho'|\rho}$ for the $d+1$ depth identity $\rho'|\rho$.

Enc(mpk, ek_σ, rcv, m) → ct: The encryption algorithm takes mpk, ek_σ, a target receiver identity rcv, and a plaintext m, and outputs a ciphertext m.

Dec(mpk, dk_ρ, snd, ct) → m/$\bot$: The decryption algorithm takes mpk, dk_ρ, a target sender identity snd, and ct, and outputs m or $\bot$.

Correctness. For correctness, we require that for all $\lambda \in \mathbb{N}$, (mpk, msk) ← Setup($1^\lambda, k, l$), σ, snd, ρ, rcv $\in \mathcal{ID}$ such that $\sigma =$ snd $\wedge \rho =$ rcv, ek$_\sigma$ ← SKGen(mpk, msk, σ), dk$_\rho$ ← RKGen(mpk, msk, ρ), and m $\in \mathcal{M}$,

$$\Pr[\text{Dec}(\text{mpk}, \text{dk}_\rho, \text{snd}, \text{Enc}(\text{mpk}, \text{ek}_\sigma, \text{rcv}, \text{m})) = \text{m}] = 1.$$

Moreover, we also require the distribution of ek$_{\sigma'|\sigma}$ ← SKDel(mpk, ek$_{\sigma'}, \sigma$) (resp., dk$_{\rho'|\rho}$ ← RKDel(mpk, dk$_{\rho'}, \rho$)) is identical to the one from SKGen(mpk, msk, $\sigma'|\sigma$) (resp., RKGen(mpk, msk, $\rho'|\rho$)).

Security. Next, we define security requirements (hib-cca-priv security, hib-tcca-priv security, hib-cpa-priv security, and hib-auth security) for HIB-ME. hib-cca-priv security is based on [12,19], While hib-cpa-priv security is based on [3], and hib-auth security is based on [14], hib-tcca-priv security is original meaningful privacy definition. While CCA security is the most desirable security, we can consider a weaker version that $\mathcal{A}$ cannot get the (secret) encryption key of the target sender σ^*. In the tweaked CCA security experiment, $\mathcal{A}$ can no longer compute encryption using the challenge (secret) encryption key. Hence $\mathcal{A}$ is given access to encryption oracle $\mathcal{O}_{\text{Enc}}$.

Definition 4 (Privacy). *Let* HIB-ME *be an (k, l)-level* HIB-ME *scheme. We define the advantage of each privacy game as*

$$\text{Adv}^{\text{priv}}_{\text{HIB-ME},\mathcal{A}}(\lambda, k, l) := \left| \Pr \left[b' = b \; \middle| \; \begin{array}{l} b \leftarrow_\$ \{0,1\}, \mathcal{L}_{\text{ek}}, \mathcal{L}_{\text{dk}}, \mathcal{L}_{\text{ct}} := \emptyset; \\ (\text{mpk}, \text{msk}) \leftarrow \text{Setup}(1^\lambda, k, l); \\ (\sigma_0^*, \sigma_1^*, \text{rcv}_0^*, \text{rcv}_1^*, \text{m}_0^*, \text{m}_1^*) \leftarrow \mathcal{A}^{\mathcal{O}}(\text{mpk}); \\ \text{ek}_{\sigma_b^*} \leftarrow \text{SKGen}(\text{mpk}, \text{msk}, \sigma_b^*); \\ \text{ct}_b^* \leftarrow \text{Enc}(\text{mpk}, \text{ek}_{\sigma_b^*}, \text{rcv}_b^*, \text{m}_b^*); \\ b' \leftarrow \mathcal{A}^{\mathcal{O}}(\text{ct}_b^*); \end{array} \right. \right] - \frac{1}{2} \right|.$$

In addition, we define eight type of oracles as follows:

- **Sender Key Generate** $\mathcal{O}_{\text{SKGen}}(\text{mpk}, \text{msk}, \cdot)$: On input σ, the challenger runs ek$_\sigma$ ← SKGen(mpk, msk, σ) and updates $\mathcal{L}_{\text{ek}} := \mathcal{L}_{\text{ek}} \cup \{(\sigma, \text{ek}_\sigma)\}$.
- **Receiver Key Generate** $\mathcal{O}_{\text{RKGen}}(\text{mpk}, \text{msk}, \cdot)$: On input ρ, the challenger runs dk$_\rho$ ← RKGen(mpk, msk, ρ) and updates $\mathcal{L}_{\text{dk}} := \mathcal{L}_{\text{dk}} \cup \{(\rho, \text{dk}_\rho)\}$.
- **Sender Key Delegate** $\mathcal{O}_{\text{SKDel}}(\text{mpk}, \cdot, \cdot)$: On input σ' such that $(\sigma', \cdot) \in \mathcal{L}_{\text{ek}}$ and σ, the challenger extracts ek$_{\sigma'}$ from $\mathcal{L}_{\text{ek}}$, runs ek$_{\sigma'|\sigma}$ ← SKDel(mpk, ek$_{\sigma'}$, σ), and updates $\mathcal{L}_{\text{ek}} := \mathcal{L}_{\text{ek}} \cup \{(\sigma'|\sigma, \text{ek}_{\sigma'|\sigma})\}$.
- **Receiver Key Delegate** $\mathcal{O}_{\text{RKDel}}(\text{mpk}, \cdot, \cdot)$: On input ρ' such that $(\rho', \cdot) \in \mathcal{L}_{\text{dk}}$ and ρ, the challenger extracts dk$_{\rho'}$ from $\mathcal{L}_{\text{dk}}$, runs dk$_{\rho'|\rho}$ ← RKDel(mpk, dk$_{\rho'}, \rho$), and updates $\mathcal{L}_{\text{dk}} := \mathcal{L}_{\text{dk}} \cup \{(\rho'|\rho, \text{dk}_{\rho'|\rho})\}$.
- **Sender Key Reveal** $\mathcal{O}_{\text{ek}}(\cdot)$: On input σ such that $(\sigma, \cdot) \in \mathcal{L}_{\text{ek}}$, the challenger extracts ek$_\sigma$ from $\mathcal{L}_{\text{ek}}$ and returns ek$_\sigma$ to $\mathcal{A}$. In addition, the challenger updates $\mathcal{L}_{\text{ek}} := \mathcal{L}_{\text{ek}} \setminus \{(\sigma, \text{ek}_\sigma)\}$.
- **Receiver Key Reveal** $\mathcal{O}_{\text{dk}}(\cdot)$: On input ρ such that $(\rho, \cdot) \in \mathcal{L}_{\text{dk}}$, the challenger extracts dk$_\rho$ from $\mathcal{L}_{\text{dk}}$ and returns dk$_\rho$ to $\mathcal{A}$. In addition, the challenger updates $\mathcal{L}_{\text{dk}} := \mathcal{L}_{\text{dk}} \setminus \{(\rho, \text{dk}_\rho)\}$.

- **Encrypt** $\mathcal{O}_{\mathsf{Enc}}(\mathsf{mpk}, \cdot, \cdot, \cdot)$: On input σ such that $(\sigma, \cdot) \in \mathcal{L}_{\mathsf{ek}}$, rcv, and m, the challenger extracts ek_σ from $\mathcal{L}_{\mathsf{ek}}$, runs ct $\leftarrow \mathsf{Enc}(\mathsf{mpk}, \mathsf{ek}_\sigma, \mathsf{rcv}, \mathsf{m})$, and returns ct *to* $\mathcal{A}$. In addition, the challenger updates $\mathcal{L}_{\mathsf{ct}} := \mathcal{L}_{\mathsf{ct}} \cup \{(\sigma, \mathsf{rcv}, \mathsf{m}, \mathsf{ct})\}$.
- **Decrypt** $\mathcal{O}_{\mathsf{Dec}}(\mathsf{mpk}, \cdot, \cdot, \cdot)$: On input ρ such that $(\rho, \cdot) \in \mathcal{L}_{\mathsf{dk}}$, snd, and ct, the challenger returns $\bot$ if $\mathsf{snd} = \sigma^* \land \rho = \mathsf{rcv}^* \land \mathsf{ct} = \mathsf{ct}_b^*$. Otherwise, it extracts dk_ρ from $\mathcal{L}_{\mathsf{dk}}$, runs m $\leftarrow \mathsf{Dec}(\mathsf{mpk}, \mathsf{dk}_\rho, \mathsf{snd}, \mathsf{ct})$, and returns m *to* $\mathcal{A}$.

Now, we say that HIB-ME *satisfies*:

1. hib-cpa-priv *if for all* PPT *adversary* $\mathcal{A}$ *that can access to* $\mathcal{O} := \{\mathcal{O}_{\mathsf{SKGen}}, \mathcal{O}_{\mathsf{RKGen}}, \mathcal{O}_{\mathsf{SKDel}}, \mathcal{O}_{\mathsf{RKDel}}, \mathcal{O}_{\mathsf{ek}}, \mathcal{O}_{\mathsf{dk}}\}$, *it holds that* $\mathsf{Adv}^{\mathsf{priv}}_{\mathsf{HIB\text{-}ME}, \mathcal{A}}(\lambda, k, l) = \mathsf{negl}(\lambda)$ *with restriction* $(\mathsf{rcv}^*, \cdot) \notin \mathcal{L}_{\mathsf{dk}} \land (\mathtt{prefix}(\mathsf{rcv}^*), \cdot) \in \mathcal{L}_{\mathsf{dk}}$.
2. hib-cca-priv *if for all* PPT *adversary* $\mathcal{A}$ *that can access to* $\mathcal{O} := \{\mathcal{O}_{\mathsf{SKGen}}, \mathcal{O}_{\mathsf{RKGen}}, \mathcal{O}_{\mathsf{SKDel}}, \mathcal{O}_{\mathsf{RKDel}}, \mathcal{O}_{\mathsf{ek}}, \mathcal{O}_{\mathsf{dk}}, \mathcal{O}_{\mathsf{Dec}}\}$, *it holds that* $\mathsf{Adv}^{\mathsf{priv}}_{\mathsf{HIB\text{-}ME}, \mathcal{A}}(\lambda, k, l) = \mathsf{negl}(\lambda)$ *with restriction* $(\mathsf{rcv}^*, \cdot) \in \mathcal{L}_{\mathsf{dk}} \land (\mathtt{prefix}(\mathsf{rcv}^*), \cdot) \in \mathcal{L}_{\mathsf{dk}}$.
3. hib-tcca-priv *if for all* PPT *adversary* $\mathcal{A}$ *that can access to* $\mathcal{O} := \{\mathcal{O}_{\mathsf{SKGen}}, \mathcal{O}_{\mathsf{RKGen}}, \mathcal{O}_{\mathsf{SKDel}}, \mathcal{O}_{\mathsf{RKDel}}, \mathcal{O}_{\mathsf{ek}}, \mathcal{O}_{\mathsf{dk}}, \mathcal{O}_{\mathsf{Enc}}, \mathcal{O}_{\mathsf{Dec}}\}$, *it holds that* $\mathsf{Adv}^{\mathsf{priv}}_{\mathsf{HIB\text{-}ME}, \mathcal{A}}(\lambda, k, l) = \mathsf{negl}(\lambda)$ *with restriction* $(\sigma^*, \cdot) \in \mathcal{L}_{\mathsf{ek}} \land (\mathtt{prefix}(\sigma^*), \cdot) \in \mathcal{L}_{\mathsf{ek}} \land (\mathsf{rcv}^*, \cdot) \in \mathcal{L}_{\mathsf{dk}} \land (\mathtt{prefix}(\mathsf{rcv}^*), \cdot) \in \mathcal{L}_{\mathsf{dk}}$.

Definition 5 (Authenticity). *Let* HIB-ME *be an* (k, l)-*level HIB-ME scheme. We say that* HIB-ME *satisfies* hib-auth *security if for all* PPT *adversary* $\mathcal{A}$, *it holds that*

$$\mathsf{Adv}^{\mathsf{hib\text{-}auth}}_{\mathsf{HIB\text{-}ME}, \mathcal{A}}(\lambda, k, l) := \Pr \left[\begin{array}{l} (\mathsf{snd}^*, \cdot) \in \mathcal{L}_{\mathsf{ek}} \land \\ (\mathsf{snd}^*, \mathsf{m}^*) \notin \mathcal{L}_{\mathsf{ct}} \land \\ \mathsf{Dec}(\mathsf{mpk}, \mathsf{dk}_{\rho^*}, \mathsf{snd}^*, \mathsf{ct}^*) \neq \bot \end{array} \middle| \begin{array}{l} \mathcal{L}_{\mathsf{ek}}, \mathcal{L}_{\mathsf{dk}}, \mathcal{L}_{\mathsf{ct}} := \emptyset; \\ (\mathsf{mpk}, \mathsf{msk}) \leftarrow \mathsf{Setup}(1^\lambda, k, l); \\ (\mathsf{snd}^*, \rho^*, \mathsf{ct}^*, \mathsf{m}^*) \leftarrow \mathcal{A}^{\mathcal{O}}(\mathsf{mpk}); \end{array} \right]$$

$$= \mathsf{negl}(\lambda),$$

with restriction $(\mathsf{snd}^*, \cdot) \in \mathcal{L}_{\mathsf{ek}} \land (\mathtt{prefix}(\mathsf{snd}^*), \cdot) \in \mathcal{L}_{\mathsf{ek}} \land (\mathsf{snd}^*, \rho^*, \cdot, \mathsf{ct}^*) \notin \mathcal{L}_{\mathsf{ct}}$. *Where* $\mathcal{A}$ *can access* $\mathcal{O} := \{\mathcal{O}_{\mathsf{SKGen}}, \mathcal{O}_{\mathsf{RKGen}}, \mathcal{O}_{\mathsf{SKDel}}, \mathcal{O}_{\mathsf{RKDel}}, \mathcal{O}_{\mathsf{ek}}, \mathcal{O}_{\mathsf{dk}}, \mathcal{O}_{\mathsf{Enc}}\}$ *defined in Definition 4.*

3.2 Construction from Anonymous HIBE and HIBS

In this section, we show a construction of CPA secure HIB-ME scheme. We can obtain hib-cpa-priv and hib-auth secure (k, l)-level HIB-ME scheme HIB-ME from k-level HIBS and $l+1$-level HIBE. The main idea of the construction is extension of Wang et al.'s sign-then-encrypt IB-ME scheme [24].

Construction. Fix integers $k \geq 1$, $l \geq 1$. Let HIBE = ($\mathsf{Setup}_{\mathsf{HIBE}}$, $\mathsf{KGen}_{\mathsf{HIBE}}$, $\mathsf{KDel}_{\mathsf{HIBE}}$, $\mathsf{Enc}_{\mathsf{HIBE}}$, $\mathsf{Dec}_{\mathsf{HIBE}}$) be an $l + 1$-level HIBE scheme, and HIBS = ($\mathsf{Setup}_{\mathsf{HIBS}}$, $\mathsf{KGen}_{\mathsf{HIBS}}$, $\mathsf{KDel}_{\mathsf{HIBS}}$, $\mathsf{Sign}_{\mathsf{HIBS}}$, $\mathsf{Ver}_{\mathsf{HIBS}}$) be a k-level HIBS scheme. Then, our (k, l)-level HIB-ME scheme HIB-ME = (Setup, SKGen, SKDel, RKGen, RKDel, Enc, Dec) is described as follows:

$\mathsf{Setup}(1^\lambda, k, l)$: It runs $(\mathsf{mpk}_{\mathsf{HIBS}}, \mathsf{msk}_{\mathsf{HIBS}}) \leftarrow \mathsf{Setup}_{\mathsf{HIBS}}(1^\lambda, k)$ and $(\mathsf{mpk}_{\mathsf{HIBE}}, \mathsf{msk}_{\mathsf{HIBE}}) \leftarrow \mathsf{Setup}_{\mathsf{HIBE}}(1^\lambda, l + 1)$. Then, it outputs $(\mathsf{mpk}, \mathsf{msk})$ where $\mathsf{mpk} := (\mathsf{mpk}_{\mathsf{HIBS}}, \mathsf{mpk}_{\mathsf{HIBE}})$ and $\mathsf{msk} := (\mathsf{msk}_{\mathsf{HIBS}}, \mathsf{msk}_{\mathsf{HIBE}})$.

SKGen(mpk, msk, σ): It runs $\mathsf{ek}_\sigma \leftarrow \mathsf{KGen}_{\mathsf{HIBS}}(\mathsf{mpk}_{\mathsf{HIBS}}, \mathsf{msk}_{\mathsf{HIBS}}, \sigma)$ and outputs ek_σ.

SKDel(mpk, $\mathsf{ek}_{\sigma'}, \sigma$): It runs $\mathsf{ek}_{\sigma'|\sigma} \leftarrow \mathsf{KDel}_{\mathsf{HIBS}}(\mathsf{mpk}_{\mathsf{HIBS}}, \mathsf{ek}_{\sigma'}, \sigma)$ and outputs $\mathsf{ek}_{\sigma|\sigma'}$.

RKGen(mpk, msk, ρ): It runs $\mathsf{dk}_\rho \leftarrow \mathsf{KGen}_{\mathsf{HIBE}}(\mathsf{mpk}_{\mathsf{HIBE}}, \mathsf{msk}_{\mathsf{HIBE}}, \rho)$ and outputs dk_ρ.

RKDel(mpk, $\mathsf{dk}_{\rho'}, \rho$): It runs $\mathsf{dk}_{\rho'|\rho} \leftarrow \mathsf{KDel}_{\mathsf{HIBE}}(\mathsf{mpk}_{\mathsf{HIBE}}, \mathsf{dk}_{\rho'}, \rho)$ and outputs $\mathsf{dk}_{\rho|\rho'}$.

Enc(mpk, ek_σ, rcv|σ, m): It runs $\Sigma \leftarrow \mathsf{Sign}_{\mathsf{HIBS}}(\mathsf{mpk}_{\mathsf{HIBS}}, \mathsf{ek}_\sigma, m\|\mathsf{rcv})$ and $\mathsf{ct} \leftarrow \mathsf{Enc}_{\mathsf{HIBE}}(\mathsf{mpk}_{\mathsf{HIBE}}, \mathsf{rcv}|\sigma, m\|\Sigma)$, and outputs ct.

Dec(mpk, dk_ρ, snd, ct): It runs $\mathsf{dk}_{\rho|\mathsf{snd}} \leftarrow \mathsf{KDel}_{\mathsf{HIBE}}(\mathsf{mpk}_{\mathsf{HIBE}}, \mathsf{dk}_\rho, \mathsf{snd})$ $m\|\Sigma \leftarrow \mathsf{Dec}_{\mathsf{HIBE}}(\mathsf{mpk}, \mathsf{dk}_{\rho|\sigma}, \mathsf{ct})$. If $\mathsf{Ver}_{\mathsf{HIBS}}(\mathsf{mpk}_{\mathsf{HIBS}}, \mathsf{snd}, \Sigma, m\|\rho) = 1$, it outputs m. Otherwise, it outputs $\bot$.

Correctness. If the ciphertext $\mathsf{ct} \leftarrow \mathsf{Enc}_{\mathsf{HIBE}}(\mathsf{mpk}_{\mathsf{HIBE}}, \mathsf{rcv}|\mathsf{snd}, m\|\Sigma)$ generated correctly, $\mathsf{Ver}_{\mathsf{HIBS}}(\mathsf{mpk}_{\mathsf{HIBS}}, \mathsf{snd}, \sigma, m\|\rho)$ always outputs 1 due to the correctness of HIBS. Hence, if HIBE satisfies correctness, HIB-ME also satisfies correctness.

Security. Here, we show that our scheme satisfies security requirements.

Theorem 1. *Suppose that the HIBE scheme HIBE is IND-hID-CPA secure. If there exists an adversary $\mathcal{A}$ that breaks hib-cpa-priv security if HIB-ME, there exists an adversary $\mathcal{B}$ that breaks IND-hID-CPA security of HIBE such that*

$$\mathsf{Adv}^{\mathsf{hib\text{-}cpa\text{-}priv}}_{\mathsf{HIB\text{-}ME}, \mathcal{A}}(\lambda, k, l) = \mathsf{Adv}^{\mathsf{ind\text{-}hid\text{-}cpa}}_{\mathsf{HIBE}, \mathcal{B}}(\lambda, l+1)$$

where k (resp., l) is the maximum depth of senders (resp., receivers). The running time of $\mathcal{B}$ is about that of $\mathcal{A}$.

Proof. Let $\mathcal{A}$ be an adversary that breaks the hib-cpa-priv security of HIB-ME. We show an adversary $\mathcal{B}$ that breaks the IND-hID-CPA security of HIBE by using $\mathcal{A}$. The description of $\mathcal{B}$ is as follows.

1. Upon receiving $\mathsf{mpk}_{\mathsf{HIBE}}$, $\mathcal{B}$ generates $(\mathsf{mpk}_{\mathsf{HIBS}}, \mathsf{msk}_{\mathsf{HIBS}}) \leftarrow \mathsf{Setup}_{\mathsf{HIBS}}(1^\lambda, k)$, picks coin $\hat{b} \leftarrow_\$ \{0, 1\}$, and prepares $\mathcal{L}_{\mathsf{ek}}, \mathcal{L}_{\mathsf{dk}} := \emptyset$. Then, $\mathcal{B}$ executes $\mathcal{A}$ on input mpk := $(\mathsf{mpk}_{\mathsf{HIBE}}, \mathsf{mpk}_{\mathsf{HIBS}})$.
2. When $\mathcal{A}$ makes some oracle queries, $\mathcal{B}$ answers as follows:
   (a) When $\mathcal{A}$ makes a sender key generation (resp., delegation) query on input σ (resp., σ' such that $(\sigma', \cdot) \in \mathcal{L}_{\mathsf{ek}}$ and σ), $\mathcal{B}$ runs $\mathsf{ek}_\sigma \leftarrow \mathsf{KGen}_{\mathsf{HIBS}}(\mathsf{mpk}_{\mathsf{HIBS}}, \mathsf{msk}_{\mathsf{HIBS}}, \sigma)$ (resp., $\mathsf{ek}_{\sigma'|\sigma} \leftarrow \mathsf{KDel}_{\mathsf{HIBS}}(\mathsf{mpk}_{\mathsf{HIBS}}, \mathsf{ek}_{\sigma'}, \sigma$ where $\mathsf{ek}_{\sigma'}$ extracted from $\mathcal{L}_{\mathsf{ek}}$) and updates $\mathcal{L}_{\mathsf{ek}} := \mathcal{L}_{\mathsf{ek}} \cup \{(\sigma, \mathsf{ek}_\sigma)\}$ (resp., $\mathcal{L}_{\mathsf{ek}} := \mathcal{L}_{\mathsf{ek}} \cup \{(\sigma'|\sigma, \mathsf{ek}_{\sigma'|\sigma})\}$).
   (b) When $\mathcal{A}$ makes a receiver key generation (resp., delegation) query on input ρ (resp., ρ' such that $(\rho', \cdot) \in \mathcal{L}_{\mathsf{dk}}$ and ρ), $\mathcal{B}$ queries ρ (resp., ρ' and ρ) to its challenger and updates $\mathcal{L}_{\mathsf{dk}} := \mathcal{L}_{\mathsf{dk}} \cup \{(\rho, \bot)\}$ (resp., $\mathcal{L}_{\mathsf{dk}} := \mathcal{L}_{\mathsf{dk}} \cup \{(\rho'|\rho, \bot)\}$).

(c) When $\mathcal{A}$ makes a sender key reveal query on input σ such that $(\sigma, \cdot) \in \mathcal{L}_{\mathsf{ek}}$, $\mathcal{B}$ extracts ek_σ from $\mathcal{L}_{\mathsf{ek}}$, and returns ek_σ to $\mathcal{A}$. In addition, $\mathcal{B}$ updates $\mathcal{L}_{\mathsf{ek}} := \mathcal{L}_{\mathsf{ek}} \setminus \{(\sigma, \mathsf{ek}_\sigma)\}$.
(d) When $\mathcal{A}$ such that $(\rho, \cdot) \in \mathcal{L}_{\mathsf{dk}}$, $\mathcal{B}$ queries to its challenger to obtain dk_ρ and returns it to $\mathcal{A}$. In addition, $\mathcal{B}$ updates $\mathcal{L}_{\mathsf{dk}} := \mathcal{L}_{\mathsf{dk}} \setminus \{(\rho, \bot)\}$.
(e) When $\mathcal{A}$ makes challenge ciphertext query on input (σ_0^*, σ_1^*), $(\mathsf{rcv}_0^*, \mathsf{rcv}_1^*)$, and $(\mathsf{m}_0^*, \mathsf{m}_1^*)$, $\mathcal{B}$ computes $\Sigma \leftarrow \mathsf{Sign}_{\mathsf{HIBS}}(\mathsf{mpk}_{\mathsf{HIBS}}, \mathsf{ek}_{\sigma_b^*}, \mathsf{m}_b^* \| \mathsf{rcv}^*)$ and makes a challenge ciphertext query on input $(\mathsf{rcv}_0^* | \sigma_b^*, \mathsf{rcv}_1^* | \sigma_b^*)$ and $(\mathsf{m}_0^* \| \Sigma, \mathsf{m}_1^* \| \Sigma)$ to obtain ct^*, and returns it to $\mathcal{A}$.
3. Finally, when $\mathcal{A}$ outputs b', $\mathcal{B}$ outputs the same.

From above construction, $\mathcal{B}$ perfectly simulates the hib-cpa-priv game against $\mathcal{A}$. Moreover, since $(\mathsf{rcv}_0^*, \cdot) \notin \mathcal{L}_{\mathsf{dk}} \wedge (\mathsf{rcv}_1^*, \cdot) \notin \mathcal{L}_{\mathsf{dk}}$ implies $(\mathsf{rcv}^*, \cdot) \notin \mathcal{L}_{\mathsf{sk}} \wedge (\mathsf{rcv}_1^*, \cdot) \notin \mathcal{L}_{\mathsf{sk}}$, $\mathcal{B}$ is admissible. Therefore, if $\mathcal{A}$ breaks the hib-cpa-priv security, $\mathcal{B}$ also breaks the IND-hID-CPA security, that is,

$$\mathsf{Adv}^{\mathsf{hib\text{-}cpa\text{-}priv}}_{\mathsf{HIB\text{-}ME}, \mathcal{A}}(\lambda, k, l) = \mathsf{Adv}^{\mathsf{ind\text{-}hid\text{-}cpa}}_{\mathsf{HIBE}, \mathcal{B}}(\lambda, l).$$

$\square$

Theorem 2. *Suppose that the HIBS scheme HIBS is EUF-hID-CMA secure. If there exists an adversary $\mathcal{A}$ that breaks hib-auth security of HIB-ME, there exists an adversary $\mathcal{B}$ that breaks EUF-hID-CMA security of HIBS such that*

$$\mathsf{Adv}^{\mathsf{hib\text{-}auth}}_{\mathsf{HIB\text{-}ME}, \mathcal{A}}(\lambda, k, l) = \mathsf{Adv}^{\mathsf{euf\text{-}hid\text{-}cma}}_{\mathsf{HIBS}, \mathcal{B}}(\lambda, k)$$

where k (resp., l) is the maximum depth of senders (resp., receivers). The running time of $\mathcal{B}$ is about $\mathcal{A}$.

Proof. Let $\mathcal{A}$ be an adversary that breaks the hib-cpa-priv security of HIB-ME. We show an adversary $\mathcal{B}$ that breaks the EUF-hID-CMA security of HIBS by using $\mathcal{A}$. The description of $\mathcal{B}$ is as follows.

1. Upon receiving $\mathsf{mpk}_{\mathsf{HIBS}}$, $\mathcal{B}$ generates $(\mathsf{mpk}_{\mathsf{HIBE}}, \mathsf{msk}_{\mathsf{HIBE}}) \leftarrow \mathsf{Setup}_{\mathsf{HIBE}}(1^\lambda, l+1)$ and prepares $\mathcal{L}_{\mathsf{ek}}, \mathcal{L}_{\mathsf{dk}}, \mathcal{L}_{\mathsf{ct}} := \emptyset$. Then, $\mathcal{B}$ executes $\mathcal{A}$ on input $\mathsf{mpk} := (\mathsf{mpk}_{\mathsf{HIBE}}, \mathsf{mpk}_{\mathsf{HIBS}})$.
2. When $\mathcal{A}$ makes some oracle queries, $\mathcal{B}$ answers as follows:
   (a) When $\mathcal{A}$ makes a sender key generation (resp., delegation) query on input σ (resp., σ' such that $(\sigma', \cdot) \in \mathcal{L}_{\mathsf{ek}}$) and σ), $\mathcal{B}$ queries σ (resp., σ' and σ) to its challenger and updates $\mathcal{L}_{\mathsf{ek}} := \mathcal{L}_{\mathsf{ek}} \cup \{(\sigma, \bot)\}$ (resp., $\mathcal{L}_{\mathsf{ek}} := \mathcal{L}_{\mathsf{ek}} \cup \{(\sigma' | \sigma, \bot)\}$).
   (b) When $\mathcal{A}$ makes a receiver key generation (resp., delegation) query on input ρ (resp., ρ' such that $(\rho', \cdot) \in \mathcal{L}_{\mathsf{dk}}$ and ρ), $\mathcal{B}$ runs $\mathsf{dk}_\rho \leftarrow \mathsf{KGen}_{\mathsf{HIBE}}(\mathsf{mpk}_{\mathsf{HIBE}}, \mathsf{msk}_{\mathsf{HIBE}}, \rho)$ (resp., $\mathsf{dk}_{\rho' | \rho} \leftarrow \mathsf{KDel}_{\mathsf{HIBE}}(\mathsf{mpk}_{\mathsf{HIBE}}, \mathsf{dk}_{\rho'}, \rho)$ where $\mathsf{dk}_{\rho'}$ extracted from $\mathcal{L}_{\mathsf{ek}}$) and updates $\mathcal{L}_{\mathsf{dk}} := \mathcal{L}_{\mathsf{dk}} \cup \{(\rho, \mathsf{dk}_\rho)\}$ (resp., $\mathcal{L}_{\mathsf{dk}} := \mathcal{L}_{\mathsf{dk}} \cup \{(\rho' | \rho, \mathsf{dk}_{\rho' | \rho})\}$).
   (c) When $\mathcal{A}$ makes a sender key reveal query on input σ such that $(\sigma, \cdot) \in \mathcal{L}_{\mathsf{ek}}$, $\mathcal{B}$ extracts ek_σ from $\mathcal{L}_{\mathsf{ek}}$, and returns ek_σ to $\mathcal{A}$. In addition, $\mathcal{B}$ updates $\mathcal{L}_{\mathsf{ek}} := \mathcal{L}_{\mathsf{ek}} \setminus \{(\sigma, \bot)\}$.

(d) When $\mathcal{A}$ such that $(\rho, \cdot) \in \mathcal{L}_{\mathsf{dk}}$, $\mathcal{B}$ queries to its challenger to obtain dk_ρ and returns it to $\mathcal{A}$. In addition, $\mathcal{B}$ updates $\mathcal{L}_{\mathsf{dk}} := \mathcal{L}_{\mathsf{dk}} \setminus \{(\rho, \mathsf{dk}_\rho)\}$.
(e) When $\mathcal{A}$ makes encryption query on input σ, rcv, and m, $\mathcal{B}$ queries σ, rcv, and m|rcv and obtains Σ. Then, $\mathcal{B}$ computes ct $\leftarrow$ Enc$_{\mathsf{HIBE}}$(mpk$_{\mathsf{HIBE}}$, rcv$|\sigma, \mathsf{m}|\Sigma)$ and returns ct to $\mathcal{A}$. In addition, $\mathcal{B}$ updates $\mathcal{L}_{\mathsf{ct}} := \mathcal{L}_{\mathsf{ct}} \cup \{(\sigma, \mathsf{rcv}, \mathsf{m}, \mathsf{ct})\}$.

3. Finally, when $\mathcal{A}$ outputs snd*, ρ^*, and ct, $\mathcal{B}$ extracts dk_{ρ^*} from $\mathcal{L}_{\mathsf{dk}}$, computes m$^*|\Sigma^* \leftarrow$ Dec$_{\mathsf{HIBE}}$(mpk$_{\mathsf{HIBE}}$, dk_{ρ^*}, ct). If Ver$_{\mathsf{HIBS}}$(mpk$_{\mathsf{HIBS}}$, snd*, m$^*|$rcv$^*, \Sigma^*) = 1$, $\mathcal{B}$ submits snd*, m$^*|$rcv*, Σ^* as forgery to its challenger. Otherwise, $\mathcal{B}$ halts.

From above construction, $\mathcal{B}$ perfectly simulates the hib-auth game against $\mathcal{A}$. Moreover, since (snd$^*, \cdot) \in \mathcal{L}_{\mathsf{ek}}$ implies (snd$^*, \cdot) \notin \mathcal{L}_{\mathsf{sk}}$ and (snd$^*, \rho^*, \mathsf{m}^*, \cdot) \notin \mathcal{L}_{\mathsf{ct}}$ implies (snd$^*, \mathsf{m}^*|\rho^*, \Sigma^*) \notin \mathcal{L}_\Sigma$, $\mathcal{B}$ is admissible. Therefore, if $\mathcal{A}$ breaks the hib-auth security, $\mathcal{B}$ also breaks the EUF-hID-CMA security, that is,

$$\mathsf{Adv}^{\mathsf{hib\text{-}auth}}_{\mathsf{HIB\text{-}ME}, \mathcal{A}}(\lambda, k, l) = \mathsf{Adv}^{\mathsf{euf\text{-}hid\text{-}cma}}_{\mathsf{HIBS}, \mathcal{B}}(\lambda, k).$$

□

Remark 1. We can obtain mismatch case privacy using computational reusable extractor using the same techniques of [7,12,14].

4 Applications of HIB-ME

In this section, we show some applications of HIB-ME. In Sect. 4.1, we show how to achieve a full-fledged CCA secure (H)IB-ME scheme by employing CHK transformation [9]. In Sect. 4.2, we remove the ciphertext overhead of the one-time signature and prove that our tweaked CHK transformation uplifts CPA secure IB-ME to tweaked CCA secure IB-ME using authenticity.

4.1 Construction with Native CHK Paradigm

In this section, we give the formal description of our CCA secure (k,l)-level HIB-ME scheme from an $(k, l+1)$-level HIB-ME scheme and a strong one-time signature scheme. Roughly, toward CCA security, we extend the technique by Canetti et al. [9].

Construction. Fix integers $k \geq 1$ and $l \geq 2$. Let HIB-ME$'$ = (Setup$'$, SKGen$'$, SKDel$'$, RKGen$'$, RKDel$'$, Enc$'$, Dec$'$) be a $(k, l+1)$-level HIB-ME scheme with a sender identity space $\mathcal{ID}$ and a receiver identity space $\mathcal{ID} = \{0,1\}|\mathcal{ID}$. Let Sig = (KGen, Sign, Ver) be a strong one-time signature scheme with a verification key space $\mathcal{ID}$. Then, our (k,l)-level HIB-ME scheme HIB-ME = (Setup, SKGen, SKDel, RKGen, RKDel, Enc, Dec) is described as follows:

Setup$(1^\lambda, k, l)$: It runs (mpk, msk) $\leftarrow$ Setup$'(1^\lambda, k, l+1)$ and outputs (mpk, msk).
SKGen(mpk, msk, σ): It runs ek$_\sigma \leftarrow$ SKGen$'$(mpk, msk, σ) and outputs ek$_\sigma$.
SKDel(mpk, sk$_{\sigma'}, \sigma$): It runs ek$_{\sigma'|\sigma} \leftarrow$ SKDel$'$(mpk, ek$_{\sigma'}, \sigma$) and outputs ek$_{\sigma'|\sigma}$.

RKGen(mpk, msk, ρ): It runs $dk_\rho \leftarrow$ RKGen$'$(mpk, msk, $0.\rho$) and outputs dk_ρ.
RKDel(mpk, $dk_{\rho'}$, ρ): It runs $dk_{\rho'|\rho} \leftarrow$ RKDel$'$(mpk, $dk_{\rho'}$, $0.\rho$) and outputs $dk_{\rho'|\rho}$.
Enc(mpk, ek_σ, rcv, m): It runs (sk, vk) $\leftarrow$ KGen(1^λ) and sets rcv$' :=$ 1.vk$|$0.rcv.
    Then, it runs ctxt $\leftarrow$ Enc$'$(mpk, ek_σ, rcv$'$, m) and $\Sigma \leftarrow$ Sign(sk, ctxt), and outputs ct $:=$ (ctxt, vk, Σ).
Dec(mpk, dk_ρ, snd, m): It checks whether $0 =$ Ver(vk, ctxt, Σ) holds. If this is the case, then it returns $\bot$. Otherwise, it generates $dk_{0.\rho|1.vk} \leftarrow$ RKDel$'$(mpk, dk_ρ, 1.vk). Finally, it runs m $\leftarrow$ Dec$'$(mpk, $dk_{0.\rho|1.vk}$, snd, ctxt) and outputs the plaintext m.

Correctness. If the ciphertexct ct $=$ (ctxt, vk, Σ) is generated correctly, Ver(vk, ctxt, Σ) always outputs 1 due to the correctness of Sig. Hence, if HIB-ME$'$ satisfies correctness, HIB-ME also satisfies correctness.

Security. Here, we show that our scheme satisfies security requirements.

Theorem 3. *Suppose that the HIBME scheme* HIB-ME$'$ *is* hib-cpa-priv *secure and the Signature scheme* Sig *is* sEUF-CMA *secure. If there exists an adversary $\mathcal{A}$ that breaks the* hib-cca-priv *security of* HIB-ME, *there exists an adversary $\mathcal{B}_1$ that breaks the* sEUF-CMA *security of* Sig, $\mathcal{B}_2$ *that breaks* hib-cpa-priv *security of* HIB-ME$'$ *such that*

$$\text{Adv}_{\text{HIB-ME},\mathcal{A}}^{\text{hib-cca-priv}}(\lambda, k, l) \leq \text{Adv}_{\text{Sig},\mathcal{B}_1}^{\text{seuf-cma}}(\lambda) + \text{Adv}_{\text{HIB-ME}',\mathcal{B}_2}^{\text{hib-cca-priv}}(\lambda, k, l+1),$$

where k (resp, l) is the maximum depth of senders (resp., receivers). The running time of $\mathcal{B}$ is about that of $\mathcal{A}$.

Proof. To prove the theorem, we consider the following sequence of games Game$_i$ for $i \in \{0, \ldots, 3\}$ and define

$$\epsilon_i := \Pr\left[b = b' \mid \text{Game}_i^\mathcal{A}(\lambda, k, l)\right].$$

Game$_0$: This is the original hib-cca-priv security game. By definition, we have

$$\left|\epsilon_0 - \frac{1}{2}\right| := \text{Adv}_{\text{HIB-ME},\mathcal{A}}^{\text{hib-cca-priv}}(\lambda, k, l).$$

Game$_1$: In previous game, the challenger picks (vk*, sk*) in the challenge phase. But in this game, the challenger runs (vk*, sk*) $\leftarrow$ KGen(1^λ) in the setup phase. Since there is no difference from $\mathcal{A}$'s viewpoint, we have

$$\epsilon_1 = \epsilon_0.$$

Game$_2$: In this game, we change the behavior of the pre-challenge decryption oracle. Specifically, when $\mathcal{A}$ makes a decryption query on input (snd, ρ, ct $=$ (ctxt, vk, Σ)), the challenger always returns $\bot$ to $\mathcal{A}$ if vk $=$ vk*.

Let Forge be $\mathcal{A}$ sends valid signature Σ such that Ver(vk*, Σ^*, m) to decryption oracle. The two games become different if Forge occurs. Thus, $|\epsilon_2 - \epsilon_1| \leq$ Pr [Forge].

To estimate $\Pr[\mathsf{Forge}]$, we show that if $\mathcal{A}$ triggers the event Forge, we can construct an adversary $\mathcal{B}_1$ that breaks the sEUF-CMA security of Sig. The construction of $\mathcal{B}_1$ is as follows.

1. Upon receiving vk^*, $\mathcal{B}_1$ runs $(\mathsf{mpk}, \mathsf{msk}) \leftarrow \mathsf{Setup}'(1^\lambda, .k, l+1)$. Next, $\mathcal{B}_1$ sets $\mathcal{L}_{\mathsf{ek}}, \mathcal{L}_{\mathsf{dk}} := \emptyset$ and picks $\hat{b} \leftarrow \{0,1\}$. Then, $\mathcal{B}_1$ executes $\mathcal{A}$ on input mpk.
2. When $\mathcal{A}$ makes some oracle queries, $\mathcal{B}_1$ answers as follows:
   (a) When $\mathcal{A}$ makes sender (resp., receiver) key generation query on input σ (resp., ρ), $\mathcal{B}_1$ runs $\mathsf{ek}_\sigma \leftarrow \mathsf{SKGen}'(\mathsf{mpk}, \mathsf{msk}, \sigma)$ (resp., $\mathsf{dk}_\rho \leftarrow \mathsf{RKGen}'(\mathsf{mpk}, \mathsf{msk}, 0.\rho)$) and updates $\mathcal{L}_{\mathsf{ek}} := \mathcal{L}_{\mathsf{ek}} \cup \{(\sigma, \mathsf{ek}_\sigma)\}$ (resp., $\mathcal{L}_{\mathsf{dk}} := \mathcal{L}_{\mathsf{dk}} \cup \{(\rho, \mathsf{dk}_\rho)\}$).
   (b) When $\mathcal{A}$ makes sender (resp., receiver) key delegation query on input σ' such that $(\sigma', \cdot) \in \mathcal{L}_{\mathsf{ek}}$ (resp., ρ' such that $(\rho', \cdot) \in \mathcal{L}_{\mathsf{dk}}$) and σ (resp., ρ), $\mathcal{B}_1$ extracts $\mathsf{ek}_{\sigma'}$ from $\mathcal{L}_{\mathsf{ek}}$ (resp., $\mathsf{dk}_{\rho'}$ from $\mathcal{L}_{\mathsf{dk}}$), runs $\mathsf{ek}_{\sigma'|\sigma} \leftarrow \mathsf{SKDel}'(\mathsf{mpk}, \mathsf{ek}_{\sigma'}, \sigma)$ (resp., $\mathsf{dk}_{\rho'|\rho} \leftarrow \mathsf{RKDel}'(\mathsf{mpk}, \mathsf{dk}_{\rho'}, 0.\rho)$), and updates $\mathcal{L}_{\mathsf{ek}} := \mathcal{L}_{\mathsf{ek}} \cup \{(\sigma'|\sigma, \mathsf{ek}_{\sigma'|\sigma})\}$ (resp., $\mathcal{L}_{\mathsf{dk}} := \mathcal{L}_{\mathsf{dk}} \cup \{(\rho'|\rho), \mathsf{dk}_{\rho'|\rho}\}$).
   (c) When $\mathcal{A}$ makes sender (resp., receiver) key reveal query on input σ such that $(\sigma, \cdot) \in \mathcal{L}_{\mathsf{ek}}$ (resp., ρ such that $(\rho, \cdot) \in \mathcal{L}_{\mathsf{dk}}$), $\mathcal{B}_1$ extracts ek_σ from $\mathcal{L}_{\mathsf{ek}}$ (resp., dk_ρ from $\mathcal{L}_{\mathsf{dk}}$), returns ek_σ (resp., dk_ρ to $\mathcal{A}$, and updates $\mathcal{L}_{\mathsf{ek}} := \mathcal{L}_{\mathsf{ek}} \setminus \{(\sigma, \mathsf{ek}_\sigma)\}$ (resp., $\mathcal{L}_{\mathsf{dk}} := \mathcal{L}_{\mathsf{dk}} \setminus \{(\rho, \mathsf{dk}_\rho)\}$).
   (d) When $\mathcal{A}$ makes decryption query on input $(\mathsf{snd}, \rho, \mathsf{ct} := (\mathsf{ctxt}, \mathsf{vk}, \Sigma))$, $\mathcal{B}_1$ works as follows:
      – if $\mathsf{vk} = \mathsf{vk}^*$: $\mathcal{B}_1$ checks whether $\mathsf{Ver}(\mathsf{vk}^*, \Sigma, \mathsf{ctxt}) = 1$ or not. If so, $\mathcal{B}_1$ outputs (Σ, ctxt) as forgely and halts. Otherwise, $\mathcal{B}_1$ returns $\bot$.
      – if $\mathsf{vk} \neq \mathsf{vk}^*$: $\mathcal{B}_1$ checks whether $\mathsf{Ver}(\mathsf{vk}^*, \Sigma, \mathsf{ctxt}) = 1$ or not. If so, $\mathcal{B}_1$ extracts dk_ρ from $\mathcal{L}_{\mathsf{dk}}$, runs $\mathsf{dk}_{0.\rho|1.\mathsf{vk}} \leftarrow \mathsf{RKDel}(\mathsf{mpk}, \mathsf{dk}_\rho, 1.\mathsf{vk})$, $\mathsf{m} \leftarrow \mathsf{Dec}(\mathsf{mpk}, \mathsf{dk}_{0.\rho|1.\mathsf{vk}}, \mathsf{snd}, \mathsf{ctxt})$, and returns m to $\mathcal{A}$. Otherwise, $\mathcal{B}_1$ returns $\bot$.
   (e) When $\mathcal{A}$ makes challenge query on input $(\sigma_0^*, \sigma_1^*), (\mathsf{rcv}_0^*, \mathsf{rcv}_1^*), \mathsf{m}_0^*, \mathsf{m}_1^*$, $\mathcal{B}_1$ extracts ek_{σ^*} from $\mathcal{L}_{\mathsf{ek}}$, and runs $\mathsf{ctxt}_{\hat{b}}^* \leftarrow \mathsf{Enc}(\mathsf{mpk}, \mathsf{ek}_{\sigma_{\hat{b}}^*}, 0.\mathsf{rcv}_{\hat{b}}^*|1.\mathsf{vk}^*, \mathsf{m}^*)$. Next, $\mathcal{B}_1$ sends $\mathsf{ctxt}_{\hat{b}}^*$ to its challenger and obtains Σ^*. Then, $\mathcal{B}_1$ returns $\mathsf{ct}^* = (\mathsf{ctxt}_{\hat{b}}^*, \mathsf{vk}^*, \Sigma^*)$ to $\mathcal{A}$.
3. Finally, when $\mathcal{A}$ outputs b', $\mathcal{B}_1$ halts.

From the above construction, $\mathcal{B}_1$ perfectly simulates hib-cca-priv game for $\mathcal{A}$. Since $(\mathsf{ctxt}_{\hat{b}}^*, \Sigma'*) \neq (\mathsf{ctxt}, \Sigma)$ holds from the requirements for decryption queries by $\mathcal{A}$, the tuple of a message and a signature (ctxt, Σ) output by $\mathcal{B}_1$ satisfies the winning conditions of the experiment sEUF-CMA game. Therefore, we have $\Pr[\mathsf{Forge}] = \mathsf{Adv}_{\mathsf{Sig}, \mathcal{B}_1}^{\mathsf{seuf-cma}}(\lambda)$, i.e.,

$$|\epsilon_2 - \epsilon_1| = \mathsf{Adv}_{\mathsf{Sig}, \mathcal{B}_1}^{\mathsf{seuf-cma}}(\lambda).$$

Finally, to estimate $\epsilon_2 = \frac{1}{2}$, we construct an adversary $\mathcal{B}_2$ that breaks the hib-cpa-priv of HIB-ME$'$ using an adversary $\mathcal{A}$ that breaks Game$_2$. The construction of $\mathcal{B}_2$ is as follows.

1. Upon receiving mpk, $\mathcal{B}_2$ runs $(\mathsf{sk}^*, \mathsf{vk}^*) \leftarrow \mathsf{KGen}(1^\lambda)$. Next, $\mathcal{B}_2$ sets $\mathcal{L}_{\mathsf{ek}}, \mathcal{L}_{\mathsf{dk}} := \emptyset$ and picks $\hat{b} \leftarrow \{0,1\}$. Then, $\mathcal{B}$ executes $\mathcal{A}$ on input mpk.

2. When $\mathcal{A}$ makes some oracle queries, $\mathcal{B}_2$ answers as follows:
   (a) When $\mathcal{A}$ makes a sender (resp., receiver) key generation query on input σ (resp., ρ), $\mathcal{B}_2$ makes a sender (resp., receiver) key generation query to its challenger on input σ (resp., ρ), and updates $\mathcal{L}_{\text{ek}} := \mathcal{L}_{\text{ek}} \cup \{(\sigma, \bot)\}$ (resp., $\mathcal{L}_{\text{dk}} := \mathcal{L}_{\text{dk}} \cup \{(\rho, \bot)\}$).
   (b) When $\mathcal{A}$ makes a sender (resp., receiver) key delegation query on input σ' such that $(\sigma', \cdot) \in \mathcal{L}_{\text{ek}}$ and σ (resp., ρ' such that $(\rho', \cdot) \in \mathcal{L}_{\text{dk}}$ and ρ), $\mathcal{B}_2$ makes a sender (resp., receiver) key delegation query to its challenger on input σ' and σ (resp., $0.\rho'$ and $0.\rho$), and updates $\mathcal{L}_{\text{ek}} := \mathcal{L}_{\text{ek}} \cup \{(\sigma'|\sigma, \bot)\}$ (resp., $\mathcal{L}_{\text{dk}} := \mathcal{L}_{\text{dk}} \cup \{(\rho'|\rho, \bot)\}$).
   (c) When $\mathcal{A}$ makes a sender (resp., receiver) key reveal query on input σ such that $(\sigma, \cdot) \in \mathcal{L}_{\text{ek}}$ (resp., ρ such that $(\rho, \cdot) \in \mathcal{L}_{\text{dk}}$), $\mathcal{B}_2$ makes a sender (resp., receiver) key reveal query to its challenger on input σ (resp., ρ), receives ek_σ (resp., dk_ρ), and returns as it is to $\mathcal{A}$. In addition, $\mathcal{B}_2$ updates $\mathcal{L}_{\text{ek}} := \mathcal{L}_{\text{ek}} \setminus \{(\sigma, \bot)\}$ (resp., $\mathcal{L}_{\text{dk}} := \mathcal{L}_{\text{dk}} \setminus \{(\rho, \bot)\}$).
   (d) When $\mathcal{A}$ makes decryption query on input snd, ρ and ct $=$ (ctxt, vk, Σ), $\mathcal{B}_2$ returns $\bot$ if vk $=$ vk* or Ver(vk, Σ, ctxt) $= 0$. Otherwise, $\mathcal{B}_2$ makes a receiver key delegation query on input $0.\rho$ and $1.$vk, and a receiver key reveal query on input $0.\rho|1.$vk to receive $\text{dk}_{0.\rho|1.\text{vk}}$. Then, $\mathcal{B}$ runs m $\leftarrow$ Dec(mpk, snd, $\text{dk}_{0.\rho|1.\text{vk}}$, ctxt) and returns m to $\mathcal{A}$.
3. When $\mathcal{A}$ makes the challenge ciphertext query on input (σ_0^*, σ_1^*), $(\text{rcv}_0^*, \text{rcv}_1^*)$ and $(\text{m}_0^*, \text{m}_1^*)$, $\mathcal{B}_2$ sets $\text{rcv}_0' := 0.\text{rcv}_0^*|1.\text{vk}^*$ and $\text{rcv}_1' := 0.\text{rcv}_1^*|1.\text{vk}^*$, and makes the challenge ciphertext query on input (σ_0^*, σ_1^*), (ρ_0', ρ_1') and $(\text{m}_0^*, \text{m}_1^*)$ to receives ctxt*. Then, $\mathcal{B}_2$ runs $\Sigma^* \leftarrow$ Sign(sk*, ctxt*) and returns ct$^* :=$ (ctxt*, vk*, Σ^*) to $\mathcal{A}$.
4. When $\mathcal{A}$ makes some oracle queries, $\mathcal{B}_2$ answers as follows. (Except decryption oracle query, $\mathcal{B}_2$ behaves the same way as in the pre-challenge query.)
   (a) When $\mathcal{A}$ makes a decryption query on input snd, ρ and ct, $\mathcal{B}_2$ returns $\bot$ if vk $=$ vk*. Otherwise, $\mathcal{B}_2$ makes a receiver key delegation query on input $0.\rho$ and $1.$vk, and a receiver key reveal query on input $0.\rho|1.$vk, and receives $\text{dk}_{0.\rho|1.\text{vk}}{}^2$. Then, $\mathcal{B}_2$ runs m $\leftarrow$ Dec(mpk, $\text{dk}_{0.\rho|1.\text{vk}}$, snd, ctxt). and returns m to $\mathcal{A}$.
5. Finally, when $\mathcal{A}$ outputs b', $\mathcal{B}_2$ outputs the same way.

From above construction, $\mathcal{B}_2$ perfectly simulates Game$_2$ for $\mathcal{A}$ and the challenge bits of $\mathcal{B}_2$ and $\mathcal{A}$ correspond. Therefore, we have

$$\left| \epsilon_2 - \frac{1}{2} \right| = \text{Adv}^{\text{hib-cpa-priv}}_{\text{HIB-ME}', \mathcal{B}_2}(\lambda, k, l+1).$$

Putting everything together, we have

$$\text{Adv}^{\text{hib-cca-priv}}_{\text{HIB-ME}, \mathcal{A}}(\lambda, k, l) = \text{Adv}^{\text{seuf-cma}}_{\text{Sig}, \mathcal{B}_1}(\lambda) + \text{Adv}^{\text{hib-cpa-priv}}_{\text{HIB-ME}', \mathcal{B}_2}(\lambda, k, l+1).$$

□

---

[2] If vk $\neq$ vk*, since $0.\text{rcv}_0^*|1.$vk (resp. $0.\text{rcv}_1^*|1.$vk) is different from $0.\text{rcv}_0^*|1.\text{vk}^*$ (resp., $0.\text{rcv}_1^*|1.$vk) and it do not leaks about $0.\text{rcv}_0^*|1.\text{vk}^*$ (resp., $0.\text{rcv}_1^*|1.$vk), $\mathcal{B}_2$ can query $0.\text{rcv}_0^*|1.$vk (resp., $0.\text{rcv}_1^*|1.$vk) to receiver key reveal query.

Theorem 4. *Suppose that the HIB-ME scheme HIB-ME′ is hib-auth secure. If there exists an adversary $\mathcal{A}$ that breaks the hib-auth security of HIB-ME, there exists an adversary $\mathcal{B}$ that breaks the hib-auth security of HIB-ME′ such that*

$$\mathsf{Adv}^{\mathsf{hib\text{-}auth}}_{\mathsf{HIB\text{-}ME},\mathcal{A}}(\lambda, k, l) = \mathsf{Adv}^{\mathsf{hib\text{-}auth}}_{\mathsf{HIB\text{-}ME}',\mathcal{B}}(\lambda, k, l+1).$$

where k (resp., l) is the maximum depth of senders (resp., receivers). The running time of $\mathcal{B}$ is about that of $\mathcal{A}$.

Proof. To prove the theorem, we construct an adversary $\mathcal{B}$ that breaks hib-auth of HIB-ME′ using $\mathcal{A}$ that breaks hib-auth of HIB-ME. The construction of $\mathcal{B}$ is as follows.

1. Upon receiving mpk, $\mathcal{B}$ executes $\mathcal{A}$ on input mpk.
2. When $\mathcal{A}$ makes some oracle queries, $\mathcal{B}$ answers as follows.
    (a) When $\mathcal{A}$ makes a sender (resp., receiver) key generation query on input σ (resp., ρ), $\mathcal{B}$ makes a sender (resp., receiver) key generation query to its challenger on input σ (resp., ρ), and updates $\mathcal{L}_{\mathsf{ek}} := \mathcal{L}_{\mathsf{ek}} \cup \{(\sigma, \bot)\}$ (resp., $\mathcal{L}_{\mathsf{dk}} := \mathcal{L}_{\mathsf{dk}} \cup \{(\rho, \bot)\}$).
    (b) When $\mathcal{A}$ makes a sender (resp., receiver) key delegation query on input σ' such that $(\sigma', \cdot) \in \mathcal{L}_{\mathsf{ek}}$ and σ (resp., ρ' such that $(\rho', \cdot) \in \mathcal{L}_{\mathsf{dk}}$ and ρ), $\mathcal{B}$ makes a sender (resp., receiver) key delegation query to its challenger on input σ' and σ (resp., $0.\rho'$ and $0.\rho$), and updates $\mathcal{L}_{\mathsf{ek}} := \mathcal{L}_{\mathsf{ek}} \cup \{(\sigma'|\sigma, \bot)\}$ (resp., $\mathcal{L}_{\mathsf{dk}} := \mathcal{L}_{\mathsf{dk}} \cup \{(\rho'|\rho, \bot)\}$).
    (c) When $\mathcal{A}$ makes a sender (resp., receiver) key reveal query on input σ such that $(\sigma, \cdot) \in \mathcal{L}_{\mathsf{ek}}$ (resp., ρ such that $(\rho, \cdot) \in \mathcal{L}_{\mathsf{dk}}$), $\mathcal{B}$ makes a sender (resp., receiver) key reveal query to its challenger on input σ (resp., ρ), receives ek_σ (resp., dk_ρ), and returns as it is to $\mathcal{A}$. In addition, $\mathcal{B}$ updates $\mathcal{L}_{\mathsf{ek}} := \mathcal{L}_{\mathsf{ek}} \setminus \{(\sigma, \bot)\}$ (resp., $\mathcal{L}_{\mathsf{dk}} := \mathcal{L}_{\mathsf{dk}} \setminus \{(\rho, \bot)\}$).
    (d) When $\mathcal{A}$ makes a encryption query on input σ such that $(\sigma, \cdot) \in \mathcal{L}_{\mathsf{ek}}$, rcv such that $(\mathsf{rcv}, \cdot) \in \mathcal{L}_{\mathsf{dk}}$, and message m, $\mathcal{B}$ runs $(\mathsf{sk}, \mathsf{vk}) \leftarrow \mathsf{KGen}(1^\lambda)$ and sets $\mathsf{rcv}' = 0.\mathsf{rcv}|1.\mathsf{vk}$. Next, $\mathcal{B}$ sends a encryption query on input σ, rcv′, and m to obtain ctxt. Then, $\mathcal{B}$ computes $\Sigma \leftarrow \mathsf{Sign}(\mathsf{sk}, \mathsf{ctxt})$ and returns $\mathsf{ct} = (\mathsf{ctxt}, \mathsf{vk}, \Sigma)$. In addition, $\mathcal{B}$ updates $\mathcal{L}_{\mathsf{ct}} := \mathcal{L}_{\mathsf{ct}} \cup \{(\sigma, \mathsf{rcv}, \mathsf{m}, \mathsf{ct})\}$.
3. Finally, when $\mathcal{A}$ submits $(\mathsf{snd}^*, \rho^*, \mathsf{ct}^* = (\mathsf{ctxt}^*, \mathsf{vk}^*, \Sigma^*))$ as a forgery, $\mathcal{B}$ submits the same $(\mathsf{snd}^*, 0.\rho^*|1.\mathsf{vk}, \mathsf{ctxt}^*)$ if $\mathsf{Ver}(\mathsf{vk}, \Sigma^*, \mathsf{ctxt}^*) = 1$.

We can verify that $\mathcal{B}$ perfectly simulates the hib-auth game. Therefore, if $\mathcal{A}$ breaks the hib-auth security of HIB-ME, $\mathcal{B}$ also breaks the hib-auth security of HIB-ME′. Thus, we have

$$\mathsf{Adv}^{\mathsf{hib\text{-}auth}}_{\mathsf{HIB\text{-}ME},\mathcal{A}}(\lambda, k, l) = \mathsf{Adv}^{\mathsf{hib\text{-}auth}}_{\mathsf{HIB\text{-}ME}',\mathcal{B}}(\lambda, k, l+1).$$

□

4.2 Construction with Tweaked CHK Paradigm

In this section, we provide a construction of tweaked CCA secure (H)IB-ME. Our tweaked CCA secure (H)IB-ME scheme can be obtained solely based on a CPA secure (H)IB-ME scheme. Notably, compared to the previous CCA secure (H)IB-ME scheme in Sect. 4.1, our tweaked CCA secure (H)IB-ME scheme does not need a strong one-time signature scheme which incurs a ciphertext overhead (with the length of a verification key and a signature). Note that, in the (ordinary) IBE setting, the non-adaptive CCA security (a.k.a. the CCA1 security) can only be achieved with a similar construction, while in the IB-ME setting, we can achieve more reasonable security notion (adaptive security but with query limitations).

Construction. Fix integers $k \geq 1$ and $l \geq 2$. Let HIB-ME$'$ = (Setup$'$, SKGen$'$, SKDel$'$, RKGen$'$, RKDel$'$, Enc$'$, Dec$'$) be a $(k, l+1)$-level HIB-ME scheme with a sender identity space $\mathcal{ID}$ and a receiver identity space $\mathcal{ID}' = \{0,1\}.\mathcal{ID}$. Then, we show how to construct (k,l)-level HIB-ME scheme HIB-ME = (Setup, SKGen, SKDel, RKGen, RKDel, Enc, Dec). Setup algorithm Setup, sender key generation algorithm SKGen, sender key delegation algorithm SKDel, receiver key generation algorithm RKGen, and receiver key delegation algorithm RKDel is the same as construction in Sect. 4.1. Now, we show encryption algorithm Enc and decryption algorithm Dec as follows:

Enc(mpk, ek$_\sigma$, rcv, m): It sets rcv$'$:= 0.rcv|1.snd, runs ct $\leftarrow$ Enc$'$(mpk, ek$_\sigma$, rcv$'$, m), and outputs ct.

Dec(mpk, dk$_\rho$, snd, ct): It runs dk$_{0.\rho|1.\text{snd}}$ $\leftarrow$ RKDel(mpk, dk$_\rho$, 1.snd) and m $\leftarrow$ Dec$'$(mpk, dk$_{0.\rho|1.\text{snd}}$, snd, m), and outputs m.

Correctness. Obviously, if HIB-ME$'$ satisfies correctness, HIB-ME satisfies correctness.

Security. Here, we show that our scheme satisfies security requirements.

Theorem 5. *Suppose that the HIB-ME scheme HIB-ME$'$ satisfies* hib-cpa-priv *security and* hib-auth *security. If there exists an adversary $\mathcal{A}$ that breaks the* hib-tcca-priv *security of HIB-ME, there exists an adversary $\mathcal{B}_1$ that breaks the* hib-cpa-priv *security of HIB-ME$'$ and $\mathcal{B}_2$ that breaks the* hib-auth *security of HIB-ME$'$ such that*

$$\text{Adv}_{\text{HIB-ME}, \mathcal{A}}^{\text{hib-tcca-priv}}(\lambda, k, l) \leq \text{Adv}_{\text{HIB-ME}', \mathcal{B}_1}^{\text{hib-cpa-priv}}(\lambda, k, l+1) + \text{Adv}_{\text{HIB-ME}', \mathcal{B}_2}^{\text{hib-auth}}(\lambda, k, l+1)$$

where k (resp., l) is the maximum depth of senders (resp., receivers). The running time of $\mathcal{B}$ is about of $\mathcal{A}$.

Proof. To prove the theorem, we consider the following sequence of games Game$_i$ for $i \in \{0,1\}$ and define

$$\epsilon_i := \Pr\left[b = b' \mid \text{Game}_i^{\mathcal{A}}(\lambda, k, l)\right].$$

Game$_0$: This is the original hib-tcca-priv security game. By definition, we have

$$\left|\epsilon_0 - \frac{1}{2}\right| := \mathsf{Adv}^{\text{hib-tcca-priv}}_{\text{HIB-ME},\mathcal{A}}(\lambda, k, l).$$

Game$_1$: Same as Game$_0$, except that, when $\mathcal{A}$ makes a decryption query $(\rho, \mathsf{snd}, \mathsf{ct})$, the challenger returns as

$$\begin{cases} \mathsf{m} & \text{if } (\mathsf{snd}, \rho, \mathsf{m}, \mathsf{ct}) \in \mathcal{L}_{\mathsf{ct}} \\ \mathsf{Dec}(\mathsf{mpk}, \mathsf{dk}_{0.\rho|1.\mathsf{snd}}, \mathsf{snd}.\mathsf{ct}) & \text{if } \mathsf{snd} \neq \sigma^* \vee \rho \neq \mathsf{rcv}^* \\ \bot & \text{othweise} \end{cases}$$

to $\mathcal{A}$.

Let Forge be $\mathcal{A}$ sends valid ciphertext tuple snd, such that $\mathsf{snd} \in \mathcal{L}_{\mathsf{ek}}$, ρ such that $\rho \in \mathcal{L}_{\mathsf{dk}}$, ct such that $\mathsf{Dec}(\mathsf{mpk}, \mathsf{dk}_\rho, \mathsf{snd}, \mathsf{ct}) \neq \bot \wedge (\mathsf{snd}, \mathsf{rcv}, \cdot, \mathsf{ct}) \notin \mathcal{L}_{\mathsf{ct}}$ to decryption query. The two games become different if Forge occurs. Thus $|\epsilon_1 - \epsilon_0| = \Pr[\mathsf{Forge}]$.

To estimate $\Pr[\mathsf{Forge}]$, we show that if $\mathcal{A}$ triggers the event Forge, we can construct an adversary $\mathcal{B}_2$ that breaks hib-auth security of HIB-ME′. The construction of $\mathcal{B}_2$ is follows.

1. Upon receiving mpk, $\mathcal{B}_2$ sets $\mathcal{L}_{\mathsf{ek}}, \mathcal{L}_{\mathsf{dk}}, \mathcal{L}_{\mathsf{ct}} := \emptyset$ and picks $\hat{b} \leftarrow_\$ \{0,1\}$. Then, $\mathcal{B}$ executes $\mathcal{A}$ on inputs mpk.
2. When $\mathcal{A}$ makes some oracle queries, $\mathcal{B}_2$ answers as follows.
   (a) When $\mathcal{A}$ makes a sender (resp., receiver) key generation query on input σ (resp., ρ), $\mathcal{B}_2$ makes a sender (resp., receiver) key generation query to its challenger on input σ (resp., ρ), and updates $\mathcal{L}_{\mathsf{ek}} := \mathcal{L}_{\mathsf{ek}} \cup \{(\sigma, \bot)\}$ (resp., $\mathcal{L}_{\mathsf{dk}} := \mathcal{L}_{\mathsf{dk}} \cup \{(\rho, \bot)\}$).
   (b) When $\mathcal{A}$ makes a sender (resp., receiver) key delegation query on input σ' such that $(\sigma', \cdot) \in \mathcal{L}_{\mathsf{ek}}$ and σ (resp., ρ' such that $(\rho', \cdot) \in \mathcal{L}_{\mathsf{dk}}$ and ρ), $\mathcal{B}_2$ makes a sender (resp., receiver) key delegation query to its challenger on input σ' and σ (resp., $0.\rho'$ and $0.\rho$), and updates $\mathcal{L}_{\mathsf{ek}} := \mathcal{L}_{\mathsf{ek}} \cup \{(\sigma'|\sigma, \bot)\}$ (resp., $\mathcal{L}_{\mathsf{dk}} := \mathcal{L}_{\mathsf{dk}} \cup \{(\rho'|\rho, \bot)\}$).
   (c) When $\mathcal{A}$ makes a sender (resp., receiver) key reveal query on input σ such that $(\sigma, \cdot) \in \mathcal{L}_{\mathsf{ek}}$ (resp., ρ such that $(\rho, \cdot) \in \mathcal{L}_{\mathsf{dk}}$), $\mathcal{B}_2$ makes a sender (resp., receiver) key reveal query to its challenger on input σ (resp., ρ), receives ek_σ (resp., dk_ρ), and returns as it is to $\mathcal{A}$. In addition, $\mathcal{B}_2$ updates $\mathcal{L}_{\mathsf{ek}} := \mathcal{L}_{\mathsf{ek}} \setminus \{(\sigma, \bot)\}$ (resp., $\mathcal{L}_{\mathsf{dk}} := \mathcal{L}_{\mathsf{dk}} \setminus \{(\rho, \bot)\}$).
   (d) When $\mathcal{A}$ makes a encryption query on input σ such that $(\sigma, \cdot) \in \mathcal{L}_{\mathsf{ek}}$, rcv such that $(\mathsf{rcv}, \cdot) \in \mathcal{L}_{\mathsf{dk}}$, and message m, $\mathcal{B}$ sets $\mathsf{rcv}' = 0.\mathsf{rcv}|1.\sigma$. Next, $\mathcal{B}$ sends a encryption query on input σ, rcv′ and m to obtain ct, and returns ct. In addition, $\mathcal{B}$ updates $\mathcal{L}_{\mathsf{ct}} := \mathcal{L}_{\mathsf{ct}} \cup \{(\sigma, \mathsf{rcv}, \mathsf{m}, \mathsf{ct})\}$.
   (e) When $\mathcal{A}$ makes a decryption query on input snd such that $(\mathsf{snd}, \cdot) \in \mathcal{L}_{\mathsf{ek}}$, ρ such that $(\rho, \cdot) \in \mathcal{L}_{\mathsf{dk}}$, ct, if $(\mathsf{snd}, \rho, \cdot, \mathsf{ct}) \in \mathcal{L}_{\mathsf{ct}}$, $\mathcal{B}$ extracts m from $\mathcal{L}_{\mathsf{ct}}$ and returns m. Otherwise, $\mathcal{B}$ obtains $\mathsf{dk}_{0.\rho|1.\mathsf{snd}}$ by making a receiver key reveal query on input $0.\rho|1.\mathsf{snd}$. If $\mathsf{Dec}(\mathsf{mpk}, \mathsf{dk}_{0.\rho|1.\mathsf{snd}}, \mathsf{snd}, \mathsf{ct}) \neq \bot$, $\mathcal{B}$ outputs $(\mathsf{snd}, 0.\rho|1.\mathsf{snd}, \mathsf{ct})$ as forgery and terminates. Otherwise, $\mathcal{B}$ returns $\bot$ to $\mathcal{A}$.

3. When $\mathcal{A}$ makes the challenge ciphertext query on input (σ_0^*, σ_1^*), $(\mathsf{rcv}_0^*, \mathsf{rcv}_1^*)$, and $(\mathsf{m}_0^*, \mathsf{m}_1^*)$, $\mathcal{B}_2$ sets $\mathsf{rcv}_0' = 0.\mathsf{rcv}_0^*|1.\sigma_0^*$ and $\mathsf{rcv}_1' = 0.\mathsf{rcv}_1^*|1.\sigma_1^*$, makes a encryption query on input (σ_0^*, σ_1^*), $(\mathsf{rcv}_0', \mathsf{rcv}_1')$, and $(\mathsf{m}_0^*, \mathsf{m}_1^*)$ and obtains ct^*. Then, $\mathcal{B}_2$ returns ct^* to $\mathcal{A}$ and updates $\mathcal{L}_{\mathsf{ct}} := \mathcal{L}_{\mathsf{ct}} \cup \{(\sigma^*, \mathsf{rcv}^*, \mathsf{m}^*, \mathsf{ct}^*)\}$.
4. Finally, $\mathcal{A}$ outputs $b' \in \{0, 1\}$, $\mathcal{B}_2$ halts.

From the above construction, $\mathcal{B}_2$ perfectly simulates hib-tcca-priv game for $\mathcal{A}$. Since $\mathcal{B}$ can reveal the target receiver's decryption key in hib-auth game, $\mathcal{B}_2$ satisfies the winning conditions of hib-auth game. Therefore, we have $\Pr[\mathsf{Forge}] = \mathsf{Adv}^{\mathsf{hib}\text{-}\mathsf{auth}}_{\mathsf{HIB}\text{-}\mathsf{ME}', \mathcal{B}_2}(\lambda, k, l+1)$, i.e.,

$$|\epsilon_1 - \epsilon_0| = \mathsf{Adv}^{\mathsf{hib}\text{-}\mathsf{auth}}_{\mathsf{HIB}\text{-}\mathsf{ME}', \mathcal{B}_2}(\lambda, k, l+1).$$

Finally, to estimate $|\epsilon_1 - \frac{1}{2}|$, we construct an adversary $\mathcal{B}_1$ that breaks the hib-cpa-priv using an adversary $\mathcal{A}$ that breaks Game_1. The construction of $\mathcal{B}_1$ is as follows.

1. Upon receiving mpk, $\mathcal{B}_1$ sets $\mathcal{L}_{\mathsf{ek}}, \mathcal{L}_{\mathsf{dk}}, \mathcal{L}_{\mathsf{ct}} := \emptyset$ and executes $\mathcal{A}$ on input mpk.
2. When $\mathcal{A}$ makes some oracle queries, $\mathcal{B}_1$ answers as follows.
   (a) When $\mathcal{A}$ makes a sender (resp., receiver) key generation query on input σ (resp., ρ), $\mathcal{B}_1$ makes a sender (resp., receiver) key generation query to its challenger on input σ (resp., ρ), and updates $\mathcal{L}_{\mathsf{ek}} := \mathcal{L}_{\mathsf{ek}} \cup \{(\sigma, \bot)\}$ (resp., $\mathcal{L}_{\mathsf{dk}} := \mathcal{L}_{\mathsf{dk}} \cup \{(\rho, \bot)\}$).
   (b) When $\mathcal{A}$ makes a sender (resp., receiver) key delegation query on input σ' such that $(\sigma', \cdot) \in \mathcal{L}_{\mathsf{ek}}$ and σ (resp., ρ' such that $(\rho', \cdot) \in \mathcal{L}_{\mathsf{dk}}$ and ρ), $\mathcal{B}_1$ makes a sender (resp., receiver) key delegation query to its challenger on input σ' and σ (resp., $0.\rho'$ and $0.\rho$), and updates $\mathcal{L}_{\mathsf{ek}} := \mathcal{L}_{\mathsf{ek}} \cup \{(\sigma'|\sigma, \bot)\}$ (resp., $\mathcal{L}_{\mathsf{dk}} := \mathcal{L}_{\mathsf{dk}} \cup \{(\rho'|\rho, \bot)\}$).
   (c) When $\mathcal{A}$ makes a sender (resp., receiver) key reveal query on input σ such that $(\sigma, \cdot) \in \mathcal{L}_{\mathsf{ek}}$ (resp., ρ such that $(\rho, \cdot) \in \mathcal{L}_{\mathsf{dk}}$), $\mathcal{B}_1$ makes a sender (resp., receiver) key reveal query to its challenger on input σ (resp., ρ), receives ek_σ (resp., dk_ρ), and returns as it is to $\mathcal{A}$. In addition, $\mathcal{B}_1$ updates $\mathcal{L}_{\mathsf{ek}} := \mathcal{L}_{\mathsf{ek}} \setminus \{(\sigma, \bot)\}$ (resp., $\mathcal{L}_{\mathsf{dk}} := \mathcal{L}_{\mathsf{dk}} \setminus \{(\rho, \bot)\}$).
   (d) When $\mathcal{A}$ makes a encryption query on input σ such that $(\sigma, \cdot) \in \mathcal{L}_{\mathsf{ek}}$, rcv such that $(\mathsf{rcv}, \cdot) \in \mathcal{L}_{\mathsf{dk}}$, and message m, $\mathcal{B}$ sets $\mathsf{rcv}' = 0.\mathsf{rcv}|1.\sigma$. Next, $\mathcal{B}$ sends a sender key reveal query on input σ to obtain ek_σ. Then, $\mathcal{B}$ computes $\mathsf{ct} \leftarrow \mathsf{Enc}(\mathsf{mpk}, \mathsf{ek}_\sigma, \mathsf{rcv}', \mathsf{m})$ and returns ct to $\mathcal{A}$. In addition, $\mathcal{B}$ updates $\mathcal{L}_{\mathsf{ct}} := \mathcal{L}_{\mathsf{ct}} \cup \{(\sigma, \mathsf{rcv}, \mathsf{m}, \mathsf{ct})\}$.
   (e) When $\mathcal{A}$ makes a decryption query on input snd, ρ and ct, if $(\mathsf{snd}, \rho, \cdot, \mathsf{ct}) \in \mathcal{L}_{\mathsf{ct}}$, $\mathcal{B}$ extracts m from $\mathcal{L}_{\mathsf{ct}}$ and returns m to $\mathcal{A}$. Otherwise, if $\rho = \mathsf{rcv}^* \land \mathsf{snd} \neq \sigma^*$, $\mathcal{B}_1$ returns $\bot$ to $\mathcal{A}$. Otherwise, $\mathcal{B}_1$ makes a receiver key reveal query on $0.\rho|1.\mathsf{snd}$ to obtain $\mathsf{dk}_{0.\rho|1.\mathsf{snd}}$. Then, $\mathcal{B}_1$ computes $\mathsf{m} \leftarrow \mathsf{Dec}(\mathsf{mpk}, \mathsf{dk}_{0.\rho|1.\mathsf{snd}}, \mathsf{snd}, \mathsf{ct})$ and returns m to $\mathcal{A}$.
3. When $\mathcal{A}$ makes the challenge ciphertext query on input σ^*, rcv^* and m^*, $\mathcal{B}_1$ sets $\mathsf{rcv}' := 0.\mathsf{rcv}^*|1.\mathsf{snd}^*$, makes the challenge query on input σ^*, rcv', m^* and receives ct^*. Then, $\mathcal{B}_1$ returns ct^* to $\mathcal{A}$.
4. Finally, $\mathcal{A}$ outputs $b' \in \{0, 1\}$, $\mathcal{B}_1$ outputs the same guess.

From the above construction, $\mathcal{B}_1$ perfectly simulates Game_1 fro $\mathcal{A}$ and the challenge bits of $\mathcal{B}_1$ and $\mathcal{A}$ correspond. Therefore, we have

$$\left|\epsilon_1 - \frac{1}{2}\right| = \mathsf{Adv}^{\text{hib-cpa-priv}}_{\text{HIB-ME}',\mathcal{A}}(\lambda, k, l+1)$$

Putting everything together, we have

$$\mathsf{Adv}^{\text{hib-tcca-priv}}_{\text{HIB-ME},\mathcal{A}}(\lambda, k, l) = \mathsf{Adv}^{\text{hib-cpa-priv}}_{\text{HIB-ME}',\mathcal{B}_1}(\lambda, k, l+1) + \mathsf{Adv}^{\text{hib-auth}}_{\text{HIB-ME}',\mathcal{B}_2}(\lambda, k, l+1).$$

□

Theorem 6. *Suppose that the HIB-ME scheme* HIB-ME′ *satisfies* hib-auth *security. If there exists an adversary* $\mathcal{A}$ *that breaks the* hib-auth *security of* HIB-ME, *there exists an adversary* $\mathcal{B}$ *that breaks the* hib-auth *security of* HIB-ME′ *such that*

$$\mathsf{Adv}^{\text{hib-auth}}_{\text{HIB-ME},\mathcal{A}}(\lambda, k, l) = \mathsf{Adv}^{\text{hib-auth}}_{\text{HIB-ME}',\mathcal{B}}(\lambda, k, l+1)$$

where k (resp., l) is the maximum depth of senders (resp., receivers). The running time of $\mathcal{B}$ is about of $\mathcal{A}$.

Proof. To prove the theorem, we construct an adversary $\mathcal{B}$ that breaks hib-auth of HIB-ME′ using $\mathcal{A}$ that breaks hib-auth of HIB-ME. The construction of $\mathcal{B}$ is as follows.

1. Upon receiving mpk, $\mathcal{B}$ executes $\mathcal{A}$ on input mpk.
2. When $\mathcal{A}$ makes some oracle queries, $\mathcal{B}$ answers as follows.
   (a) When $\mathcal{A}$ makes a sender (resp., receiver) key generation query on input σ (resp., ρ), $\mathcal{B}$ makes a sender (resp., receiver) key generation query to its challenger on input σ (resp., ρ), and updates $\mathcal{L}_{\text{ek}} := \mathcal{L}_{\text{ek}} \cup \{(\sigma, \bot)\}$ (resp., $\mathcal{L}_{\text{dk}} := \mathcal{L}_{\text{dk}} \cup \{(\rho, \bot)\}$).
   (b) When $\mathcal{A}$ makes a sender (resp., receiver) key delegation query on input σ' such that $(\sigma', \cdot) \in \mathcal{L}_{\text{ek}}$ and σ (resp., ρ' such that $(\rho', \cdot) \in \mathcal{L}_{\text{dk}}$ and ρ), $\mathcal{B}$ makes a sender (resp., receiver) key delegation query to its challenger on input σ' and σ (resp., $0.\rho'$ and $0.\rho$), and updates $\mathcal{L}_{\text{ek}} := \mathcal{L}_{\text{ek}} \cup \{(\sigma'|\sigma, \bot)\}$ (resp., $\mathcal{L}_{\text{dk}} := \mathcal{L}_{\text{dk}} \cup \{(\rho'|\rho, \bot)\}$).
   (c) When $\mathcal{A}$ makes a sender (resp., receiver) key reveal query on input σ such that $(\sigma, \cdot) \in \mathcal{L}_{\text{ek}}$ (resp., ρ such that $(\rho, \cdot) \in \mathcal{L}_{\text{dk}}$), $\mathcal{B}$ makes a sender (resp., receiver) key reveal query to its challenger on input σ (resp., ρ), receives ek_σ (resp., dk_ρ), and returns as it is to $\mathcal{A}$. In addition, $\mathcal{B}$ updates $\mathcal{L}_{\text{ek}} := \mathcal{L}_{\text{ek}} \setminus \{(\sigma, \bot)\}$ (resp., $\mathcal{L}_{\text{dk}} := \mathcal{L}_{\text{dk}} \setminus \{(\rho, \bot)\}$).
   (d) When $\mathcal{A}$ makes a encryption query on input σ such that $(\sigma, \cdot) \in \mathcal{L}_{\text{ek}}$, rcv such that $(\text{rcv}, \cdot) \in \mathcal{L}_{\text{dk}}$, and message m, $\mathcal{B}$ runs $(\mathsf{sk}, \mathsf{vk}) \leftarrow \mathsf{KGen}(1^\lambda)$ and sets $\text{rcv}' = 0.\text{rcv}|1.\mathsf{vk}$. Next, $\mathcal{B}$ sends a encryption query on input σ, rcv′, and m to obtain ct. Then, $\mathcal{B}$ computes $\Sigma \leftarrow \mathsf{Sign}(\mathsf{sk}, \mathsf{ct})$ and returns $\mathsf{ct} = (\mathsf{ct}, \mathsf{vk}, \Sigma)$. In addition, $\mathcal{B}$ updates $\mathcal{L}_{\text{ct}} := \mathcal{L}_{\text{ct}} \cup \{(\sigma, \text{rcv}, \mathsf{m}, \mathsf{ct})\}$.
3. Finally, when $\mathcal{A}$ submits $(\mathsf{snd}^*, \rho^*, \mathsf{ct}^* = (\mathsf{ct}^*, \mathsf{vk}^*, \Sigma^*))$ as a forgery, $\mathcal{B}$ submits the same $(\mathsf{snd}^*, 0.\rho^*|1.\mathsf{vk}, \mathsf{ct}^*)$ if $\mathsf{Ver}(\mathsf{vk}, \Sigma^*, \mathsf{ct}^*) = 1$.

We can verify that $\mathcal{B}$ perfectly simulates the hib-auth game. Therefore, if $\mathcal{A}$ breaks the hib-auth security of HIB-ME, $\mathcal{B}$ also breaks the hib-auth security of HIB-ME'. Thus, we have

$$\mathsf{Adv}^{\text{hib-auth}}_{\text{HIB-ME},\mathcal{A}}(\lambda, k, l) = \mathsf{Adv}^{\text{hib-auth}}_{\text{HIB-ME'},\mathcal{B}}(\lambda, k, l+1).$$

□

Acknowledgments. The authors would like to thank anonymous reviewers for their constructive and valuable comments. This work was supported by JSPS KAKENHI Grant Number JP23K24846, Japan. Sohto Chiku was partially supported by JSPS KAKENHI Grant Number JP25KJ1319, Japan. Keisuke Hara was partially supported by JSPS KAKENHI Grant Number JP24K20776 and JST-CREST JPMJCR22M1, Japan.

References

1. Agrawal, S., Boneh, D., Boyen, X.: Efficient lattice (H)IBE in the standard model. In: Gilbert, H. (ed.) EUROCRYPT 2010. LNCS, vol. 6110, pp. 553–572. Springer, Heidelberg (2010). https://doi.org/10.1007/978-3-642-13190-5_28
2. Ateniese, G., Francati, D., Nuñez, D., Venturi, D.: Match me if you can: matchmaking encryption and its applications. In: Boldyreva, A., Micciancio, D. (eds.) CRYPTO 2019. LNCS, vol. 11693, pp. 701–731. Springer, Cham (2019). https://doi.org/10.1007/978-3-030-26951-7_24
3. Ateniese, G., Francati, D., Nuñez, D., Venturi, D.: Match me if you can: matchmaking encryption and its applications. J. Cryptol. **34**(3), 16 (2021). https://doi.org/10.1007/s00145-021-09381-4
4. Belfiore, R.C., Cosmo, A.D., Ferrara, A.L.: Identity-based matchmaking encryption from standard lattice assumptions. In: Pöpper, C., Batina, L. (eds.) ACNS 2024, Part II. LNCS, vol. 14584, pp. 163–188. Springer, Cham (2024). https://doi.org/10.1007/978-3-031-54773-7_7
5. Blazy, O., Kiltz, E., Pan, J.: (Hierarchical) identity-based encryption from affine message authentication. In: Garay, J.A., Gennaro, R. (eds.) CRYPTO 2014. LNCS, vol. 8616, pp. 408–425. Springer, Heidelberg (2014). https://doi.org/10.1007/978-3-662-44371-2_23
6. Boneh, D., Franklin, M.: Identity-based encryption from the Weil pairing. In: Kilian, J. (ed.) CRYPTO 2001. LNCS, vol. 2139, pp. 213–229. Springer, Heidelberg (2001). https://doi.org/10.1007/3-540-44647-8_13
7. Boyen, X., Li, Q.: Identity-based matchmaking encryption with enhanced privacy — a generic construction with practical instantiations. In: Tsudik, G., Conti, M., Liang, K., Smaragdakis, G. (eds.) ESORICS 2023. LNCS, vol. 14345, pp. 425–445. Springer, Cham (2023). https://doi.org/10.1007/978-3-031-51476-0_21
8. Boyen, X., Waters, B.: Anonymous hierarchical identity-based encryption (without random Oracles). In: Dwork, C. (ed.) CRYPTO 2006. LNCS, vol. 4117, pp. 290–307. Springer, Heidelberg (2006). https://doi.org/10.1007/11818175_17
9. Canetti, R., Halevi, S., Katz, J.: Chosen-ciphertext security from identity-based encryption. In: Cachin, C., Camenisch, J.L. (eds.) EUROCRYPT 2004. LNCS, vol. 3027, pp. 207–222. Springer, Heidelberg (2004). https://doi.org/10.1007/978-3-540-24676-3_13

10. Cash, D., Hofheinz, D., Kiltz, E., Peikert, C.: Bonsai trees, or how to delegate a lattice basis. J. Cryptol. **25**(4), 601–639 (2012). https://doi.org/10.1007/s00145-011-9105-2
11. Chen, J., Li, Y., Wen, J., Weng, J.: Identity-based matchmaking encryption from standard assumptions. In: Agrawal, S., Lin, D. (eds.) ASIACRYPT 2022, Part III. LNCS, vol. 13793, pp. 394–422. Springer, Heidelberg (2022). https://doi.org/10.1007/978-3-031-22969-5_14
12. Chiku, S., Hashimoto, K., Hara, K., Shikata, J.: Identity-based matchmaking encryption, revisited: strong security and practical constructions from standard classical and post-quantum assumptions. Cryptology ePrint Archive, Paper 2023/1435 (2023). https://eprint.iacr.org/2023/1435
13. Ducas, L., Lyubashevsky, V., Prest, T.: Efficient identity-based encryption over NTRU lattices. In: Sarkar, P., Iwata, T. (eds.) ASIACRYPT 2014. LNCS, vol. 8874, pp. 22–41. Springer, Heidelberg (2014). https://doi.org/10.1007/978-3-662-45608-8_2
14. Francati, D., Guidi, A., Russo, L., Venturi, D.: Identity-based matchmaking encryption without random oracles. In: Adhikari, A., Küsters, R., Preneel, B. (eds.) INDOCRYPT 2021. LNCS, vol. 13143, pp. 415–435. Springer, Cham (2021). https://doi.org/10.1007/978-3-030-92518-5_19
15. Fujisaki, E., Okamoto, T.: How to enhance the security of public-key encryption at minimum cost. In: Imai, H., Zheng, Y. (eds.) PKC 1999. LNCS, vol. 1560, pp. 53–68. Springer, Heidelberg (1999). https://doi.org/10.1007/3-540-49162-7_5
16. Gentry, C., Silverberg, A.: Hierarchical ID-based cryptography. In: Zheng, Y. (ed.) ASIACRYPT 2002. LNCS, vol. 2501, pp. 548–566. Springer, Heidelberg (2002). https://doi.org/10.1007/3-540-36178-2_34
17. Horwitz, J., Lynn, B.: Toward hierarchical identity-based encryption. In: Knudsen, L.R. (ed.) EUROCRYPT 2002. LNCS, vol. 2332, pp. 466–481. Springer, Heidelberg (2002). https://doi.org/10.1007/3-540-46035-7_31
18. Kiltz, E., Neven, G.: Identity-based signatures. In: Cryptology and Information Security Series on Identity-Based Cryptography, vol. I, pp. 31–44, January 2008
19. Lin, S., Li, Y., Chen, J.: CCA-secure identity-based matchmaking encryption from standard assumptions. In: Ge, C., Yung, M. (eds.) Information Security and Cryptology, pp. 253–273. Springer, Singapore (2024). https://doi.org/10.1007/978-981-97-0942-7_13
20. Prest, T., et al.: FALCON. Technical report, National Institute of Standards and Technology (2022). https://csrc.nist.gov/Projects/post-quantum-cryptography/selected-algorithms-2022
21. Sakai, R., Ohgishi, K., Kasahara, M.: Cryptosystems based on pairing. In: The 2000 Symposium on Cryptography and Information Security, January 2000
22. Seo, J.H., Kobayashi, T., Ohkubo, M., Suzuki, K.: Anonymous hierarchical identity-based encryption with constant size ciphertexts. In: Jarecki, S., Tsudik, G. (eds.) PKC 2009. LNCS, vol. 5443, pp. 215–234. Springer, Heidelberg (2009). https://doi.org/10.1007/978-3-642-00468-1_13
23. Shi, E., Waters, B.: Delegating capabilities in predicate encryption systems. In: Aceto, L., Damgård, I., Goldberg, L.A., Halldórsson, M.M., Ingólfsdóttir, A., Walukiewicz, I. (eds.) ICALP 2008. LNCS, vol. 5126, pp. 560–578. Springer, Heidelberg (2008). https://doi.org/10.1007/978-3-540-70583-3_46
24. Wang, Y., Wang, B., Lai, Q., Zhan, Y.: Identity-based matchmaking encryption with stronger security and instantiation on lattices. Theoret. Comput. Sci. **1029**, 115048 (2025). https://doi.org/10.1016/j.tcs.2024.115048. https://www.sciencedirect.com/science/article/pii/S0304397524006650

Silentium: Implementation of a Pseudorandom Correlation Generator for Beaver Triples

Vincent Rieder

University of Stuttgart, Stuttgart, Germany
vincent.rieder@online.de

Abstract. Secure Multi-Party Computation is a privacy-enhancing technology that allows several parties to securely compute on distributed private data. In the line of the well established SPDZ protocol, the by far most expensive task is the generation of Beaver triples in the so called offline phase. Silentium is our implementation of an actively secure offline phase in the form of a Pseudorandom Correlation Generator for Beaver triples (Bt-PCG, Boyle et al. CRYPTO 2020), which, as any PCG, is designed to have low communication. Compared to previous offline phases, their Bt-PCG reduces the communication costs by three orders of magnitude. However, so far efficiency was only estimated. With Silentium, we demonstrate that their Bt-PCG can achieve even better running times than state-of-the-art offline phase implementations in the MP-SPDZ library. To actually achieve such a performance, Silentium comprises a systematic parallelization strategy and implementation-friendly decomposition scenarios of the Bt-PCG into structured modules. Looking forward for large-scale applications on the cloud, Silentium is designed to be versatile to support hardware acceleration in future.

Keywords: Secure Multi-Party Computation · Beaver Triples · Pseudorandom Correlation Generators

1 Introduction

Secure multi-party computation (MPC) is a privacy-enhancing technology that allows several parties to evaluate a public function without leaking private inputs and outputs. Silentium is our implementation of a recent protocol for silent MPC [9], i.e., we bring forward practical MPC solutions with low communication. Our motivation is MPC on cloud servers, e.g., with the Carbyne Stack platform[1] based on the SPDZ protocol [13]. On the cloud, typically communication is a bottleneck due to high latency. More generally, the cloud setting is promising to outsource large-scale and industrial applications, e.g., privacy-preserving

---

[1] https://carbynestack.io/.

machine learning. In this sense, the attractiveness of MPC on the cloud is determined not only by communication but also computation. Concretely, Silentium is our implementation of a recent Pseudorandom Correlation Generator (PCG) for the generation of Beaver triples [9], the most expensive, and cryptographically challenging, task in the line of the SPDZ protocol. While this PCG, as any PCG, is designed to have low communication, so far concrete efficiency was only estimated. With Silentium[2] we prove that this novel PCG is indeed attractive in practice.

1.1 Silentium as Offline Phase in the Line of SPDZ

The basic MPC framework of our work is the SPDZ protocol [13]. Protocols in the line of SPDZ can be seen as standard approach for MPC over arithmetic circuits (encoding the real-world function to evaluate). The crucial point of the SPDZ protocol is the preprocessing model [3] with two phases. In this model, the actual secure function evaluation (online phase) consumes distributed correlated randomness that is provided by a preceding, input-independent, offline phase. While this separation allows the construction of online phases with little overhead compared to an unprotected (local) function evaluation, the construction of actively secure offline phases is challenging in terms computation and communication. For SPDZ the offline phase mainly refers to the generation of Beaver triples, also known as authenticated multiplication triple, each supporting one multiplication in the online phase. For the cloud context, Silentium targets for large-scale applications, that means for the generation of millions of Beaver triples.

In the last years, the initial offline phase for SPDZ was improved in several directions [3,12,13], with ready-to-use implementations in the MP-SPDZ library [17]. While these typically rely on homomorphic encryption, Silentium can be seen as an alternative offline phase implementation, following the recent design of Pseudorandom Correlation Generators [8]. Concretely we implement a PCG for Beaver triples (Bt-PCG) [9], which is the only attractive PCG for Beaver triples (Appendix A.1). In general, PCGs come with low-communication by design [1, 6,25]. Specifically, for the Bt-PCG the generation of one million Beaver triples (100 MB of correlated randomness) takes a few MB of communication, while the protocols in MP-SPDZ take a few GB of communication. In pure numbers, this reduction promises a game changing advantage in the aforementioned MPC cloud context. With Silentium we demonstrate that on the same time, the Bt-PCG is computationally as good as the protocols in MP-SPDZ.

1.2 Technical Context

To distinguish our work from other MPC approaches, we mention three main MPC assumption of Silentium. Firstly, following the SPDZ protocol, Silentium is

---

[2] Silentium (latin for silence) denotes periods of silence in monasteries with special rules to bring communication to a minimum, in analogy to the design of PCGs.

in the domain of MPC over arithmetic circuits based on additive secret-sharing, in contrast to MPC over binary circuits based on e.g. garbled circuits [27]. Secondly, following the Bt-PCG, Silentium is restricted to the two-party setting, which is already sufficient to outsource a secure computation for any number of parties to (two) cloud servers [3]. Finally, we consider the actively secure Bt-PCG formulation [9], i.e., with strong security guarantees even if one malicious party might actively deviate from the MPC protocol. Active security provides a stronger legal basis compared to only passive security, which is a relevant factor for industrial applications. The technical roots of Silentium are further discussed in Appendix A, where we relate Silentium with the competitive MP-SPDZ library and the PCG primitive as theoretical basis. Hereby, we explain what actually hides beyond the term Bt-PCG, which in the domain of active security has to be read with some care with respect to the theoretical (passively secure) PCG definition [8,9].

1.3 Contribution

Silentium is the first implementation of the Bt-PCG [9] (to the best of our knowledge), proving the competitiveness with MP-SPDZ. Effectively, our best setup of the Bt-PCG runs 34% faster than respective benchmarks for LowGear, the fastest offline phase in MP-SPDZ. For fairness, we do not claim to be in fact better: Firstly, we stress that our benchmarks are only preliminary, rather than a comprehensive comparison, e.g., with respect to the selection of parameters. Secondly, while Silentium is standalone offline phase of based on the rather new PCG paradigm, the protocols in MP-SPDZ are much more established and mature in practice.

Silentium takes a two-folded approach to achieve good performance for the Bt-PCG. As a theoretical contribution, Silentium actually comprises a whole framework with systematic strategies for parallelization and decomposition (Sect. 1.4). On the practical side, Silentium comprises more than 20.000 lines of code, which, for good efficiency on hardware level, are mainly written in C language. The purse number of lines of code can be justified by the novelty and size of many building blocks, the implementation of the Silentium framework, and a versatile design. The most outstanding components are:

- At the core is the first implementation of an actively secure protocol to generate authenticated secret-shared scaled unit vectors (SUVs) [9,23].
- An implementation of the Number Theoretic Transform (NTT) [20] for the extraordinary large degree 2^{20}, based on a from scratch 128-bit field arithmetic implementation. This setting is Bt-PCG specific and much more extensive compared to usual cryptography NTT applications (with degree up to 2^{15} on smaller fields, e.g. [2]).
- Two libraries for MPC online phases (as necessary for the Bt-PCG itself): For SPDZ [13], i.e., for arithmetic operations, and for TinyOT [14,21], i.e., for binary operations. We stress that the overhead for their respective offline phases, which are not (yet) covered by Silentium, is expected to be small [9,23].

Looking forward to large-scale MPC deployments on the cloud, we design the Silentium framework to be versatile. One goal is to prepare Silentium for special purpose hardware acceleration and thus even better performance for large-scale applications. For example, Silentium allows to easily exchange different components like the field implementation, enabling future use of specialized hardware implementations. A further aspect of versatility is the challenge to find optimal parameters configurations, which we address with our decomposition framework.

1.4 Technical Overview and Paper Outline

After setting up the notation for additive secret-sharing (Sect. 2), Sect. 3 introduces further building blocks and describes the Bt-PCG. In Sect. 4, we then perform a cost analysis of the Bt-PCG, identifying relevant cost metrics and suitable actions concerning communication, computation, internal MPC operations, and memory consumption. Based on this analysis, we then derive the Silentium framework. Concretely, we introduce different techniques and scenarios to decompose the Bt-PCG into modules of implementation-friendly size (Sect. 5). At the core is a parallelization strategy for speed-up, operating on two levels:

- **High-level multi-tasking:** Different modules are supposed to run on different computation units like cores. This allows to balance high memory consumption.
- **Low level multi-threading:** Within each module, we synchronize identical task to run arithmetic operations in parallel on hardware level, and to reduce the number of communication rounds.

In Sect. 6 we make one further step towards an versatile implementation by formalizing the modules as small executable programs. The interested reader can find conceptual details of our C implementation in the full paper version [24]. As evaluation of this implementation, Sect. 7 provides running times in comparison to MP-SPDZ benchmarks. The interested reader can find an internal evaluation of the Silentium features the full paper version [24]. With Sect. 8 we conclude the paper with a list of possible future work.

2 Preliminaries: Additive Secret-Sharing

In general, we write $\mathbb{F}$ for a large finite field, where the bit size ν is a security parameter. We write $x \leftarrow S$ to denote that x is sampled uniformly random from a set S. We use upper indices S^c to denote c independent instances of S.

In SPDZ [13] the secure arithmetic circuit evaluation operates on additive secret-sharing with authentication for active security. We write $[x]$ for a secret-shared value $x \in \mathbb{F}$, where both parties P_σ hold a private share x_σ and a private message authentication code (MAC) x'_σ such that $x = x_0 + x_1$ and $\mathrm{m}x = x'_0 + x'_1$, where $\mathrm{m} = \mathrm{m}_0 + \mathrm{m}_1 \in \mathbb{F}$ is an additively shared global MAC key [12]. We write $x' = \mathrm{m} \cdot x$ for short. The MAC is used to ensure active security, i.e., on each secret-shared value $[x]$ that is revealed as output, a MAC check is performed to ensure that the value x was computed as intended without any corruption.

Note that due to linearity of $[\cdot]$, the online phase evaluation of addition gates in an arithmetic circuit can be done locally without communication. In contrast, multiplications are interactive, consuming one Beaver triple $[x], [y], [z]$, where $x, y \leftarrow \mathbb{F}, z = x \cdot y$. Silentium is an offline phase for the generation of Beaver triples[3], making itself use of secret-sharing $[\cdot]$. Hereby, we extend the notation $[\cdot]$ to vectors and polynomials over $\mathbb{F}$, where all coefficients are secret-shared individually. We denote an authenticated secret-shared scaled unit vector, i.e., a secret-shared element in $\mathbb{F}^N$, where exactly one position α has a non-zero payload A, as SUV.

Apart from SPDZ for arithmetic circuits, Silentium uses secret-sharing in the sense of the TinyOT protocol [21] for actively secure evaluation of binary circuits, operating on authenticated secret-shared bits $[\cdot]_2$. We extend this to bit-wise secret-shared integers $[\cdot]_2$.

3 Description of the Bt-PCG

The purpose of the Bt-PCG [9] is to generate a large batch of N many uniformly random Beaver triples. As any PCG (Appendix A) the Bt-PCG consists of an interactive seed generation phase (Sect. 3.1) proceeded by a local expansion phase (Sect. 3.2). In Sect. 3.3 we draw a whole picture, Fig. 1, and we conclude the description of the Bt-PCG with a discussion of secure parameters choices (Sect. 3.4).

We distinguish between between a direct and indirect Bt-PCG variation, see Appendix A.3 for the relation to the initial Bt-PCG description [9,23]. While the direct PCG is more compact with respect to computation in the local phase, the indirect Bt-PCG is more compact with respect to memory requirements between the interactive and local phase. Whether to use the direct or indirect Bt-PCG is a design choice of the real-world deployment. While the direct Bt-PCG contains less computational steps, the indirect Bt-PCG has the advantage of the seed compression. The latter is not only useful to reduce storage in large-scale applications, but also if the interactive phase is schedule independently of the MPC online phase, e.g., on cloud servers.

3.1 Interactive Phase and Generation of SUVs

The core of the interactive phase is a novel protocol Π_{SUV} for the generation of SUVs [9]. We always consider Π_{SUV} in optimized form [23]. Given an integer position α, the task of Π_{SUV} is to generate a random SUV with position α and payload A without revealing information about α, A, m. For this, Π_{SUV} processes the position bit-wise secret shared with $[\cdot]_2$, whereas the payload A and MAC

---

[3] We do not explicitly consider the generation of random share $[a]$ (to input private values in the online phase), since this is a sub-task of generating Beaver triples.

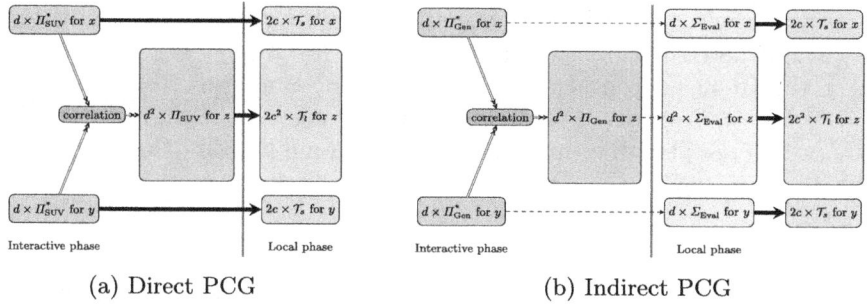

Fig. 1. Visualization of the Bt-PCG. An execution starts with the Π^*_{SUV} (resp. Π^*_{Gen}) for x, y and ends with the output $[x] \cdot [y] = [z]$ of the LPN transformation $\mathcal{T}$. Double arrows represent the flow of secret-shared positions and payloads, thick arrows represent the flow of large vectors, and dashed arrows the flow of small DPF keys.

key m, are both secret-shared with $[\cdot]$. The choice of $[\cdot]_2, \cdot [\cdot]$ is due to protocol details [9]. As key feature, the communication of Π_{SUV} only operates on the level of the position and payload, instead of the full SUV of large degree N. This is the core of the global PCG design for low communication.

To describe the indirect Bt-PCG, we also consider a two-step separation of Π_{SUV} over the interactive and local phase. As part of the interactive phase, this approach takes a key generation protocol Π_{Gen}, which generates two private keys that are much smaller than the respective SUV. The keys are made such that the parties can expand them into their share of the SUV with a local (non-interactive) algorithm Σ_{Eval}. Hereby, Π_{Gen} is similar to Π_{SUV}, differing only in the output format, and Σ_{Eval} can be seen as a localization of Π_{SUV}, where all information received by interaction is encoded into the private keys. Note that the literature mainly focuses on Π_{SUV}, leaving the description of the two-step approach with $\Pi_{\text{Gen}}, \Sigma_{\text{Eval}}$ is a straightforward modification [9,23].

As variations of Π_{SUV} and Π_{Gen}, we additionally use protocols $\Pi^*_{\text{SUV}}, \Pi^*_{\text{Gen}}$ that do not expect a secret-shared position and payload as input, but rather include to sample fresh values in an efficient way [23].

3.2 Local Phase and Ring-LPN Transformation

The local phase relies on a special purpose coding-theoretic assumption, which we refer as ring-LPN assumption [9]. The assumption itself is out of the scope of its work, for Silentium the underlying polynomial transformation is sufficient. For this, let $R = \mathbb{F}[X]/F$ be the polynomial ring modulo F, where $F \in \mathbb{F}[X]$ has degree N and is fully reducible into different linear factors, i.e., there exists a ring isomorphism $\psi : R \cong \mathbb{F}^N$, where we identify polynomials in R with their N-dimensional coefficient vectors. For example, if F is the cyclotomic polynomial $F = X^N + 1$, than ψ is efficiently computable with the NTT [20]. Let furthermore $R_q \subset R$ be the set of q-sparse polynomials, i.e., N dimensional vectors with q

arbitrary non-zero positions and respective arbitrary payloads. Let $\langle x, y \rangle_c = \sum_{i=0}^{c-1} x_i y_i$ denote the c-dim scalar product over R.

For the Bt-PCG, consider vectors $u, v \leftarrow \mathcal{H}_q^c$ and respective MACs $u' = \mathrm{m} \cdot u, v' = \mathrm{m} \cdot v$. We write $\otimes$ for tensor products, e.g., $w = u \otimes v \in R^{c \times c}$ is given by $w_{i,j} = u_i \cdot v_j$. Then the ring-LPN assumption implies that the distribution

$$\{x, x', y, y', z, z' \mid \rho \leftarrow R^c, u \leftarrow R_q^c, v \leftarrow R_q^c, u' = \mathrm{m} \cdot u, v' = \mathrm{m} \cdot v,$$
$$w = u \otimes v, w' = \mathrm{m} \cdot w, x = \langle \rho, u \rangle_c, x' = \langle \rho, u' \rangle_c, y = \langle \rho, v \rangle_c, \quad (1)$$
$$y' = \langle \rho, v' \rangle_c, z = \langle \rho \otimes \rho, w \rangle_{c \times c}, z' = \langle \rho \otimes \rho, w' \rangle_{c \times c}\}$$

over R^6 is computationally indistinguishable from sampling $[x], [y], [z]$, where $x, y \xleftarrow{\$} R, z = x \cdot y$. Hence, after applying ψ, Eq. (1) describes nothing else than to sample N independent Beaver triples over $\mathbb{F}$. We denote the respective map

$$u \mapsto \psi(\langle u, \rho \rangle)), \quad v \mapsto \psi(\langle v, \rho \rangle)), \quad w \mapsto \psi(\langle w, \rho \otimes \rho \rangle)$$
$$u' \mapsto \psi(\langle u', \rho \rangle)), \quad v' \mapsto \psi(\langle v', \rho \rangle)), \quad w' \mapsto \psi(\langle w', \rho \otimes \rho \rangle) \quad (2)$$

as ring-LPN transformation $\mathcal{T}$. We write $\mathcal{T}_s, \mathcal{T}_l$ for the individual maps with small c- or large c^2-dimensional input vectors, respectively.

3.3 Visualization of the Bt-PCG

Given the previous two sections, we now can draw a complete picture of the Bt-PCG (Fig. 1). First observe that due to linearity, the parties can locally apply $\mathcal{T}_s, \mathcal{T}_l$ to transform a secret-shared version of $w = u \otimes v$ into a batch of N many pseudo-random Beaver triples $[x], [y], [z]$. This already induces the task of the interactive phase, namely to generate a respective triple $[u], [v], [w]$ of secret-shared sparse vectors (SSVs), that are correlated by a polynomial tensor product. These SSV can be generated with Π_{SUV}, since the SSVs can be decomposed into vectors of SUVs $\bar{u}, \bar{v}, \bar{w}$ with coefficients $u_i^k \cdot v_j^l = w_{i,j}^{k,l}, 0 \le i, j < c, 0 \le k, l < q$, where for the w component the degree of the vectors is increased to $2N$. We refer to the SUVs in $\bar{u}, \bar{v}$ as *small* SUVs and to the SUVs in $\bar{w}$ as *large* SUVs (resp. for SSVs).

Altogether, the direct Bt-PCG proceeds as follows (Fig. 1a). In the interactive phase, the computation starts with calls of Π_{SUV}^* to generate the small SSVs $[u], [v]$ with uniformly random payloads $[\alpha]_2, [\beta]_2$ and payloads $[A], [B]$. Afterwards, positions and payloads $[\gamma]_2, [C]$ of the SSVs $[w]$ are computed. This is done with d^2 secret-shared integer additions for $[\gamma]_2$ (with TinyOT AND gates [9,21]) and d^2 secret-shared multiplications for $[C]$ (consuming Beaver triples). Afterwards, Π_{SUV} is used to generate the d^2 many respective SSVs $[w]$. In a separate local phase, the parties can then call $\mathcal{T}_s, \mathcal{T}_l$ on their shares of u, v, w, giving them secret-shares of N Beaver triples $[x], [y], [z]$.

For the indirect approach, Fig. 1b, the difference is that $\Pi_{\mathrm{SUV}}, \Pi_{\mathrm{SUV}}^*$ calls are replaced by $\Pi_{\mathrm{Gen}}, \Pi_{\mathrm{Gen}}^*$ protocol calls. This replaces the output SSVs by a set of respective SUV keys, altogether referred as PCG seed. It is then part of the local phase to recompute the SSVs shares with Σ_{Eval} before running $\mathcal{T}$.

3.4 Bt-PCG Parameter Choices

To complete the description of the Bt-PCG we comment on the parameter choices for N, c, t. One point is that the Bt-PCG can be slightly improved by replacing the set R_q of sparse vectors, by a set $R_{b,t}$ of regular sparse vectors, where the polynomial is split into b many t sparse blocks. The concrete advantage of this regular variant is that the degree of the SUVs is reduced to $N_b = N/b$ ($2N/b$ respectively), which reduces the costs for the SUV generation in terms of communication, memory consumption, and runtime, while on the other side the security level of the ring-LPN assumption is only slightly decreased [9].

All available parameter recommendations [9] are for fixed $N = 2^{20}, \nu \approx 124, F = X^N + 1$ and different $\lambda = 80, 128, c = 2, 4, 8$ and $d = c \cdot b \cdot t = 32, 40, 64, 96, 156$, where b is a power of 2 in order to divide N_b (see Sect. 7 for concrete combinations). The general relation is that larger values for c allow to use smaller values for $b \cdot t$. We stress that there are no further derivations beyond the initial discussion on the ring-LPN assumption [9]. Due to out versatile design, Silentium is adaptive to future results on the ring-LPN assumption.

4 Analysis of the Bt-PCG

The Bt-PCG employs a wide variety of tools and cryptographic primitives, which makes it hard to predict bottlenecks and to detect possible improvements in theory only. During the process of implementing we identified several bottlenecks- The following lists metrics describing these bottlenecks. Furthermore, for each metric, we derive countermeasures towards an efficient implementation.

The following is a summary of the metrics, for more details, see the full paper version [24]. Concrete values for the cost analysis can be found in the Appendix, Table 3. At this point, we note that a reasonable choice is $N = 2^{20}$ on a bit field size of 128 (due to security [9]). In other words, each individual SUV has a size of more than 30 MB per party, making the Bt-PCG very heavy.

Metric 1. Communication: By design, the Bt-PCG achieves low communication of $\mathcal{O}(\log(N))$ (Metric 1.a), which we do not further address since it is already highly optimized [9,23]. Instead of the amount, it turns out that the number of communication rounds is critical (Metric 1.b), with many message taking only a few bits.

Derived Countermeasures: Synchronization to pack several messages into larger batches that can be exchanged in one communication round.

Metric 2. Computation (Interactive Phase): The computational costs of the interactive phase are dominated by $\mathcal{O}(N)$ calls to a PRG (Metric 2a) and multiplications over $\mathbb{F}$ (Metric 2b) in Π_{SUV} ($\Pi_{\text{Gen}}, \Sigma_{\text{Eval}}$ respectively).

Derived Countermeasures: Use single instruction many data (SIMD) hardware instructions for the PRG and $\mathbb{F}$. Synchronization of communication rounds to increase the parallelization rate for the operations in between.

Metric 3. MPC Operations: Most of the interactive parts are in terms of MPC operations (TinyOT, SPDZ). Hereby, these MPC operations are embedded into the Bt-PCG, excluding generic MPC implementations.

Derived Countermeasures: From scratch implementation of the MPC operations (for now only their online phase). This allows not only to address the other derived countermeasures, but allows for Bt-PCG specific optimization.

Metric 4. Memory Consumption: By design, the indirect Bt-PCG compress the target correlation into small seeds. However, during runtime the direct and indirect Bt-PCG contains a blow-up of pseudo-randomness in terms of the intermediate SSVs, where each SUV already takes 20 MB.

Derived Countermeasure: Compact data representation enabling fast memory access. Time-scheduling and decomposition strategy for the SSV generation to balance high memory consumption.

Metric 5. Computation (Local Phase): The transformation $\mathcal{T}$ in the local phase employs ψ and ring multiplications, with extraordinary NTT degree 2^{20}.

Derived Requirements: Careful selection of NTT algorithms and their implementation, i.e., parallelization and fast memory access. Versatile design of Silentium in preparation of hardware acceleration.

4.1 General Challenges of an Implementation

On the global Bt-PCG level, we identify the following challenges with the metrics and their countermeasures:

- There is a trade-off between parallelization and large memory consumption. How can we find a suitable granularity of tasks?
- The Bt-PCG contains several heavy tasks that are the one hand supposed to run in parallel and on the other hand are time-wise dependent. How can we realize respective time-scheduling of tasks?
- The Bt-PCG employs very different primitives that however rely on common functions, like MPC operations and field arithmetic. How can we connect the different blocks in Fig. 1 with little overhead?
- How do the recommendations for c, b, t, Sect. 3.4 affect the performance in practice?

Derived Methods: We provide several techniques to decompose the Bt-PCG into handful sizes with the goal to have a suitable granularity for parallelization and time-scheduling of tasks (Sect. 5). To control the interfaces of the modules, we equip the modules with additional structure (Sect. 6). In our implementation modules share common functionalities and data structures with a focus on compact memory representation and synchronization (see full version [24]). All our constructions are independent of specific parameter choices.

5 Decomposition of the Bt-PCG

Silentium comprises a framework to decompose the Bt-PCG into implementation-friendly modules. Starting point of all our decomposition scenarios is the visualization in Fig. 1, which already contains a task-oriented decomposition but without taking care about the aspects of our analysis in Sect. 4. We provide further decomposition techniques in terms of modules as containers for several instances of one task. Hereby we distinguish between different module categories like COR, SUV, GEN, EVAL, LPN, similar as in Fig. 1. For example, a module of the category SUV has the task to generate a given number of SUV instances, while a module of the category LPN has the task to apply the transformation $\mathcal{T}_s, \mathcal{T}_l$ to a specified set of input vectors. In this sense, a decomposition scenario describes how to cluster the relevant instances (e.g. all $2d + d^2$ SUVs to be generated, all d correlation steps, all calls to ψ) into a set of modules. Hereby, setting the number and sizes of modules is a tool for balancing different tasks and costs, e.g., to perform a trade-off between low-level and high-level parallelization. Individual modules are supposed to run on different computation units (high level parallelization), while the low-level parallelization takes place inside the modules.

In Sect. 5.1, we differentiate between module categories for different tasks. Due to Metric 4, one aspect is, where to perform the aggregation of SUVs to SSVs (Sect. 5.2). In Sect. 5.3, we discuss decomposition steps for the block of large SUVs, which can be seen as a blueprint for other decomposition techniques.

5.1 The Module Categories

In the following we formalize the different module categories and discus respective decomposition steps.

The Correlation COR: The task of COR is to compute the positions γ and payloads C of the large SUV instances (Sect. 3.3), which in fact takes secure circuit evaluations with SPDZ (positions) and TinyOT (payloads) [9]. To separate cryptographic techniques we actually use two the module categories, namely POS, correlating the positions, and PAYL, correlating the payloads. Than, for high-level parallelization both module categories can run on parallel cores, using different communication channels. For low-level parallelization, we propose to run all d additions/multiplications in parallel with synchronous communication to address Metric 1b (see the full version [24] for details).

In a further step, the tensor sum and product might be distributed to several modules by splitting the d-dimensional tensor operations into k instances of smaller $\tilde{d}$-dimensional tensor operations, where $d = k \cdot \tilde{d}$. However, we stress that for reasonable Bt-PCG parameters ($d < 100$) a further decomposition tends to be disadvantageous, since, if the actual computational steps become smaller, the time to setup the modules during runtime, e.g., communication channels, becomes more and more dominant.

Modules for the SUV Generation: For the generation of the vectors of SUVs $\bar{u}, \bar{v}, \bar{w}$, we distinguish between the module category SUV, for the direct Bt-PCG and the module categories GEN, EVAL for the indirect Bt-PCG. We treat SUV* and Gen* as corner cases of SUV, GEN (see Sect. 6 and [23]). In the following we focus on SUV and treat all categories equal to simplify the description. Still in practice one might distinguish especially between the interactive SUV, GEN and local category EVAL. For example, the key generation runs faster since there are no latency issues, hence parallelization is less critical. The versatile module design allows such a separation (Sect. 6).

One module refers to several SUV instances, or their respective key encoding. In practice, we distribute the SUVs into at least three modules, separating the terms u, v, w as already done in Fig. 1. In Sect. 5.3, we further decompose the SUV module referring to the w component of size d^2, addressing the metrics 1 and 4. A similar decomposition scenario can be applied to the smaller components u, v of size d. However, we skip the details, since for our current implementation we see no strong need. Depending on parameter choices, such a decomposition might have even disadvantages since the modules become too small, as for the correlation modules.

LPN Modules: For the LPN category, we distinguish between the three components x, y, z of the target Beaver triples, as already done in Fig. 1. Although the costs for the z component are quadratic in c, we do not apply any further decomposition. The point is that the LPN transformation is non-interactive; controlling the Metrics 4 and 5 is less critical than controlling for example latency issues in the interactive phase. Instead, for now, we focus on an efficient implementation of the large degree polynomial operations.

MAC Checks: The MPC operations in the POS, PAYL, SUV, GEN categories require MAC checks for authentication against malicious parties (Sect. 2). While one option is to introduce an extra module for MAC checks, we take the opposite approach and include the MAC checks into the individual modules. The advantage is that this isolation avoids the overhead of coordinating the opened values, see Metric 3, during the Bt-PCG execution.

5.2 Aggregation of SUVs to SSVs

While the SUV protocol from Sect. 3.1 generates individual SUVs, the LPN transformation $\mathcal{T}$ operates on SSVs. At some point this requires to aggregate the vectors $\bar{u}, \bar{v}, \bar{w}$ of SUVs into vectors u, v, w of SSVs, which is a very critical part of the Bt-PCG. While the memory consumption of the intermediate SUVs is very critical in pure numbers (Metric 4), the aggregation itself is intensive in terms of memory access, i.e., to read in the SUVs and to concatenated them following the polynomial tensor product modulo F.

An open question is where to perform the aggregation: As part of SUV, EVAL or as part of LPN? In case of the direct Bt-PCG: As part of the interactive-

or local phase? Since the aggregation is a purely arithmetic tasks, it naturally belongs to the local phase. In the interactive phase, the aggregation might introduce latency. However, for memory efficiency, the aggregation should run as early as possible, i.e., in the interactive phase as part of the SUV generation. In fact, this would reduce the amount of data to be send and stored between different module executions (Metric 4a vs. Metric 4b), respectively the interactive and local phase.

Our design choices is to perform the aggregation in the SUV, EVAL modules, where decomposition of the large SUV instances into several modules respects the aggregation step (Sect. 5.3). For each module, all SUV instance are generated at once, which addresses Metric 1b and 2. However, this implies that the memory consumption for Metric 4b reaches a maximum with respect to the number of SUV instances. In particular, large memory consumption is already an issue inside the SUV module and not only between different module categories. Hence, it is only consequent to perform the aggregation as final step of $\Pi_{\text{SUV}}, \Sigma_{\text{Eval}}$ without further delay.

5.3 Decomposition of the Large SUV Component

The generation of the SUV for the z component as visualized in Fig. 1 demands for a further decomposition, e.g., since the Metrics 2 and 4 scale with d^2 and are prohibitively large for low-level parallelization. The opposite to Fig. 1 would be to decompose the Bt-PCG down to the level of its noise entries, i.e., referring to each of the SUVs in $\bar{w}$ as individual modules, which are then processed individually. As discussed for the small SUV instances, POS, PAYL, this goes however too far.

The optimal solution is somewhere in between, depending on the parameters c, b, t, N. In the following we describe such decompositions for SUV, the other categories GEN, EVAL are similar. Note that SUV includes the aggregation step, where the factor c, of the parameter product $d = c \cdot b \cdot t$, has a special role since it separates individual SSVs. As a natural consequence, we map all SUVs referring to one SSV into the same module.

As a first step, we propose a decomposition with c many modules of size $s = c(bt)^2$, see Fig. 2a. For the Bt-PCG parameter recommendations, it holds $128 \leq s \leq 11552$. Since each of the $2N$ dimensional SUVs takes 67 MB (for $b = 1$), even for $s = 128$ the memory consumption is still prohibitively large for low-level parallelization. Hence we propose to continue the decomposition and to use c^2 many modules of size $(bt)^2$ (Fig. 2b).

Separating the large SUV instances as in Fig. 2a and 2b results in reasonable modules sizes with respect to memory. However, the number of SUV modules is given by c in the first scenario Fig. 2a and by c^2 in the second scenario Fig. 2b, where the recommendations are $c \in \{2, 4, 8\}$. While the first scenario with $c = 2$ employs two parallel computation units for the z component (in the sense of our high-level parallelization), the scenario with $c = 8$ would employ 64 parallel computation units. Even if these are available for the Bt-PCG deployment, setting up 64 modules and coordinating the parallel units, adds some overhead. To address this, we propose to take only c modules of size $s = (bt)^2$, which all run

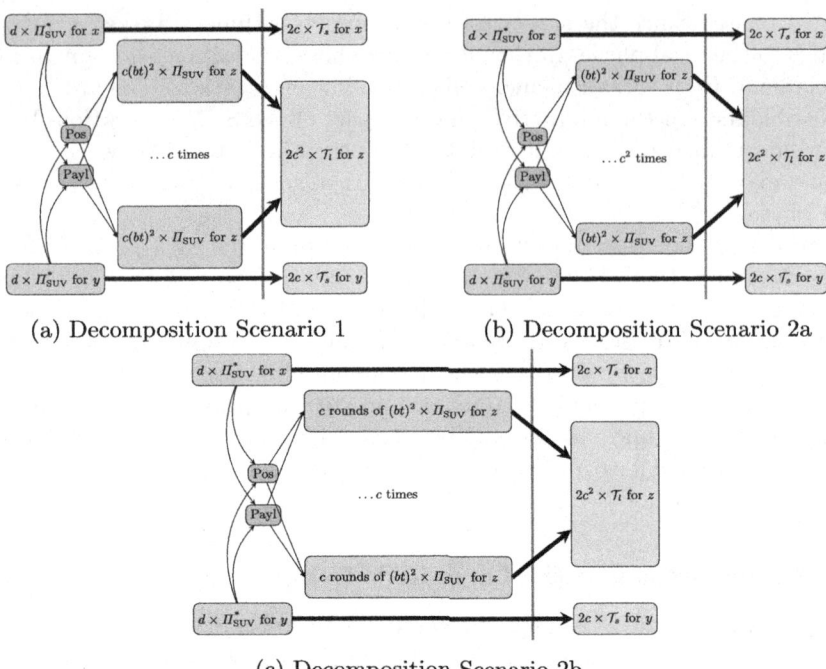

Fig. 2. Decomposition scenarios of the Bt-PCG. An execution starts with the Π^*_{SUV} executions and ends with the output the LPN transformation $\mathcal{T}$. Thin arrows represent the flow of positions or payloads, thick arrows represent vectors of SSVs.

on c rounds (Fig. 2c). The concrete advantage is that compared to a separation to independent modules, the iterative calls share the same infrastructure like communication channels and memory, which reduces the setup costs.

6 Structured Modules and Bt-PCG Programs

The decomposition scenarios, as visualized in Fig. 2 are static in the sense that they do not specify how to schedule the high-level parallelization or how to link the modules at runtime. In preparation of our implementation, the purpose of this section is to formulate a Bt-PCG execution in terms of our module concept. Our implementation is then a straightforward translation into a Bt-PCG script, calling small C programs, one for each module. Hereby, the decomposition scenario is determined by the script, while the Bt-PCG parameters are passed in at run time.

6.1 Bt-PCG Programs

We now sketch one exemplary program for the decomposition scenario Fig. 2c, formalizing the description from Sect. 3.3 in terms of our module concept. To keep the interactive phase as compact as possible we assume to have a strict time-wise separation of the interactive and local phase. Before starting the program, the parties agreed on Fig. 2b, and global PCG parameters N, c, b, t.

- Before running the Bt-PCG make sure to provide ρ and to have sufficiently many correlated randomness available for the internal SPDZ and TinyOT operations. For now, we only provide an insecure fake generation, where one party samples and distributes all correlated randomness. While this is sufficient for testing, a real offline phase for the Bt-PCG is future work.
- **Small SUV instances:** Run the two SUV modules for the x, y component. Since they are independent of each other, they are scheduled parallel, using two different communication channels. According to Sect. 5.3, we model the optimization by SUV* as a specification of SUV modules, which needs to be set by the Bt-PCG program. Each SUV* protocol gives to kinds of outputs. A set of c SSVs, which are large in size for a later use in the local phase; and d secret-shares of positions and payloads, which are subsequently processed in the correlation step.
- **Correlation Step:** Execute the POS and PAYL modules, in parallel. The output are blocks of secret-shared positions and payloads, referring to the blocks of the SUV modules for z. Note that hereby, we implicitly assume that the POS and PAYL modules take care about splitting the output data into respective blocks, which allows a better memory management by implementation specific implementations at an early stage. As a consequence, the Bt-PCG program needs to further specify the two correlation modules, i.e. they require all three parameters c, b, t (not only d) and the decomposition scenario of the z component.
- **Large SUV instances:** Run all large SUV modules, in parallel. Ideally, all modules are scheduled at once, such that the Bt-PCG requires no further coordination and such that there is less latency to wait for all modules to finish in the end. At this point, the transition form Fig. 2b to Fig. 2c becomes relevant: If the number of modules in Fig. 2b is too large for a given number of computation units, one can delegate the coordination of sequential SUV instance calls to the execution inside modules.
- **Local Phase:** Locally run the LPN for the x, y component in parallel, followed by one call for the z component. The point of separating the module for z is that our implementation of LPN internally distributes operations between different computations units (for each of the c^2 SSV), which would be in concurrence to run all three LPN modules at once.

We stress that it is part of the Bt-PCG program to split the correlated randomness into respective blocks following the decomposition. Hereby a security restriction is that each entry of the correlated randomness can be only used once. Furthermore, for efficiency reasons one might assign exactly as much correlated randomness as needed by a module execution, even if this depends on the PCG parameter choices.

6.2 Structured Modules

For an implementation, the module categories SUV, GEN, EVAL, POS, PAYL, LPN are often not precise enough, for example SUV does not distinguish between Π_{SUV} and Π^*_{SUV} or other algorithmic branches, which might be selected depending on available resources. We now describe a respective configuration, either at compile time, i.e., one can select between different module programs for the Bt-PCG program, or at runtime, which can be controlled by program variables. For the latter we extend the modules from Sect. 5 to structured modules. The general template of a structured module is depicted in Fig. 3, where for practical reasons we distinguish between the following variable types:

Variables of a Structured Module

Program: Algorithm $\mathcal{A}$ or protocol $\mathcal{P}$, together with flavors
Configuration: type (small or large), linking mode $\mathcal{L}$
PCG Parameters: $N = 2^n, c, b, t$ and a relevant fraction c_0, b_0, t_0
Files: input files, output files, correlated randomness
Setup: arithmetic data, communication channel
Iteration: r (see Section 5.3, scenario Fig. 2c)

Fig. 3. List of module variables

Program Variables: The program variable specifies the algorithm (LPN, EVAL), or protocol (SUV, GEN, POS, PAYL) that runs inside each module. For generality, one program can have different flavors. Static global flavors, e.g., the choice of the finite field or F, are better addressed at compile-time, while smaller adaptive flavors, e.g., to turn off/on a specific resource or further specify arithmetic choices, might be set at run-time.

Configuration Variables: The main tool to differentiate between different modules are the configuration variables. The type variable differentiates between small and large instances, e.g., between the components x, y and z, which for example comes with different degrees, N or $2N$, and either refers to d or d^2. Furthermore, the type specifies whether to run SUV or SUV* (Gen, Gen*), which in fact only changes the input/output format. In general, the configuration variables simplify the deployment of the Bt-PCG, since there is no need to provide different programs that are almost identical up to a few sub-routines.

PCG Parameters: To set the context, the modules get the global PCG parameters $N = 2^n, c, b, t$ (Sect. 3.4). For example, the value n and b determine the SUV degree N_b to run the SUV generation. However, each module only processes specific instances of one task (e.g. referring to a specific set of SUVs or positions), and these need to be specified as well. For example in Fig. 2c, the large SUVs run on $c(bt)^2$. This can be specified by additionally passing in $b_0 = b, t_0 = t$, and, to indicate that the module execution refers to only one SSV, $c_0 = 1$. Although we do not cover such decompositions in Sect. 5, this can be technically be similarly used to split along the variables b, t. Note that the fractional parameters c_0, b_0, t_0 only describe the scope of the internal instances. We model the proper linking to specific items implicitly through the input variables.

File Variables: The file variable describe the input and output of each module, covering secret-shared positions and payloads, SUVs, DPF keys, the MAC, as well as files with correlated randomness or the LPN parameter ρ. Note that the PCG parameters and configuration variables only specify the task, but that they do not map to specific instances of SUVs, SSVs etc. Instead, the idea is that the file variable include this information, i.e., they only contain data for the relevant instances. It is hence the task of the Bt-PCG program to assign the file variables accordingly, using a proper indexing. Instead, the technical splitting (and merging) of the data into (from) blocks is part of the module executions, e.g., the correlation steps returns individual files referring to each SUV module execution. Still during the correlation, all d^2 positions/payloads are computed in parallel.

Setup Variables: With setup variables we refer to information that is relevant from the perspective of an implementation, e.g., setting up communication channels or providing arithmetic data. Apart from small values like an identifier of the parties and their communication ports, the prime or polynomial F, this might even refer to larger data like lookup tables for the NTT.

Iteration r: In Sect. 5.3 we propose to run the SUV modules on several iteration c in order to reduce setup costs and the number of communication channels. The iteration variable r sets the respective number of iterations. For simplicity we let all iterations refer to the same variables, with the exception that the file variables need to be extended to cover r rounds.

7 Evaluation

The goal of Silentium is to be competitive with previous offline phase implementations in MP-SPDZ [17]. This Section provides benchmarks for a comparison. For a comprehensive evaluation of our decomposition methods and the individual modules, we refer to the evaluation in the full paper version [24]. For all our benchmarks we use two servers in a LAN setting, with 24 cores, 2.80 GHz, and 256 GB RAM.

As already known from theory, the Bt-PCG reduces the communication costs by three orders of magnitude, which for 2^{20} triples means a reduction from a few GB to a few MB, see Tables 1 and 2. To compare the running times, we run several Beaver triple generation protocols in MP-SPDZ [12,17] on the same local servers as our Bt-PCG benchmarks (Table 1). It turns out that our work outperforms the protocols in MP-SPDZ. While the benchmarks for MP-SPDZ range between 400 and 7400 triples per second, our Bt-PCG implementation achieves a throughput between 2900 and 11200 triples per second (Table 2), for the same security level $\lambda = 128$. LowGear is the only protocol that runs faster than some of our Bt-PCG programs. For the limitations of our comparison, we refer to Sect. 1.3.

Table 2 provides further data (see the full version [24] for more details) for different combination of parameters and decomposition, which we derive from the parameters of the theoretical Bt-PCG evaluation [9] and concrete memory limitations of our implementation. This might give an intuition how performance is determined by the small and large SUV instances, or how performance differs between the module categories SUV, GEN, EVAL. An important takeaway from Table 2 is that the time-relation between the interactive phase and local phase highly depends on the parameters and the direct or indirect Bt-PCG approach. All these freedoms need to be considered when it comes to a deployment.

Table 1. Throughput in triples per second, and communication in GB per triple 2^{20} triples for different protocols in MP-SPDZ [17] (named as in [19]). All protocols are with respect to a 128 bit field and 128 bit computational security. (S)HE refers to (somewhat) homomorphic encryption, and OT to oblivious transfer extension.

Protocol	MP-SPDZ Program	Primitives	tr/s	GB
SPDZ 1 [13]	simple-offline.x	SHE	2800	4
High Gear [19]	simple-offline.x -g	semi-HE	2700	4
Low Gear [19]	pairwise-offline.x	semi-HE	7400	2
SPDZ 2 [12]	cnc-offline.x	SHE	300	59
MASCOT [18]	ot-offline.x	OT	1900	47

8 Conclusion and Open Topics

Our work confirms that the Bt-PCG [9] is competitive with previous offline phases in MP-SPDZ [17], which is especially attractive for real-world applications in the cloud context. Towards such applications, we conclude with a list of further optimizations and issues that Silentium leaves open:

- Our benchmarks are on two local servers. How is the performance on two distant (cloud) severs with higher latency? While he Bt-PCG benefits from low communication, delays induced by high memory consumption might become more significant.
- In Sect. 5, we focus on those decomposition scenarios that we actually implement, leaving details about further decomposition techniques as future work. Is it possible to differentiate the decomposition scenarios for different hardware environments and network settings? How can one find the best decomposition scenario in a given context?

Table 2. Running times for the generation of $N = 2^{20}$ Beaver triples for different parameters with the direct and indirect Bt-PCG, including explicit numbers for the parallel execution of the SUV, GEN, EVAL modules with respect to small and large SUV instances. The local percentage is the percentage the local phase takes of the full running time. The last section gives the performance in terms of triples per second (tr/s, rounded) and communication per 2^{20} triples in MB for the direct Bt-PCG. We do not explicitly list the time to run the Cor modules since it takes only about 1 s for all scenarios.

						SUV		GEN	EVAL	LPN		direct		indirect		direct	
λ	d	c	b	t	Fig. 2	small	large	large	large	small	large	total	local	total	local	tr/s	MB
80	32	8	4	1	2b	15	190	159	69	11	78	293	30%	333	49%	3600	0.8
128	40	8	1	5	2b	17	257	188	105	11	78	362	24%	402	50%	2900	1.2
80	40	4	2	5	2b	10	180	111	106	6	20	217	12%	255	53%	4800	1.2
80	32	8	2	2	2b	8	134	115	36	11	78	230	38%	250	51%	4600	0.7
80	32	8	4	1	1	7	32	26	13	11	78	127	69%	135	76%	8300	0.7
80	32	8	4	1	2b	5	102	96	19	11	78	194	45%	208	52%	5400	0.7
128	64	4	8	2	2b	6	112	65	69	6	20	144	17%	165	58%	7300	2.8
128	64	4	16	1	2b	4	63	39	35	6	20	94	28%	106	59%	11200	2.7

- Future work might continue the initial security analysis of the new ring-LPN assumption [9], especially with the goal to provide further parameter sets for the Bt-PCG.
- Silentium does not cover the preprocessing for the internal MPC (TinyOT, SPDZ), which needs to be addressed for any real-world deployment.
- We see high potential in hardware acceleration for arithmetic operations ($\mathcal{T}$, the NTT, PRG) on GPUs or FPGAs for better multi-threading. Hereby, a challenge might be the high data transfer between different devices, especially with respect to latency in the interactive phase.
- Can the techniques of Silentium be applied to other PCGs? Can the modular approach of Silentium be used to compose other types of correlated randomness efficiently (e.g. circuit-depending tuples or multi-party triples).

Acknowledgements. This work has been done as part of the CRYPTECS project that received funding from the German Federal Ministry of Education and Research under Grant Agreement No. 16KIS1441 and from the French National Research Agency under Agreement Grant No. ANR-20-CYAL-0006. The author has no competing interest to declare that are relevant to the content of this article.

A thanks goes to the Robert Bosch GmbH, Research Campus Renningen, where this project was located. A special thanks goes to the master students Daniele de Bernardini, Giulia Salvatori and Enrico Sorbera for supporting in coding.

A Technical Background

A.1 PCGs in the Cloud Context

In general, PCGs [8] are a recent primitive for MPC offline phases with a focus on low communication. PCGs [5,8] can be seen as a distributed generalization of PRGs to expand small seeds into a large batch of correlated pseud-randomness that is close to a given distributed target correlation. A PCG consists of two stages: In a first step, private seeds are generated, which in our use case of an MPC offline phase takes place as actively secure seed generation protocol. In a second step, the seeds can be locally, i.e., without further communication, expanded into a large amount of correlated randomness, e.g., 2^{20} of Beaver triples in case of the Bt-PCG [9]. The point about PCGs is to be compressive in terms of small private seeds, which typically is achieved with an encoding of the target correlation under variations of the learning with error assumption [22]. While the compressive property is challenging to achieve it has two practical advantages, that especially apply to MPC in the cloud context:

- **Low Communication:** When carefully constructed, the small seeds can be generated with low communication, which typically is achieved with function secret sharing [10,11] in the form of distributed point functions (DPF) [15].
- **Reduced Storage:** The storage costs for the seed between the interactive and local phase is cheap, which becomes relevant for large-scale applications with many PCG iterations. Concretely, small seeds enable efficient MPC deployments, where the interactive phase of the PCGs can be scheduled ways before the PCG local phase and the MPC online phase. A dynamic cloud deployment can benefit from that freedom, and for example schedule seed generations at times where high bandwidth is available. Instead, dynamic resource allocation on the cloud allows to schedule local phases just in advance of an MPC online phase activation, which might depend on short-notice user inputs.

A.2 PCGs for Beaver Triples

It is well known that PCGs in general can achieve very good performances [4,6,7,25,26]. However, the construction of PCGs for Beaver triples turns out to be more challenging compared to other forms of correlated randomness like VOLE. The point is that the non-linear multiplicative property of Beaver triples is in contrast with many linear building blocks in the toolbox of PCGs. Apart from initial, but inefficient, approaches [8], there exists only the Bt-PCG construction [9] for two-party Beaver triples with two follow-up works about optimizations [23] and the multi-party setting [1]. Impressively, for the Bt-PCG the generation of 2^{20} Beaver triples (128 bit field) takes only 0.5 to 30 MB per party, which is three orders of magnitude better than for the protocols in MP-SPDZ. However, there exists no implementation, mainly since the Bt-PCG is based on two special purpose primitives [9]. The first is an actively secure generation protocol for authenticated secret-shared scaled unit vectors (SUVs) [23]. So far, concrete efficiency is only based on related work [7]. The second primitive is the ring-LPN assumption over large fields, generalizing the binary-ring LPN assumption [16]. Hereby the challenge is that the ring-LPN assumptions requires large degree polynomial arithmetic, e.g., the Number Theoretic Transforms with degree 2^{20} over a 128-bit field, which is far beyond sizes for comparable applications like the lattice based protocols standardized by NIST[4].

A.3 Indirect and Direct PCG

The initial presentation of the Bt-PCG [9,23] only considers the direct Bt-PCG, without actually naming it as PCG. This has technical reasons since the initial PCG definition [8] is hard to formalize for active security. More concretely, the mechanism for active security at Π_{SUV} introduces a technical leakage. While this leakage is not critical with respect to security, it makes a formalization in terms of the initial PCG definition very challenging. Still in practice, we do not see a point in not using an indirect, two-step approach, or why not to call the whole construction as PCG. What the indirect PCG actually does compared to the PCG all depends on the different output structure of Π_{SUV} and Π_{Gen}. Since the communicated messages are identical, there is nothing to discuss about security (following the simulation based privacy formalization from the UC framework as used for PCGs [9]). Furthermore, Σ_{Eval} has no effect on the security and privacy, since it is only local.

Table 3. Different cost metrics for the direct Bt-PCG. The absolute numbers are per party and with respect to $N = 2^{20}, \nu = 128$, and different parameters (c, b, t).

Nr.	Metric	Asymptotic costs	(8,1,4)	(8,4,1)	(2,1,76)
1a	communication	$\mathcal{O}(d^2(n_b\lambda + \nu))$	0.8 MB	0.8 MB	23.1 MB
1b	exchanged messages	$\mathcal{O}(d^2 n_b)$	$123 \cdot 10^3$	$113 \cdot 10^3$	$2702 \cdot 10^3$
2a	PRG calls (interactive phase)	$\mathcal{O}(d^2 N_b)$	$4.5 \cdot 10^9$	10^9	$87 \cdot 10^9$
2b	$\mathbb{F}$ mults. (interactive phase)	$\mathcal{O}(d^2 N_b)$	$9 \cdot 10^9$	$2 \cdot 10^9$	$195 \cdot 10^9$
3a	opened values	$\mathcal{O}(d^2 n_b)$	$57 \cdot 10^3$	$55 \cdot 10^3$	$1275 \cdot 10^3$
3b	consumed correlated randomness	$\mathcal{O}(d^2(n_b\lambda + \nu))$	1.2 MB	1.2 MB	32.7 MB
4a	size of SSVs $\bar{u}, \bar{v}, \bar{w}$	$\mathcal{O}(d^2 N_b \nu)$	35 GB	9 GB	780 GB
4b	size of SUVs u, v, w	$\mathcal{O}(c^2 N_b \nu)$	1342 MB	1342 MB	134 MB
4c	size of PCG seed	$\mathcal{O}(d^2(n_b\lambda + \nu))$	0.3 MB	0.2 MB	8.7 MB
5	ring mults. ($\mathcal{O}(N \log N)$ $\mathbb{F}$ mults.)	$\mathcal{O}(c^2)$	144	144	12

---

[4] https://csrc.nist.gov/projects/post-quantum-cryptography.

References

1. Abram, D., Scholl, P.: Low-communication multiparty triple generation for SPDZ from Ring-LPN. In: Hanaoka, G., Shikata, J., Watanabe, Y. (eds.) PKC 2022. LNCS, vol. 13177, pp. 221–251. Springer, Cham (2022). https://doi.org/10.1007/978-3-030-97121-2_9
2. Alkadri, N.A., Buchmann, J., El Bansarkhani, R., Krämer, J.: A framework to select parameters for lattice-based cryptography. Cryptology ePrint Archive, Paper 2017/615 (2017)
3. Bendlin, R., Damgård, I., Orlandi, C., Zakarias, S.: Semi-homomorphic encryption and multiparty computation. In: Paterson, K.G. (ed.) EUROCRYPT 2011. LNCS, vol. 6632, pp. 169–188. Springer, Heidelberg (2011). https://doi.org/10.1007/978-3-642-20465-4_11
4. Bombar, M., Couteau, G., Couvreur, A., Ducros, C.: Correlated pseudorandomness from the hardness of quasi-abelian decoding. In: Handschuh, H., Lysyanskaya, A. (eds.) CRYPTO 2023. LNCS, vol. 14084, pp. 567–601. Springer, Cham (2023). https://doi.org/10.1007/978-3-031-38551-3_18
5. Boyle, E., Couteau, G., Gilboa, N., Ishai, Y.: Compressing vector OLE. In: Proceedings of the 2018 ACM SIGSAC Conference on Computer and Communications Security. Association for Computing Machinery, New York, NY, USA (2018)
6. Boyle, E., et al.: Correlated pseudorandomness from expand-accumulate codes. In: Dodis, Y., Shrimpton, T. (eds.) CRYPTO 2022. LNCS, vol. 13508, pp. 603–633. Springer, Cham (2022). https://doi.org/10.1007/978-3-031-15979-4_21
7. Boyle, E., et al.: Efficient two-round OT extension and silent non-interactive secure computation. In: Proceedings of the 2019 ACM SIGSAC Conference on Computer and Communications Security. Association for Computing Machinery, New York, NY, USA (2019)
8. Boyle, E., Couteau, G., Gilboa, N., Ishai, Y., Kohl, L., Scholl, P.: Efficient pseudorandom correlation generators: silent OT extension and More. In: Boldyreva, A., Micciancio, D. (eds.) CRYPTO 2019. LNCS, vol. 11694, pp. 489–518. Springer, Cham (2019). https://doi.org/10.1007/978-3-030-26954-8_16
9. Boyle, E., Couteau, G., Gilboa, N., Ishai, Y., Kohl, L., Scholl, P.: Efficient pseudorandom correlation generators from ring-LPN. In: Micciancio, D., Ristenpart, T. (eds.) CRYPTO 2020. LNCS, vol. 12171, pp. 387–416. Springer, Cham (2020). https://doi.org/10.1007/978-3-030-56880-1_14
10. Boyle, E., Gilboa, N., Ishai, Y.: Function secret sharing. In: Oswald, E., Fischlin, M. (eds.) EUROCRYPT 2015. LNCS, vol. 9057, pp. 337–367. Springer, Heidelberg (2015). https://doi.org/10.1007/978-3-662-46803-6_12
11. Boyle, E., Gilboa, N., Ishai, Y.: Function secret sharing: improvements and extensions. In: Proceedings of the 2016 ACM SIGSAC Conference on Computer and Communications Security. Association for Computing Machinery, New York, NY, USA (2016)
12. Damgård, I., Keller, M., Larraia, E., Pastro, V., Scholl, P., Smart, N.P.: Practical covertly secure MPC for dishonest majority – or: breaking the SPDZ limits. In: Crampton, J., Jajodia, S., Mayes, K. (eds.) ESORICS 2013. LNCS, vol. 8134, pp. 1–18. Springer, Heidelberg (2013). https://doi.org/10.1007/978-3-642-40203-6_1
13. Damgård, I., Pastro, V., Smart, N., Zakarias, S.: Multiparty computation from somewhat homomorphic encryption. In: Safavi-Naini, R., Canetti, R. (eds.) CRYPTO 2012. LNCS, vol. 7417, pp. 643–662. Springer, Heidelberg (2012). https://doi.org/10.1007/978-3-642-32009-5_38

14. Frederiksen, T.K., Keller, M., Orsini, E., Scholl, P.: A unified approach to MPC with preprocessing using OT. In: Iwata, T., Cheon, J.H. (eds.) ASIACRYPT 2015. LNCS, vol. 9452, pp. 711–735. Springer, Heidelberg (2015). https://doi.org/10.1007/978-3-662-48797-6_29
15. Gilboa, N., Ishai, Y.: Distributed point functions and their applications. In: Nguyen, P.Q., Oswald, E. (eds.) EUROCRYPT 2014. LNCS, vol. 8441, pp. 640–658. Springer, Heidelberg (2014). https://doi.org/10.1007/978-3-642-55220-5_35
16. Heyse, S., Kiltz, E., Lyubashevsky, V., Paar, C., Pietrzak, K.: Lapin: an efficient authentication protocol based on Ring-LPN. In: Canteaut, A. (ed.) FSE 2012. LNCS, vol. 7549, pp. 346–365. Springer, Heidelberg (2012). https://doi.org/10.1007/978-3-642-34047-5_20
17. Keller, M.: MP-SPDZ: a versatile framework for multi-party computation. In: Proceedings of the 2020 ACM SIGSAC Conference on Computer and Communications Security. Association for Computing Machinery, New York, NY, USA, (2020)
18. Keller, M., Orsini, E., Scholl, P.: MASCOT: faster malicious arithmetic secure computation with oblivious transfer. In: Proceedings of the 2016 ACM SIGSAC Conference on Computer and Communications Security, pp. 830–842. Association for Computing Machinery, New York, NY, USA (2016)
19. Keller, M., Pastro, V., Rotaru, D.: Overdrive: making SPDZ great again. In: Nielsen, J.B., Rijmen, V. (eds.) EUROCRYPT 2018. LNCS, vol. 10822, pp. 158–189. Springer, Cham (2018). https://doi.org/10.1007/978-3-319-78372-7_6
20. Longa, P., Naehrig, M.: Speeding up the number theoretic transform for faster ideal lattice-based cryptography. In: Foresti, S., Persiano, G. (eds.) CANS 2016. LNCS, vol. 10052, pp. 124–139. Springer, Cham (2016). https://doi.org/10.1007/978-3-319-48965-0_8
21. Nielsen, J.B., Nordholt, P.S., Orlandi, C., Burra, S.S.: A new approach to practical active-secure two-party computation. In: Safavi-Naini, R., Canetti, R. (eds.) CRYPTO 2012. LNCS, vol. 7417, pp. 681–700. Springer, Heidelberg (2012). https://doi.org/10.1007/978-3-642-32009-5_40
22. Regev, O.: On lattices, learning with errors, random linear codes, and cryptography. J. ACM (2009)
23. Rieder, V.: Generation of authenticated secret-shared scaled unit vectors for beaver triples. In: Eichlseder, M., Gambs, S. (eds.) SAC 2024. LNCS, vol. 15516, pp. 54–83. Springer, Cham (2025). https://doi.org/10.1007/978-3-031-82852-2_3
24. Rieder, V.: Silentium: implementation of a pseudorandom correlation generator for beaver triples. Cryptology ePrint Archive, Paper 2025/1013 (2025)
25. Schoppmann, P., Gascón, A., Reichert, L., Raykova, M.: Distributed vector-OLE: improved constructions and implementation. In: Proceedings of the 2019 ACM SIGSAC Conference on Computer and Communications Security, CCS 2019, pp. 1055–1072. Association for Computing Machinery, New York, NY, USA (2019)
26. Yang, K., Weng, C., Lan, X., Zhang, J., Wang, X.: Ferret: fast extension for correlated OT with small communication. In: Proceedings of the 2020 ACM SIGSAC Conference on Computer and Communications Security. Association for Computing Machinery, New York, NY, USA (2020)
27. Yao, A.C.-C.: How to generate and exchange secrets. In: 27th Annual Symposium on Foundations of Computer Science (SFCS 1986), pp. 162–167 (1986)

Towards Privacy and Integrity: SNARK-Driven Verifiable FHE for Outsourced Computation

Rohitkumar R. Upadhyay[1]($^\boxtimes$)[🆔], Sahadeo Padhye[1][🆔], Rajeev Anand Sahu[2][🆔], and Vishal Saraswat[2][🆔]

[1] Department of Mathematics, Motilal Nehru National Institute of Technology Allahabad, Prayagraj 211004, Uttar Pradesh, India
math4rohit@gmail.com, sahadeo@mnnit.ac.in
[2] Bosch Global Software Technologies, Bengaluru 560095, Karnataka, India
{rajeevanand.sahu,vishal.saraswat}@in.bosch.com

Abstract. Fully Homomorphic Encryption (FHE) enables secure computation on encrypted data, preserving confidentiality without requiring decryption. However, FHE alone cannot guarantee the integrity of results computed by potentially untrusted servers, necessitating mechanisms to verify correctness. Succinct Non-Interactive Arguments of Knowledge (SNARKs) have emerged as a powerful tool to address this challenge, enabling efficient verification of computations while maintaining data privacy. This paper provides a systematization of knowledge (SoK) of SNARK-based approaches for verifiable FHE, focusing on recent advancements in designing SNARK-friendly homomorphic schemes and the integration of homomorphic signatures and Message Authentication Codes (MACs), many of which leverage SNARKs for enhanced security. We analyze the trade-offs between privacy, efficiency, and compatibility with modern FHE schemes, offering insights into their practical deployment. Our SoK highlights the transformative potential of these techniques for privacy-preserving applications, including secure cloud computing, machine learning, and distributed data processing.

Keywords: Fully Homomorphic Encryption · Verifiable Computation · SNARKs · Homomorphic Signatures · Homomorphic MACs · Privacy-Preserving Computing

1 Introduction

In an era where data-driven applications dominate industries from healthcare to finance, the outsourcing of computationally intensive tasks to remote servers has become ubiquitous. This trend, however, introduces significant risks, as clients must trust untrusted entities to process sensitive data accurately and securely. Verifiable computation has emerged as a cornerstone of modern cryptography, aiming to ensure both the *privacy* of data and the *correctness* of results in such adversarial settings. This dual objective is critical for applications requiring confidentiality and integrity, such as privacy-preserving cloud computing, secure machine learning, and decentralized data processing.

Two pivotal cryptographic primitives underpin this challenge: Fully Homomorphic Encryption (FHE) and zero-knowledge Succinct Non-Interactive Arguments of Knowledge (zk-SNARKs). FHE, pioneered by Gentry [34], enables arbitrary computations on encrypted data without decryption, making it a cornerstone for privacy-preserving outsourcing. Yet, its malleability allowing undetectable ciphertext modifications leaves computational integrity vulnerable. In contrast, zk-SNARKs provide succinct, efficiently verifiable proofs of correctness for complex computations, encoding circuits as polynomial identities or quadratic constraints like Rank-1 Constraint Systems (R1CS) [46,49]. The central question driving this field is: *can FHE and zk-SNARKs be synergistically combined to achieve verifiable computation over encrypted data, ensuring both privacy and integrity?*

A parallel research avenue focuses on *authenticated homomorphic computation*, augmenting FHE with mechanisms to verify result integrity without decryption. Homomorphic Message Authentication Codes (MACs) [15,25,33] and homomorphic signatures [8] attach authentication tags that persist through homomorphic operations. Three paradigms have emerged:

– **Encrypt-and-MAC (EaM):** Generates a ciphertext and an unencrypted MAC tag from the same plaintext, requiring the MAC to support homomorphic operations and ensure semantic security [43].
– **Encrypt-then-MAC (EtM):** Applies a MAC to FHE ciphertexts, using homomorphic hash functions or pseudorandom functions (PRFs) to align with ciphertext operations, thus relaxing privacy requirements for the MAC [5,25].
– **MAC-then-Encrypt (MtE):** Authenticates plaintexts before encryption, with verification post-decryption, often at high computational cost due to recomputation requirements [15,33].

Homomorphic signatures further enable *public verification*, allowing clients to sign data before outsourcing, with servers updating signatures during computation. Fully Homomorphic Signatures (FHS) support arbitrary functions, and recent constructions leverage SNARKs for recursive verifiability and compact proofs [37]. These schemes often rely on extractable SNARKs and recursive composition, necessitating strong assumptions like the Knowledge of Exponent Assumption (KEA) or Algebraic Group Model (AGM), and typically require a trusted setup, introducing potential security concerns.

Combining FHE with zk-SNARKs presents significant technical challenges, primarily due to algebraic incompatibilities. FHE schemes, grounded in lattice assumptions, operate over polynomial rings $\mathcal{R}_Q = \mathbb{Z}_Q[X]/\langle X^N + 1\rangle$ [45], with schemes like BGV [12], BFV [11,24], CKKS [20], and TFHE [22] employing diverse moduli Q-large and composite for BGV/BFV/CKKS, or smaller for TFHE. Conversely, SNARKs operate over prime-order fields $\mathbb{F}_p$ with large primes (e.g., 256-bit p) [27,38]. Emulating ring arithmetic in SNARK circuits is computationally intensive, and FHE maintenance operations such as modulus switching, key switching, rescaling, or bootstrapping are non-arithmetic, posing significant representation challenges in SNARK-friendly constraints like R1CS or Customizable Constraint Systems (CCS) [49].

Two primary approaches have emerged to address these challenges:

- **Plaintext-Domain Verification:** Schemes like [2,28] verify computations over plaintexts under FHE, avoiding emulation of non-arithmetic operations. Utilizing the HE-IOP paradigm [2], these methods apply FHE to the information-theoretic phase of SNARKs, such as the Fast Reed-Solomon Interactive Oracle Proof (FRI) [4], enabling full FHE functionality, including bootstrapping. However, they often require private verification, limiting public applicability, and may risk information leakage if verification outcomes are exposed, potentially enabling decryption oracle attacks.
- **Ciphertext-Domain Verification:** General-purpose SNARKs verify computations directly over ciphertexts [25,41], ensuring end-to-end privacy but incurring significant efficiency costs due to algebraic mismatches. Specialized SNARKs, such as [6,29], support native ring operations, with lattice-based SNARKs [39] offering post-quantum security and compatibility with smaller moduli. However, these schemes often involve large trusted setups, designated-verifier models, or restrictions to constant-depth circuits.

1.1 Applications of Verifiable Fully Homomorphic Encryption

Verifiable FHE enables secure outsourced computation across diverse domains, including cloud computing, machine learning, decentralized systems, and secure multi-party computation (MPC). For example, in privacy-preserving cloud computing, clients can encrypt sensitive data using FHE schemes such as BGV [12] or CKKS [20] and delegate computations to untrusted servers. Correctness is ensured through SNARKs [29] or homomorphic MACs [15]. In secure machine learning, hospitals can train models on encrypted patient data, utilizing SNARK proofs [2] to verify gradient computations, although scalability challenges remain with private verification schemes [14]. In decentralized systems, such as blockchain, verifiable FHE supports private smart contracts, with the Encrypt-then-MAC paradigm [25] aligning well with FHE's algebraic structure, despite limitations posed by trusted setups [29]. In MPC, which often builds on FHE [51,52], verifiable FHE facilitates collaborative computations, such as secure auctions, with lattice-based SNARKs [39] providing post-quantum security. However, high computational costs for maintenance operations [41] necessitate optimizations like proof batching [6].

Practical deployment of verifiable FHE requires balancing efficiency, security, and scalability, particularly for real-time or iterative applications like machine learning and blockchain-based smart contracts. Innovative techniques, such as folding schemes (e.g., LatticeFold [7]) and proof batching, reduce verification overhead, while alternative proof systems, such as Quasi-Adaptive NIZKs [40], offer potential efficiency gains. Nevertheless, reliance on trusted setups, strong cryptographic assumptions, and the computational burden of SNARKs highlight the need for novel FHE-tailored cryptographic primitives.

1.2 Our Contribution

This paper surveys the landscape of verifiable FHE, providing a comprehensive analysis of techniques that integrate FHE with zk-SNARKs, homomorphic MACs, and signatures. We offer a detailed taxonomy of authentication mechanisms, an in-depth study of

SNARK-based FHS, a comparative evaluation of plaintext- and ciphertext-domain verification, and a discussion of applications and future directions, guiding the development of secure, scalable protocols for privacy-preserving computation.

2 Preliminaries

2.1 Succinct Non-interactive ARgument of Knowledge (SNARK)

We define a *Succinct Non-interactive ARgument of Knowledge (SNARK)* in the preprocessing model with a designated verifier. A SNARK consists of the following three probabilistic polynomial-time (PPT) algorithms:

- **Setup**($1^\lambda, CS$) → (crs, st): Given a security parameter λ and a constraint system CS (e.g., in R1CS form), this algorithm outputs a common reference string (CRS) crs and a verification state st.
- **Prover**(crs, $\mathbf{x}, \mathbf{w}$) → π: Given the CRS crs, a public statement $\mathbf{x}$, and a witness $\mathbf{w}$ satisfying $CS(\mathbf{x}, \mathbf{w}) = 1$, this algorithm produces a proof π.
- **Verifier**(st, $\mathbf{x}, \pi$) → b: Given the verification state st, a statement $\mathbf{x}$, and a proof π, this algorithm outputs a verification bit $b \in \{0, 1\}$, indicating acceptance (1) or rejection (0).

These algorithms must satisfy the standard correctness properties of *completeness* and *knowledge soundness*:

Completeness. A SNARK scheme is *complete* if, for all λ, any valid statement-witness pair $(\mathbf{x}, \mathbf{w})$ satisfying $CS(\mathbf{x}, \mathbf{w}) = 1$, and (crs, st) ← Setup($1^\lambda, CS$), it holds that:

$$\Pr\left[\text{Verifier}(\text{st}, \mathbf{x}, \pi) = 1 \mid \pi \leftarrow \text{Prover}(\text{crs}, \mathbf{x}, \mathbf{w}) \right] = 1.$$

Knowledge Soundness. A SNARK satisfies *knowledge soundness* if for every PPT adversarial prover Prover*, there exists a PPT extractor Extr such that for any security parameter λ, R1CS instance CS, and auxiliary input z, we have

$$\Pr\left[\begin{array}{c} \text{Verifier}(\text{st}, \mathbf{x}, \pi^*) = 1 \\ \wedge\ CS(\mathbf{x}, \mathbf{w}^*) \neq 1 \end{array} \;\middle|\; \begin{array}{c} (\text{crs}, \text{st}) \leftarrow \text{Setup}(1^\lambda, CS) \\ (\pi^*, \mathbf{x}) \leftarrow \text{Prover}^*(\text{crs}; z) \\ \mathbf{w}^* \leftarrow \text{Extr}(\text{crs}; z) \end{array} \right] \leq \text{negl}(\lambda).$$

Succinctness. A SNARK is *succinct* if the proof size is poly($\lambda + \log |CS|$), and the verifier runs in time poly($\lambda + |\mathbf{x}| + \log |CS|$).

2.2 Fully Homomorphic Encryption (FHE)

FHE is a cryptographic primitive that enables computations on encrypted data without decryption. The result remains encrypted, decrypting to the same output as if the computation were performed on plaintext. This property supports secure data processing in untrusted environments, such as cloud computing, preserving data privacy. Applications include secure outsourcing in healthcare, finance, and machine learning.

The concept of homomorphic encryption was introduced by Rivest et al. in 1978 [48], with early schemes limited to either additive or multiplicative operations. In 2009, Gentry [34] proposed the first FHE scheme, capable of evaluating arbitrary circuits on encrypted data, marking a significant milestone for secure computation.

An FHE scheme evaluates a circuit C on encrypted inputs, producing an encrypted output that decrypts to $C(m)$ for a plaintext m. We describe the BGV scheme [12] as an example, noting that BFV [11,24] and CKKS [20] share similar algebraic foundations. For simplicity, we present a symmetric-key version; public-key variants follow standard transformations.

Algebraic Setup. Let $\mathcal{R} = \mathbb{Z}[X]/\langle X^N + 1 \rangle$ for $N = 2^k$, a cyclotomic ring. Define the ciphertext modulus $Q = \prod_{i=0}^{L} q_i$ with distinct primes q_i, yielding $\mathcal{R}_Q = \mathbb{Z}_Q[X]/\langle X^N + 1 \rangle$. Ciphertexts are polynomials in $\mathcal{R}_Q[Y]$, represented as $c(Y) = \sum_{i=0}^{u-1} c_i Y^i$, where Y is an indeterminate for bookkeeping. Let t be the plaintext modulus, defining $\mathcal{R}_t = \mathbb{Z}_t[X]/\langle X^N + 1 \rangle$. An error distribution χ_{err} over $\mathcal{R}$ has standard deviation σ. A ciphertext $c(Y)$ decrypts to $m \in \mathcal{R}_t$ if:

$$c(\text{sk}) \mod Q = te + m, \quad e \in \mathcal{R},$$

where e is a small error term ensuring $(c(\text{sk}) \mod Q) \mod t = m$.

FHE Scheme Algorithms. An FHE scheme HE includes:

- **HE.ParamGen**($1^\lambda, L$): Outputs parameters (N, Q, σ, t) for λ-bit security and circuit depth L, defining rings $\mathcal{R}$, $\mathcal{R}_Q$, and $\mathcal{R}_t$.
- **HE.KeyGen**(1^λ): Generates secret key sk and relinearization key rlk under params.
- **HE.Enc**$_{\text{sk}}(m)$: Encrypts $m \in \mathcal{R}_t$ by sampling $a \leftarrow \mathcal{R}_Q$, $e \leftarrow \chi_{\text{err}}$, and computing $b = -a \cdot \text{sk} + te + m$. Outputs $c(Y) = b + aY$.

Homomorphic Operations. For ciphertexts $c_i(Y) = \text{HE.Enc}(m_i)$, the evaluation HE.Eval$(C, \{c_i\})$ yields $c'(Y)$ such that HE.Dec$(c') = C(\{m_i\})$. Key operations are:

- **HE.Add**(c_0, c_1): Computes $c_{\text{add}}(Y) = c_0(Y) + c_1(Y)$, decrypting to $m_0 + m_1$ with linear noise growth.
- **HE.Mult**(c_0, c_1): Computes $c_{\text{mult}}(Y) = c_0(Y) \cdot c_1(Y)$, a degree-2 polynomial, decrypting to $m_0 \cdot m_1$ with quadratic noise growth.
- **HE.MultPtxt**(c_0, m_1): Computes $c_{\text{multPtxt}}(Y) = m_1 \cdot c_0(Y)$, maintaining degree with linear noise growth.

Noise Management. To ensure correctness after multiplications, FHE employs:

- **Relinearization:** Reduces ciphertext degree using rlk, e.g., converting $c(Y) = c_0 + c_1 Y + c_2 Y^2$ to $c'(Y) = c_0' + c_1' Y$.
- **Modulus Switching:** Scales modulus Q to $Q^\star = Q/q_i$, reducing noise to maintain decryption accuracy.

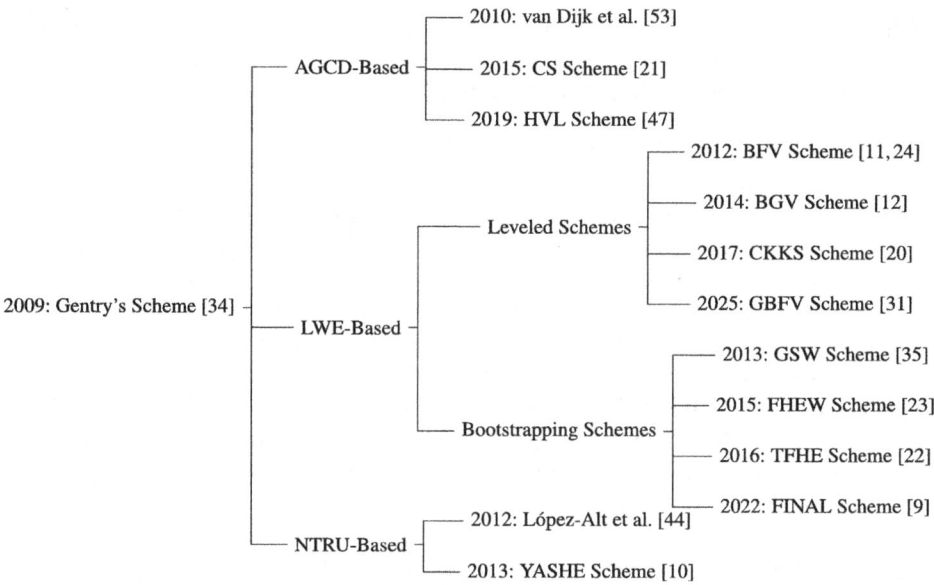

Fig. 1. Timeline of FHE schemes

Figure 1 traces the evolution of FHE schemes from Gentry's 2009 breakthrough [34], which used ideal lattices. This spurred advancements in AGCD-based schemes (e.g., CS, HVL), LWE-based leveled schemes (e.g., BFV, BGV, CKKS), and bootstrapping-efficient schemes (e.g., GSW, FHEW, TFHE). Recent schemes like GBFV and FINAL emphasize practical efficiency. Despite theoretical advances, FHE faces challenges like large ciphertexts and computational overhead, driving ongoing research for optimized implementations.

3 Verifiable FHE by Authentication Mechanisms

Traditional FHEs provide robust privacy guarantees, but they do not ensure the integrity of computed results inherently. Authentication mechanisms such as Message Authentication Codes (MACs) and homomorphic signatures have been developed to verify the correctness of computations performed on encrypted data. This section explores the integration of these mechanisms with FHE, detailing their evolution, key paradigms, and theoretical advancements in ensuring both privacy and integrity.

3.1 Homomorphic MACs

Homomorphic MACs extend traditional MACs to support homomorphic operations, allowing verification of computations on authenticated data without requiring decryption or recomputation. These MACs are designed to remain valid under specific operations (e.g., addition and multiplication), ensuring the integrity for FHE-evaluated ciphertexts of FHE ciphertexts. Three primary paradigms have emerged for integrating MACs with FHE, each offering distinct trade-offs in expressiveness, verification efficiency, and compatibility with modern FHE schemes.

- **Encrypt-and-MAC (EaM):** In this approach, a ciphertext and a MAC tag are generated from the same plaintext and processed independently. The MAC must support the same homomorphic operations as the FHE scheme and ensure semantic security since it is not encrypted. Li et al. [43] proposed an EaM scheme using multilinear maps, supporting addition and multiplication. However, this construction does not account for critical FHE maintenance operations such as relinearization, modulus switching, or key switching. Extending the expressive power of EaM-based MACs while preserving strong security properties remains a significant challenge.
- **Encrypt-then-MAC (EtM):** Here, data is first encrypted using FHE, and a MAC is then applied to the resulting ciphertext. The MAC does not need to preserve privacy but must support homomorphic operations over ciphertexts, including FHE maintenance operations. Fiore et al. [25] implemented this using bilinear pairings, leveraging homomorphic hash functions and amortized PRFs [5] to bridge the algebraic gap between ciphertext rings and pairing groups. However, their construction is limited to quadratic circuits (i.e., circuits with at most one multiplication gate), and its applicability to deeper circuits remains uncertain.
- **MAC-then-Encrypt (MtE):** In this paradigm, the plaintext is first authenticated with a MAC, and the authenticated data is then encrypted using FHE. Since MAC verification occurs on plaintexts, the MAC does not need to support ciphertext maintenance operations. Gennaro and Wichs [33] proposed an early MtE-based integrity scheme, but it required recomputation for verification, rendering it inefficient. Catalano and Fiore [15] improved verification efficiency but were limited to bounded-depth circuits. More recently, Chatel et al. [17] introduced a generalized scheme supporting arbitrary circuits, compatible with modern FHE schemes, marking a significant advancement.

3.2 Homomorphic Signatures

Homomorphic signature schemes enable the derivation of a valid signature for a computed message $f(m_1, \ldots, m_n)$ given signatures $\sigma_1, \ldots, \sigma_n$ for inputs $m_1, \ldots, m_n$. Verification ensures that the derived signature σ_f corresponds to $f(m_1, \ldots, m_n)$ under a public verification key. Unforgeability guarantees that no adversary can produce a valid signature on an incorrect result $y \neq f(m_1, \ldots, m_n)$, thus authenticating both the input messages and the computation.

A scheme supporting both addition and multiplication is termed *fully homomorphic*, enabling evaluation of any polynomial or Boolean function. Early constructions were limited in scope: Agrawal et al. [1] proposed an additive-only homomorphic MAC, while Boneh and Freeman [8] extended this to constant-degree polynomials. Catalano et al. [16] enhanced efficiency for specific functions. Gennaro and Wichs [33] introduced the first fully homomorphic MAC based on FHE, followed by Catalano and Fiore's more efficient schemes for certain function classes [15]. Gorbunov et al. [37]

developed the first leveled Fully Homomorphic Signature (FHS) scheme, supporting arbitrary circuits up to a predefined depth.

3.3 FHS from SNARKs

Gennaro and Wichs [33] and Gorbunov et al. [37] conjectured that Fully Homomorphic Signatures (FHS) could be constructed using SNARKs for NP. Although no complete proof was provided, this conjecture has inspired approaches combining SNARKs with standard digital signatures.

One such construction operates as follows. Let $\Sigma = $ (KeyGen, Sign, Verify) be a standard digital signature scheme. Given signed messages $\{(m_i, \sigma_i)\}_{i \in [n]}$, a prover computes $y = f(m_1, \ldots, m_n)$ and generates a SNARK proof for the NP statement:

$$\exists \{m_i, \sigma_i\} \text{ such that } f(m_1, \ldots, m_n) = y \text{ and Verify}(\text{vk}, m_i, \sigma_i) = 1 \; \forall i.$$

The SNARK proof serves as a signature on y, leveraging SNARK succinctness for short, efficiently verifiable signatures. The extractability of SNARKs ensures that the unforgeability of the FHS reduces to that of the underlying signature scheme.

This construction supports *single-step* computation. For *multi-hop* computation—where further functions are applied to previously signed outputs—recursive SNARKs are employed. Signatures are organized into levels:

- **Level-0:** Standard signatures $\sigma_i = \text{Sign}(\text{sk}, m_i)$.
- **Level-j:** A SNARK proof attesting that $y = g(m_0, m_1)$ for a gate g, applied to messages m_0, m_1 with signatures σ_0, σ_1 at level $j - 1$, such that

$$\text{Verify}(\text{vk}, m_b, \sigma_b) = 1 \quad \text{for } b \in \{0, 1\}.$$

Security in this recursive setting relies on SNARK extractability at each level, requiring extractors to run in time $t_\mathcal{A} + \text{poly}(\lambda)$. Currently, only SNARKs based on strong assumptions, such as the Knowledge of Exponent Assumption (KEA) or the Algebraic Group Model (AGM), satisfy this requirement.

4 Verifiable FHE from SNARKs

The integration of FHE with SNARKs has emerged as a powerful approach to achieve verifiable computation (VC) on encrypted data, ensuring both privacy and correctness. This section explores the evolution of this field, detailing foundational contributions, modern advancements, and the two primary paradigms SNARK-FHE and FHE-SNARK that define the landscape of verifiable FHE.

The journey begins with early efforts to combine FHE and verifiable computation. Gennaro, Gentry, and Parno [32] laid a foundational result by proposing a non-interactive VC scheme that merges garbled circuits with FHE. Their construction supports arbitrary functions while preserving input and output privacy against an untrusted server. However, it relies on the full power of FHE to evaluate garbled circuits homomorphically, incurring significant computational overhead due to the complexity of the operations involved.

Building on this, Goldwasser et al. [36] introduced a VC protocol using a succinct single-key functional encryption scheme. While preserving input privacy, their approach does not protect output privacy and is limited to functions with single-bit outputs. The scheme employs multiple instances of attribute-based encryption for expressive predicates, but its constrained output space limits its practicality for general-purpose computations.

Fiore, Gennaro, and Pastro [25] advanced the field by combining FHE with a VC scheme tailored for quadratic functions. Leveraging homomorphic MACs, their construction is efficient for computations of multiplicative depth one. However, it requires a secret MAC key for verification, restricting its use to scenarios where the client and verifier are the same or share keys. Despite offering input and output privacy, the designated-verifier model and depth limitation hinder broader applicability.

A significant milestone came with Parno et al.'s Pinocchio system [46], a practically efficient SNARK that inspired further research into verifiable encrypted computation. Building on this, Fiore, Nitulescu, and Pointcheval [26] proposed a scheme supporting public verifiability and higher-degree arithmetic circuits. Their approach reduces verification of computations over polynomial rings to scalar arithmetic circuits using SNARKs, enabling modular composition and zero-knowledge evaluation at random points. However, it is limited to inefficient FHE schemes over specific polynomial rings and does not support advanced FHE operations like bootstrapping or rescaling.

More recently, Ganesh et al. [29] introduced Rinocchio, a SNARK designed for arithmetic over polynomial rings $\mathbb{R}_q = \mathbb{Z}_q[x]/R(x)$, aligning closely with modern FHE schemes. Representing computations as Quadratic Ring Programs (QRP), Rinocchio supports FHE-specific operations like modulo switching. However, it remains a designated-verifier scheme and lacks input hiding and zero-knowledge guarantees.

The theoretical framework for verifiable FHE was formalized in [41], utilizing the Rinocchio SNARK [29] and the BGV FHE scheme. By operating over the same ring $\mathcal{R}_Q$, this approach eliminates the need to simulate arithmetic, allowing a single proof to verify the entire computation. A zero-knowledge variant of Rinocchio enables private server inputs, while a Regev-style RLWE encoding optimizes batching of N plaintexts into a single ciphertext, significantly improving efficiency over earlier constructions [41].

In contrast, Atapoor et al. [3] also adopt the BGV scheme for its simplicity, noting compatibility with BFV or CKKS schemes. Their innovation lies in leveraging the factorization $Q = \prod_{i=0}^{L} q_i$, where each q_i is a small prime (approximately 30 bits). Using the Chinese Remainder Theorem (CRT), they establish the isomorphism:

$$\mathcal{R}_Q = \frac{\mathbb{Z}_Q[X]}{\langle X^N + 1 \rangle} \cong \prod_{i=0}^{L} \mathcal{R}_{q_i} = \prod_{i=0}^{L} \frac{\mathbb{Z}_{q_i}[X]}{\langle X^N + 1 \rangle}. \tag{1}$$

Operating over smaller rings $\mathcal{R}_{q_i}$ avoids the inefficiency of multi-precision arithmetic over large Q. They propose generating SNARK proofs over fields $\mathbb{Z}_{q_i}$ to verify computations in $\mathcal{R}_{q_i}$, reducing proofs to polynomial reductions modulo $X^N + 1$. To address the mismatch with typical SNARKs over large prime fields $\mathbb{F}_p$ (e.g., $p \approx 2^{256}$), they employ a lattice-based SNARK [39] that supports smaller moduli and offers post-quantum security.

BGV's maintenance operations, such as modulus switching and key switching, pose challenges due to their non-arithmetic nature. To address this, Atapoor et al. structure the computation as layered circuits, with each layer ending in a single multiplication and synchronized outputs serving as inputs to maintenance operations across all $\mathcal{R}_{q_i}$. The computation over $\mathcal{R}_Q$ is expressed as:

$$C_0 \circ M_1 \circ \cdots \circ M_{L-1} \circ C_{L-1} \circ M_L \circ C_L,$$

where C_i denotes the i-th computation layer and M_i the maintenance operations. SNARK proofs are generated for C_L over each $\mathbb{Z}_{q_j}$, and for M_{i+1} and $C_i \circ M_{i+1}$ for $j = 0, \ldots, L$ and $i = 0, \ldots, L-1$, with optimizations to minimize the number of proofs.

Two distinct paradigms have emerged for verifiable computation with FHE: SNARK-FHE and FHE-SNARK.

- **SNARK-FHE (SNARK outside FHE):** The server performs homomorphic computations on encrypted data using FHE and generates a SNARK proof to attest correctness [3,25,41]. This approach simulates secure two-party computation, ensuring verifiability without compromising verifier privacy.
- **FHE-SNARK (FHE outside SNARK):** The server uses FHE to homomorphically evaluate both the target computation and the proof-generation algorithm, producing a ciphertext that decrypts to a valid SNARK proof [2,28]. This may permit limited leakage of verification outcomes.

Functionally, SNARK-FHE avoids the one-bit leakage possible in FHE-SNARK, offering stronger verifier privacy. However, it incurs significant overhead due to the need to encode complex FHE operations (e.g., bootstrapping, gadget decomposition) within SNARK-friendly arithmetic. FHE schemes supporting strong privacy (e.g., IND-CPA-D security [42]) require frequent bootstrapping or conservative parameters, degrading performance [18,19].

The efficiency gap between paradigms stems from algebraic mismatches. FHE ciphertexts operate in cyclotomic rings $R_q = \mathbb{Z}_q[X]/(X^N + 1)$, with large q (e.g., 2^{32} or 2^{64}) and N (e.g., 2048 or 32768), while SNARKs typically use prime fields $\mathbb{F}_p$ with $p \approx 2^{128}$ or 2^{256}. Simulating FHE operations in SNARKs is computationally expensive. Conversely, FHE-SNARK aligns plaintext arithmetic with FHE's capabilities, enabling efficient proof generation within the encrypted domain, often outperforming SNARK-FHE by orders of magnitude.

5 Analysis of Verifiable FHE Computations

Verifiable FHE computation schemes can be broadly categorized into two types: those generating proofs over plaintexts under homomorphic encryption (HE) and those operating directly on ciphertexts. Both approaches aim to achieve succinct verification, where the verifier's workload is sublinear in the computation size, a crucial requirement for practical deployment.

Plaintext-based approaches, such as HE-IOPs described in [2], generate proofs over encrypted plaintexts. Recent advancements [2,28,30] optimize this method by applying HE solely to the information-theoretic component of a SNARK, such as the Fast

Reed-Solomon Interactive Oracle Proof (FRI) protocol [4]. This avoids emulating the full HE stack within the SNARK, improving efficiency and supporting all HE operations, including bootstrapping. However, plaintext-based schemes face notable limitations. They are incompatible with approximate HE schemes like CKKS [20] due to misaligned plaintext spaces with IOP-based proof systems. Additionally, verification requires decrypting the proof, which may leak the result unless the verifier remains private. This reliance on a weak adversary model limits security, as exposure of the verification result could compromise the IND-CPA security of the HE scheme.

The second approach proves the correctness of homomorphic computations directly over ciphertexts using general-purpose SNARKs or other verifiable computation (VC) systems [25]. This method offers stronger privacy guarantees, even against adaptive adversaries with access to a verification oracle, and supports a wider range of HE schemes, including CKKS. However, ciphertext-based proofs impose significant computational overhead on the prover. A key challenge is aligning the algebraic structure of HE ciphertexts typically elements of polynomial rings $R_q = \mathbb{Z}_q[X]/(X^N + 1)$ with SNARKs, which are optimized for large prime fields. Furthermore, HE maintenance operations (e.g., modulus switching, key switching, rescaling) involve non-arithmetic steps, such as rounding or division, which are costly to emulate in SNARK circuits. For example, [41] estimates that proving a single ciphertext multiplication requires approximately three billion R1CS constraints.

To address these inefficiencies, specialized SNARKs for R_q have been developed. Bois et al. [6] proposed a scheme supporting efficient verification of algebraic operations over R_q, but it is limited to constant-depth circuits and basic RingLWE-based HE schemes [13]. Rinocchio [29] enhances support for complex computations over R_q, but it relies on costly bit-decomposition for non-arithmetic operations, assumes non-falsifiable security models, requires a secret key for verification, and depends on a large trusted setup.

5.1 Comparison of State-of-the-Art Schemes

Table 1 presents a comparative analysis of recent verifiable computation schemes designed for RingLWE-based homomorphic encryption (HE). The comparison spans key dimensions, including support for ciphertext-level arithmetic and maintenance operations, compatibility with different HE schemes, verifier type (public or private), and the overall architectural integration of SNARK and FHE components.

In this context, "Ctxt" refers to ciphertext-level operations. **Arithmetic** includes basic homomorphic operations such as ciphertext addition and multiplication. **Maintenance** encompasses advanced operations required for HE scheme functionality, such as modulus switching and key switching. Regarding architecture, **SNARK-FHE** schemes implement FHE functionality within a SNARK circuit, whereas **FHE-SNARK** schemes apply SNARKs to computations performed homomorphically within FHE.

General-purpose SNARK-based constructions, such as that of Knabenhans et al. [41], provide broad compatibility by simulating FHE operations within SNARKs. However, this generality incurs high computational cost. More specialized approaches, including Bois et al. [6] and Ganesh et al. [29], provide native support for ciphertext

Table 1. Comparison of verifiable fully homomorphic encryption (FHE) schemes.

Scheme	Ctxt Arithmetic	Ctxt Maintenance	Supported HE Schemes	Verifier Type	Type
Knabenhans et al. [41]	✗	✗	Any	Public	SNARK-FHE
Bois et al. [6]	✓	✗	Exact	Public	SNARK-FHE
Ganesh et al. [29]	✓	✗	Any	Private	SNARK-FHE
Atapoor et al. [3]	✓	✓	Exact	Private	SNARK-FHE
Garg et al. [30]	✓	✓	Exact	Private	FHE-SNARK
Aranha et al. [2]	✓	✓	Exact	Private	FHE-SNARK
Cascudo et al. [14]	✓	✓	Any	Public	SNARK-FHE
Gama et al. [28]	✓	✓	Exact	Private	FHE-SNARK

arithmetic over R_q, though they lack support for maintenance operations and differ in verifier requirements (public vs. private).

The scheme proposed by Atapoor et al. [3] advances this line by adding native support for ciphertext maintenance, albeit requiring a private verifier. FHE-SNARK designs such as those by Garg et al. [30] and Aranha et al. [2] achieve full HE functionality with efficient, non-interactive verification, suitable for client-side verifiability.

Cascudo et al. [14] offers a compelling design point by supporting public verification, efficient ciphertext maintenance, and compatibility with arbitrary Ring LWE-based schemes positioning it as a strong candidate for practical and scalable verifiable HE.

5.2 Limitations and Future Research Directions

Verifiable FHE is a rapidly evolving field with significant potential but notable challenges. Current constructions, such as those in [3], leverage SNARKs like [39], which offer faster prover and verifier times compared to classical SNARKs [38]. However, limitations include high setup costs, large memory footprints due to proof and Common Reference String (CRS) sizes, and designated-verifier restrictions. Additionally, the lack of reusable knowledge soundness where multiple proofs under the same CRS and secret key are insecure against a verification oracle restricts flexibility.

Future research should focus on developing SNARKs tailored for verifiable FHE, addressing these challenges while aligning with the parameter regime of [3]. Incorporating proof batching mechanisms could reduce verifier workload by consolidating multiple SNARK proofs. Additionally, replacing recursive proofs with folding schemes, as proposed in [50], could enhance efficiency for Incrementally Verifiable Computation (IVC). For instance, LatticeFold [7] supports Customizable Constraint Systems (CCS) [49], enabling succinct expression of complex non-ring operations, such as modular reductions or numerical approximations.

The inherent costs of FHE, including high memory usage and limited throughput, combined with SNARK overhead, render current verifiable FHE constructions inefficient for real-world applications. Reducing SNARK-related costs to be negligible relative to FHE is a critical goal. Since most SNARKs are designed for blockchain or general-purpose verifiability, developing SNARKs optimized for verifiable FHE could yield significant improvements. Exploring alternative Non-Interactive Zero-Knowledge (NIZK) proof systems, such as Quasi-Adaptive NIZKs [40], may also provide context-specific advantages. Ultimately, designing novel cryptographic primitives tailored for verifiable FHE could offer a transformative solution, enhancing both efficiency and security.

6 Conclusion

In this SoK, we have reviewed the integration of Fully Homomorphic Encryption (FHE) with verifiable computation techniques, including Succinct Non-Interactive Arguments of Knowledge (SNARKs), homomorphic Message Authentication Codes (MACs), and homomorphic signatures, to ensure both privacy and integrity in outsourced computations. Our analysis covered plaintext- and ciphertext-domain verification approaches, evaluating their efficiency, privacy guarantees, and compatibility with FHE schemes like BGV and CKKS. Plaintext methods offer efficiency but require private verification, while ciphertext approaches provide stronger privacy at higher computational cost. Despite progress, challenges such as SNARK overhead and algebraic mismatches persist. Future research should prioritize optimized SNARKs, proof batching, and novel cryptographic primitives to enable scalable, secure verifiable FHE for applications like cloud computing and secure machine learning.

Acknowledgment. The authors gratefully acknowledge the financial support from the Centre International de Mathématiques Pures et Appliquées (CIMPA), the Cryptology Research Society of India (CRSI), and Bosch Global Software Technologies (BGSW) Bangalore, India, which enabled Rohitkumar R. Upadhyay to participate in the conference and present this work.

References

1. Agrawal, S., Boneh, D.: Homomorphic MACs: MAC-based integrity for network coding. In: Abdalla, M., Pointcheval, D., Fouque, P.-A., Vergnaud, D. (eds.) ACNS 2009. LNCS, vol. 5536, pp. 292–305. Springer, Heidelberg (2009). https://doi.org/10.1007/978-3-642-01957-9_18
2. Aranha, D.F., Costache, A., Guimarães, A., Soria-Vazquez, E.: Heliopolis: verifiable computation over homomorphically encrypted data from interactive oracle proofs is practical. In: Chung, K.M., Sasaki, Y. (eds.) ASIACRYPT 2024. LNCS, vol. 15488, pp. 302–334. Springer, Singapore (2025). https://doi.org/10.1007/978-981-96-0935-2_10
3. Atapoor, S., Baghery, K., VL Pereira, H., Spiessens, J.: Verifiable FHE via lattice-based snarks. IACR Commun. Cryptol. (CiC) 1(1) (2024)
4. Ben-Sasson, E., Bentov, I., Horesh, Y., Riabzev, M.: Fast Reed-Solomon interactive oracle proofs of proximity. In: 45th International Colloquium on Automata, Languages, and Programming (ICALP 2018), pp. 14–1. Schloss Dagstuhl–Leibniz-Zentrum fuer Informatik (2018)
5. Benabbas, S., Gennaro, R., Vahlis, Y.: Verifiable delegation of computation over large datasets. In: Rogaway, P. (ed.) CRYPTO 2011. LNCS, vol. 6841, pp. 111–131. Springer, Heidelberg (2011). https://doi.org/10.1007/978-3-642-22792-9_7
6. Bois, A., Cascudo, I., Fiore, D., Kim, D.: Flexible and efficient verifiable computation on encrypted data. In: Garay, J.A. (ed.) PKC 2021. LNCS, vol. 12711, pp. 528–558. Springer, Cham (2021). https://doi.org/10.1007/978-3-030-75248-4_19

7. Boneh, D., Chen, B.: Latticefold: a lattice-based folding scheme and its applications to succinct proof systems. Cryptology ePrint Archive (2024)
8. Boneh, D., Freeman, D.M.: Homomorphic signatures for polynomial functions. In: Paterson, K.G. (ed.) EUROCRYPT 2011. LNCS, vol. 6632, pp. 149–168. Springer, Heidelberg (2011). https://doi.org/10.1007/978-3-642-20465-4_10
9. Bonte, C., Iliashenko, I., Park, J., Pereira, H.V., Smart, N.P.: Final: faster FHE instantiated with NTRU and LWE. In: Agrawal, S., Lin, D. (eds.) ASIACRYPT 2022. LNCS, vol. 13792, pp. 188–215. Springer, Cham (2022). https://doi.org/10.1007/978-3-031-22966-4_7
10. Bos, J.W., Lauter, K., Loftus, J., Naehrig, M.: Improved security for a ring-based fully homomorphic encryption scheme. In: Stam, M. (ed.) IMACC 2013. LNCS, vol. 8308, pp. 45–64. Springer, Heidelberg (2013). https://doi.org/10.1007/978-3-642-45239-0_4
11. Brakerski, Z.: Fully homomorphic encryption without modulus switching from classical GapSVP. In: Safavi-Naini, R., Canetti, R. (eds.) CRYPTO 2012. LNCS, vol. 7417, pp. 868–886. Springer, Heidelberg (2012). https://doi.org/10.1007/978-3-642-32009-5_50
12. Brakerski, Z., Gentry, C., Vaikuntanathan, V.: (leveled) Fully homomorphic encryption without bootstrapping. ACM Trans. Comput. Theory (TOCT) **6**(3), 1–36 (2014)
13. Brakerski, Z., Vaikuntanathan, V.: Fully homomorphic encryption from ring-LWE and security for key dependent messages. In: Rogaway, P. (ed.) CRYPTO 2011. LNCS, vol. 6841, pp. 505–524. Springer, Heidelberg (2011). https://doi.org/10.1007/978-3-642-22792-9_29
14. Cascudo, I., Costache, A., Cozzo, D., Fiore, D., Guimarães, A., Soria-Vazquez, E.: Verifiable computation for approximate homomorphic encryption schemes. Cryptology ePrint Archive (2025)
15. Catalano, D., Fiore, D.: Practical homomorphic MACs for arithmetic circuits. In: Johansson, T., Nguyen, P.Q. (eds.) EUROCRYPT 2013. LNCS, vol. 7881, pp. 336–352. Springer, Heidelberg (2013). https://doi.org/10.1007/978-3-642-38348-9_21
16. Catalano, D., Fiore, D., Warinschi, B.: Homomorphic signatures with efficient verification for polynomial functions. In: Garay, J.A., Gennaro, R. (eds.) CRYPTO 2014. LNCS, vol. 8616, pp. 371–389. Springer, Heidelberg (2014). https://doi.org/10.1007/978-3-662-44371-2_21
17. Chatel, S., Knabenhans, C., Pyrgelis, A., Hubaux, J.P.: Verifiable encodings for secure homomorphic analytics. arXiv preprint arXiv:2207.14071 (2022)
18. Checri, M., Sirdey, R., Boudguiga, A., Bultel, J.P.: On the practical CPA^D security of "exact" and threshold FHE schemes and libraries. In: Reyzin, L., Stebila, D. (eds.) CRYPTO 2024. LNCS, vol. 14922, pp. 3–33. Springer, Cham (2024). https://doi.org/10.1007/978-3-031-68382-4_1
19. Cheon, J.H., Choe, H., Passelègue, A., Stehlé, D., Suvanto, E.: Attacks against the ind-cpad security of exact FHE schemes. In: Proceedings of the 2024 on ACM SIGSAC Conference on Computer and Communications Security, pp. 2505–2519 (2024)
20. Cheon, J.H., Kim, A., Kim, M., Song, Y.: Homomorphic encryption for arithmetic of approximate numbers. In: Takagi, T., Peyrin, T. (eds.) ASIACRYPT 2017. LNCS, vol. 10624, pp. 409–437. Springer, Cham (2017). https://doi.org/10.1007/978-3-319-70694-8_15
21. Cheon, J.H., Stehlé, D.: Fully homomophic encryption over the integers revisited. In: Oswald, E., Fischlin, M. (eds.) EUROCRYPT 2015. LNCS, vol. 9056, pp. 513–536. Springer, Heidelberg (2015). https://doi.org/10.1007/978-3-662-46800-5_20
22. Chillotti, I., Gama, N., Georgieva, M., Izabachène, M.: Faster fully homomorphic encryption: bootstrapping in less than 0.1 seconds. In: Cheon, J.H., Takagi, T. (eds.) ASIACRYPT 2016, Part I. LNCS, vol. 10031, pp. 3–33. Springer, Heidelberg (2016). https://doi.org/10.1007/978-3-662-53887-6_1
23. Ducas, L., Micciancio, D.: FHEW: bootstrapping homomorphic encryption in less than a second. In: Oswald, E., Fischlin, M. (eds.) EUROCRYPT 2015. LNCS, vol. 9056, pp. 617–640. Springer, Heidelberg (2015). https://doi.org/10.1007/978-3-662-46800-5_24

24. Fan, J., Vercauteren, F.: Somewhat practical fully homomorphic encryption. Cryptology ePrint Archive (2012)
25. Fiore, D., Gennaro, R., Pastro, V.: Efficiently verifiable computation on encrypted data. In: Proceedings of the 2014 ACM SIGSAC Conference on Computer and Communications Security, pp. 844–855 (2014)
26. Fiore, D., Nitulescu, A., Pointcheval, D.: Boosting verifiable computation on encrypted data. In: Kiayias, A., Kohlweiss, M., Wallden, P., Zikas, V. (eds.) PKC 2020, Part II. LNCS, vol. 12111, pp. 124–154. Springer, Cham (2020). https://doi.org/10.1007/978-3-030-45388-6_5
27. Gabizon, A., Williamson, Z.J., Ciobotaru, O.: Plonk: Permutations over Lagrange-bases for oecumenical noninteractive arguments of knowledge. Cryptology ePrint Archive (2019)
28. Gama, M., Beni, E.H., Kang, J., Spiessens, J., Vercauteren, F.: Blind zksnarks for private proof delegation and verifiable computation over encrypted data. Cryptology ePrint Archive (2024)
29. Ganesh, C., Nitulescu, A., Soria-Vazquez, E.: Rinocchio: snarks for ring arithmetic. J. Cryptol. **36**(4), 41 (2023)
30. Garg, S., Goel, A., Wang, M.: How to prove statements obliviously? In: Reyzin, L., Stebila, D. (eds.) CRYPTO 2024. LNCS, vol. 14929, pp. 449–487. Springer, Cham (2024). https://doi.org/10.1007/978-3-031-68403-6_14
31. Geelen, R., Vercauteren, F.: Fully homomorphic encryption for cyclotomic prime moduli. In: Fehr, S., Fouque, P.A. (eds.) EUROCRYPT 2025. LNCS, vol. 15603, pp. 366–397. Springer, Cham (2025). https://doi.org/10.1007/978-3-031-91131-6_13
32. Gennaro, R., Gentry, C., Parno, B.: Non-interactive verifiable computing: outsourcing computation to untrusted workers. In: Rabin, T. (ed.) CRYPTO 2010. LNCS, vol. 6223, pp. 465–482. Springer, Heidelberg (2010). https://doi.org/10.1007/978-3-642-14623-7_25
33. Gennaro, R., Wichs, D.: Fully homomorphic message authenticators. In: Sako, K., Sarkar, P. (eds.) ASIACRYPT 2013. LNCS, vol. 8270, pp. 301–320. Springer, Heidelberg (2013). https://doi.org/10.1007/978-3-642-42045-0_16
34. Gentry, C.: Fully homomorphic encryption using ideal lattices. In: Proceedings of the Forty-First Annual ACM Symposium on Theory of Computing, pp. 169–178 (2009)
35. Gentry, C., Sahai, A., Waters, B.: Homomorphic encryption from learning with errors: conceptually-simpler, asymptotically-faster, attribute-based. In: Canetti, R., Garay, J.A. (eds.) CRYPTO 2013, Part I. LNCS, vol. 8042, pp. 75–92. Springer, Heidelberg (2013). https://doi.org/10.1007/978-3-642-40041-4_5
36. Goldwasser, S., Kalai, Y.T., Popa, R.A., Vaikuntanathan, V., Zeldovich, N.: How to run Turing machines on encrypted data. In: Canetti, R., Garay, J.A. (eds.) CRYPTO 2013, Part II. LNCS, vol. 8043, pp. 536–553. Springer, Heidelberg (2013). https://doi.org/10.1007/978-3-642-40084-1_30
37. Gorbunov, S., Vaikuntanathan, V., Wichs, D.: Leveled fully homomorphic signatures from standard lattices. In: Proceedings of the Forty-Seventh Annual ACM Symposium on Theory of Computing, pp. 469–477 (2015)
38. Groth, J.: On the size of pairing-based non-interactive arguments. In: Fischlin, M., Coron, J.-S. (eds.) EUROCRYPT 2016, Part II. LNCS, vol. 9666, pp. 305–326. Springer, Heidelberg (2016). https://doi.org/10.1007/978-3-662-49896-5_11
39. Ishai, Y., Su, H., Wu, D.J.: Shorter and faster post-quantum designated-verifier zksnarks from lattices. In: Proceedings of the 2021 ACM SIGSAC Conference on Computer and Communications Security, pp. 212–234 (2021)
40. Jutla, C.S., Roy, A.: Shorter quasi-adaptive NIZK proofs for linear subspaces. J. Cryptol. **30**(4), 1116–1156 (2017)
41. Knabenhans, C., Viand, A., Merino-Gallardo, A., Hithnawi, A.: VFHE: verifiable fully homomorphic encryption. In: Proceedings of the 12th Workshop on Encrypted Computing and Applied Homomorphic Cryptography, pp. 11–22 (2023)

42. Li, B., Micciancio, D.: On the security of homomorphic encryption on approximate numbers. In: Canteaut, A., Standaert, F.-X. (eds.) EUROCRYPT 2021. LNCS, vol. 12696, pp. 648–677. Springer, Cham (2021). https://doi.org/10.1007/978-3-030-77870-5_23
43. Li, S., Wang, X., Zhang, R.: Privacy-preserving homomorphic MACs with efficient verification. In: Jin, H., Wang, Q., Zhang, L.-J. (eds.) ICWS 2018. LNCS, vol. 10966, pp. 100–115. Springer, Cham (2018). https://doi.org/10.1007/978-3-319-94289-6_7
44. López-Alt, A., Tromer, E., Vaikuntanathan, V.: On-the-fly multiparty computation on the cloud via multikey fully homomorphic encryption. In: Proceedings of the Forty-Fourth Annual ACM Symposium on Theory of Computing, pp. 1219–1234 (2012)
45. Lyubashevsky, V., Peikert, C., Regev, O.: On ideal lattices and learning with errors over rings. In: Gilbert, H. (ed.) EUROCRYPT 2010. LNCS, vol. 6110, pp. 1–23. Springer, Heidelberg (2010). https://doi.org/10.1007/978-3-642-13190-5_1
46. Parno, B., Howell, J., Gentry, C., Raykova, M.: Pinocchio: nearly practical verifiable computation. Commun. ACM **59**(2), 103–112 (2016)
47. Pereira, H.V.L.: Efficient AGCD-based homomorphic encryption for matrix and vector arithmetic. In: Conti, M., Zhou, J., Casalicchio, E., Spognardi, A. (eds.) ACNS 2020. LNCS, vol. 12146, pp. 110–129. Springer, Cham (2020). https://doi.org/10.1007/978-3-030-57808-4_6
48. Rivest, R.L., Adleman, L., Dertouzos, M.L., et al.: On data banks and privacy homomorphisms. Found. Secure Comput. **4**(11), 169–180 (1978)
49. Setty, S., Thaler, J., Wahby, R.: Customizable constraint systems for succinct arguments. Cryptology ePrint Archive (2023)
50. Thibault, L.T., Walter, M.: Towards verifiable FHE in practice: proving correct execution of TFHE's bootstrapping using plonky2. Cryptology ePrint Archive (2024)
51. Upadhyay, R.R., Padhye, S.: Multi-key fully homomorphic encryption scheme over the integers. In: Roy, N.R., Tanwar, S., Batra, U. (eds.) REDCYSEC 2023. LNCS, vol. 896, pp. 203–215. Springer, Singapore (2023). https://doi.org/10.1007/978-981-99-9811-1_16
52. Upadhyay, R.R., Padhye, S.: Efficient and secure MPC through integration of FHE and proxy re-encryption. SN Comput. Sci. **6**(2), 1–10 (2025)
53. van Dijk, M., Gentry, C., Halevi, S., Vaikuntanathan, V.: Fully homomorphic encryption over the integers. In: Gilbert, H. (ed.) EUROCRYPT 2010. LNCS, vol. 6110, pp. 24–43. Springer, Heidelberg (2010). https://doi.org/10.1007/978-3-642-13190-5_2

SPIQE – Secure Protocol Implementations in the Quantum Era

Public Key Linting for ML-KEM and ML-DSA

Evangelos Karatsiolis[1], Franziskus Kiefer[2], Juliane Krämer[3], Mirjam Loiero[1], Christian Tobias[1], and Maximiliane Weishäupl[3](✉)

[1] MTG AG, Darmstadt, Germany
[2] Cryspen, Berlin, Germany
[3] University of Regensburg, Regensburg, Germany
maximiliane.weishaeupl@ur.de

Abstract. With the advancing standardization of post-quantum cryptographic schemes, the need for preparing the IT security infrastructure for integrating post-quantum schemes increases. The focus of this work is a specific part of the IT security infrastructure, namely public key infrastructures. For public certification authorities, it is crucial to guarantee the quality of public keys certified by them. To this end, linting is deployed, which describes the process of analyzing the content of a certificate with respect to predefined rules, the so-called lints.

In this work, we initiate the study of lints for post-quantum cryptography. As a starting point, we choose lattice-based schemes and analyze the public keys of the NIST standards ML-KEM and ML-DSA. We base our analyses on the NIST FIPS standards and IETF documents. We formally describe the identified lints and classify them with respect to the property of the public key that the lint checks. We implement the lints for a common X.509 certificate linter and provide an open-source tool.

Keywords: ML-KEM · ML-DSA · PQC · X.509 · Linting

1 Introduction

A public key infrastructure (PKI) is an important building block to secure our current IT systems and services. In a PKI, a public certification authority (CA) issues certificates to entities to enable protocols like TLS (to secure the Internet) or S/MIME (to secure email communication). The operations of such CAs are crucial for the security and proper functioning of those protocols as well as to establish trust among users. Several policies and requirements about those operations exist and failing to comply with them would lead to an incident. A list of such incidents can be found in the CA/Incident Dashboard[1]. A significant number of these incidents is related to the content of the certificate and could be avoided, if proper mechanisms like certificate linting would always be deployed.

Linting is the process of analyzing the content of a certificate and checking whether it adheres to certain rules: The CA creates the certificate and then

---

Work of Maximiliane Weishäupl was funded by the German Federal Ministry of Research, Technology and Space (BMFTR) under the project Quant-ID (16KISQ111).
[1] https://wiki.mozilla.org/CA/Incident_Dashboard.

initiates the linting process. During linting, the certificate is checked for each rule that is implemented by the underlying linting library. If the check for one rule fails, the linting fails. Then, the CA discards the certificate and notifies the key owner who requested the certificate. Thus, only certificates without lint errors are sent to a certificate transparency (CT) log server and are finally issued. This helps CAs avoid misissuance and report incidents. To avoid errors, linting checks should be applied at an early stage. Ballot SC-75 of CA/Browser Forum[2] renders pre-sign linting mandatory from March 2025. The CA/Browser Forum also states that validating the key material presented by the key owner is a responsibility of the CA and specifies that certain checks must be performed to identify weak keys. Currently, RSA and elliptic curve keys as well as certain vulnerabilities are covered by this requirement. Linting is an appropriate mechanism to implement these checks and comply with the CA/Browser Forum requirements.

Linting is well understood for classical cryptographic schemes like RSA or elliptic-curve cryptography. For post-quantum cryptographic algorithms, however, linting has not been studied yet, although with the introduction of the standards ML-KEM, ML-DSA, and SLH-DSA,[3] the wait for standardized post-quantum cryptography (PQC) is over and the demand for using PQC in practice will increase. Hence, our current IT infrastructure has to be prepared for integrating post-quantum schemes. In this work, we contribute to this endeavor by initiating the research on linting for post-quantum cryptography. As a starting point, we analyze the public key material of lattice-based schemes. We analyze the public keys of the standards ML-KEM [16] and ML-DSA [15], which are based on the algorithms CRYSTALS-KYBER [19] and CRYSTALS-DILITHIUM [13], respectively.[4] We focus on ML-KEM and ML-DSA as a starting point as these are the "primary algorithms to be implemented for most use cases"[5] according to NIST and because they are new to current PKIs. Thus, we provide CAs with a method and a tool to check the public keys of these novel schemes and increase assurance about the quality of the certificates they issue.

Note that next to the public key material, which is the focus of this paper, there are multiple other factors that can compromise the security of the schemes. For the lattice problem ring-LWE, for instance, it was shown that a wrong choice of the underlying ring can result in weak instances [6,8]. Furthermore, LWE with unusually small secrets or binary errors can be attacked [1,2]. In this work, however, only potential impairments of the public key are of interest.

---

[2] https://cabforum.org/2024/06/27/ballot-sc-75-pre-sign-linting/.
[3] https://groups.google.com/a/list.nist.gov/g/pqc-forum/c/s_Wez9FanHw/m/ipiYjLSdBAAJ.
[4] Handling of bad key material has also already been discussed in NIST's pqc-forum, albeit with a focus on private keys: https://groups.google.com/a/list.nist.gov/g/pqc-forum/c/9nVfHKtid-k?pli=1.
[5] https://www.nist.gov/news-events/news/2022/07/pqc-standardization-process-announcing-four-candidates-be-standardized-plus.

Related Work. Several certificate linters already exist. They contain lints for algorithms from classical cryptography and target checking compliance rather than cryptographic aspects. In this work, we present results for two prominent lattice-based schemes, i.e., focus on PQC algorithms and particularly their cryptographic aspects. We observe that these new algorithms require linting for new cases, such as randomness distributions that have been less of an issue before. Therefore, a direct comparison is only possible to a limited degree.

A widely used linter is ZLint [11,22]. ZLint lints both certificates and revocation lists. It mainly focuses on checking compliance with various specifications about the contents of certificates and revocation lists. Examples are checks about the encoding of fields and extensions, correctness of data, or the absence or presence of certain data. Also, a few lints that check the cryptographic properties of certain schemes exist, e.g., a lint that checks whether an RSA modulus can be factored using Fermat's factorization method[6]. Another certificate linter is pkilint [7], which also lints some PKI protocol messages like online status validation of certificates, i.e., OCSP responses [17]. pkilint is currently under active development. During the writing of this work it added support for linting PQC-certificates, similar to the interoprability lints discussed in Sect. 4.1. Lastly, two other certificate linters exist, certlint [5] and x509lint [12], which are not being developed actively.

JZLint [14] is a port of Zlint in the programming language Java. It contains most of the lints of ZLint and adds further lints. Together with ZLint, it can be used to perform differential testing for both libraries but also the underlying programming languages and the libraries they use. JZLint also lints other PKI objects like OCSP responses. JZLint is the target software platform where we have integrated our PQC linting work.

Project Wycheproof [21] tests crypto libraries against known attacks. It is a collection of unit tests that check for expected behavior of cryptographic algorithms. The tests covered in Wycheproof comprise (amongst others) known-answer tests, timing attacks, wrong exceptions, and default values (as, e.g., weak or deprecated algorithms). Wycheproof differs from linting considerably: While Wycheproof focuses on cryptographic libraries and the implementation of cryptographic algorithms, certificate linting checks static data objects like public key certificates. Testing of private keys is not covered in Wycheproof, but may be done by linting. Also, linting checks single objects (e.g., a single public key) whereas Wycheproof can be used to create a set of objects of the same type and check for patterns. The correct encoding of public keys (unreduced values, non-invertible matrices used, etc.) is checked in both scenarios. At the time of writing, Wycheproof works on the integration of post-quantum algorithms.

---

[6] https://github.com/zmap/zlint/blob/master/v3/lints/community/lint_rsa_fermat_factorization.go.

Contribution. We initiate[7] the study on PQC linting by identifying lints for ML-KEM and ML-DSA. These algorithms are in the early stages of deployment in the Internet and mechanisms to evaluate the quality of their public keys increase assurance for their use. Based on existing formal descriptions of lints, we provide refined formal descriptions. We introduce a classification of lints that depends on the property of the public key that the lint checks. Moreover, we identify several lints that cannot be checked by the CA, but must be performed at the application side. We call such lints application lints and explain why these are different from the lints checked by a CA. The structural similarities of ML-DSA and ML-KEM public keys also transfer to their respective lints. Due to space limitations, we focus on linting ML-KEM in this submission and refer to the full version of the paper (in the IACR eprint archive) for the ML-DSA lints. An overview of our ML-KEM lints can be found in Table 1.

We provide an open source implementation of the ML-KEM lints. Additionally, we implement a linting tool in Java which incorporates these implementations in order to lint certificates employing PQC algorithms. This tool can be used by entities issuing certificates, for example public CAs. The implementation is provided under https://github.com/MTG-AG/jzlint and https://github.com/cryspen/libcrux/.

Note that we see our work only as a first step: Our results can be used for ML-KEM and ML-DSA only. Both for other lattice-based schemes and other post-quantum schemes in general, each scheme has to be analyzed thoroughly to identify useful lints. In particular, the code-based KEM HQC, which was recently selected for standardization[8] by NIST, requires a separate analysis. In this work, we showcase that linting of lattice-based algorithms is often more complex than for classical cryptography, and we expect the same to be true for other post-quantum schemes. Moreover, currently different approaches are discussed for the migration from classical to post-quantum cryptography. It is very likely that composite, i.e., hybrid algorithms will be used, consisting of a classical and a post-quantum algorithm. This adds complexity to the cryptographic algorithms and the public key infrastructure used. Hence, for hybrid algorithms more complex lints will have to be identified.

Organization. This work is organized as follows: In Sect. 2, we describe the used notation and provide background on ML-KEM. In Sect. 3, we explain our methodology, which comprises the formal description of lints, our strategy for finding lints, and their implementation. In Sect. 4, we present the lints for ML-KEM that we identified. We provide the formal description of all our ML-KEM lints in Appendix A. For background on ML-DSA and the identified ML-DSA lints, we refer to the full version (in the IACR eprint archive) of the paper.

---

[7] Concurrent to this research, the certificate linter pkilint added support for X.509 certificates using the PQC schemes ML-KEM, ML-DSA, and SLH-DSA.

[8] https://www.nist.gov/news-events/news/2025/03/nist-selects-hqc-fifth-algorithm-post-quantum-encryption.

2 Background

In this section, we provide necessary background information on ML-KEM. We start with describing the notation in Sect. 2.1 and then present ML-KEM in Sect. 2.2.

2.1 Notation

Throughout this work, we write $\mathbb{B} := \{0,1\}^8$ for the set of bytes and we use $||$ to denote the concatenation of bit and byte strings. For a bitstring $b \in \{0,1\}^n$ and $i \leq j \leq n$, the notation $b[i,j]$ will be used for $b[i]||b[i+1]||\ldots||b[j]$ where $b[k]$ denotes the k-th bit of b (note that indexing starts at 1). By $[[\cdot]]$ we denote the boolean predicate, that evaluates the expression inside the brackets. We denote the modulus by q and write $\mathbb{Z}$ for the ring of integers and $\mathbb{Z}_q$ for the finite field with q elements. Following the notation from FIPS 203 and 204 [15,16], the symbol '$\circ$' will be used to denote the multiplication in $\mathbb{Z}_q^{256}$ while '$\cdot$' is used in all other cases. For a positive integer n, we consider the polynomial rings $R = \mathbb{Z}[X]/(X^n + 1)$ and $R_q = \mathbb{Z}_q[X]/(X^n + 1)$. For a matrix A and a vector b we denote by $A[i,j]$ and $b[i]$ the entry at the position (i,j) and i, respectively. The public key matrix from ML-KEM will be denoted by $\hat{A}$, which is a square matrix of dimension k. Lastly note that we will use H and G as notation for hash functions and XOF for extendable-output functions.

2.2 ML-KEM

ML-KEM is a NIST standard for key-encapsulation mechanisms (KEM) using module lattices. It is based on the KEM CRYSTALS-Kyber, which was submitted to NIST's PQC standardization process and selected for standardization.

In the following section, we provide the algorithms from the standard FIPS 203 [16] that are relevant for our work and short high-level descriptions of them. In the standard, key generation, en- and decapsulation are divided into external and internal components. The former generate randomness, check whether the randomness generation was successful, and finally call their internal counterparts, which then perform the actual steps of the procedures. Since the public key is relevant solely for the internal components, we will describe only those in detail. Further, we focus particularly on the key generation and the encapsulation as we are linting the public key. Next to this, we describe the subalgorithms used to encode, decode, and expand the public key, as we give lints for the public key in all of its forms. Lastly, we give an overview on which lints concern which components of the public key in Algorithm 2; the corresponding lint identifiers are listed on the very right of each affected line in the pseudocode.[9] Following NIST's notation, we call ML-KEM public keys also encapsulation keys.

---

[9] Note that this does not include interoperability and generic lints as those cannot be assigned to certain components of a public key.

Algorithm 1. ML-KEM.KeyGen_internal(d, z)

Uses randomness to generate an encapsulation key and a corresponding decapsulation key.
Input randomness $d, z \in \mathbb{B}^{32}$
Output encapsulation key $ek \in \mathbb{B}^{384k+32}$, decapsulation key $dk \in \mathbb{B}^{768k+96}$
1: $(ek_{\text{PKE}}, dk_{\text{PKE}}) \leftarrow$ K-PKE.KeyGen(d)
2: $ek \leftarrow ek_{\text{PKE}}$
3: $dk \leftarrow (dk_{\text{PKE}} \| ek \| H(ek) \| z)$
4: **return** (ek, dk)

On a high level, ML-KEM is constructed in two steps: Firstly, a public key encryption scheme K-PKE is described and secondly, this scheme is turned into a KEM via an application of the FO-transform. This structure is also reflected in the algorithms for ML-KEM, which call the corresponding algorithms of the underlying PKE.

In Algorithm 1 the internal ML-KEM key generation is described and in Algorithm 2 the one of K-PKE is depicted. Essentially, an ML-KEM encapsulation key is obtained by generating an LWE sample $\hat{t} = \hat{A} \circ \hat{s} + \hat{e}$ for a random matrix $\hat{A}$ and s, e sampled from a centered binomial distribution. More precisely, the ML-KEM encapsulation key consists of an encoded version of $\hat{t}$ together with a seed ρ that can be used to generate the matrix $\hat{A}$. Note that the NTT is used to switch between representations of the elements as polynomials and vectors over $\mathbb{Z}_q$ (following the notation of the standard, we denote $\hat{f} = \text{NTT}(f)$).

In Algorithm 3 the internal ML-KEM encapsulation is described and in Algorithm 4 the encryption of the underlying PKE is given. The encapsulation returns a key K and a ciphertext. The former is computed as the hash of a randomly chosen message m and the encapsulation key, while the latter is obtained using the encryption of K-PKE. During this encryption, the matrix $\hat{A}$ and vector $\hat{t}$ are retrieved from the encapsulation key and used to compute another noisy linear equation incorporating the message m (during decapsulation, the vector $\hat{s}$ that is contained in the ML-KEM decapsulation key can be used to recover m and then in turn K).

In the key generation and the encapsulation, the encapsulation key is encoded and decoded, respectively. We describe the corresponding procedures in Algorithm 5 and 6. Further, the algorithm used to generate the matrix $\hat{A}$ from the seed ρ is given in Algorithm 7. Note that, for the rest of the paper, we will use the descriptors *encoded*, *extracted*, and *expanded* to refer to the encapsulation key after encoding, decoding, and expansion (i.e., the generation of A out of ρ). Lastly, the most important parameters are $q = 3329 = 2^8 \cdot 13 + 1$, $n = 256$, and $k \in \{2, 3, 4\}$.

Algorithm 2. K-PKE.KeyGen(d)

Uses randomness to generate an encryption key and a corresponding decryption key.
Input: randomness $d \in \mathbb{B}^{32}$
Output: encryption key $ek_{\text{PKE}} \in \mathbb{B}^{384k+32}$, decryption key $dk_{\text{PKE}} \in \mathbb{B}^{384k}$
1: $(\rho, \sigma) \leftarrow G(d\|k)$ ▷ DIM_02, DIS_01, DIS_02, DIS_03
2: $N \leftarrow 0$
3: **for** $(i \leftarrow 0; i < k; i{+}{+})$ **do** ▷ DIM_03
4:     **for** $(j \leftarrow 0; j < k; j{+}{+})$ **do**
5:         $\hat{A}[i,j] \leftarrow \text{SampleNTT}(\rho\|j\|i)$ ▷ DOM_01, DIS_04, DIS_05, DIS_06
6:     **end for**
7: **end for**
8: **for** $(i \leftarrow 0; i < k; i{+}{+})$ **do**
9:     $s[i] \leftarrow \text{SamplePolyCBD}_{\eta_1}(\text{PRF}_{\eta_1}(\sigma, N))$
10:    $N \leftarrow N + 1$
11: **end for**
12: **for** $(i \leftarrow 0; i < k; i{+}{+})$ **do**
13:    $e[i] \leftarrow \text{SamplePolyCBD}_{\eta_1}(\text{PRF}_{\eta_1}(\sigma, N))$
14:    $N \leftarrow N + 1$
15: **end for**
16: $\hat{s} \leftarrow \text{NTT}(s)$
17: $\hat{e} \leftarrow \text{NTT}(e)$
18: $\hat{t} \leftarrow \hat{A} \circ \hat{s} + \hat{e}$ ▷ DIM_04, DOM_02
19: $ek_{\text{PKE}} \leftarrow \text{ByteEncode}_{12}(\hat{t})\|\rho$ ▷ DIM_01
20: $dk_{\text{PKE}} \leftarrow \text{ByteEncode}_{12}(\hat{s})$
21: **return** $(ek_{\text{PKE}}, dk_{\text{PKE}})$

3 Methodology

In this section, we present the methodology of our work. In Sect. 3.1, we explain our strategy for finding lints. In Sect. 3.2, we describe the formal description of lints that we use in this work, introduce the concepts of lint classes and application lints, and comment on the completeness of the lints and lint classes studied in this work. In Sect. 3.3, we provide details of the implementation.

3.1 Finding Lints

As a strategy for finding lints we consider the public key in all of its occurring forms, each time checking whether all rules are fulfilled and if the properties of an honestly generated key are given. On a first level, we consider the certificate, then secondly the actual public key—in encoded form, after decoding, and lastly fully expanded. We pay special attention to the algorithms that have the public key as input to assess the consequences of a malformed public key.

Algorithm 3. ML-KEM.Encaps_internal(ek, m)

Uses the encapsulation key and randomness to generate a shared key and a ciphertext.
Input: encapsulation key $ek \in \mathbb{B}^{384k+32}$, randomness $m \in \mathbb{B}^{32}$
Output: key $K \in \mathbb{B}^{32}$, ciphertext $c \in \mathbb{B}^{32(d_u k + d_v)}$
1: $(K, r) \leftarrow G(m \parallel H(ek))$
2: $c \leftarrow $ K-PKE.Encrypt(ek, m, r)
3: **return** (K, c)

Next to this, we take into account the input validation checks described in FIPS 203 and existing ML-KEM test vectors discussed in the pqc-forum.[10]

3.2 Formal Description of Lints

Lint Names. Every lint has a unique name, which is necessary to both identify it and offer a mechanism to reference it. This is helpful to keep track of the lints that have been executed and the result of the linting. The name of the lint consists of a label specifying the severity of a lint failure and a short description of what this lint checks. For our lints the label is always e_ to identify an error, because failing one of our lints always results in an error.

The formal description used in this work follows the notation of zlint which is extensively used by public CAs. On the one hand it is a practical representation of lints and on the other hand—since it is widely used—it facilitates integration of our post-quantum lints into existing processes. The formal description of all our lints is shown in Appendix A.

In addition to its name, each lint has an ID that consists of three parts: first the algorithm is referenced, e.g., ML_DSA. This is followed by the abbreviation of the lint's classification—details on the lint classes can be found in the next paragraph. The last part of the ID is a number, starting at 01 for each combination of scheme and class and incremented by 1 for each additional lint. Additionally to the ID, a citation is always present to point to an external document, usually a specification, from which the lint requirements have been derived and where more context about the lint can be found. Lastly, each lint has a description to briefly describe the requirement on the certificate or public key that is checked by the lint. In this description also a short background on the check is given.

Lint Classes. We assign each lint to one of five classes: interoperability (INTER), dimension (DIM), domain (DOM), distribution (DIS), and generic (GEN). The class name tells what kind of property of the key the lint checks: The interoperability lints focus on certificate properties which assist applications in properly communicating among each other. The dimension lints test the size of the public key (in encoded form as well as after extraction and expansion),

---

[10] https://groups.google.com/a/list.nist.gov/g/pqc-forum/c/aCAX-2QrUFw/m/rLoIz6duCwAJ.

Algorithm 4. K-PKE.Encrypt(ek_{PKE}, m, r)

Uses the encryption key to encrypt a plaintext message using the randomness r.
Input: encryption key $ek_{\text{PKE}} \in \mathbb{B}^{384k+32}$, message $m \in \mathbb{B}^{32}$, randomness $r \in \mathbb{B}^{32}$
Output: ciphertext $c \in \mathbb{B}^{32(d_u k + d_v)}$
1: $N \leftarrow 0$
2: $\hat{t} \leftarrow \text{ByteDecode}_{12}(ek_{\text{PKE}}[0 : 384k])$
3: $\rho \leftarrow ek_{\text{PKE}}[384k : 384k + 32]$
4: **for** $(i \leftarrow 0; i < k; i++)$ **do**
5:     **for** $(j \leftarrow 0; j < k; j++)$ **do**
6:         $\hat{A}[i,j] \leftarrow \text{SampleNTT}(\rho||j||i)$
7:     **end for**
8: **end for**
9: **for** $(i \leftarrow 0; i < k; i++)$ **do**
10:     $y[i] \leftarrow \text{SamplePolyCBD}_{\eta_1}(\text{PRF}_{\eta_1}(r, N))$
11:     $N \leftarrow N + 1$
12: **end for**
13: **for** $i \leftarrow 0$ to $k - 1$ **do**
14:     $e_1[i] \leftarrow \text{SamplePolyCBD}_{\eta_2}(\text{PRF}_{\eta_2}(r, N))$
15:     $N \leftarrow N + 1$
16: **end for**
17: $e_2 \leftarrow \text{SamplePolyCBD}_{\eta_2}(\text{PRF}_{\eta_2}(r, N))$
18: $\hat{y} \leftarrow \text{NTT}(y)$
19: $u \leftarrow \text{NTT}^{-1}(\hat{A}^\top \circ \hat{y}) + e_1$
20: $\mu \leftarrow \text{Decompress}_1(\text{ByteDecode}_1(m))$
21: $v \leftarrow \text{NTT}^{-1}(\hat{t}^\top \circ \hat{y}) + e_2 + \mu$
22: $c_1 \leftarrow \text{ByteEncode}_{d_u}(\text{Compress}_{d_u}(u))$
23: $c_2 \leftarrow \text{ByteEncode}_{d_v}(\text{Compress}_{d_v}(v))$
24: **return** $c \leftarrow (c_1 \parallel c_2)$

while the domain lints check whether the type of the objects is correct. Examples for this are if the public key matrix has the right number of rows and columns and entries from the correct space. For some of the objects distribution properties are claimed, which are verified by distribution lints. Lastly, lints that can be defined for any scheme are referred to as generic.

Application Lints. While studying lints for ML-KEM and ML-DSA, we realized that not all identified lints can be verified by a CA during the linting process. To explain these lints, we first recapitulate how the certificate request to a public CA and the linting process proceed, as is shown in Fig. 1. In the certificate use part of Fig. 1, the use of the certificate by anyone is depicted. We call this the application side since an application, like an email client or a browser, extracts the public key from the certificate in order to, e.g., verify a digital signature. In the case of ML-KEM and ML-DSA, apart from extracting the public key from the certificate, the application must perform further operations, like expanding the key. At this particular time, the CA has neither access to the public key, nor can it influence the cryptographic library used by the application. There-

Algorithm 5. ByteEncode$_d(F)$

Encodes an array of d-bit integers into a byte array, for $1 \leq d \leq 12$.
Input: integer array $F \in \mathbb{Z}_m^{256}$, where $m = 2^d$ if $d < 12$ and $m = q$ if $d = 12$
Output: byte array $B \in \mathbb{B}^{32d}$
1: **for** $(i \leftarrow 0; i < 256; i{+}{+})$ **do**
2: $\quad a \leftarrow F[i]$
3: $\quad$ **for** $(j \leftarrow 0; j < d; j{+}{+})$ **do**
4: $\quad\quad b[i \cdot d + j] \leftarrow a \mod 2$
5: $\quad\quad a \leftarrow (a - b[i \cdot d + j])/2$
6: $\quad$ **end for**
7: **end for**
8: $B \leftarrow$ BitsToBytes(b)
9: **return** B

Algorithm 6. ByteDecode$_d(B)$

Decodes a byte array into an array of d-bit integers, for $1 \leq d \leq 12$.
Input: byte array $B \in \mathbb{B}^{32d}$
Output: integer array $F \in \mathbb{Z}_m^{256}$, where $m = 2^d$ if $d < 12$ and $m = q$ if $d = 12$
1: $b \leftarrow$ BytesToBits(B)
2: **for** $(i \leftarrow 0; i < 256; i{+}{+})$ **do**
3: $\quad F[i] \leftarrow \sum_{j=0}^{d-1} b[i \cdot d + j] \cdot 2^j \mod m$
4: **end for**
5: **return** F

---

fore, some lints must be performed at the application side (if at all), where the public key is used. We call such a lint an *application lint*. For example, only after expanding the key, the ML_KEM_DIM_02 lint, which checks whether the seed contained in the ML-KEM encapsulation key has the correct length, can be performed, cf. Sect. 4.2. Application lints should also be covered by known answer tests on the cryptographic implementation and should therefore only fail in exceptional cases. They may fail when, e.g., (i) unpacked keys are used, i.e., the keys are never serialized to the format standardized by NIST[11], or (ii) the implementation used by the application is flawed. In the latter case, failure of the application lint does not necessarily imply that the original serialized key used is faulty. This should not be interpreted as a recommendation against using unpacked or seed-only keys. However, it raises a counter point to a popular opinion that using seed-only keys is preferable. While seed-only keys have many advantages, faulty implementations may expand seeds to weak keys. In our implementation, which targets CAs, we do not explicitly implement such application lints. Table 1 indicates which lints are application lints.

---

[11] For ML-KEM, many implementations will use such unpacked keys due to performance reasons. The key format for these is not standardized, which again introduces the potential for invalid keys.

Algorithm 7. SampleNTT(B)

On input a 32-byte seed and two indices, it outputs a pseudorandom element of $\mathbb{Z}_q^{256}$.
Input: byte array $B \in \mathbb{B}^{34}$ ▷ a 32-byte seed along with two indices
Output: array $\hat{a} \in \mathbb{Z}_q^{256}$
1: $ctx \leftarrow$ XOF.Init()[12]
2: $ctx \leftarrow$ XOF.Absorb(ctx, B)
3: $j \leftarrow 0$
4: **while** $j < 256$ **do**
5:     $(ctx, C) \leftarrow$ XOF.Squeeze($ctx, 3$)
6:     $d_1 \leftarrow C[0] + 256 \cdot (C[1] \mod 16)$
7:     $d_2 \leftarrow \lfloor C[1]/16 \rfloor + 16 \cdot C[2]$
8:     **if** $d_1 < q$ **then**
9:         $\hat{a}[j] \leftarrow d_1$
10:        $j \leftarrow j + 1$
11:    **end if**
12:    **if** $d_2 < q$ and $j < 256$ **then**
13:        $\hat{a}[j] \leftarrow d_2$
14:        $j \leftarrow j + 1$
15:    **end if**
16: **end while**
17: **return** $\hat{a}$

Completeness of Lints and Lint Classes. While all of our lints can be sorted into the described classes, we do not exclude the possibility of further lints arising that require the introduction of new classes. Regarding the existing classes, we consider the dimension and domain check lints to be complete, as we give the corresponding checks for all states (encoded, extracted, expanded) of the public key. The same is not true for the distribution lints, which are easily seen to be incomplete. The kinds of lints we describe to test for randomness do not detect all cases of non-uniformness, e.g., there are no pattern tests. This incompleteness is due to the fact that many known distribution tests are not suited to be used as lints as the latter are supposed to be small and easily verifiable checks. However, we provide a first set of randomness lints that meet these requirements while excluding some obvious cases of non-uniformity. For the remaining classes (interoperability and generic), it is hard to define completeness as they comprise more generic concepts. In general, we want to emphasize that we view our paper as a starting point for post-quantum linting with the objective that more lints can be added over time using the proposed formal description.

3.3 Implementation

Lints are implemented in Java and Rust. Lints which examine the properties of the certificate related to the public key, like the key usage, rather than properties

---

[12] The functions Init(), Absorb(), and Squeeze() relate to the SHAKE128 API. Details can be found in [16].

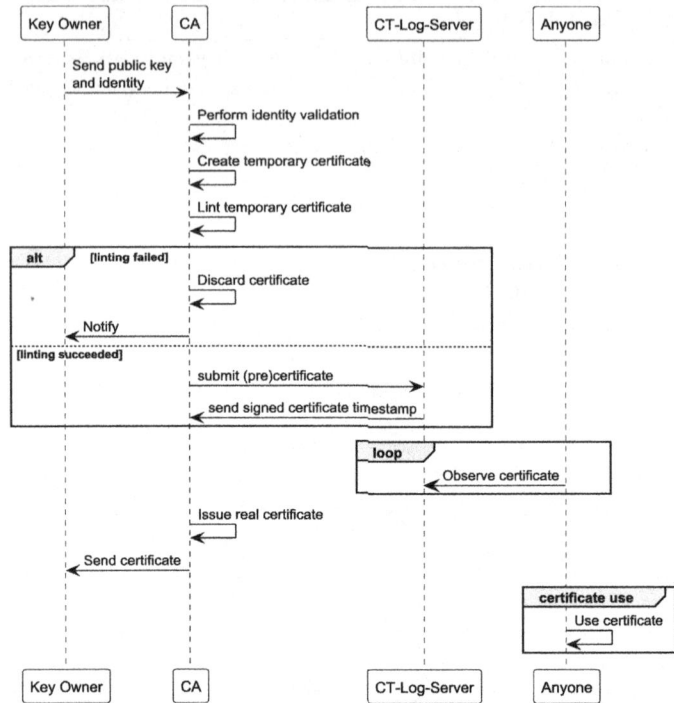

Fig. 1. Simplified certificate request and linting process. The user sends the public key to the CA. If the linting fails, the CA notifies the user to correct the request, especially the error in the public key. If linting is successful, then the certificate is submitted to a certificate transparency (CT) log server. A CT log server holds a large number of certificates and provides public accessibility to them.

of the public key itself are implemented in Java. This is done using methods provided by BouncyCastle [3], an open-source cryptographic library.

Lints that check the correctness of the key within the certificate are implemented in Rust. Rust allows us to enforce the size of inputs on the type level, such that dimension lints get covered by the API and do not need additional checks. The caller needs to ensure that the array is of the correct size and the compilation will fail, or the conversion of the unsized slice to the fixed-sized array will fail even calling the implementation if the key has the wrong size. The lint GEN_02 corresponds to the domain check described in FIPS 203 [16] for ML-KEM and is implemented as such. We further implement the distribution checks on the seed. They are implemented in order and hence fail with the first offending lint.

Listing 1.1 shows how our linting tool can be called from the command line to lint a certificate. The output of this call is given in Listing 1.2 (cf. Appendix B). Some lints (like e_ml_dsa_key_usage) are not applicable (na), since the key contained in the certificate is an ML-KEM key, while all others are a pass since the public key contained in the certificate is a valid one and does not contain any errors. In our implementation, test vectors for keys with and without errors exist.

Listing 1.1. Calling the command-line tool. It uses Java to start the tool. The certificate mlkem.crt, which contains an ML-KEM public key signed with ML-DSA, is provided. The flag -includeSources PQC is used to include lints only from this paper. Lastly, flag -p provides an easy-to-read output of the tool.

```
java -jar jzlint-cli-X.Y.Z.jar \
mlkem.crt -p -includeSources PQC
```

The lints for ML-DSA are essentially identical to those for ML-KEM, and their implementation is deferred to future work, as it does not add significant value to the work. The implementation is provided under https://github.com/MTG-AG/jzlint and https://github.com/cryspen/libcrux/.

4 Lints for ML-KEM

In this section, we present all lints that we have identified for ML-KEM. An overview of the lints is given in Table 1. The lints for ML-DSA are similar to the ones for ML-KEM and can be found in the full version (in the IACR eprint archive) of the paper. The formal description of the lints for ML-KEM is provided in Appendix A.

The main sources for the ML-KEM lints are the NIST standard FIPS 203 [16] and the IETF draft [20]. We also take into account known ML-KEM test vectors that are relevant for linting the public keys.[12]

While the standard FIPS 203 describes multiple tests for input validation, not all of them are relevant for public key linting. The tests *seed consistency* and *pair-wise consistency* are not applicable in our setting, as a CA does not obtain the randomness (used during key generation) and the secret key, but only the public key. For the same reason, the *ciphertext type check*, *decapsulation key type check*, and *hash check* do not apply. The remaining two tests, the *type check* and the *modulus check* concern the public key and are implemented as lints in our work: The *type check* (ML_KEM_DIM_01) concerns the size of the encoded encapsulation key and is hence assigned to the dimension check lints in Sect. 4.2. The *modulus check* (ML_KEM_GEN_02) relates to the de- and encoding process and is presented as a generic lint in Sect. 4.5. The lints related to the IETF draft focus on certificate properties that target interoperability, like the encoding of the algorithms used to identify the cryptographic schemes and parameters or meaningful values for the usage of the key.

In the following sections we mark the lints that we implement, i.e., all lints that are not application lints, by appending the symbol * to the lint identifier.

---

[12] There was a discussion about this topic in the pqc-forum https://groups.google.com/a/list.nist.gov/g/pqc-forum/c/aCAX-2QrUFw/m/rLoIz6duCwAJ.

Table 1. Lints for ML-KEM extracted from [16,20]. The first column shows the name of the lint, and column two shows what the lint checks. Column three shows the identifier of the lint, where the prefix ML_KEM_ needs to be added. Column four shows a ✓ if the lint is an application lint and an ✗ otherwise. Column five shows whether the public key is linted in encoded (enc), extracted (extr), or expanded (exp) form. All lints are described formally in Appendix A, and their implementation is presented in Sect. 3.3.

Lint	Classification	Identifier	Application lint?	Form of public key
key usage	interoperability	INTER_01	✗	-
pk aid enc	interoperability	INTER_02	✗	-
ek length	dimension	DIM_01	✗	enc
ek seed length	dimension	DIM_02	✗	enc[a]
ek matrix dimension	dimension	DIM_03	✓	exp
ek vector dimension	dimension	DIM_04	✓	extr
ek matrix entries	domain	DOM_01	✓	exp
ek vector entries	domain	DOM_02	✓	extr
ek seed entry frequency	distribution	DIS_01	✗	enc
ek seed entry run	distribution	DIS_02	✗	enc
ek seed small/large entries	distribution	DIS_03	✗	enc
ek matrix entry frequency	distribution	DIS_04	✓	exp
ek matrix entry run	distribution	DIS_05	✓	exp
ek matrix small/large entries	distribution	DIS_06	✓	exp
known enc key	generic	GEN_01	✗	enc/extr/exp
ek encoding	generic	GEN_02	✗	enc

[a] Note that for ML-KEM the encapsulation key is $\text{ByteEncode}_{12}(\hat{t}) \| \rho$, i.e., to check properties of the seed ρ it is not necessary to decode.

The Binding Notions. Recently, there have been many discussions about the binding properties of ML-KEM[12] and it was shown that the scheme does not achieve three of the binding notions [10,18]. For these three notions (and more generally, for the so-called MAL notions), the adversary can maliciously generate key pairs. Depending on the attack, however, a key pair cannot always be recognized as faulty—even given both the public *and* the secret key. We are not aware of binding attacks against ML-KEM that can be solely detected given the public keys (and hence through public key linting). However, if such arise in the future, corresponding lints should be added to the collection below.

---

[12] https://groups.google.com/a/list.nist.gov/g/pqc-forum/c/8cNYhg23B9k/m/KoAO1xmUAAAJ.

4.1 Interoperability Lints

ML_KEM_INTER_01*. In a certificate the key usage extension [4, Sec. 4.2.1.3] specifies for which types of use, like digital signature or encryption of data, the certificate's public key can be used. This lint checks that the values of the key usage extension are compatible with the ML-KEM algorithm. Only values related to key encryption are compatible.

ML_KEM_DIM_02. This lint checks that the encoding of the algorithm identifier of the ML-KEM public key in a certificate is correct. This means that the object identifier is one of ML-KEM-512, ML-KEM-768, or ML-KEM-1024 and that the parameters of the algorithm are absent.

4.2 Dimension Check Lints

ML_KEM_DIM_01*. This lint checks the length of the encoded encapsulation key ek. The correct length is $384k + 32$ bytes for $k \in \{2,3,4\}$ depending on the ML-KEM parameter set (see Algorithm 2). If the encoded encapsulation key is too long, the computation $G(m||H(ek))$ used to derive the shared key K and randomness r (see Algorithm 3, l.1), can become inefficient. If it is too short, the seed ρ and vector $\hat{t}$, contained and extracted, respectively, from the encoded key will not have full length (see Algorithm 4)—possible consequences of this are described in the corresponding application lints.

ML_KEM_DIM_02. This lint checks the length of the seed ρ that is contained in the encoded ML-KEM encapsulation key ek. The seed makes up the last 32 bytes of the encoded encapsulation key, i.e., $\rho \in \mathbb{B}^{32}$ (see Algorithm 2). A too long seed can slow down the XOF computation in SampleNTT (see Algorithm 7).

The two lints below check the dimensions of the matrix $\hat{A}$ and the vector $\hat{t}$. Depending on the implementation, $\hat{A}$ and $\hat{t}$ of the wrong dimension can impair functionality but also security, as encapsulation and decapsulation key are related via $\hat{A}$ and $\hat{t}$. More precisely $\hat{t} = \hat{A} \circ \hat{s} + \hat{e}$ for e an error term sampled from a centered binomial distribution and $dk = \text{ByteEncode}_{12}(\hat{s})$ (see Algorithm 2).

ML_KEM_DIM_03. This lint checks the dimensions of the matrix $\hat{A}$, that is obtained by expanding the seed ρ, which is in turn part of the encoded ML-KEM encapsulation key ek. The matrix is computed as $\hat{A}[i,j] = \text{SampleNTT}(\rho||j||i)$ and should have $k \in \{2,3,4\}$ rows and columns (see Algorithm 2).

ML_KEM_DIM_04. This lint checks the size of the vector $\hat{t}$, which is contained in the extracted ML-KEM encapsulation key. The correct length of $\hat{t} = \text{ByteDecode}_{12}(ek[0 : 384k])$ is k for $k \in \{2,3,4\}$ (see Algorithm 2).

4.3 Domain Check Lints

ML_KEM_DOM_01. This lint checks if expanding the seed ρ, that is part of the encoded ML-KEM encapsulation key ek, yields a matrix with entries over the correct space. More precisely, we consider $\hat{A}$ with $\hat{A}[i,j] = \text{SampleNTT}(\rho||j||i)$ and test whether $\hat{A}[i,j] \in \mathbb{Z}_q^{256}$ for $q = 3329$ (see Algorithm 7).

Depending on the concrete implementation, a matrix $\hat{A}$ that is not reduced modulo q can cause interoperability problems. We give an example, in which encapsulation using $\hat{A}$ will result in a ciphertext c that leads to implicit rejection during decapsulation with overwhelming probability. For this, assume that $\hat{A}$ has entries greater q. During an ML-KEM encapsulation, $\text{NTT}^{-1}(\hat{A}^\top \circ \hat{y})$ is used in the underlying encryption $c = \text{K-PKE.Encrypt}(ek, m, r)$ (see Algorithms 3, 4). Here y is sampled from a centered binomial distribution, hence we can assume $\hat{A}^\top \circ \hat{y}$ to still have entries greater q. Note that we assume that the implementation does not explicitly reduce $\hat{A}^\top \hat{y}$—this is sensible as $\hat{A}^\top \hat{y}$ is directly inputted into NTT^{-1}, which contains a reduction modulo q (see [16, Algorithm 10]). Then during decapsulation, the value $\text{NTT}(\text{NTT}^{-1}(\hat{A}^\top \circ \hat{y}))$ is computed (see [16, Algorithm 15, 1.6]), which is reduced modulo q and hence different from $\hat{A}^\top \circ \hat{y}$. However, then $m' = \text{K-PKE.Decrypt}(\text{dk}, c)$ is likely to differ from m. This implies that the re-encrypt step will fail with overwhelming probability, which in turn induces implicit rejection (see [16, Algorithm 18]).

ML_KEM_DOM_02. This lint checks if the vector $\hat{t}$ contained in the extracted ML-KEM public key has entries from the correct space. We test whether $\hat{t}[i] \in \mathbb{Z}_q^{256}$ for $q = 3329$ and $\hat{t} = \text{ByteDecode}_{12}(ek[0:384k])$ (see Algorithm 6).

4.4 Distribution Lints

The following lints concern the distribution of the components contained in (and computed from) the public key, more precisely the seed ρ, the matrix $\hat{A}$, and the vector $\hat{t}$ (see Algorithms 2, 4). As ρ and $\hat{A}$ are assumed to be pseudorandom in FIPS 203 [16], we give three lints that exclude some obvious cases of non-uniformness for the entries of ρ and $\hat{A}$. Note that non-randomness of the public key matrix can negatively influence security. For example, in the extreme case that a sparse matrix is used, hardness of the standard LWE problem is not guaranteed, as is the case if binary matrices are used [9].

To determine the rejection value x for which a lint should output an error, we roughly use the following procedure: We choose the bound $\alpha = 2^{-128}$ and compute x as a value such that for uniformly distributed values, the probability that the lint outputs an error is smaller α. Details on the computation of the rejection values can be found in Appendix C.

ML_KEM_DIS_01*. This lint checks if the seed ρ, that is contained in the encoded ML-KEM encapsulation key ek, contains the same element an amount of times that is unlikely for a pseudorandomly sampled value from $\mathbb{B}^{32}$. The lint outputs an error if there are at least $x = 20$ occurrences of the same element.

ML_KEM_DIS_02*. This lint checks if the seed ρ, that is contained in the encoded ML-KEM encapsulation key ek, contains a long run of the same element, which is unlikely for a pseudorandomly sampled value from $\mathbb{B}^{32}$. An error is outputted if the length of the longest run of the same element has length at least 18.

ML_KEM_DIS_03*. This lint checks if the seed $\rho \in \mathbb{B}^{32}$, that is contained in the encoded ML-KEM encapsulation key ek, has too small or too large entries. An error is outputted if N_s, the number of entries smaller than 128, and N_g, the number of entries greater than 128, fulfill $N_s \geq x$ or $N_g \geq x$ for $x = 29$.

Note that for this lint we cannot achieve a probability smaller 2^{-128} (unless we reject no seeds at all) due to the fact that only 32 elements are drawn. Hence we change the bound α to $\frac{1}{2^{18}}$ to obtain a sensible rejection bound. In particular, this means that this lint will output an error far more often than the other distribution lints. Thus, before deploying the lint, its relevance should be weighed against the disadvantage of more false positives—taking into account the use case at hand. Here, one should be aware that the frequent rejection of valid keys, can weaken the perceived reliability of a CA. In our implementation, lints can be configurably disabled. Thus, one CA can easily exclude this particular lint to avoid rejecting valid keys, while another CA, which is interested in performing this check, may include it.

Remark. Note that during the computation of the matrix $\hat{A}$, the seed ρ is expanded using an extendable-output function XOF (see Algorithm 2). However, XOF does not have a fixed output length, but will produce more bytes until $\hat{A}$ is filled with entries that have the desired properties (being reduced modulo q, see Algorithm 7). Hence, for seeds ρ such that $\mathrm{XOF}(\rho)$ has many large entries, the generation of $\hat{A}$ will take longer. This in turn would influence efficiency of encapsulation and decapsulation in a negative manner.

The following three lints test the uniformness of the entries in the matrix A that is contained in the expanded public key. Note that these lints can only output an error in exceptional cases, e.g., if "weak seeds" for SampleNTT exist. By this, we mean seeds ρ for which the matrix expansion using SampleNTT yields a matrix that is biased in some way—which in turn can enable attacks, as the one for sparse or binary matrices [9]. However, we are not aware of any existing examples of such weak seeds, and consider this as an open question that has to be further analyzed in the future.

ML_KEM_DIS_04. This lint checks if the matrix $\hat{A}$ that is generated from the seed ρ (contained in the encoded ML-KEM encapsulation key ek) contains each element from $\mathbb{Z}_q$ only a number of times that is likely for a pseudorandomly generated matrix. The matrix $\hat{A}$ is computed as $\hat{A}[i,j] = \mathrm{SampleNTT}(\rho||j||i)$ for $i, j \in \{1, \ldots, k\}$ and $k \in \{2, 3, 4\}$ and has entries in $\mathbb{Z}_q^{256}$ with $q = 3329$. The lint outputs an error if there are at least x occurrences of the same element from $\mathbb{Z}_q$, where $x \in \{26, 31, 36\}$ (corresponding to the three parameter sets).

ML_KEM_DIS_05*. This lint checks if the matrix $\hat{A}$ that is generated from the seed ρ (contained in the encoded ML-KEM encapsulation key ek) contains a long run of the same element, which is unlikely for a pseudorandomly generated matrix. The matrix $\hat{A}$ is computed as $\hat{A}[i,j] = \text{SampleNTT}(\rho||j||i)$ for $i,j \in \{1,\ldots,k\}$ and $k \in \{2,3,4\}$ and has entries in $\mathbb{Z}_q^{256}$ with $q = 3329$. The lint outputs an error if the length of the longest run[12] of the same element from $\mathbb{Z}_q$ has length at least $x = 13$.

ML_KEM_DIS_06*. This lint checks whether the matrix $\hat{A}$ that is generated from the seed ρ (contained in the encoded ML-KEM encapsulation key ek) has too small or too large entries. The matrix $\hat{A}$ is computed as $\hat{A}[i,j] = \text{SampleNTT}(\rho||j||i)$ for $i,j \in \{1,\ldots,k\}$ and $k \in \{2,3,4\}$ and has entries in $\mathbb{Z}_q^{256}$. Note that we can consider $\hat{A}$ to be a $(256k \times 256k)$-matrix over $\mathbb{Z}_q$. The lint outputs an error if the number of entries N_s smaller than $\frac{q}{2}$ and then the number N_g of ones greater than $\frac{q}{2}$ fulfill $N_s \geq x$ or $N_g \geq x$ for $x \in \{720, 1466, 2467\}$ (depending on the parameter set).

4.5 Generic Lints

ML_KEM_GEN_01*. The lint checks for public keys of publicly known key pairs, e.g., key pairs that are published for demonstration purposes (in standards, specifications, etc.) or stem from key leaks. Public keys of such key pairs should not be used in practice, as the corresponding secret keys are publicly available.

ML_KEM_GEN_02*. This lint checks if first decoding and then encoding the encapsulation key ek will give back the same ek.[12] First, we observe that this is not automatically given. [16, Section 7.2]: ByteDecode_{12} takes a byte array of length 384 as input and computes from each 12-bit segment of this input an integer smaller than $2^{12} = 4096$. The resulting values are reduced modulo $q = 3329$ and ByteDecode_{12} outputs the corresponding element in $(\mathbb{Z}_q)^{256}$. Now assume the input B to ByteDecode_{12} is chosen in a way such that at least one of its 12-bit segments will yield a value $3329 \leq x < 4096$. Note that this can easily be achieved by setting $B = (255, 255, \ldots, 255)$. However, such an output cannot be produced by ByteEncode_{12}, i.e., $\text{ByteEncode}_{12}(\text{ByteDecode}_{12}(B)) \neq B$. Moreover, in this case the input B cannot be the result of an honest ML-KEM key generation as first applying ByteEncode_{12} and then ByteDecode_{12} is the identity mapping. Thus, this test is of great importance, as it can identify encapsulation keys that might have the correct length, but still do not stem from an honest key generation.

---

[12] Note that the ordering of the elements in the matrix should coincide with the order in which the entries of $\hat{A}$ are generated during the key generation.

[12] Note that for ML-DSA no such lint is necessary as pkEncode can hit the full output space, which equals the input space of pkDecode. In contrast for ML-KEM, one can input values into ByteDecode_{12} that are never outputted by ByteEncode_{12}.

5 Conclusion

In this paper, we initiated the study of lints for PQC and gave the first lints for the lattice-based standards ML-KEM and ML-DSA. Additionally, we provided a general framework consisting of formal descriptions and a classification for lints.

While linting is not novel, applying it to post-quantum schemes is. From this, challenges that did not occur when linting classical schemes arise. One of them is due to the fact that for post-quantum schemes, security is often related to certain elements looking random or following a pre-defined distribution. While there are also vulnerabilities in classical schemes that are due to badly distributed elements (e.g., the RSA primes p and q being too close), such issues occur even more predominantly in post-quantum schemes. Hence, finding ways to check distribution properties using lints, i.e., small and easily verifiable checks, is one of the challenges that has to be met when linting post-quantum schemes. Therefore, we introduced the class of distribution lints and equipped it with first lints for ML-KEM and ML-DSA. However, these lints do not detect all cases of non-uniformness and further lints should be added in the future.

Another hurdle stems from the usage of seeds, as is also done in ML-KEM and ML-DSA. Instead of saving the public key in the form that is used for computations during the verification of signatures, only the seed from which this full version can be expanded, is saved. Hence, properties of the expanded public key cannot be checked by the CA when seeds are used, and the correctness of the expanded public key depends on the implementation of the expansion algorithm used by the party expanding the seed. In practice, different or even faulty implementations of the expanding functions might be used, which can lead to different results when expanding the same seed, and thereby induce, among others, interoperability problems. Thus, the usage of seeds requires testing of the implementations used for expanding, which lies outside the scope of linting, which is the responsibility of the CA. More generally, the decision between using seeds or "full" keys relates to a trade-off between implementation testing and key linting.

Since linting heavily depends on scheme-specific details, one cannot give a complete set of lints covering all lattice-based or even post-quantum schemes, both now and in the future. Instead, with the ongoing standardization and increased usage of PQC, dedicated analyses of the relevant schemes have to be carried out. The lints we gave for ML-KEM and ML-DSA serve as a starting point and example for future analyses, and the provided framework guides the introduction of further lints in the future.

A Formal Description of Lints for ML-KEM

Name	e_ml_kem_key_usage
ID	ML_KEM_INTER_01
Citation	[20, Sec. 4]
Description	A certificate with an ML-KEM public key must only have the keyEncipherment key usage value.

Name	e_ml_kem_public_key_aid_encoding
ID	ML_KEM_INTER_02
Citation	[20, Sec. 4]
Description	The algorithm identifier in the public key of a certificate with an ML-KEM public key must have the correct encoding.

Name	e_ml_kem_ek_length
ID	ML_KEM_DIM_01
Citation	[16]
Description	An encoded ML-KEM encapsulation key must be of the correct length.

Name	e_ml_kem_ek_seed_length
ID	ML_KEM_DIM_02
Citation	[16]
Description	The seed contained in the ML-KEM encapsulation key must be of the correct length.

Name	e_ml_kem_ek_matrix_dimension
ID	ML_KEM_DIM_03
Citation	[16]
Description	The matrix expanded from the seed, that is contained in the ML-KEM encapsulation key, must have the correct dimensions.

Name	e_ml_kem_ek_vector_dimension
ID	ML_KEM_DIM_04
Citation	[16]
Description	The vector contained in the extracted ML-KEM encapsulation key, must have the correct dimension.

Name	e_ml_kem_ek_matrix_entries
ID	ML_KEM_DOM_01
Citation	[16]
Description	The matrix expanded from the seed, that is contained in the ML-KEM encapsulation key, must have entries from the correct space.

Name	e_ml_kem_ek_vector_entries
ID	ML_KEM_DOM_02
Citation	[16]
Description	The vector contained in the extracted ML-KEM encapsulation key, must have entries from the correct space.

Name	e_ml_kem_ek_seed_entry_frequency
ID	ML_KEM_DIS_01
Citation	[16]
Description	The seed contained in the ML-KEM encapsulation key must not have too many occurrences of the same element.

Name	e_ml_kem_ek_seed_entry_run
ID	ML_KEM_DIS_02
Citation	[16]
Description	The seed contained in the ML-KEM encapsulation key must not have a too long run of the same element.

Name	e_ml_kem_ek_seed_sl_entries
ID	ML_KEM_DIS_03
Citation	[16]
Description	The seed contained in the ML-KEM encapsulation key must not have too small or too large entries.

Name	e_ml_kem_ek_matrix_entry_frequency
ID	ML_KEM_DIS_04
Citation	[16]
Description	The matrix expanded from the seed, that is contained in the ML-KEM encapsulation key must not have too many occurrences of the same element.

Name	e_ml_kem_ek_matrix_entry_run
ID	ML_KEM_DIS_05
Citation	[16]
Description	The matrix expanded from the seed, that is contained in the ML-KEM encapsulation key must not have a too long run of the same element.

Name	e_ml_kem_ek_matrix_sl_entries
ID	ML_KEM_DIS_06
Citation	[16]
Description	The matrix expanded from the seed, that is contained in the ML-KEM encapsulation key must not have too small or too large entries.

Name	e_known_encoded_key
ID	ML_KEM_GEN_01
Citation	Databases, documents etc., containing public keys whose private key is suspected to be known.
Description	A public key whose corresponding private key is known to be compromised, is weak, or is leaked must not be placed in a certificate.

Name	e_ml_kem_ek_encoding
ID	ML_KEM_GEN_02
Citation	[16]
Description	An ML-KEM encryption key must be correctly encoded.

B Postponed Listing

Listing 1.2. Output of the tool in JSON format. Each key is the name of the lint and in the result key the result of the linting process for this lint is given. For example, the public key in the certificate passed the lint e_ml_kem_ek_seed_entry_run.

```
{
    "e_ml_kem_ek_encoding" : {
        "result" : "pass"
    },
    "e_ml_kem_ek_seed_entry_run" : {
        "result" : "pass"
    },
    "e_ml_kem_ek_length" : {
        "result" : "pass"
    },
    "e_ml_dsa_signature_aid_encoding" : {
        "result" : "pass"
    },
    "e_known_encoded_key" : {
        "result" : "pass"
    },
    "e_ml_dsa_key_usage" : {
```

```
            "result" : "na"
        },
        "e_ml_dsa_public_key_aid_encoding" : {
            "result" : "na"
        },
        "e_ml_kem_ek_seed_sl_entries" : {
            "result" : "pass"
        },
        "e_ml_kem_ek_seed_entry_frequency" : {
            "result" : "pass"
        },
        "e_ml_kem_key_usage" : {
            "result" : "pass"
        },
        "e_ml_kem_public_key_aid_encoding" : {
            "result" : "pass"
        }
    }
}
```

C Computation of Rejection Values

For all lints described below, we want to determine the rejection value x in a way such that for uniformly sampled values, the probability that the lint outputs an error is smaller $\alpha = 2^{-128}$.

C.1 Entry-Frequency-Lints

These lints check whether a string of length n with entries from a set M of size m, contains the same element an amount of times that is unlikely for pseudo-randomly sampled values.

Let E denote the event that the lint outputs an error, i.e., there is some element that appears at least x times. Further, for each $\mu \in M$, consider the event E_μ that the value μ appears at least x times. Then, for a uniformly sampled string, we obtain the following upper bound

$$\Pr(E) = \Pr\left(\bigcup_\mu E_\mu\right) \leq \sum_\mu \Pr(E_\mu)$$

$$= \sum_\mu \left(\sum_{i=x}^n \binom{n}{i} \left(\frac{1}{m}\right)^i \left(1 - \frac{1}{m}\right)^{n-i}\right)$$

$$= m \cdot \underbrace{\left(\sum_{i=x}^n \binom{n}{i} \left(\frac{1}{m}\right)^i \left(1 - \frac{1}{m}\right)^{n-i}\right)}_{=:P}.$$

For concrete values for n and m, this formula allows to determine x such that $P \leq \frac{1}{m} \cdot \alpha$, which yields the desired rejection value.

C.2 Entry-Run-Lints

These lints check whether a string of length n with entries from a set M of size m, contains a long run (i.e., consecutive occurrences) of the same element, which is unlikely for pseudorandomly sampled values.

Let E denote the event that the lint outputs an error, i.e., that the longest run has length at least x. Further, for each $i \in \{1, \ldots, n\}$, consider the event E_i that, starting in position i of the string, there is a run of length at least x. Note that $\Pr(E_i) = m \cdot \left(\frac{1}{m}\right)^x = \frac{1}{m^{x-1}}$ as there are m possibilities for the element in the run, and the probability that this element appears at x chosen positions is $\left(\frac{1}{m}\right)^x$.[12] Then, for a uniformly sampled string, we obtain

$$\Pr(E) = \Pr\left(\bigcup_i E_i\right) \leq \sum_i \Pr(E_i)$$
$$\leq \sum_i \frac{1}{m^{x-1}} = \frac{n}{m^{x-1}}.$$

Thus, for $x \geq \log_m(n 2^{128}) + 1$, it holds that $\Pr(E) \leq \alpha$, which yields the desired rejection value.

C.3 Small/Large-Entries-Lints

These lints check whether a string of length n with entries from $M = \{1, \ldots, m\}$, has too small or too large entries—which is unlikely to hold for pseudorandomly sampled values.

Denote by N_s the number of entries that belong to the first $\lfloor \frac{m}{2} \rfloor$ elements of M and by N_g the number of ones that belong to the last $\lfloor \frac{m}{2} \rfloor$ elements of M.[12] Let E denote the event that the lint outputs an error, i.e., that $N_s \geq x$ or $N_g \geq x$. Note that this condition can be reformulated into $x \leq N_s$ or $N_s \leq n - x$ holding. Then, for a uniformly sampled string, we obtain

$$\Pr(E) = \left(\sum_{i=x}^{n} \binom{n}{i} \left(\frac{1}{2}\right)^i \left(1 - \frac{1}{2}\right)^{n-i}\right) + \left(\sum_{i=0}^{n-x} \binom{n}{i} \left(\frac{1}{2}\right)^i \left(1 - \frac{1}{2}\right)^{n-i}\right).$$

For concrete values for n and m, this formula allows to determine x such that $\Pr(E) \leq \alpha$, which yields the desired rejection value.

---

[12] Note that this computation holds only if a run of length x starting at positions i is possible, otherwise the probability is 0.

[12] We assume wlog that m is even as the odd case can be reduced to the even case using the estimate $\Pr(E$ in the odd case$) \leq \Pr(E$ in the even case$)$.

References

1. Albrecht, M.R.: On dual lattice attacks against small-secret LWE and parameter choices in HElib and SEAL. In: Coron, J.-S., Nielsen, J.B. (eds.) EUROCRYPT 2017, Part II. LNCS, vol. 10211, pp. 103–129. Springer, Cham (2017). https://doi.org/10.1007/978-3-319-56614-6_4
2. Arora, S., Ge, R.: New algorithms for learning in presence of errors. In: Aceto, L., Henzinger, M., Sgall, J. (eds.) ICALP 2011, Part I. LNCS, vol. 6755, pp. 403–415. Springer, Heidelberg (2011). https://doi.org/10.1007/978-3-642-22006-7_34
3. Bouncy Castle – Open-source cryptographic APIs. https://www.bouncycastle.org/
4. Boeyen, S., Santesson, S., Polk, T., Housley, R., Farrell, S., Cooper, D.: Internet X.509 Public Key Infrastructure Certificate and Certificate Revocation List (CRL) Profile. RFC 5280, May 2008
5. Bowen, P.: certlint. https://github.com/amazon-archives/certlint. GitHub repository
6. Castryck, W., Iliashenko, I., Vercauteren, F.: Provably weak instances of ring-LWE revisited. In: Fischlin, M., Coron, J.-S. (eds.) EUROCRYPT 2016, Part I. LNCS, vol. 9665, pp. 147–167. Springer, Heidelberg (2016). https://doi.org/10.1007/978-3-662-49890-3_6
7. DigiCert. pkilint. https://github.com/digicert/pkilint. GitHub repository
8. Elias, Y., Lauter, K.E., Ozman, E., Stange, K.E.: Provably weak instances of ring-LWE. In: Gennaro, R., Robshaw, M. (eds.) CRYPTO 2015, Part I. LNCS, vol. 9215, pp. 63–92. Springer, Heidelberg (2015). https://doi.org/10.1007/978-3-662-47989-6_4
9. Herold, G., May, A.: LP solutions of vectorial integer subset sums – cryptanalysis of Galbraith's binary matrix LWE. In: Fehr, S. (ed.) PKC 2017, Part I. LNCS, vol. 10174, pp. 3–15. Springer, Heidelberg (2017). https://doi.org/10.1007/978-3-662-54365-8_1
10. Krämer, J., Struck, P., Weishäupl, M.: Binding security of implicitly-rejecting KEMs and application to BIKE and HQC. Cryptology ePrint Archive, Paper 2024/1233 (2024)
11. Kumar, D., et al.: Zlint: tracking certificate misissuance in the wild. In: 2018 IEEE Symposium on Security and Privacy (SP) (2018)
12. Kurt Roeckx. x509lint. https://github.com/kroeckx/x509lint. GitHub repository
13. Lyubashevsky, V., et al.: CRYSTALS-DILITHIUM. Technical report, National Institute of Standards and Technology (2020). https://csrc.nist.gov/projects/post-quantum-cryptography/post-quantum-cryptography-standardization/round-3-submissions
14. MTG AG. JZLint. https://github.com/MTG-AG/jzlint. GitHub repository
15. National Institute of Standards and Technology. Module-Lattice-Based Digital Signature Standard (2024). https://doi.org/10.6028/NIST.FIPS.204
16. National Institute of Standards and Technology. Module-Lattice-based Key-Encapsulation Mechanism Standard (2024). https://doi.org/10.6028/NIST.FIPS.203
17. Santesson, S., Myers, M., Ankney, R., Malpani, A., Galperin, S., Adams, C.: X.509 Internet Public Key Infrastructure Online Certificate Status Protocol - OCSP. RFC 6960, June 2013
18. Schmieg, S.: Unbindable Kemmy Schmidt: ML-KEM is neither MAL-BIND-k-CT nor MAL-BIND-k-PK. Cryptology ePrint Archive, Paper 2024/523 (2024)

19. Schwabe, P., et al.: CRYSTALS-KYBER. Technical report, National Institute of Standards and Technology (2020). https://csrc.nist.gov/projects/post-quantum-cryptography/post-quantum-cryptography-standardization/round-3-submissions
20. Turner, S., Kampanakis, P., Massimo, J., Westerbaan, B.: Internet X.509 Public Key Infrastructure - Algorithm Identifiers for Module-Lattice-Based Key-Encapsulation Mechanism (ML-KEM). Internet-Draft draft-ietf-lamps-kyber-certificates-03, Internet Engineering Task Force, March 2024. Work in Progress
21. Wycheproof. https://github.com/C2SP/wycheproof. GitHub repository
22. ZLint. https://github.com/zmap/zlint. GitHub repository

Author Index

A

Aggarwal, Akshit   III-207, III-213
Aghili, Farhad   III-141
Arya, Kislay   I-3
Aung, Yan Lin   I-204
Azzabi, Radhouene   III-162

B

Balachandran, Vivek   III-179, III-197
Balodis, Rihards   I-266
Barbu, Guillaume   II-3
Basurto-Becerra, Abraham   I-77
Battagliola, Michele   II-251
Bhattacharya, Sarani   I-3

C

Cao, Yunfei   II-41, II-118
Celms, Edgars   I-266
Che, Anda   II-229
Chen, Luoqi   II-81
Chetry, Reejit   I-113
Chiku, Sohto   II-274
Chithambara Moorthii, J.   I-113
Chowdhury, Siddhartha   I-3

D

D'Alconzo, Giuseppe   II-251
Damie, Marc   III-109
Dehghantanha, Ali   III-70
Del Bino, Leonardo   III-191
Ding, Yaoling   II-23
Dong, Ye   I-204

E

Edu, Jide   I-185
Eisenbarth, Thomas   III-43

F

Felde, Hendrik Meyer Zum   III-162
Fu, Haoyue   II-118

Fujino, Takeshi   I-94
Fukuda, Yuta   I-94

G

Gangemi, Andrea   II-251
Gansel, Antoine   I-245
Gao, Jing   II-23
Gay, Maël   I-58
Geloczi, Emiliia   I-222
Gil, Amaia   III-162
Goldmann, Mirko   III-191
Gong, Weiping   II-23
Gong, Zheng   II-81, II-211
Gonzalez, Ruben   II-173
Goswami, Bhanprakash   I-113
Gouy-Pailler, Cédric   III-162
Grémy, Laurent   II-3

H

Hahn, Florian   III-109
Haiqi, He   III-179
Hao, Xinpeng   II-152
Hara, Keisuke   II-274
Hara, Yuko   I-144, III-223
He, Junlin   II-132
He, Yituo   II-152
Hirata, Haruka   I-144
Hoffmann, Clément   II-101
Holler, Benedikt   I-222
Hristoskova, Anna   III-141
Hu, Xi   II-41

I

Ise, Kenshiro   III-223

J

Janetschek, Matthias   I-163
Jia Jing, Caleb Lee   III-179
Jing, Jiwu   II-132, II-229

K

Kalnina, Elina   I-266
Kalvin, Lee Ling Yi   III-121
Karatsiolis, Evangelos   II-337
Karayalçin, Sengim   I-40
Katzenbeisser, Stefan   I-222
Khairallah, Mustafa   I-22
Kharitonov, Alexander   I-58
Kiefer, Franziskus   II-337
Kiggins, Andrew   I-185
Kissner, Michael   III-191
Kou, Chunjing   II-132
Kozlovics, Sergejs   I-266
Kozlovičs, Sergejs   III-185
Krämer, Juliane   I-245, II-337
Kristen, Meret   III-218

L

Le Jeune, Laurens   III-141
Lehmann, Gilles   III-162
Lescuyer, Roch   II-3
Li, Juanru   II-152
Li, Meixuan   III-121
Li, Yang   I-144, III-207, III-213
Li, Zhen   II-193
Limbasiya, Trupil   I-204
Lin, Zihe   II-23
Liu, Anjiang   II-193
Liu, Zhenyuan   I-124
Loiero, Mirjam   II-337
Long, Chongyu   II-229

M

Malmqvist, Lars   III-52
Malnicof, Andrew   I-124
Mandal, Upasana   I-3
Maurer, Felix   III-43
Merkle, Florian   I-163
Mexis, Nico   I-222
Mishra, Rina   III-89
Miyahara, Daiki   I-144
Momin, Charles   II-101
Mottok, Jürgen   III-218
Mouiche, Inoussa   III-3
Mukhopadhyay, Debdeep   I-3

N

Nambiar, Sanjana   III-23
Nocker, Martin   I-163

O

Odoh, Kenneth   III-202
Opmane, Inara   I-266

P

Padhye, Sahadeo   II-318
Peng, Jin   II-211
Peters, Thomas   II-101
Petručeça, Krišjānis   III-185
Petrucena, Krisjanis   I-266
Picek, Stjepan   I-40, I-77
Pöhls, Henrich C.   I-222
Polian, Ilia   I-58
Pöpper, Christina   III-23

Q

Qian, Yuhan   II-23

R

Rabieinejad, Elnaz   III-70
Raj, Amal   III-197
Rencis, Edgars   I-266
Rezaeezade, Azade   I-77
Rieder, Vincent   II-296

S

Saad, Sherif   III-3
Sahu, Rajeev Anand   II-318
Sakiyama, Kazuo   I-144
Sander, Jonas   III-43
Saraswat, Vishal   II-318
Sarkar, Tishya Sarma   I-3
Schaumont, Patrick   I-124
Schoenauen, Thibaud   II-101
Schöttle, Pascal   I-163
Schumacher, Tim   I-245
Schwartzentruber, Jeff   III-70
Shanmugam, Dillibabu   I-124
Shikata, Junji   II-274
Shukla, Shubhi   I-3
Spadafora, Chiara   II-251
Standaert, François-Xavier   II-101
Struck, Patrick   I-245
Suri, Manan   I-113
Swain, Srinibas   III-207, III-213

T

Tang, Yufeng   II-81
Tippmann, Maximilian   I-245

Author Index

Tobias, Christian II-337

U
Upadhyay, Rohitkumar R. II-318

V
van Dartel, Bram III-109
Varshney, Gaurav III-89
Viksna, Juris I-266
Vīksna, Juris III-185

W
Walther, Thomas I-245
Wang, An II-23, II-193
Wang, Cheng I-204
Wang, Dachao II-211
Wang, HengSheng II-61
Wang, Wei II-61
Wang, WeiJia II-193
Weishäupl, Maximiliane II-337
Welling, Tarick I-58
Wen, ShuShang II-61

Wu, Jingjie II-23

X
Xiang, Hong II-41, II-118
Xing, Haoyang II-229

Y
Yamasaki, Hirokatsu I-94
Yap, Trevor I-22
Yoshida, Kota I-40, I-94
Yousaf, Awais III-121
Yu, Yu II-152

Z
Zarrinkalam, Fattane III-70
Zhang, Congyi II-118
Zhao, Liangju II-81
Zhao, Yiyan II-132
Zheng, Fangyu II-132, II-229
Zhong, Yuchen II-23
Zhou, Jianying I-204, III-121

Made in the USA
Monee, IL
03 May 2026

49438491R00214